The Historical Atlas of the Civil War

A CARTOGRAPHICA BOOK

This updated edition published in 2010 by:
CHARTWELL BOOKS, INC.
A Division of BOOK SALES, INC.
276 Fifth Avenue Suite 206
New York, New York 10001, USA

Reprinted in 2011 twice

ISBN-13: 978-0-7858-2703-0
ISBN-10: 0-7858-2703-X

QUMCMINI

This book is produced by
Cartographica Ltd
6 Blundell Street
London N7 9BH

Design & Cartography:
Red Lion Mapping

Printed in Singapore by
Star Standard Industries Pte Ltd.

The Historical Atlas of the Civil War

CHARTWELL
BOOKS, INC.

CONTENTS

INTRODUCTION
10—15

ORIGINS OF THE CIVIL WAR
16—21

EXPANDING TERRITORIES
22—25

SLAVERY AND EMANCIPATION 1775—1860
26—29

THE MISSOURI COMPROMISE
30—35

THE GADSDEN PURCHASE, JUNE 24, 1853
36—37

POPULATION GROWTH AND IMMIGRATION 1783—1860
38—41

AGRICULTURE, INDUSTRY, AND RAILROADS
42—49

TWO PRESIDENTS: THEIR SIMILARITIES AND DIFFERENCES
50—53

THE DRIFT INTO WAR: FORT SUMTER, 1861
54—59

ENLISTMENT AND CONSCRIPTION
60—63

AFRICAN AMERICAN SOLDIERS
64—67

THE OPENING CAMPAIGNS, 1861—62
68—73

BLOCKADING THE SOUTHERN SEAPORTS, APRIL 19, 1861
74—77

THE FIRST BATTLE OF BULL RUN, JULY 21, 1861
78—83

THE BATTLE OF WILSON'S CREEK, AUGUST 10, 1861
84—87

LINES OF COMMUNICATION
88—91

THE STRATEGIES OF WAR
92—95

THE FALL OF NEW ORLEANS, 1862
96—97

THE OPPOSING ARMIES
98—101

NEW MEXICO CAMPAIGN
102—105

KENTUCKY DURING THE CIVIL WAR
106—109

NORTHWESTERN ARKANSAS
110—113

FORTS HENRY AND DONELSON
114—119

THE NORTH CAROLINA CAMPAIGN
120—121

CORINTH AND ISLAND NO.10
122—125

THE HAMPTON ROADS, MARCH 8—9, 1862
126—129

SHENANDOAH, JACKSON'S VALLEY: PHASE I
130—133

THE PENINSULA CAMPAIGN
134—139

THE BATTLE OF SHILOH
140—145

LOWER MISSISSIPPI VALLEY, APRIL — JULY, 1862
146—149

JACKSON'S VALLEY, PHASE II
150—155

LIFE AT THE FRONT
156—159

SEVEN DAYS' BATTLES
160—163

CONFEDERATE INVASION OF KENTUCKY
164—169

SECOND BATTLE OF BULL RUN
170—171

ANTIETAM
172—179

EMANCIPATION PROCLAMATION
180—181

FREDERICKSBURG
182—183

BATTLE OF STONE'S RIVER
184—187

THE FIRST VICKSBURG CAMPAIGN
188—191

WASHINGTON AT WAR
192—197

WARFARE WITH THE INDIANS
198—203

The Campaigns of 1863
204—205

Vicksburg and Port Hudson
206—215

Charleston
216-217

Chancellorsville, and the Death of "Stonewall" Jackson
218—221

The Battle of Gettysburg, July 1—3, 1863
222—229

Morgan and Quantrill
230—231

The Knoxville Campaign, August 15 — December 4, 1863
232—235

Operations in Virginia, October 9 — November 26, 1863
236—237

Chickamauga and Chattanooga
238—245

The Campaigns of 1864
246—249

Meridian and Olustee
250—255

The Red River Campaign, March 10 — May 22, 1864
256—259

Forrest's Operations in Mississippi and Tennessee
260—263

State of Arkansas, March 29 – May 3, 1864
264—265

Sherman's Atlanta, Phase I
266—269

The Wilderness
270—273

Sheridan's Raids
274—277

Drewry's Bluff
278—279

Spotsylvania Phase I and II
280—283

North Anna
284—285

Cold Harbor
286—287

The Advance, Assaults and Siege of Petersburg
288—295

Atlanta
296—299

The Battle of Mobile Bay
300—301

Missouri
302—303

Shenandoah Valley, 1864
304—307

Hood's Tennessee Campaign
308—311

Siege of Richmond
312—315

Sherman's March from Atlanta to the Sea
316—321

The Battle of Nashville
322—325

Prisoners of War
326—329

The Campaigns of 1865
330—333

Texas and New Mexico
334—335

Fort Fisher
336—337

Sherman's Carolinas Campaign
338—343

The Fall of Petersburg and Richmond
344—347

Military Discipline
348—349

Firepower of the Armies
350—353

Guerrilla Troops
354—357

The War at Sea
358—365

Medical Facilities
366—367

Aftermath of War and Reconstruction
368—377

The Cost of War
378—379

Epilogue
380—383

FURTHER READING
384

INDEX
385—399

ACKNOWLEDGEMENTS
400

MAP LIST

Major Battle Sites 12/13
Major Battle Sites 15
Presidential Election, 1860 19
The Secession Vote, 1860-61 21
Seceding States 21
Go West! 23
Territorial Expansion 24
Cotton Belt, 1801—60 27
Number of Slaves per Slaveholder, per County, 1860 27
Missouri Compromise, 1820 31
Compromise of 1850 32/33
Kansas-Nebraska Act, 1854 35
Urban Population by State, 1800 and 1860 39
European Immigration to the United States, 1841-1860 40
Three Largest Sources in Each Top Ten U.S. State by Number of Foreign-born 41
Railroads and Canals, 1860 43
Farmland by Value, 1860 44/45
Agriculture, Raw Material, and Industry, 1860 47
Charleston Harbor, December 1860 - April 1861 55
Slave "Contraband" Camps, 1861-63 65
Black Soldiers in the Union Army 66
Major African American Battle Sites in the Civil War 67
The Campaigns of 1861-62 69
Philippi Races, June 3, 1861 71
Northern Virginia, June 10 - October 12, 1861 72
Western Virginia, 1861 73
South Atlantic Coast, August 27 - November 7, 1861 75
Port Royal, November 7, 1861 77
Bull Run (First Manassas), July 21, 1861 80/81
Battle of Wilson's Creek, August 10, 1861 85
Clashes in Missouri, July 5 - November 7 87
Strategic Railroads and the Civil War 89
Mobile Bay to New Orleans 97
Enlistment Rate of Union Soldiers, by State, 1861-65 99
Valverde, February 21 103
Glorieta Pass, March 26-28, 1862 103
Pigeon's Ranch, March 28, 1862 104
New Mexico Campaign, July 1861 - July 1862 105
Eastern Kentucky and Tennessee, January 10 - June 18, 1862 107
Battle of Middle Creek, August 10 108
Operations in Missouri and Arkansas 112
Battle of Pea Ridge, March 7—8, 1862 112
Battle of Prairie Grove, December 7—8, 1862 113
Fort Henry and Fort Donelson Campaign, February 4-14, 1862 116/17
North Carolina Campaign, February 8 - April 25 121
Military and Naval Movements, March - June 123
Defences of Corinth, April 8 - May 30 124
Hampton Roads, March 8-9, 1862 127

Jackson's Shenandoah Valley Campaign:Phase I, March 23 - May 25 133
McClellan's Peninsula Campaign, March - June 136
Yorktown to Williamsburg, April 5 - May 4 137
Shiloh Campaign, April 6, 1862 141
Lower Mississippi Valley, April - July, 1862 147
Battle of Baton Rouge, August 5, 1862 148
Jackson's Shenandoah Valley Campaign: Phase II, May 30 - June 9 154
Battle of Port Republic, June 9 155
Skirmish at Port Republic, June 8 155
Seven Days' Battles, June 25-28 162
Seven Days' Battles, June 29 - July 1 63
Forrest's Raids in Middle Tennessee, July 9—27 165
Morgan's Raids in Kentucky, July 4-22 166
Confederate Invasion of Kentucky, August 14 - October 8 169
Second Battle of Manassas (Bull Run) Campaign, August 8-30 171
Antietam Campaign, September 4-20 173
Sedgwick's Attack, September 17, 1862 174
Antietam, September 17, 1862 175
Battle of Fredericksburg, December 11-13 183
Murfreesboro (Stone's River), December 31 - January 2 187
Chickasaw Bayou, December 29, 1862 188
Arkansas Post, January 11 190
Grant's First Vicksburg Campaign 191
Defenses of Washington 195
Indian Territories, 1861—65 199
Indian Wars in the West, 1850—1900 202
The Campaigns of 1863 205
Milliken's Bend to Port Gibson, January 30 - May 1 208
Grant's Second Vicksburg Campaign, May 2—17 210/211
Siege and Capture of Vicksburg, May 18 - July 4, 1863 213
Port Hudson Campaign, May 8 - July 9 215
Charleston Campaign, April 7 - September 24 217
Chancellorsville Campaign, April 27 - May 4 219
Chancellorsville, May 2—5 220
Salem Church, May 4 221
Gettysburg, July 1, 1863 223
Gettysburg, July 2, 1863 225
Gettysburg, July 3, 1863 227
Quantrill's Raid, August 19-23 231
Knoxville Campaign, August 15 - December 4 234/235
Operations in Virginia, October 9 November 26 237
Chickamauga Campaign, September 10-18 239
Chickamauga, September 19-20 240
The Campaigns of 1864 247
The Confederate Sunset, 1864-65 249
Sherman's Occupation of Meridian, February 24-26 252
Operations in Mississippi, February to March 253
Battle of Olustee, February 20 255
The Red River Campaign, March 20 - May 22 256/257
Forrest's Operations in Mississippi and Tennessee, 10 March - 4 November, 1864 261
Attack on Johnsville, November 4 262
Steele's Arkansas Campaign, March 1 - May 3 265
Atlanta Campaign Phase I, May 7—20 267
Advance on Atlanta, May 21 - July 9, 1864 268
Cassville, May 18—19 269
Dallas, May 28 269
Pickett's Mill, May 27 269
Kennesaw Mountain, June 27 269
The Wilderness, May 5 271
The Wilderness, May 6 273
Sheridan's Raid, May 9—24 275
Sheridan's Raid, June 7—28 277
Battle of Drewry's Bluff, May 16 279
Spotsylvania, May 8—12 281
Spotsylvania, May 13—19 282—283
Cold Harbor, June 3 287
Assault on Petersburg 292—293
Advance to Petersburg 294
Siege of Petersburg 295
Siege of Atlanta, from July 29 299
Mobile Bay, August 3-5, 1864 301
Price's Raid in Missouri, September - October 303
Operations in the Shenandoah Valley, May - June 305
Sheridan and Early in the Shenandoah valley 307
Hood's Tennessee Campaign 310/311
Operations Against Richmond 313
Attack on Fort Harrison 315
Battle at Chaffin's Bluff, September 29 315
Battle of Darbytown Road 315
Sherman's March from Atlanta, November 14 - December 21 318/319
Defenses of Savannah, December 10—13 321
Battle of Nashville, December 15—16, 1864 323
The Campaigns of 1865 331
Texas and Part of New Mexico 334/335
Fort Fisher 337
Sherman in the Carolinas, January - May 339
Averasboro, March 16 340
Battle of Bentonville, March 19—21 342/343
Fall of Petersburg and Richmond, march 25 - April 2 345
Confederate Trade, 1862-65 359
Activities of the U.S. Sanitary Commission 367
Reestablishment of Conservative Governments, 1869-77 370
Election of the 42nd Congress, 1870 371
Homesteading, 1863-1950 372/373
David C. Barrow's Syll's Fork Plantation, Oglethorpe County, Georgia, 1860 374

KEY TO MAPS

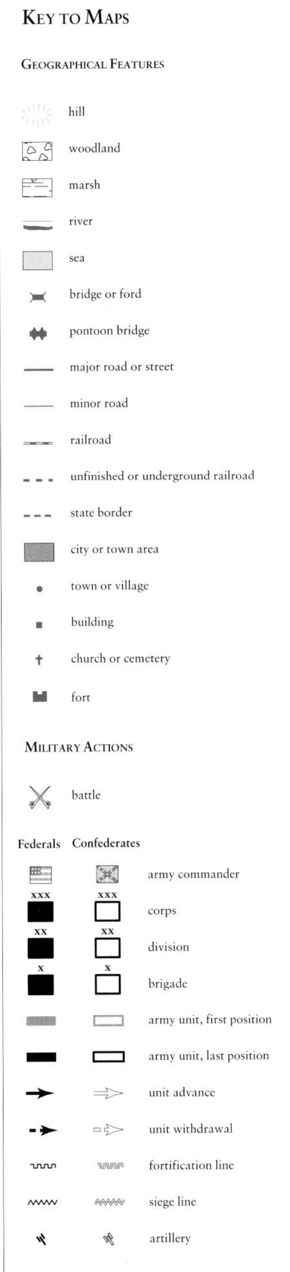
KEY TO MAPS
GEOGRAPHICAL FEATURES
hill
woodland
marsh
river
sea
bridge or ford
pontoon bridge
major road or street
minor road
railroad
unfinished or underground railroad
state border
city or town area
town or village
building
church or cemetery
fort
MILITARY ACTIONS
battle
Federals
Confederates
army commander
XXX
corps
XX
division
X
brigade
army unit, first position
army unit, last position
unit advance
unit withdrawal
fortification line
siege line
artillery

INTRODUCTION

THE AMERICAN CIVIL WAR WAS THE DEFINING MOMENT IN THE HISTORY OF THE UNITED STATES. MANY NATIONS, HAVING WON BY FORCE OF ARMS THEIR FREEDOM FROM A COLONIAL POWER, HAVE SUBSEQUENTLY BEEN SPLIT BY INTERNAL RIVALRIES, TORN APART IN INTERNECINE CONFLICT. YET NO OTHER NATION HAS CAUSED ITSELF MORE SUFFERING AND ULTIMATELY PRESERVED ITS UNITY; NONE HAS SIMILARLY BEEN STRENGTHENED BY ITS ORDEAL WHILE PERPETUATING MANY OF THE DIFFERENCES THAT PITCHED IT INTO CRISIS.

Opposite page: A living history event held in modern Maryland, commemorating one of the many battles of the Civil War. In this particular scene, Confederate infantry attacks a Union battle line.

At the root of the conflict was a dispute over slavery—23 Northern states opposed it, while the 11 in the South of the Union believed that forced labor was essential to their economic wellbeing and, in order to preserve it, they tried to form a breakaway nation known as the Confederate States of America. Yet it would be an oversimplification to suggest that one faction was enlightened and liberal, while the other was benighted and reactionary—at the time, few people on either side believed that the enslaved African Americans should have the same status as white people. The war may ultimately have contributed to the enhancement of the rights of man, regardless of race, color, creed, and ethnicity, but that was not what it was primarily about. The Civil War—also known as the "War Between Brothers"—was a conflict of firsts.

The Civil War was the first to make extensive use of trench warfare (a strategy subsequently developed to an infernal low point in World War I), the first in which ironclad warships, submarines, machine guns, and aerial reconnaissance were employed, the first whose course was influenced by railroads, and the first to be covered in detail by newspapers and recorded photographically. Never before had men been able to kill each other from a distance, without physical confrontation—for that reason, it is sometimes known as the first technological war.

Right: This map shows the major battle sites of the Civil War. Note the large number of key engagements that were fought in the heart of the South, deep in Confederate territory, particularly along the Mississippi River and around Atlanta, Georgia.

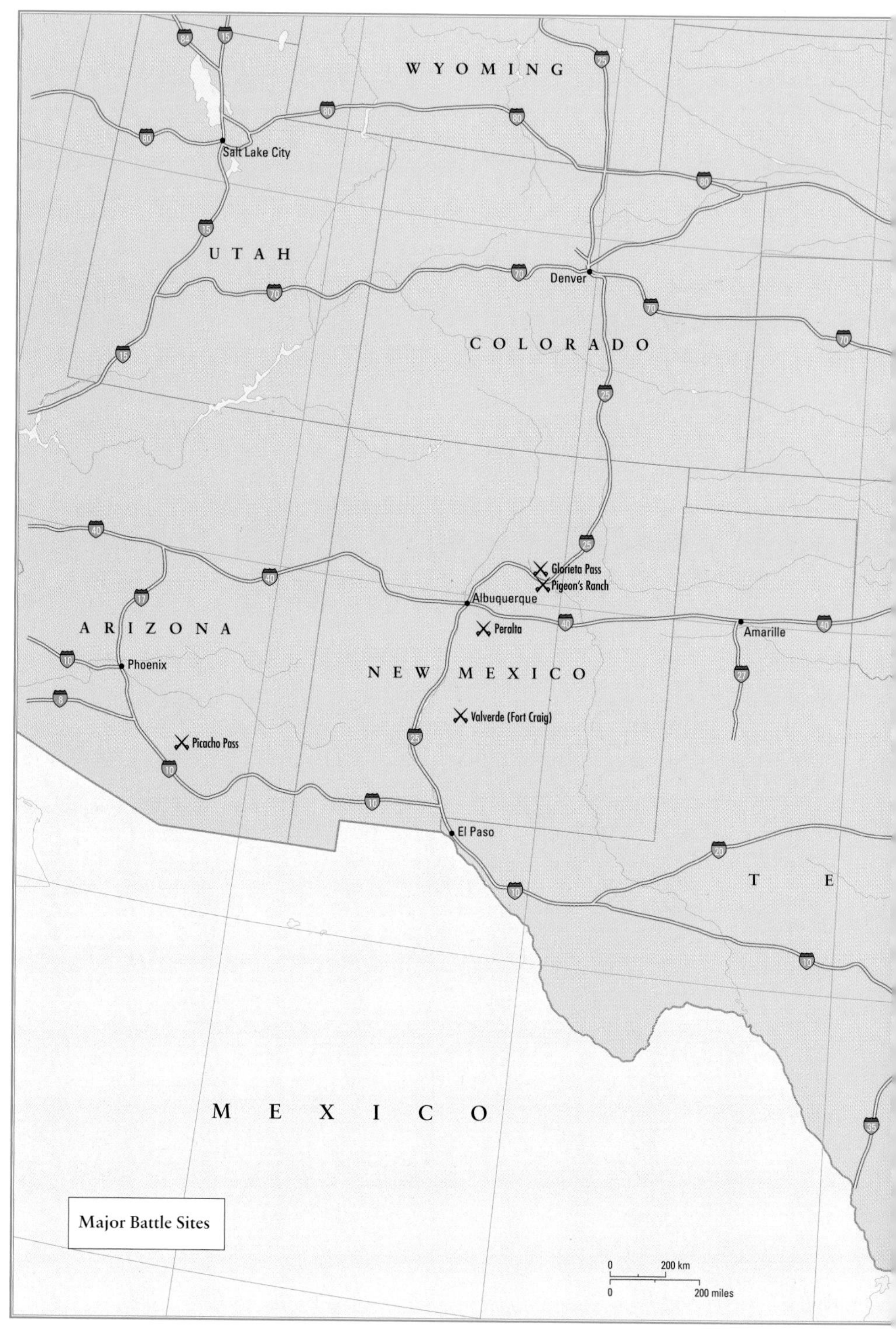

IOWA
MICHIGAN
OHIO
INDIANA
ILLINOIS
MISSOURI
KENTUCKY
WEST VIRGINIA
VIRGINIA
NORTH CAROLINA
SOUTH CAROLINA
TENNESSEE
ARKANSAS
MISSISSIPPI
ALABAMA
GEORGIA
LOUISIANA
FLORIDA
PA
NY
Gulf of Mexico
Milwaukee
Chicago
Detroit
Cleveland
Pittsburg
Columbus
Indianapolis
Cincinnati
Bloomington
St. Louis
Louisville
Lexington
Nashville
Memphis
Little Rock
Chattanooga
Birmingham
Atlanta
Macon
Montgomery
Jackson
New Orleans
Houston
Dallas
Tulsa
Kansas City
Greensboro
Charlotte
Columbia
Jacksonville
Orlando
Independence
Lexington
Marshall
Centralia Massacre
Boonville
Westport
Blackwater
Marais des Cygnes
Mine Creek (Little Osage River)
Pilot Knob (Fort Davidson)
Baxter Spring Massacre
Carthage
Wilson's Creek
Newtonia
Cabin Creek
Chustenahlak
Round Mountain
Pea Ridge (Elkhorn Tavern)
Old Fort Wayne (Beatties Prairie)
Prairie Grove
Honey Springs
Belmont
New Madrid
Island No.10
Fort Henry
Fort Donelson
Johnsonville
Parker's Crossroads
Plum Point Bend
Fort Pillow
Shiloh
Corinth
Iuka
Booneville
Brices Crossroads
Tupelo
Okolona
Helena
St. Charles
Jenkin's Ferry
Pine Bluff
Arkansas Post
Marks Mills
Poison Spring
Ft. Pemberton
Chickasaw Bayou
Big Black River Bridge
Champion Hill
Vicksburg
Grand Gulf
Raymond
Port Gibson
Mansfield (Sabine Crossing)
Pleasant Hill
Blair's Landing
Monett's Ferry (Cane River Crossing)
Henderson's Hill
Fort De Russy
Yellow Bayou
Port Hudson
Baton Rouge
Bayou Carencro
Irish Bend
Sabine Pass
Galveston
Fort Esperanza
Palmito Ranch
Ship Island
Fort St. Philip and Fort Jackson
Fort Blakely
Spanish Port
Mobile Bay
Ebenezer Church
Selma
Columbus
Huntsville
Hartsville
Lebanon
La Vergne
Franklin
Thompson's Station
Spring Hill
Stone's River (Murfreesboro)
Hoover's and Liberty Gaps
Missionary Ridge
Lookout Mtn.
Orchard Knob
Chickamauga
Dalton
Resaca
Cassville
Pickett's Mill
New Hope Church
Dallas
Ezra Church
Kennesaw Mountain
Peachtree Creek
Jonesboro
Lovejoy's Station
Griswoldville
Munfordville
Perryville (Chaplin Hills)
Logan's Crossroads (Mill Spring)
Cynthiana
Mount Sterling
Richmond
Prestonburg
Knoxville
Rogersville
Blue Springs
Blountsville
Telford's Station
Salineville
Philippi
Corrick's Ford
New Market
Camp Alleghany
Cheat Mtn.
McDowell
Charleston
Carnifex Ferry
Gauley Bridge
Droop Mtn.
Waynesboro
Princeton
Dublin
Wytheville
Marion
Salisbury
Fort Sumter
Battery Wagner
Secessionville
Fort Beauregard
Honey Hill
Fort Walker
Fort Pulaski
Fort McAllister ("Montauk" and "Nashville")
Jacksonville
Olustee
Fort Marion

Opposite page: This detailed map shows the locations of the major Civil War confrontations in the state of Virginia. They include the First and Second Bull Runs, both Confederate victories. Also marked is the site of the Battle of Gettysburg, in neighboring Pennsylvania, a pivotal Union victory in 1863.

Of the thousands of contemporary chroniclers and later historians who have written about the Civil War, few have reached the same conclusion about its significance and true purpose. That may be confusing for modern students, but it is also a fair reflection of the complexity of the conflict. The one thing the Civil War was not—and it is easy to overlook this in hindsight—was a foregone conclusion. The Southern cause was not a romantic folly that was doomed to failure from the outset—the seceding states had a captive labor force and the prospect of foreign assistance, neither of which was available to the North. They were, in addition, fighting mainly on home territory and their generals, at least at the start of the war, were better regarded than their northern counterparts. The North, however, had a stronger industrial base and a bigger population. Either side could have won the war, and the course of the conflict was determined by human inspiration, willpower, genius, and error rather than by fate. However, the longer the war went on, the less likely it became that the seceding states would triumph.

The American Civil War lasted for four years, from April 1861 to April 1865. In terms of casualties, it was the most damaging conflict in U.S. history—from a total U.S. population of around 31 million in 1860 (a figure that includes nearly four million slaves), more than 630,000 people were killed. Almost half a million others were wounded. The devastation of land and property was immense—the worst affected areas took more than a generation to recover.

At the end of the Civil War, the United States was reunited and the slaves were emancipated. Yet, as one Northern newspaper editor observed, "Cannon conquer but they do not necessarily convert." The victors needed to reincorporate the vanquished into the fabric of the nation, but their disdain for the rebels and the losers' bitterness delayed the process for many years. The Civil War marked one of the most permanent changes in American history, transforming the country economically, politically, and socially. It increased northern prosperity, but totally destroyed the South's entire society and consequently its economy. Reconstruction—the name given to the Federal attempts to solve the economic, political, and social problems arising from the readmission to the Union of the states that had seceded at the start of the war—officially lasted until 1877. Despite the Emancipation Proclamation and the Thirteenth amendment ratified by Abraham Lincoln in 1865, many blacks would continue to experience limited freedom and prejudice. In the view of many, the problems that had caused the war remained unresolved for nearly a century, until the civil rights' movement of the 1960s. It would take many years for the nation to recover from the repercussions of a four-year war.

This book provides a detailed account of the course of the Civil War, illustrated with photographs and high-grade maps that clearly show the movements of armies and navies as well as the demography of the period. It also signposts the location of some of the monuments and reenactment sites that help to keep alive the memory of the sacrifice and suffering of a nation that almost tore itself apart through war. The Civil War left America with a haunting memory, apparent in the ranked rows of white headstones that line many wartime cemeteries, but it is its recovery from this period that should be revered. The book provides an overview on how America pulled itself back from this brink of destruction to reform with renewed cohesion and resolve, and to create the nation it is today.

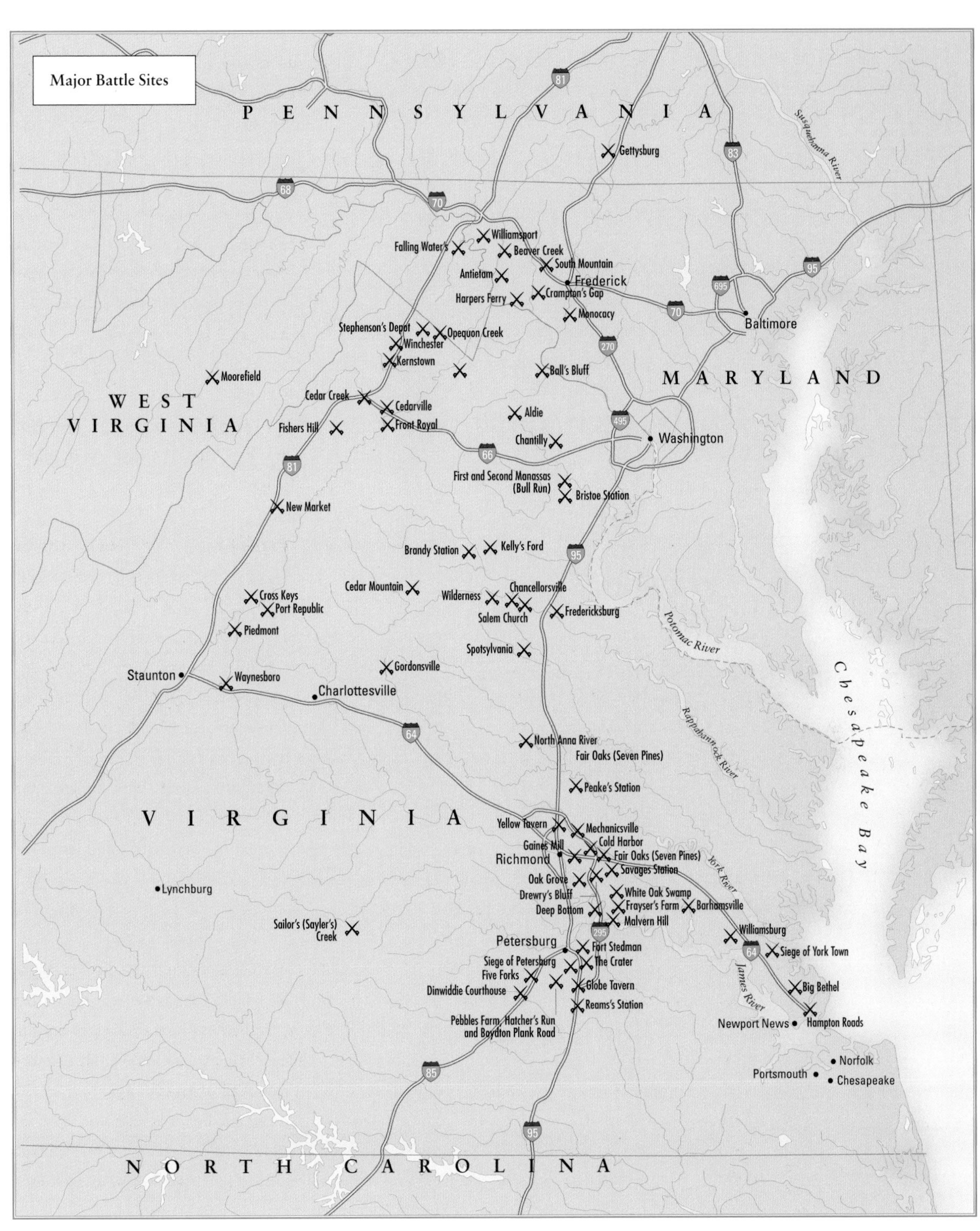
Major Battle Sites
PENNSYLVANIA
MARYLAND
WEST VIRGINIA
VIRGINIA
NORTH CAROLINA
Gettysburg
Williamsport
Falling Waters
Beaver Creek
South Mountain
Antietam
Frederick
Harpers Ferry
Crampton's Gap
Monocacy
Baltimore
Stephenson's Depot
Opequon Creek
Winchester
Kernstown
Ball's Bluff
Moorefield
Cedar Creek
Cedarville
Front Royal
Fishers Hill
Aldie
Chantilly
Washington
First and Second Manassas (Bull Run)
Bristoe Station
New Market
Brandy Station
Kelly's Ford
Cedar Mountain
Cross Keys
Port Republic
Wilderness
Chancellorsville
Salem Church
Fredericksburg
Piedmont
Spotsylvania
Gordonsville
Staunton
Waynesboro
Charlottesville
North Anna River
Fair Oaks (Seven Pines)
Peake's Station
Yellow Tavern
Mechanicsville
Gaines Mill
Cold Harbor
Richmond
Fair Oaks (Seven Pines)
Savages Station
Oak Grove
White Oak Swamp
Drewry's Bluff
Frayser's Farm
Barhamsville
Deep Bottom
Malvern Hill
Lynchburg
Sailor's (Sayler's) Creek
Williamsburg
Petersburg
Fort Stedman
Siege of York Town
Siege of Petersburg
The Crater
Five Forks
Globe Tavern
Dinwiddie Courthouse
Big Bethel
Reams's Station
Pebbles Farm, Hatcher's Run and Boydton Plank Road
Newport News
Hampton Roads
Norfolk
Portsmouth
Chesapeake
Susquehanna River
Potomac River
Rappahannock River
York River
James River
Chesapeake Bay
81
83
68
70
95
695
270
495
66
64
295
85

ORIGINS OF THE CIVIL WAR

THE ROOTS OF THE CIVIL WAR (1861–1865) CAN BE TRACED BACK TO THE AMERICAN REVOLUTION (1775–1783), IN WHICH THIRTEEN OF BRITAIN'S NORTH AMERICAN COLONIES WON THEIR FREEDOM AND ESTABLISHED THE UNITED STATES AS AN INDEPENDENT NATION.

Above: Fighting during Shays's Rebellion, an uprising in 1786–87 led by American officer Daniel Shays to protest against the harsh punishments suffered by debtors during the post-Revolutionary economic recession.

The Americans were anxious to banish forever subjugation of the kind they had endured under British rule, so they tried to ensure that none of the component states of their new nation could ever become more powerful than any other. The idea that every state should retain its sovereignty within the United States was enshrined in the Articles of Confederation, work on which began in 1776. The document was completed and adopted by the Congress in the following year, and fully ratified by all the states on March 1, 1781.

The Articles of Confederation were idealistic, and idealism is often hard to reconcile with political necessity. The main flaw in the document was that it gave the U.S. Congress the right to collect taxes and requisition troops from the states, but no power to enforce such demands. Meanwhile, the states guarded their independence jealously, and objected to any move that they thought might restrict their freedom.

In 1786, there was an armed uprising in Massachusetts in which Daniel Shays led a force of more than 1,200 to oppose an increase in federal taxes. Shays's Rebellion was put down quite easily, but it demonstrated that the Articles of Confederation were unworkable. They were superseded the following year by the U.S. Constitution. The Constitution strengthened the national government but

Left: A series of postcards showing the tragic progress of a black slave from work on a Southern plantation to his death in battle on the side of the Union during the Civil War.

did not alleviate the tension between states' rights and federal rights. On the contrary, it served to greatly exacerbate them.

The 55 state delegates to the Constitutional Convention, held in Philadelphia, Pennsylvania, in the summer of 1787, disagreed over several questions, one of the most contentious of which was slavery. Some delegates wanted to abolish it or—failing that—to restrict the number of permitted slaves to a proportion of each state's free population.

Opposition to slavery was concentrated in the Northern states. Rhode Island had abolished slavery in 1774; it had been followed three years later by Vermont, and then by Pennsylvania (1780), Massachusetts (1781), New Hampshire (1783), and Connecticut (1784).

Above: United States Senator Stephen A. Douglas *(top)* who was responsible for the Fugitive State Law of 1850, as well as a number of other compromise measures between the slave states and the free states; and two of the vote-splitting 1860 Presidential candidates, John C. Breckinridge *(middle)* and John Bell *(bottom)*.

Delegates from the South—the economy of which was dependent on the use of forced labor—threatened to walk out of the convention if any such restrictions were imposed on them. Cotton was the backbone of the Southern economy, which gave rise to the phrase "King Cotton." The Southern states relied on slaves as a workforce for cotton production, and after the invention of the cotton gin in 1793, cotton became the dominant cash crop in the agricultural economy of the South, surpassing tobacco. It soon comprised half of the total U.S. exports.

Even at this early stage of U.S. history it can be seen that there was a potentially irreconcilable difference between two large groups. The Union was preserved by the implementation of what became known as the Great Compromise, one of the terms of which was that the Congress should allow the importation of slaves to continue for 21 years. At the end of that period, in 1808, the Congress carried out its original intention and banned the human traffic from abroad but, within the Southern states, the buying and selling of slaves continued.

Tensions between the two halves of the United States increased in the 19th century as the North became industrialized and needed a larger work force to operate its new machinery. Northern politicians called for the abolition of slavery, not simply on humanitarian grounds, but because they wanted to attract laborers from the South—which remained predominantly agricultural—to better-paid jobs in the new factories.

The North also wanted trade tariffs to reduce competition from foreign goods. The South protested such proposals because it relied heavily on imports. The Tariff of 1828 was labeled the Tariff of Abominations by its Southern detractors, who saw it as a means for Northern states to protect their own industry from competing prices of European products.

Northern opposition to slavery gathered momentum during the first half of the 19th century. New York abolished the practice in 1799 and New Jersey in 1804. Although the U.S. Congress tried to maintain a balance between slave states and free states, most of the important additions to the Union in the first half of the 19th century were free and starting to reap the financial benefits of the Industrial Revolution—Ohio (1803), Indiana (1816), Illinois (1818), Maine (1820), Michigan (1837), Wisconsin (1848), and California (1850). The slave states that joined in the same period—Louisiana (1812), Mississippi (1817), Alabama (1819), Arkansas (1836), and Florida (March 1845)—were less powerful, which partly explains the enthusiasm of the South's backing for the annexation of Texas, a vast and mighty slave state, in December of 1845.

The general trend of these developments greatly worried the South. By this time slavery had become so ingrained in its economy that to get rid of it entirely would necessarily result in a major economic problems. The South was also concerned with the growth of the Anti-slavery Society, which was formed in 1831 in New York by William Lloyd Garrison and Arthur Tappan. The famous freed slave Frederick Douglass was also a key leader of the society and regularly spoke at meetings. Douglass would later go on to write *Narrative of the Life of Frederick Douglass*, a memoir and treatise on abolition considered to be one of the abolitionist movement's most influential pieces of literature. By 1840, the Anti-slavery Society had a nationwide membership of more than 250,000. The South feared that it was increasingly being left behind and possibly even in danger of subjugation by the North.

In 1850, in an attempt to reach a compromise between slave and free states, the Congress passed the Fugitive State Law, which allowed anyone who was suspected of being a runaway slave to be arrested without warrant and turned over to his or her master. Since the ownership of slaves was established by sworn testimony alone, a market developed in which African Americans were sold to the highest bidder. Not all of them were slaves, however; many free blacks were kidnapped for profit. Abolitionists regarded the law as an outrage, and responded by setting up the Underground Railroad, a network of safe houses and sympathizers who helped to spirit runaways from slavery in the South to freedom in the North.

The ideological gulf that existed between the North and the South widened in 1854, when the U.S. Senate permitted Kansas and Nebraska, the two latest applicants for statehood, to decide for themselves whether to adopt or reject slavery. This led to controversy when the number of votes cast in the 1855 elections to the Kansas legislature was three times higher than the number of registered voters. Most of the extra 4,000 were slave owners from neighboring Missouri who had crossed the line to ensure that the new state adopted their own approach.

The following year, the Congress proposed that the people living in the Louisiana Purchase (Louisiana, Arkansas, Oklahoma, Kansas, Missouri, Nebraska, Iowa, the Dakotas, Montana, and parts of Minnesota, Colorado, and Wyoming) should be allowed to own slaves. One of the main opponents of this move was Illinois lawyer Abraham Lincoln, who argued that the territories must be kept free for "poor people to go and better their condition."

Below: Map showing the voting in the 1860 U.S. Presidential election. Note the divisions in the opposition to the Republicans that enabled the party to notch up its first President only four years after its formation.

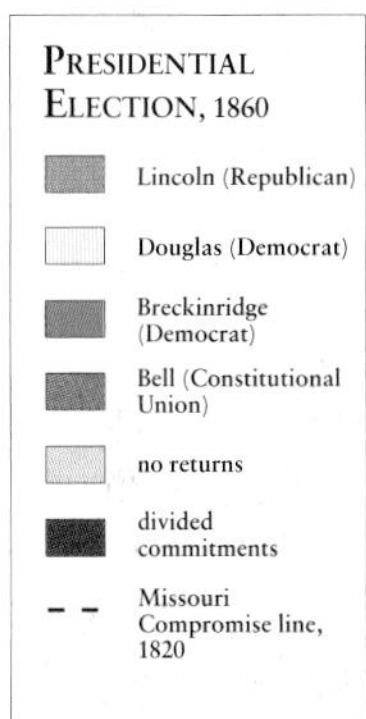

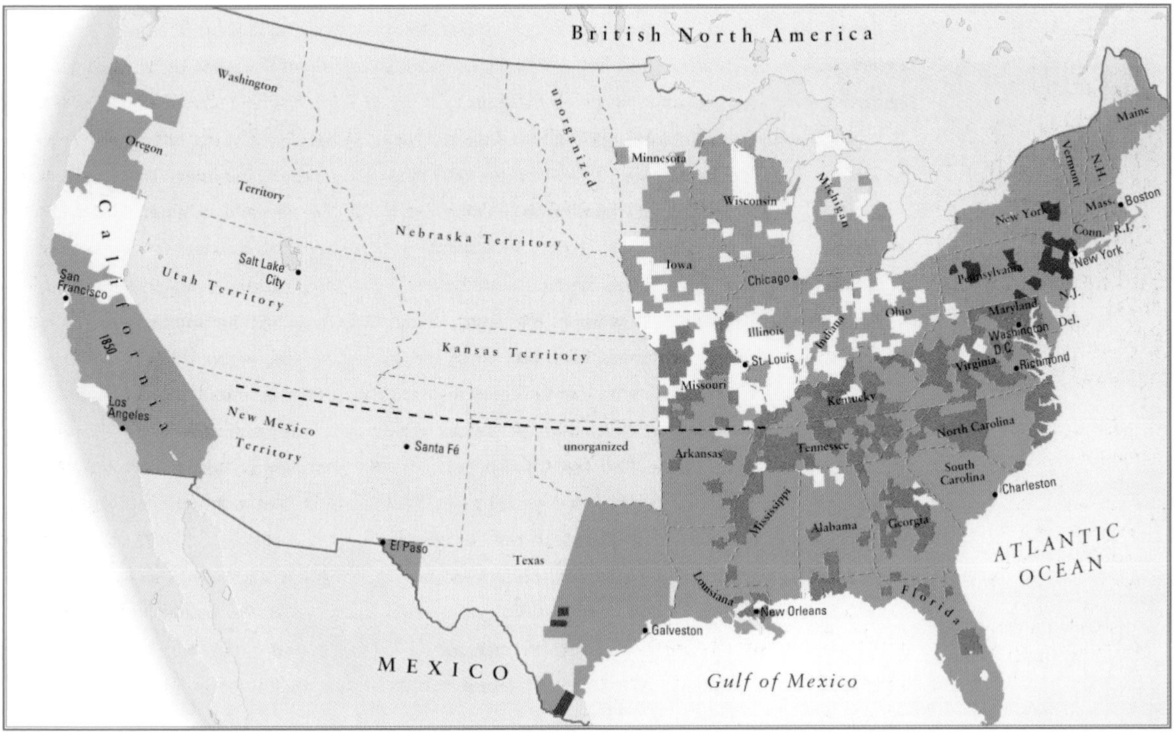

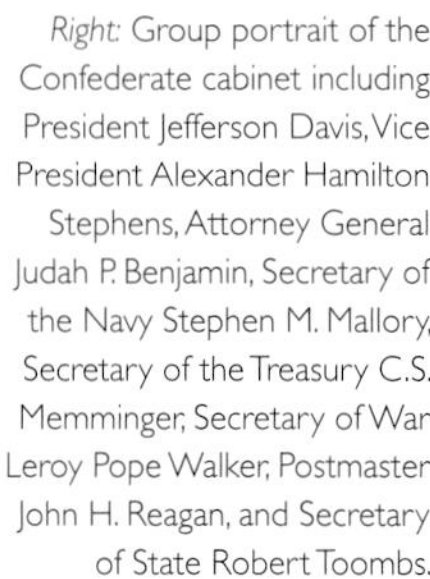

Right: Group portrait of the Confederate cabinet including President Jefferson Davis, Vice President Alexander Hamilton Stephens, Attorney General Judah P. Benjamin, Secretary of the Navy Stephen M. Mallory, Secretary of the Treasury C.S. Memminger, Secretary of War Leroy Pope Walker, Postmaster John H. Reagan, and Secretary of State Robert Toombs.

Opposite page: The United States did not divide neatly along the Mason–Dixon line. As these maps clearly demonstrate, some counties of the Confederacy never seceded at all.

Lincoln further alienated Southern opinion in 1858, when he declared in a speech that slavery was "a moral, a social, and a political wrong." When he was adopted as the Republican Party's presidential candidate for the 1860 election, crisis loomed. The South looked to the Democrats to defend its interests, but the party nominated Stephen A. Douglas, a Senator from Illinois who believed in compromise on the slavery issue. The Southern wing of the party broke away and fell behind two competing candidates: John C. Breckinridge of Kentucky and John Bell of Tennessee.

With opposition to the Republicans hopelessly divided, Lincoln won a major victory, carrying 18 free states. Of the slave states, 13 went to Breckinridge, three to Bell, and one to Douglas. Lincoln selected a strong cabinet that included all his major rivals for the Republican nomination: Seward as Secretary of State, Salmon P. Chase as Secretary of Treasury, and Edward Bates as Attorney General. Lincoln's victory in this election would change the racial future of the United States.

As Lincoln celebrated his victory, the South decided that it had no future in the United States. The new U.S. administration was only three months old when the slave states set up a new nation of their own, the Confederate States of America under President Jefferson Davis. The Union resisted this attempt at secession and the nation subsided into four years of bloody Civil War. The cost of the conflict was astonishing, and in some ways the United States still struggles to come to terms with its impact and consequences—for many, the purpose and meaning of the war remain puzzling, even with the benefit of hindsight. In human terms, of over 1.5 million soldiers in the Federal (Northern) armies, nearly 360,000 were killed and over 275,000 wounded. Of around 800,000 men in the Confederate forces, 258,000 died and 225,000 were wounded. The damage caused to the economy and to the social cohesion of the United States could still be detected over a century after the South had been forced back into the fold.

VIRGINIA
NORTH CAROLINA
TENNESSEE
SOUTH CAROLINA
ARKANSAS
GEORGIA
MISSISSIPPI
ALABAMA
TEXAS
LOUISIANA
FLORIDA
The Secession Vote, 1860–61
for Secession
against Secession
divided
no return
N
0 100 km
0 100 miles

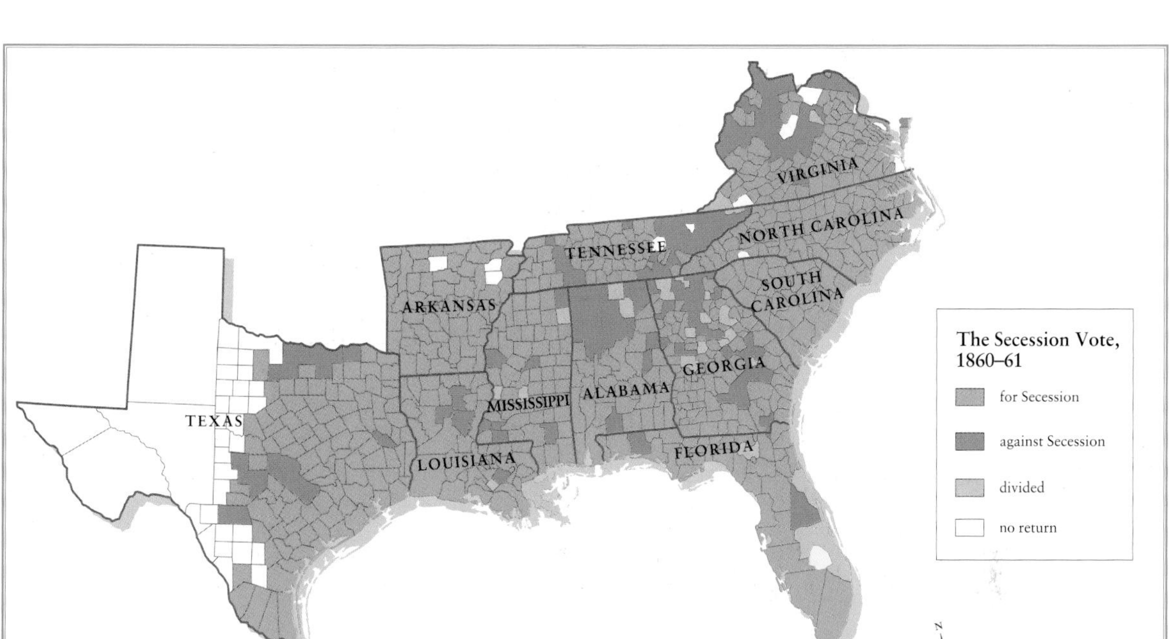

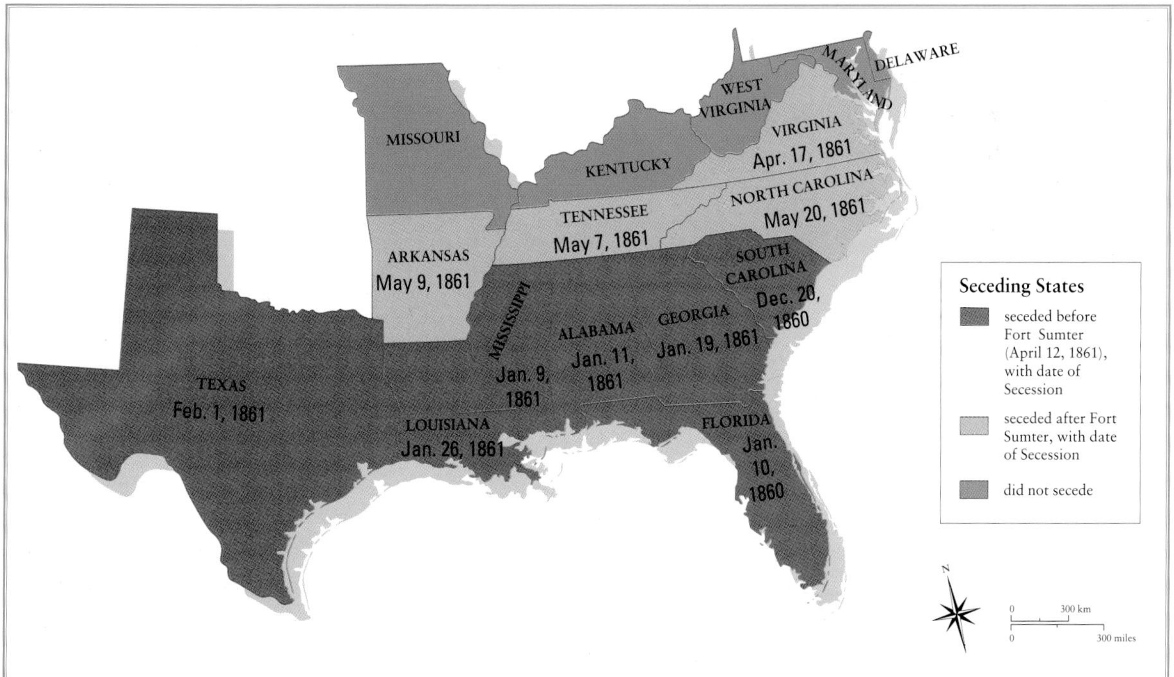

DELAWARE
MARYLAND
WEST VIRGINIA
MISSOURI
VIRGINIA
Apr. 17, 1861
KENTUCKY
NORTH CAROLINA
May 20, 1861
TENNESSEE
May 7, 1861
ARKANSAS
May 9, 1861
SOUTH CAROLINA
Dec. 20, 1860
MISSISSIPPI
Jan. 9, 1861
ALABAMA
Jan. 11, 1861
GEORGIA
Jan. 19, 1861
TEXAS
Feb. 1, 1861
LOUISIANA
Jan. 26, 1861
FLORIDA
Jan. 10, 1860
Seceding States
seceded before Fort Sumter (April 12, 1861), with date of Secession
seceded after Fort Sumter, with date of Secession
did not secede
N
0 300 km
0 300 miles

EXPANDING TERRITORIES

IN 1803, THE UNITED STATES ALMOST DOUBLED ITS AREA BY BUYING FROM FRANCE THE WESTERN HALF OF THE MISSISSIPPI RIVER BASIN. AFTER THIS IMMENSE LEAP WESTWARD, AMERICANS BEGAN LAYING CLAIM TO LANDS RIGHT UP TO THE BANKS OF THE RIO GRANDE AND BECAME PREOCCUPIED WITH EXTENDING THEIR TERRITORY ALL THE WAY TO THE PACIFIC OCEAN.

Above: Based on an 1872 oil painting by John Gast, this lithograph, entitled American Progress, depicts an allegorical female figure leading pioneers and railroads into the West.

Opposite page: This map shows the sites of the principal 19th-century battlefields in the territorial struggle between Native Americans and European settlers, and highlights the main established trails followed by pioneers, in addition to the spread of the railroads across the vast country.

The 828,000 square miles (2,144,000 sq km) acquired from France by the United States in the Louisiana Purchase cost less than three cents per acre, and, given the enormous potential of the area, ranks as one of the greatest bargains of all time.

Settlers had been traveling across the North American continent since the explorers Lewis and Clark first blazed their trails between 1804 and 1806, but 1843 saw the start of the largest peacetime migration in history, as 1,000 pioneers with more than 100 wagons and 5,000 head of livestock assembled at Independence, Missouri, in the hope of making a better life out West. Hot on their heels came the railroads, which also began to spread inexorably westward.

In 1845, journalist John L. O'Sullivan described the American ambition as "our manifest destiny to overspread the continent allotted by Providence." The phrase "manifest destiny" was popularized by politicians and became the term most commonly used to describe and excuse the whole period of antebellum territorial expansion, which would see pioneers and U.S. forces fight numerous battles against Indian tribes living in these new territories.

Another significant development in the United States' territorial expansion occurred more than two decades earlier, in 1821, when Mexico gained independence from Spain. The new republic was split by internal rivalries, and its central government in the capital, Mexico City, exercised little

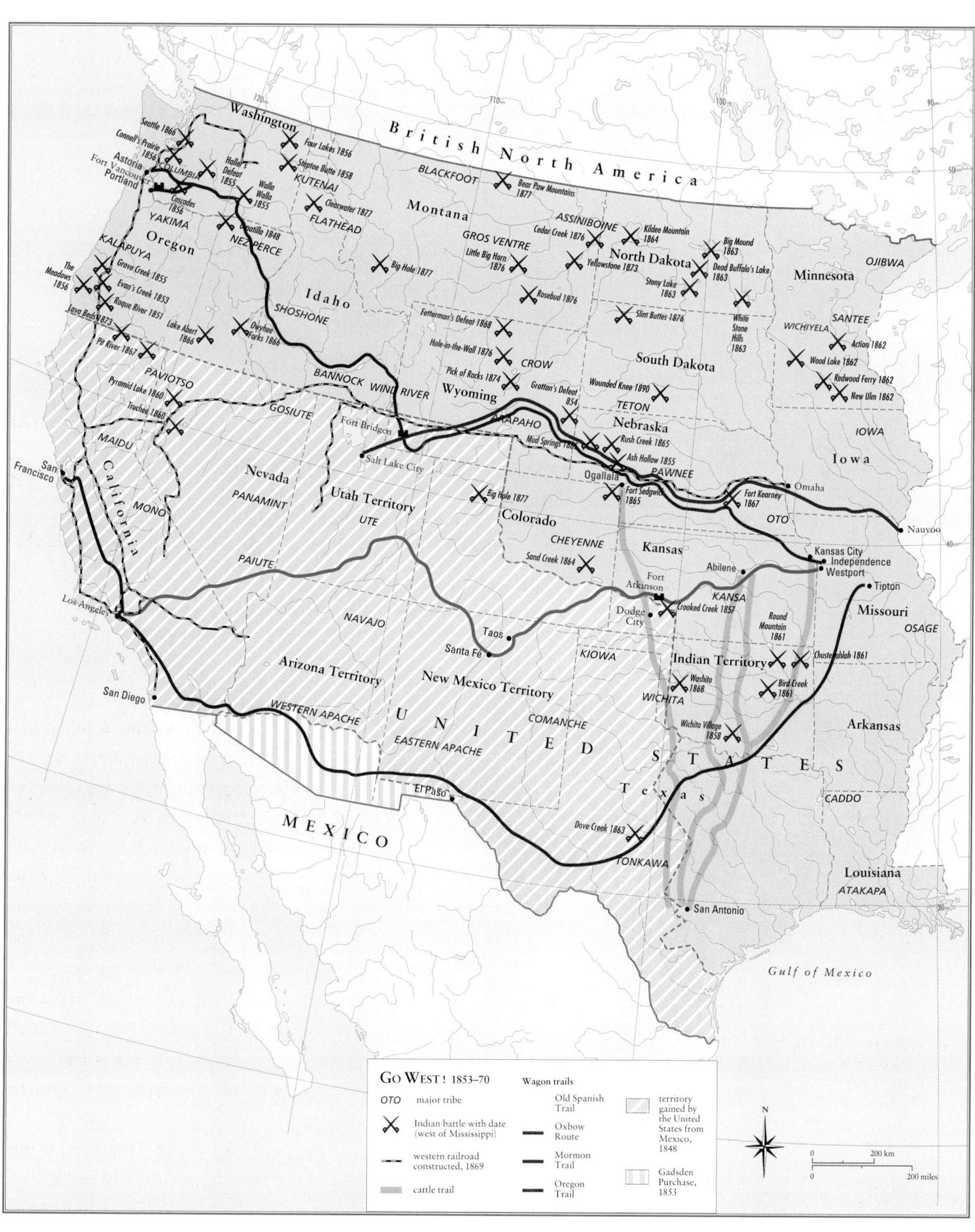
GO WEST! 1853–70
OTO major tribe
Indian battle with date (west of Mississippi)
western railroad constructed, 1869
cattle trail
Wagon trails
Old Spanish Trail
Oxbow Route
Mormon Trail
Oregon Trail
territory gained by the United States from Mexico, 1848
Gadsden Purchase, 1853
British North America
UNITED STATES
MEXICO
Gulf of Mexico
Washington
Oregon
Idaho
Montana
Wyoming
North Dakota
South Dakota
Nebraska
Minnesota
Iowa
Kansas
Missouri
Colorado
Nevada
California
Utah Territory
Arizona Territory
New Mexico Territory
Indian Territory
Texas
Arkansas
Louisiana

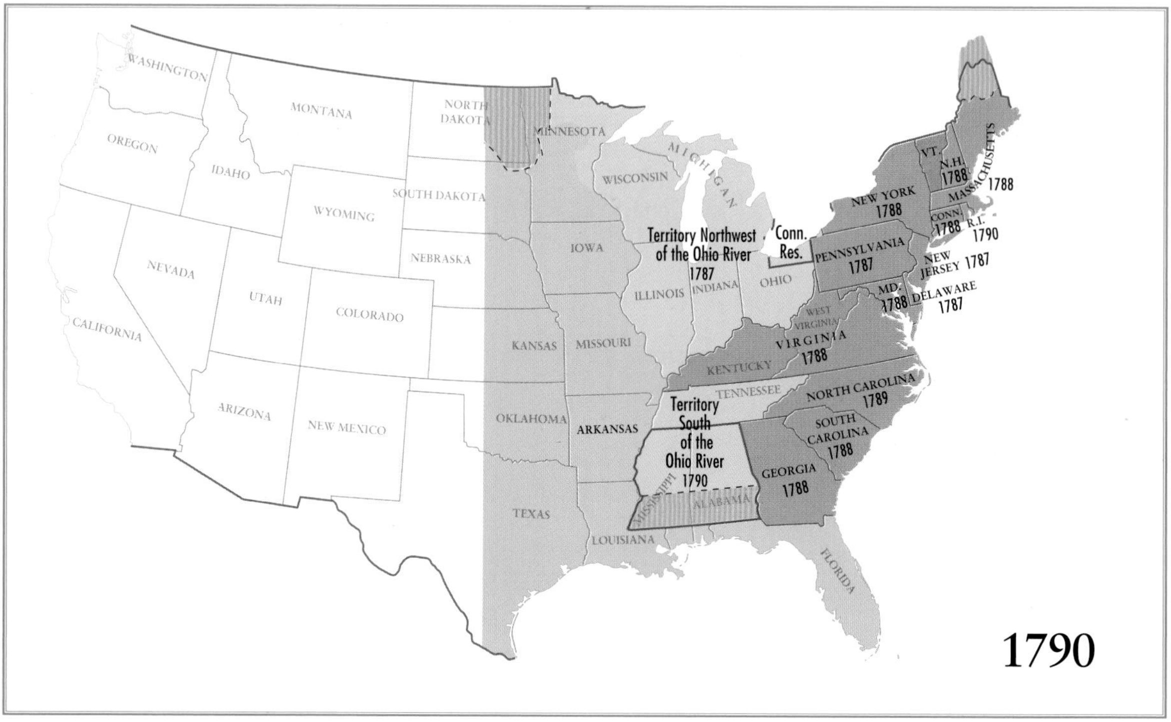
WASHINGTON
OREGON
MONTANA
IDAHO
NORTH DAKOTA
SOUTH DAKOTA
WYOMING
NEBRASKA
NEVADA
UTAH
COLORADO
CALIFORNIA
ARIZONA
NEW MEXICO
MINNESOTA
WISCONSIN
MICHIGAN
IOWA
Territory Northwest of the Ohio River 1787
Conn. Res.
ILLINOIS
INDIANA
OHIO
KANSAS
MISSOURI
OKLAHOMA
ARKANSAS
TEXAS
LOUISIANA
Territory South of the Ohio River 1790
MISSISSIPPI
ALABAMA
TENNESSEE
KENTUCKY
WEST VIRGINIA
VIRGINIA 1788
NORTH CAROLINA 1789
SOUTH CAROLINA 1788
GEORGIA 1788
FLORIDA
NEW YORK 1788
PENNSYLVANIA 1787
VT.
N.H. 1788
MASSACHUSETTS 1788
CONN. 1788
R.I. 1790
NEW JERSEY 1787
MD. 1788
DELAWARE 1787
1790

Washington Territory
Oregon
Nebraska Territory
Unorganized Territory
Minnesota
Wisconsin
Michigan
Utah Territory
California
Kansas Territory
New Mexico Territory
Unorganized Territory
Texas
Iowa
Illinois
Indiana
Ohio
Missouri
Arkansas
Louisiana
Mississippi
Alabama
Georgia
Florida
Tennessee
Kentucky
Virginia
North Carolina
South Carolina
Pennsylvania
New York
Maine
Vt.
N.H.
Mass.
Conn.
R.I.
New Jersey
Md.
Delaware
Territorial Expansion to 1860
State
Territory
Unorganized territory
Gadsden Purchase 1853
N
0 300 km
0 300 miles

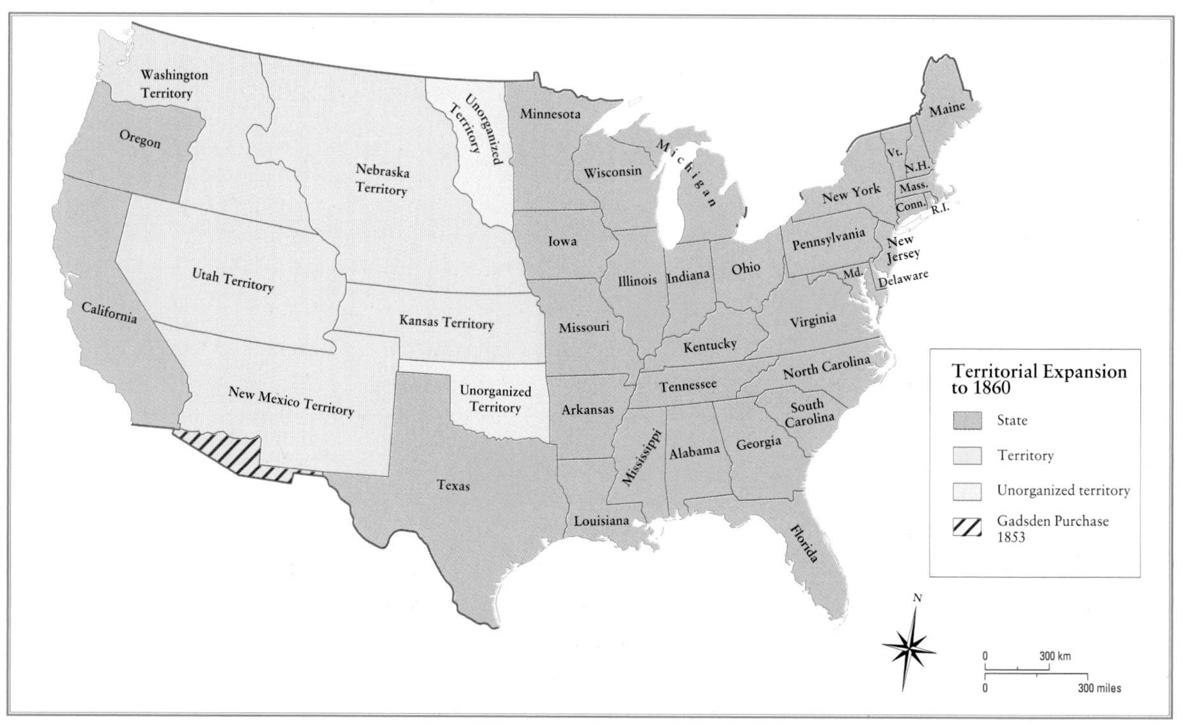

real control of its outlying provinces. In 1833, one of Mexico's largest and most powerful regions declared independence as the breakaway Republic of Texas.

Opposite page: These maps show some of the intermediate stages of the westward expansion that rapidly transformed the central belt of North America into the United States between 1790 and 1860.

The Texans—who consisted of Anglo-American settlers as well as Spanish Mexicans—wanted to escape the clutches of the unstable Mexican state, but they were by no means all convinced that independence was the way forward. Indeed, they had attempted to join the United States in 1836, but the move had been blocked by two U.S. Presidents—Andrew Jackson and Martin Van Buren. However, Washington softened its attitude when Britain—still smarting from the loss of territory after the Revolutionary War—supported Texan independence. Determined to prevent any resurgence of European colonial power in the region, annexation was approved in 1845, and in December of that year Texas became the 28th state of the Union. (The 27th state, Florida, had joined the United States nine months previously.)

The entry of Texas into the Union brought U.S. forces face to face with their Mexican counterparts across the Rio Grande. The former accused the latter of territorial incursions, providing the United States with a pretext for the Mexican War of 1846–1848, which ended when U.S. General Winfield Scott captured Mexico City. According to the terms of the ensuing Treaty of Guadalupe Hidalgo, Mexico agreed to renounce its claims to Texas and also ceded vast swathes of its northern territories to the victors. One part of the new U.S. acquisition became the state of California in 1850. The later Gadsden Purchase of 1853 saw a further chunk of Mexican land acquired by the United States.

The last state to join the Union before the Civil War was Kansas, previously the Territory of Kansas, which became a fully fledged part of the United States on January 29, 1861. The question of whether it should join the 18 free states or be allied with the 15 slave states turned out to be one of the sparks that ignited the "War Between Brothers".

The remaining area of what is now the contiguous United States was still divided in 1861 into four vast regions that were under de facto U.S. control but awaiting full accession to the Union. They were Nebraska Territory, New Mexico Territory, Utah Territory, and Washington Territory. There were also two extensive unorganized territories—one later became the states of North Dakota and South Dakota, while the other became Oklahoma.

At the outbreak of the Civil War in 1861, the United States consisted of 19 free states, 15 slave states, and several territories. Eleven slave states withdrew from the Union and made up the Confederate States of America. This happened officially in early February, 1861, at Montgomery, Alabama, when the eleven states met to create a new nation, the Confederate States of America. The remaining 23 states and the territories fought for the Union. The provisional constitution adopted by the Confederate States of America was similar to that of the United States, but it of course allowed for the keeping of slaves.

The flags of both these States were not dissimilar. The Union's National Flag was the Stars and Stripes, and at the beginning of the war "Old Glory" had 33 stars, typically placed in rows, in the blue canton. By the war's end, it had 35 stars, Kansas and West Virginia having been admitted to the Union in 1861 and 1863. The first National Flag of the Confederate States of America—the Stars and Bars could not always be distinguished from the Stars and Stripes of the Union flag. As a result, a battle flag was created, consisting of a blue cross containing white stars on a red background.

SLAVERY AND EMANCIPATION, 1775–1860

IN THE EARLY DAYS OF EUROPEAN COLONIZATION, SLAVERY WAS NOT—AS IT LATER BECAME—CONFINED TO THE SOUTHERN PARTS OF NORTH AMERICA, BUT WAS PRACTICED THROUGHOUT THE CONTINENT. THAT IT ENDED IN MOST OF THE BRITISH COLONIES WAS A DIRECT RESULT OF THE AMERICAN REVOLUTION.

Opposite page: These maps show the principal areas of cotton production and the greatest strongholds of slavery; it is clear that the former was heavily dependent on the latter.

The abolition of slavery in the northern United States was subsequently depicted as a consequence of the broader struggle for freedom for all and the agitation for human rights. However, although it is true that there was a degree of high-mindedness on both sides during the War of Independence, emancipation was to a large extent inspired by economic necessity, rather than a primarily moral stance.

By 1770, one of the major difficulties of slavery was the diminishing supply of people. Vast swathes of West Africa had been depopulated over the previous century, with the result that the cost of new slaves had risen prohibitively. Many traders were forced out of business. When Vermont banned slavery seven years later, it had very few slaves anyway, and the issue had lost much of its former sensitivity. Thirty years previously, it would have been a different story, as much of the colonies' wealth was founded on the work done by forced labor.

The War of Independence presented African Americans with an unforeseen opportunity as both sides offered them freedom as an incentive to join their ranks. The colonies forestalled opposition from slave owners with various forms of compensation,usually land—in New York, one slave master acquired 500 acres for every slave he allowed to enlist for three years in the rebel army. Around 5,000 black people fought on the side of the rebels, although a much greater number found the inducements more attractive from King George's men. Win or lose, the British had no reason to keep black people in servitude—on the contrary, the more of them who were free, the less the rebels' power. That formed a bond between the imperialists and the slaves—when the British

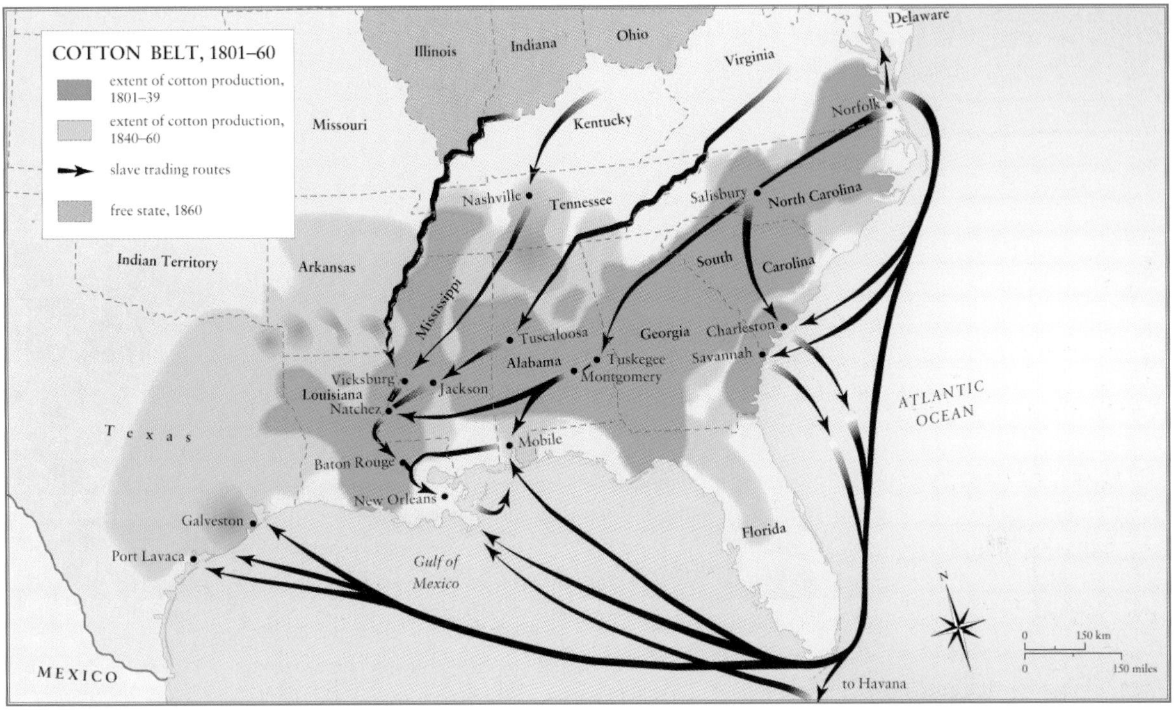

COTTON BELT, 1801–60

extent of cotton production, 1801–39

extent of cotton production, 1840–60

slave trading routes

free state, 1860

Delaware
Illinois
Indiana
Ohio
Virginia
Missouri
Kentucky
Norfolk
Nashville
Tennessee
Salisbury
North Carolina
Indian Territory
Arkansas
South
Carolina
Mississippi
Tuscaloosa
Georgia
Charleston
Alabama
Tuskegee
Savannah
Vicksburg
Louisiana
Natchez
Jackson
Montgomery
ATLANTIC OCEAN
Texas
Mobile
Baton Rouge
New Orleans
Galveston
Florida
Port Lavaca
Gulf of Mexico
N
0 150 km
0 150 miles
MEXICO
to Havana

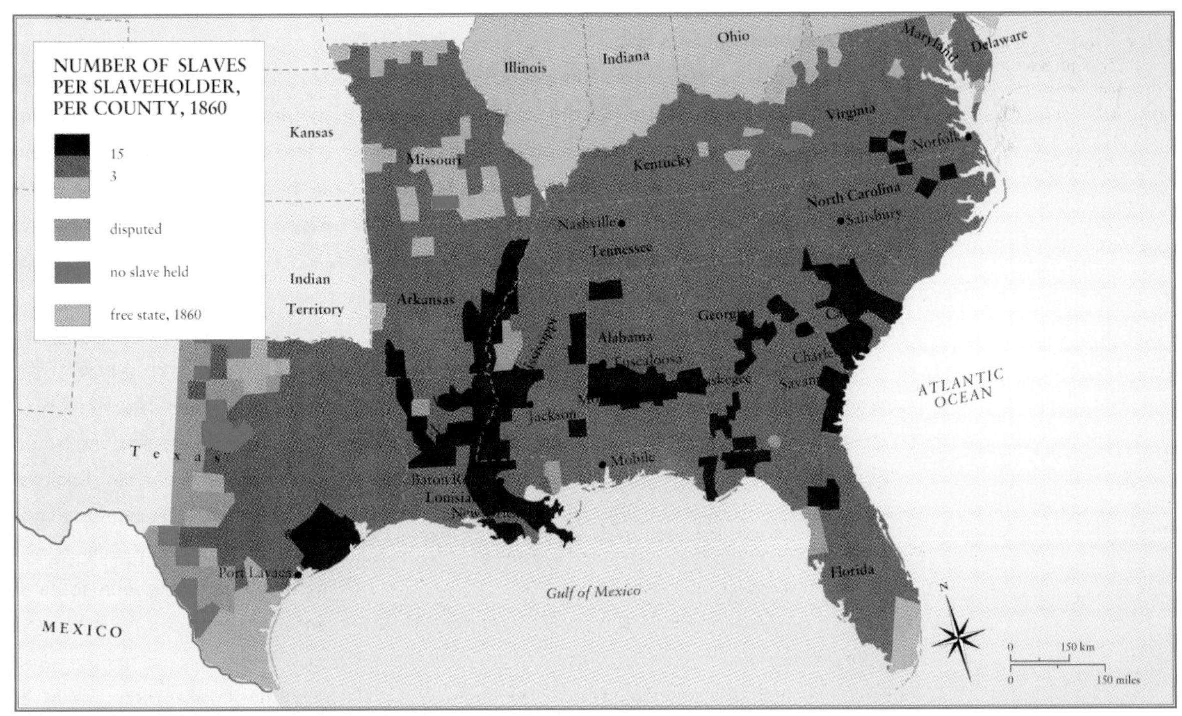

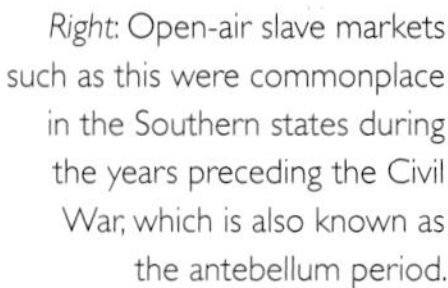

Right: Open-air slave markets such as this were commonplace in the Southern states during the years preceding the Civil War, which is also known as the antebellum period.

withdrew, 3,000 black former slaves accompanied them out of North America.

The Northern colonies' white working classes felt threatened by the liberation of slaves and reacted by making it almost impossible for black people to take their jobs. In fact, the decline in slavery in the North created a lucrative new form of human traffic as black Americans were sold back into servitude in the South.

By the 1790 census, 94 percent of the 698,000 slaves in the United States lived south of the Mason-Dixon Line. It is thought that at this time most of the South's work force had been purchased from the North which, though now "emancipated," had caused, directly and indirectly, large numbers of African Americans to quit their former homes. Meanwhile, Northern ports handled most of the traffic going out from the Southern plantations—principally cotton and tobacco—and took a cut from the transshipment of imported raw materials. Thus the North had the best of two worlds: it could claim, not unreasonably, to have abolished slavery, but it was not a free or desirable place for African Americans to live in; it had almost no slaves of its own, but maintained a high living standard off the backs of Southerners, not only the slaves themselves but also their owners.

About 3,500,000 slaves and 135,000 free blacks lived in the Confederate States at the outbreak of war. Their lives would undergo many changes throughout the course of the conflict. While their owners were away fighting, slaves continued to work on plantations under the direction of the mistress of the household or hired overseers, some of whom were black. They engaged in tanning, boiling sea water to obtain salt, making soap, spinning, weaving, and other such chores. A few accompanied their masters to war as body servants, and generally remained loyal to them although ownership of body servants became less and less practical as the war wore on. Stories of slaves bringing their wounded masters in for medical treatment were common. At Sharpsburg, one got a horse to bring his master in—then remounted and rode to the Union lines. Black labor also made a significant contribution to the Confederate cause. Although many plantation owners resisted the use of their slaves, many were impressed to build fortifications, repair railroads, and perform essential public work jobs. They also drove supply wagons and served as cooks for the military on occasion; they did yeoman service as orderlies and nurses in hospitals. Indeed, in the last year of the war, the Confederacy opened the ranks of the army to blacks, but the decision came so late that few were enrolled. Fair-skinned blacks passing as white may have been in the Confederate army, though.

While Southern whites feared insurrection, none occurred. Minor incidents did happen, but were easily quashed. On the whole slaves adopted a passive attitude to the conflict, generally preferring to let the whites fight it out among themselves.

Still, the war altered the institution of slavery in both obvious and subtle ways. The customary relationship changed; whites appeared less like masters, blacks less like slaves when the master was away at war and the prospect of liberation was plausible. Women and elderly overseers, not experienced in management, could provide little in the way of leadership. Blacks developed a new consciousness of the leverage their labor gave them in a time of crisis. A few instances occurred where they demanded, and received, wages.

Slaves reacted more as individuals than as a group during the war. Many slaves deserted as the Union army approached, while some remained loyal to their masters to the end. Some told Union soldiers where plantation owners had hidden property, and some volunteered intelligence to Union officers. General Grant, for example, received from a slave important information that helped him cross the Mississippi River near Vicksburg.

A frequently overlooked element of the war is the role played by the South's skilled white laborers, who manned its essential industries, and without whom it could not have continued the war. Skilled workers were in a much greater bargaining position than unskilled ones, who could be easily replaced by blacks—a strike by white graveyard workers in Richmond ended with the strikers driving off the blacks and going back to work. Mass meetings were held to support price controls, and unions experimented with political pressure and collective bargaining, but with little success. Confederate workers never considered themselves part of a proletarian movement.

Below: Slaves leaving a field carrying large baskets of cotton. Being a very labor-intensive crop, landowners in Georgia required workers in record numbers. Darker skinned slaves were sent to work out in the fields and those with lighter skins were engaged as domestic servants.

THE MISSOURI COMPROMISES

THE MISSOURI COMPROMISES OF 1820 AND 1850 WERE REACHED IN ORDER TO MAINTAIN THE BALANCE BETWEEN FREE STATES AND SLAVE STATES. ALTHOUGH BY THEIR NATURE IMPERMANENT, THEY SUCCESSFULLY POSTPONED THE CIVIL WAR FOR MORE THAN A GENERATION. WITH THE KANSAS-NEBRASKA ACT IN 1854, HOWEVER, THE UNITED STATES TEETERED CLOSER TO THE BRINK OF CONFLICT.

Above: Speaker of the House, Henry Clay addresses the U.S. Senate. The statesman helped gain Congressional approval for the Missouri Compromise of 1820.

By 1819, the 22 United States were equally divided—half of them were slave states, the other 11 were free states. In the same year, the population of Missouri—originally a part of the 1803 Louisiana Purchase—first exceeded 60,000, the minimum required for statehood.

The imminent incorporation of the territory into the Union reignited the controversy about slavery that had generated varying degrees of heat since before the American Revolution. At the 1787 Constitution Convention, the South—where slavery had already become an indispensable part of the fabric of society—lobbied successfully for every state to determine its own policy in the matter. That worked well for the founding members but it did not address the question of what to do about new applicants.

After having put off discussions of the matter for nearly 30 years, Congress was forced to respond to Missouri's application for statehood. During a debate in the House in February 1819, Representative James Tallmadge, Jr., from New York, proposed that, as a condition of entry, no more slaves should be introduced into Missouri, which already had around 10,000 of them, and that those already in servitude should be freed on attaining the age of 25 years. The amendment provoked a

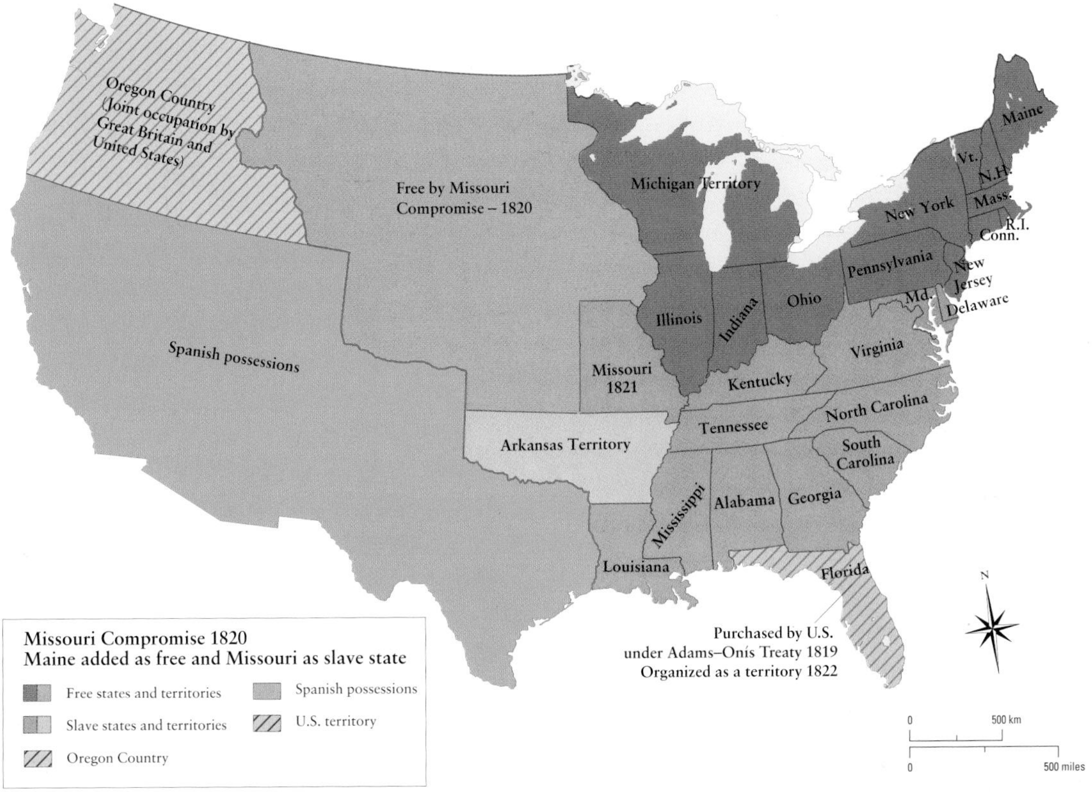

Above: Map showing the line of the Missouri Compromise of 1820; to the north of it were free states; to the south of it, slavery was permitted.

bitter debate; it was eventually passed, but, ominously, only because every representative voted on sectional lines—the enfranchised population of the North was growing much faster than that of the South, and so the free states were in the majority.

That might have been the tipping point, had it not been for the Upper House, which, composed of two senators from each state, regardless of population, was the only part of the legislature that could maintain the historic balance. Predictably, there was impasse, and the bill was blocked. Congress then adjourned but when it reconvened in December 1819 the debate was resumed with even greater ferocity. Northern congressmen wanted to stop the westward spread of slavery as a step toward abolishing it altogether; their Southern counterparts were equally adamant that, if and when they were allowed to settle in the new state, they should be allowed to take their belongings with them, and their prize possessions were slaves.

With no resolution in sight, the Speaker of the House, Henry Clay, proposed a deal that, he hoped, would satisfy both North and South and prevent the possible dissolution of the Union. His idea was that the northeastern portion of Massachusetts should be split to create a new political entity, Maine, which would be admitted as a free state to counterbalance the entry of Missouri as a slave state, thus preserving the equilibrium of both the Senate and the nation.

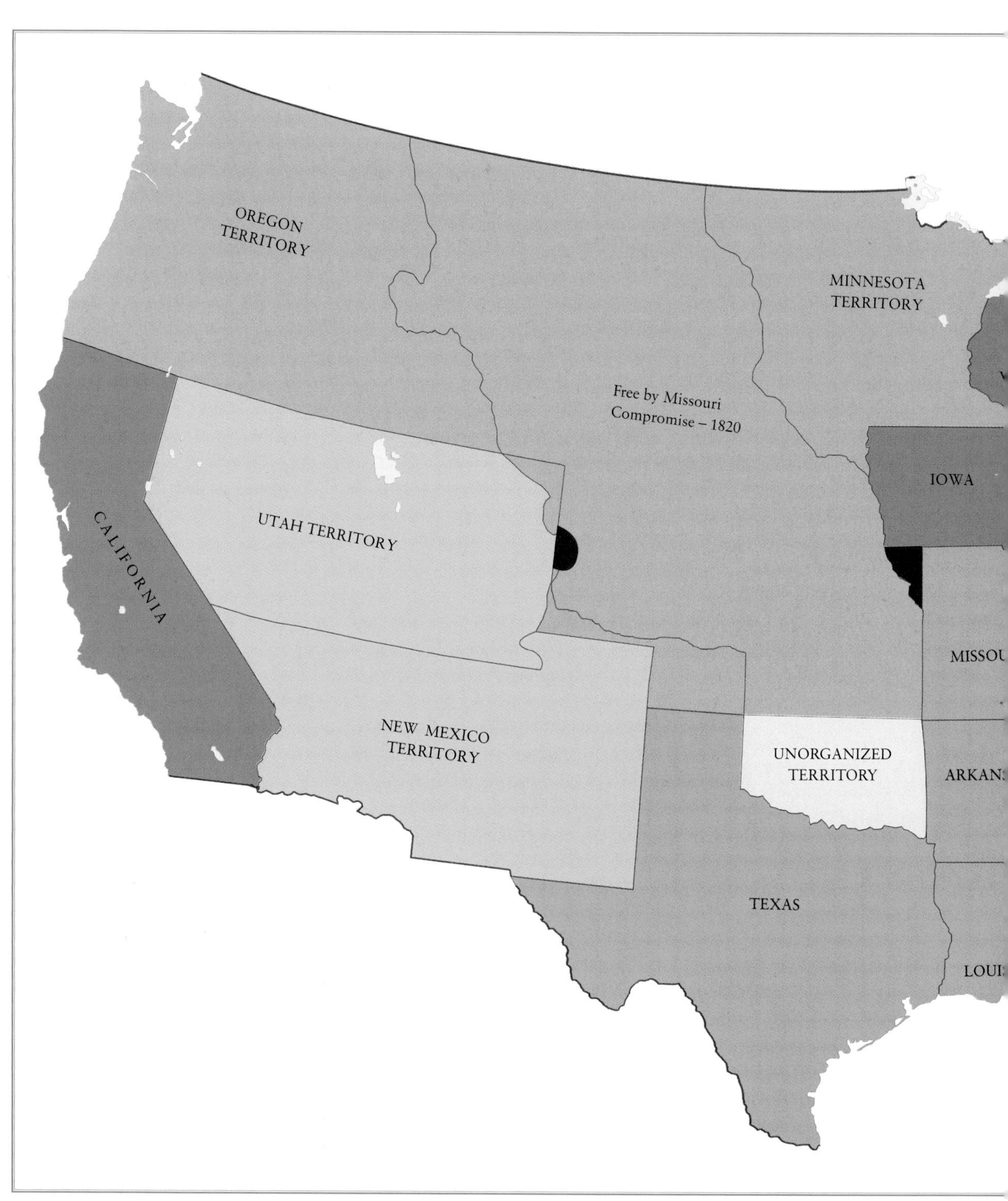
OREGON TERRITORY
MINNESOTA TERRITORY
Free by Missouri Compromise – 1820
IOWA
UTAH TERRITORY
CALIFORNIA
NEW MEXICO TERRITORY
UNORGANIZED TERRITORY
TEXAS

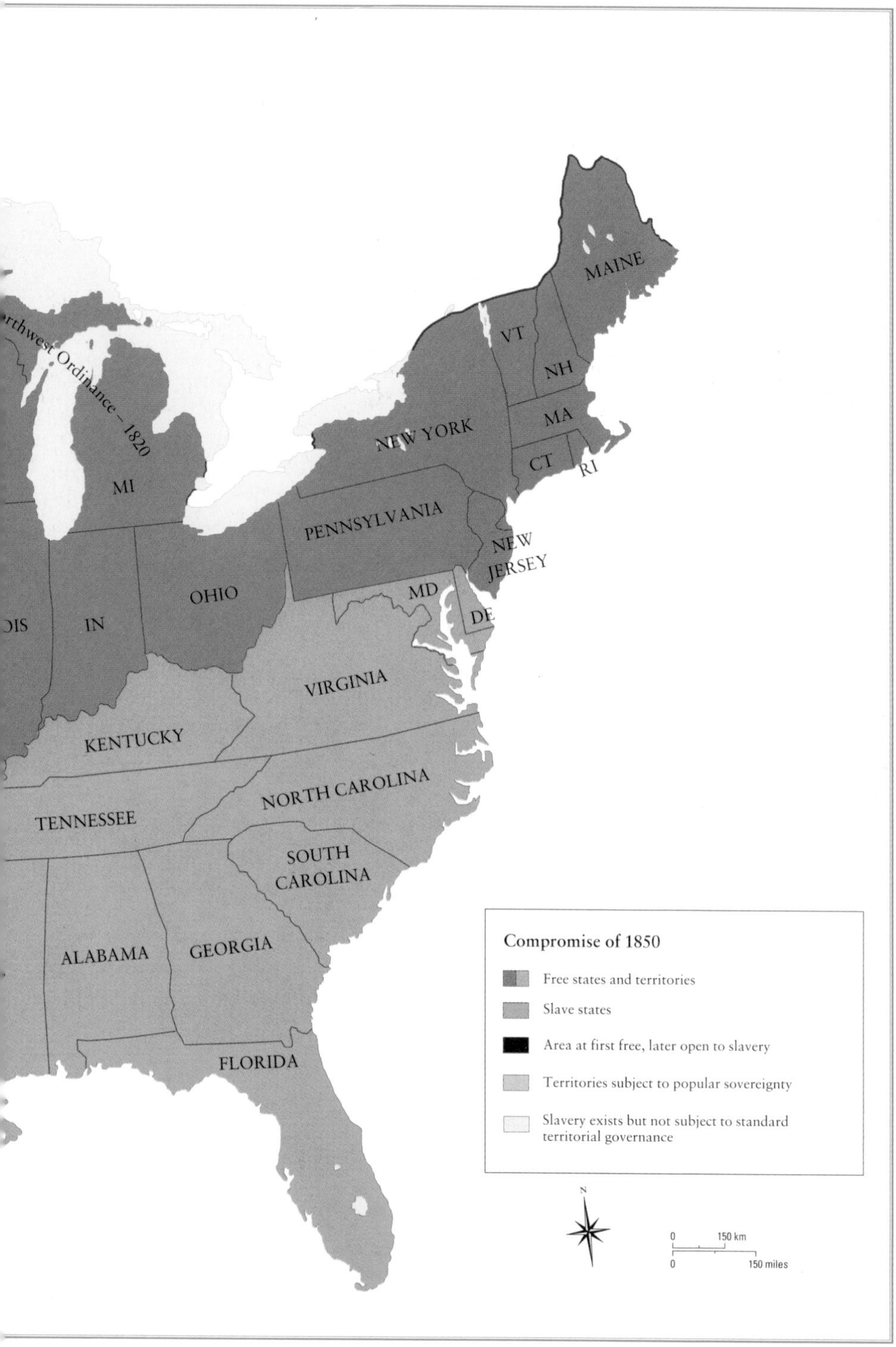

Left: This map shows the situation in the United States after the Compromise of 1850.

Compromise of 1850

- Free states and territories
- Slave states
- Area at first free, later open to slavery
- Territories subject to popular sovereignty
- Slavery exists but not subject to standard territorial governance

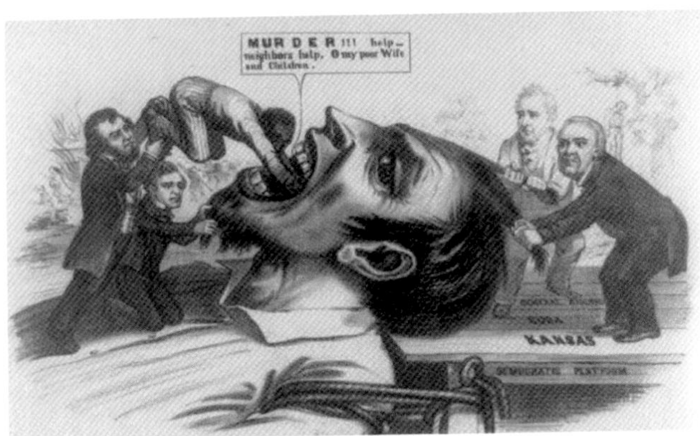

Above: Two wry views of the slavery question during the period of the Missouri Compromises. The cartoon of 1854 *(top)* shows a member of the Free Soil Party (one of the shortlived precursors of the Republican Party) being force-fed a black man (symbolizing slavery) by Stephen A. Douglas. The political cartoon *(bottom)* criticizes the Democratic Party for supporting the Kansas-Nebraska Act during the 1856 Presidential campaign.

Jesse B. Thomas, a senator from Illinois, supported Clay's motion and introduced a new idea, that, in future, states should only ever be admitted in pairs, one from each side of a dividing line across North America on the latitude of 36° 30°, along which ran the southern border of Missouri. States to the north of that line would be free; those to the south of it would be slave states. That, in outline, was the Missouri Compromise. On March 15, 1821, Maine became the 23rd state of the Union; it was joined on August 10 by Missouri, the 24th. In signing the laws that admitted them both, U.S. President James Monroe believed that he had ended the controversy once and for all, and indeed for the next 40 years many Americans regarded the Missouri Compromise as a sacred accord that would bind the United States together in perpetuity.

However, Thomas Jefferson, the third President of the United States, now in old age, took an apocalyptic view. He wrote to a friend: "This momentous question, like a firebell in the night, awakened and filled me with terror. I considered it at once as the knell of the Union." He also described the Missouri Compromise as "a reprieve only; not a final sentence."

The United States then entered a period of territorial expansion, gaining Texas in 1845 and a vast tract of land in the Southwest after the Mexican War of 1846–1848. Commercial interests soon began competing for the right to build a transcontinental railroad that would link the Atlantic and Pacific oceans. The principle was agreed by almost everyone, but the route was a matter of dispute. The Southern states naturally wanted the line to link them to both coasts and facilitate the spread of slavery into the newly acquired lands.

The North, however, had other ideas and in 1853 one of its leading politicians, U.S. Senator Stephen A. Douglas, introduced a bill in Congress to enable the construction of a railroad between California and his own home city of Chicago, Illinois. In the face of implacable opposition from the Southern states, Douglas then redrafted his legislation: he now proposed that the territories of Kansas and Nebraska should be incorporated into the United States, and that as they advanced to statehood the settlers in both regions should exercise what he called "popular sovereignty" to determine for themselves whether to adopt or outlaw slavery. Under further pressure from the South, Douglas then wrote in a further concession: that the Missouri Compromise should be repealed.

The consensus view in Congress was that, left to themselves, the people of Kansas would follow the lead of neighboring Missouri and become a slave state, while those of Nebraska would line up with the North and be a free state. Confident that the status quo would thus be maintained without

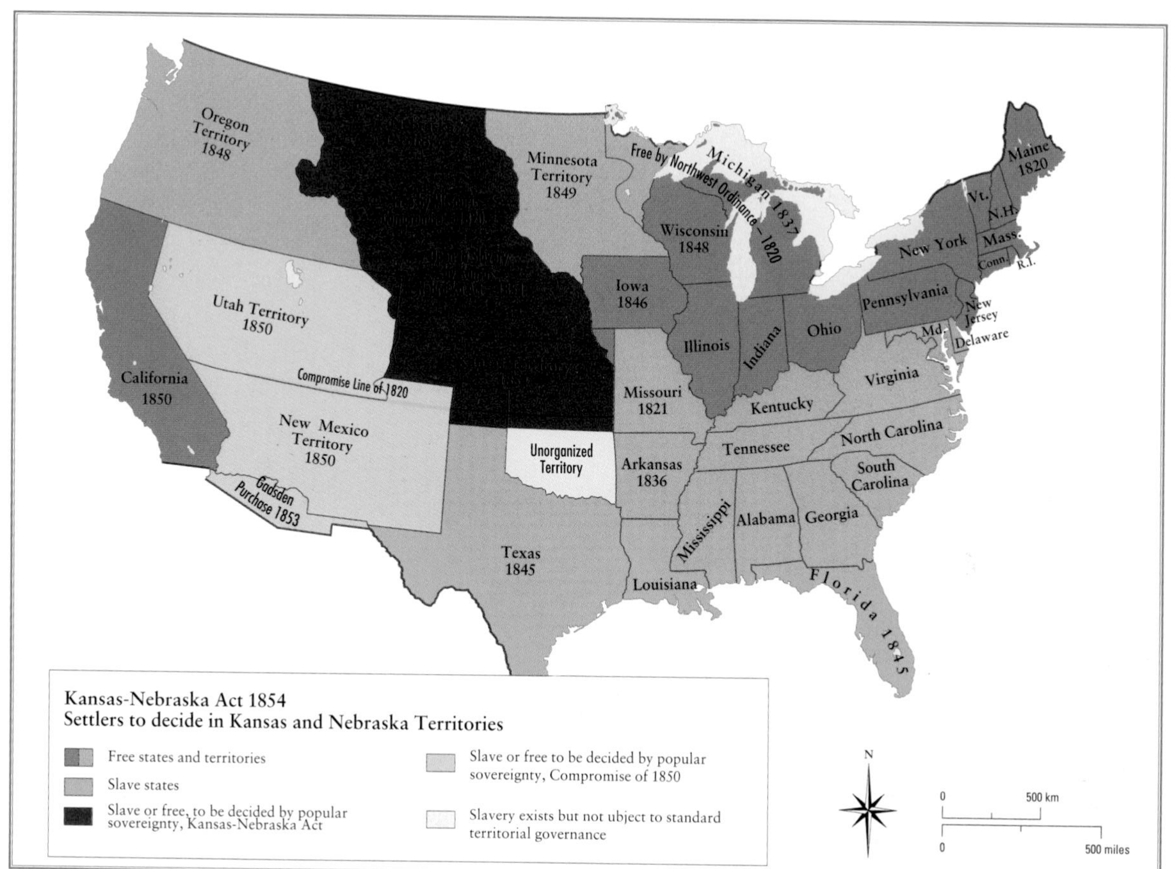

Above: This map shows the United States after the Kansas–Nebraska Act.

the coercion of either party, Congress passed the Kansas–Nebraska Act in May 1854 by 37 to 14 in the Senate and 113 to 100 in the House.

The new law soon caused the dissolution of the Whig Party, which had previously united otherwise disparate interest groups in North and South. Appalled by their representatives' support for the act, Southern Democrats abstained, while Northern Democrats deserted in droves to two new political groupings, the Know-Nothing Party, which promoted American nativism, and the Republican Party, which took its name in memory of Jefferson.

In the 1854 elections, the number of northern Democrats in the House of Representatives fell from 92 to just 23, while opponents of the Kansas–Nebraska Act elected no less than 150 congressmen. This was no one-time protest vote, however; resentment continued to fester, and the opponents of slavery eventually united to bring about the election of the first U.S. Republican President, Abraham Lincoln, whose triumph caused the secession of the South and the formation of the Confederacy. Meanwhile, in Kansas, the act resulted in years of violence, a period known as "Bleeding Kansas," as slavers and abolitionists struggled for supremacy. Kansas was finally admitted to the Union as a free state in 1861.

THE GADSDEN PURCHASE, JUNE 24, 1853

IN 1853, AS A FURTHER PART OF THE GREAT WESTWARD EXPANSION, THE UNITED STATES BOUGHT FROM MEXICO A STRIP OF LAND, 460 MILES (735KM) LONG AND 130 MILES (208KM) WIDE AT ITS BROADEST POINT, STRETCHING ALONG THE BORDER BETWEEN THE TWO COUNTRIES WITH THE INTENTION OF BUILDING A TRANSCONTINENTAL RAILROAD.

Above: President Franklin Pierce's popularity in the North waned after he came out in favor of the Kansas-Nebraska Act, which allowed those territories to decide whether they would allow slavery within their boundries.

The United States wanted the land for a transcontinental railroad. Although other routes were possible between New Orleans, which was then the preferred eastern terminus of the proposed line, and the Pacific coast in recently acquired California, this was the flattest of all the viable options.

The chief U.S. negotiator was James Gadsden (1788–1858), whose personal preference was for an east-west rail link that took a more northerly course to and from Charleston in his native South Carolina. However, he did not allow his own wishes to interfere with his duties as U.S. Minister to Mexico. After discussions with Mexican President Antonio López de Santa Anna, a price of $10 million was agreed. At around 53 cents per acre, this was nearly 18 times more expensive than the Louisiana Purchase, and the land gained was around 27 times smaller. However, the U.S. Senate decided that it was good value as an essential stepping stone on the route to the Manifest Destiny and ratified the purchase, which was signed by President Franklin Pierce on June 24, 1853.

Not that the acquisition pleased everyone. Many Americans wanted to press for a much larger territory—including most of the northern Mexican states of Coahuila, Chihuahua, Sonora, Nuevo

Left: A portrait of the Mexican President Antonio Lopez de Santa Anna in his military costume. After negotiations with Gadsden, Santa Anna sold the United States a strip of Mexican land for $10 million as part of the U.S.'s great westward expansion.

León, and Tamaulipas, as well as all of the Baja California peninsula—but the U.S. Congress was persuaded not to pursue those objectives by northern senators who argued that such lands would be turned into yet more slave states.

In 1854, one of the disappointed parties, filibuster William Walker, led a band of armed men from California to Sonora, where they declared the independent Republic of Sonora, which staked claim to both the Mexican province of that name and Baja California. In the absence of support from Washington, D.C., the occupiers were easily driven back across the border by the Mexican army.

The displeasure of southern Americans was nothing compared to the outrage felt in Mexico. Even though the nation lost only a small portion of its territory through the Gadsden Purchase, many Mexicans regarded the deal as yet another example of Santa Anna's profligacy, and their opposition hastened the end of the President's political career.

The Gadsden Purchase was first incorporated into the U.S. New Mexico Territory; Fort Buchanan was established there in Sonoita Creek to protect it. However, the difficulties of protecting the remote land—the nearest major settlement was Santa Fe, more than 200 miles (320km) to the north—led to calls for the creation of a new territory, but Congress failed to pass enabling legislation because the Northern states were concerned about the large number of slave owners who had already settled in the region. In 1861, after the outbreak of the Civil War, the Confederacy incorporated most of the Gadsden Purchase into its declared Territory of Arizona. In 1863, the Union occupied the western half of the New Mexico Territory and made the 1851 purchase a part of its Arizona Territory.

The irony of the Gadsden Purchase was that the first North American transcontinental railroad, completed in 1869, was built along a much more northerly route between Sacramento, California, and Omaha, Nebraska. There was no railroad across the strip until 1881.

POPULATION GROWTH AND IMMIGRATION 1783–1860

BETWEEN BRITISH RECOGNITION OF U.S. INDEPENDENCE IN 1783 AND THE OUTBREAK OF THE CIVIL WAR IN 1861, THE POPULATION OF THE FLEDGLING NORTH AMERICAN NATION INCREASED ALMOST TENFOLD.

The total number of inhabitants recorded in 1790, the year of the first U.S. census, was 3,929,214, more than 80 percent of whom were white and of British extraction. By 1860, the number of Americans had increased to 31,443,321 from a wide range of national and ethnic backgrounds; that total included 4,441,830 blacks.

The causes of the increase were mainly natural growth—throughout the period, the population, exclusive of newcomers, doubled every 25 years—but immigration and, to a lesser extent, the acquisition of territory also contributed.

Although the general tide was bringing vast numbers of people into the United States, there was some emigration, too. After the American Revolution, an estimated 60,000 people left the country for Canada or returned to Britain, from which they or their forebears had come.

In the early years of independence, most immigrants were black men and women brought forcibly from Africa to work as slaves. Non-black immigration was little more than a trickle—only around 6,000 arrivals a year, most of whom were refugees from the revolution in Haiti that began in 1791. European immigration was negligible because the French Revolution of 1789 and the Napoleonic Wars of 1792–1814 had caused the virtual suspension of transatlantic travel from the continent.

Opposite page: These maps show how the population of the United States became more urbanized and concentrated in the northeast of the country during the first 60 years of the 19th century.

In 1808, the U.S. Congress banned any further importation of black slaves from abroad. Nevertheless, the 1810 census revealed that one in five Americans was now of African heritage, and that the total number of black people had topped the million mark.

White immigration got into full swing in the 1820s and was now better documented than ever

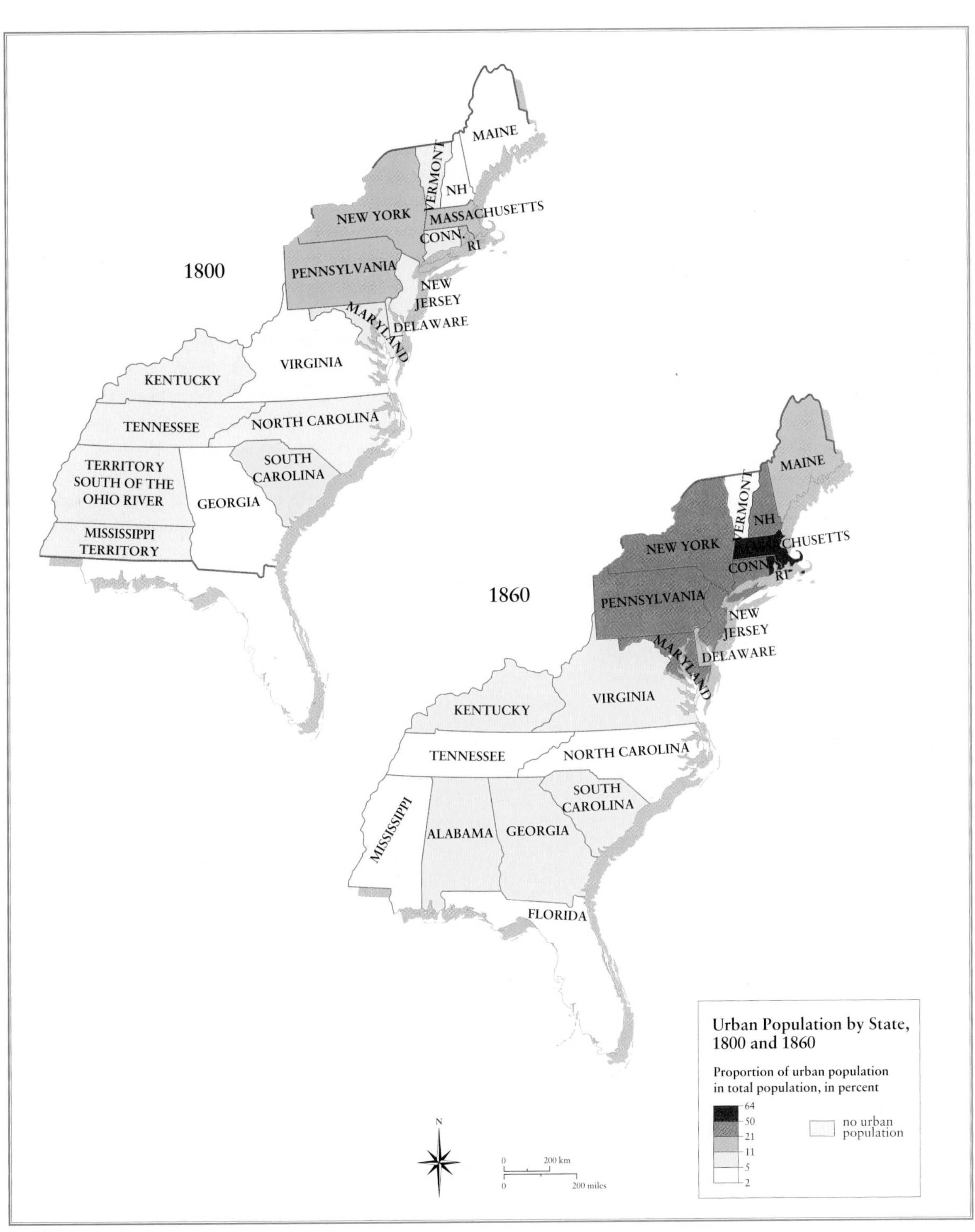
1800
MAINE
VERMONT
NH
NEW YORK
MASSACHUSETTS
CONN.
RI
PENNSYLVANIA
NEW JERSEY
MARYLAND
DELAWARE
VIRGINIA
KENTUCKY
TENNESSEE
NORTH CAROLINA
SOUTH CAROLINA
TERRITORY SOUTH OF THE OHIO RIVER
GEORGIA
MISSISSIPPI TERRITORY
1860
MAINE
VERMONT
NH
NEW YORK
CHUSETTS
CONN
RI
PENNSYLVANIA
NEW JERSEY
MARYLAND
DELAWARE
VIRGINIA
KENTUCKY
TENNESSEE
NORTH CAROLINA
SOUTH CAROLINA
MISSISSIPPI
ALABAMA
GEORGIA
FLORIDA
Urban Population by State, 1800 and 1860
Proportion of urban population in total population, in percent
64
50
21
11
5
2
no urban population
N
0 200 km
0 200 miles

before. That decade saw a total of 143,000 incomers, but they contributed only around one in 10 of the total increase in a population that by 1830 had reached 12,866,020.

Between 1831 and 1840, nearly 600,000 people immigrated to the United States. Most came from Europe, particularly from Ireland (207,000) after its British rulers relaxed travel restrictions. The next largest group was German (152,000), followed by 76,000 Britons and 46,000 French. Many were fugitives from poverty, attracted to the New World by the prospect of better wages and the availability of cheap land. By 1840, the total population of the United States exceeded 17 million.

This influx was almost insignificant by comparison with what happened over the next 10 years, during which 1,713,000 new immigrants settled in the United States. The largest group was from Ireland, where the famine of 1845–1849 sent at least three-quarters of a million malnourished natives of every social class in search of a better life on the far side of the Atlantic Ocean. The British gave the fugitives incentives to settle in Canada rather than in the United States, and although some of the Irish initially took up the offer, many of them later crossed the southern border and settled principally in Boston and New York.

Most of the Irish were Roman Catholics, and their arrival en masse in the United States reduced the predominant Protestant religionists from around 95 percent to 90 percent of the population. This development fueled fears that the country might be swamped by people whose commitment to American values was sometimes doubted and who were suspected of being directly controlled by the Pope. The resultant rise of anti-immigrant feeling spawned the Know-Nothing Party, a political group whose name was a reference to its early days as a clandestine movement, when members were supposed to deny all knowledge of its existence. When it went public in 1852, it achieved huge popularity, but split two years later over the question of slavery. Anti-slavery Know-Nothings defected to the Republicans, while the remainder transferred their allegiance to the pro-slavery Democrats.

In 1848, much of mainland Europe was afflicted by extremely bad harvests and a series of abortive revolutions. These crises drove another three-quarters of a million people onto transatlantic boats. That total comprised around 437,000 Germans and 77,000 French immigrants, as well as

Below: This map shows the numbers of immigrants who left Europe for a new life in America. By 1860, the population of the United States had increased to 31 million, a huge increase from the 7 million recorded in 1810.

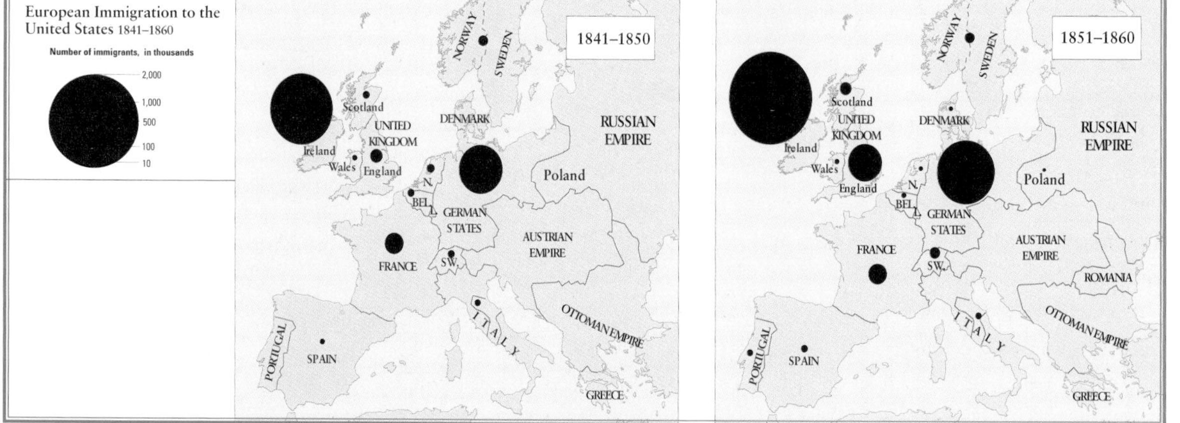

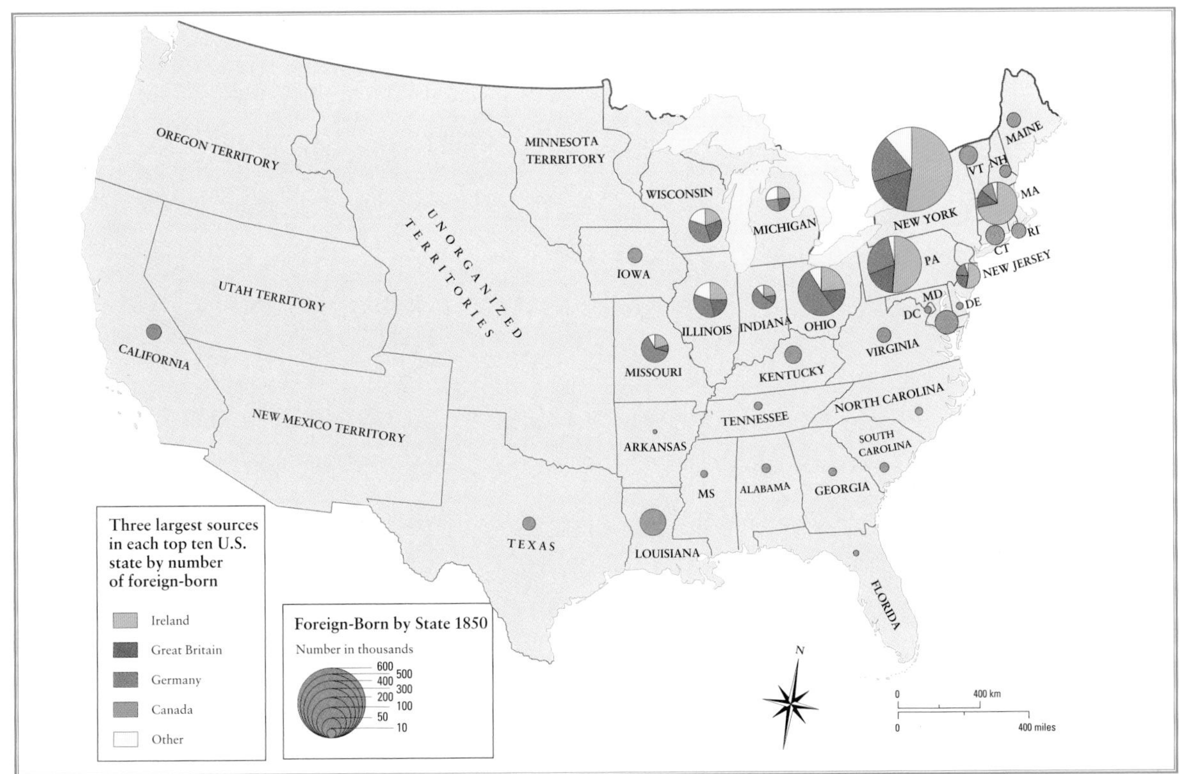

Above: Immigration was encouraged to the United States in the mid-nineteenth century, particularly due to letters sent to relatives back home urging them to follow. There was also a lot of active recruitment of passengers from steamship companies and railroad workers by railroad companies. The above map shows the number of foreign-born by state in 1850.

267,000 Britons. All three nationalities were attracted the by promise of freedom and opportunity in the new continent, and they knew that their assimilation would be eased by relatives and other compatriots who had settled there successfully following earlier waves of immigration. The California Gold Rush, which began in January of that year, was yet another major draw for them and also lured large numbers of fortune-seekers from much farther afield, including Australia, China, Mexico, and South America.

Another significant addition to the population came after U.S. victory in the Mexican War (1846–1848) led to the acquisition of a vast new chunk of territory—the future states of Arizona, California, New Mexico, and Texas—and its 80,000 inhabitants.

By 1850, the U.S. population was 23,191,876, a 35 percent increase on the total just ten years previously. Immigration was much reduced during the last decade before the Civil War, but the population still grew remarkably. The census of 1860 recorded yet another 35 percent rise, with African Americans now comprising 14.1 percent of the population: 3,953,760 of them were slaves, while 488,070 were free men and women.

During the period, immigrants to the United States might land almost anywhere along the eastern seaboard, especially at Baltimore, Boston, New Orleans, and Philadelphia. New York was also busy, but it did not start to achieve its paramount status until 1855, when the nation's first formal immigration facilities were established at Castle Garden on the southern tip of Manhattan Island.

AGRICULTURE, INDUSTRY, AND RAILROADS

BY THE TIME THE COLONIES DECLARED INDEPENDENCE FROM BRITAIN IN 1776, NEW ENGLAND HAD ALREADY BECOME PROMINENT IN THE PRODUCTION OF IRON. THE METAL GAVE THE REGION AN OVERWHELMING AND PERMANENT ADVANTAGE OVER THE REST OF THE UNION IN THE ENSUING INDUSTRIAL REVOLUTION AND THE BURGEONING PROGRESS OF THE RAILROADS. IN THE SOUTH, HOWEVER, THE VALUABLE RESOURCE, COTTON, WAS KING.

Above: In 1843, Nashville became the permanent state capital of Tennessee. In this 1864 photograph of the railroad yard and depot, the Capitol can be seen in the distance.

Opposite page: The U.S. railroads and canal system were at their densest in the northeast but by 1860 they had become well developed along the shores of the Great Lakes as far west as Chicago, and were beginning to increase rapidly in the South.

At the start of the Civil War, most of the north of the United States was industrialized, with extensive food-growing farmland in the western parts of its territory and in the Piedmont Plateau of Pennsylvania which, until the settlement of the Midwest, had the most productive soil in the United States. Meanwhile, agriculture remained the mainstay of the economy of the South, where the most productive areas were the alluvial plain of the lower Mississippi River and the chalky black soils of Alabama, Mississippi, and Texas.

The northeastern United States were always at the center of the nation's manufacturing industries, beginning in the early 19th century with the production of small arms, and later developing into the great steelworks in which were constructed the heavy machinery that would facilitate U.S. economic development and expansion across North America. The iron and steel

DAKOTA TERRITORY
MINNESOTA
WISCONSIN
MICHIGAN
NEBRASKA TERRITORY
IOWA
KANSAS
MISSOURI
INDIAN TERRITORY
TEXAS
ARKANSAS
LOUISIANA
MISSISSIPPI
ALABAMA
GEORGIA
FLORIDA
TENNESSEE
KENTUCKY
ILLINOIS
INDIANA
OHIO
WEST VIRGINIA (1861)
VIRGINIA
NORTH CAROLINA
SOUTH CAROLINA
PENNSYLVANIA
NEW YORK
MARYLAND
DELAWARE
N.J.
CON.
R.I.
MASS.
VERMONT
N.H.
MAINE
Madison
Milwaukee
Chicago
Detroit
Toledo
Cleveland
Buffalo
Dunkirk
Davenport
Ft. Wayne
Indianapolis
Springfield
St. Joseph
St. Louis
Cincinnati
Columbus
Louisville
Lexington
Pittsburgh
Harrisburg
Baltimore
Washington
Wilmington
Philadelphia
Trenton
New York
New Haven
Hartford
Providence
Worcester
Boston
Albany
Rutland
Concord
Portland
Bangor
Richmond
Norfolk
Bristol
Nashville
Memphis
Little Rock
Corinth
Chattanooga
Charlotte
Wilmington
Columbia
Atlanta
Charleston
Savannah
Montgomery
Vicksburg
Mobile
New Orleans
Houston
Jacksonville
Railroads and Canals, 1860
railroad
canal
Union states
Confederate states
N
0 200 km
0 200 miles

industries developed so rapidly, particularly in Pennsylvania, that, by the 1850s, the United States was competing on almost level terms internationally with Britain, which had become the world's leading toolmaker.

Among the most influential products of the industrialization of the North were the railroads, which quickly spread out across the United States. Although the early plans for a national rail system were government-inspired, the lines were eventually constructed by private enterprise. The earliest was the Baltimore and Ohio Railroad, begun in 1827 to link Baltimore, Maryland, and Washington, D.C. The railroads made an immediate impact, opening up many ports to productive hinterlands that had previously been unexploited. Parts of Massachusetts, for example, were on the point of being abandoned as unworkable when the construction of railroads enabled their transformation into some of the most valuable real estate in the Union. There was later a proliferation of lines, most of them short, especially in the South. Among the earliest were the Tuscumbia-Courtland-Decatur Railroad in Alabama and the Pontchartrain Railroad in New Orleans, Louisiana, which opened in 1830 and 1831 respectively. Although the railroads caused irreparable damage to the profitability of the barges and riverboats that, along with the horse, had previously been the only practical means of transcontinental transportation, they made a monumental contribution to the coalescence of the contiguous states and later, as detailed elsewhere, played significant role in the outcome of the Civil War.

In the Southern states, on either side of the railroad tracks, most of the country was farmland. Although rice and oranges were grown in the humid southeastern coastal region, the principal crop throughout most of the region was originally tobacco. However, by the start of the 19th century, this had lost its overall preeminence to cotton. This development was made possible by the introduction of the cotton gin, a revolving cylinder on which the fibers of the plant were mounted and then pulled through a set of wire teeth that were too closely aligned to permit the passage of the seeds. Previously, the seeds had had to be removed by hand, a laborious and time-consuming occupation. Invented in 1793 by Eli Whitney, the cotton gin was introduced just in time for American producers to capitalize on trade with Britain, where the recent development of mechanized spinning techniques had created a massive new market for U.S. exports. From that moment on, in nearly all parts of the South apart from Virginia, which kept faith with tobacco, cotton became the principal crop, and it was often cultivated to the exclusion of all other plants. The region was henceforth effectively a monoculture.

There was great truth in the contemporary slogan "Cotton is King,"

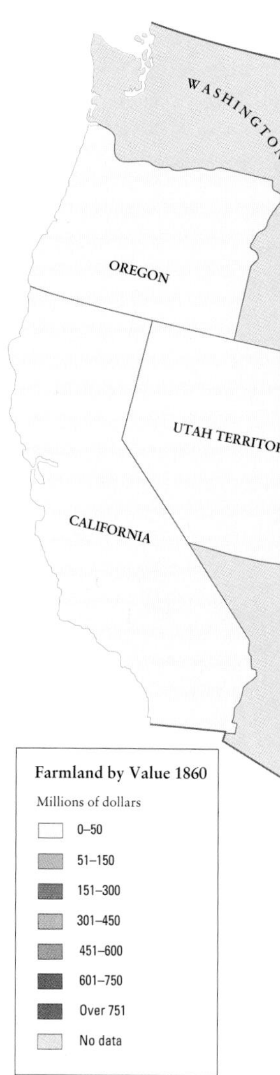

which originated as the title of an influential book of 1855 by antislavery journalist David Christy and was later popularized by Senator James Henry Hammond of South Carolina, who in 1858 used it as the clinching line of a statement that began, "Without the firing of a gun, without the drawing of a sword, should they [the Northerners] make war upon us [Southerners], we could bring the whole world to our feet. What would happen if no cotton was furnished for three years?... England would topple headlong and carry the whole civilized world with her. No, you dare not make war on cotton! No power on earth dares make war upon it."

While heavy industry fueled the North, the economic boom in the South was caused by the rising level of global demand for cotton. By 1860, the Southern states exported two-thirds of the world's cotton, and the prosperity thus created contributed significantly to the Confederacy's optimistic

Below: In 1860 the majority of Southern states concentrated on cotton farming—a prosperous crop—hence the higher value of farmland in the South.

assessment of its chances of success when it seceded from the Union in the following year.

The cotton trade also ensured that slavery, which was already widespread, became institutionalized and an immovable cornerstone of the whole antebellum economy below the Mason-Dixon line. Although cotton gins could be operated by horses or water, as well as by humans, the actual cultivation of the crop continued along old-established, labor-intensive lines. Farmworkers prepared beds for the cotton by cleaning out the stalks left over from the previous harvest; they beat the small stalks down with clubs but had to remove the larger ones (sometimes more than five feet tall) by hand. Manure or commercial fertilizer was then deposited as deeply as possible in the furrows, which were between three and six feet apart; this part of the process was again performed manually. So, too, was the planting, which normally took place in April. The cotton plants bloomed in June, and around six weeks later the bolls (seed pods containing the fibers) opened. Cotton-picking began around August 20th every year; again, the whole process was performed by hand. Most of the crop was ginned immediately. Production levels were unsustainable without vast numbers of workers; if the workers had to be paid, the business would have been unsustainable. The South, which had once regarded slavery as a necessary evil, began to see it as an essential good.

Improved production methods and increased demand necessitated improvements in the transportation network between the fields and the customers. Existing roads were widened and new ones built to take horsedrawn wagon trains laden with bales. Cities grew up around the river ports and railroad stations that provided links between the South and the Northeast and Midwest. The demand for labor created a prosperous slave trade, as vast numbers of African Americans were brought in to fill vacancies, principally in Georgia and South Carolina, and in other Southern states.

In addition to the great plantations, with their rich and powerful white owners and their impoverished black slaves, there were large numbers of smaller cotton plantations owned by the descendants of the yeoman farmers who the Founding Fathers had imagined would constitute the backbone of European settlement in North America. Yet, so far from sharing in the general prosperity, many of these people were subsistence farmers; some were unable to compete at all, and had to diversify into food crops for which there was a strictly limited demand, because most of the South's sustenance came from the North of the country. Thus it was not just the Confederacy that relied on cotton. The North supplied all the things that the South could not produce itself—principally foodstuffs and machinery—so it was the whole of the U.S. economy that depended on the crop. The North also profited through the export of Southern cotton, most of which left the United States through Union seaports.

As the Civil War loomed, the South began to use the economic power that it derived from the cotton trade to negotiate with foreign powers without reference to the Federal government. Confederate leaders tried to use cotton to bring Britain and France into the conflict on their side. They wanted to enlist the help of the two great European nations to break the maritime blockade by which the Union hoped to deny the Southern states access to the export market. The pressure was particularly intense on Britain, 75 percent of whose cotton came from the United States and 20 percent of whose population earned its living from related service industries.

Opposite page: This map shows a breakdown of the raw material industry in America in 1860. Note the large number of cotton plantations in the South.

However, at the outbreak of the Civil War, Britain happened to have a surplus of cotton.

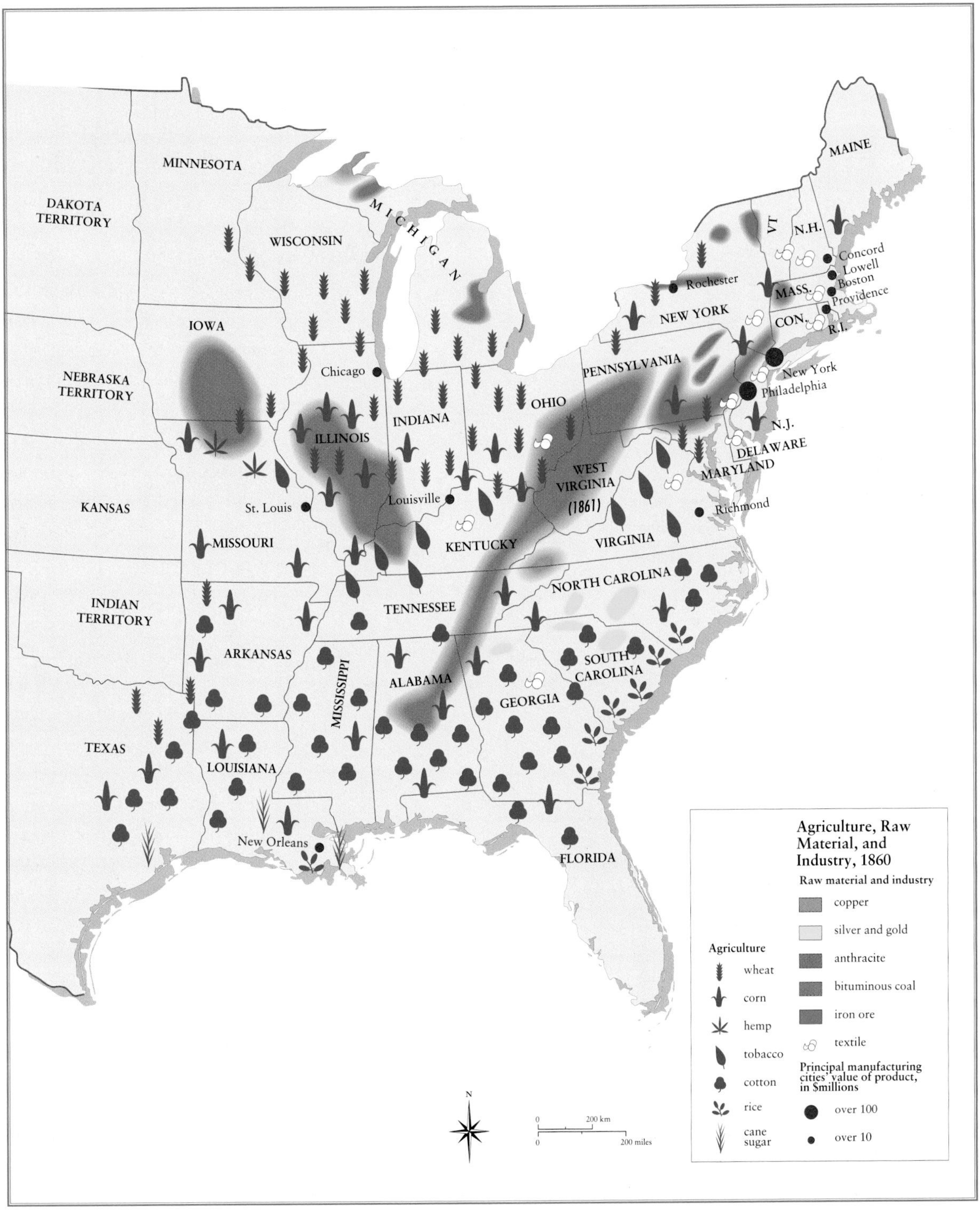

MINNESOTA
DAKOTA TERRITORY
WISCONSIN
MICHIGAN
IOWA
NEBRASKA TERRITORY
Chicago
ILLINOIS
INDIANA
OHIO
KANSAS
St. Louis
Louisville
MISSOURI
KENTUCKY
INDIAN TERRITORY
ARKANSAS
TENNESSEE
MISSISSIPPI
ALABAMA
TEXAS
LOUISIANA
New Orleans
GEORGIA
FLORIDA
SOUTH CAROLINA
NORTH CAROLINA
VIRGINIA
WEST VIRGINIA (1861)
Richmond
MARYLAND
DELAWARE
N.J.
PENNSYLVANIA
Philadelphia
New York
NEW YORK
Rochester
CON.
R.I.
MASS.
VT
N.H.
MAINE
Concord
Lowell
Boston
Providence
N
0 200 km
0 200 miles
Agriculture, Raw Material, and Industry, 1860
Raw material and industry
copper
silver and gold
anthracite
bituminous coal
iron ore
textile
Principal manufacturing cities' value of product, in $millions
over 100
over 10
Agriculture
wheat
corn
hemp
tobacco
cotton
rice
cane sugar

Partly for that reason, and partly because the British government was by that time opposed to slavery, their intervention in the conflict was not as realistic a prospect as the South had hoped; Britain never even gave diplomatic recognition to the Confederacy, let alone gave serious consideration to intervening in the Civil War. France was similarly unsympathetic to appeals from the rebel government in Richmond, Virginia.

Although the South failed to secure overseas military aid, and was never recognized by any foreign power, it fared better in its search for external financial backing, which was forthcoming from a wide range of sources with cotton as the security on the loans.

During the Civil War, in the absence of allies, the South attempted to make itself self-sufficient. Confederate leaders encouraged farmers to plant more foodstuffs—beans, corn, and wheat—by imposing limits on the amount of cotton that they were allowed to grow, sometimes reducing the permitted output by as much as 80 percent. The farmers responded favorably, but they still failed to produce as much food as the government wanted. Hence the Confederate policy proved self-defeating. The change of agricultural priorities reduced the production of cotton throughout the Civil War. In 1861, the Southern states produced 4.5 million bales; the number then dropped year on year to 1.5 million bales in 1862, 500,000 bales in 1863, and 300,000 bales in 1864. As output fell, the world market price rose. Unscrupulous exporters soon reached the conclusion that the potential profits were worth the risk of trying to break the blockade, but because their activities were illegal, the Confederate government derived no benefit from their illicit trade.

The South's cotton power was further undermined by the war strategy of the North. At the start of the conflict, the Confederacy banned the export of cotton to the Union. President Abraham Lincoln then authorized traders to follow Union armies into the South and help themselves to the cotton they found there. President Jefferson Davis responded by instructing plantation owners to destroy any of their own crops that were in danger of falling into enemy hands. Some Southerners obeyed his orders to the letter, dutifully setting fire to their own sole source of income before withdrawing to safety behind their army's lines. However, many others realized that the Northerners were often prepared to pay for their cotton, or to trade it for food and other vitals that were in desperately short supply. Thus there developed another clandestine market from which the Confederate government derived no revenue.

Although the antebellum North was generally industrial and the prewar South mainly agricultural, that is to some extent a simplification of a complex picture that was further complicated during the Civil War itself. For example, the Union ban on cotton imports from the South stimulated nationwide demand for one of Ohio's major products, wool, which was used to make army uniforms and blankets. This new market partly compensated for the damage caused to the Ohio economy by the loss of the Confederate states as an outlet for its main peacetime product, corn. By 1860, cotton ruled the South, which annually exported two-thirds of the world supply of the "white gold." It also ruled the West because each year these sections sold $30 million worth of food supplies to Southern cotton producers. Cotton ruled the Northeast because the domestic cotton industry there produced $100 million worth of cloth each year. In addition, the North sold to the cotton growing South more than $150 million worth of manufactured goods every year, and Northern

Above: This illustration gives a strong impression of the life endured by black people before the Civil War. At the height of the plantation system in 1850, when cotton had become the major cash crop of the south, 1.8 million of the 2.5 million slaves in the United States were involved in its production.

ships transported cotton and cotton products worldwide.

The Civil War caused the destruction of much of the South's cropland, the break-up of the vast old plantations, and the loss of innumerable heads of livestock. The vanquished states took many years to recover because their agricultural infrastructure was too dependent on a monoculture (usually of cotton, rice or tobacco, depending on the region) to adapt to the requirements of the postbellum period. The South also struggled to cope with the emancipation of the slaves, although it circumvented Federal legislation through the introduction of Jim Crow laws, which led, after the end of Reconstruction in 1877, to the introduction of a new system of government that was founded economically on sharecropping (tenant farmers), politically on a one-party system (the Democrats), and socially on racial segregation.

TWO PRESIDENTS: THEIR SIMILARITIES & DIFFERENCES

THE LEADERSHIP OF NORTH AND SOUTH REFLECTED BOTH THE SIMILARITIES AND DIFFERENCES BETWEEN PRESIDENTS ABRAHAM LINCOLN AND JEFFERSON DAVIS. BOTH WERE WESTERNERS, BORN A HUNDRED MILES APART IN KENTUCKY. BOTH WERE MIDDLE CLASS IN ORIGIN, AND BOTH WERE A COMPLEX MIXTURE OF IDEALISM AND OPPORTUNISM, WHICH AFFECTED THEIR PROSECUTION OF THE WAR.

Abraham Lincoln was a practical, ingenuous man who read utilitarian books and was not interested in intellectual pursuits for their own sake. His law partner, William H. Herndon, remembered a man who relished power and the management of people. Lincoln used humility as a tool to obtain political advantage, and had confidence in his considerable abilities. His rural brand of shrewdness made him calculating and forward-looking, especially with regard to his political future; yet he preferred a simple, direct approach to problems and policies. Although Lincoln was not awkward or without social graces, he was never lionized by Washington society. He had little experience as an administrator, but he had tremendous latent ability and was a quick learner. His deliberate balancing within his administration of the diversity of prevalent ideologies with which he was not in conflict gave him access to talents he did not possess. Men such as Treasury Secretary Salmon P. Chase and Secretary of War Edwin Stanton exerted considerable influence. Friction would develop from every direction, but Lincoln controlled it through a policy of quiet manipulation—at which he excelled—or by direct exercise of authority.

Lincoln held office in Illinois' House of Representatives in the 1830s under Whig sponsorship, before graduating in the 1840s to the U.S. House of Representatives. His distinguished service contributed to his selection to oppose Senator Stephen A. Douglas, a powerful Democrat with presidential ambitions, in the 1858 senatorial elections. The way Lincoln backed Douglas into a corner on the issue of popular sovereignty

Above: Abraham Lincoln (*left*) and Jefferson Davis. The presidents of the warring states were opposed in ideology but remarkably similar in character and temperament.

in the Western territories in the celebrated Lincoln-v-Douglas debates showed his mettle and soon became the stuff of national folklore. Although he did not win the election, he received national exposure and an approving eye from the growing Abolitionist movement. However, Lincoln's political beliefs were as mixed as his personality. His political conversion was a combination of opportunism and ideological growth. Lincoln believed the unity of the nation to be sacred. He supported an antislavery policy, but its details were vague and he was not in a hurry to enforce it at the expense of the Union. This changed as the war progressed and he accepted the growing influence of the Abolitionist wing of the Republican Party on appointments and on shifts in policy.

Jefferson Davis's family moved south from Kentucky and in time attained a modest fortune. They became part of the Southern landed aristocracy, with all its pretensions and charm. Davis developed in a way quite different from Lincoln; he was not a self-made man but the product of a system producing a gracious living from managerial toil. He even experienced the tragedy so popular in Southern folklore when his wife of three months—Sarah Knox Taylor, the daughter of President Zachary Taylor—died after contracting malaria in Cuba, in June 1835. A complex mixture of principle and ambition, Davis creatively mastered one challenge after another during a long career in government. His protracted period of public service, both in Congress and in the executive. meant that he was completely at home in the urbane and sophisticated atmosphere of Washington.

He was elected to the United States House of Representatives, and then to the Senate, before serving a term as United States Secretary of War. Such was the extent of his service that, by the time he was chosen to lead the fledgling Confederacy, Davis was widely regarded as the "foremost man in the South." As President of the Confederacy Davis showed his diligence and attention to detail, the fruits of the education he had received at West Point, which then as now was one of the best available. But in the long run, his insistence on handling even the smallest detail harmed his person, his reputation, and the Confederate war effort. A courageous man, he did not let ill health—resulting from a congenital defect, aggravated by malaria—become an excuse for shirking responsibility or making tough decisions. He was moralistic, hardworking and confident. His intense loyalty proved to be both a strength and a weakness; he would not countenance criticism of those in whom he believed and was obstinate about his appointees and policies. Davis's belief in the rightness of the Southern cause and in States' Rights never wavered. Indeed, it increased during the war. This did not prevent him from centralizing the Confederate Government when prosecution of the war demanded it. He was more flexible on the fundamental questions of State powers versus those of the national government than about the details of policies and relationships with people. Unlike others, Davis could see that the Southern way of life would be lost unless the war could be won. The public perception of Davis was one of aloofness, but this was a misinterpretation of the dignified reserve and courtly manner which endeared him to the critical patricians of Richmond. Among friends and family, he was warm and devoted, and he loved children.

Both men were given more power than any president to that time; Davis was less successful than Lincoln in using it. Davis was unable to negotiate a workable alliance between the conflicting ideologies in the South. Maybe no one could; the plantation mentality, which viewed any change in the political and social structure as treason, weakened the Confederacy toward the end of the war.

Lincoln, too, was confronted by ideologues, while less sincerely motivated men wielded enormous power in the shadows behind him. The most influential members of his Cabinet were from the northeast and from the radical wing of the party, and their authority was enhanced by the outbreak of war. Lincoln maneuvered adroitly between Peace Democrats and radical Abolitionists by using both institutional inducements and personal prestige in whatever combinations were required.

The Confederacy, a new nation, and its inaugural president, Jefferson Davis, needed to devise a complete set of laws and governmental institutions by which to abide. A convention was called in Montgomery, Alabama, at that time the capital of the Confederacy, to draft a constitution for the new nation. There, 50 representatives from seceded States participated in a 35-day meeting, which proceeded logically and carefully to determine the boundaries of its authority, create the framework of a provisional government and draft a permanent constitution while acting as a provisional Congress. The United States Constitution was, as one might have expected, used as a basic framework for the Confederate Constitution, but a number of modifications enthroned the Southern concept of government. States would possess a "sovereign and independent character" even though a "permanent federal government" was to be established. The people elected to office would, it was hoped, devise a workable compromise between the two.

In some respects the Confederate document improved on the United States Constitution. It established item veto by the president and required two-thirds approval of appropriations not requested by the president; it provided for a district court structure and a procedure in the event of presidential disability; and it prohibited tariffs. While it contained a prohibition against any new extension of the slave trade, it protected slavery in the States and territories of the Confederacy. Confederate presidents would be elected for six-year terms but could not stand for reelection. Congress could, if desired, offer seats to members of the president's cabinet so that it could hear from them first hand. In putting together a cabinet, Davis was constrained by the same type of regional considerations that had influenced American politics since the Revolution.

Constitutional issues also were important in the North. Lincoln assumed more power than any previous president. By classifying secession as insurrection, he was able to assume emergency powers and commit the

United States to war long before Congress acted. In the interest of national security, he followed a rule of "military necessity" during the war, which suspended civil liberties and instituted summary arrest of persons suspected of opposing the war effort.

Although Lincoln was lenient toward malefactors charged under his proclamations, including those in the military, the suspension of habeas corpus and abrogation of constitutional rights by commanders of the military departments were controversial actions. Some constitutional issues were not settled until after the war. In the meantime, thousands were arrested and imprisoned citizens were forced to take loyalty oaths, and simple economic rights were violated.

Lincoln did not aspire to dictatorship; his aggressive actions accomplished quickly what would have taken Congress months to do and Congress ultimately acquiesced in all of them. However, he was not above using military actions to serve political ends.

The contrast between the two leaders shows clearly in the places which retain their memories. The log cabin in which President Lincoln is believed to have been born is preserved in a handsome marble structure on 100 acres of his father's farm near Hodgenville, Kentucky. Davis's birthplace no longer exists, but a 351-ft (107m) high monument to his memory has been erected at Fairfield, Connecticut. Lincoln's law office in Springfield, Illinois, from which he moved into a political career, is typical of the small, unpretentious Midwest town office of the era. His home has a plain exterior and a homespun interior that matched his personality. The agony Davis suffered after the war as a prisoner at Fort Monroe, Virginia, is reflected in the Casemate Museum there, while his tastes in home life are evident at both the White House of the Confederacy, his first official residence, in Montgomery, Alabama, and at Bellevue, near Mobile, where he spent the last years of his life. The war destroyed both men. Lincoln had been assassinated by the time Davis was captured. Davis survived imprisonment to provide his account of the ideological and economic conflict that ravaged whole states and sent at least half a million young men and uncounted numbers of civilians to their graves.

Left: Photograph of Abraham Lincoln's boyhood home in Kentucky.

THE DRIFT INTO WAR: FORT SUMTER, 1861

RELUCTANCE AND ANTICIPATION PERVADED THE AIR OF CHARLESTON, SOUTH CAROLINA, ON THE NIGHT OF APRIL 12, 1861. THE SHORELINE WAS RINGED WITH MORTARS AND CANNON, AIMED AT FORT SUMTER ON A MANMADE ISLAND AT THE HARBOR ENTRANCE. WITH WAR IMMINENT, CITIZENS OF NORTH AND SOUTH BOTH EXHIBITED ENTHUSIASM FOR CONFLICT WITH A DESIRE NOT TO BE BLAMED FOR STARTING IT.

Above: Fort Sumter in Charleston Harbor was one of a series of fortifications constructed after the War of 1812 to protect the U.S. coastline from foreign invaders, but the first shots ever fired at it came from American guns.

Great effort to avoid armed confrontation was coming to nothing. Politicians in both North and South had exerted enormous efforts to resolve the conflict between the two regions over slavery, economic competition, and jealousy, and especially the divisive tariff issue, which was almost as abrasive as the more emotional slavery question. South Carolina had endured the affront to its sovereignty by "foreign" (i.e. Union) forces stationed on its soil since December 20, 1860, when the State seceded from the United States and then joined the Confederated States of America.

Confederate President Jefferson Davis had sent word from Montgomery, Alabama, to exercise caution. U.S. officials likewise were hesitant to provoke the fight that seemed inevitable. When a relief ship sent to Fort Sumter in January by the outgoing President James Buchanan was fired upon by Confederate shore batteries, it turned back. Newly elected president, Abraham Lincoln, backed up a tough Inaugural Address asserting Federal authority over the seceding States with almost a month of inaction. When he decided to send a relief expedition of three ships to the fort, he advised the South Carolina governor, Francis Pickins, that only supplies would be landed, not reinforcements, unless

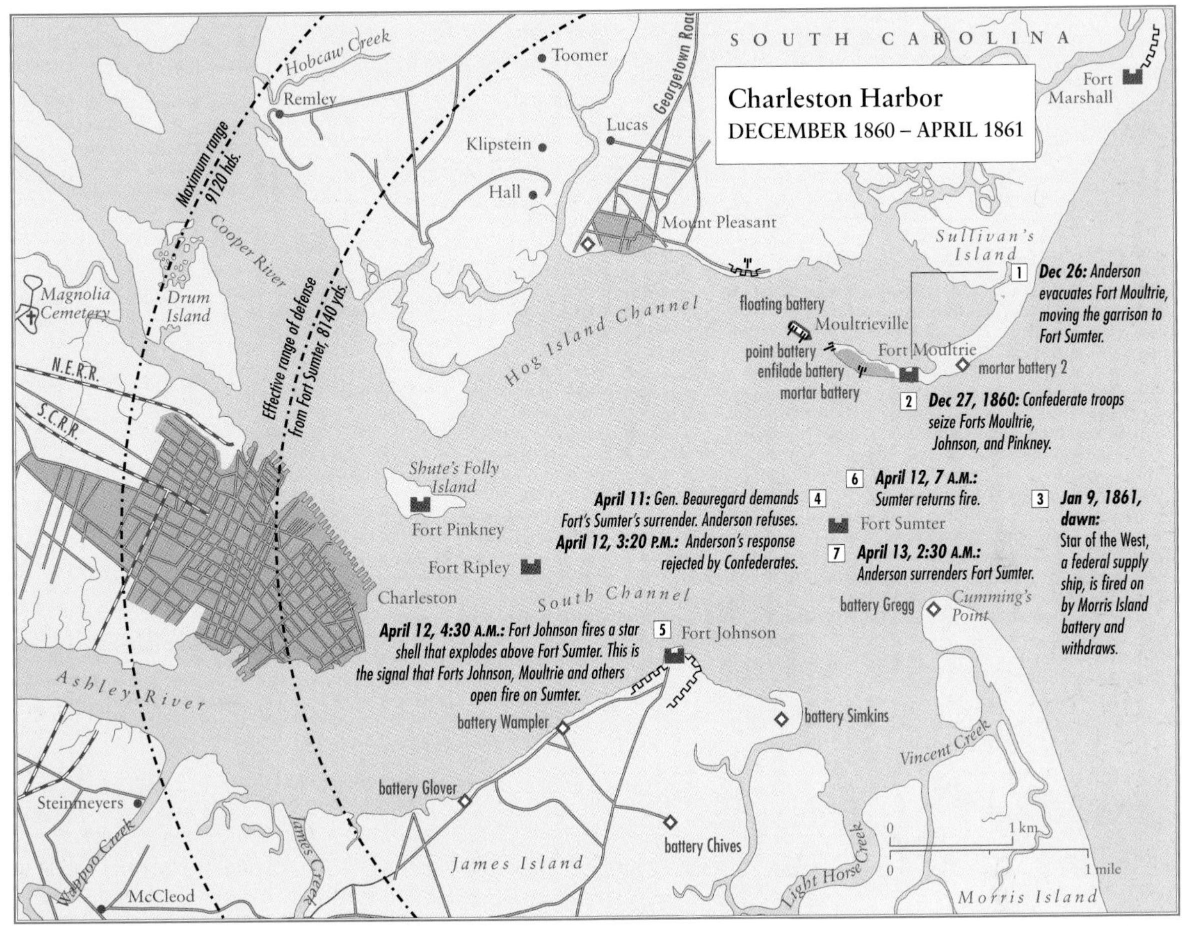

Above: Map showing the events in and around Charleston Harbor that tipped the United States from uneasy peace into a state of war.

the expedition met resistance. All of this, however, was outweighed by mutual mistrust and strategic considerations.

Both sides had misled the other on occasion and those three small Federal ships now posed a major problem for the Confederacy. Fort Sumter was brand new (its present occupants were its first) and formidable, with 50-ft (15.2-m) high brick walls, 12ft (3.6m) thick at their base. It mounted 60 guns, but only a garrison of 85 men. The commander, Major Robert Anderson, had orders to remain, but admitted to Confederate emissaries that, without supplies, he could not resist the powerful array of 43 guns and mortars at Forts Johnson and Moultrie, located on each side of the entrance to the narrow harbor; Castle Pinckney, a small island in the inner harbor off the Battery; an innovative floating battery near Moultrieville; and temporary gun emplacements at other strategic locations along the shoreline. His supplies would be exhausted by April 15 and then he would have to capitulate.

The three relief ships, the steamship Baltic, the USS Pawnee, and the five-gun revenue cutter Harriet Lane could alter the situation. If their mission succeeded, South Carolina officials foresaw

Above: Robert Anderson *(top)*, the Federal commander of Fort Sumter, who surrendered his garrison of about 85 men to 5,500 Confederate troops under P. G. T. Beauregard. Edmund Ruffin *(below)*, farmer, slaveholder, and political activist, advocated States' Rights and secession, and was an avowed enemy of the North for its invasion of his beloved Virginia. Legend has it that he fired the first shot at Fort Sumter.

the possibility of continued Federal occupation of the fort, which guarded one of the most important harbors in the new Confederacy; it could not remain in unfriendly hands.

By the spring, excitement had been building in Charleston for some time. State officials had been upset by Major Anderson's Christmas 1860 decision to occupy the fort, believing they had an agreement with President Buchanan that Federal troops would remain at the more vulnerable Forts Moultrie and Johnson. To many minds, the decision made war inevitable. Confederate forces had responded by moving into the former Federal mainland bases and began fortifying the entire shoreline. Crowds gathered to watch the emplacement of new cannon, and to look at the beleaguered fort.

When the Confederate cannon finally opened fire at 4.10 a.m. on April 13, it was like an early Fourth of July. Charleston's civilians, roused from their slumbers by the booming of the guns, climbed to their roofs to watch the palpitating light of muzzle flashes and the explosion of shells. Spectators would be prominent through the 34 hours the fort was under siege. For men such as Brigadier General P. G. T. Beauregard of Louisiana, a former West Point commandant picked by Confederate President Davis to command the attack, there was less elation than a sense of relief that the waiting was over and that the final act of dissolution was occurring, mixed with the nagging uncertainty that affects all soldiers at such times.

A tragicomedy was being acted out. An ardent civilian secessionist from Virginia (still in the Union at that point), Edmund Ruffin, was accorded the honor of touching off the first shot—although there is no definitive evidence that he actually did so. Fort Sumter did not immediately return the fire, but waited until after daybreak. Major Anderson's soldiers leisurely breakfasted before manning their posts, and then spaced their firing to conserve ammunition.

Confederate batteries, which opened the battle with an intense bombardment, alternated between sporadic firing and flurries during the 34 hours the fort held out. In a day and a half of firing, more than 2,000 rounds were fired from Fort Sumter, with the Confederates firing 3,500 more, but no one was killed and only eight men, four on each side, were wounded. The only fatality came as Major Anderson saluted the flag before evacuating the fort. A cartridge bag exploded, killing a gun-crew member, Private Daniel Hough. The relative light damage sustained by the fort in this first battle was just the beginning. As the war went on, repossession of Fort Sumter became a Union obsession, partly because the naval blockade of the harbor was unsuccessful. There were three small attacks from sea, all ending ingloriously, even the one in April 1863 that utilized a fleet of nine ironclad vessels.

Union guns threw seven million pounds of metal at the fort, but, despite this, only 52 Confederate soldiers were killed. Action elsewhere on the Atlantic Coast and on Western rivers would find winning combinations of seapower and land forces against forts, but Fort Sumter, even though subjected to sustained Union bombardment after 1863 from Morris Island, remained in Confederate hands until Charleston was taken from the rear on February 17, 1865, during Major General William T. Sherman's celebrated march to the sea. By that time, however, the fort was just a pile of broken bricks—a sign, also observed elsewhere during the war, that the advent of rifled cannon had made large, fixed fortifications somewhat obsolete.

The Confederate attack on Fort Sumter was not much of a contest; both sides were fatalistic about the outcome, and the action in retrospect seems more pro forma than contemporaries judged from news accounts at the time. The naval relief expedition, through a series of misunderstandings caused by secrecy and disagreement, waited just outside the harbor while Sumter was being forced to surrender. Indeed, the spark that set off the Civil War could easily have happened in Florida, instead of South Carolina. Fort Pickens, on Santa Rosa Island off Pensacola, was one of the key coastal forts that President Buchanan promised not to reinforce and Lincoln was determined to hold. For a time it was a powder keg with a short fuse.

Numerous historians have pointed to similarities between the little-known events in Florida on the eve of war and the famous events in South Carolina at Charleston. At the same time as Florida's vote on secession in early January 1861, Federal officials decided to destroy the Chattahoochee Arsenal and reinforce the Pensacola Forts. To prevent this, Florida seized the arsenal from a sergeant and three men took possession of the navy yard and concentrated a sizable force near Fort Barrancas. Confederates also took control of Fort Marion (Castillo de San Marcos) in St. Augustine from a single caretaker.

Fort Pickens was unfinished at the time, but was more strategically located than Fort Barrancas on the mainland, which Lieutenant Adam J. Slemmer had orders to hold. Slemmer decided to move his 46 soldiers and 35 ordinary seamen to the more defensible fort on Santa Rosa Island, which also could be reinforced from the sea. The same decision made by Major Anderson at Fort Sumter and a war of nerves with Confederate forces on the mainland began. President Buchanan, as fearful of starting a war at Pensacola as he was at Charleston, agreed to maintain the status quo and the Confederates held their fire. Lincoln, after taking office, decided to reinforce the fort and, within a week after the bombardment of Fort Sumter, more than 2,000 soldiers had been

Below: This late-19th century oil painting depicts Fort Sumter under attack by Confederate forces at the outbreak of the Civil War.

Above: The Confederate flag flies over battle-scarred Fort Sumter, after the Union occupants had turned it over to the enemy.

sent to defend the position. Ironically the officer carrying orders to reinforce the fort had received a pass through the Confederate lines from the new commander of the Pensacola region, General Braxton Bragg. Confederates raided the island and guns from the battered Confederate Fort McRee, burned Warrington and Wolsey, and fired at construction in the navy yard, but neither side had an advantage.

Fort Jefferson and Key West also remained in Union hands throughout the war, the first because it was (and still is) inaccessible, and the second because of the cleverness of Captain James M. Brannan, commanding the 44 soldiers on the island. Brannan's men were quartered away from Fort Taylor, the only place they could defend, so the captain moved them secretly in small groups and at night, through the hostile city to the fort. The attempt to take the State capital at Tallahassee late in the war started from Key West. Fort Jefferson, the largest of the coastal forts built by the United States in the early nineteenth century, is now a national monument as well known for legends of pirates and sunken gold as it is for war stories. Fort Pickens is now part of the Gulf Islands National Seashore. The ruins and museum relate the lively history of the fort, which included imprisonment of the Indian Chief Geronimo after his capture. Fort Barrancas, located on the grounds of the Pensacola Naval Air Station, is restored and included with the Water Battery in a guided historical tour. Old Christ Church, the oldest remaining church building in Florida which was used by Union soldiers as a barracks and hospital, houses the Pensacola Historical Museum. A number of other antebellum structures survive, including the 1810 Charles Lavalle House and the 1825 Lighthouse, still owned by the Coast Guard.

Fort Moultrie has been restored to reflect its entire martial history, starting with the Revolutionary War, but key features remain from its strategic role during the Civil War. The masonry fort that exists today had been given its basic shape by the time of the Civil War, but was reinforced with sand and wood to reduce the effect of explosions. The right section of the curved forward edge holds Civil War batteries, which indicate the alterations made by Confederates in response to technological changes in coast artillery. Along Cannon Walk, outside the walls of the fort, are a series of cannon which highlight the evolution of seacoast defence weaponry during and after the Civil War. The site of old Fort Johnson, on the other side of the harbor, is now occupied by a research center and is not open to the public.

Like others on the east coast, Fort Sumter has accretions from later wars, when the forts were used by coastal artillery; however, even today, it still shows the wear and tear of Civil War action. A tour boat from the mainland deposits visitors at a dock on the left flank from where they enter the fort through a sally port, built since the Civil War. Casemates, or rooms in the walls of the fort, demonstrate the practice of gunnery as it existed in the mid 1860s. Along the right flank are eleven 100-pound Parrot guns, a rifled cannon that was extremely popular throughout the Civil War. A mountain howitzer near the Right Gorge Angle, intended to defend the fort against a surprise landing by Union forces, reveals how the Confederates were forced to improvize. Several projectiles still protrude from the wall of the left flank, stark reminders of the shelling by Union batteries in 1863.

The original shape of the five-sided brick fort, one of the series of fortifications authorized by Congress after the War of 1812 with Great Britain, remains. One of the flagpoles, replacing the one that was shot away during the Confederate bombardment, was erected in 1928 to honor Major Anderson and his men. The fort's museum contains a variety of relics, and tells certain episodes of the fort's history in diorama and pictorial display form. A ground-level view from the esplanade along the Gorge exterior reveals the way the fort dominates the entrance to the harbor.

Below: The Federal government formally took possession of Fort Sumter on February 22, 1865 with a gala flag raising cermemony.

Enlistment & Conscription

In the first wave of enthusiasm, thousands enlisted in both the Union and Confederate armies for short periods, without concern for reward. Eventually, however, as the conflict wore on, inducements became necessary for longer periods, and this lead to numerous abuses—and in the end conscription became necessary.

Above: Intended to romanticize the Civil War and boost morale, this painting shows gaudily dressed Union soldiers marching away from the banks of the Potomac River with the Capitol building clearly recognizable in the background.

Girls who loved uniforms helped recruitment, by making imaginative displays of flags, and giving patriotic speeches at holiday picnics and in public squares. Bounties provided one of the most effective inducements, and sizable sums were offered. Some men made a career of enlisting, skipping out, and then reenlisting under another name many times over. Although a large number were caught, several reenlisters got away with (time and again) and so the practice continued. States generally took the lead in forming new units. In most states, however, anyone who was persuasive or clever enough was usually allowed to form his own unit. Usually these weren't companies but ambitious individuals, who had enough prestige and money to get things started in a community, and sometimes formed whole regiments.

The North, with its larger population and greater level of immigration, had an advantage under the volunteer system. The United States Congress authorised increasing the Regular Army to 40,000, but Federal recruiting officers were so ineffective that it never totalled more than 26,000 at any time during the war. Regular officers were appointed to most major field commands but were seldom placed in command of individual volunteer units or used to train volunteers.

Although the heritage of volunteering was strong in America—and was producing armies

Left: This contemporary illustration shows a Union recruitment drive through the streets of Philadelphia, Pennsylvania.

larger than the county had ever known before—it soon became obvious that, even with financial inducements, the volunteer system could not provide the ever-increasing number of soldiers and sailors needed to satisfy the insatiable demands of war. Conscription, enacted first by the Confederate Congress on April 16, 1862, and a year later by the Union, added a new dimension to the way.

The Confederate draft, the first national conscription law in American history, authorised impressments of all males between 18 and 35 (later extended to between 17 and 50) not legally exempt. The exception list was extensive, with state governors making liberal use of their powers to confer exemptions to satisfy domestic political needs.

The Union draft law permitted buying an exemption for $300, the amount usually paid as a bounty. As a result, the initial draft call raised $15 million for the Federal Treasury. The law also allowed hiring a substitute—those who could afford it were allowed to hire someone to fight in their stead—which created a perception (also prevalent in the South) that this was a "rich man's war and a poor man's fight." This controversial feature of the act was not canceled until 1864.

Resistance movements came into being. Georgia's Governor Joe Brown was a fervent and particularly outspoken opponent of conscription, who made extensive use of his privilege of granting exemptions and even went so far as to challenge the constitutionality of the law in court. Opposition wasn't restricted to the south. The Federal draft sparked off riots in New York, Hartford, and other cities. Troops had to be pulled back from the fighting front to put down rioting in New York, which lasted for five days and cost 1,200 lives, many of them black.

Although many conscripts made good soldiers, just as many resented being forced to serve and were of questionable military value. Volunteers denigrated the conscripts so badly that serious tensions arose at times, with conscripts returning the dislike. Many hired substitutes, some of whom were immigrants seeking a start in a new country and often performed admirable service; others, however, quickly deserted. Men were supposed to receive physicals before entering service, but these were often perfunctory. In some instances, inductees were simply asked by a doctor if they were in good health.

Company officers were elected by the men forming a unit, and so the person organizing the unit frequently was the man chosen to command it. These men had little experience in drilling, much less in directing a unit on the battlefield, and they had to learn along with those in the ranks. In some instances, officers marched alongside privates to learn drill from experienced sergeants, but most tried to tough it out by reading books, including *Hardee's Tactics* (used by both sides), and by personal bravery. In the Union army, regimental and brigade commanders were elected by the officers of the smaller units. Volunteer units were integrated into armies and corps under the command of professional soldiers appointed by presidents and war departments.

The practice of electing officers prevailed throughout the war. It worked better in the South, which had a much stronger military tradition, than in the North. Attrition, resignations ,and weeding out by senior military commanders solved some, but not all, of the worst problems. Incompetence plagued the Union army throughout the war, even at the highest levels. Although some Confederate senior commanders were accused of incompetence, in general the quality of leadership was superior to that in the Union army.

The officers were a mixed lot. Vanity, politics, even personal greed interfered with the performance of their duties. Hot tempers sometimes created ludicrous—sometimes dangerous—situations; differences over authority or remarks about courage often led to disputes. Union General William "Old Bill" Nelson was shot by a general whom he had slapped during an argument. In September 1883, Confederate Brigadier General John S. Marmaduke challenged Brigadier General Lucius M. Walker to a duel and killed him; Walker allegedly had impugned his courage.

Although some officers were popular with their troops, most were regarded by enlisted men in both armies as pampered, overbearing, and dictatorial. Even the best officers sometimes were affected. In June 1863, General Nathan Bedford Forrest was shot by an aggrieved subordinate; but he stabbed his assailant fatally and himself recovered to continue to lead his cavalry in bold forays against the Union.

The war had a leveling effect. As it wore on, those who remained alive began advancing through the ranks so that many who enlisted as privates became lieutenants and higher-ranking officers.

Above: A Union recruitment tent in a park in Manhattan, New York City.

Left: A parody of a Confederate recruitment office. Note the anti-Union slogans on the placards and the figure depicting "Old Abe" referring to United States President Lincoln hanging from a noose on the wall.

AFRICAN AMERICAN SOLDIERS

FROM THE OUTBREAK OF THE CIVIL WAR, THE RECRUITMENT OF BLACK TROOPS WAS A MATTER OF STRONG FEELING AND INTENSE DISAGREEMENT, EVEN AMONG PEOPLE ON THE SAME SIDE OF THE CONFLICT. IN THE SOUTHERN SLAVE STATES, THE POTENTIAL PROBLEMS INHERENT IN GIVING AFRICAN AMERICANS WEAPONS TO FIGHT WITH WERE APPARENT.

Above: A group of contrabands. Despite the best Union efforts to care for these runaways, the conditions in the holding camps were often extremely unhealthy —the worst reported a 25 per cent mortality rate over a two-year period.

It was considered by many, that even if slaves were capable of bearing the responsibility of fighting in a war (which their owners doubted), they might be tempted to flee or even turn on their owners. But such misgivings were not confined to the Confederacy. In the North, even some of the most implacable opponents of slavery were uncertain whether black people should be allowed to take an active part in the war. There was a widespread feeling that, although the conflict was largely about slavery, the slaves should not be involved in its resolution—it was to be a war between white people to determine how black people should henceforth be treated.

The engagement at Fort Sumter on April 12, 1861, which marked the opening of the Civil War, prompted a great rush by free blacks in the North to enlist in the Union army. However, they were all turned away because of a Federal law that forbade African Americans from bearing arms—notwithstanding that the legislation had been conveniently overlooked during the American Revolution and the War of 1812.

Abolitionists called for a rethink of this policy. One prominent African American, Frederick Douglass, wrote, "Let the slaves and free colored people be called into service and formed into a liberating army." For the first year of the war, the Lincoln administration refused to budge, partly for fear that a change in the law would prompt the secession of the five slave states—Delaware, Kentucky, Maryland, Missouri, and West Virginia—that had joined the Union at the start of the war. When two Union generals—John C. Frémont in Missouri and David Hunter in South Carolina—took the decision to issue emancipation proclamations on their own initiative, their orders were promptly countermanded by Washington, D.C.

However, by the middle of 1862, the growing number of contrabands (escaped Southern slaves who put themselves at the disposal of the Union) and the diminishing number of white volunteers inspired a wholesale change in government attitudes. On July 17, Congress passed the Confiscation Act and Militia Act, which for the first time guaranteed freedom for former slaves and enabled them to enlist in the Union forces. Two days later, the North officially abolished slavery. Immediately, black regiments began forming under white officers throughout the Northern states and in the Southern territories under Union control.

After the Battle of Antietam on September 17, 1862, when Federal forces turned back Robert E. Lee's advance into Maryland, Lincoln called on the Confederate states to surrender and rejoin the Union by the end of the year, otherwise their slaves would be declared free men—It should be restated that the President was not implacably opposed to slavery; his principal avowed objective had always been to do whatever it took to preserve the Union, whether by preserving slavery, destroying it, or by keeping it in some states and abolishing it in others. However, when none of the seceding states responded positively to his ultimatum, the way forward was clear. On January 1, 1863, Lincoln issued the Emancipation Proclamation, which freed all Confederate slaves and thus incited them to desert the South.

Below: Map showing the location of the contraband camps where fugitive Southern slaves took refuge within the Union, which refused to send them back to their Confederate masters.

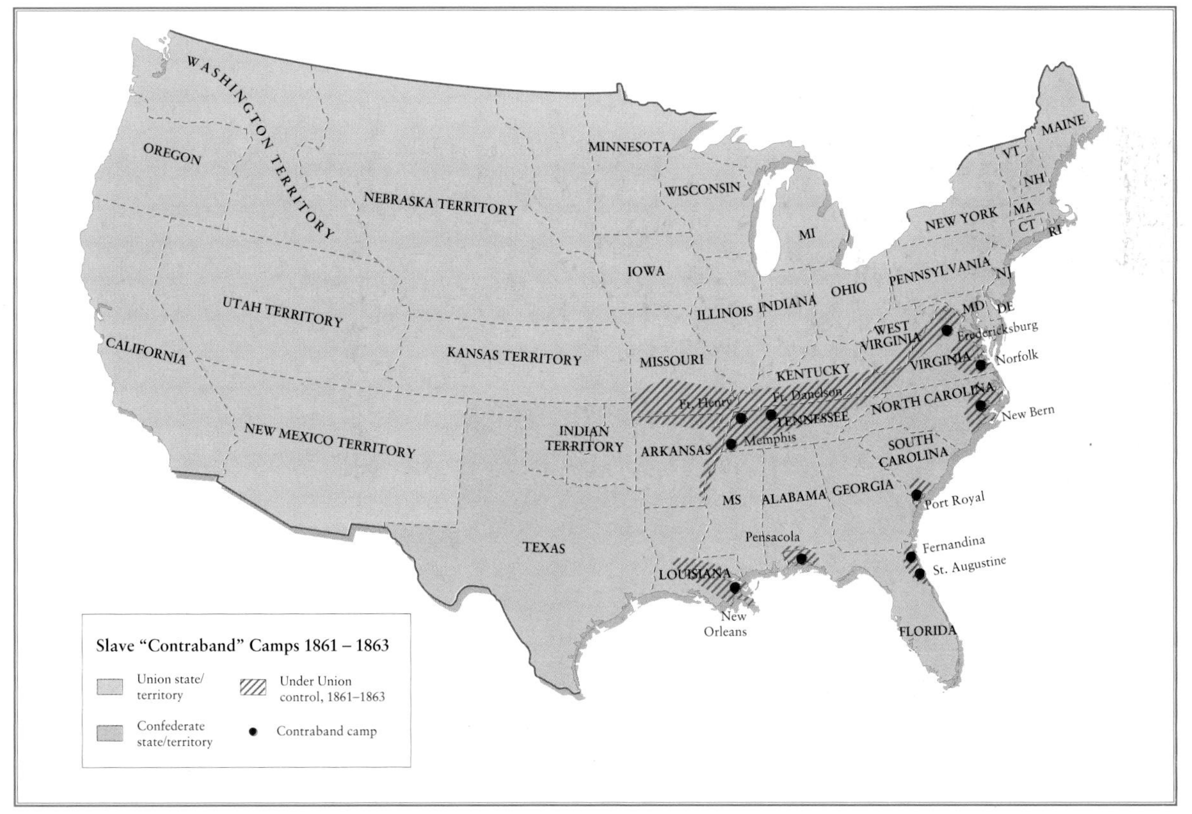

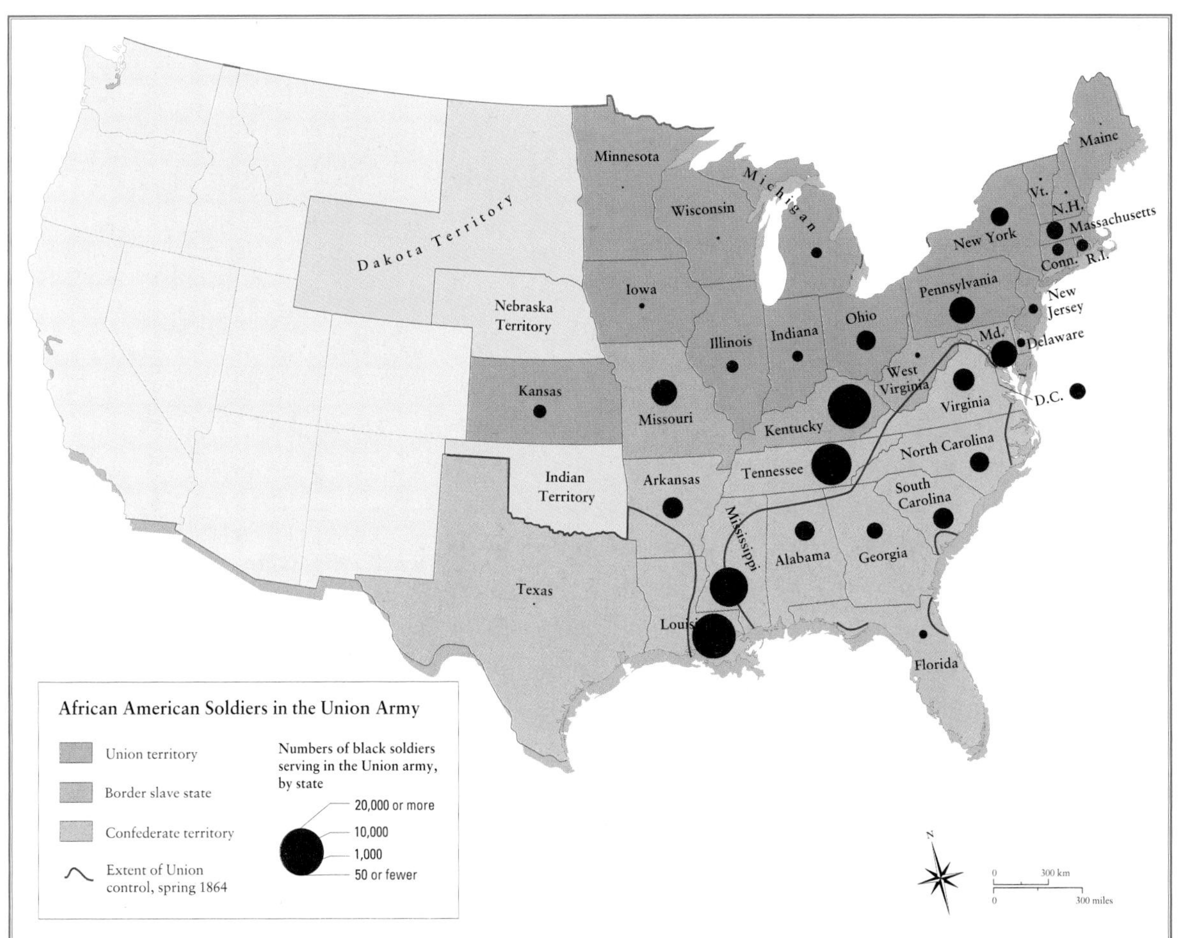

Above: The Union had tremendous success with African American recruitment. By the end of 1863, there were 20 regiments of United States Colored Troops (USCTs), and a year later there were 50. By the end of the Civil War, 10 percent of the Federal army was black.

African Americans then joined the Union army, slowly at first, but ultimately volunteering in their tens of thousands, encouraged by promises of full citizenship in return for victory. To cope with the growing number of recruits, particularly from among former slaves who were liberated when the Mississippi Valley came under Union control, the Federal government set up the Bureau of Colored Troops. All black soldiers were designated USCTs (United States Colored Troops). They were not welcomed, however, and neither were they granted comparable status with their white counterparts. Discrimination abounded, and many Union commanders, doubting that their new recruits were capable of active service, used African Americans solely as menial labor.

It was not until the summer of 1863 that black soldiers were allowed to take the field. Their first engagement came on July 18 of that year, when the 54th Massachusetts Volunteers—a segregated regiment—charged the Confederate stronghold at Fort Wagner, South Carolina. Although the assault was a failure—the unit lost two-thirds of its white officers and half of its black troops—the incident had great symbolic significance because it demonstrated to doubters that black men could fight.

Although black soldiers were henceforth allowed to serve and fight and die on the same footing

as their white comrades in arms, they were not paid the same for doing so. The average monthly wage for white soldiers was $13, plus a $3.50 clothing allowance; black soldiers received just $10 a month, but less a $3 clothing reduction. The 54th Massachusetts, having been promised equal pay, protested the injustice by refusing to accept any money at all. It took until June 1864 for Congress to finally grant black troops the same wages as white troops. In the event of capture by the Confederacy, white Union soldiers were treated as prisoners of war, but black soldiers were either executed or sent into slavery. There were many atrocities, the most notorious of which occurred in April 1864, when 200 of the 262 black Union troops defending Fort Pillow, Tennessee, were massacred after being taken prisoner during a Confederate attack. "Remember Fort Pillow" became the rallying cry of African American regiments during the final year of the war.

Despite the poor treatment they received, African Americans—supportive of the Union cause and fearful of the alternative to victory—still flocked to the Federal army and eventually comprised ten percent of its total manpower. By the end of the Civil War, approximately 179,000 black troops had enlisted, although no more than 100 of them were made officers. Many served with distinction—notably at Milliken's Bay and Port Hudson, Louisiana; Petersburg, Virginia; and at Nashville, Tennessee—and, by the end of the war, 16 of them had been awarded the Medal of Honor for feats of valor. Nearly 40,000 African Americans were killed in the Civil War—although around three quarters of them died from infection and disease.

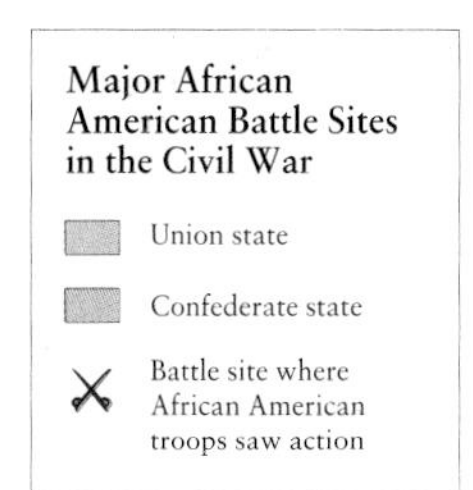

Above: African Americans served with valor and distinction in the Civil War. For all that, they were paid less than their white brothers-in-arms and fewer than 100 of them were commissioned as officers.

Meanwhile, the Union navy—confronted from the outbreak of the Civil War with a potentially catastrophic manpower shortage—adopted a more liberal attitude, recruiting African Americans from the outset. By the end of the conflict, some 15 percent of the North's sailors (around 18,000 men) were black, although none was an officer.

In the South, at the start of the war, it was axiomatic that blacks should not—indeed, in the eys of many, could not—fight. In the words of Georgia politician Howell Cobb: "The moment you resort to Negro soldiers your white soldiers will be lost to you. If slaves will make good soldiers, our whole theory of slavery is wrong."

As the tide of the war turned against the Confederacy, its generals pressurized President Jefferson Davis to allow the recruitment of slaves. Although he reluctantly agreed, by the time the Confederate Congress had authorized the necessary enabling legislation, on March 13, 1865, it was too late: the Civil War ended less than two months later.

THE OPENING CAMPAIGNS, 1861–62

BOTH THE UNION AND THE CONFEDERACY ENTERED THE CIVIL WAR WITH A SOMEWHAT UNREALISTIC CONFIDENCE THAT VICTORY WOULD BE RELATIVELY EASY AND THAT THE OPPOSING SIDE WAS NOT REALLY SERIOUS IN ITS STATED INTENTIONS. BOTH THOSE ASSUMPTIONS, HOWEVER, WERE SOON PROVED FALSE AT THE FIRST BATTLE OF BULL RUN, VIRGINIA, IN JULY 1861.

Above: Confederate General Thomas J. "Stonewall" Jackson pushed his men, but shared their hardships. His Stonewall Brigade continued to serve with distinction after his death.

Opposite page: Map showing the major campaigns of the Civil War during 1861–62.

The first major campaigns of the Civil War started in the summer of 1861 and involved untrained forces on both sides. A Union army, led by Brigadier General Irvin McDowell, marched on Richmond, Virginia—the new Confederate capital—but was defeated at the First Battle of Bull Run, Manassas. Although the rout ended in a Southern victory, it left the Confederates so damaged and exhausted by their exertions in achieving it that they failed to press home their advantage. This allowed the Union forces to regroup after leaving the field in disarray. From that point on, the earlier and rather naîve expectations of a brief campaign began to fade and both sides in the conflict became acutely aware that they were committed for the long haul.

In the light of this new knowledge, in July 1861, the Union blockaded the coast of the Confederacy, which responded by building a fleet of small, fast ships that could outmaneuver the enemy vessels. Prior to the events at Manassas, however, the western counties of Virginia, now the State of West Virginia, had become an early major area of contention. Mountainous West Virginia was divided by the war. These counties had always been suspicious of the lowlands, which controlled the

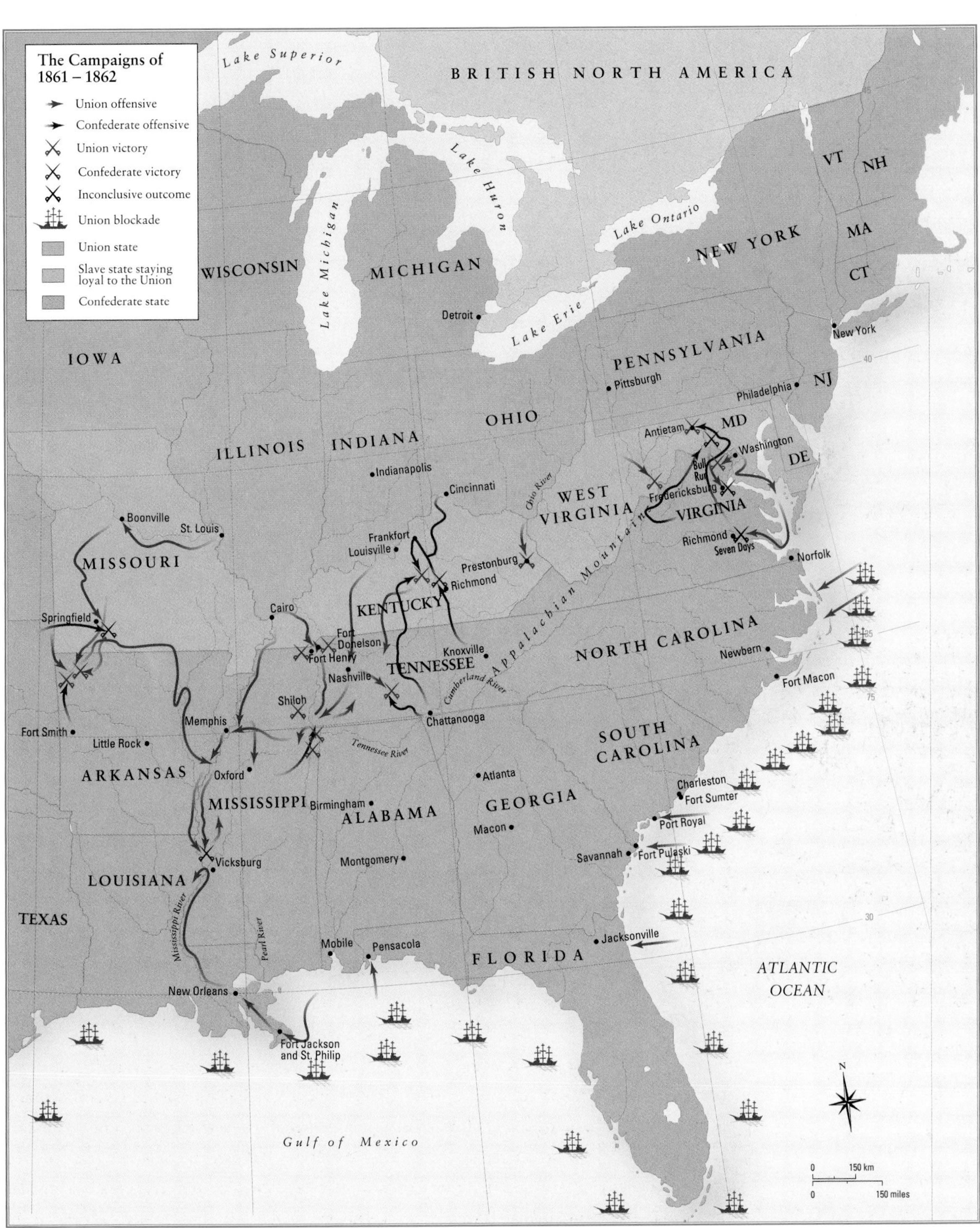
The Campaigns of 1861 – 1862
Union offensive
Confederate offensive
Union victory
Confederate victory
Inconclusive outcome
Union blockade
Union state
Slave state staying loyal to the Union
Confederate state
Lake Superior
BRITISH NORTH AMERICA
Lake Huron
Lake Michigan
Lake Ontario
Lake Erie
VT
NH
MA
CT
NEW YORK
WISCONSIN
MICHIGAN
Detroit
New York
IOWA
PENNSYLVANIA
Pittsburgh
Philadelphia
NJ
OHIO
ILLINOIS
INDIANA
Antietam
MD
Washington
DE
Bull Run
Fredericksburg
Indianapolis
Cincinnati
Ohio River
WEST VIRGINIA
VIRGINIA
Boonville
St. Louis
Frankfort
Louisville
Richmond
Seven Days
MISSOURI
Prestonburg
Norfolk
Richmond
Appalachian Mountains
Springfield
Cairo
KENTUCKY
Fort Donelson
Fort Henry
Knoxville
NORTH CAROLINA
Newbern
TENNESSEE
Nashville
Cumberland River
Fort Macon
Shiloh
Memphis
Chattanooga
Fort Smith
Little Rock
Tennessee River
SOUTH CAROLINA
ARKANSAS
Oxford
Atlanta
Charleston
Fort Sumter
MISSISSIPPI
Birmingham
ALABAMA
GEORGIA
Port Royal
Macon
Savannah
Fort Pulaski
Vicksburg
Montgomery
LOUISIANA
TEXAS
Mississippi River
Pearl River
Mobile
Pensacola
FLORIDA
Jacksonville
ATLANTIC OCEAN
New Orleans
Fort Jackson and St. Philip
Gulf of Mexico
N
0 150 km
0 150 miles

Above: Federal guns bombard Confederate troops at the Battle of Philippi. A relatively bloodless battle, that took place in Virginia June 3, 1861. It was one of the first battles of the war.

government in far-away Richmond. The inhabitants of the mountainous parts of western Virginia were, for the most part, mainly small farmers and miners who owned few slaves and thus had little reason to sympathize with the slave-holding Confederacy—their loyalty was to themselves more than to any cause or government. Yet some of the South's greatest heroes came from the area. General Thomas J. "Stonewall" Jackson was born at Clarksburg and raised at Jackson Mill near Weston, and many mountain men followed him into Confederate gray. The infamous Confederate spies Belle Boyd and Nancy Hart were also West Virginians.

Virginia tried to hold on to the area. The first fighting in West Virginia occurred when Union forces engaged Confederate artillery at Sewell's (or Seawell's) Point. However, the distinction of staging the first battle goes to Philippi, where a splendid old covered bridge over the Tygart River used by both armies still remains.

The Battle of Philippi, on June 3, 1861 was an easy Union victory, since Union forces under Colonel B.F. Kelly surprised newly recruited Confederates under Colonel G.A. Porterfield and sent them scurrying, some woken from their sleep and still in their bed clothes. Nicknamed the "Philippi Races" because it was so one-sided, the battle helped pro-Unionists maintain control of West Virginia and may have given McDowell's army a feeling of overconfidence.

General Jackson, in particular, thought that the valleys along the forks of the Potomac River had immense strategic value. Even the dead of winter could not keep Jackson idle, and reinforced by 7,000 men under Brigadier General W. W. Loring, he moved to Romney, 35 miles (56km) from Winchester, which was defended by now-Brigadier General Kelley with 5,000 men. Jackson's move was hampered by the softness of his troops, a lack of equipment and the reluctance of Loring, but he nevertheless managed to destroy the Baltimore & Ohio Railway bridge over the Great Cacapon River and to occupy Romney, which Kelley had evacuated.

Jackson left Loring to hold Romney and returned to Winchester with his "Stonewall Brigade." Loring's imaginary fear that he would be cut off, fed by the grumbling of the officers at Romney, led the Confederate Secretary of War Judah P. Benjamin to tell Jackson "to order him back immediately." Jackson dutifully obeyed orders, and duly submitted his resignation or alternatively requested to be returned to duty at the Virginia Military Institute. Neither request was accepted, but Benjamin was less eager to inject politics into military affairs thereafter.

The Federal arsenal at Harper's ferry, Jefferson County, at the confluence of the Potomac and Shenandoah rivers—and the object of John Brown's famous raid in 1859—was considered a prize. It was taken by the Confederates on several occasions, only to be abandoned to the Federals because the surrounding hills, looking down on the town, made it almost indefensible.

In further clashes, the Gauley Bridge over the New River, in Fayette County, West Virginia, was

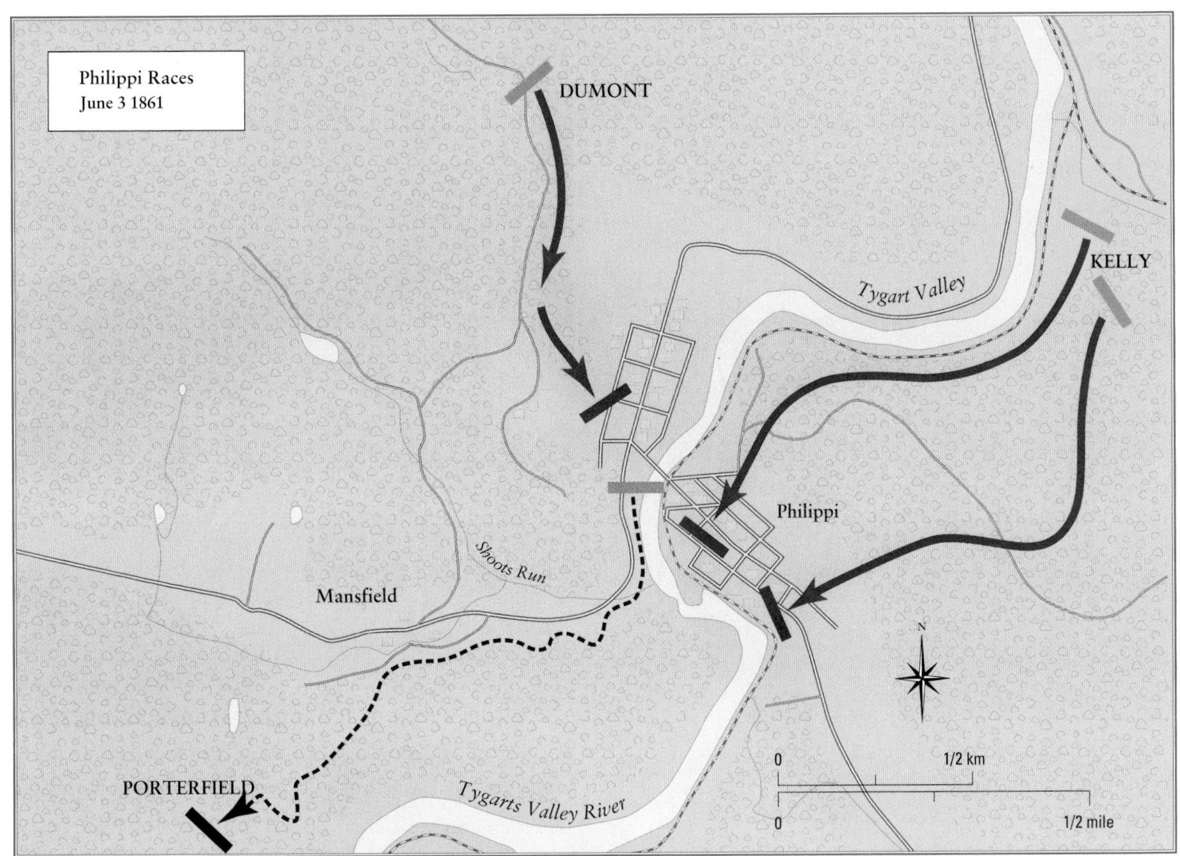

Above: The Battle of Philippi, also called The Philippi Races, was fought on June 3, 1861, in and around Philippi, Virginia (now West Virginia) as part of the Western Virginia Campaign. The first organized land action in the Eastern Theater of war, it is often dismissed as a skirmish rather than a significant battle, although it resulted in a resounding victory for the Union forces.

the scene of heavy fighting in 1861, when troops under the command of Brigadier General William S. Rosecrans defeated Confederates, who destroyed the bridge to protect their retreat.

A Confederacy that was short on manpower, as well as everything else, could not spare the means to hold West Virginia against a Federal army that numbered more than 27,000 at times. Federal interest was political, and in time West Virginians were induced to hold a constitutional convention in Wheeling and secede from Virginia. On July 14, 1862, Congress voted West Virginia into the Union as a separate State. West Virginians thus fought on both sides for most of the war, as the Confederate monument in Union, West Virginia, shows.

While the earliest fighting of the war occurred in West Virginia, the 26 sparsely settled counties were later spared from becoming a major scene of battle by their difficult terrain, which restricted maneuvering by large units, their isolation, and their poverty.

In the early part of 1862, the main action of the Civil War occurred in the Western theater, between the Appalachian Mountains and the Mississippi River, where a Union thrust led to the fall of Fort Henry and Fort Donelson, in Stewart County, Tennessee, two victories that did a great deal to restore shaky Northern morale.

In April, the two sides clashed again at the Battle of Shiloh—also known as the Battle of Pittsburg

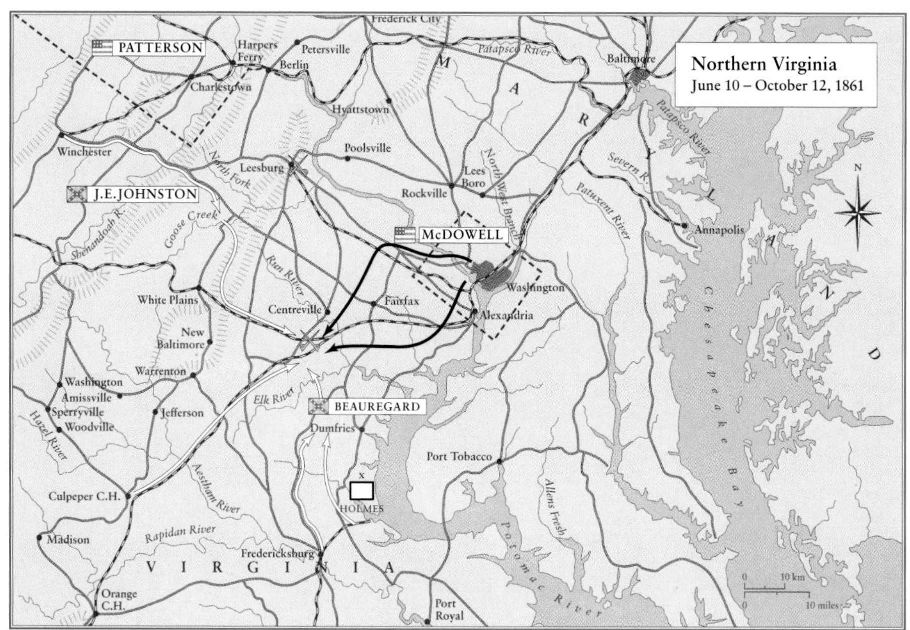

Right: On July 21, McDowell's Federal forces, some 37,000-strong, met the combined forces of Beauregard and Johnstone at Manassas Junction. The Battle of Bull Run ensued. The Federals withdrew in confusion toward the Washington defenses. On October 21, reconnaissance by the Union into northern Virginia resulted in a clash at Ball's Bluff, in which the Federal forces were surprised and defeated by a Confederate brigade.

Landing—in northwestern Tennessee, which ended in a Union victory but at immense cost to both sides. It was the bloodiest battle to date in the country's history. In the same month, a daring Union naval assault up the mouth of the Mississippi River led to the capture of New Orleans and Baton Rouge, Louisiana—this, together with the coastal blockade, was part of the Union's "Anaconda Plan," proposed by General-in-Chief Winfield Scott, which was designed to cut off all trade routes into and out of the South.

Meanwhile, March 1862 marked the start of the Peninsular Campaign, through which the Union aimed to capture Richmond, Virginia, by advancing westward down the finger of land on the Atlantic coast between the James River and the York River. The campaign was a partial success; when it ended in July, after the Seven Days' Battles—a series of six major battles over the seven days from June 25 to July 1, 1862—the Union had driven the Confederates back into Richmond, although the Confederate capital itself remained unscathed.

In May, Confederate forces under General Jackson stormed through Virginia's Shenandoah Valley and drove the Union army back across the Potomac River.

In August, the Union was again defeated at the Second Battle of Bull Run, which was fought on almost exactly the same ground as the first. Determined to press home his advantage and drive the Union forces out of the South, Confederate commander Robert E. Lee then led his troops into western Maryland. There he was confronted by Federal forces at the Battle of Antietam, which was brief but the bloodiest of the entire Civil War, with more than twelve thousand Union dead and over thirteen thousand Confederate. At the end of that landmark battle, Lee withdrew to Virginia.

On this occasion, however, it was the Union that failed to press home its advantage—much to the annoyance of President Abraham Lincoln—and it suffered another disheartening setback

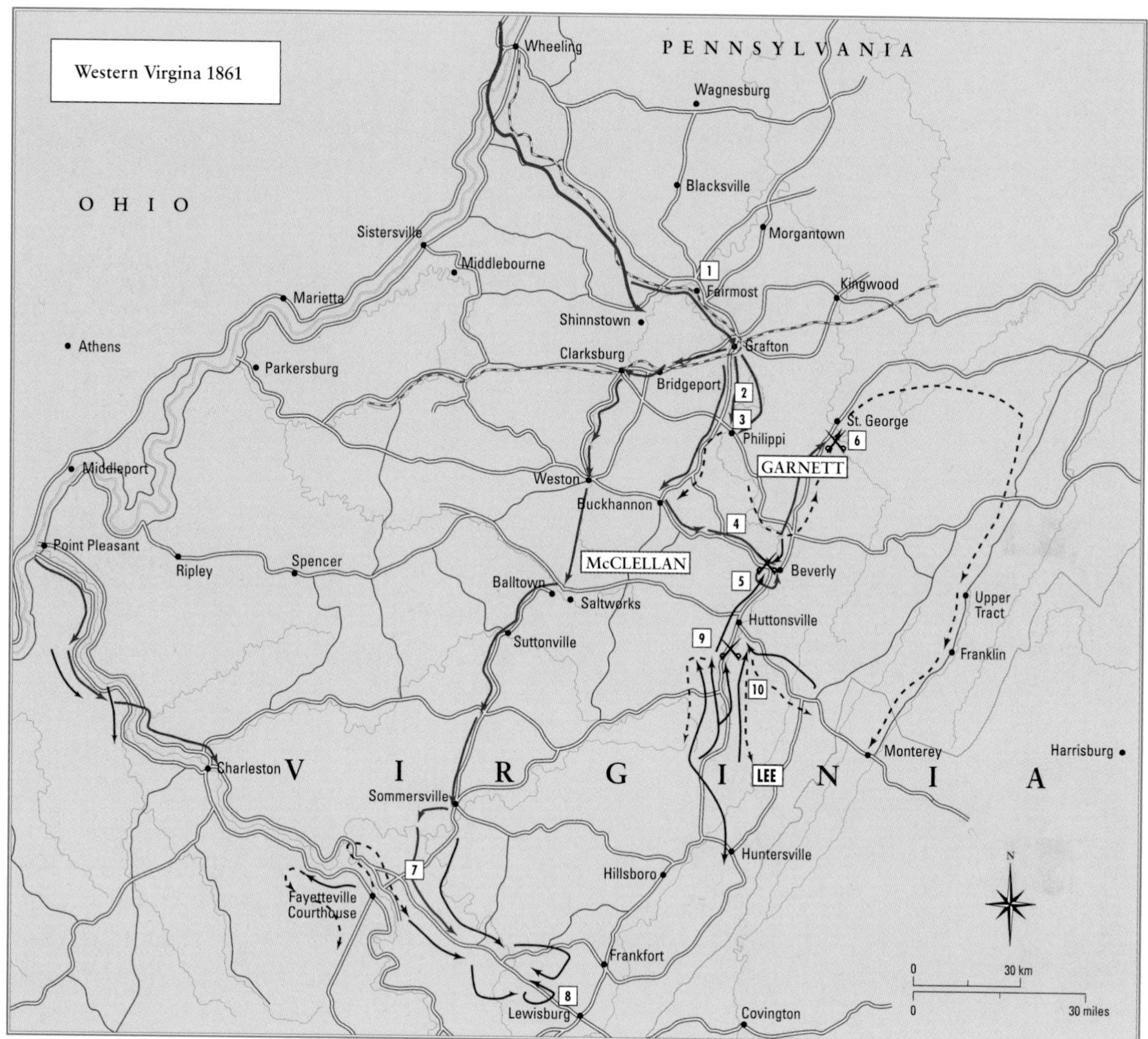

against entrenched Southern forces at the Battle of Fredericksburg, Virginia, in December 1862. The battle, between Lee's Confederate Army of Northern Virginia and the Union Army of the Potomac, commanded by Major General Ambrose E. Burnside, is remembered as one of the most one-sided battles of the American Civil War.

Above: The Confederacy was desperate to maintain its hold on Western Virginia. Though the Northerners had invaded quite successfully, they knew that if they failed to take this section of Virginia, they would have a very limited corridor through which to transport supplies to their troops in the west.

At the end of 1862, the forces in the East had reached deadlock and the Federal advance in the West had stalled. Union morale was at an unprecedented low, but this was the darkest hour before the first glimmering of dawn.

Unnoticed at first, the North's superior manpower and economic resources were beginning to tell on the stretched Southern forces—the longer the War went on, the likelier it was that the richer side would prevail.

BLOCKADING THE SOUTHERN SEAPORTS, APRIL 19, 1861

JUST ONE WEEK AFTER THE ATTACK ON FORT SUMTER, PRESIDENT ABRAHAM LINCOLN ORDERED A BLOCKADE OF ALL CONFEDERATE SEAPORTS FROM SOUTH CAROLINA TO TEXAS—THE ANACONDA PLAN—WITH THE INTENTION OF STRANGLING THE REBELS OF FOREIGN TRADE, AND CAUSING PRIVATION AND HARDSHIP AMONG SOLDIERS AND CIVILIANS ALIKE. BREAKING THE BLOCKADE BECAME A PRIORITY AND AN URGENT NECESSITY FOR THE SOUTH.

Above: 1861 cartoon map of the proposed Anaconda Strategy. It involved Union Troops capturing the Mississippi River and establishing a blockade, thus dividing the Confederacy.

Opposite page: Map of Union naval blockades along the coast of North Carolina and South Carolina.

After the fall of Fort Sumter, President Lincoln issued a call for 75,000 volunteers and militia to restore the union, an action that precipitated further acts of secession, including those of Virginia and Tennessee, which would soon become major Civil War battlegrounds. Baltimore citizens stoned troops being sent to protect the national capital of Washington, but Maryland remained in the Union. Neither side had been prepared for war, but both acted quickly. Alexandria, Virginia, across the Potomac River from the national capital at Washington, was occupied by Federal troops on May 28. The Union remained in control of Fortress Monroe in Hampton, Virginia, and began probing Confederate defensive positions. At Big Bethel,

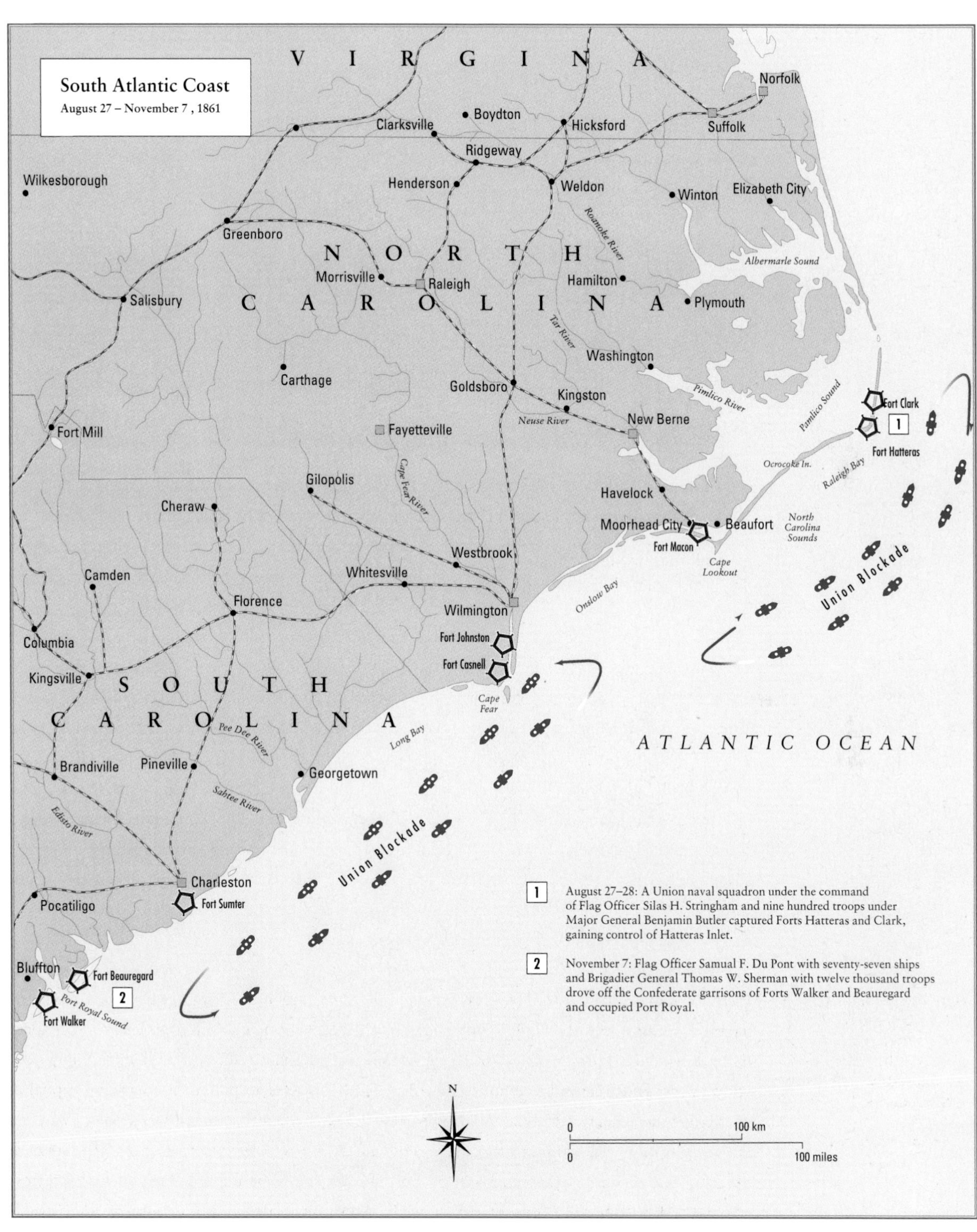
South Atlantic Coast
August 27 – November 7 , 1861
VIRGINIA
NORTH CAROLINA
SOUTH CAROLINA
Norfolk
Suffolk
Boydton
Clarksville
Hicksford
Ridgeway
Henderson
Weldon
Winton
Elizabeth City
Wilkesborough
Greenboro
Morrisville
Raleigh
Hamilton
Plymouth
Albermarle Sound
Roanoke River
Salisbury
Tar River
Washington
Carthage
Goldsboro
Kingston
Pimlico River
Pamlico Sound
Fort Clark
Fort Hatteras
Fort Mill
Fayetteville
Neuse River
New Berne
Ocrocoke In.
Raleigh Bay
Gilopolis
Cape Fear River
Havelock
Cheraw
Moorhead City
Beaufort
Fort Macon
North Carolina Sounds
Cape Lookout
Westbrook
Camden
Whitesville
Onslow Bay
Union Blockade
Florence
Wilmington
Columbia
Fort Johnston
Fort Casnell
Kingsville
Cape Fear
Pee Dee River
Long Bay
ATLANTIC OCEAN
Brandiville
Pineville
Georgetown
Sahtee River
Edisto River
Union Blockade
Charleston
Fort Sumter
Pocatiligo
Bluffton
Fort Beauregard
Port Royal Sound
Fort Walker
1
2
August 27–28: A Union naval squadron under the command of Flag Officer Silas H. Stringham and nine hundred troops under Major General Benjamin Butler captured Forts Hatteras and Clark, gaining control of Hatteras Inlet.
November 7: Flag Officer Samual F. Du Pont with seventy-seven ships and Brigadier General Thomas W. Sherman with twelve thousand troops drove off the Confederate garrisons of Forts Walker and Beauregard and occupied Port Royal.
N
0
100 km
0
100 miles

Right: View of Hatteras, location of an early amphibious battle where Federal defenses quickly fell victim to Union forces. The Hatteras Inlet proved to be of immense strategic importance as it allowed access to much of the North Carolina coast which eventually also fell to Union occupation.

4,000 untested Federals failed to dislodge 1,500 equally green Confederates on June 10 1861. The first Confederate battle casualty was Henry Lawson Wyatt of North Carolina.

A Union strategy soon developed, with a major element being the attempt to control the coast of the South, through blockade and occupation of strategic points, and thereby to strangle the Confederacy. Accordingly, fighting on North Carolina soil began on the coast.

In the first amphibious operation of the Civil War, in August 1861, Union troops took Cape Hatteras, a strategic elbow island on the North Carolina Outer Banks, whose offshore waters were known for their peculiar currents and violent storms. During a two-day battle, hastily constructed Forts Hatteras and Clark guarding Hatteras Inlet were reduced by gunfire from a fleet of eight warships. Then, the two troopships carried 900 of General Benjamin F. Butler's soldiers from Fortress Monroe in Virginia to capture the forts and take more than 600 Confederate prisoners. The loss of Hatteras was a severe blow to Confederate efforts to keep imports flowing through North Carolina because it deprived blockade runners of the entrance to Pamlico Sound.

Comments by Confederate prisoners after the battle indicate that they placed too much confidence in newly invented water-mines installed at Hatteras Inlet, which were expected to deal with the Federal fleet, including the flagship USS *Minnesota*.

A *Washington Star* article belittled the inventor of the mines, Matthew Fontaine Maury, as a "trickster" and Confederates as "credulous enough to put faith in his pretentions to the extent of that by his wonderful submarine batteries and other kickshaws he could blow sky-high any of Uncle Sam's vessels that might seek an entrance into Hatteras Inlet."

The Confederates chose Roanoke Island, lying behind the Outer Banks and between Pamlico and Albemarle Sounds as a substitute defensive position, hoping it would limit the effectiveness of Federal possession of Hatteras. They strongly fortified the island and the adjacent mainland with three forts and three independent batteries, holding more than 38 cannons of various sizes and types, and a squadron of eight gunboats. These were manned by 4,000 officers and men, and protected by a double row of stakes and some sunken ships across the inland passage, Croatan Sound. These measures did not prove to be sufficient when General McClellan, preparing for his Peninsular Campaign, decided that possession of Roanoke Island, and thus complete Federal control of the North Carolina Sounds, would constitute a continuing threat to Richmond's lines of communication.

An expedition of 12,000 men and 19 shallow-draft gunboats was delayed by damage in a mid-January storm off Hatteras Inlet, but succeeded in capturing their objective on February 8, 1862, with forces under the command of Brigadier General Ambrose E. Burnside.

The occupation of Port Royal Sound and Hilton Head Island in South Carolina was another early achievement of the Union army. Hilton Head was the headquarters of the Union Army Department of the South, commanded by Brigadier General Thomas W. Sherman (also known as "The Other" Sherman), and therefore was a major staging base for the coastal operations in South Carolina, Georgia, and Florida. During one memorable attack on this fort, the Union flagship *Harvest Moon* was sunk by Confederate mines.

Remnants of Confederate Fort Walker, which quickly succumbed to Union naval fire because it was improperly constructed and armed, still survive on today's fashionable resort island, giving little indication of the extreme isolation and harsh conditions that must have existed there during the Civil War period.

Below: Map illustrating a successful United States Navy operation to capture Port Royal. It sustained and stregthened their control of Southern ports.

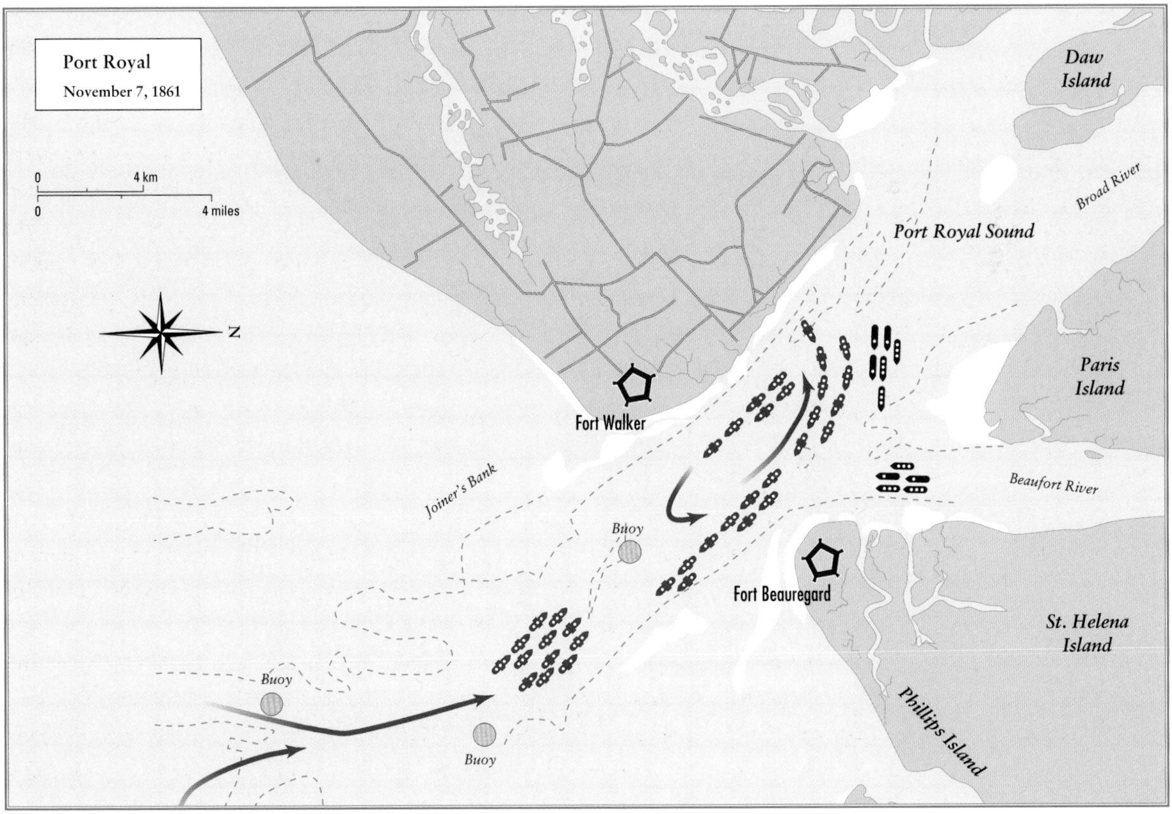

The First Battle of Bull Run, July 21, 1861

The Battle of Manassas, or bull run, is regarded as the first clash in history between two civilian armies: the Confederacy, as a new nation, entered the Civil War without a professional army, while the Union army at the outset had only 16,000 regulars, most engaged in protecting the Western frontier, or holed up in East coast forts.

Above: Thomas J. "Stonewall" Jackson was a gifted military tactition and an innovative commander. His successful leadership in the first Battle of Bull Run earned him the promotion to Major General.

A stern-faced statue of Major General Thomas J. "Stonewall" Jackson, his taut muscles pressing against his uniform, perpetually surveys the battlefield of Manassas (Bull Run) from a vantage point on Henry Hill. The statue is a veritable symbol of power, and it stands on the ridge where the Confederate leader received, during the heat of battle, one of the most famous nicknames in history. But even such a heroic representation does not do justice to that imperturbable, demanding leader who inspired his men to prodigious feats. He was a superior tactician whose campaigns would later be studied by officers from many nations, and a firm believer that once he had done his best, the outcome of the battle rested in God's hands. Jackson's solidity was crucial to the Confederate victory in the first major land conflict of the Civil War because, at a critical moment, he provided a rallying point for Southern soldiers who only a few weeks earlier had been ploughing fields or totting accounts.

It was inevitable that fighting would occur at Manassas, barely 25 miles (40km) from Washington, D.C. Although Virginia had worked for reconciliation between the Union and seceding States, when President Lincoln issued a call for 75,000 militia and volunteers to put down the rebellion, she then cast her lot with the Confederacy. Her geographic location on the border made her a likely battleground, especially after Richmond became the Confederate capital. Manassas was a transportation hub astride the approaches to both Richmond and the fertile Shenandoah Valley; General Robert E. Lee, who had turned down command of United States forces to join his native State and initially served as adviser to Confederate President Davis, immediately recognized the importance of the junction. Federal forces posted there could pose a double-edged threat to Virginia, while protecting the national capital, whose safety was one of President Abraham Lincoln's major concerns.

Neither side was prepared for war, but neither hesitated. The first battle of Manassas aroused the same enthusiasm and confidence, on both sides, that excited both populations before Fort Sumter. Federals were so confident of success that they openly boasted of driving Confederate forces back to Richmond. Curious civilians, including some members of Congress, mingled unhindered with the Union units, often visiting the camps. Many of them brought picnic baskets, as though on a holiday, and some of the ladies had finery with them so that they could attend the victory ball which was to be held in Alexandria.

The Battle of First Manassas on July 21, 1861, was the largest that had ever been fought up to that time in the Western Hemisphere. There were two distinct phases of battle. The morning phase basically involved a Union flanking movement that initiated the fighting, while Confederate forces were forming to attack the Union army near Centreville. Confederates defended the Stone Bridge across Bull Run as a key point in their line. However, Union Brigadier General Irwin McDowell chose a flanking movement across fords of the stream. Sudley Ford was the principal crossing point, but became clogged as thirsty soldiers stopped for water on a hot day—one of numerous delays that affected the outcome of the battle. The crossing at Farm Pond, a little known ford which a loyalist farmer pointed out to Federal forces, went better. Confederate Colonel Nathan "Shanks" Evans became one of the unsung heroes of the action by correctly diagnosing Union movements and moving his forces from the bridge to Mathews Hill to cope with the first Union assault. Mathews Hill quickly developed as the principal site of the morning fighting, with Confederates defending successive positions such as the unfinished railroad grade of the Manassas Gap Independent Line. At Sudley Church, worshippers gathering for a church service were surprised to see Federal troops marching by; the church was used later as a Union hospital.

The Confederates gradually were forced back to Henry Hill, which has a spectacular view over Bull Run and to the mountains to the west. There, the second, and decisive, phase of the battle occurred in the afternoon. During seesaw fighting on the slope around the Henry House and the Robinson House, owned by a freed slave at the time of the fighting, Federal troops made five partially successful assaults only to be driven back each time by rallying Confederates. On the eastern edge of Henry Hill, Jackson earned the name "Stonewall" from General Bernard Bee, who later was fatally wounded, as he exhorted his South Carolinians to rally around Jackson, who was standing like a "stone wall."

The Rebel Yell, the battle cry which would remain a fixture throughout the war, came into being as Beauregard, Jackson and others brought their troops to an emotional pitch in the late afternoon. The final clash began at about 4p.m. and ended in a disorderly defeat of the Federals. The bridge

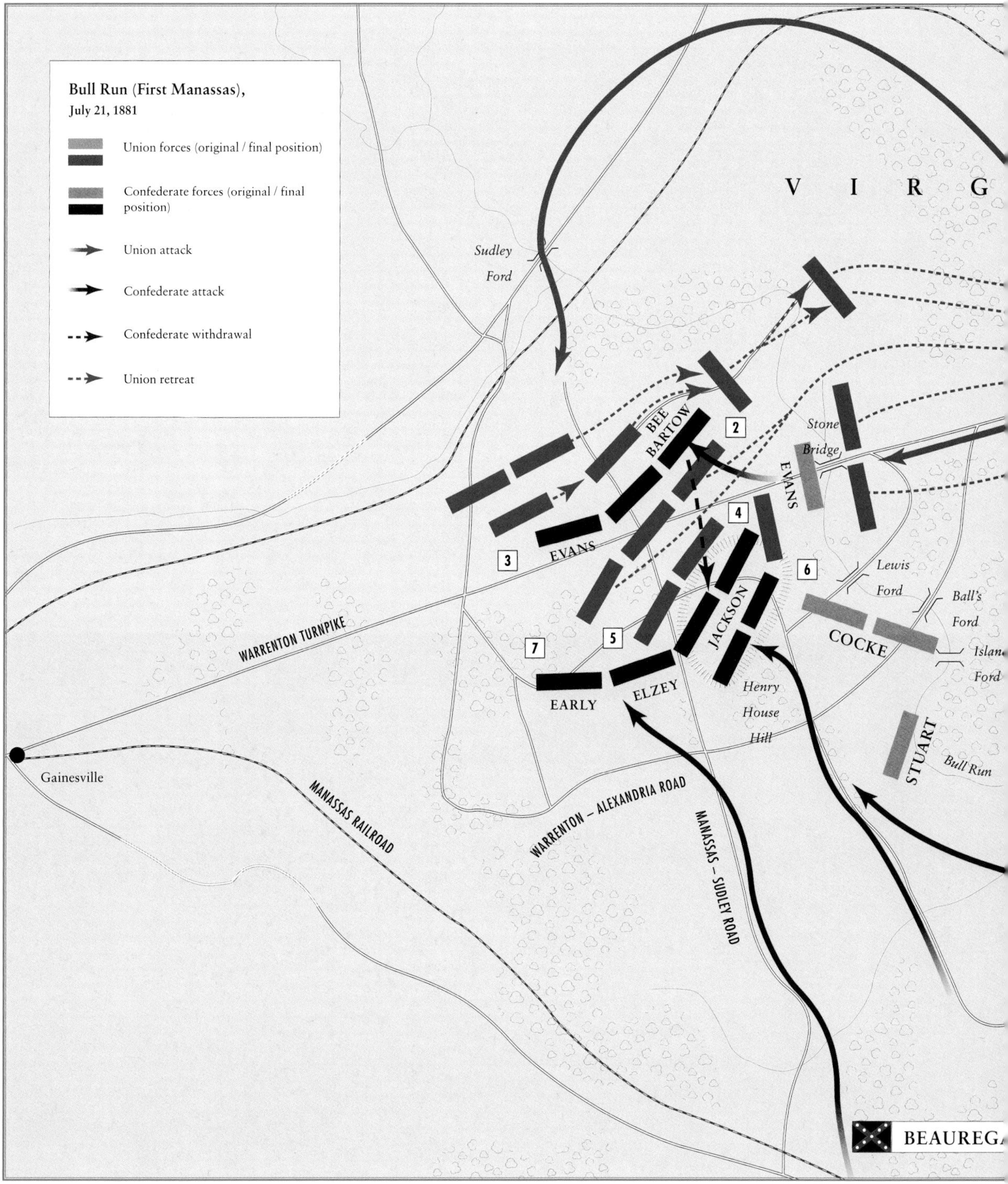

Bull Run (First Manassas),
July 21, 1881

- Union forces (original / final position)
- Confederate forces (original / final position)
- Union attack
- Confederate attack
- Confederate withdrawal
- Union retreat

V I R G

Sudley Ford

BEE
BARTOW
EVANS
EVANS
JACKSON
COCKE
STUART
EARLY
ELZEY

2
3
4
5
6
7

Stone Bridge
Lewis Ford
Ball's Ford
Islan
Ford
Henry House Hill
Bull Run

WARRENTON TURNPIKE
Gainesville
MANASSAS RAILROAD
WARRENTON – ALEXANDRIA ROAD
MANASSAS – SUDLEY ROAD

BEAUREGA

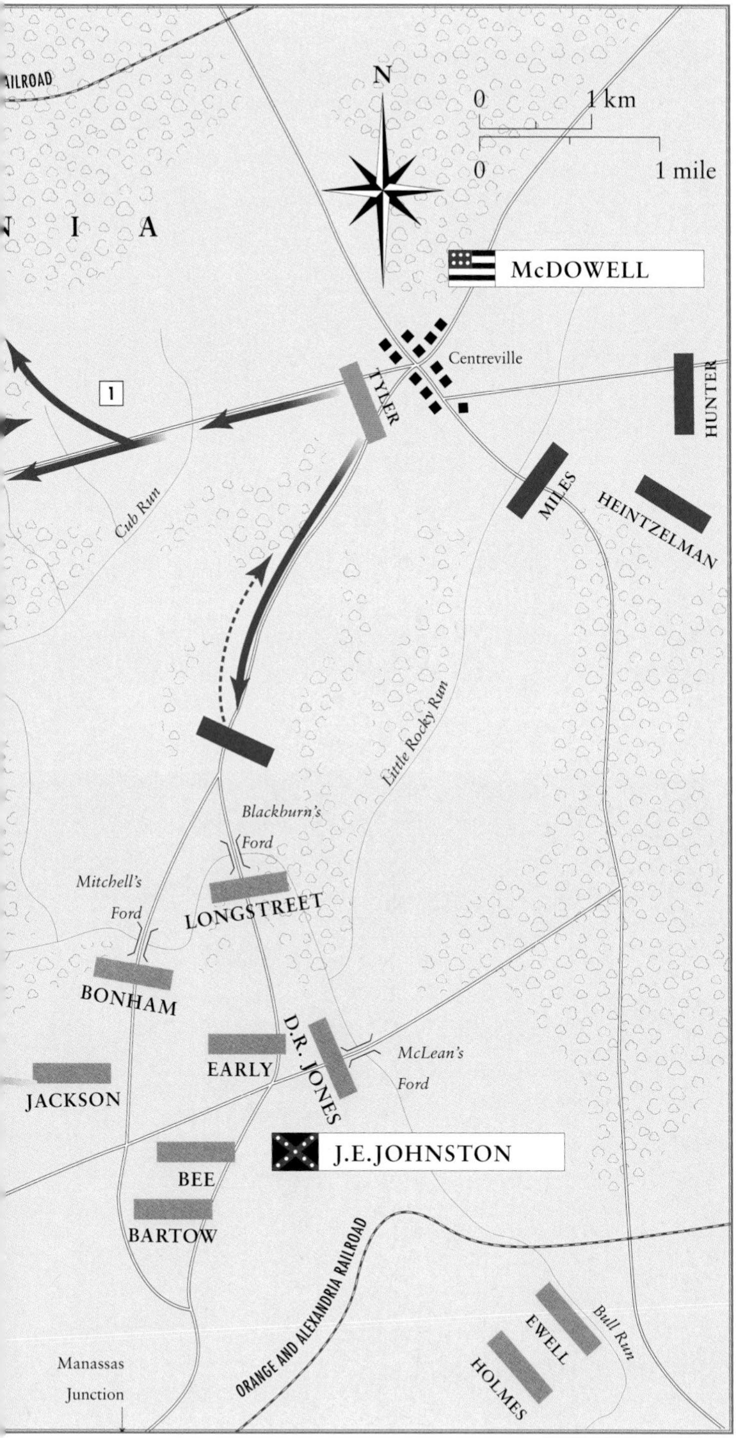

AILROAD
N
0 1 km
0 1 mile
I A
McDOWELL
Centreville
1
TYLER
HUNTER
MILES
HEINTZELMAN
Cub Run
Little Rocky Run
Blackburn's Ford
Mitchell's Ford
LONGSTREET
BONHAM
D.R. JONES
McLean's Ford
EARLY
JACKSON
J.E.JOHNSTON
BEE
BARTOW
ORANGE AND ALEXANDRIA RAILROAD
Bull Run
EWELL
HOLMES
Manassas Junction

1 **July 20, night:** Intending to outflank the Confederate left, McDowell moves 10,000 men from Centreville heading west and south.

2 **July 21, 8:30 A.M.:** The Confederate defenders of Stone Bridge learn the Union troops are at Sudley Ford. Brig. Gen. N. G. Evans moves a portion of his command to meet the Federal retreat.

3 **A.M.:** Evans opposes Union moves.

4 Outnumbered, Evans's force withdraws to Henry House Hill, where it makes a stand.

5 **Afternoon:** For several hours, the front line pushes up and down on Henry House Hill.

6 Confederates withdraw from Henry House Hill. Gen. Thomas Jackson leads in fresh Confederate troops.

7 **4 P.M.:** Confederate attack forces Union to retreat toward Centreville.**July 20, night:** Intending to outflank the Confederate left, McDowell moves 10,000 men from Centreville heading west and south.

Left: The First Battle of Bull Run, otherwise named the First Battle of Mannassas, was the first major conflict of the American Civil War. The Union Army consisted of 28, 000 men with barely any training, who faced 33, 000 Confederate soldiers who were equally as inexperienced. Heavy losses were sustained on both sides before the Federals made a hasty retreat back to Washington.

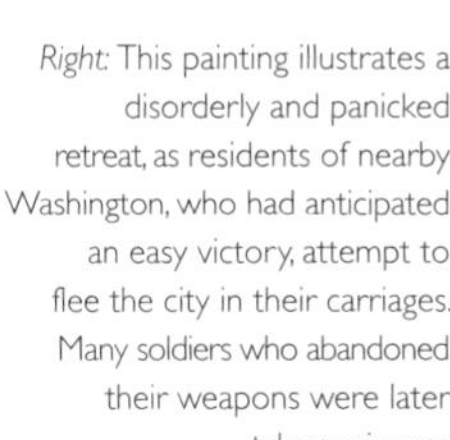

Right: This painting illustrates a disorderly and panicked retreat, as residents of nearby Washington, who had anticipated an easy victory, attempt to flee the city in their carriages. Many soldiers who abandoned their weapons were later taken prisoner.

across Bull Run, regarded as a prize at the outset of the battle, became an obstacle as the Federals retreated in headlong disorder. As McDowell wrote later, "the retreat soon became a rout, and this soon degenerated still further into a panic." One who helped to create the panic was a firebrand who had been present at the siege of Fort Sumter: ardent secessionist Edmund Ruffin. He fired the final shot of the battle at soldiers fleeing across the Stone Bridge.

The flight toward Washington was panicky, with soldiers and civilians mingling on the dusty roads. What had started with such enthusiasm and promise had ended in disaster, and Washington itself was in jeopardy. It was saved by the exhaustion of the Confederate forces, and the uncertainty of Southerners about how their devotion to secession could justify an offensive stance.

Many of the intangibles that affect the outcome of combat were present at First Manassas. General McDowell's plan to flank the Confederate position was basically sound, but delays in moving units, faulty logistics and preparation, the inexperience of his troops and officers, and bad judgement during the course of the battle proved costly.

Confederate execution was not perfect, either, but was better, while the South possessed more effective intelligence and communications. The deference shown by the senior Brigadier General Joseph E. Johnston to Beauregard upon arriving on the scene, because Beauregard was familiar with the situation, was unusual in a war where the egos of the officers loomed large. After the war, Johnston and Beauregard would duel in print about what happened and its significance.

The battle was, in a significant way, an object lesson in the changes taking place in warfare—the emerging preeminence of firepower and manoeuvre. This first battle would turn on the strategic value of the railroads to move men and supplies quickly and prove their worth in modern warfare. It saw the first use of the telegraph in war, opening a new era in one of the major requirements in combat—communications. Confederate use of signal flags represented a new form of battlefield communication. Professor Thaddeus Lowe, who already had demonstrated to Union leaders how balloons could provide combat observation, encountered the hazards of the road as his partially inflated balloon snagged on trees along the road to Manassas. His balloon tracked the movement of Confederate forces after the battle. Balloons would be used often during the early stage of the war, and in May 1862 a Union general became the first to direct artillery fire from aloft.

More variations of weapons were used in the Civil War than in any previous conflict. While the Civil War did produce innovations in weapons and tactics—breech-loading rifles, rifled artillery, the first use of machine guns in combat, submarines, land and sea mines and hand grenades among them—it was basically a proving ground for existing technology and so was of considerable interest to the European powers. Military writers in Great Britain, France and Germany would recognize it as the first total war, fought with the might produced by the Industrial Revolution, and as a glimpse of the warfare of the future.

Well into the 20th century, military authors would draw on the tactical improvisation of Confederate and Union generals and the prodigious engineering feats performed by both sides. First Manassas produced the first winner of the Congressional Medal of Honor, an award created during the Civil War. The honor went to Adelbert Ames of East Thomaston, Maine, who commanded an artillery section, although he would not receive it until 33 years after the event.

THE BATTLE OF WILSON'S CREEK, AUGUST 10, 1861

"IT WAS A MIGHTY MEAN FOWT FIGHT," ONE OF THE CONFEDERATES WROTE HOME AFTER THE BATTLE OF WILSON'S CREEK. THAT WAS AN UNDERSTATEMENT, YET THAT BATTLE WAS NOT EVEN THE BEST EXAMPLE OF THE INTENSITY OF THE CIVIL WAR CLASHES IN MISSOURI. THE TERRITORY HAD BEEN ABLAZE LONG BEFORE THE REST OF THE COUNTRY DISSOLVED INTO CIVIL WAR.

Above: General Nathaniel Lyon (July 14, 1818–August 10, 1861), from Ashford, Connecticut, was the first Union general to be killed in the American Civil War and is noted for his actions in the state of Missouri at the beginning of the conflict.

Opposite page: Map detailing the Battle of Wilson's Creek. The Confederates attacked three times but failed to break Union lines.

Missouri's petition for Statehood precipitated the great national debate on the extension of slavery and the Missouri Compromise, which admitted Missouri to the Union in 1821 as a slave state, was only a temporary solution. The attempt to extend slavery into neighboring Kansas in the 1850's bled both states, as slavery and antislavery partisans fought openly and in the process devastated a good portion of the border region.

The assault on Fort Sumter in 1861 intensified a fight that had been going on sporadically for seven years and added to the carnage. Although newly elected Governor Claiborne Fox Jackson and many other legislators favored secession, both the State legislature and a convention called to decide the issue voted against it. Federal troops under General Nathaniel Lyon, disarmed the State guard and helped the Unionists install a new government at Jefferson City. At a meeting in Cassville, the Jackson faction approved an ordinance of secession and petitioned for admission to the Confederacy. Missouri men enrolled in substantial numbers on both sides. One estimate is 100,000 in the Union army and 30,000 in the Confederate army. Some served as far away as Virginia. More than 1,100 military activities of all kinds rank the state as one of the greatest battlegrounds of the war, even though only a few of the incidents were large enough to be classified as battles. Union records indicate 13,885 died in blue uniform alone. Although Missouri's loss in Confederate grey would be

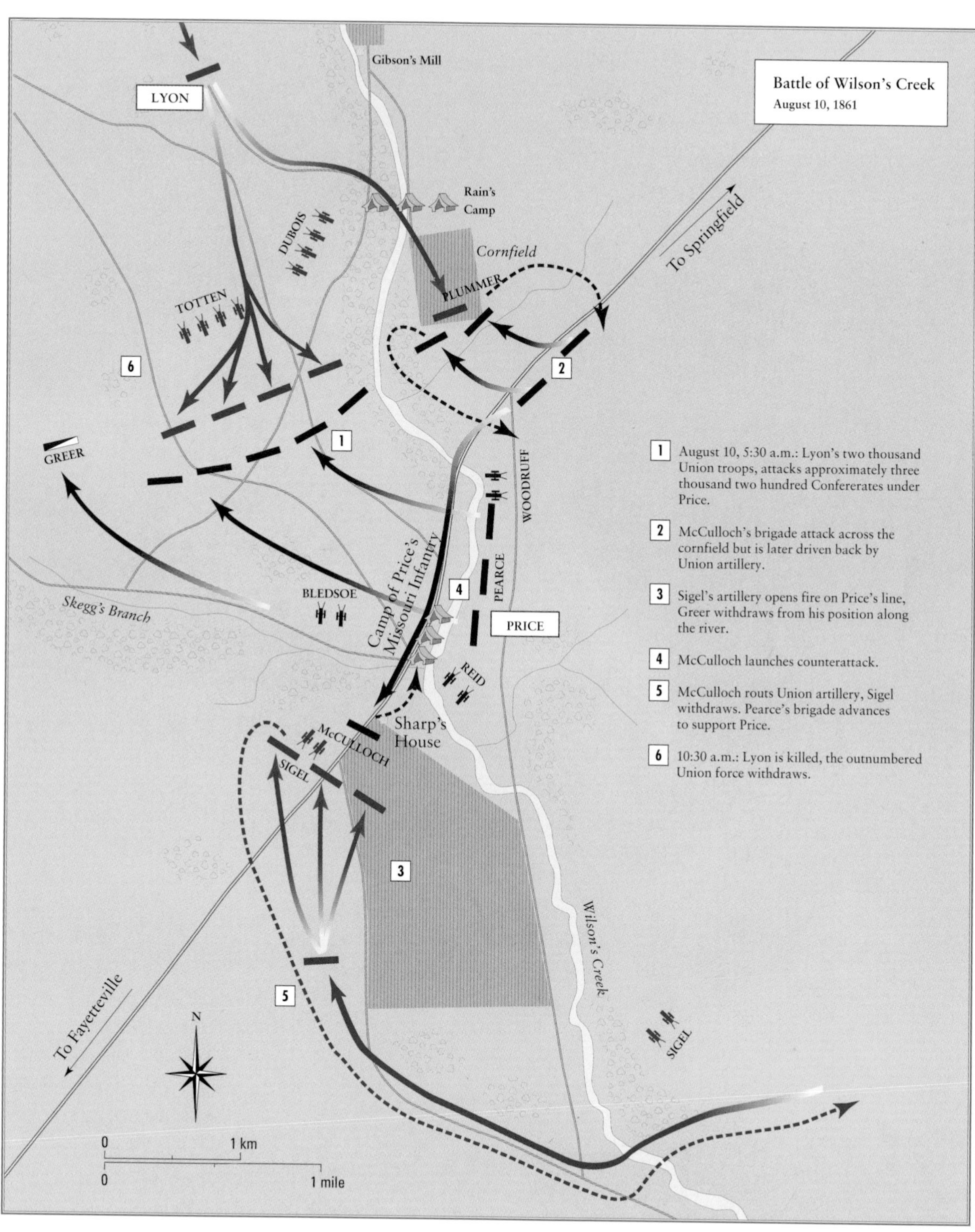
Battle of Wilson's Creek
August 10, 1861
Gibson's Mill
LYON
Rain's Camp
Cornfield
To Springfield
DUBOIS
TOTTEN
PLUMMER
GREER
WOODRUFF
BLEDSOE
Skegg's Branch
Camp of Price's Missouri Infantry
PEARCE
PRICE
REID
Sharp's House
McCULLOCH
SIGEL
Wilson's Creek
To Fayetteville
N
0 1 km
0 1 mile
1 August 10, 5:30 a.m.: Lyon's two thousand Union troops, attacks approximately three thousand two hundred Confererates under Price.
2 McCulloch's brigade attack across the cornfield but is later driven back by Union artillery.
3 Sigel's artillery opens fire on Price's line, Greer withdraws from his position along the river.
4 McCulloch launches counterattack.
5 McCulloch routs Union artillery, Sigel withdraws. Pearce's brigade advances to support Price.
6 10:30 a.m.: Lyon is killed, the outnumbered Union force withdraws.

less, it was substantial. The Civil War experience in Missouri was divided between guerrilla action and regular warfare, both vicious. Antislavery and proslavery guerrillas roamed the state, looting, burning and killing.

Regular warfare was often just as bitter. General Lyon, who in the early stages controlled all Federal units in Missouri, was determined to drive the secessionist from the State. He rejected pleas from Governor Jackson to allow the state to remain neutral and began a campaign against Jackson and the state militia before they could unite with Confederate units. Lyon moved his troops by steamboat up the Missouri River to Boonville and, on June 17, 1861, drove the state guard from the town in the first regular battle in Missouri. A few weeks later, on July 5, 1861, Federal units under Colonel Franz Sigel, a refugee from the German Revolution of 1848, attempted to block Jackson's rendezvous with Confederate forces in southwest Missouri but were defeated at Carthage and hurried back to the safety of Springfield. The Carthage fighting is shown on a mural, in the Jefferson County Courthouse, which depicts the history of the city and is entitled, "Forage in Fire." Although the battlefield is not intact, interpretive signs beginning about eight miles (12.8km) north of the city and extending to Carter Park in Carthage trace the events of the battle. The fighting and the damage to Carthage had a curious side effect; a teenage observer named Myra Belle Shirley later became the famous Belle Starr, Confederate spy and eventual outlaw. The Battle of Wilson's Creek, the largest fought in Missouri, was not long in coming. In southwest Missouri, the State guard under Major General Sterling Price was joined by Confederate troops from Texas, Arkansas, and Louisiana bringing the total to about 12,000 men. Lyon, spoiling for a fight, was encamped 75 miles (120.7km) away at Springfield. The Confederates were eager to trap Lyon and thus regain control of the state; but Lyon, though outnumbered, hoped to surprise the advancing Confederates by attacking first. Lyon mauled the Confederate vanguard at Dug Springs but was forced to fall back to Springfield in the face of superior numbers. The confederate army followed and camped on the fields and bluffs overlooking Wilson's Creek, with Price eager to attack and McCulloch hesitant. McCulloch, had a low opinion of the effectiveness of the Missouri guard, agreed to act only after Price offered to place his entire command under McCulloch.

Lyon again decided on a surprise attack, and sent Colonel Sigel on a wide flanking movement against the Southern right. The Confederates, who also had planned a surprise attack on August 9, 1861, but called it off because of rain, did not reset their pickets and were surprised by Lyon's attack at 5 a.m. on the morning of August 10. They immediately lost several key positions, including the crest of a ridge that would became known before the battle was over as Bloody Hill. Arkansas artillery was able to halt the attack and gave Price time to form a new battle line on the south slope of the hill. The fighting on that ridge, much of it at close quarters, raged for five hours in the firing was so intense it could be heard in Springfield. With its leader, Lyon, dead and ammunition almost exhausted, the Federal army, leaving many of its dead behind, retreated to Springfield and then to Rolla, where it entrained for St. Louis. The victorious Confederate army, though superior in numbers, for some unknown reason did not pursue. Casualties on both sides exceeded 2,500. The bodies of 30 Union soldiers, buried in a sinkhole on the ridge by the Confederates, later were reinterred along with almost 1,600 others from both sides in Springfield National Cemetery.

Lexington, Missouri, a busy river port with pro-Southern proclivities, preserves both the battlefield and bitter memories of Federal occupiers, who seized nearly a million dollars from the bank. The battle on September 18–20, 1861, was a leisurely one, even by Civil War standards, as the larger Confederate forces surrounded the Union position before making a major attack, and nearby Union units failed to join their beleaguered comrades due to lack of communications. It is remembered as the "Battle of the Hemp Bales," a name derived from the wet bales which Confederates used as movable breastworks when assaulting the Union fortifications. Union cannon set fire to several buildings in the town and chipped a piece from the courthouse column. A farmer, lunch pail in hand, joined Price's besieging forces and industriously shot heads which appeared above the Union defenses until lunchtime, contentedly ate his meal, and then went back to his grisly task. Original earthworks and trenches remain. The Anderson House, constructed in 1853 and used alternately as a hospital by both sides, is preserved as a museum and contains Civil War relics and period furnishings. The unusual battle was a victory for the Confederates under General Price; the Union surrendered the entire garrison, 1,000 horses, 3,000 muskets, 100 wagons and five pieces of artillery. One Union officer surrendered his sword to his brother, who served on Price's staff—a good example of why the conflict is sometimes called The War Between Brothers. Price was chivalrous, allowing the Union officers to keep their guns and horses and permitting the Irish regimental band to parade its colors before stacking arms. The Confederate army remained at Lexington for two weeks before marching south again.

Below: Map pinpointing the military clashes in Missouri that lead to the deaths of over 2, 500 soldiers, General Lyon among them. It was the first major battle that took place west of the Mississippi River.

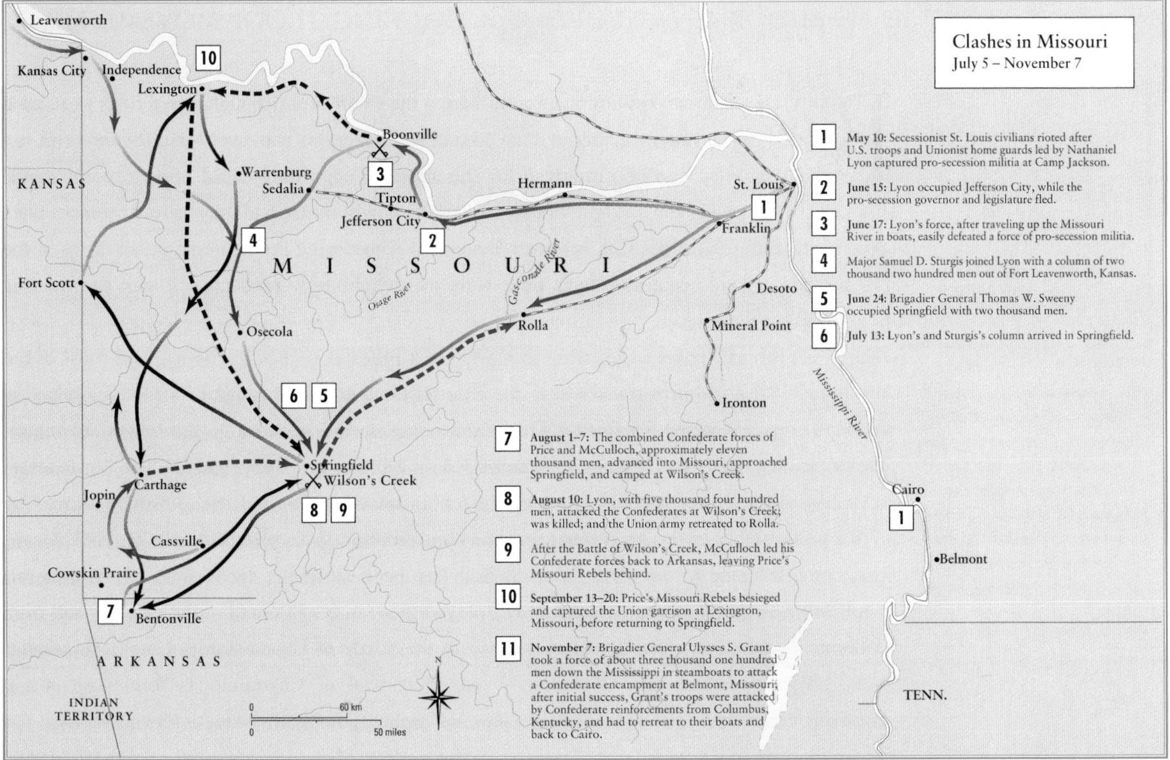

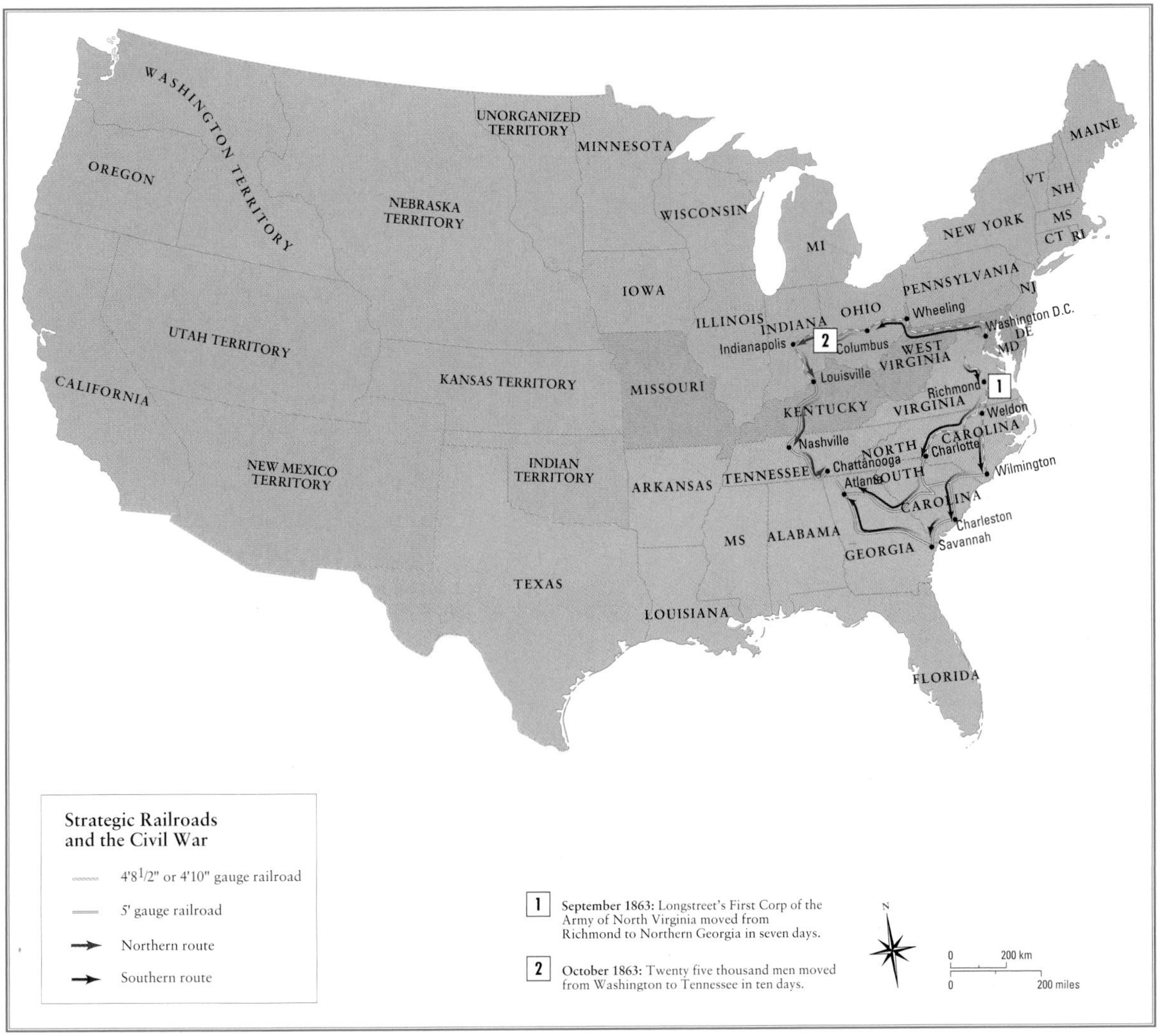

Strategic Railroads and the Civil War

4'8 1/2" or 4'10" gauge railroad

5' gauge railroad

Northern route

Southern route

1 **September 1863:** Longstreet's First Corp of the Army of North Virginia moved from Richmond to Northern Georgia in seven days.

2 **October 1863:** Twenty five thousand men moved from Washington to Tennessee in ten days.

Braxton Bragg.

Although the Confederacy made better use of its railroads, the Southern system was in many ways a military strategist's nightmare. The network comprised 113 separate, independent companies, many of which had been commercial rivals in the antebellum period. As a result, they nearly all had their own terminals, and consequently troops and equipment transported by rail often had to be unloaded onto wagons at each major terminus, taken by road all the way across town, and then painstakingly reloaded onto another train on another line at a different station. These were costly and time-consuming undertakings; a trip from the Mississippi to the Eastern seaboard involved seven separate lines.

The most important lines were the Richmond, Fredericksburg and Potomac, which played a major role in the defense of Virginia, and the Baltimore and Ohio, which probably suffered greater damage

Above: In 1863, the railroad network was used to transfer huge numbers of Confederate troops over great distances in record time, making the "Iron Horse" one of the most valuable tools of the Civil War, and the tracks themselves the prime target of enemy control.

Above: Professor Thaddeus Lowe pioneered the use of the gas balloon in the Civil War. His observation balloon, *Intrepid* was inflated using the aeronaut's revolutionary portable gas generators *(right)*. Hydrogen was created by dropping iron filings into containers of sulfuric acid, and the gas piped into the envelope of varnished silk. The process took two days. Balloons flew to an altitude of 2,000 feet (610 m), sometimes tethered to floating launchpads.

Lines of Communication

The Civil War was the first conflict in which technological advances played an active role. Not only were the railroads an important means of transporting men and equipment to and from the battlefield, but also telegraphy was widely used for long distance communication, while gas balloons provided an airborne platform for tracking troop movements.

Both sides improved communications during the Civil War. Although signal flags were used widely in combat, starting at First Manassas, telegraph was used extensively—and the railroads began to be employed for the strategic edge they could offer to combatants. Although rail lines had been used previously in warfare, nowhere else had they proved their strategic value. At the outbreak of the war, however, instead of considering the strategic possibilities of the railroads, the private owners on both sides were overwhelmingly preoccupied with profiteering out of troop movements.

The Northern rail system had twice as many track miles as that of the South, and most of the Union lines had a uniform track width, the international standard gauge of 4ft 8½ inches (144 cm). However, it was the South that first began using its rail network to the better advantage, notwithstanding that it was smaller and comprised multiple incompatible gauges. The Confederate leadership realized that it could compensate for its relatively limited manpower resources by quickly transporting troops on trains from one confrontation to another. On July 21, 1861, Union forces were defeated at the First Battle of Bull Run because of the speed with which generals Joseph Johnson and Thomas J. Jackson redeployed thousands of Confederate troops by rail from the Shenandoah Valley. The Southern victory at the Battle of Chickamauga Creek (September 19-20, 1863)—by which the Confederacy gained control of Chattanooga, Tennessee, a rail center or tremendous tactical importance—would probably not have been achieved without the transfer by train of General James Longstreet's forces from Virginia to reinforce those of General than any other U.S. line, being taken and retaken, destroyed, and rebuilt, several times as opposing armies advanced and retreated back and forth.

Toward the end of the Civil War, as the Confederate armies were pushed back deeper and deeper into the Southern heartland, they applied a scorched-earth policy to the railroads they were forced to abandon. Advancing Union troops often had to rebuild the lines virtually from scratch.

Technology also moved away from terra firma. Professor Thaddeus S. C. Lowe claimed that he was the first prisoner of war to be taken from a balloon, when a flight he had begun in Ohio set down in South Carolina. He was arrested and released only after a local citizen identified him as a scientist, not a spy. Lowe demonstrated his gas balloons for President Lincoln, but got hung on a tree while trying to reach the battlefield at First Manassas (Bull Run). However, he made good use of the balloon for observation after the battle. Balloons were used by both sides on other occasions—a Union officer became the first to use one to direct artillery fire. The North also first employed balloons for airborne strikes, the soldiers on board shooting at people on the ground below. The South later adopted them, too, but they were never popular with either side because, although maneuverable, they were difficult to control, and of course they were hugely vulnerable to a shot that punctured their gas bags.

Above: Samuel Finley Breese Morse invented the telegraphic communication system using electrical pulses sent along a wire. Known as Morse Code, the system proved invaluable for sending messages quickly over long distances, and became a vital part of railroad equipment.

The Union Army formed a Balloon Corps of several gas balloons. The aerostats were kept inflated for weeks, and transported by rail, boat, or carried cross-country; trees obstructing their path were felled.

The new technology that had the greatest influence on the Civil War was the electric telegraph. This recent invention (Samuel Morse had filed the first U.S. patent in 1837) enabled field commanders to remain in constant touch with their headquarters, and to react more quickly than ever before to the swirling tide of battle. The Confederacy adopted it first, on April 19, 1862, and the Union became wired up a year later. The electric telegraph transformed both Lincoln and his Confederate counterpart Jefferson Davis from pure politicians into commanders-in-chief who were involved with the conduct of the war on a daily basis. More importantly, the telegraph enabled generals to coordinate the deployment of units that were hundreds of miles apart. Telegraph lines were also used to eavesdrop on and mislead opponents. Operators would tap into enemy telegraph lines to intercept orders and to send misleading information regarding troop movements and potential battle plans.

Although telegraph was used to communicate between reconnaissance balloon and the ground, there was also great synergy between the telegraph system and the railroads: most of the wires were erected along the trackbeds, and the Union converted some of its passenger cars into rolling transmitter centers. Telegraph operators became some of the most important participants in the war; on the Union side, they were exempted from military service.

Civilian operators played an integral role in the operation of field armis, striking their tents and putting their wagons into line when armies moved. In laying and maintaining wire at army and corps headquarters, they faced many of the hazards of combat. These civilians strung about 15,000 miles (24,000 km) of wire and transmitted and received an estimated 3,000 messages a day during the war.

THE STRATEGIES OF WAR

THE CIVIL WAR BEGAN WITH NEITHER SIDE HAVING A WELL-DEVELOPED STRATEGY, AND CONSEQUENTLY THE BUILDING PROCESS WAS LONG AND INVOLVED MANY SHIFTS. BOTH SIDES MOVED FROM ONE STRATEGY TO ANOTHER, IN RESPONSE TO EVENTS AND THE GRUELING DEMANDS OF THE MOST DESTRUCTIVE WAR IN AMERICAN HISTORY. NOT EVEN THE RULES OF WARFARE WERE CLEARLY UNDERSTOOD AT THE START OF THE CONFLICT.

The use of railroads, for transporting troops and supplies at speed, and the telegraph, for swiftly communicating message, added new dimensions to warfare, as previously described. They greatly expanded the battlefield by facilitating coordinated campaigns, increasing the area from which armies could draw supplies and creating a close working relationship between field commanders and their political superiors. While these elements made it easier to overcome geographical distances in one sense, at the same time they gave new importance to the control of particular features such as rivers.

The leading strategists of the era were Antoine Henri Jomini and Karl von Clausewitz. While the concept of grand strategy was foreign to most West Point graduates who would assume the highest rank, they were familiar with the works of Swiss-born Jomini, the foremost authority on warfare in the period when most of them were studying at "the Point." The influence of Jomini on the generals of both sides is still being debated by military analysts and historians but—whether intentional or not—their actions followed his thinking on objectives, the offensive, mass, economy of force, and the unity of command.

Jomini's concept of warfare, derived from the Napoleonic Wars, involved the concept of theaters of operation; the Union did not fully recognize until 1864 the interdependence of the Eastern and Western theaters. In a primitive way that was heavily colored by political considerations, President

Abraham Lincoln foresaw the need to coordinate actions on all fronts, but was mesmerized by the idea of a crushing blow to subjugate the South.

General Ulysses S. Grant was the first to make destruction of the opposing army and its civilian supports primary objectives. His coordinated advance on all fronts in 1864, which prevented Confederate armies from reinforcing each other, was aimed at not just destroying those armies, but also the supporting industrial infrastructure, not to mention civilian will to continue the war.

Above: Eastern European soldier and prominent military theorist Carl Philipp Gottlieb von Clausewitz (1780–1831). He wrote a meticulous and philiosophical book about war in all its aspects. His theories about "total war" proved true in respect to the American Civil War.

Confederate policy more closely reflected Jomini's views, but in limited ways and often for non-Jominian reasons. Jomini's concept of territorial objectives coincided with political realities in the Confederacy, which dictated an attempt to defend every mile of its border and to maintain its influence in Border States, even if it did not have the ability to separate them from the Union.

The consequent dispersion of Southern forces reflected the pre-Jominian cordon system of defense and prevented the concentration that Jomini demanded. Here, again, conditions dictated the strategy of defense. The South, whose main objective was separation from the Union, entered the war with a strictly defensive policy. It did not want to force other States to leave the Union.

The Confederacy were never really able to create a uniform strategy that they could apply to both fronts. Only in the waning months of the war, when all was lost, did General Robert E. Lee reluctantly accept overall command.

Jomini's influence was greater on battlefield tactics, where concentration of forces on interior lines was practised where feasible. His emphasis on defense as the strongest tactical position found a ready audience. General Lee was the foremost builder of defensive works during the war, but both he and President Jefferson Davis saw the tactical advantage of attacking, in the Napoleonic fashion, with divided armies and exposed flanks. Lee took calculated risks and divided his forces on numerous occasions; he subdivided an already divided army to achieve the brilliant flanking victory at Chancellorsville.

Clausewitz, whose book *On War* appeared in 1832, would eventually eclipse Jomini and others as military mentor to the world. However, he had not been widely studied in the United States and, therefore, had limited influence on the Civil War. Nevertheless, the frustrations of a long war and the terrible toll of the casualties produced definite Clausewitzian results, including the gradual deterioration of moral restraint.

Northern determination to win produced the "total war" which Clausewitz had predicted, based on his interpretation of the Napoleonic Wars. The carnage caused by frontal assault and stand-and-fire tactics made many converts to his principle of maneuver. Even General Grant, who suffered 61,000 casualties in his Virginia campaign of 1864–5 (more than Lee's entire army), turned more and more to flanking maneuvers as the casualties mounted.

Clausewitz's dictum that war is an extension of policy—an "affair of the people"— gained importance as the Civil War progressed. In the North political objectives, including the Emancipation Proclamation, assumed such importance that Lincoln came to believe they would determine the outcome of the conflict. The weaknesses of the Confederate political system, in which states vied with the central government for control of resources and events, were one of the causes of defeat. The psychological factors which Clausewitz cited played an increasingly significant role in the decline of the resistance put up by the South.

But Clausewitz stressed wars with limited objectives. While both sides entered the conflict with limited objectives, the North soon adopted a more comprehensive policy of crushing Confederate leadership and changing the political system in Southern States. This was enshrined into law by Congress as early as 1862. Grant took this to the ultimate—the ability of both the Confederate army and the Southern people to make war was to be crushed. He was so effective in achieving this end that an Italian general, writing in the twentieth century, listed the "American War of Secession" among the"wars of destruction."

To attain such results, according to Clausewitz, the North needed an army capable of defeating the enemy, avoiding self-exhaustion, and holding off foreign intervention—all of which the Union managed to achieve.

Right: Portrait of Dennis Hart Mahan (1802–1871). An American professor. He studied advanced engineering techniques in Europe before returning to New York City. His writings on miliary engineering and defensive fortifactions were influential during the Civil War.

Grant and Lincoln were demonstrating almost instinctively Clausewitzian views when they advocated the complete and utter destruction of the enemy army, and not the capture of territory, as the primary military objective. However, possession of Richmond, the Confederate capital, became an obsession with Lincoln that he was never quite able to overcome. As a result, Grant had to consider Richmond, and its potential capture, in all his planning as general-in-chief.

Dennis H. Mahan, a respected professor of engineering, natural philosophy and the art of war at West Point in the prewar years, exerted a powerful influence on his former students, especially during the early stages of the war. Mahan's *Outpost*—the official title was *Advanced-Guard, Outpost and Detachment Service of Troops, with the Essential Principles of Strategy and Grand Tactics for the Use of Officers of Militia and Volunteers*—was in the mind or knapsack of many officers and was felt often on the field of battle. Mahan's books were reproduced during the Union and Confederacy.

Above: Scene on the battlefield. Confederate troops launching at a Union defensive force.

Mahan emphasized a combat condition that influenced a number of Civil War battles—that on occassion commanders must make decisions based on incomplete information. For him swiftness (of thought and action) was everthing. The value of speed in marches and maneuvers, which was one of Mahan's main teachings, was ably demonstrated by Confederate Lieutenant General Thomas J. "Stonewall" Jackson. On the opposing side, many a Union general also learned the validity of Mahan's judgement that "the very elements of nature seem to array themselves against a slow and over-prudent general."

But, of course, books, essays and observations can carry the soldier only so far. Invariably, experience is the greatest instructor of all. A great, and extremely unhappy, learning opportunity awaited the eager minions of war.

The Fall of New Orleans, 1862

New Orleans was the largest city in the Deep South. It owed its fortune to the slave trade. When attacked from the sea by a Union fleet, the city was rapidly overcome and never regained its former status.

By the early 1860s New Orleans was the sixth largest city in the United States. It was the commercial heart of the Deep South with a population approaching 170,000. It had grown rich as a result of the slave trade and had the nation's largest slave market in the nation. Each year 1.4 million bales of cotton passed through the port - over half of the entire United States cotton crop.

In January 1861 the State of Louisiana voted to secede from the Union and accepted the constitution of the Confederate States of America. As a result, with its enormous wealth, New Orleans soon became a major source of troops, armament and supplies to the Confederate States Army.

From the outset its importance and its location near the mouth of the Mississippi, made New Orleans a prime target for the Union who realized that its capture would choke off a major source of income and supplies to the fledgling Confederacy.

In January 1862 Admiral Farragut was given command of the West Gulf Blockading Squadron with the task of securing coastline, the river and the port and he gathered together a fleet, including four heavy ships, a number of gunboats and a flotilla of twenty mortar boats.

The city was defended by two permanent forts, Fort Jackson and Fort St Philip, plus a number of lesser fortifications. The forts were well armed and commanded good views of the river and the surrounding flats. The Confederates also had some improvised ironclads and gunboats of various sizes but these were all outnumbered and out gunned by the Union fleet.

On April 16, the Union fleet steamed up to a position below the forts and two days later the

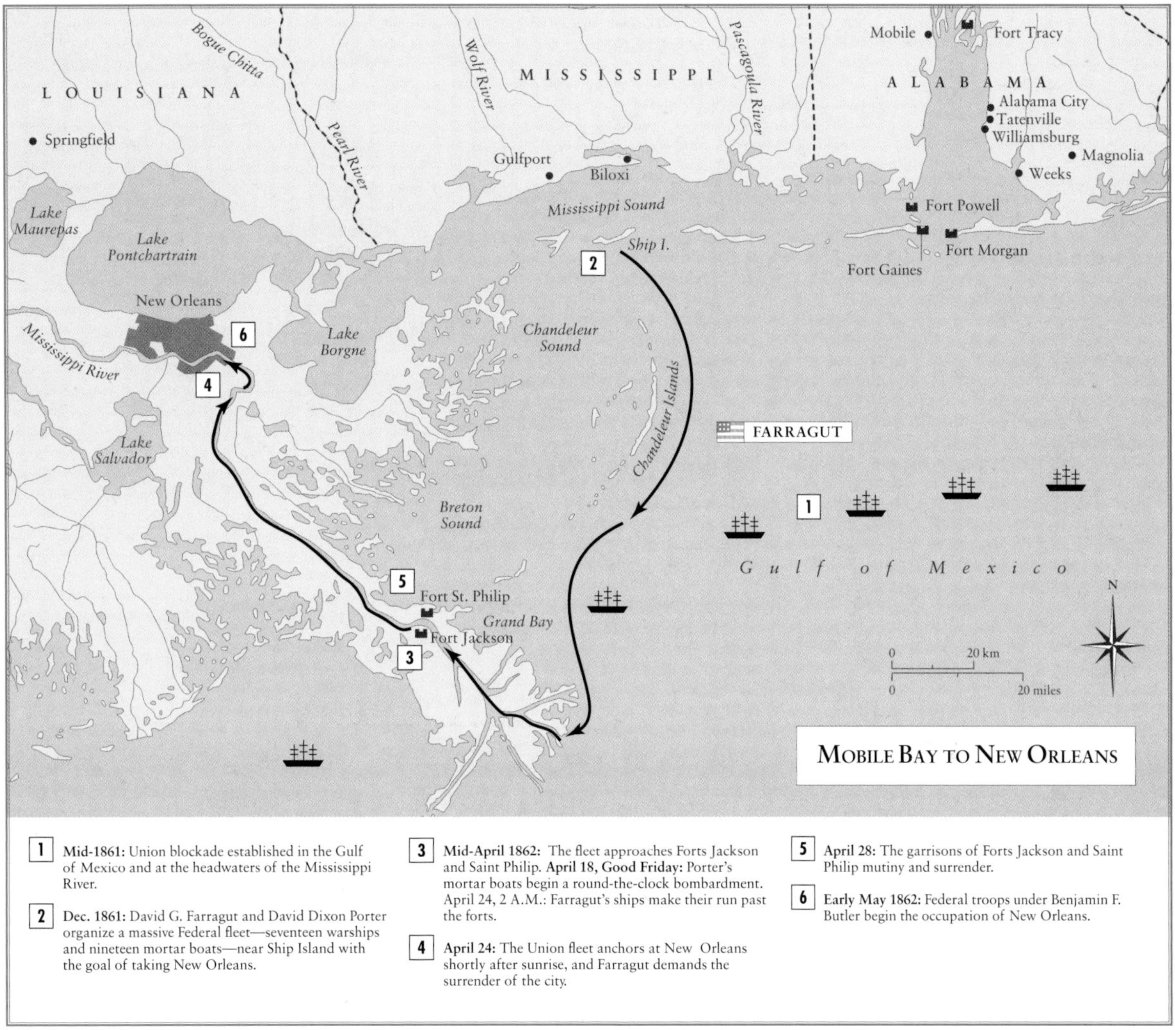

MOBILE BAY TO NEW ORLEANS

1 **Mid-1861:** Union blockade established in the Gulf of Mexico and at the headwaters of the Mississippi River.

2 **Dec. 1861:** David G. Farragut and David Dixon Porter organize a massive Federal fleet—seventeen warships and nineteen mortar boats—near Ship Island with the goal of taking New Orleans.

3 **Mid-April 1862:** The fleet approaches Forts Jackson and Saint Philip. **April 18, Good Friday:** Porter's mortar boats begin a round-the-clock bombardment. April 24, 2 A.M.: Farragut's ships make their run past the forts.

4 **April 24:** The Union fleet anchors at New Orleans shortly after sunrise, and Farragut demands the surrender of the city.

5 **April 28:** The garrisons of Forts Jackson and Saint Philip mutiny and surrender.

6 **Early May 1862:** Federal troops under Benjamin F. Butler begin the occupation of New Orleans.

Above: Map of Union Naval officer David Farragut's approach to New Orleans. In order to reach it via the Mississippi, he had to force his way past two Confederate forts that were blocking the entry.

attack began. Although the Union fleet suffered losses, Fort Jackson was seriously damaged, but the defenses were by no means crippled. A formidable obstacle was the boom that had been set up between the two forts. This effectively held attacking ships under close fire should they attempt to run past. Meanwhile the bombardment continued.

Eventually, on the night of April 23rd, two gun boats managed to race in and break a gap in the boom. At 2.00 am on April 24 Farragut led his fleet forward. There followed a period of fierce fighting at close quarters, but eventually the Union fleet forced its way past. At noon on April 25 Farragut anchored his in front of the city, which finally surrendered on April 28 1862. The Union occupation began.

The Opposing Armies

Soldiers on both sides of the conflict seemed to sense that they were living through an exceptional period of history. Many recorded their experiences in letters home to their loved ones and battle scenes were photographed, creating extensive and informative accounts of their activities.

Above: A cataclysmic clash between armies at the Siege of Corinth (also known as the First Battle of Corinth), fought from April 29 to June 10, 1862, in Corinth, Mississippi.

Billy Yank" and "Johnny Reb" as the Union and Confederate Soldiers were known, were similar, but not cut of the same cloth. They came from the same native stock, with a sprinkling of immigrant blood, and they retained their attachment to their native states. Both rushed off to fight with romantic notions of war that soon were destroyed. Both were confident of success at the start, and both experienced periods of doubt but doggedly persevered in the face of adversity. The differences between Billy and Johnny lay in their backgrounds and attitudes and in the abilities of their governments to support them.

The average Billy Yank was a youthful soldier. The enthusiastic first wave of volunteers came mostly from the 18 to 21 years age group. The average age of the Union Soldier was only about 26 at the end of the war: 98 percent of those who fought were between 18 and 45. Most were under six feet (1.8m) tall and weighed under 150 pounds (68kg).

Drummer boys, 13 years of age and younger, beat commands while shot and shell burst around them. Many of them died; one, named Johnny Clem, survived and ultimately became a general long after the war. Officers were slightly older; on average Senior officers were mostly in their

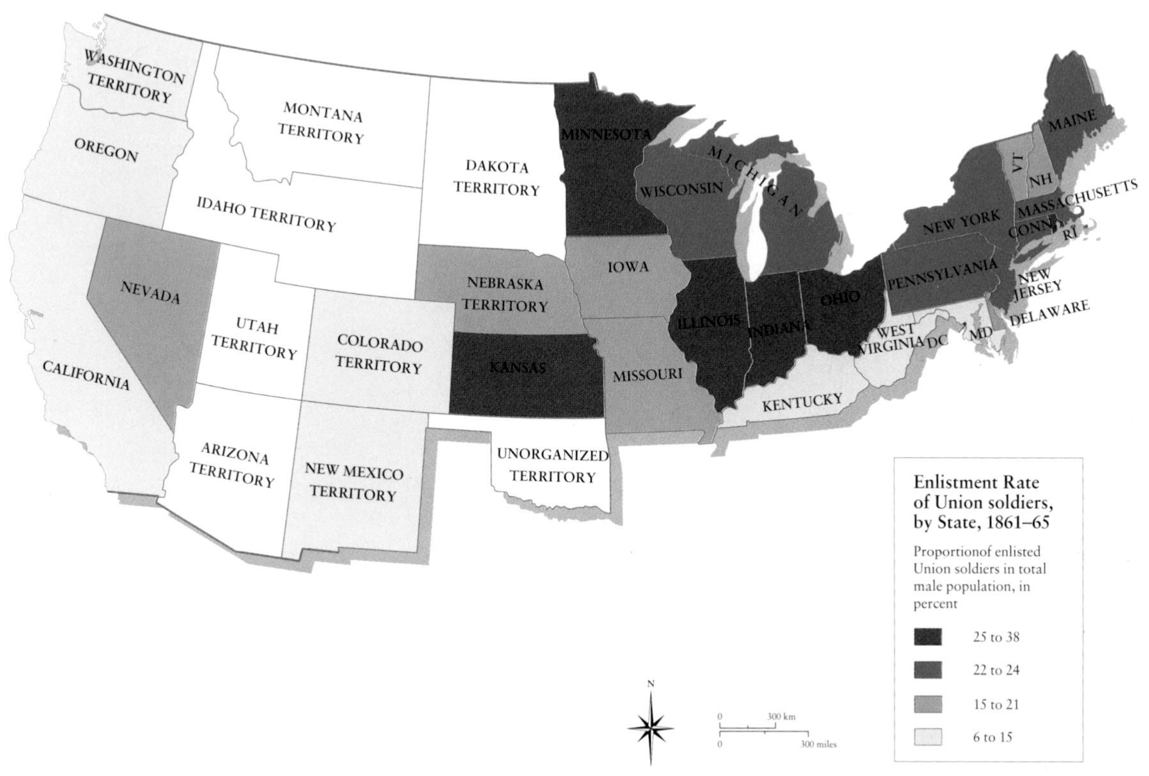

Above: A map detailing the enlistment rate of Union Soldiers. By the end of the war the average age of a soldier was 26.

forties—General Ulysses S. Grant was 39 when the war started, but General George A. McClellan was only 35. A few attained senior rank at a very early age. Arthur McArthur, Medal of Honour winner at Missionary Ridge and father of the celebrated Second World War general, was only 18 years of age when he was commissioned lieutenant colonel. The enfant terrible of the military, George Armstrong Custer, was only 24 when he received a general's star.

The "Men in Blue" came from all jobs and professions—more than 300 in fact. Farmers were the largest group, followed by carpenters, shoemakers and clerks. There were rich, uppercrust socialites, and there were illiterates. One of the Indians who served was Lieutenant Ely S. Parker, a Seneca chief who was Grant's aide in the last stage of the war. About 200,000 blacks were enrolled, and at least 500,000 soldiers—nearly 20 percent of the 2,865,028 men called into Federal service—were recent immigrants. The Irish Brigade was perhaps the most famous, but Germans, especially, also formed the rank and file of whole units.

Most men who entered the Federal service were not prepared for the different kind of life led by soldiers. Submission to military authority was hard for farm boys and city youth accustomed to control only by a loving family and the weather or constraints of the job. It was especially difficult

Right: Men of the 114th Pennsylvania Infantry assembled at the siege of Petersburg in the final days of the war.

for them to subdue their belief in meritocracy and give blind obedience to any men wearing shoulder straps, regardless of their ability and leadership qualities. They served best in units organized by their own states, to which they retained a strong attachment—regional affiliations were fostered whenever possible.

The Union soldier typically rushed to defend the national flag. While he opposed slavery in principle he had little knowledge of it. The crusade against slavery was never popular with the soldiers at the front; some of them often denigrated blacks and, when the Emancipation Proclamation was first issued in September, 1862, bitterly denounced the "Negro war."

Johnny Reb was young, too. Most Southern soldiers were between 18 and 30 years of age, and about three-fourths of them had rural backgrounds. Many were illiterate, and no effort was made by the military to educate them. The peculiar spellings in letters to the folks at home revealed an absence of dictionaries and a general acceptance of phonetic spelling. Most Southern soldiers were unmarried but, like soldiers in every war, carried a photo or memory of a dream girl back home. Most were native Southerners with only about four per cent being foreign born as there were fewer immigrants in the South. Foreign nationals did sometimes assist. In New Orleans, foreigners who loved the city's robust ambience formed a unit to help defend the city. Indians—mostly Creeks, Cherokees, Chickasaws, Choctaws and Seminoles—served with distinction in the Southern army, and Stand Watie, a Cherokee, rose to the rank of general.

The Southern soldier was an individualist who never really adjusted to military life. He chafed under camp routine and military discipline, and preferred to do things his own way; but performed well in combat, where action replaced routine and individualism was rewarded. The Southern soldier was not fighting for slavery; fewer than 25 per cent owned slaves or came from slave-owning families. To him, the attack on Fort Sumter was defensive because his "nation" already had been invaded. Letters back home usually reflected a belief that he was fighting for "freedom."

Neither the North nor the South had an army of any consequence at the start of the war. The United States army at the time numbered about 16,000 men, most of them manning frontier posts or coastal forts. The Confederacy began from scratch, but was aided by a stronger tradition of military service. Many of the best qualified officers in the U.S. Army came from the South, and most of them resigned to enter Confederate service. Both armies, therefore, had to depend on volunteers. Militia units were the first to be called to service in the war, sometimes augmented by new recruits on the eve of entering Federal service. Lincoln's initial call for three months was woefully inadequate, and later calls were for six months or a year. Trouble sometimes erupted because commanders would not let men go home at the end of their enlistment periods.

Above: Portrait of a Confederate soldier wearing a homemade shirt as a uniform. Unusual uniforms proved deadly on the battlefield because they provided the enemy with an easy target.

No matter how long they had been in existence, these units were unprepared for war. They had received only rudimentary training, were equipped with antiquated weapons and were filled with romantic notions of warfare, reflected in their fanciful uniforms. Units marched off to war dressed in bright colors and unusual designs. Although impressive on parades, these uniforms were a hindrance on the battlefield. Billowing red Zouave-style pantaloons and fezes created easy targets at First Manassas and impeded the troops' movement when fording streams and climbing forested hills. While New York's Highlanders left their kilts and bonnets at home, they were ill dressed for combat in tartan trews (trousers). The Emerald Guards of Mobile, Alabama, wore bright green uniforms, and the Granville Rifles of North Carolina wore red flannel shirts and black trousers. A mixture of blue and grey in the uniforms of both armies was confusing. When the Orleans Grand Battalion of New Orleans, wearing blue uniforms, went into battle at Shiloh, they were mistaken by other Confederates as the enemy and fired upon.

The fanciful uniforms were quickly discarded in both armies in favour of the more practical blue and grey. The legendary "butternut grey" of the Confederates was an accident; it was nearest to the official cadet grey that could be achieved by homemade dyes when regular dyes could not be brought through the Union blockade. Although the double breasted jacket remained the official uniform for both sides, it was usually discarded in the field in favour of the more practical single-breasted style. Soldiers of both armies wore wool uniforms with frock coats or short jackets all year, a morale-sapping experience in hot summer weather in the South. The roadside often became strewn with abandoned clothing and equipment on a hot march. In the winter, the soldiers wore overcoats or capes, but these were not always available to the men in the Confederate army. The men lived, marched, fought and were buried in the same uniforms. Annual cash payments were made to soldiers to replace lost or damaged components.

Rank insignia was slightly different in the two armies, but the table of organization was basically the same. The Confederate army was created on the same pattern as the United States army. Union officers wore shoulder straps showing their rank, while non-commissioned officers wore chevrons on their sleeves.

Corps badges originated in the Union army in an attempt to alleviate confusion and identify stragglers. They first appeared in General Philip Kearny's Third Corps in 1862 and were made standard almost a year later.

New Mexico Campaign

At the outbreak of the Civil War, the New Mexico Territory (now the states of New Mexico and Arizona) was a sparsely settled, lightly defended area with considerable appeal to the Confederacy. It extended almost to the West Coast, had sizable stocks of weapons and supplies at Union forts, and was the gateway to great mineral wealth, both inside and outside its boundaries.

Opposite page: (above) Map showing the progress of the first major conflict of the New Mexico Campaign, Valverde, which ended with the Confederates driving the Unionists back to their starting point at Fort Craig. *Below:* The Battle of Glorieta, was the decisive battle of the New Mexico Campaign, and was intended to stop the Confederates from invading the West.

Texans invaded the territory soon after the war began and precipitated a showdown that involved maneuvers as much as fighting, but which from time to time produced spirited battles between the small forces involved. At first, the Confederates met with success against small Union forces divided among a number of posts. Mesilla was proclaimed capital of the Confederate territory after the surrender of Fort Fillmore.

Union defenders traded land for time and concentration of forces, surrendering forts and towns in the southern part of the territory as 3,700 Confederates advanced northward along the banks of the Rio Grande River.

The first major conflict occurred on February 21, 1862, at Valverde, about six miles (10km) north of Fort Craig and three miles (5km) east of Route 85, a hundred miles south of Albuquerque, when the invading Confederates threatened the fort's supply lines. Union troops sent to keep the Confederates from crossing the river drove them back, and gradually the forces of both sides were committed piecemeal as the fighting continued. A feature of the battle was "one of the most gallant and furious charges...ever witnessed in the annals of battles" by Texas lancers—Confederates on the frontier were armed with whatever weapons were available. They were beaten back with heavy losses. In the end, the battle was decided by a furious Confederate charge against the artillery on one Union flank. Colonel Edward R.S. Canby, who commanded the Union forces, then pulled them back to the fort.

The ratio of casualties to the number of men involved was high on both sides, but the

Confederate victory produced sizable stores of small arms and supplies, in addition to the captured cannon. A truce was declared for two days while both armies treated their wounded and buried their dead, after which Colonel Canby again refused to surrender the fort. The Confederate commander, Brigadier General Henry H. Sibley, then bypassed the fort and marched on to capture Albuquerque and Santa Fe.

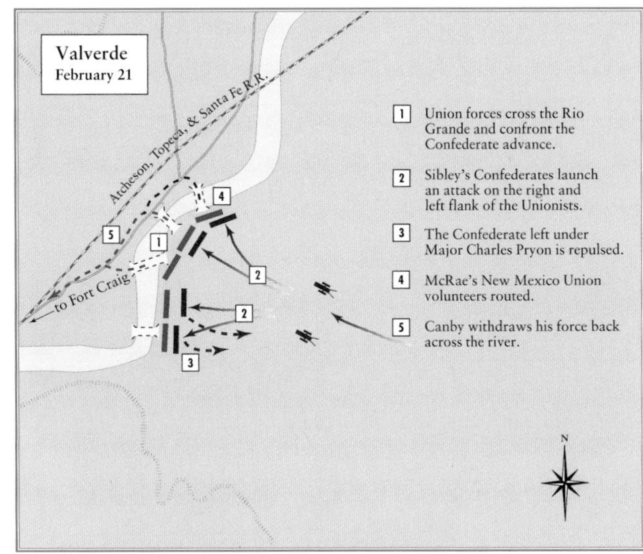

The most significant Civil War battle in the New Mexico Territory, at Pigeon's Ranch 19 miles southeast of Santa Fe, is sometimes called the "Gettysburg of the West." It is reenacted each year by history organizations.

Army records list two battles, but the first encounter on March 26, 1862, at Apache Canyon was only a preliminary to the Battle of Glorieta two days later. The site of the latter is preserved, but only partly developed for visitors. The ruins of a three-room adobe ranch structure remain to mark the site where Confederate and Union forces fought a furious hand-to-hand battle over rugged terrain. Although Union forces retreated to their base at the Kozlowski Ranch after the battle, the Confederates could not pursue because their supply train had been destroyed by an isolated cavalry.

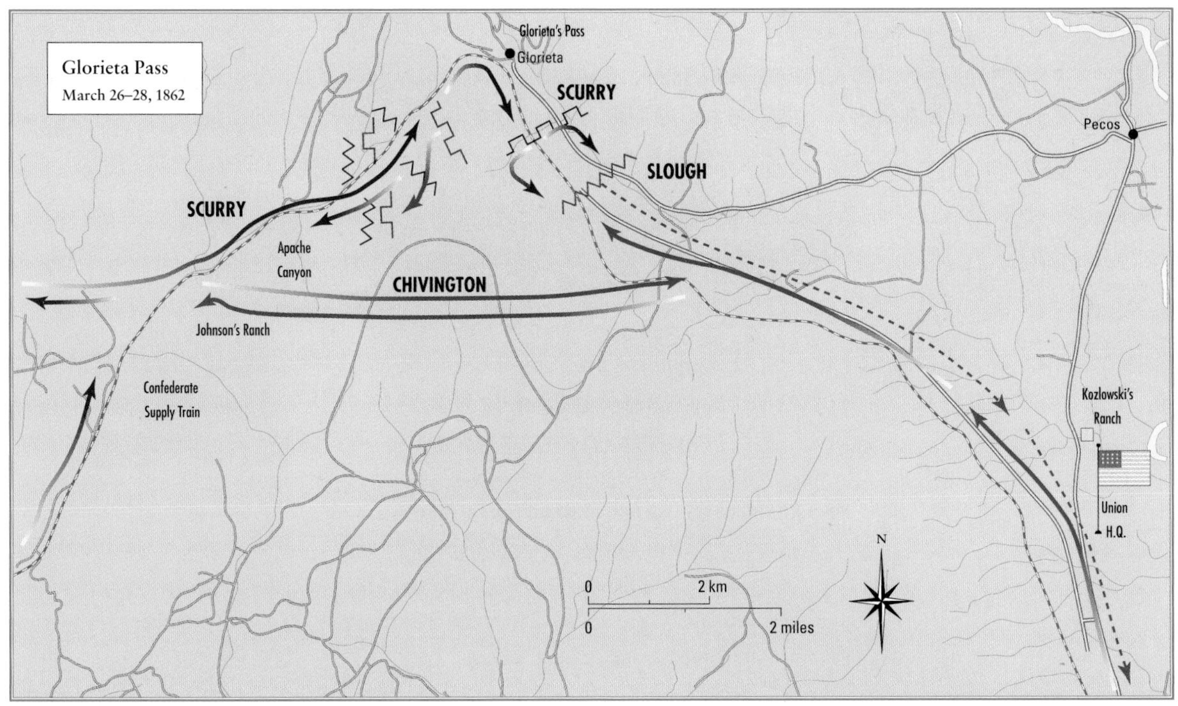

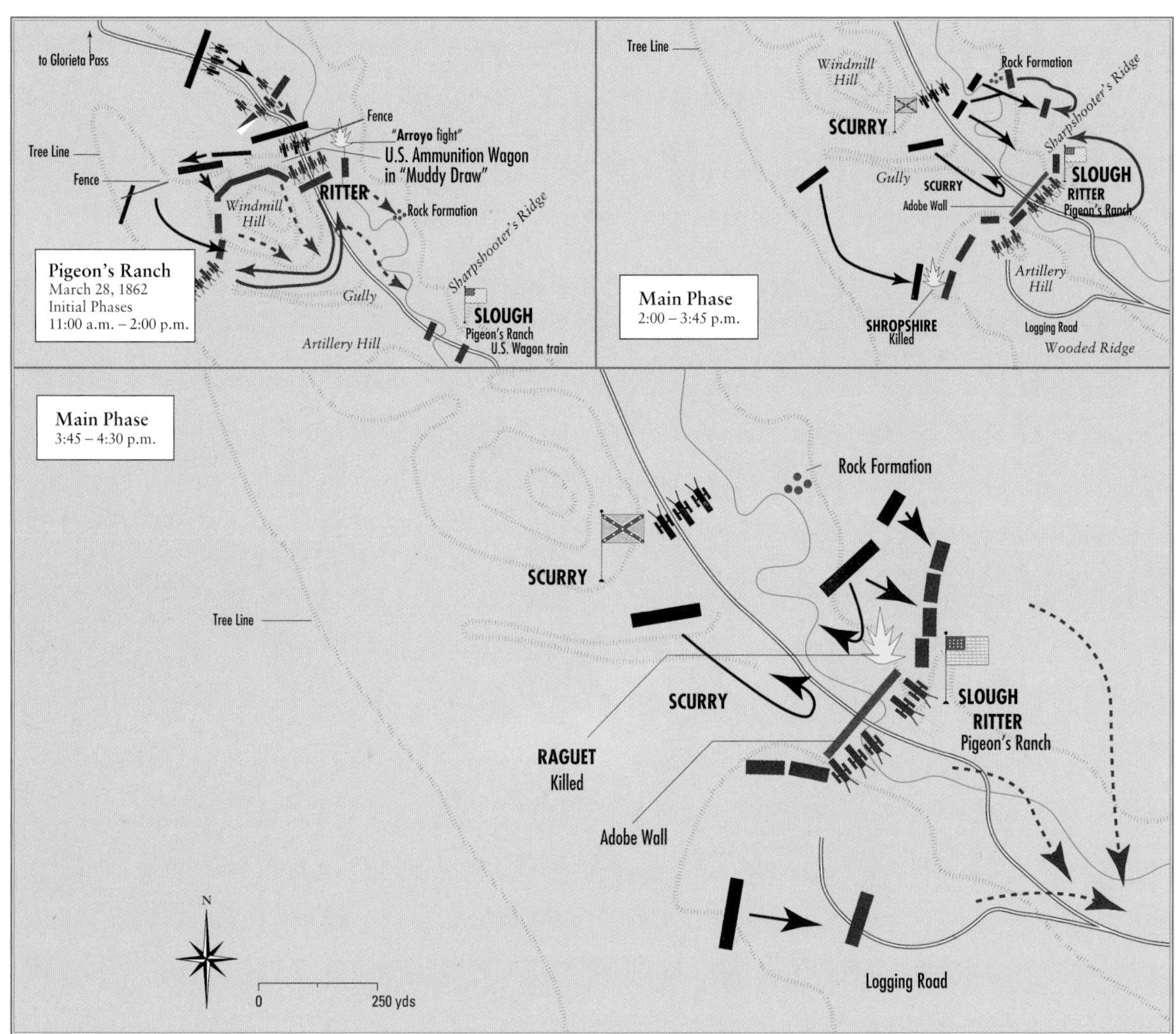

Above and opposite page: These maps (clockwise from top left) chart the progress of the attack by Colonel Scurry's Confederates of Colonel Slough's Unions at Pigeon's Range, near Glorieta. The map opposite details an overview of the New Mexico Campaign, fought between July 1861 and July 1862.

Fort Union, the Union's principal bastion against the Confederate invasion, was untouched. At Fort Union National Monument, a self-guided one-and-a-quarter mile trail leads to adobe and brick ruins, while the Visitors' Centre highlights the history of the three forts that protected the region from 1851–91, including undeveloped remains of the Civil War earthen fort. Those who fell in New Mexico battles are buried in the Santa Fe National Cemetery.

The loss of their supplies and ammunition at Glorieta Pass forced the Confederates to retreat to Santa Fe and then to their base at Albuquerque. As further Union reinforcements arrived from Colorado, and the California Column moved from southern California into the southern part of the territory, Brigadier General Sibley abandoned Albuquerque, and, after an indecisive battle at Peralta, retreated to his base at Fort Bliss, Texas.

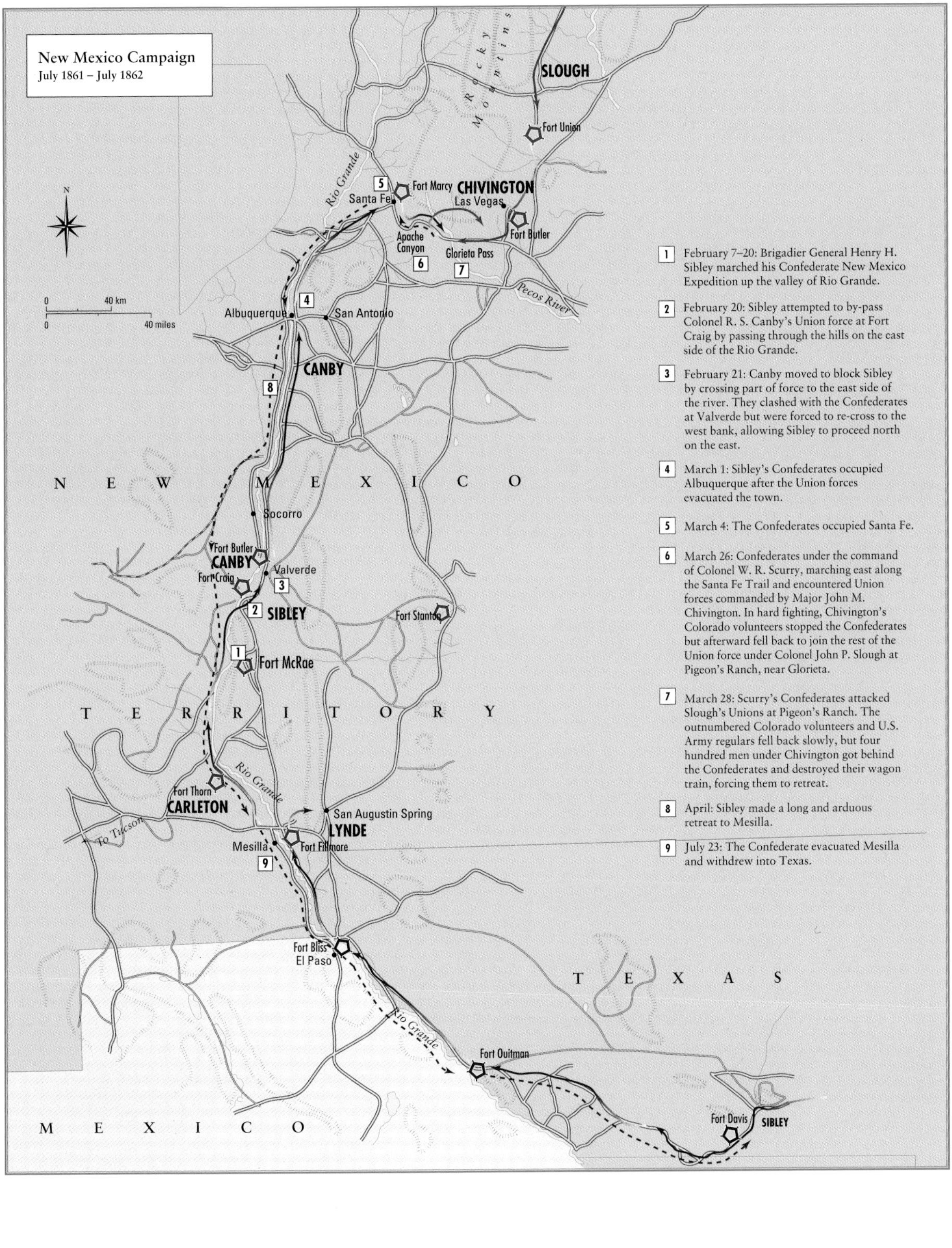

New Mexico Campaign
July 1861 – July 1862

1. February 7–20: Brigadier General Henry H. Sibley marched his Confederate New Mexico Expedition up the valley of Rio Grande.
2. February 20: Sibley attempted to by-pass Colonel R. S. Canby's Union force at Fort Craig by passing through the hills on the east side of the Rio Grande.
3. February 21: Canby moved to block Sibley by crossing part of force to the east side of the river. They clashed with the Confederates at Valverde but were forced to re-cross to the west bank, allowing Sibley to proceed north on the east.
4. March 1: Sibley's Confederates occupied Albuquerque after the Union forces evacuated the town.
5. March 4: The Confederates occupied Santa Fe.
6. March 26: Confederates under the command of Colonel W. R. Scurry, marching east along the Santa Fe Trail and encountered Union forces commanded by Major John M. Chivington. In hard fighting, Chivington's Colorado volunteers stopped the Confederates but afterward fell back to join the rest of the Union force under Colonel John P. Slough at Pigeon's Ranch, near Glorieta.
7. March 28: Scurry's Confederates attacked Slough's Unions at Pigeon's Ranch. The outnumbered Colorado volunteers and U.S. Army regulars fell back slowly, but four hundred men under Chivington got behind the Confederates and destroyed their wagon train, forcing them to retreat.
8. April: Sibley made a long and arduous retreat to Mesilla.
9. July 23: The Confederate evacuated Mesilla and withdrew into Texas.

N
0 40 km
0 40 miles
Rocky Mountains
SLOUGH
Fort Union
Rio Grande
Fort Marcy CHIVINGTON
Santa Fe
Las Vegas
Fort Butler
Apache Canyon
Glorieta Pass
Pecos River
Albuquerque
San Antonio
CANBY
NEW MEXICO TERRITORY
Socorro
Fort Butler
CANBY
Fort Craig
Valverde
SIBLEY
Fort Stanton
Fort McRae
Fort Thorn
CARLETON
To Tucson
San Augustin Spring
LYNDE
Mesilla
Fort Fillmore
Fort Bliss
El Paso
TEXAS
Fort Quitman
Fort Davis
SIBLEY
MEXICO

KENTUCKY DURING THE CIVIL WAR

POPULAR SENTIMENT IN KENTUCKY WAS AGAINST BOTH SECESSIONISTS AND COERCION, AND AT FIRST BOTH STATE AND NATIONAL OFFICIALS PROCEEDED GINGERLY. GOVERNOR BERIAH MAGOFFIN, U.S. SENATOR JOHN C. BRECKINRIDGE, AND ABOUT HALF OF THE STATE LEGISLATURE ACCEPTED THE IDEA OF SECESSION AS A RIGHT, BUT ALMOST EVERYONE FAVORED NEUTRALITY. LINCOLN ACTED TO END THE STANDOFF.

The Commonwealth of Kentucky held a key position in the Civil War, which President Lincoln understood as early as 1861 when he wrote to a friend: "I think to lose Kentucky is nearly the same as to lose the whole game. Kentucky gone, we cannot hold Missouri, nor, as I think, Maryland. These all against us, and the job on our hands is too large for us. We would as well consent to separation at once, including the surrender of the capital." The Confederacy, too, recognized the necessity of winning Kentucky, the ninth most populous state at the time, to its cause. Like most border states, Kentucky was sharply divided, but the division was not always what might be expected. The Commonwealth had been formed from Virginia as a slave state, and thus maintained cultural and political ties with the South.

Furthermore, the commercial life of Kentucky was oriented toward the Mississippi River and its tributaries. The presidents of both sides during the Civil War were native sons: Abraham Lincoln was born at Sinking Spring Farm near Hodgenville and Jefferson Davis was born at Fairview. Yet, in the election of 1860, Lincoln and the Republican Party were so unpopular that he failed to carry a single county. This tangled political situation induced some big slave owners to defend the Union, while a few antislavery partisans fought to defend state's rights. Although Kentucky officially remained within the Union, many citizens were so dissatisfied with the status that they formed a rival Provisional

Government, which was formally admitted to the Confederacy. The "Kentucky colonel" thus wore blue and gray with equal ease, but would have preferred to remain neutral. Kentucky was an early and an often-used battleground; 453 military activities of all types occurred in the State, but only two of them qualify as battles. A number of places lay claim to the first armed clash; but the distinction probably has to be shared by several communities, including Columbus and Hickman, where action followed occupation. Many Southern sympathizers went south to serve the Confederacy, and both sides

Below: The Battle for Kentucky: Both sides vied for control of the decisive and strategically placed territory that was occupied by the Union.

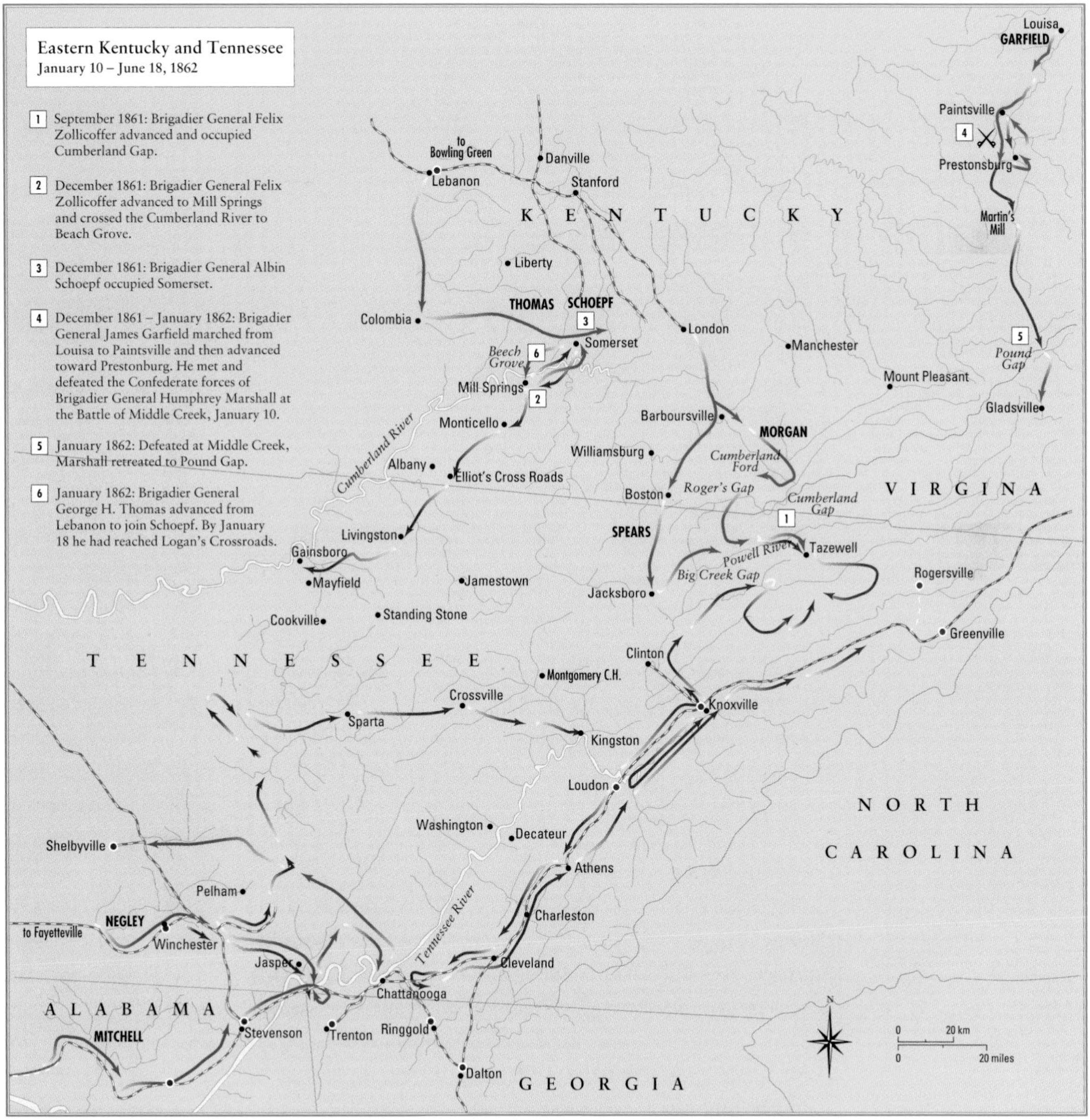
Eastern Kentucky and Tennessee
January 10 – June 18, 1862
1 September 1861: Brigadier General Felix Zollicoffer advanced and occupied Cumberland Gap.
2 December 1861: Brigadier General Felix Zollicoffer advanced to Mill Springs and crossed the Cumberland River to Beach Grove.
3 December 1861: Brigadier General Albin Schoepf occupied Somerset.
4 December 1861 – January 1862: Brigadier General James Garfield marched from Louisa to Paintsville and then advanced toward Prestonburg. He met and defeated the Confederate forces of Brigadier General Humphrey Marshall at the Battle of Middle Creek, January 10.
5 January 1862: Defeated at Middle Creek, Marshall retreated to Pound Gap.
6 January 1862: Brigadier General George H. Thomas advanced from Lebanon to join Schoepf. By January 18 he had reached Logan's Crossroads.
K E N T U C K Y
T E N N E S S E E
V I R G I N A
N O R T H C A R O L I N A
A L A B A M A
G E O R G I A
Louisa
GARFIELD
Paintsville
Prestonsburg
Martin's Mill
Pound Gap
Gladsville
Mount Pleasant
to Bowling Green
Lebanon
Danville
Stanford
Liberty
THOMAS
SCHOEPF
Colombia
Somerset
Beech Grove
Mill Springs
Monticello
London
Manchester
Barboursville
MORGAN
Williamsburg
Cumberland Ford
Cumberland River
Albany
Elliot's Cross Roads
Boston
Roger's Gap
Cumberland Gap
SPEARS
Tazewell
Powell River
Big Creek Gap
Jacksboro
Rogersville
Livingston
Gainsboro
Mayfield
Jamestown
Standing Stone
Cookville
Clinton
Montgomery C.H.
Greenville
Crossville
Sparta
Kingston
Knoxville
Loudon
Washington
Decateur
Athens
Shelbyville
Pelham
NEGLEY
to Fayetteville
Winchester
Jasper
Tennessee River
Charleston
Cleveland
Chattanooga
MITCHELL
Stevenson
Trenton
Ringgold
Dalton
N
0 20 km
0 20 miles

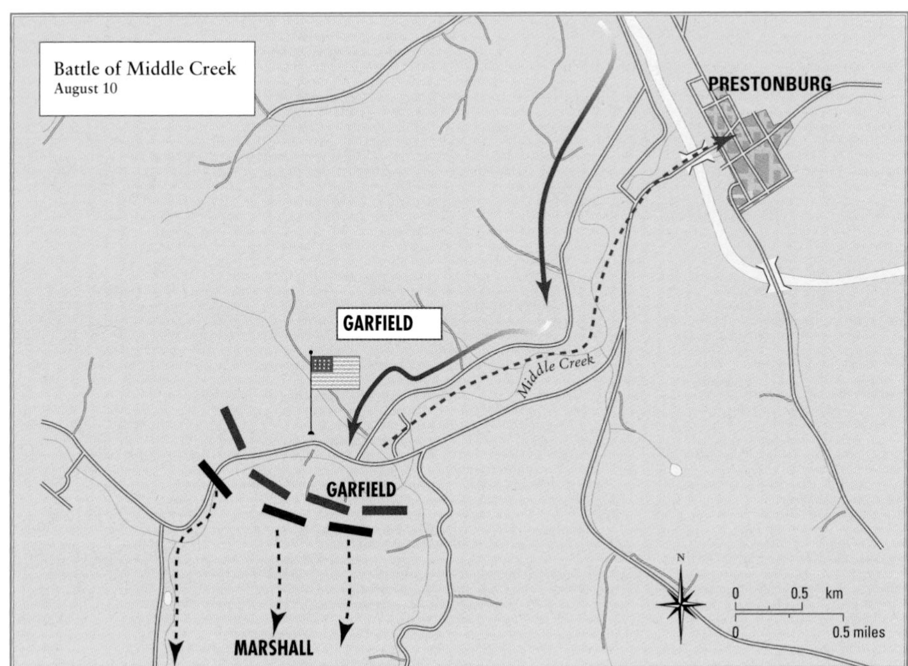

Right: The Battle of Middle Creek gave the Union armies a strategic inroads to invade Tennesse. 65 (combined) casualties and losses were reported in this battle.

recruited troops—illegally—in the State of Kentucky during that period. However, when the citizens of Kentucky elected a majority of Unionists to Congress in 1861, Abraham Lincoln ended the standoff by denouncing neutrality and opening Camp Dick Robinson to recruit soldiers. "I hope to have God on my side," Lincoln told a friend, "but I must have Kentucky." In September 1861, General Grant was ordered to occupy the pro-Southern city of Columbus, located at a strategic point on the Mississippi River, but Confederates in Tennessee did not wait for him to arrive. They moved in and fortified it so well it became known as the "Gibraltar of the West." Unionist members of the State legislature, taking control of the state away from the governor, called for Federal assistance and endorsed military action against seceding states. Confederate sympathizers held a convention in Logan County and asked to be admitted to the Confederacy. Columbia-Belmont Battlefield State Park preserves part of the huge chain that Confederates stretched across the river in an attempt to block Union gunboats, restored earthworks, and numerous Civil War relics, some of which are located in the park's museum. With Columbus in Confederate hands, General Ulysses S. Grant occupied Paducah instead, and turned it into a base from which he pushed south along the Mississippi River.

Although the state was occupied by Union forces, whole sections cheered when Confederates rode in. Kentuckians were required by Union generals to repeat loyalty oaths frequently. Citizens accused of engaging in disloyal activities, criticizing the war, or displaying Confederate flags or symbols were jailed and their property seized. Voters were given a loyalty test before voting.

At home, few Kentuckians escaped the internecine warfare that developed between the Home Guard, created to control pro-Confederate elements, and the Partizan units formed by Confederate sympathizers in self-defence. Both forces engaged, without concern for flag, as much in plunder as in defending a helpless public. In western Kentucky, Union General E.A. Paine achieved a reputation that rivalled Butler's during a 51-day reign of terror against civilians that included arbitrary arrests, confiscation, plunder, and pillage. He levied taxes on the whole areas—$300,000 on the Purchase area and $85,000 on the citizens of McCracken County—and on individuals. When citizens could not pay, their land was confiscated. He imposed a tax on tobacco shipments by anyone who was not an "unconditional" Union supporter and seized the rent of properties of suspected pro-Southerners. There was a suspicion that he killed 40 men. Paine's actions caused such a furore that the United States Senate investigated them. He fled to Illinois, but was returned for trial by a court martial on charges of malfeasance, extortion, oppression, and murder. He was convicted of only one small charge and was let off with a reprimand in official orders. The "great hog swindle" in Kentucky, also perpetrated under military orders, was an attempt to counter a sharp rise in the price of processed pork.

It was decreed that hogs could be sold only to army agents, who paid less than the market price. Farmers who tried to sell hogs quietly on the private market were imprisoned and the hogs confiscated. Packing houses not given government contracts closed for lack of meat to process. Public reaction was so strong that the scheme was abandoned, but not before Kentucky farmers had lost $300,000.

Although malfeasance of this type was generally dealt with leniently, official policy never condoned such activities. Furthermore, such deviations must be balanced against the many honorable decisions made by military commanders. General Grant not only rejected the bid of his own father for government contracts, but successfully resisted the efforts of would-be profiteers at Cairo, Illinois, despite intercession by Leonard Sweatt of Chicago, a personal friend of Lincoln and a major stockholder in the Illinois Central Railroad. Grant told Sweatt he would seize the railroad if Sweatt interfered. Property rights were seldom observed where slaves were concerned. Slaves were frequently taken by the military, first to do manual labor and then to serve in the army. Loyalist owners were given receipts, while Confederate sympathizers received nothing. As the Union army moved south, slaves by the thousands left the plantations to migrate northward. Those passing through Kentucky and other states where slavery was still legal sometimes were taken into custody and returned to their owners upon payment of a fee. Slaves not reclaimed could be sold at auction.

The Perryville battlefield, located in farming county about two miles (3km) from the town with the same name, is preserved as a State park. Perryville, fought on October 8, 1862, was the largest and bloodiest battle fought in Kentucky, with over 7,500 casualties, and it sealed the state within the Union. In 1862, Confederate General Braxton Bragg devised a two-pronged plan which would enable his Army of Tennessee to "liberate" Kentucky. It stared successfully with 12,000 men under General Kirby Smith advancing from Knoxville as far as Lexington. Bragg moved his army from Chattanooga toward Louisville, an important Union base. Capture of Louisville would put Bragg to the rear of the Union Army of Ohio, commanded by Major General Don Carlos Buell, and give the Confederacy control of the state. Bragg would have a defensible river boundary and be in a position to advance to the Great Lakes, cutting the North in two. It was a good plan, but suffered from lack of coordination and was much too ambitious for the resources at Bragg's command. He counted on Kentuckians rallying to his colors, thus providing additional forces. They did not: most of them cautiously waited to see whether he could clear Buell from the State.

NORTHWESTERN ARKANSAS

ARKANSAS WAS IMPORTANT THROUGHOUT THE CIVIL WAR BECAUSE OF ITS STRATEGIC POSITION ON THE MISSISSIPPI. THE CONFEDERATE STATE SAW NUMEROUS SKIRMISHES ALONG THE WEST BANK OF THE RIVER, BUT ITS TWO MAIN BATTLES TOOK PLACE IN THE NORTHWEST DURING THE EARLY PART OF THE CONFLICT.

Above: The official battle flag of the Confederate States of America. Although the flag had many similar forms over the years of the war, this design was adopted officially in 1863.

The first was the Battle of Pea Ridge or Elkhorn Tavern, which was fought on March 6–8, 1862. The build-up to this confrontation began when the Union Army of the Southwest under Samuel R. Curtis drove Confederate Brigadier General Sterling Price and his 8,000 men across the southern border of Missouri and into the Boston Mountains. There the rebels were joined by Earl Van Dorn's Confederate Army of the West, and the joint forces decided to turn on their pursuers.

On March 5, in darkness and bitter cold, Van Dorn led his men on a 55-mile (89-km) trek around Curtis's troops in preparation for an attack the following morning from the north. During the maneuver, Van Dorn fell into a freezing stream; by daybreak he had developed a fever and, when battle was joined, had to command his troops from a field ambulance.

The encounter took place in a hollow, where the morning mist was soon thickened by gunsmoke: visibility was poor throughout the first day, at the end of which the advantage lay with the

Left: Confederate General Earl Van Dorn (1820-1863). After failing to destroy the Union control of northwestern Arkansas and later losing the Second Battle of Corinth, he was never again trusted to lead a Confederate Army. Instead he was given command of a cavalry in 1863. He was murdered later that year by a man claiming that Van Dorn had been having an affair with his wife.

Confederates. However, on the second morning of the battle, Curtis counterattacked and followed up with an intense artillery barrage. Van Dorn withdrew, leaving an estimated 4,600 casualties in the field. Among those killed were Confederate brigadier generals Ben McCulloch and James McQueen McIntosh.

After this Union victory, Curtis decided to press on toward the state capital, Little Rock, but he abandoned his advance after a setback at the Battle of Whitney's Lane on May 19, 1862, and set up supply lines on the Mississippi River at Helena, Arkansas. He then ordered one of his accompanying generals, John M. Schofield, to drive any remaining Confederate forces out of the region. Schofield divided his Army of the Frontier into two divisions, one of which went to Springfield, Missouri, while the other, under General James G. Blunt, set off into northwest Arkansas.

Noticing that the Union forces had become vulnerably disconnected, Confederate General Thomas C. Hindman led a force to Fort Smith, Arkansas. On November 28, 1862, 2,000 men in a Confederate cavalry detachment went out from there to distract the Union troops

Right: Map showing the movements of armies in Missouri and Arkansas—including plotting the Battle of Pea Ridge.

Below: The map shows Union control and dominant presence in Missouri.

Opposite page: This map shows that, despite the Battle of Prairie Grove ending in tactical stalemate, Union forces actually exercised control over northwest Arkansas as as well..

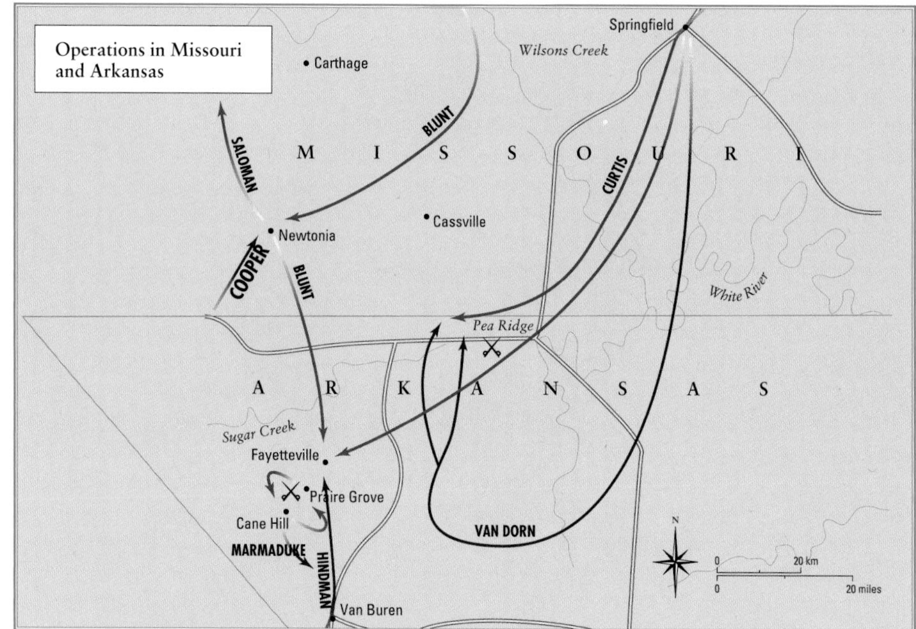

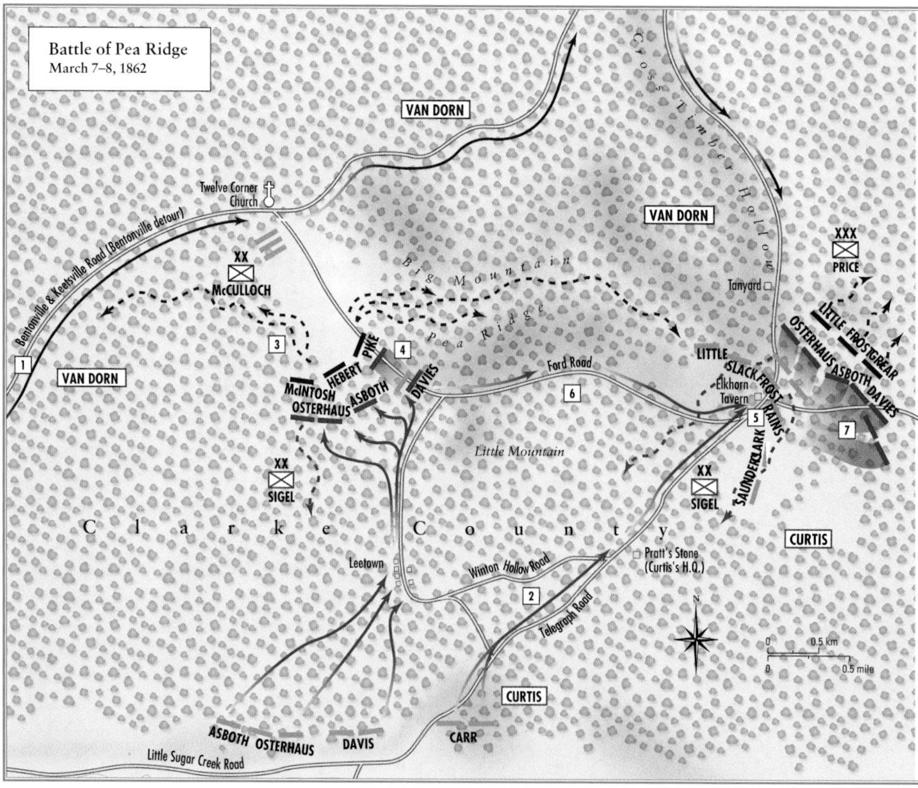

Battle of Pea Ridge
March 7–8, 1862

1 During the night of 6–7 March, Major General Earl Van Dorn marched his Confederate army via the Bentonville Detour in order to get in rear of the Union army of Major General Samuel R. Curtis.

2 **7 March:** After his scouts detected Van Dorn's march, Curtis gradually shifted troop to his right and rear to meet the Confederate threat.

3 **7 March:** Van Dorn ordered Brigadier General Benjamin McCulloch's division to attack along the Ford Road. McCulloch achieved some initial success.

4 **7 March:** After the death of McCulloch his men became demoralized and retreated.

5 **7 March:** Advancing from Cross Timbers Hollow, Major General Sterling Price's division, under Van Dorn personal supervision attacked toward Elkhorn Tavern and drove the Union troops of Brigadier General Eugene A. Carr's division back some distance before running low on ammunition.

6 **8 March:** Early in the morning the Union troops from the Leetown sector marched eastward to join Carr's division near Elkhorn Tavern.

7 **8 March:** After an artillery bombardment, Curtis launched an all-out assault that routed the Confederates.

from the movements of the main rebel army. Blunt managed to drive Marmaduke back at the Battle of Cane Hill.

On December 3, Hindman advanced his main force of 11,000 men and 22 cannon over the Boston Mountains toward Blunt's division. Blunt telegraphed General Francis J. Herron, commander of the Springfield division, for assistance, then set up defensive positions at Cane Hill and waited to see which would come first—the reinforcements or the enemy onslaught.

When Hindman realized that further Union troops were on their way, he abandoned his initial plan to attack Blunt from the east and decided instead to move north and intercept Herron. Marmaduke's advanced cavalry sighted the Union reinforcements on the march south of Fayetteville, Arkansas.

Instead of attacking immediately, Hindman set up defensive positions on top of a low ridge near Prairie Grove, Arkansas. There, on December 7, 1862, a Union artillery barrage drove many of the Confederate troops off the brow of the hill. Seizing his opportunity, Herron immediately began the ascent even though Blunt's men had still not arrived. The Confederates counterattacked from three sides and drove the Union forces back down the slope. However, they then broke lines and pursued the withdrawing forces, and in so doing ran straight into Union artillery fire, sustaining terrible losses. At almost exactly the same time, Blunt's forces joined the battle and drove the surviving Confederates back up the hill. The rebel force withdrew that night in disarray, leaving the Union in effective control of northwest Arkansas.

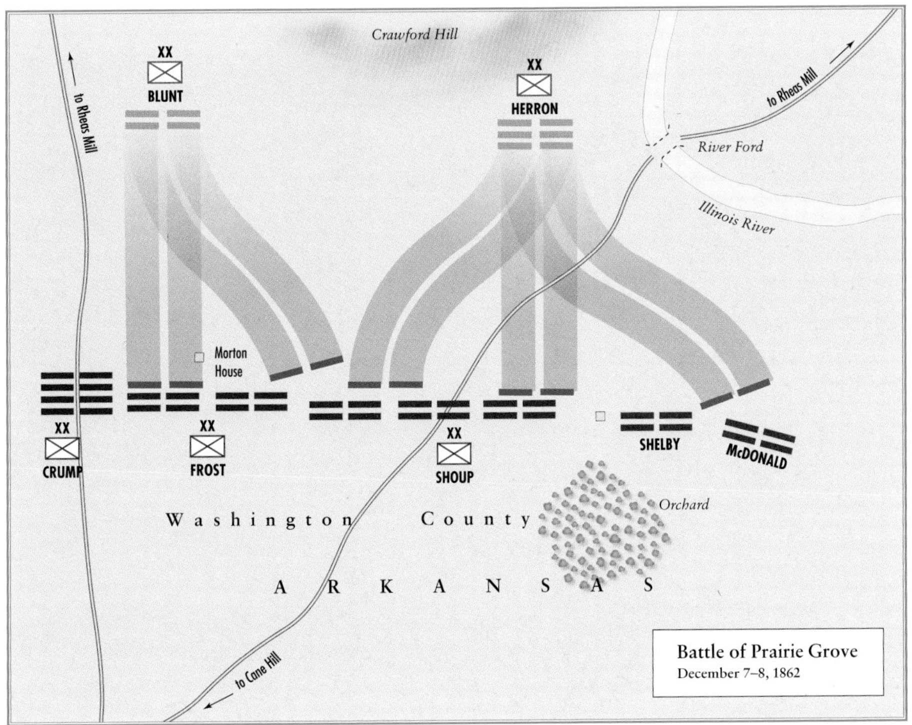

Battle of Prairie Grove
December 7–8, 1862

Forts Henry & Donelson

The concept of "Unconditional Surrender," was first accepted in early 1862 when the North achieved its first major victory with the capture of Forts Henry and Donelson in northwest Tennessee. Far greater battles would follow in the State, one of which could have prolonged the war, but these seizures established the pattern of pressure warfare that would dominate in the Western Theatre.

This and subsequent events would not only provide the military leadership the North desperately needed, but would establish Grant as perhaps the first modern general. Forts Henry and Donelson were part of the Southern attempt to defend extensive borders at all points against greatly superior forces and industrial capacity, an effort that dispersed the limited resources of the Confederacy. Neither fort could survive without support, and with Union naval forces in command of the Tennessee and Cumberland Rivers, they were quickly cut off by the superior land forces Grant led down from their base in Cairo, Illinois. In the first use of rivers for a major operation during the war, Fort Henry was attacked and surrendered to the naval commander after most of its guns were disabled. The bulk of the troops at nearby Fort Donelson missed an opportunity to evacuate overland, mainly because of the indecisiveness of the commanders, and thus were trapped.

The strength of the fort was never tested in land combat. Union forces had penetrated only about half of the outer defences when the isolated Confederates surrendered on February 16,1862; an attempt to break out had failed largely because Confederate troops, on the verge of victory, were ordered back to their entrenchments. Several thousand Confederates did escape, including about 700 cavalrymen and determined foot soldiers under Colonel Nathan Bedford Forrest, who would soon become a legend in his own time. When surrender became inevitable,

Above: Bombardment and the capture of Fort Henry, Tennessee 1862. An important victory for the Union Army led by General Ullysses S. Grant.

Next page: Map charting General Grants's progress west where he was eventually able to launch an assualt on Fort Henry and then Fort Donelson.

the two ranking Confederate generals left with some of their men on ships which arrived with 400 new recruits.

The loss of the forts was a stunning defeat for the Confederacy. With the capture of Forts Henry and Donelson, Grant had seized the initiative, made inevitable the evacuation of heavily fortified Columbus in Kentucky, and in fact, forced the Confederates out of Kentucky, broken their defence line in northern Tennessee, and permanently changed the strategic situation in the West. The surrender was celebrated throughout the North by the ringing of bells. Union forces had fared badly in other early battles, and this was a refreshing change.

Confederate Brigadier General Simon Bolivar Buckner, to whom command had been passed, surrendered to Grant at the Dover Hotel which had been his headquarters. Many Confederate soldiers stacked arms near the hotel and left from the landing for Northern prison camps. The meetings between Grant and Buckner were poignant; the officers had known each other at West Point, and Buckner had helped Grant out of a financial difficulty in New York prior to the war.

The loss of Forts Henry and Donelson subjected Tennessee to a long period of seesaw warfare that devastated the state. Tennessee was the primary battleground of the Western Theatre. Federal forces insecurely occupied the northern section of the State, including its capital, Nashville, and the Southerners created a new defensive line in the southern part of the State. A total of 1,462 military activities of all kinds, at least 454 of them significant, took place in Tennessee—more than in any other state except Virginia.

The best generals adapted quickly. Confederate General Robert E. Lee's early and continued

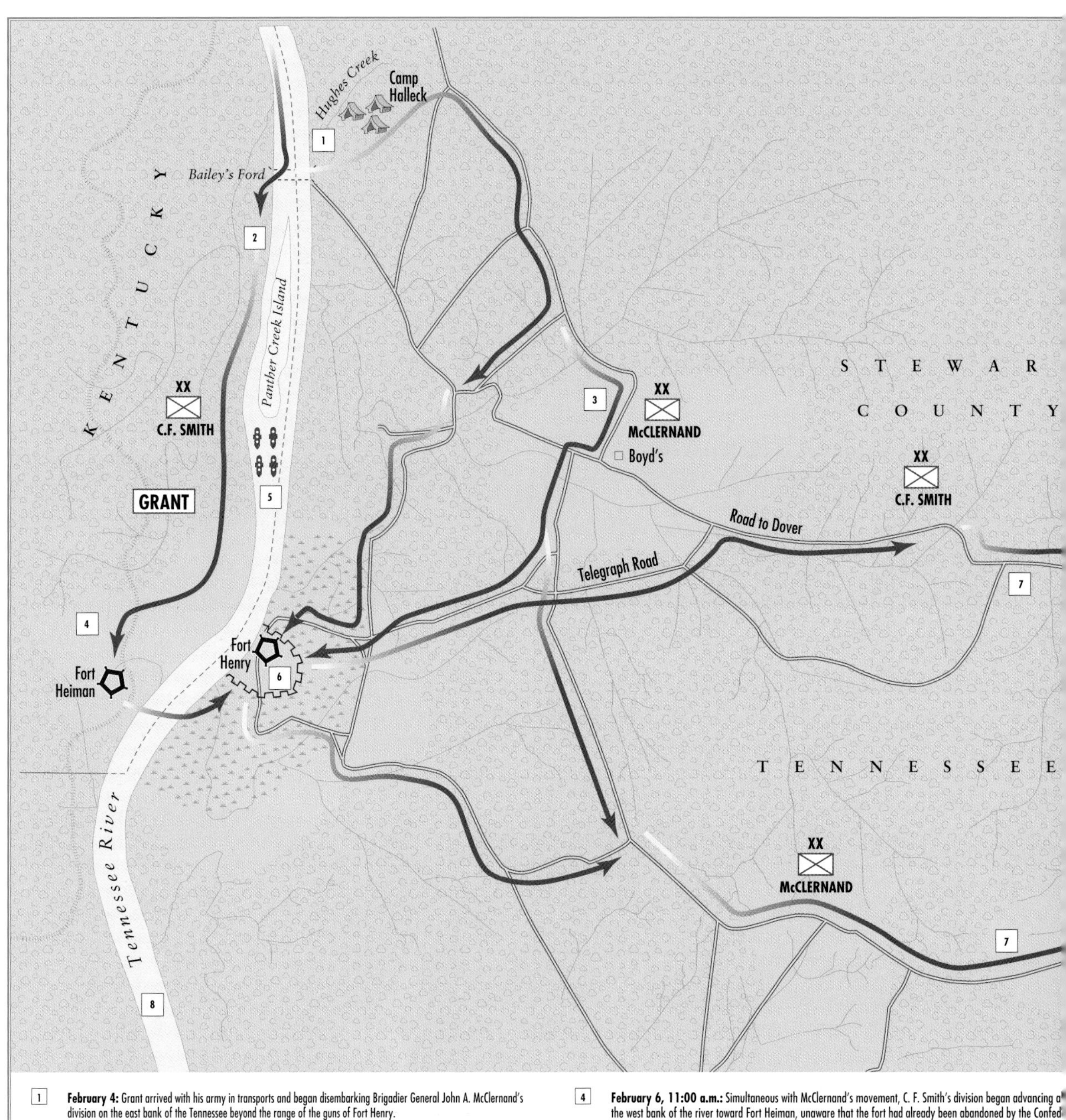

1 **February 4:** Grant arrived with his army in transports and began disembarking Brigadier General John A. McClernand's division on the east bank of the Tennessee beyond the range of the guns of Fort Henry.

2 **February 5:** Disembarkation continued, as Grant had Brigadier General C. F. Smith's division land on the west bank of the river. February 6, 11:00 a.m.: As ordered by Grant, McClernand's division left is camps, marching toward the rear of Fort Henry.

3 **February 6, 11:00 a.m.:** As ordered by Grant, McClernand's division left is camps, marching toward the rear of Fort Henry.

4 **February 6, 11:00 a.m.:** Simultaneous with McClernand's movement, C. F. Smith's division began advancing a the west bank of the river toward Fort Heiman, unaware that the fort had already been abandoned by the Confed

5 **February 6, 11:00 a.m.–1:55 p.m.:** While the ground troops toiled over muddy roads, Flag Officer Andrew H Foote's gunboat flotilla proceeded up the river at the hour Grant had appointed. Foote's gunboats shelled the fort until it surrendered.

6 **February 6, 6:00 p.m.:** After a miserable day of slogging over soggy roads, Grantis troops finally reached and occupied Fort Henry.

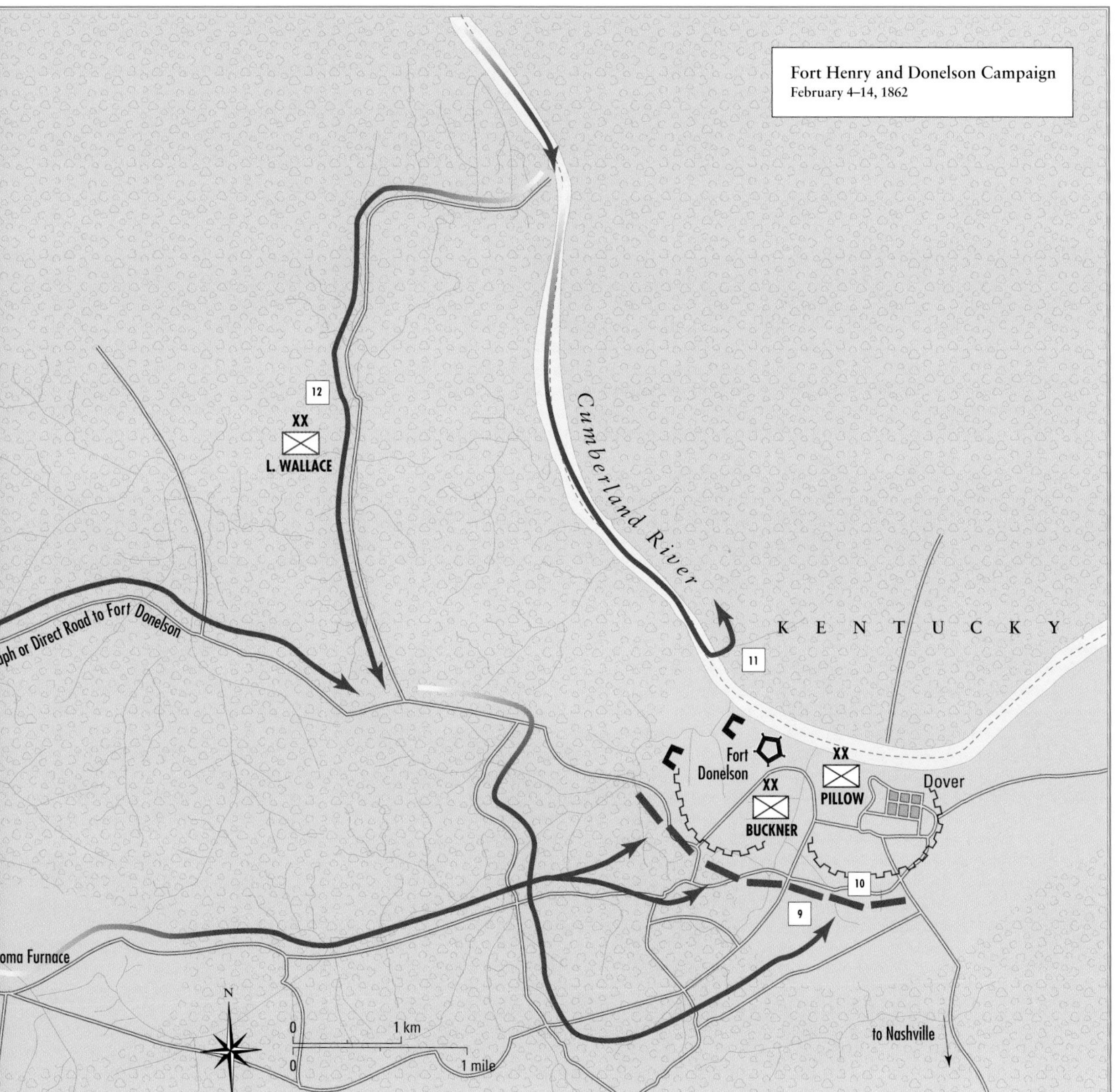

February 11: Determined to take Fort Donelson as well, Grant advanced leading elements of his force to within seven miles of that Confederate stronghold.

Foote sent his three "timberclad" gunboats on a raid up the Tennessee River while he led the four ironclad boats back down the Tennessee and then up the Cumberland to join Grant at Fort Donelson.

February 12: Grant arrived in front of Fort Donelson with the divisions of McClernand and Smith. His force was inadequate to invest the fort completely, and he was outnumbered by the Confederate garrison inside the defenses.

10 **February 13:** Smith and McClernand both launched local unauthorized attacks on the defenses of Fort Donelson, which the Confederates easily repulsed. That night a winter storm brought snow and intense cold.

11 **February 14, 2:00 p.m.:** Foote led his gunboats in an attack on Fort Donelson, but heavy and accurate Confederate fire disabled all four boats and wounded Foote. The gunboats had accomplished nothing.

12 **February 14:** Lew Wallace's brigade arrived from Fort Heiman, and Grant combined it with additional troops arriving on transports by river to form a third division under Wallace's command. With these new troops Grant for the first time enjoyed numerical superiority over the defenders of Fort Donelson.

US
US
US
US

emphasis on breastworks and other temporary defensive structures did not result entirely from his engineering background; he was actually aware of the damage that increased firepower did to his troops.

Union General Ullysses S. Grant, despite complaints which persisted throughout his career that he was a "butcher" unconcerned about the lives of his men, was an early exponent of manoeuvre. He in effect flanked Fort Donelson by taking Fort Henry first and ravaged the hinterland of Vicksburg before settling down to besiege the city. In his drive to take Richmond, he consistently flanked Lee's smaller army. General William Tecumseh Sherman's favorite manoeuvre, his famous March to the Sea notwithstanding, was the flanking movement. But, both Lee and Grant were capable of ignoring the lesson they had learned when greater considerations were at stake. Grant believed that "if men make war in slavish observance of the rules, they will fail."

The effect on United States military doctrine was considerable. The ascendancy of the offensive in U.S. Army tactics, while not transmitted in an unbroken line, dates from the Civil War Period. The concept of "unconditional surrender" would surface again in World War II. The objective of "total war" during the Civil War was to hasten the military victory; the consequences were not considered. That narrow definition of strategy prevailed in the United States until after World War II. By the end of the Civil War, the foundation stones of modern warfare were in place.

Left: The capture of Fort Donelson. Due to the Confederate surrender, the Federal Army took over 12,000 of their soldiers as prisoner. Note the soldier to the right of the picture raising the flag for the Union in defiance of Confederate Ensign.

THE NORTH CAROLINA CAMPAIGN

SUCH HAD BEEN THE SUCCESS OF THE UNION'S COASTAL CAMPAIGNS IN 1861 THAT IT WASTED NO TIME IN RESTARTING OPERATIONS IN 1862. BY JANUARY 2, 26 WARSHIPS WERE STEAMING SOUTH FROM VIRGINIA TO NORTH CAROLINA.

Their target was once again Hatteras Inlet where Union forces had already destroyed two Confederate batteries. This time their aim was to sail through the narrow inlet into the sounds beyond, which the Federals had identified as a prime location for blockade running by Confederates, who could hide out in among the many narrow waterways and islands.

Planning for how to negotiate the sounds' geographical peculiarities had been poor, however. The waters beyond the inlet were far too shallow to be negotiated by warships, obliging the fleet's leader, Flag Officer Louis M. Goldsborough, to send for smaller, more maneuverable craft, which took several weeks to arrive.

Union troops were not able to enter the sounds until February 7. Once there, however, they made good progress, heading north to Roanoke Island where 7,500 troops under the command of Brigadier General Ambrose Burnside quickly overwhelmed a number of Confederate forts. Further victories for the North followed in swift succession, each of which would serve to tighten the coastal blockade Elizabeth City fell easily on February 10, as did Winton on February 18,. and New Bern on March 14.

The capture of the Union's next target would require a little greater effort, however. Union troops reached Fort Macon, which guarded Beaufort Inlet, on March 23. When their demand for the fort's surrender was ignored, a siege began. During the month the Confederates held out, the Union forces were all the time being steadily reinfoced. On April 25, deadlock was broken by a huge Union bombardment—from both land and sea—which reduced the fort to rubble and precipitated an immediate Confederate surrender.

Above: Map of the North Carolina campaign, the Union's attempt to prevent the Confederates from breaking their coastal blockade.

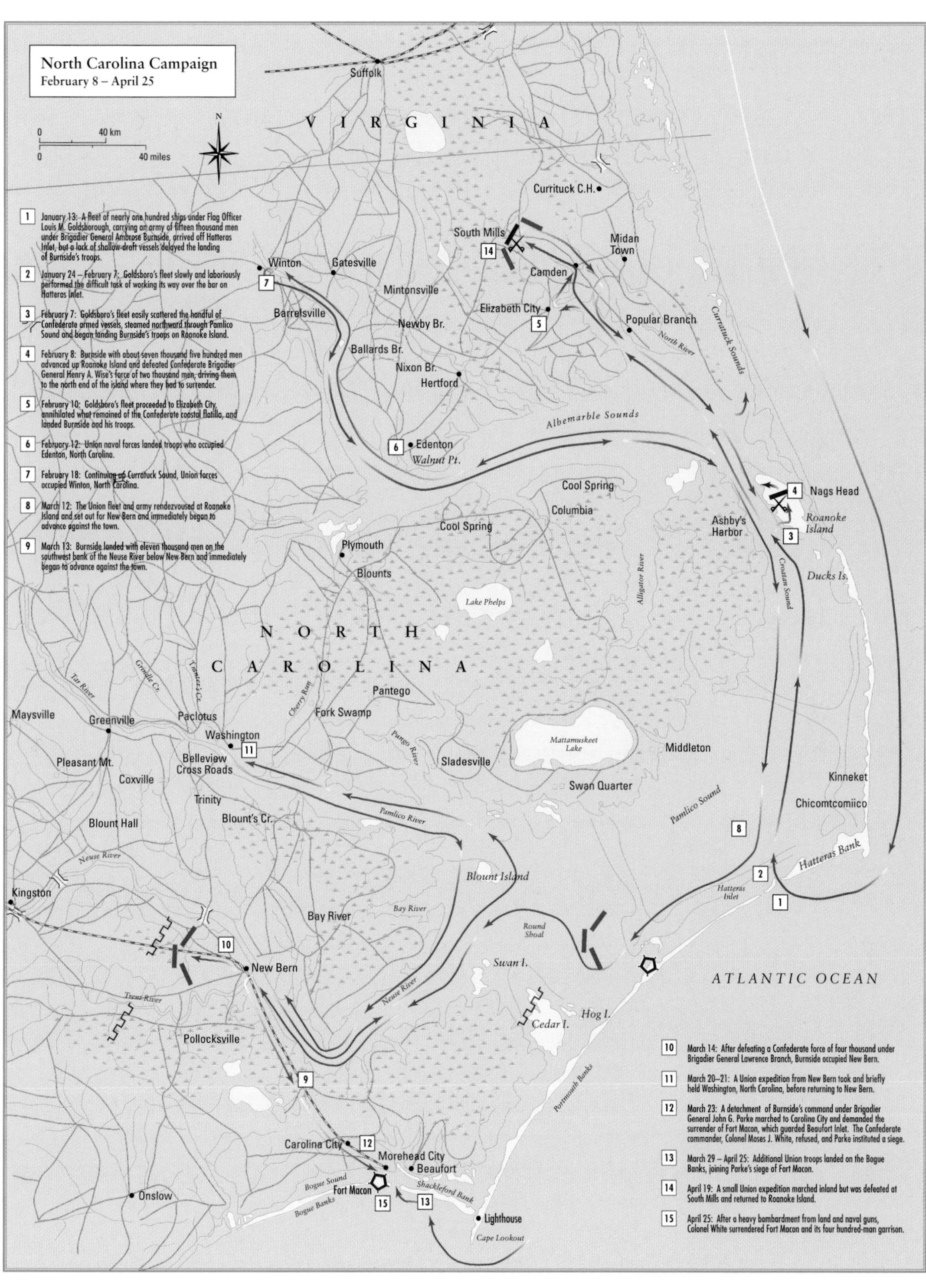
North Carolina Campaign
February 8 – April 25
0 40 km
0 40 miles
N
VIRGINIA
NORTH CAROLINA
ATLANTIC OCEAN
Suffolk
Currituck C.H.
South Mills
Midan Town
Camden
Winton
Gatesville
Mintonsville
Barrelsville
Elizabeth City
Popular Branch
Newby Br.
Ballards Br.
Nixon Br.
Hertford
North River
Currituck Sounds
Albemarle Sounds
Edenton
Walnut Pt.
Nags Head
Cool Spring
Columbia
Ashby's Harbor
Roanoke Island
Plymouth
Blounts
Lake Phelps
Alligator River
Croatan Sound
Ducks Is.
Tar River
Grindle Cr.
Cherry Run
Pantego
Fork Swamp
Maysville
Greenville
Paclotus
Washington
Pleasant Mt.
Belleview Cross Roads
Coxville
Pungo River
Sladesville
Mattamuskeet Lake
Middleton
Swan Quarter
Kinneket
Chicomtcomiico
Trinity
Blount's Cr.
Blount Hall
Pamlico River
Pamlico Sound
Hatteras Bank
Hatteras Inlet
Neuse River
Blount Island
Kingston
Bay River
Round Shoal
New Bern
Swan I.
Trent River
Cedar I.
Hog I.
Pollocksville
Portsmouth Banks
Carolina City
Morehead City
Beaufort
Bogue Sound
Fort Macon
Shackleford Bank
Bogue Banks
Onslow
Lighthouse
Cape Lookout
1 January 13: A fleet of nearly one hundred ships under Flag Officer Louis M. Goldsborough, carrying an army of fifteen thousand men under Brigadier General Ambrose Burnside, arrived off Hatteras Inlet, but a lack of shallow-draft vessels delayed the landing of Burnside's troops.
2 January 24 – February 7: Goldsboro's fleet slowly and laboriously performed the difficult task of working its way over the bar on Hatteras Inlet.
3 February 7: Goldsboro's fleet easily scattered the handful of Confederate armed vessels, steamed northward through Pamlico Sound and began landing Burnside's troops on Roanoke Island.
4 February 8: Burnside with about seven thousand five hundred men advanced up Roanoke Island and defeated Confederate Brigadier General Henry A. Wise's force of two thousand men, driving them to the north end of the island where they had to surrender.
5 February 10: Goldsboro's fleet proceeded to Elizabeth City, annihilated what remained of the Confederate coastal flotilla, and landed Burnside and his troops.
6 February 12: Union naval forces landed troops who occupied Edenton, North Carolina.
7 February 18: Continuing up Curratuck Sound, Union forces occupied Winton, North Carolina.
8 March 12: The Union fleet and army rendezvoused at Roanoke Island and set out for New Bern and immediately began to advance against the town.
9 March 13: Burnside landed with eleven thousand men on the southwest bank of the Neuse River below New Bern and immediately began to advance against the town.
10 March 14: After defeating a Confederate force of four thousand under Brigadier General Lawrence Branch, Burnside occupied New Bern.
11 March 20–21: A Union expedition from New Bern took and briefly held Washington, North Carolina, before returning to New Bern.
12 March 23: A detachment of Burnside's command under Brigadier General John G. Parke marched to Carolina City and demanded the surrender of Fort Macon, which guarded Beaufort Inlet. The Confederate commander, Colonel Moses J. White, refused, and Parke instituted a siege.
13 March 29 – April 25: Additional Union troops landed on the Bogue Banks, joining Parke's siege of Fort Macon.
14 April 19: A small Union expedition marched inland but was defeated at South Mills and returned to Roanoke Island.
15 April 25: After a heavy bombardment from land and naval guns, Colonel White surrendered Fort Macon and its four hundred-man garrison.

CORINTH AND ISLAND NO.10

AFTER THE FALL OF FORT HENRY AND FORT DONELSON, REBEL FORCES UNDER GENERAL BEAUREGARD WITHDREW TO CORINTH, MISSISSIPPI—THE JUNCTION OF THE MOBILE AND OHIO AND THE MEMPHIS AND CHARLESTON LINES AND THE CONFEDERACY'S ONLY DIRECT RAIL CONNECTION WITH THE EAST. THE TOWN WAS PROTECTED FROM ATTACK DOWN THE MISSISSIPPI BY SOUTHERN FORTIFICATIONS ON ISLAND NO. 10 IN THE RIVER AND THE SURROUNDING AREA AROUND 60 MILES (97KM) DOWNSTREAM FROM COLUMBUS, KENTUCKY.

Having identified the weak point in the Southern defenses, Union Brigadier General John Pope led his troops overland from Commerce, Missouri, through swampland to confront Southern forces in New Madrid, to which they laid siege on March 3, 1862.

Confederate General John P. McCown responded with a spirited defense of the city: at one stage of the battle, Brigadier General M. Jeff Thomson took the Missouri State Guard out of Corinth on a sortie that bombarded the Northerners with heavy artillery. However, they failed to land a knockout blow and on March 13 McCown decided that his position was untenable. He evacuated the city and took his men on gunboats to Island No. 10 and to Tiptonville; the Union army entered Corinth on the following day.

On March 15, a Union flotilla under Flag Officer Andrew H. Foote came south down the river to take up a threatening position to the north of Island No. 10. After watching and waiting for nearly three weeks, on the stormy night of April 4, one of Foote's ships, the ironclad USS *Carondelet*, slipped past the gun batteries on the island and anchored off New Madrid. It was joined there two nights later by another Union vessel, the USS *Pittsburg*. The ships drew Confederate fire from Tiptonville and the surrounding area while Pope's men crossed the Mississippi and blocked the

Opposite page: A map of military and naval movements in Tennessee and surrounding states.

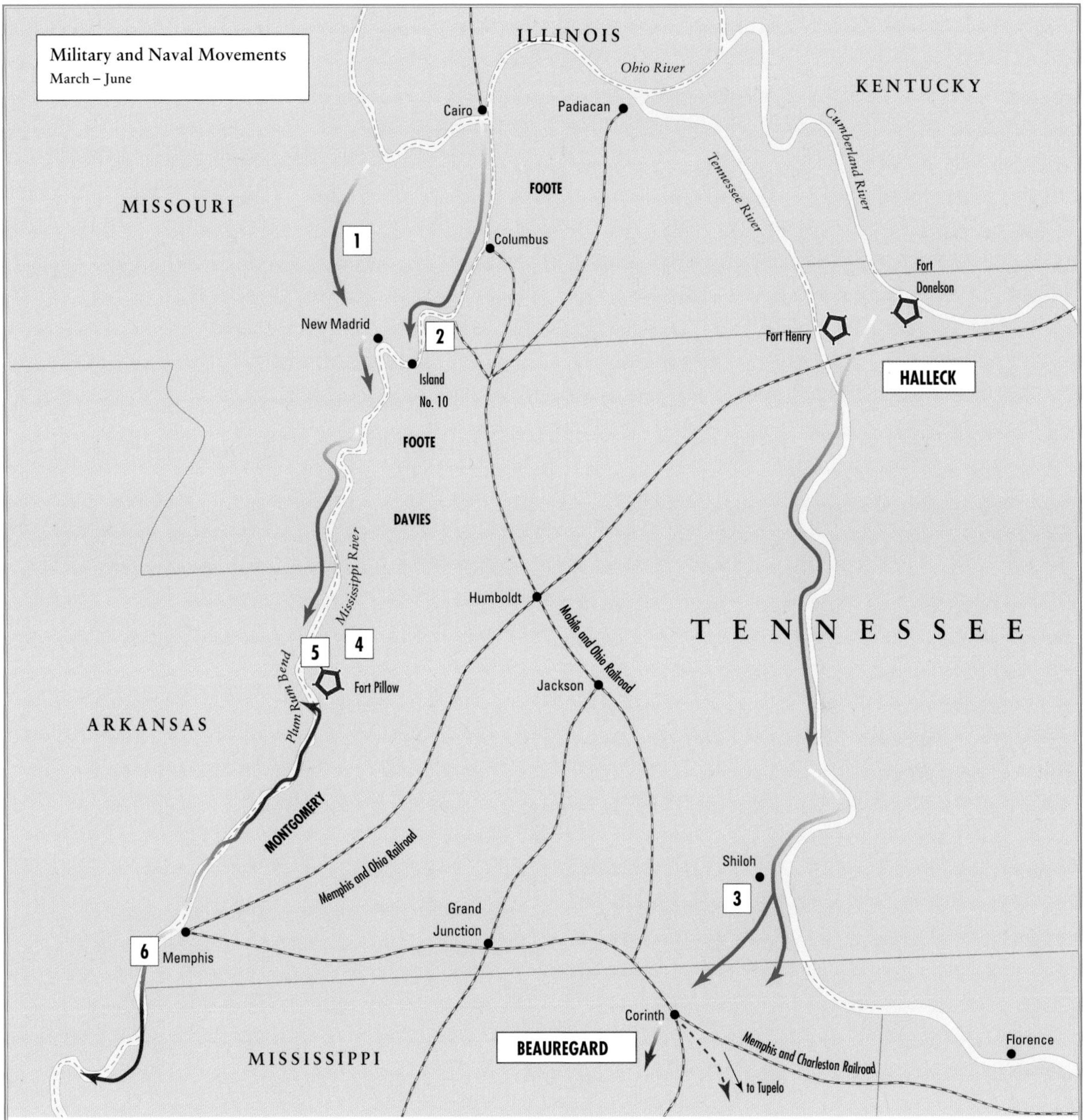

Military and Naval Movements
March – June

ILLINOIS
Ohio River
KENTUCKY
Cumberland River
Tennessee River
Cairo
Padiacan
MISSOURI
FOOTE
Columbus
Fort
Donelson
New Madrid
Island
No. 10
Fort Henry
HALLECK
FOOTE
DAVIES
Mississippi River
Humboldt
Mobile and Ohio Railroad
TENNESSEE
Plum Run Bend
Fort Pillow
Jackson
ARKANSAS
MONTGOMERY
Memphis and Ohio Railroad
Shiloh
Grand
Junction
Memphis
Corinth
BEAUREGARD
Memphis and Charleston Railroad
Florence
MISSISSIPPI
to Tupelo

1 **March:** After the fall of Fort Henry forced the Confederates to abandon their fortifications at Columbus, Halleck dispatched Brigadier General John Pope overland to attack New Madrid while the navy's gunboats, commanded by Flag Officer Andrew H. Foote proceeded down the river.

2 **March 13 – April 17:** Foote and Pope cooperated in besieging New Madrid, Island No. 10, and their associated fortifications, compelling their surrender with seven thousand men.

3 **April 29 – May 30:** Halleck's massive army advanced ponderously toward the key rail junction at Corinth, which the Confederates finally evacuated on May 30.

4 **April 14:** The Union mortar fleet began bombarding Fort Pillow.

5 **May 10:** The Confederate River Defense Fleet under command of Captain James E. Montgomery attacked the Union gunboats at Plum Run Bend north of Fort Pillow, sinking two but sustaining significant damage. Montgomery's vessels then return to Memphis.

6 **June 7:** The Union fleet under Flag Officer Charles H. Davis decisively defeated Montgomery's River Defense Fleet. Memphis surrendered.

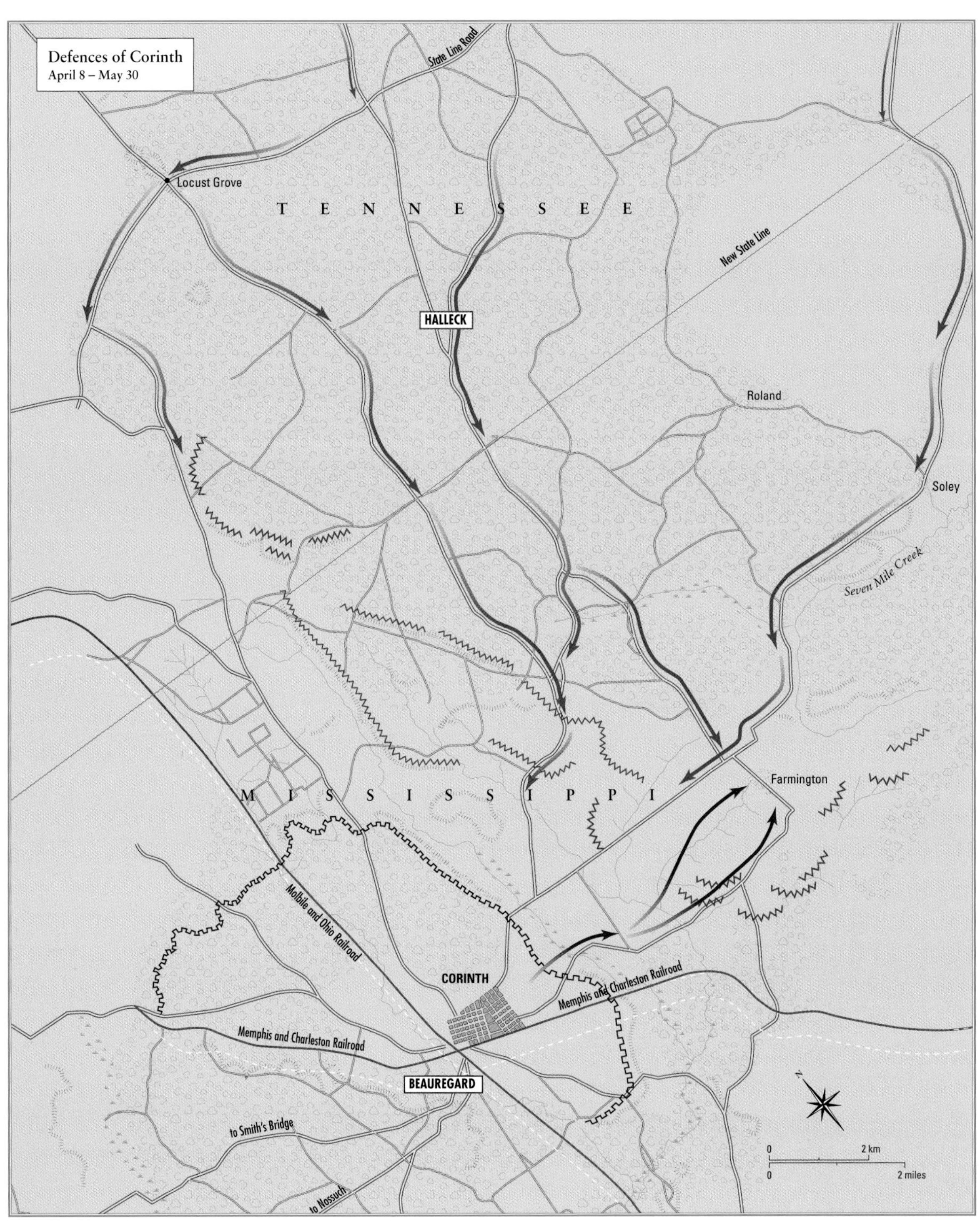
Defences of Corinth
April 8 – May 30
State Line Road
Locust Grove
TENNESSEE
New State Line
HALLECK
Roland
Soley
Seven Mile Creek
Farmington
MISSISSIPPI
Mobile and Ohio Railroad
CORINTH
Memphis and Charleston Railroad
Memphis and Charleston Railroad
BEAUREGARD
to Smith's Bridge
to Nassuch
N
0 2 km
0 2 miles

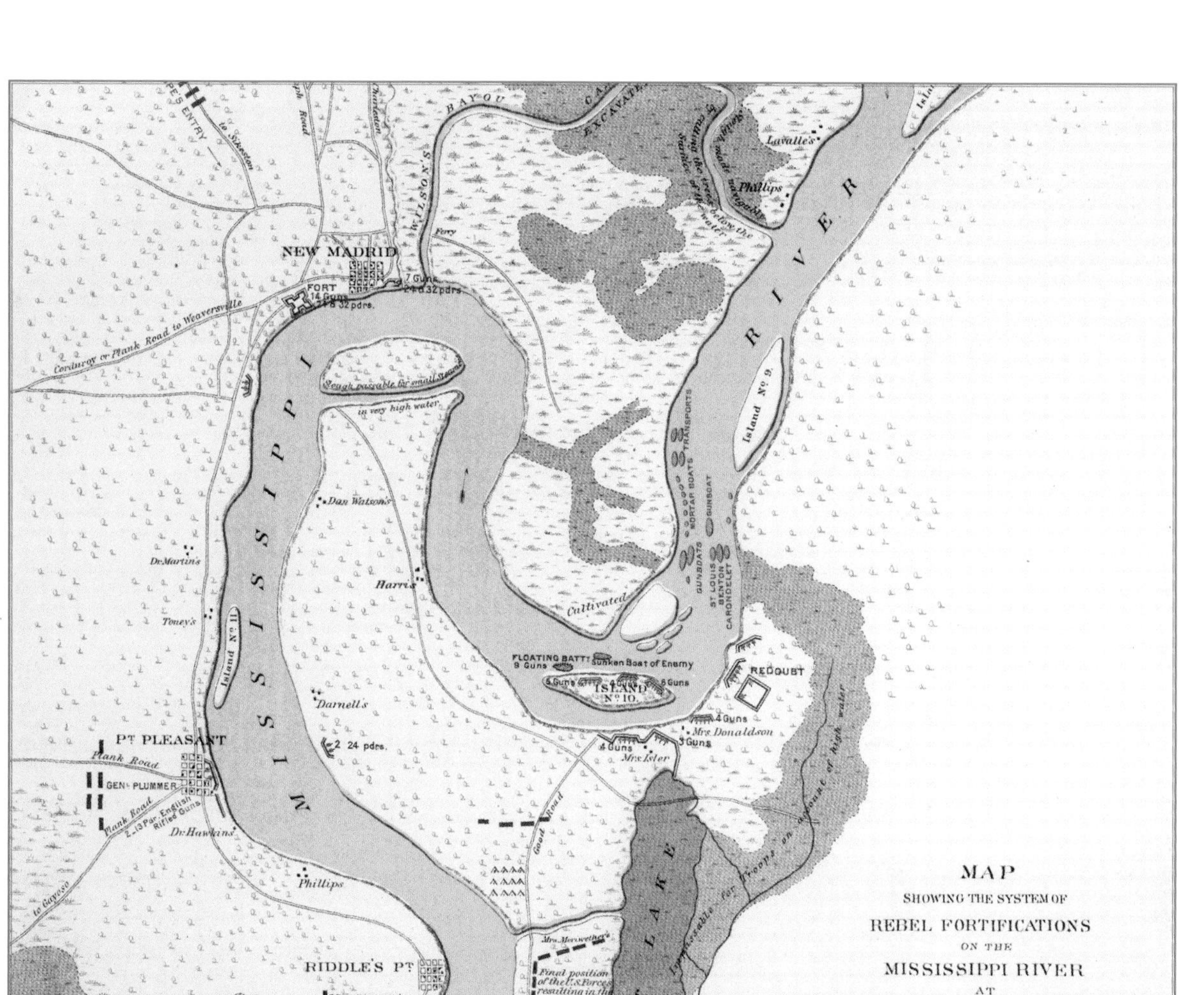

land route to and from the jetty that served the island. The vessels moved back up river to bombard the island; with its exit blocked by Pope, the garrison with its 7,000 men surrendered on April 8.

The fall of Island No. 10 opened the Mississippi River to Union troops as far south as Fort Pillow, and from there the Union was able to launch a successful attack two months later on Memphis. Before that, however, the Northern army turned its attention back to Corinth. Union Major General Henry Halleck advanced cautiously, digging entrenchments at each stop, and took three weeks to cover five miles (8km). He finally laid siege to the town on May 25, 1862. After a preliminary bombardment, Beauregard abandoned Corinth on May 30 and removed hismen to Tupelo.

Above: Map showing military activity along the Mississippi River, a Union gateway into Tennessee.

Opposite page: Map of P. G. T. Beauregard's defences in Corinth, Mississippi.

Above: This painting shows the battle between the USS *Monitor* and CSS *Virginia*, which was fought on March 9, 1862 at Hampton Roads.

The use of ironclads helped compensate for the much larger Union fleets of wooden ships, but the vessels drew too much water and were too unwieldy to be the decisive weapon envisioned by their designers. Many of them performed poorly or broke down in combat because of engine problems.

The best-known Confederate ironclad vessel was by far the CSS *Virginia*, the resurrected and converted former USS *Merrimack* (which had burned to the waterline when the Union evacuated Norfolk in April 1861). Her above-water structure was plated with two inches (5cm) of armor. On its first day out of Norfolk, the *Virginia* had a field day against the wooden Federal warships anchored off Newport News, sinking the sloop *Cumberland* (part of its anchor chain is on display in Casino Park in Newport News) and destroying the grounded frigate *Congress*. The consternation among Federal naval and army officers exceeded the damage caused by the fighting; unchallenged, the *Virginia* could endanger the Union position on the Peninsula and break the blockade. The ironclad fought only one major battle—with the USS *Monitor*, the "cheesebox on a raft," built in New York according to a radical design developed by inventor John Ericsson.

The battle, one of the most famous naval engagements in history, began on March 8, 1862, when the *Virginia* steamed out of Norfolk under command of Lieutenant George U. Morris to challenge the wooden Union fleet massing in Hampton Roads for General George B. McClellan's approaching Peninsular Campaign to take Richmond, the Confederate capital. The alarm caused by the easy sinking of the *Cumberland* and destruction of the grounded *Congress*, two powerful warships, extended all the way to Washington and raised Confederate hopes of breaking the Union blockade.

Fortunately for the Union, the strange looking *Monitor* arrived at Fortress Monroe during the night, setting the stage for the first battle of ironclads. When the *Virginia* steamed into Hampton Roads the next day to resume destruction of the Union fleet, it was engaged by the *Monitor* in a four-hour battle at close quarters which ranged back and forth in the world's largest natural harbor. For the most part shells bounced off the thick hulls of both ships. Both received some damage, but remained seaworthy; neither could gain the upper hand. The contest was a draw: the *Virginia* was slow, unwieldy, and her draft was too deep for shallow water; the *Monitor* was unwieldy, too, had difficulty with her guns and equipment, and was subject to flooding.

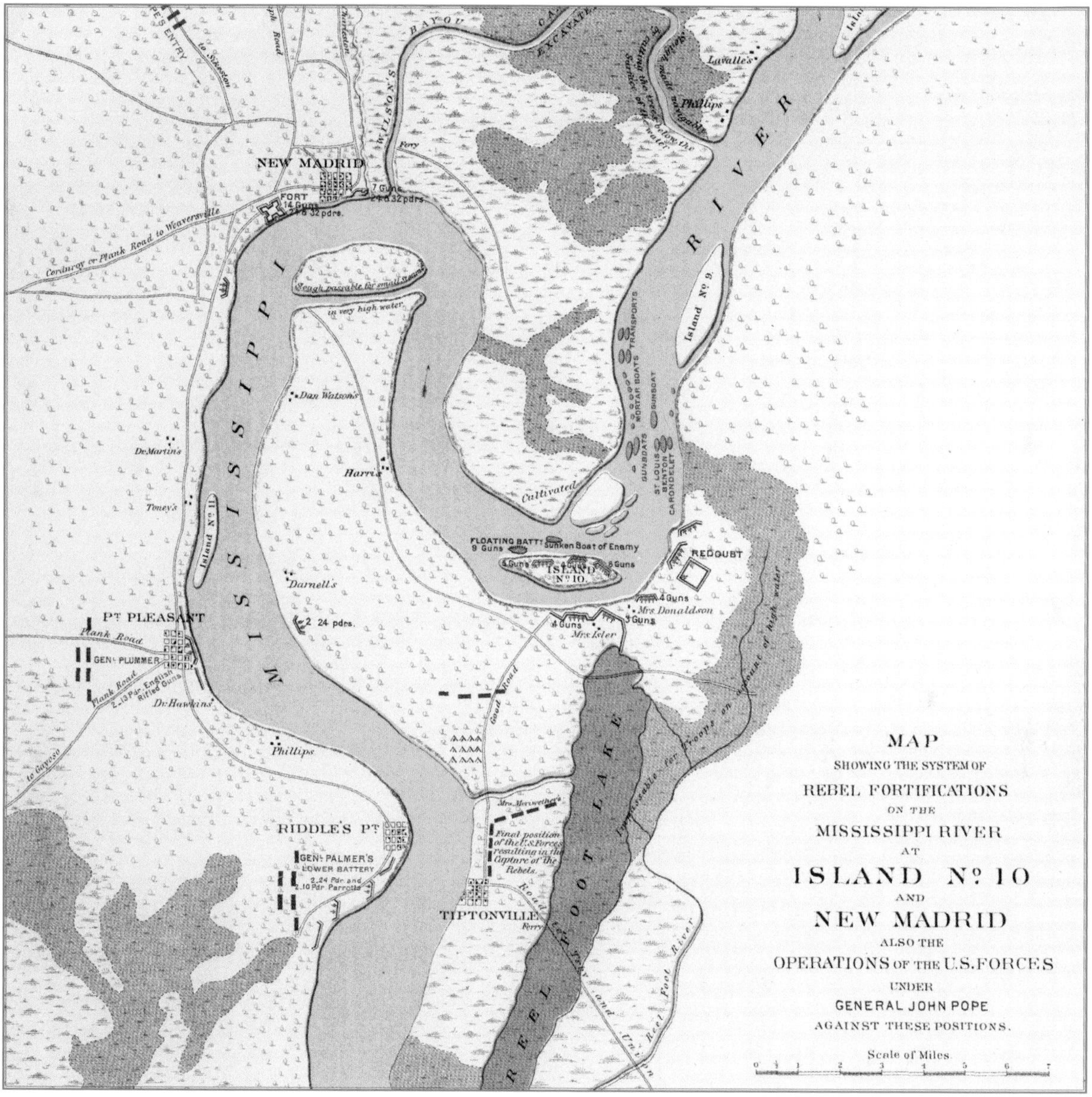

MAP
SHOWING THE SYSTEM OF
REBEL FORTIFICATIONS
ON THE
MISSISSIPPI RIVER
AT
ISLAND Nº 10
AND
NEW MADRID
ALSO THE
OPERATIONS OF THE U.S.FORCES
UNDER
GENERAL JOHN POPE
AGAINST THESE POSITIONS.

Above: Map showing military activity along the Mississippi River, a Union gateway into Tennessee.

Opposite page: Map of P. G.T. Beauregard's defences in Corinth, Mississippi.

land route to and from the jetty that served the island. The vessels moved back up river to bombard the island; with its exit blocked by Pope, the garrison with its 7,000 men surrendered on April 8.

The fall of Island No. 10 opened the Mississippi River to Union troops as far south as Fort Pillow, and from there the Union was able to launch a successful attack two months later on Memphis. Before that, however, the Northern army turned its attention back to Corinth. Union Major General Henry Halleck advanced cautiously, digging entrenchments at each stop, and took three weeks to cover five miles (8km). He finally laid siege to the town on May 25, 1862. After a preliminary bombardment, Beauregard abandoned Corinth on May 30 and removed hismen to Tupelo.

THE HAMPTON ROADS, MARCH 8-9, 1862

AT SEA, UNION FORCES ALREADY HAD IMPLEMENTED A VERSION OF THE ANACONDA PLAN, WHICH CALLED FOR OCCUPATION OF KEY POINTS ALONG THE CONFEDERATE COAST. THE NORTHERN BLOCKADE PROCLAIMED BY LINCOLN ON APRIL 19, SLOWLY STRANGLED THE FOREIGN TRADE OF THE CONFEDERACY. BREAKING THE BLOCKADE BECAME A NECESSITY FOR THE SOUTH. TECHNOLOGICAL DEVELOPMENTS WERE EMPLOYED IN VESSELS OF BOTH SIDES IN A NEW FORM OF NAVAL WARFARE.

Above: Illustration of a Confederate ironclad ship sinking The USS *Congress*. The Union created the most powerful navy afloat. However, there were instances where the Confederate Navy could not be beaten.

Nowhere was the disparity of assets during the Civil War more evident than in the naval forces. Not only did the Union possess virtually all of the prewar Navy, it had an industrial base capable of coping with wartime demands. A massive construction program made the Union navy the most powerful afloat; by the end of the war, it surpassed in number of ships even the greatest maritime power in history, Great Britain.

The Confederacy made a valiant effort to build a navy, but had no hope of achieving parity. An inadequate industrial base forced the Navy Department to improvise. It experimented with many types of vessels, but achieved its best results with ironclads. Fifty were ordered and 22 actually saw service.

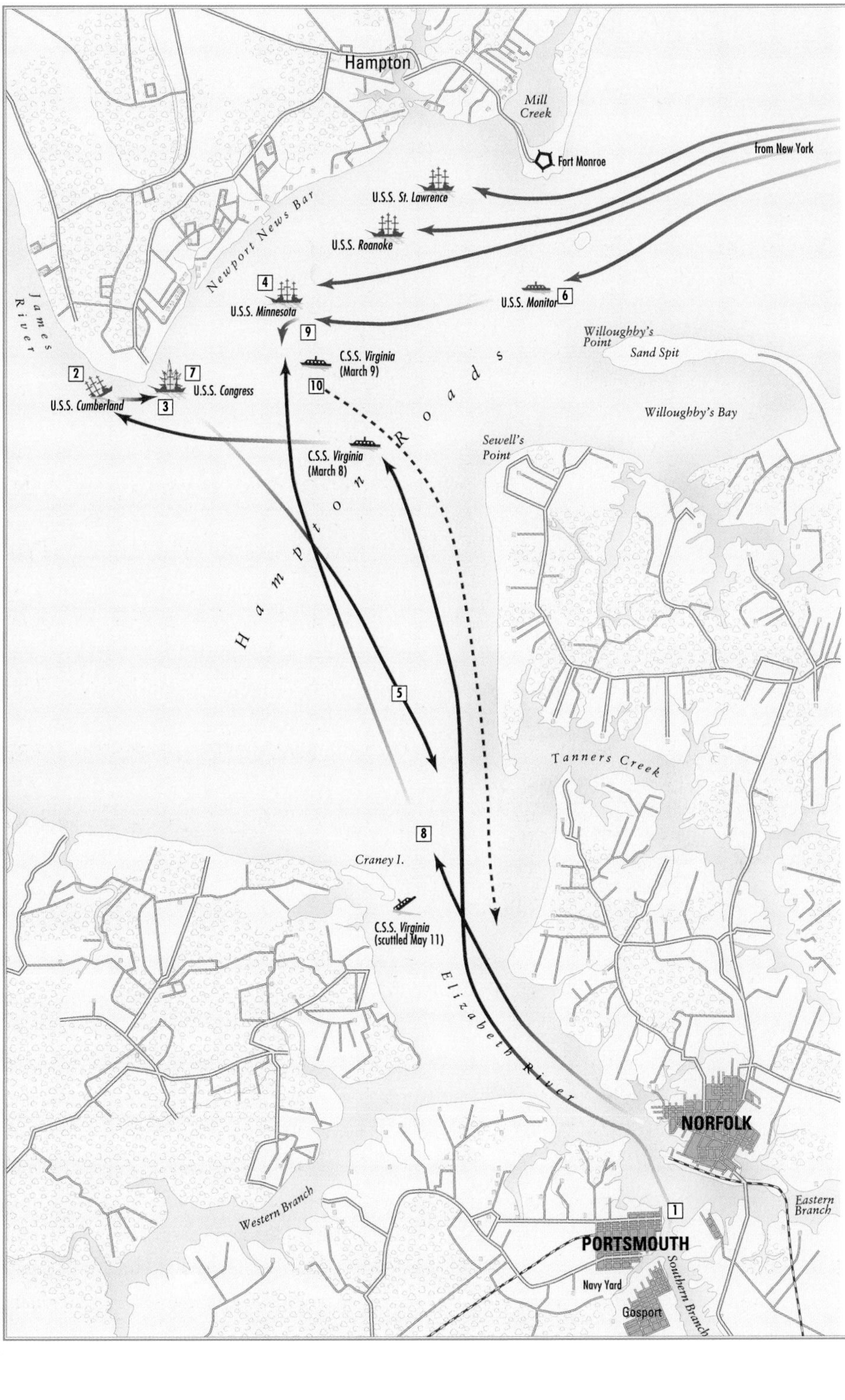

Hampton Roads
March 8–9, 1862

1. **March 8, c. 1:00 p.m.:** C.S.S. *Virginia* from Norfolk enters Hampton Roads.
2. U.S.S. *Cumberland* sinks following ramming attack by U.S.S. *Virginia*.
3. U.S.S. *Virginia* sets *Congress* on fire.
4. U.S.S. *Minnesota* runs aground while attempting to maneuver.
5. **6:06 p.m.:** C.S.S. *Virginia* returns to Norfolk for the night.
6. **9:00 p.m.:** U.S.S. *Monitor* arrives and anchors near U.S.S. *Minnesota*.
7. **March 9, 12:30 p.m.:** U.S.S. *Congress* explodes.
8. **7:00 a.m.:** C.S.S. *Virginia* returns to Hampton Roads and heads for U.S.S. *Minnesota*.
9. U.S.S. *Monitor* steams out to meet C.S.S. *Virginia* and opens fire.
10. **Until 12:15 p.m.:** Action continues. C.S.S. *Virginia* withdraws.

Left: Map illustrates the body of water known as Hampton Roads and the battle that took place between ironclad warships on March 8–9, 1862

Above: This painting shows the battle between the USS *Monitor* and CSS *Virginia*, which was fought on March 9, 1862 at Hampton Roads.

The use of ironclads helped compensate for the much larger Union fleets of wooden ships, but the vessels drew too much water and were too unwieldy to be the decisive weapon envisioned by their designers. Many of them performed poorly or broke down in combat because of engine problems.

The best-known Confederate ironclad vessel was by far the CSS *Virginia*, the resurrected and converted former USS *Merrimack* (which had burned to the waterline when the Union evacuated Norfolk in April 1861). Her above-water structure was plated with two inches (5cm) of armor. On its first day out of Norfolk, the *Virginia* had a field day against the wooden Federal warships anchored off Newport News, sinking the sloop *Cumberland* (part of its anchor chain is on display in Casino Park in Newport News) and destroying the grounded frigate *Congress*. The consternation among Federal naval and army officers exceeded the damage caused by the fighting; unchallenged, the *Virginia* could endanger the Union position on the Peninsula and break the blockade. The ironclad fought only one major battle—with the USS *Monitor*, the "cheesebox on a raft," built in New York according to a radical design developed by inventor John Ericsson.

The battle, one of the most famous naval engagements in history, began on March 8, 1862, when the *Virginia* steamed out of Norfolk under command of Lieutenant George U. Morris to challenge the wooden Union fleet massing in Hampton Roads for General George B. McClellan's approaching Peninsular Campaign to take Richmond, the Confederate capital. The alarm caused by the easy sinking of the *Cumberland* and destruction of the grounded *Congress*, two powerful warships, extended all the way to Washington and raised Confederate hopes of breaking the Union blockade.

Fortunately for the Union, the strange looking *Monitor* arrived at Fortress Monroe during the night, setting the stage for the first battle of ironclads. When the *Virginia* steamed into Hampton Roads the next day to resume destruction of the Union fleet, it was engaged by the *Monitor* in a four-hour battle at close quarters which ranged back and forth in the world's largest natural harbor. For the most part shells bounced off the thick hulls of both ships. Both received some damage, but remained seaworthy; neither could gain the upper hand. The contest was a draw: the *Virginia* was slow, unwieldy, and her draft was too deep for shallow water; the *Monitor* was unwieldy, too, had difficulty with her guns and equipment, and was subject to flooding.

The shallow-draft *Monitor* retired to its anchorage under the protecting guns of Forth Monroe and the *Virginia* returned to its Norfolk base. They never met again; the *Virginia* was burned when the Confederates abandoned Norfolk and the *Monitor* sank in a storm off the North Carolina coast while being towed to a new base of operations. Efforts to locate the *Monitor* failed until, in 1973, modern technology spotted the vessel on the bottom of the ocean.

The *Monitor*, the first ship to mount a revolving turret, was the lead ship of a whole class produced during the war. Sister vessels would serve with distinction in several future engagements. In other confrontations, the Confederacy used armament of any kind available, including bales of cotton, to strengthen its vessels against superior numbers and armament on Union ships. The "cottonclad" gunboats *Bayou City* and *Neptune* and the tenders *John F. Carr* and *Lady Gwin*, under army Major Leon Smith, helped recapture Galveston, Texas, on January 1, 1863. Union Commander William B. Renshaw's six wooden gunboats sank one of the cottonclads, but two union vessels were lost. The others put to sea when Confederate soldiers occupied the city. Cottonclad vessels failed, however, to prevent the occupation of Roanoke Island and Elizabeth City, North Carolina.

Below: Hampton Roads, Virginia: The Original *Monitor* after battle with the *Virginia*. Near the port-hole are the dents made by the guns of the Union craft.

Shenandoah, Jackson's Valley: Phase 1

The Shenandoah Valley is widely regarded as "Stonewall's Valley." No other general is so closely identified with it, and not even Robert E. Lee rivaled Jackson for the affection of its inhabitants. People sent letters to Confederate Secretary of War "Judah P. Benjamin" demanding that only Jackson defend the valley, and then filled the ranks of the Stonewall Brigade with their sons.

Mennonites who refused to fight sent wagons with supplies to Jackson's army. Citizens of towns frequently occupied by Federals turned out on their porches to wave and cheer whenever the Confederates returned. Jackson lived up to their trust in him; his 1862 Valley Campaign "whupped" an opponent three times his size so badly that Union armies were wary of valley defenders long after Jackson's death.

Jackson possessed an odd sort of charisma. He was dour and aloof, a quiet man whose life centered on his family and his Presbyterian religion. He was a gentle, affectionate father and his religion pervaded everything he did.

He once said that "every thought should be a prayer." He shared Lee's belief that duty was a calling, not an elective. Jackson was a professor at Virginia Military Institute in Lexington, Virginia, when the Civil War started, but volunteered for active duty immediately. His first command, at Harper's Ferry, was a ragtag group of undisciplined newly enlisted civilians known as the Army of the Shenandoah, who at first resented his harsh discipline and dedication to year-round warfare. Jackson remained close to his men and suffered along with them so that soldiers waking with snow on their blankets in the mountains of West Virginia might see their commander rise from the ground a few feet from them. If they had grumbled about their condition, and Jackson had heard it, he did not remonstrate. Neither did he relent; soldiers were supposed to endure hardships. They soon learned that combat and comfort did not coexist in Jackson's army and, while many thought him peculiar, they quickly came to trust and respect him. Jackson reciprocated by regarding no task beyond their capabilities.

This group, the 1st Virginia, became the Stonewall Brigade, which fought with great distinction from First Manassas to Appomattox. The men cheered when Jackson rode past them, even on secret marches, and revered him like a father even after his death. Strangely, Jackson's most famous nickname never appealed to his troops; he was "Old Jack" to most of them, and sometimes even "Old Blue Light" or "Hickory." He was even know as "Square Box" because of his large shoe size, but men of the 1st Brigade seldom referred to him as "Stonewall."

After First Manassas, where he acquired the nickname that helped make him a legend in his own lifetime, Jackson was ordered to take command of Confederate forces in the Shenandoah Valley, which were part of the Army of Northern Virginia but operated independently most of the time. He was reluctant to leave the Stonewall Brigade, and a farewell address made at the request of his soldiers told something about him and his men. Rising in his stirrups before the massed brigade, he shouted:

Below: This drawing shows "Stonewall" Jackson fighting a Union battalion at close range. The Shenandoah Valley was the site of several battles between the North and the South during the war.

Above: Lieutenant General Thomas Jonathan "Stonewall" Jackson (1824–1863), Commander of the Stonewall Brigade.

Opposite page: Jackson's Shenandoah Valley Campaign: Phase I (March 23–25 May).

"In the Army of the Shenandoah you were the First Brigade! In the Army of the Potomac you were the First Brigade! In the Second Corps of the army you are the First Brigade! You are the First Brigade in the affection of your general, and I hope by your future deed and bearing you will be handed down the posterity as the First Brigade in this our Second War of Independence. Godspeed!"

The Valley Campaign was Confederate General Thomas "Stonewall" Jackson's brilliant spring campaign of 1862 through the Shenandoah Valley of Virginia.

Jackson was given command of the valley district in November 1861, and chose to base his headquarters in Winchester. He had grown up in the valley district, so was very familiar with the terrain. However, although his troops had been reinforced, he was all too aware that he still did not have sufficient for any offensive operations.

Spring 1862 was an anxious time for the Confederacy. After its successes the previous year, nothing now seemed to go right. Major General George McClelland's massive Army of the Potomac was approaching Richmond from the southeast, while Major General Irvin McDowell's large corps was poised to take it from the north. As if this weren't enough, Major General Nathaniel Banks was threatening the Shenandoah Valley.

Jackson gathered a force of 17,000 and hoping to mask his intentions, he marched his army by a circuitous route to West View. Meanwhile Major General John Frémont decided to advance on Staunton. Jackson realized that if Frémont and Banks joined forces, he would be overwhelmed, so he decided to strike first at the Union forces at McDowell on May 8 to May 9.

On March 12 Banks occupied Winchester, but by then Jackson had withdrawn to Strasburg. Banks had been ordered to drive Jackson from the valley and then withdraw to a position near Washington D.C. Jackson's orders were to keep Banks occupied and prevent him from doing this, and from sending extra troops to McClelland. At the same time, because he was so seriously outnumbered, he had been told to avoid general combat. The First Battle took place at Kernstown, just south of Winchester on March 23. Jackson mistakenly believed that he was up against a weak Union force and although he suffered a tactical defeat, it was a strategic victory for the Confederacy because Lincoln ordered a considerable Unionist force to stay in the valley, thus subtracting about 50,000 troops from McClelland's Unionist invaders.

After fierce fighting the result was a victory for Jackson who after a two-week lull then force-marched his troops to attack the small outpost of Front Royal, at the confluence of the north and south forks of the Shenandoah River, on May 23. The aim was to cut Banks's line of communication and supply. Nearly 900 Union troops surrendered and Banks's troops were forced to retreat towards Winchester. At the Battle of Winchester on May 25, Banks' army was soundly defeated—the Union army of 8,000 men suffered 2,019 casualties, while Jackson's army of 16,000 lost just 400. Banks withdrew the remainder of his forces north across the Potomac River, pursued by Jackson' army, albeit somewhat slowly considering the exertions they have been made to endure over the course of the campaign.

Things got even better for the Confederates when their aim of tying down Union forces was greatly bolstered by Lincoln's reaction to the Shenandoah setback—which was to pour even more troops into the valley in a desperate, and ultimately doomed, attempt to defeat Jackson.

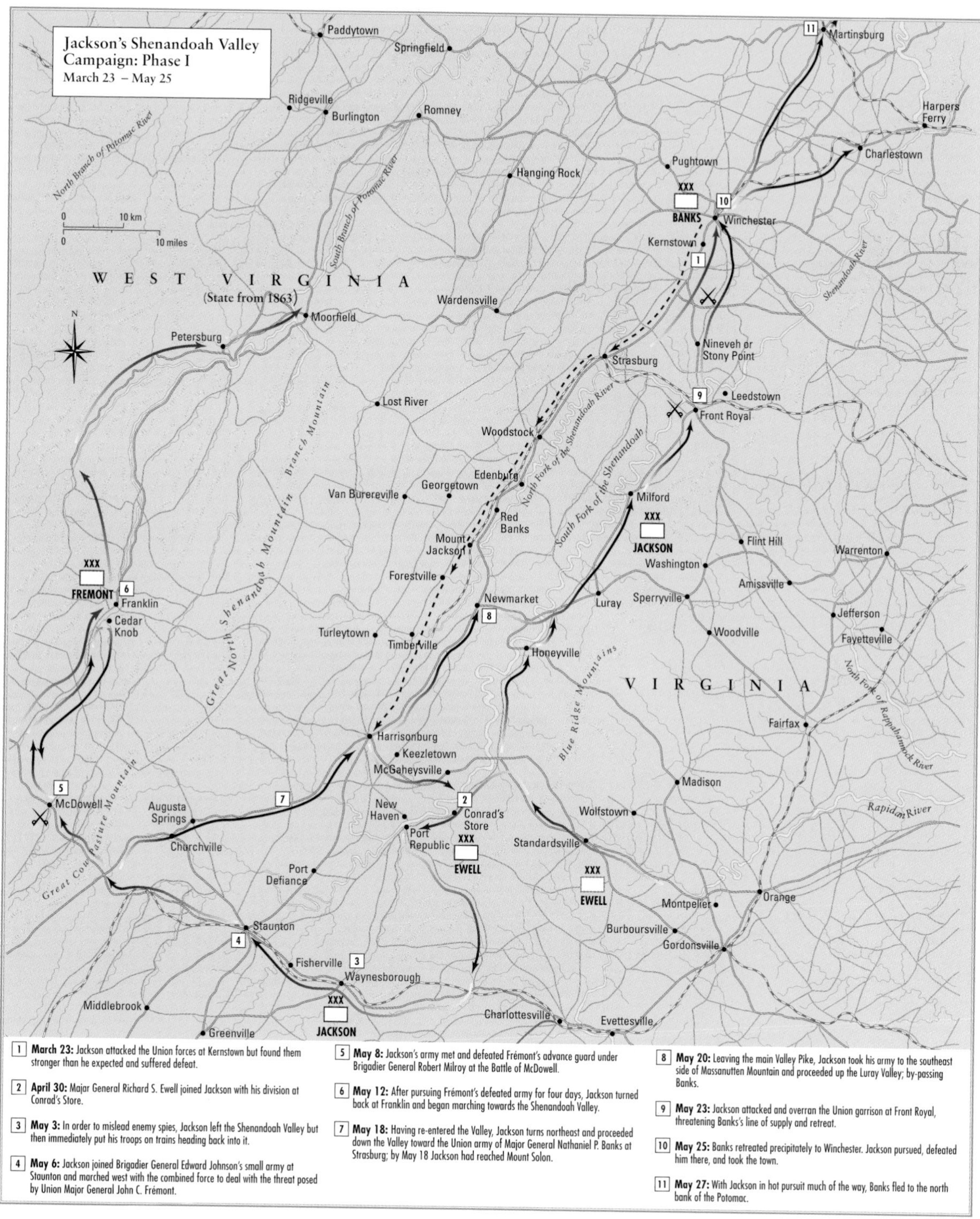
Jackson's Shenandoah Valley Campaign: Phase I
March 23 – May 25
Paddytown
Springfield
Ridgeville
Burlington
Romney
North Branch of Potomac River
South Branch of Potomac River
Hanging Rock
Pughtown
Martinsburg
Harpers Ferry
Charlestown
XXX
BANKS
Winchester
Kernstown
Shenandoah River
0 10 km
0 10 miles
W E S T V I R G I N I A
(State from 1863)
Moorfield
Wardensville
Petersburg
N
Strasburg
Nineveh or Stony Point
Leedstown
Front Royal
Lost River
Woodstock
North Fork of the Shenandoah River
South Fork of the Shenandoah
Great North Shenandoah Mountain
Branch Mountain
Edenburg
Georgetown
Van Burereville
Milford
Red Banks
Mount Jackson
XXX
JACKSON
Flint Hill
Warrenton
Washington
Forestville
XXX
FREMONT
Franklin
Cedar Knob
Newmarket
Luray
Sperryville
Amissville
Jefferson
Fayetteville
Turleytown
Timberville
Woodville
Honeyville
Blue Ridge Mountains
V I R G I N I A
North Fork of Rappahannock River
Fairfax
Harrisonburg
Keezletown
McGaheysville
Madison
McDowell
Great Cow Pasture Mountain
Augusta Springs
New Haven
Conrad's Store
Port Republic
XXX
EWELL
Wolfstown
Rapidan River
Churchville
Standardsville
Port Defiance
XXX
EWELL
Montpelier
Orange
Staunton
Burboursville
Gordonsville
Fisherville
Waynesborough
XXX
JACKSON
Middlebrook
Greenville
Charlottesville
Evettesville
1 March 23: Jackson attacked the Union forces at Kernstown but found them stronger than he expected and suffered defeat.
2 April 30: Majar General Richard S. Ewell joined Jackson with his division at Conrad's Store.
3 May 3: In order to mislead enemy spies, Jackson left the Shenandoah Valley but then immediately put his troops on trains heading back into it.
4 May 6: Jackson joined Brigadier General Edward Johnson's small army at Staunton and marched west with the combined force to deal with the threat posed by Union Major General John C. Frémont.
5 May 8: Jackson's army met and defeated Frémont's advance guard under Brigadier General Robert Milroy at the Battle of McDowell.
6 May 12: After pursuing Frémont's defeated army for four days, Jackson turned back at Franklin and began marching towards the Shenandoah Valley.
7 May 18: Having re-entered the Valley, Jackson turns northeast and proceeded down the Valley toward the Union army of Major General Nathaniel P. Banks at Strasburg; by May 18 Jackson had reached Mount Solon.
8 May 20: Leaving the main Valley Pike, Jackson took his army to the southeast side of Massanutten Mountain and proceeded up the Luray Valley; by-passing Banks.
9 May 23: Jackson attacked and overran the Union garrison at Front Royal, threatening Banks's line of supply and retreat.
10 May 25: Banks retreated precipitately to Winchester. Jackson pursued, defeated him there, and took the town.
11 May 27: With Jackson in hot pursuit much of the way, Banks fled to the north bank of the Potomac.

THE PENINSULA CAMPAIGN

"ON TO RICHMOND!" WAS THE NORTH'S BATTLE-CRY IN THE EAST, BUT IT WAS EASIER SAID THAN DONE. IN THEIR FORTIFIED LINE AROUND WASHINGTON, FEDERAL FORCES WERE ONLY 100 MILES (161KM) FROM THE CONFEDERATE CAPITAL OVER EASY TERRAIN WITH GOOD ROADS. AFTER FIRST MANASSAS, HOWEVER, IT MIGHT AS WELL HAVE BEEN THE MOON.

Richmond was in transition at the start of the Civil War. It was both a traditional Southern market-town an a developing industrial and rail centre, with a sizable immigrant population. It was at the same time the capital of the cradle of constitutional government, where memories of George Washington and Thomas Jefferson were strong.

Life in Richmond changed abruptly when Virginia joined the Confederacy. The city became a military center, with troops mustering, marching, and massing. Relocation of the capital of the Confederacy to Richmond brought new civil servants of all grades, legislators, and Cabinet officers into the city, creating shortages of housing and supplies. They were the vanguard of more than 70,000 who ultimately would work for the Confederate government. The city's "floating population" overtaxed the hotels so badly that residents took temporary visitors into their homes.

Confederate President Jefferson Davis brought a new sense of urgency to a city used to leisurely living. Large crowds gathered on the streets when he arrived; within a few hours, he was on horseback inspecting the troops. A government which had been organized in Montgomery, Alabama, set up shop quickly and began issuing purchase orders, letters of marque and military commissions, dispatching commissioners to foreign countries, and performing other tasks required of a sovereign nation.

The Confederate government also brought to Richmond a flood of "pernicious characters" —speculators, gamblers, and lawless rogues who made thievery, garrotting, and murder "nightly employments." A guard system was set up to protect the city at night, and people were challenged on almost every street corner. Gambling houses opened on Main Street and elsewhere, while brothels operated more or less openly. A "Stranger's Guide" which appeared in a Richmond newspaper observed that "very large numbers of men... frequently a very large number of barrooms in the city." Soldiers appeared regularly in court on charges of drunkenness, beating women, and attempted rape. Women followed their husbands and fiancées to the city. One was a young woman from the Deep South en route to First Manassas because her betrothed had been ordered away before their wedding and she went to find him before it was too late. A lieutenant from South Carolina, rejected by the girl he loved, killed himself by jumping out of a sixth-story window.

Richmond played a larger role in the wartime Confederacy than any other city. It was not only the Confederate and State capitals, but was also a city of refuge for civilians driven from their homes by the war. It was a hospital center for the treatment of wounded; soldiers from all over the South said "God bless the women of Virginia" for their saving work and enlifting presence in the hospitals.

Richmond became a prisoner-of-war center after the success at First Manassas. Union soldiers captured in that battle became the vanguard of thousands who would occupy crowded, makeshift quarters, and conditions became intolerable after the Union halted exchange of prisoners. The citizens of Richmond consoled themselves that conditions there were no better than those being experienced by their own solders in the field.

Despite the influx of people, Richmonders remained clannish. They were protective, as they always have been, of the favorites in their society. The fall of strategic Roanoke Island, North Carolina, was a tragedy of the first order for the Confederacy, and General Henry A. Wise came under criticism for the defeat. Richmonders were confident it was not his fault since he had insisted it could be held only with reinforcements and had been ill at the time of the invasion. An investigation placed the blame on the then Secretary of War, Judah P. Benjamin.

Civilian life revolved around the military effort throughout the city's existence as capital of the Confederacy. Political, social, literary, scientific, and religious circles were absorbed in the war. Writers of both prose and poetry were engrossed in war themes, and poets especially produced commendable works. Schools closed when classes were empty or professors were not available. Scientists worked to develop new weapons and improve old ones. Editors and ministers appealed to both God and the public for assistance; some members of both groups felt so strongly they joined the army. The local government sent out agents in an effort to purchase food.

Not everyone approved of the Confederacy. Union sympathizers spread graffiti on buildings, calling "Union men to the rescue" and "God Bless the Stars and Stripes." Occasional arrests were made and Unionists often banded together to protect each other. Those suspected of "incomprehensible neutrality" were commonly known but some innocent people no doubt were unjustly tarred.

Attempts were made to continue usual pursuits. New Year's Day 1861 was bright and balmy, and President Davis's New Year's reception for government officials, military officers, and civilian guests was a gala affair. This was the first New Year for the new Confederate nation and the people of Richmond were impressed by the grace and dignity, amiability, nobility of character, and the absence of hauteur of their new president. Davis was especially taken by three children brought to the reception by their parents in defiance of protocol. Governor John Letcher also entertained, minus the usual champagne which had been cut off by the Union blockade. The giant cut glass

Above: Union leader George Brinton McClellan (1878–1881), Major General of the Army of the Potomac *(top)*. Confederate leader Robert E. Lee (1807–1870), General of the Army of Northern Virginia *(bottom)*.

Next page: Maps detailing the Peninsula Campaign which was General McClellan's attempt to lead a Union army into Richmond, via the route with the least amount of resistance.

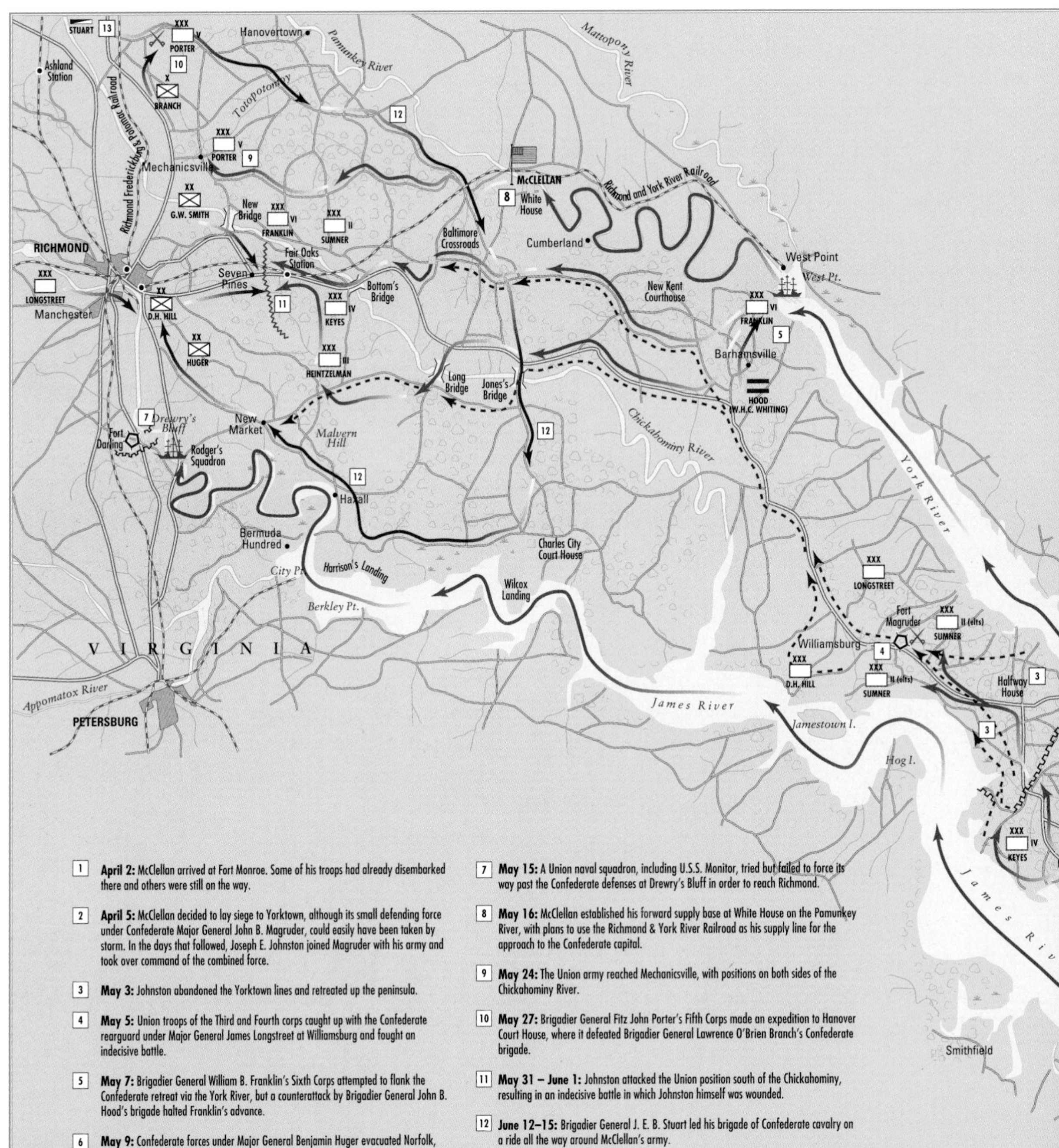

STUART 13
XXX V PORTER 10
X BRANCH
Ashland Station
Hanovertown
Pamunkey River
Totopotomoy
Mattopony River
12
Richmond Fredericksburg & Potomac Railroad
XXX V PORTER 9
Mechanicsville
McCLELLAN
8 White House
Richmond and York River Railroad
XX G.W. SMITH
New Bridge
XXX VI FRANKLIN
XXX II SUMNER
Baltimore Crossroads
Cumberland
RICHMOND
West Point
West Pt.
Fair Oaks Station
Seven Pines
Bottom's Bridge
New Kent Courthouse
XXX LONGSTREET
Manchester
XX D.H. HILL
11
XXX IV KEYES
XXX VI FRANKLIN
5
XX HUGER
Barhamsville
XXX III HEINTZELMAN
Long Bridge
Jones's Bridge
HOOD (W.H.C. WHITING)
7 Drewry's Bluff
New Market
12
Fort Darling
Rodger's Squadron
Malvern Hill
Chickahominy River
12
Haxall
York River
Bermuda Hundred
Charles City Court House
City Pt.
Harrison's Landing
Wilcox Landing
XXX LONGSTREET
Berkley Pt.
Fort Magruder
XXX II (elts) SUMNER
VIRGINIA
Williamsburg
4
XXX D.H. HILL
XXX II (elts) SUMNER
Halfway House 3
Appomatox River
James River
PETERSBURG
Jamestown I.
3
Hog I.
XXX IV KEYES
James River
Smithfield
1 April 2: McClellan arrived at Fort Monroe. Some of his troops had already disembarked there and others were still on the way.
2 April 5: McClellan decided to lay siege to Yorktown, although its small defending force under Confederate Major General John B. Magruder, could easily have been taken by storm. In the days that followed, Joseph E. Johnston joined Magruder with his army and took over command of the combined force.
3 May 3: Johnston abandoned the Yorktown lines and retreated up the peninsula.
4 May 5: Union troops of the Third and Fourth corps caught up with the Confederate rearguard under Major General James Longstreet at Williamsburg and fought an indecisive battle.
5 May 7: Brigadier General William B. Franklin's Sixth Corps attempted to flank the Confederate retreat via the York River, but a counterattack by Brigadier General John B. Hood's brigade halted Franklin's advance.
6 May 9: Confederate forces under Major General Benjamin Huger evacuated Norfolk, leading to the scuttling of the C.S.S. Virginia (formerly Merrimac) two days later.
7 May 15: A Union naval squadron, including U.S.S. Monitor, tried but failed to force its way past the Confederate defenses at Drewry's Bluff in order to reach Richmond.
8 May 16: McClellan established his forward supply base at White House on the Pamunkey River, with plans to use the Richmond & York River Railroad as his supply line for the approach to the Confederate capital.
9 May 24: The Union army reached Mechanicsville, with positions on both sides of the Chickahominy River.
10 May 27: Brigadier General Fitz John Porter's Fifth Corps made an expedition to Hanover Court House, where it defeated Brigadier General Lawrence O'Brien Branch's Confederate brigade.
11 May 31 – June 1: Johnston attacked the Union position south of the Chickahominy, resulting in an indecisive battle in which Johnston himself was wounded.
12 June 12–15: Brigadier General J. E. B. Stuart led his brigade of Confederate cavalry on a ride all the way around McClellan's army.

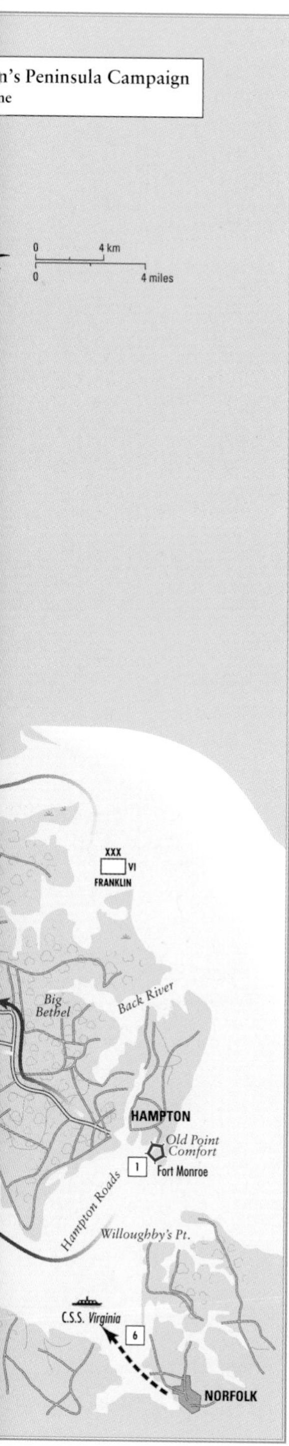

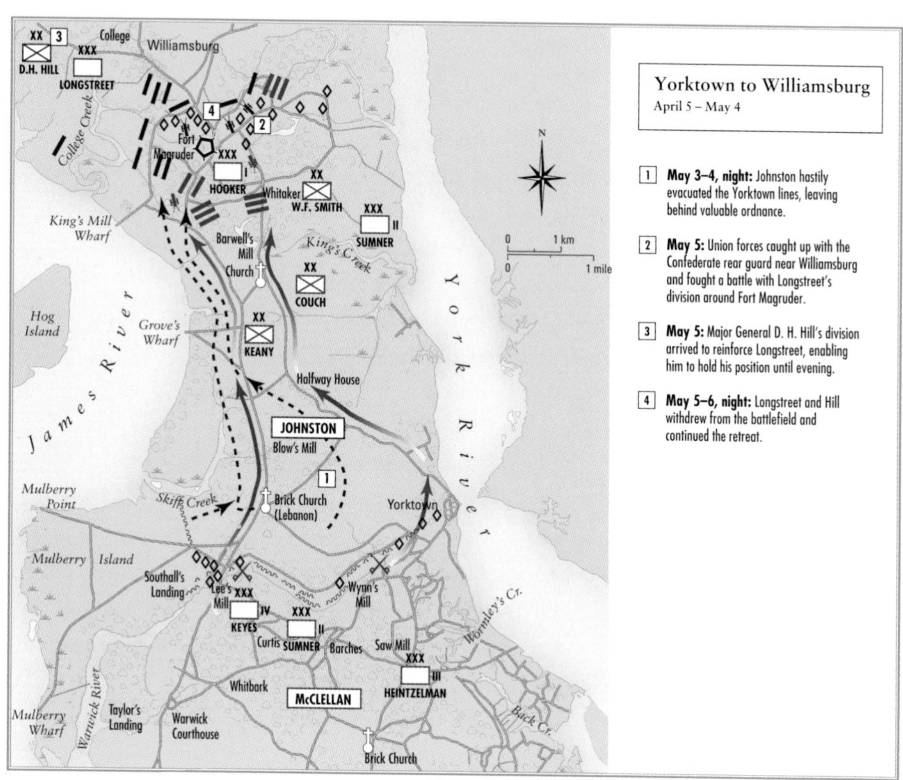

crystal punch bowl was filled with a steaming beverage derived from apples, while eggnog was also available.

Conditions steadily deteriorated. Holiday week at the close of 1861 was "sad." Supplies were short and it was patriotic to conserve, in recognition of the fact that the fare of the soldier in the field was not as bountiful as the turkey and fixings on the home table. Knitting for soldiers replaced pleasant evenings of chatting and repartee.

The nation needed new holidays. February 22, already observed as George Washington's birthday, was adopted as the national day of the Confederate States of America. Its first observance in 1862 was a formal occasion, with carriages bringing people the city for a week prior to the event. The large square in front of the Capital was crowded, but the address, like most delivered in those days, was heard by only those people within earshot of the speaker's voice.

Lincoln was kept aware of the conditions in the Confederate capital by a rapidly growing spy network. A few Union spies were discovered, including a War Department clerk who was hanged and his wife, who was expelled to the North, but some residents thought the attitude of officials toward spying was too lenient. When a woman attempted to send information to the North on how the man of the household in which she was a guest, who at the time was in Great Britain on assignment for the Confederacy, could be arrested, she was held captive in the infirmary of St. Francis instead of a prison.

Above: Photographs of the Union Army encamped near the Mississippi River.

Richmond was a prime Federal target and Lincoln chose General George B. McClellan to build and field a Union army that could take the city. "Little Mac" was better at building than marching, and devised a strategy for indirect action which would force the South to submit through control of strategic railroad junctions. He did not hasten to commit his troops to combat.

McClellan's success at turning the rabble which ran at First Manassas into the well-schooled and disciplined Army of the Potomac helped him overcome his natural caution and encouraged him into action. His optimism waned when his army of 150,000 was reduced to 105,000 men because Lincoln insisted on retaining 37,000 men, formed into the Army of Virginia, to defend Washington. (In this campaign and others, McClellan overestimated the size of the forces opposing him and doubted he had enough men of his own.) After prodding by Lincoln, McClellan set in motion a plan to approach Richmond through the Virginia Peninsula, a sliver of land lying between the James and York Rivers.

The Peninsular Campaign was an attempt to follow a line of least resistance. McClellan's plan had certain advantages. The rivers and naval superiority would protect his flanks during the advance on Richmond. Fort Monroe at the tip of the Peninsula, which, like Fort Sumter, was part of the coastal defences constructed after the War of 1812, remained in Union hands to anchor a secure supply line. The Peninsula route reduced the distance on land to Richmond by 30 miles (48km) and was only lightly defended during the period when he formulated his plan.

Intermittent skirmishing had been indecisive, however; the first land battle of the war occurred when 4,000 untested Federals failed to dislodge 1,500 equally green Confederates at Big Bethel in Hampton. Furthermore, the slightest resistance heightened McClellan's anxiety. He moved slowly and cautiously; a Confederate line of trenches, dams, and forts anchored on Yorktown and extending across the Peninsula delayed the Federal advance until Confederate General Joseph E. Johnston could bring 60,000 troops south from the Manassas line. Johnston's fighting retreat along the Peninsula included a one-day battle at Williamsburg, which enabled the bulk of his forces to settle into position and make ready for Richmond.

The fighting for Richmond began at Fair Oaks. General Johnston was wounded in his attack on McClellan, and General Robert E. Lee replaced him. It was one of the most significant events of the war; as one historian has said, Lee in command was worth another army in the field.

McClellan's army could hear the church bell ringing in Richmond, but Lee took the initiative with an imaginative and daring plan. McClellan's forces were divided by the rain-swollen Chickahominy River, which made his right flank under Brigadier General Fitz John Porter vulnerable. Lee's assault began in the Mechanicsville area northeast of Richmond. Lee watched the initial phase of the battle from the Chickahominy Bluff overlook, just off present U.S. Route 360 (Mechanicsville Road). At Beaver Dam Creek, massed Union artillery and musket fire halted the Confederate attack, but the Confederates were successful at Gaines Mill on the second day. Today, vestiges of shallow Union trenches are visible along the nature trail to Breakthrough Point.

In his first action, Lee used many of the tactics he would employ throughout the remainder of the war. He left a light defensive force between the main enemy army and Richmond and sent the remainder of his army, together with Jackson's troops brought secretly from the valley, against the vulnerable flank. Delays prevented Jackson from arriving in time for the first battle, and the stiff resistance of Porter's units kept Lee from achieving his objective. Nevertheless, Porter's orderly withdrawal began the retrograde action that would take McClellan to the banks of the James River at Harrison's Landing on Berkeley Plantation, from which the army would ultimately be withdrawn. The army camped under the protection of the Union fleet in the river.

McClellan used eighteenth-century Berkeley mansion, ancestral home of the Harrison family which produced a signer of the Declaration of Independence and two presidents, as his headquarters, a use that is overshadowed by the other historical aspects of the mansion, now owned by a descendant of a Union bugler.

Even the great victory in the Seven Days' Battles did not produce Confederate exultation. People who tried to resume their activities were absorbed by the aftermath. Since many of the soldiers involved in the fighting lived in Richmond, women eagerly sought news of their sons and husbands. When an officer rode up to tell a mother her son was alive but that his captain had been killed, the fiancée of the captain, who lived nearby, unhappily overheard the announcement.

Hospitals remained full of sick and wounded, some of them Union soldiers, and more were brought in gravediggers were overworked. Too many soldiers died to accord all of them military burial honours, but the ladies of Richmond provided flowers whenever they could. Private houses, whose tenants had fled the city to escape the war, were concerted into impromptu hospitals to handle the masses of sick and wounded created by fighting near the city. Citizens volunteered to provide bedding and services, including the preparation of food. Women not only helped the surgeons, but made the men comfortable by reading to them, listening to their stories and providing words of kindness to dying soldiers who worried about their wives and "little ones" back home.

Captured Union generals were paroled to walk unguarded through the city, while their less fortunate subordinates were herded into Libby Prison.

Left: Soldiers preparing for battle in a series of specially constructed forts trenches and breastwork.

THE BATTLE OF SHILOH

GENERAL ALBERT SIDNEY JOHNSTON, THE SECOND-HIGHEST RANKING SOLDIER IN THE CONFEDERACY, RODE ALONG THE LINE OF BATTLE-WEARY SOLDIERS AT SHILOH, TOUCHING THE BAYONETS ON THEIR RIFLES. "I WILL LEAD YOU," HE DECLARED, APPARENTLY ON AN IMPULSE. HIS WORDS WERE OF GREAT INSPIRATION TO THE ASSEMBLED MEN.

Above: Launched as a surprise attack against General Grant's Union forces, the Battle of Shiloh proved to be a decisive defeat for the Confederate army. Some of the fiercest engagements took place around an area of dense oak thicket nicknamed the "Hornet's Nest" by the Confederates because of the intensity of the artillery fire across it.

Delays and stubborn resistance by Union soldiers from behind trees had created a critical situation for Southerners trying to break the Union left flank. Inspired by Johnston, they swept forward and drove the Federals from the Peach Orchard and flaking positions before bogging down once again because of heavy casualties. It was another bloody action in one of the bloodiest battles of the Civil War. To one Federal participant, Confederate casualties looked like "a line of troops laying down to receive our fire." The most important casualty of the action would die a short time later, bleeding to death while he continued to issue orders. A severed artery in General Johnston's right leg went largely unnoticed because it bled into his boot and the severity of the injury did not become apparent until he collapsed in the saddle.

Johnston was not only courageous, but he was also an able and determined commander who provided the kind of leadership the South needed to engage superior Union manpower and resources. He was the "good soldier" who had resigned a western post to join the Confederacy. To Confederate forces in the Western Theatre of war, his death was a loss comparable to that of Jackson in the east. "The West perished with Albert Sidney Johnston and the Southern country followed," one of his subordinates wrote later.

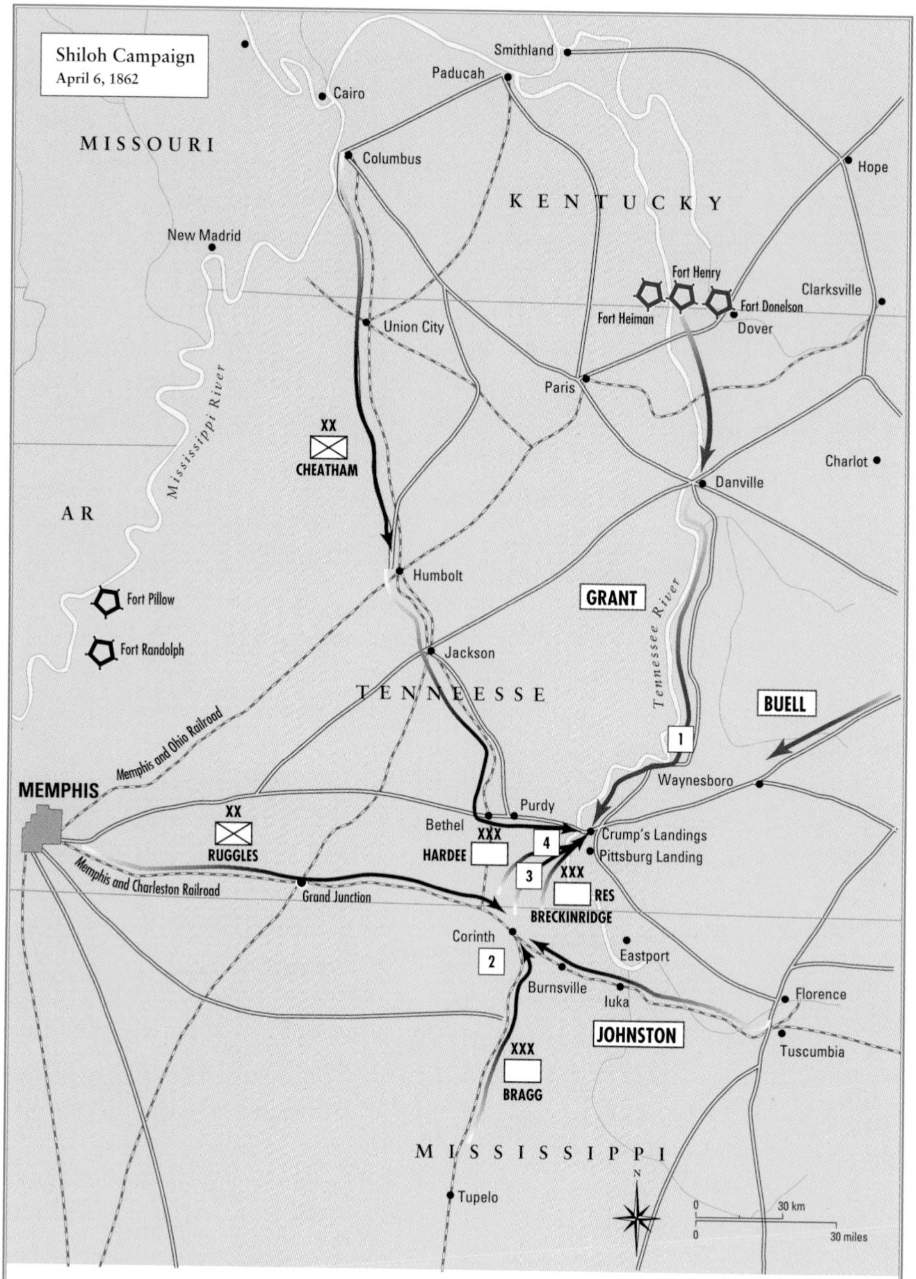

Shiloh Campaign
April 6, 1862

1 **March 1:** Grant and his fifty six thousand-strong Army of the Tennessee move into Tennessee arriving at Pittsburg Landing on April 3 to await the arrival of Buell's army.

2 **March 1:** Johnston with fifty five thousand Confederates concentrate in Corinth.

3 **April 3:** Bad weather delays Johnston's advance to Pittsburg Landing.

4 **April 6:** Johnston launches surprise attack on Grant before Buell could reinforce Grant's army.

Left: Map detailing the activities of both armies during the Shiloh Campaign. On the day of the actual Battle of Shiloh the Confederates, having suffered enormous casualties in previous conflicts, were greatly outnumbered. General Johnston was a great inspiration to his men which was crucial for their morale. He died unexpectedly from a severed artery in the midst of the battle.

Shiloh National Military Park, located on State Route 22 seven miles south of Crump, is a complete Civil War battlefield. The cemetery, historical markers, and monuments commemorate the 25,000 casualties and recall dramatic events. A stopping place on the self-guided automobile tour at the place where Johnston bled to death dramatizes the extent of heroism and disregard for personal safety shown by both sides on an almost daily basis. The shaded memorial area includes part of the trunk of the tree identified later by the Governor of Tennessee, Isham G. Harris, who was present, as the one under which the Southern commander died. Nearby is a monument made up of a cannon and cannonballs.

The Union commander at Shiloh almost became a casualty in another way. General Ulysses S. Grant considered it the most misunderstood action of war. He would dwell on this battle longer than on any other in which he participated, partly because he resented the criticism of him—evoked due to his heavy casualties—in the Northern press. Aware of the battle's importance, he would later declare that few battles of greater significance had "taken place in the history of the world." Grant may be forgiven the exaggeration as he had a personal stake; the battle tarnished his reputation and almost ended his career.

All battles are fateful, some are pivotal. Shiloh was pivotal. The Union push into the interior of the South had followed the Cumberland and Tennessee Rivers, which were easier to capture than the mighty Mississippi and which provided secure and rapid means of reinforcing and resupplying forward forces. At Shiloh, the Confederacy lost a golden opportunity to achieve a major victory in the west, where one was desperately needed. Western Tennessee was effectively lost to the Confederacy, which would spend the next three years trying to get it back. The inability of Confederate forces to clear southern Tennessee left Union armies encamped in the heart of the Confederate west and in control of large chunks of critical territory. Shiloh reduced the Confederacy's ability to control the central Mississippi River. A decisive victory at Shiloh would have improved the chances of holding Vicksburg.

Still, the results were as much psychological as military. Shiloh solidified thinking in the west the way First Manassas did in the East: the idea of quick victories and maneuvering were replaced by a realization that armies had to be defeated in head-on confrontation. Union forces found a new determination and a new confidence; command leadership was developing to augment the Federals' superior grasp of strategy. Yet Shiloh was another of those battles that almost didn't happen, and then was decided by Union units which held their ground tenaciously without being aware of their influence on the outcome.

The Northern push into southern Tennessee in the spring of 1862 threatened the vital railroad hub at Corinth, Mississippi—the Confederacy's only direct rail connection with the East. The object was to cut or to limit the use of that rail line, and for that purpose Grant's forces were to be united with those of General Don Carlos Buell from Nashville to create overwhelming superiority. General P. G. T. Beauregard was the first to see the advantage of striking Grant's camp at Pittsburg Landing before the two armies could unite, but later urged that the plan be abandoned because delays reduced the element of surprise. Yet Johnston insisted on attacking even if a "million" Federals confronted him, and fell upon the unsuspecting Union army encamped at Pittsburg Landing.

The tour of the battlefield begins with the critical phases of the battle. The first stop identifies the ridge along which Grant formed his final battle line after being driven from most of his original positions. By repulsing four frontal assaults, Union defenders at the so-called Hornet's Nest and the Sunken Road bought Grant the time he needed to organize his new defensive line to their rear and to man it with fresh troops. Confederate forces finally captured the site after Brigadier General Daniel Ruggles bombarded it with sixty-two cannon, the largest concentration of artillery yet used by that stage in the Civil War—a level of assault that earned the Hornet's Nest its nickname and gives some idea of the intensity of the fighting.

One of the stops on a driving tour of the battlefield is Shiloh Church, where the initial Confederate assault took place on April 6, 1862, and after which the battle is named. Ironically, the church survived the fighting only to be destroyed a short time later; the present brick building was erected in 1949. Equally ironic is the meaning of its name: place of peace. A small pond near the church became known as Bloody Pond. It was used by soldiers of both sides to bathe their wounds, but that did not stop other thirsty soldiers drinking from it.

Below: In a bloody scene of hand-to-hand fighting, the Fourth Brigade, led by Brigadier General Lovell Rousseau and part of the 2nd Division of the Army of the Ohio, recapture artillery from the Confederates.

The Peach Orchard comes much later in the tour, but was part of the defensive line buying time for Grant. The firing there was so intense that bullets slicing through and scattering buds on the trees created the illusion of falling snow.

Another critical point of the first day's fighting was the Union left flank, anchored on the Tennessee River, where troops reinforced by Buell's vanguard repulsed the final Confederate attack of the day. In this area, monuments have been erected by Iowa, Ohio, Wisconsin, and Arkansas. Other monuments on Federal Road were given by Pennsylvania, Indiana, and Illinois. The Missouri monument has the shape of the State.

General Beauregard, who assumed command of Confederate forces upon the death of Johnston, was unaware that Buell's forces had arrived and thought he had Grant "just where I wanted him and could finish him in the morning." Concerned about Confederate disarray produced by confused fighting, he ordered a halt to the attacks and a withdrawal to the captured enemy camps. Later, he would be accused, with some justification, of making one of the greatest mistakes of the war. On the second day of fighting, Confederates sought to recapture ground they had voluntarily evacuated the night before, now manned by Buell's fresh troops. The Water Oaks Pond stop on the park tour represents the major phases of that day. By noon, the outnumbered Confederates were near exhaustion but Beauregard organized a desperate attempt to break the Federal line at Water Oaks Pond, where heavy seesaw fighting was under way. It was a case of too little, too late, and Beauregard ordered a retreat to Corinth. The Confederate retreat was slow because the troops were exhausted, but Grant's army was in no condition to pursue in earnest.

A Confederate burial trench on the battlefield holding the bodies of 700 men emphasizes the carnage that took place. It is only one of five such trenches at the site. General Johnston's son, Colonel William Preston Johnston, said "No Confederate who fought at Shiloh has ever said that he found any point on that bloody field easy to assail." The National Cemetery, which overlooks the river near the Visitors' Center, holds 3,590 Civil War dead and additional casualties of later wars, including Vietnam. A monument marks the site where Grant located his field headquarters, while a pair of siege guns backed by gravestones create a corner of appropriate symbolism. Other major battlefield points are Pittsburg Landing, now with a beautiful view of the river; the site where Federal surgeons established one of the first tent hospitals of the Civil War, an action which no doubt saved numerous lives; and the Confederate Monument Building, which provides a valuable introduction to the battlefield tour.

Federal occupation of western Tennessee was completed with the capture of Memphis while forces crept toward Corinth to initiate a string of actions in northern Mississippi that would help seal the fate of Vicksburg, the strongest remaining Confederate bastion on the Mississippi.

Grant would be involved in all of them and ultimately in the victory in the east, but the qualities that would achieve results were only partly revealed at Shiloh. These were principally his determination and his tactical ability. He was almost naïve at times; and yet Shiloh contributed to an order of battle that would produce later results. Grant's subsequent successes ultimately would propel him into the presidency.

Another future president, General James A. Garfield, served in a subordinate command at

the battle. Perhaps the youngest soldier of the war, 10-year-old Johnny Clem, who was unofficial drummer of the 22nd Michigan, was present at the battle.

Shiloh battlefield also preserves a much older segment of history. Not far from Pittsburg Landing are two types of mounds raised by prehistoric Native Americans one a burial mound and the other a foundation for ceremonial houses.

Above: A painting depicting the 44th Indiana Infantry Regiment shooting into burning woods on April 6, 1862, during the Battle of Shiloh.

LOWER MISSISSIPPI VALLEY, APRIL-JULY, 1862

FEDERAL ATTEMPTS TO CAPTURE THE LOWER MISSISSIPPI VALLEY WERE PART OF THE ANACONDA PLAN, PROPOSED BY WINFIELD SCOTT AND ENTHUSIASTICALLY TAKEN UP BY PRESIDENT LINCOLN, TO BLOCKADE THE CONFEDERATE COAST AND TAKE CONTROL OF THE MISSISSIPPI RIVER.

Above: A Southerner by birth and upbringing yet loyal to the Union, James Glasgow Farragut (1801–1870) became a naval hero after his victories at New Orleans and Mobile Bay. He would later become the first Admiral of the U.S. Navy.

Opposite page: With his flagship *Hartford* and a fleet of wooden vessels, mortar boats, and 700 men, Farragut sailed up the Mississippi and took New Orleans on April 28, 1862.

This phase of the campaign began under cover of darkness on April 24, 1862, when Union Flag Officer David G. Farragut ran his ships with their guns blazing past the Rebel coastal stations of Fort Jackson and Fort St. Philip at the mouth of the river. Five days later, in one of the great turning points of the Civil War, Federal forces captured New Orleans, the largest Confederate city.

Farragut's flotilla consisted of his flagship, *Hartford*, together with 10 gunboats, 6 steam sloops, and a schooner. They were mounted with a total of 286 guns and 21 mortars.

Moving upriver, Farragut took Baton Rouge and Natchez and then sailed on northward around the tight loops of the lazy river. His next target was Vicksburg, the most important remaining Rebel stronghold on the Mississippi, which now held the key to control of the entire course of the river. On arrival there on May 18, 1862, Farragut demanded the immediate surrender of the city, but the resident garrison remained defiant—justifiably so, because Vicksburg stood on high bluffs overlooking the river and was protected on its northern flank by a swampy complex of bayous.

After bombarding Vicksburg and dodging return fire from the shore for more than a month, Farragut was joined on July 1, 1862, by a flotilla of gunboats and rams that had come downstream from Memphis, Tennessee, under the command of Flag Officer Charles H. Davis. Just over a fortnight later, three of Davis's vessels—the ironclad *Carondelet*, the wooden

Lower Mississippi Valley
April – July, 1862
Union movements
Confederate movements
Union fleet
Confederate C.S.S. Arkansas
1 May 18: Farragut arrives at Vicksburg and demands its surrender. Confederate commander, Brigadier General Martin L. Smith refuses.
2 May 19 – June 27: Farragut's fleet bombards Vicksburg.
3 June 28: Farragut's fleet run passed Vicksburg bombarding it even more forcefully though still without apparent effect.
4 July 1: Farragut's Gulf Squadron meets Flag Officer Charles H. Davis's river gunboat coming down the river from Memphis.
5 July 15: While a detachment of Union gunboats ascend the Yazoo River on a scouting mission, C.S.S. Arkansas steamed down the river badly damaging the gunboats, and proceeds into the Mississippi River.
6 Although badly damaged, the Arkansas steams right through the combined Union fleets and ties up safely on the Vicksburg waterfront.
7 Farragut again runs his squadron past Vicksburg, this time with the goal of destroying Arkansas. The Confederate gunboat receives only moderate additional damage.
8 July 24: Farragut gives up his attempt to capture Vicksburg and turns back toward the Gulf of Mexico.
MISSISSIPPI
Anthony's Ferry
Yazoo River
Mississippi River
Milliken's Bend
Pawpaw Island
Queen of the West
Tyler
Carondelet
Arkansas
Old Bed or False River
Flat Lake
De Soto Point
De Soto
Water Battery
Wyman's Battery
VICKSBURG
Tuscumbia Bend
Vicksburg, Shreveport & Texas Railroad
Vicksburg & Jackson Railroad
Marine Hospital Battery
St Albans Station
Canal
Bluff Batteries
LOUISIANA
Big Bayou
Madison County
Warren County
Warrenton
N
0 2 km
0 2 miles

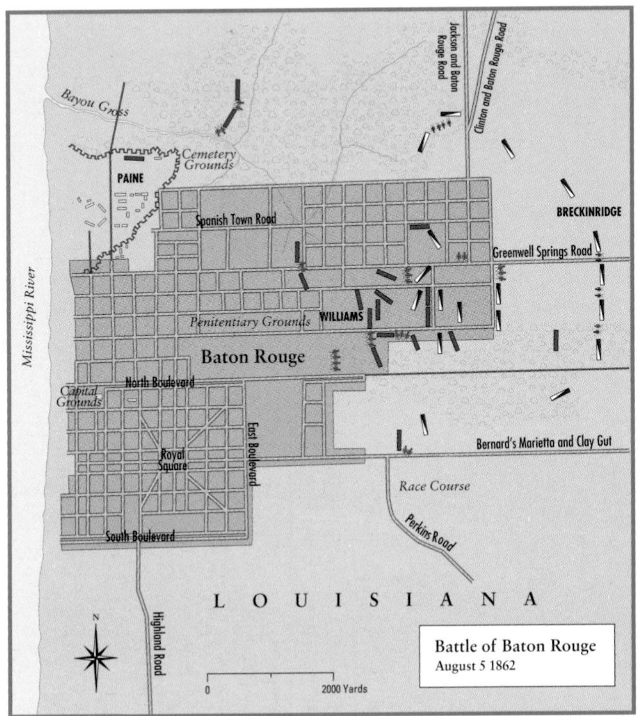

Above: After capturing Baton Rouge, the Louisiana state capital, Union forces turned their attention to Vicksburg further upriver, leaving the city vulnerable to recapture by the Confederates. In the Battle of Baton Rouge, the opposing forces vied for control of the city, but victory eventually went to the Union.

gunboat *Tyler*, and the ram *Queen of the West*—set off up the Yazoo River in search of another line of attack on the Vicksburg. At the first big bend in the river, the Union detachment encountered the CSS *Arkansas* on its way downstream. The Confederate ironclad opened fire and then chased the enemy back to Vicksburg.

The rest of the Union fleet was unprepared for the sudden appearance of a Southern warship —shots were exchanged and 18 Union men were killed and 50 wounded. However, none of the vessels was seriously damaged. The *Arkansas* put in at Vicksburg, where it received a hero's welcome from the local populace.

Later the same day, July 15, Farragut ordered his fleet to sail back past the Vicksburg defense batteries in an attempt to destroy the *Arkansas*, but by the time the attack got under way it was dark, and only one of the shells fired hit the target —it killed one man and wounded three others, but failed to cripple or sink the ship. Confederate losses for the whole day were 12 killed and 18 wounded.

The presence of the *Arkansas* on the Vicksburg waterfront changed the whole nature of the siege. No longer could the Union ships launch attacks on a more or less impromptu basis, and then withdraw out of range to regroup and rest—they now had to remain on alert and under steam at all times, in case the Rebel ship should come for them. With sickness spreading through the Union crews and the river level dropping rapidly in the midsummer heat, Farragut withdrew on July 24, 1862, to deeper water below .

After the fall of New Orleans in April, Union forces had gone on to capture Baton Rouge but when Farragut withdrew from the city the Confederate commander in Vicksburg, General Earl van Dorn, decided to mount an expedition to retake it.

He reasoned that if the *Arkansas* could reach Baton Rouge the Union gunboats that were in place to defend the city would either flee or be sunk. He dispatched General John Breckinridge with 5,000 men to lead a land attack but, by the time Breckinridge arrived, his effective force had been cut by half.

The Union garrison defending Baton Rouge was roughly the same size as Breckinridge's force. Their commander was Brigadier-General Thomas Williams. He had had advance warning of the attack and on the morning of August 5 had his men lined up in order of battle, ready for the awaited assault.

It came soon after daybreak and the Union line was forced back toward the river, which had been the Confederate plan. Unfortunately for the Confederates, however, the fleet of Union gunboats was still intact and was able to give instant protection to the retreating troops.

The grand plan for the *Arkansas* to eliminate the gunboats was a dramatic failure because the ship never arrived. Its engines were old and unreliable and when it was just a few miles short of Baton Rouge they failed completely. After drifting and wedging itself in the river bank, the vessel was stranded.

To add to the indignity, when the USS *Essex* appeared, *Arkansas's* commander discovered that not one of his guns could be aimed at the Union ship. In desperation he was forced to abandon her, blowing her up to avoid capture.

Meanwhile in Baton Rouge, the gunboats were beginning to have an effect. Just as Brigadier-General Williams was about to order a counter-attack he was shot and killed. Colonel Thomas Cahill took over and forced Breckinridge to retreat; by 10am the battle was finally over.

Losses were heavy on both sides, with 383 Union troops dead, wounded or missing, compared to the Confederate's 456; this was nearly 20 percent of their entire force.

Despite his retreat Breckinridge was still a threat and on August 20 the Union garrison withdrew to New Orleans. The Confederates then reoccupied the city until it was retaken by Union forces on December 17. It was to remain in Union hands for the rest of the war.

Left: Members of the Confederate Navy at a campsite. As the Mississippi River effectively split the Confederate territory in two, they knew that if it was taken by the enemy, they would face economic strangulation.

JACKSON'S VALLEY, PHASE II

GENERAL JACKSON'S VICTORY AT THE BATTLE OF WINCHESTER ON MAY 25, 1862, POSED A SERIOUS TACTICAL PROBLEM FOR LINCOLN. THE UNION PRESIDENT WANTED TO DEPLOY TROOPS FROM THE SHENANDOAH VALLEY TO BOLSTER THOSE OF MAJOR GENERAL GEORGE B. MCCLELLAN ON HIS DRIVE TOWARDS RICHMOND. HOWEVER, SO LONG AS JACKSON REMAINED AT LARGE, THAT WOULD PROVE IMPOSSIBLE.

Above: Portrait of respected Confederate General T. J. "Stonewall" Jackson.

Opposite page: A photograph taken at a civil war battle reenactment, giving a very realistic example of a battle scene like those at the Shenandoah Valley.

Lincoln decided that the time had come to crush, or at least rout, Jackson's forces once and for all. To that end he ordered a pincer movement on the Southern general. Major General Irvin McDowell was to march west from Fredricksburg, Virginia, while Major General Jon Frémont would march east from the mountains of West Virginia, the idea being to try and trap Jackson's army between the two sets of Union forces.

Frémont set off at a rapid pace and by the end of May was just thirty miles from Jackson's troops. McDowell was also fast closing in on the other side. Jackson, stationed at Strasburg, became aware of the encroaching danger, and, despite his troops' extreme weariness, ordered them to march southwest away from the pursuing Union hordes. He reacted just in time—had he delayed just one more day, he probably would have been caught in the Union trap.

Union forces, arriving just too late, set off in pursuit of the Confederate army. The front end of Frémont's forces was soon within touching distance of the fleeing Confederates, skirmishing fiercely with the back end of Jackson's army as they made their way along the banks of the North Fork of the Shenandoah River. Jackson' Chief of Cavalry, Colonel Turner Ashby, was killed in the fighting, just south of of Harrisonburg.

With the situation becoming ever more desperate, Jackson realised that, without concerted and co-ordinated action, his retreat was doomed to failure, as sooner or later his forces would simply be hunted down and destroyed. In order to swing the advantage in his favor he would have to stand and fight, ideally with the hope of taking his pursuers by surprise. He decided to split his forces, ordering Major General Richard S. Ewell to stay behind with 6,500 men at the important junction of Cross Keys—which Jackson knew Frémont would have to pass through—to try and halt one side of the Union advance. He then led the rest of his forces southeast to Port Republic and toward the rest of the approaching Union forces.

Despite facing a Union army of some 10,500 men, Ewell successfully held off Frémont's advance at the Battle of Cross Keys on June 8, suffering just 288 casualties compared with 684 on the Union side. After the battle, most of Ewell's troops moved south to join up with Jackson at Port Republic, leaving just a nominal force watching over Frémont at Cross Keys.

On June 9, Jackson made a bold and sudden attack on McDowell's troops as they headed down the Luray Valley. Jackson's army actually outnumbered its Unionist opposers by 5,900 men to

Right: "Stonewall" Jackson in the battle where he got his famous nickname. It was, however, unpopular with his own men who preferred to call him "Old Jack".

Left: Manassas Military Camp March, 1862. Stonewall Jackson led his troops into Manassas, Virginia, and ransacked the town, prior to moving to his campaign in the Shenandoah Valley. When Major General John Pope and his federal troops arrived, they were met by a bleak and damaged town.

3000, but it still took several hours of hard, intense fighting before the Confederate side proved victorious. The casualty numbers—which numbered 1018 on the Union side to the Conderates' 804—tell how close and competitive the battle was.

Victory at the Battle of Port Republic marked the successful completion of General Jackson's Shenandoah Campaign. Over the course of five weeks, the General had put his army through intense physical ordeals, marching them for several hundred miles—often at pace, pursued by, or in pursuit of, the enemy—and sent them out to fight in five highly significant battles, all of which they won. These facts seem all the more remarkable when it is considered that throughout this period, Union forces in the area greatly outnumbered Confederate ones, by 60,000 troops to just 17,000 It was only through shrewd tactical maneuvering that Jackson was usually able to engage in battle with greater numbers.

If anything, it could be argued that Jackson's greatest success was not the number of battles he won, the level of casualties he inflicted or the size of the territory he defended, but rather that he forced the Union forces to engage in battle at all, thereby tying down troops which the Federal side was desperate to send elsewhere—particularly to help bolster McClellan's drive toward Richmond.

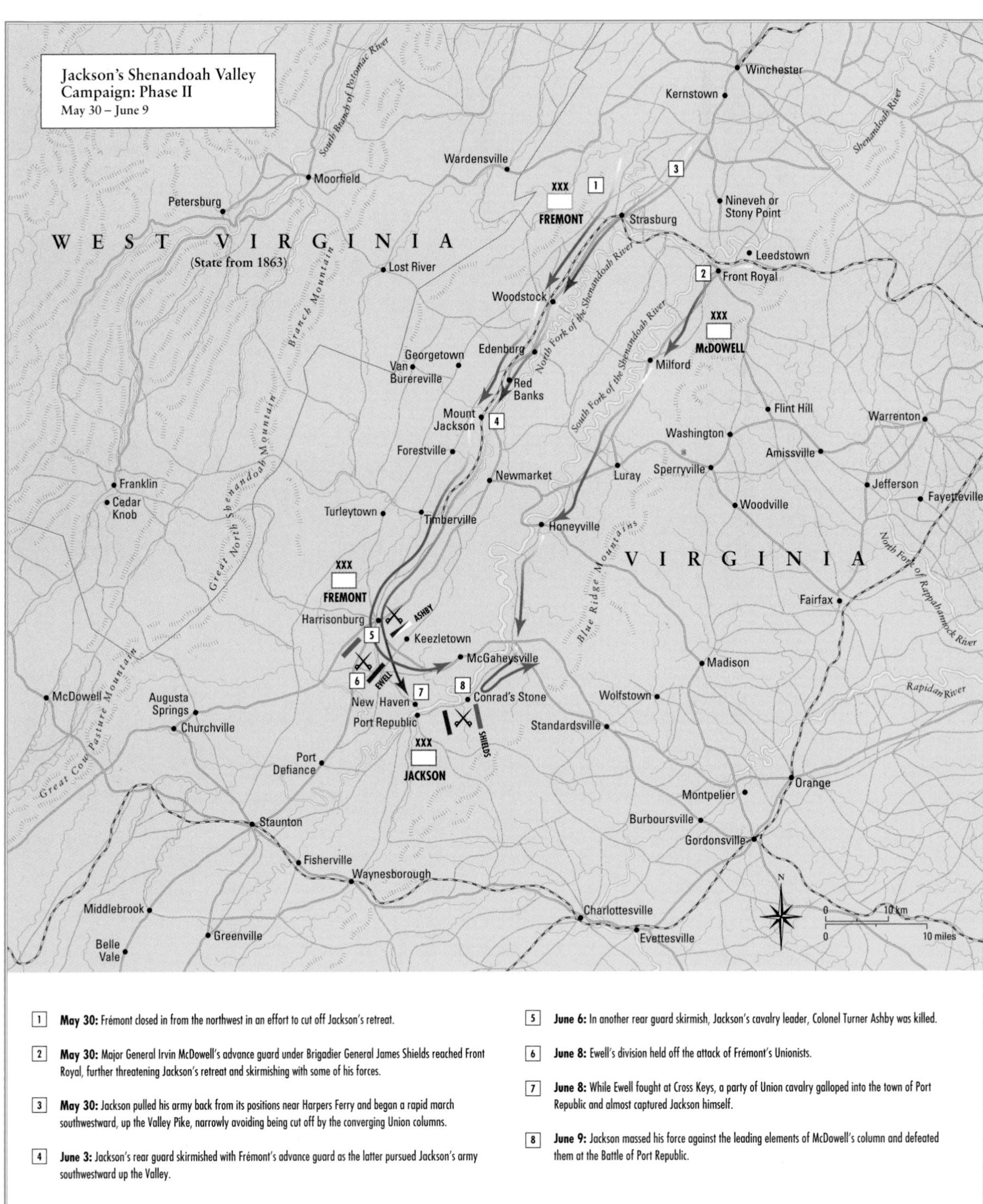

1 **May 30:** Frémont closed in from the northwest in an effort to cut off Jackson's retreat.

2 **May 30:** Major General Irvin McDowell's advance guard under Brigadier General James Shields reached Front Royal, further threatening Jackson's retreat and skirmishing with some of his forces.

3 **May 30:** Jackson pulled his army back from its positions near Harpers Ferry and began a rapid march southwestward, up the Valley Pike, narrowly avoiding being cut off by the converging Union columns.

4 **June 3:** Jackson's rear guard skirmished with Frémont's advance guard as the latter pursued Jackson's army southwestward up the Valley.

5 **June 6:** In another rear guard skirmish, Jackson's cavalry leader, Colonel Turner Ashby was killed.

6 **June 8:** Ewell's division held off the attack of Frémont's Unionists.

7 **June 8:** While Ewell fought at Cross Keys, a party of Union cavalry galloped into the town of Port Republic and almost captured Jackson himself.

8 **June 9:** Jackson massed his force against the leading elements of McDowell's column and defeated them at the Battle of Port Republic.

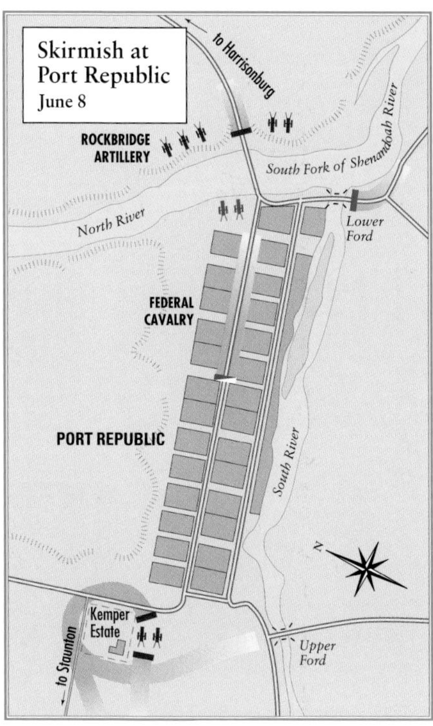

Opposite page: Phase II of Stonewall Jackson's campaign in the Shenandoah Valley.

Left: A portrait of Major General John C. Frémont. In addition to being a major general in the Union armies during the Civil War, John Charles Frémont was an explorer and surveyor, a two-time Republican candidate for the Presidency (1856 and 1864), and the governor of Arizona from 1878–1882

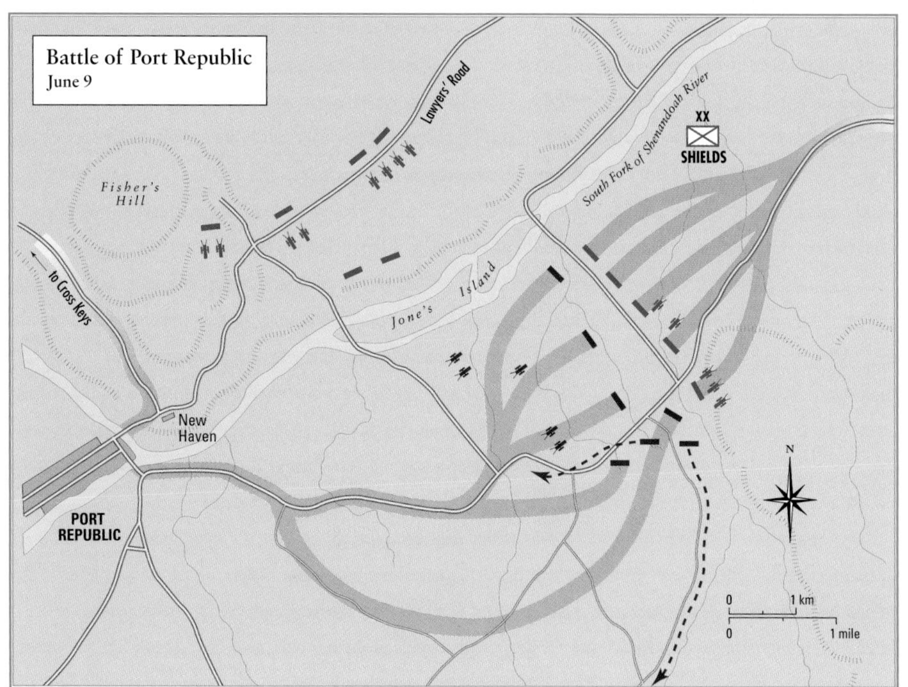

Left: Two major victories for Stonewall Jackson at Port Republic. He defeated two Union armies in this battle, then went on to reinforce General Lee's troops in Richmond for The Seven Days Battle.

LIFE AT THE FRONT

ONCE THEY ENTERED NATIONAL SERVICE, SOLDIERS BEGAN A CYCLE OF ADVENTURE AND BOREDOM SO EQUALLY DEADLY THAT MANY WONDERED WHICH WOULD KILL THEM FIRST. THE TRIP FROM HOME TO THEIR FIRST ASSIGNMENT WAS EXCITING, PARTLY BECAUSE MANY HAD NEVER TRAVELED SUCH DISTANCES ON TRAINS AND STEAMSHIPS.

A patriotic send off, with flags flying, bands playing and friends and neighbors cheering, added to the romantic notions of war. The department of the 6th Michigan Regiment from Kalamazoo rated a community celebration; the enlisted men rode in first-class railroad cars and the officers enjoyed the luxury of the directors' plush private car. New Orleans's Washington Artillery Battalion, which comprised men of wealth and high standing in the community, and served with great distinction throughout the war, was hailed at almost every stop along the long train trip to Richmond. But some new soldiers got a better introduction into what military life would be like; a San Augustine, Texas, company had to march several days to Alexandria, Louisiana, before it could ride eastward to Richmond on a train.

Camp life, whether for purposes of training or for duty, meant boring idleness and tedious chores. The men lived in tents in summer and, when possible, draughty log huts in winter while they shed their disorganized civilian ways and learned the sometimes senseless but organized routine of the military life. Their days were occupied twice-a-day drilling, policing of the camp area, guard duty (the most despised of all activities), parading, inspections, and personal care. In the Union army, as many as 26 bugle calls might summon soldiers to duty during a day, although a dozen calls were normal for infantry, a few more for artillery and cavalry.

Since recreational activities were not officially sponsored, except in rare instances, soldiers in camp made their own diversions according to their interests. They read newspapers and cheap novels when they were available; gambled; played various sports in warm weather, and engaged in snowball fights in winter; stages impromptu theatre performances; wrote letters home; sang traditional or offcolor songs and recited poetry around the camp fires; organized literary associations and listened to band concerts. When they were near towns and cities, those who could attended lodge meetings, concerts and watched prize fights. They sometimes stole off to "liberate" a chicken or pig from a nearby farmer. In the Confederate army, soldiers occasionally would work nostalgically on a nearby farm during off-duty hours. Many Union divisions printed their own newspapers, an activity that was rare in the South because paper was in short supply. Cavalry units added horse racing and shooting contests to the usual activities. Camp life was just as deadly as combat because soldiers from the farms had not been exposed to communicable diseases—such as measles, whooping cough and typhoid fever—or other diseases such as malaria and dysentery. A single measles epidemic at Camp Moore, training centre in North Louisiana, killed 600 to 700 recruits.

Below: Union Generals outside their cabin in the middle of a camp *(top)*. Union soldiers eating a meal at their camp *(bottom)*. Although official regulations prescribed adequate food to all soldiers, it was not always what was received.

Furloughs were rare. Most often they were given to ill or wounded soldiers for convalescence at home, or before reporting for new duty after being exchanged. In the Union army, they sometimes were given for political reasons; General Sherman furloughed thousands of Indiana soldiers in 1863 so they could return home and vote for Lincoln in his bid for re-election. As both North and South recognized, any army marches on its stomach. In camps, company cooks generally prepared rations. When possible, bread was prepared by regimental cooks. The Union bakery ovens of Fort Monroe, Virginia, were famous during the 1862 Peninsular Campaign; and for a time, vaults in the Capitol Building in Washington were converted into ovens that produced 16,000 loaves a day in 1861. In the field, soldiers prepared their own food or in messes (small groups).

Official regulations in both armies prescribed adequate food, but the men did not always receive what the regulations stated. In the Union army, this was a matter of expediency and quality; in the Confederate, the result of shortages. Prescribed diets in the two armies were similar, but each included regional variations and preferences in methods of preparation. Staples were fresh and salted beef and pork (the latter were sometimes so briny that soldiers soaked their rations in streams overnight to desalinate them), hardtack, softbread when in camp, and coffee

Above: Mess hall at a Union Camp. Cooks here had to make do with what supplies they were given in order to adequately feed everyone. Lack of fresh food was a major problem, and many soldiers developed scurvy.

and sugar, which experienced soldiers carried mixed together in cloth bags. Tobacco was prized.

Cornbread and beef were the mainstays of Johnny Reb's diet, supplemented as often as possible by pork, peas, flour, hardtack, potatoes, rice, molasses, coffee, sugar and fresh vegetables. Shortages were aggravated by the poor quality of food when it was available.

Troops and civilians shared hardships and good fortune. On one occasion, soldiers defending Richmond volunteered to share their rations with the poor of the city. Richmond returned the generosity while it was being besieged by sending a New Year's Day turkey to the soldiers, who drew lots to see which men should enjoy it.

Packages from home, usually shared with buddies, supplemented the fare of both armies. Union packages naturally were better stocked than those in the Confederacy, which generally contained only eggs, fresh or dried apples, apple butter, preserves and cakes. Sutlers, or merchants with semiofficial status, accompanied the Union armies and sold food and personal items to the soldiers at inflated prices. No sutlers were attached to the Confederate army, although itinerant merchants visited camps on occasion.

Equipment carried by soldiers varied according to their experience and the conditions. Essentials included blankets and rubber mats; canteens; dippers, tins, plates, knives, forks and spoons for mess; limited numbers of candles for lighting during winter encampment, often jammed into the mounting ring of a bayonet stuck into the ground; and personal grooming and sewing kits called "housewives."

Soldiers of both nations received inadequate training. The initial units to be called up were militia, which supposedly had been drilled and schooled, but their training quickly proved to be flawed. The mistakes made at First Manassas by both sides showed how green the troops were. Even as late as February 1862, when 10,000 Union soldiers overwhelmed Roanoke Island, North Carolina, a battery of Confederate cannon could not be fired because none of the men on the site knew how to service the weapons. A hastily summoned instructor from headquarters was giving instructions when the Union attack came.

Union and Confederate training camps were set up early in the war, but jurisdictional disputes limited their effectiveness. On both sides, States retained a major responsibility for training the soldiers they recruited. This consisted primarily of drilling at makeshift campsites, such as fairgrounds, often with wooden guns. When real weapons were available, they were often obsolete or unworkable. Infantrymen received basic instruction in loading musket or rifle, but seldom got enough practice to master the complicated technique. Some units received training in firing by file or by company, but the availability of ammunition for practice was limited. Sometimes shooting contests were held, and an effort was made to improve accuracy, but marksmanship was never good during the war. Bayonet drill was perfunctory; an hour for an entire brigade was not unusual.

In the Union, Federal training began when the soldiers reached large assembly points near Washington or at Cairo in Illinois or other places. These camps gave only rudimentary instruction in drill and the use of shoulder firearms. Cavalry and artillery units generally drilled on foot until they reached the Federal camps, where they received horses and heavy weapons. Cavalry training was long and difficult. It required hours of mounted and unmounted practice, as well as training in the care and treatment of horses. Easterners who entered the cavalry to escape the infantry often failed to take care of their mounts and ended up on foot or back in camp. Servicing an artillery piece was a complicated procedure that involved a team of men performing distinctive but coordinated tasks. If it were to be effective, there had to be considerable practice in maneuvering and unlimbering guns and in the aiming and firing. Training included target practice, using a tree or stump when such were available. In one instance, Battery B of the Rhode Island Light Artillery almost hit a town while aiming at a tree. The Tenth Massachusetts provoked the anger of a farmer by sighting on his pig pen.The soldiers were supposed to receive further training in their permanent units, and often they did. Training continued during lax periods after units had been sent to the front, but this usually amounted to nothing more than refreshers in close-order drill. Officers who had to instruct were often inexperienced in the fundamentals themselves.

Despite the intentions of the training system, most soldiers went into battle ill prepared. On both sides, there were instances when green soldiers were sent into combat within a week or two of induction, some without any training at all. Many an infantryman, on the eve of battle, searched for an experienced comrade who would show him which end of a bullet to insert into his rifle. It has been established that half of those who served had never fired their weapons until they reached the field. There, the most terrible teacher of all—combat itself—awaited them with a vengeance.

Left: Many soldiers found salvation in religion. Christian religious services in camps were very popular and raised morale amongst the troops.

Seven Days' Battles

Over a period of seven days, from June 25–28 and June 29–July 1, 1862, six major battles took place around Richmond, Virginia. "It was not war; it was murder," said Confederate General Daniel Hill of the final engagement.

Above: Major General Fitz John Porter, commanding the Fifth Corps of McClellan's Army of the Potomac, was a key target in Lee's strategy to defeat the Union forces.

In early June, 1862, the large, well-equipped Union Army of the Potomac, commanded by Major General George McClellan, lay just a couple of miles away from Richmond, Virginia. The town was poorly fortified, its defenders were outnumbered, demoralized, and badly coordinated. General Robert E. Lee—arguably the greatest Confederate commander and a strategic genius—adopted an audacious plan to drive the Union army from the vicinity. While a thin screen of Confederate troops maintained the lines between Richmond and most of McClellan's army, Lee would mass his army against the Union's Fifth Corps, led by Major General Fitz John Porter. Porter had been left isolated north of the Chickahominy River, largely to guard Union supply lines. To insure victory and avoid the high potential losses of a frontal attack, Lee also instructed Major General J. "Stonewall" Jackson to march his three divisions on a roundabout route to strike the Union's right flank.

On June 25, an unsuspecting McClellan launched a probe of the Confederate lines, but remained none the wiser as to Lee's strategy. On June 26, although Jackson had failed to get his troops into position, Lee's forces went ahead in a headlong assault against Porter, but were repulsed. Later that day, Jackson's approach to Porter's right flank prompted McClellan to order a withdrawal of the Fifth Corps to a strong, defensive position behind Boatswain's Creek. June 27 saw a repeat of the previous day's action, with Jackson's repeated failure to launch a flank attack—for reasons that have never been satisfactorily explained—again forcing Lee into another frontal assault. This time, however, his superior numbers and the bravery of his Texas Brigade enabled him to force Porter to retreat.

The following day there was a lull in fighting, but on June 29 Lee picked up his pursuit of McClellan's retreating army and engaged with its rear guard at Savage's Station. His final and best chance to trap and defeat the Army of the Potomac came on June 30. If he could seize the vital crossroads at the village of Glendale, he would be able to cut the army in two. Jackson was to attack from the north and the rest of the Confederates from the west. However, Jackson's attack again failed to materialize, and in fierce fighting around Glendale—in a battle known, among other names, as Glendale, Frayser's Farm and White Oak Swamp—McClellen managed to hold the crossroads for long enough to allow his army to continue its retreat.

Lee pursued McClellan to Malvern Hill, where Union forces had assumed a strong defensive position, hoping to beat down the enemy guns with his artillery and thus facilitate an infantry attack. But McClellan's powerful and well-sited artillery quickly demolished the Confederate batteries and then the advancing lines of Rebel infantry. With the Battle of Malvern Hill, the Seven Days' Battles came to an end. Fighting had been vicious and casualty figures were dreadful. McClellan's Union losses were put at 15,849 killed, wounded or captured from a total of 105,445. Lee's Confederate losses were even greater with 21,141 from an estimated strength of 80,000–90,000.

Next page: Maps detailing two of the six battles that took place between June 25–28 and June 29–July 1, 1864. The savage Seven Days' Battles ended with the Battle of Malvern Hill.

Below: After the Confederates clashed with the rear guard of McClellan's army—Major General Edwin Vose Sumner's Second Corps—at Savage's Station, the Unionists retreated, leaving behind their large field hospital with 2,500 sick and wounded Federal soldiers.

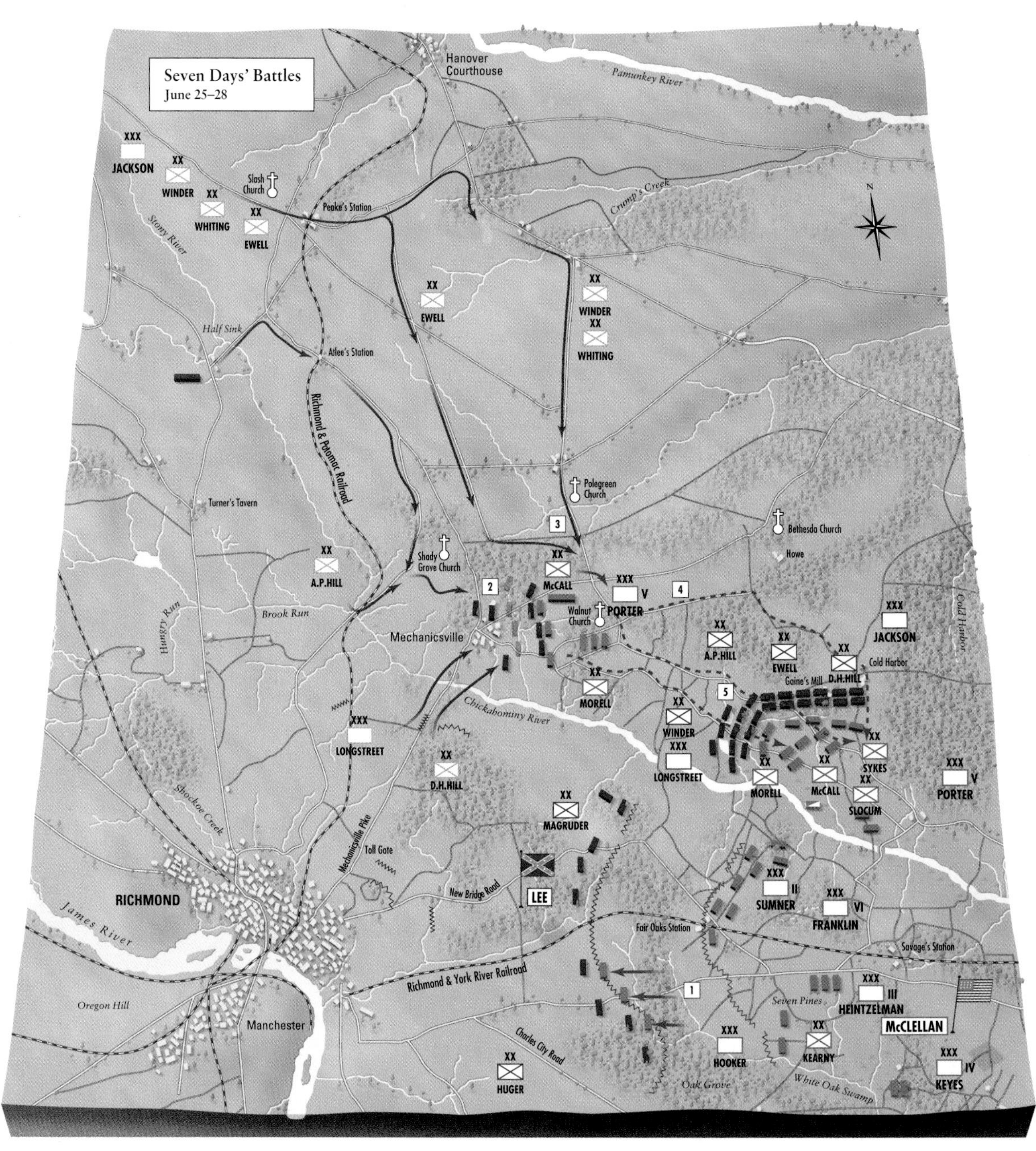

1 **June 25:** Unaware of Lee's planned offensive, McClellan launched a probe of Confederate lines south of the Chickahominy by Major General Samuel Heintzelman's Third Corps.

2 **June 26:** Lee's forces attacked Brigadier General Fitz John Porter's Fifth Corps north of the Chickahominy but suffered a bloody repulse.

3 **June 26:** Although he failed to get his wing of the army into the battle, Jackson approached Porter's right flank late in the day, posing a serious threat.

4 **June 26–27:** With his right flank threatened McClellan decided on retreat and ordered Porter to withdraw during the night to a position behind Boatswain's Creek.

5 **June 27:** With Jackson again failing to get into position, Lee launched another frontal assault against Porter and this time succeeded in breaking his lines and driving him back across the river.

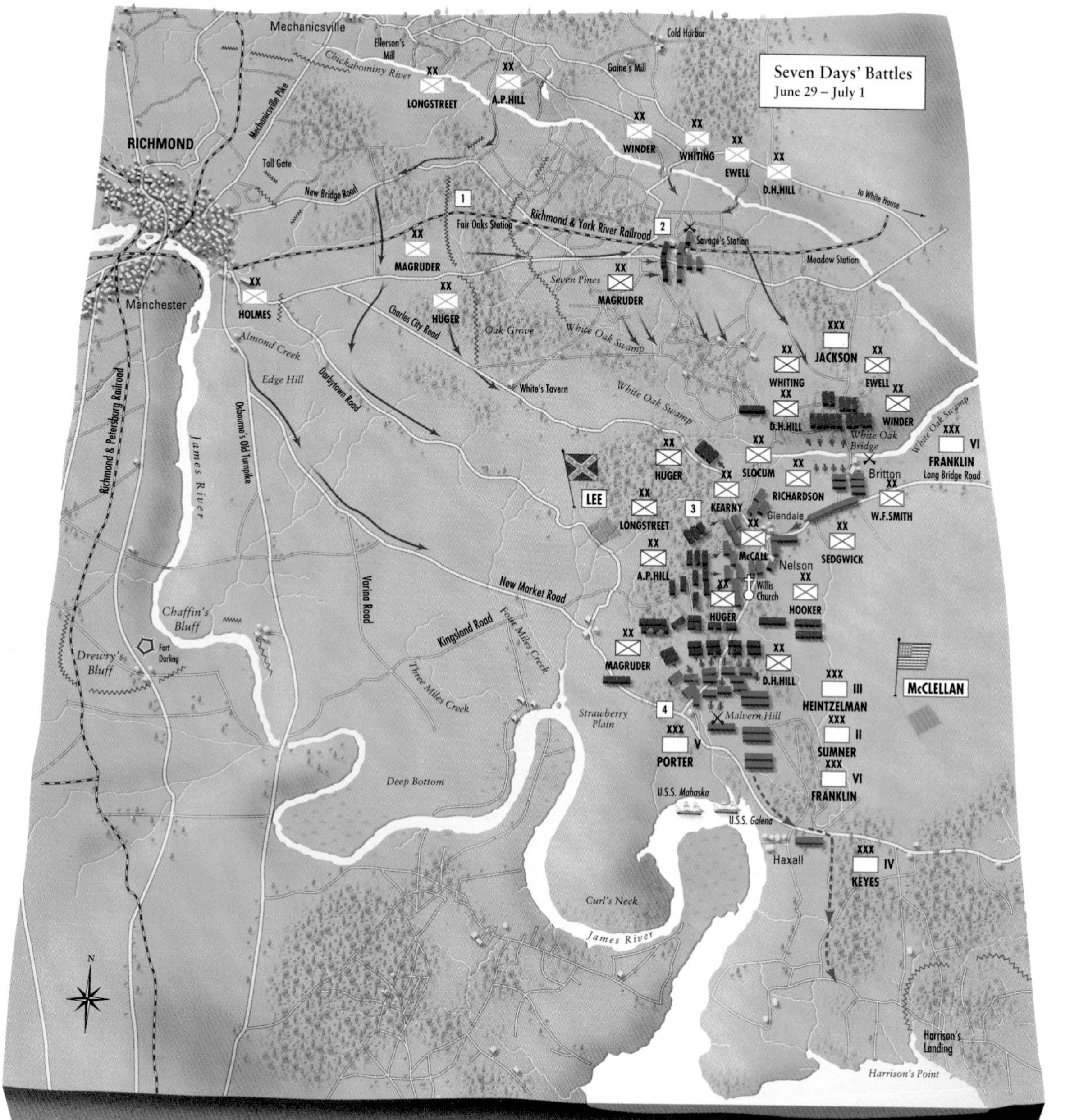

1 **June 29:** Confederate troops marched in pursuit of McClellan's retreating army south of the Chickahominy.

2 **June 29:** Confederate and Union forces clashed indecisively at Savage's Station. The Unionists withdrew, abandoning the Army of the Potomac's general hospital with two thousand five hundred sick and wounded soldiers.

3 **June 30:** Major General James Longstreet's Confederate division, supported by several others, struck at Brigadier General McCall's Union division at the crossroads of Glendale, or Frayser's Farm. The fighting was extremely intense, but the Union troops managed to hold the crossroads long enough to prevent Lee from cutting off any part of the retreating Army of the Potomac.

4 **July 1:** Lee pursued McClellan on July 1 and found him in a very strong position on Malvern Hill, where Lee launched a series of bloody and futile attacks.

CONFEDERATE INVASION OF KENTUCKY

THE SUCCESS OF COLONEL JOHN HUNT MORGAN'S RAIDS INTO KENTUCKY IN JULY 1862, AND THE HUNDREDS OF VOLUNTEERS WHO FLOCKED TO HIS SIDE AS HE LAID WASTE TO UNION-HELD POSITIONS, CONVINCED MANY ON THE CONFEDERATE SIDE THAT A SOUTHERN INVASION OF THE STATE WOULD PROVIDE A POPULAR UPRISING IN THEIR FAVOR—THEY WERE TO BE PROVED MISTAKEN.

Not all Confederate military operations were large-scale affairs. In 1862, some of its most successful actions were undertaken by raiders operating outside of the main body of the army, who launched, swift, small-scale, impromptu incursions behind Union lines. Colonel John Hunt Morgan was a renowned raider, particularly associated with activities in Kentucky during the Civil War. Morgan was actually a native of Alabama, but had moved to the blue-grass state as a child where he became captain of a militia compay, the Kentucky Rifles. Upon the outbrieak of war, he put his company at the disposal of the Confederate forces, and by February 1862, he had been placed in charge of Second Kentucky Cavalry and given the task of launching raids behind Union lines.

On July 4, Morgan and his 900 men completed their first successful raid, capturing the town of Tompkinsville. A week later he took Lebanon, and on July 17 captured Cynthiana. The Union forces were by this time in hot pursuit of Morgan. Two things, however, kept the raider from being captured. Firstly, despite the fears of those living in the big towns of Cincinnati, Lexington, and Louisville, Morgan was strictly a small-town operator, having neither the inclination nor, in truth, the resources, to tackle anything larger. Furthermore, Morgan employed a telegraph operator to tap wires and keep abreast of Union movements. He also got him to send rogue messages, providing false information about Morgan's whereabouts and even rescinding official Union orders.

By July 22, Morgan was safely back in Tennessee, having successfully evaded his Union pursuers. Although he had lost 90 men duing his operations, he had managed to recruit several hundred volunteers as Confederate sympathizers flocked to his cause.

At the same time that Morgan was making inroads into Kentucky, Colonel Nathan Bedford Forrest was undertaking a similar operation in Tennessee. With 1,400 men under his command, he launched a lightning raid on Murfreesboro on July 14, routing the Union troops stationed there, who surrendered following several hours' worth of fighting. Forrest then went on to destroy the bridges, railroads, and telegraph wires in the immediate vicinity before retreating.

These Confederate raids notwithstanding, the early summer of 1862 seemed to provide something of a lull compared to the intensity of the previous (and subsequent) fighting of the Civil War. The Union commander of the Western Theater, Henry H. Halleck, was an extremely cautious operator—something that would eventually see him recalled to Washington. Rather than launch an all out offensive, Halleck preferred to keep his troops standing by. His only significant undertaking at that time was to order Brigadier General Don Carlos Buell to repair the Memphis and Charleston Railroad all the way up to the important junction of Charleston.

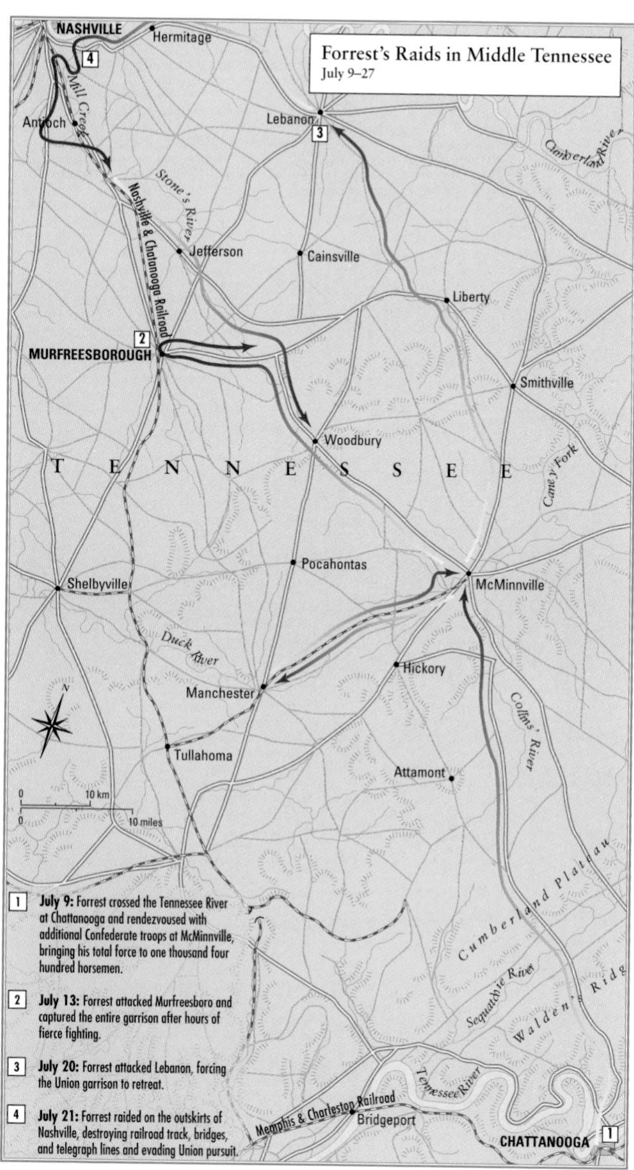

Above: Confederate Lieutenant Nathan Bedford Forrest and his cavalry brigade conducted raids against Union communication and supply lines in Tennessee.

Braxton Bragg, the commander of the Confederate army in the West, and Major General Edmond Kirby Smith, the commander of the Confederate East Tennessee forces, decided to act. Bragg's forces, in particular, began to undermine Buell's restorative efforts, immediately destroying whatever railroad his men had managed to re-lay. Bragg also sent his troops on by rail to Chatanooga to arrive head of Buell. He then planned to march out to meet Buell, hoping to catch him between his forces and those of Kirkby Smith.

It was a bold and brilliant maneuver, which was undermined only by the actions of his fellow Confederate commander. Rather than adhere to Bragg's plan, which may well have carried the day, Kirkby Smith instead decided to act according to his own volition. He had become obsessed with the idea of stirring a popular uprising in Kentucky, particular its blue-grass region, which he believed would drive the Federals from the state. Determined to release this popular fervor, he

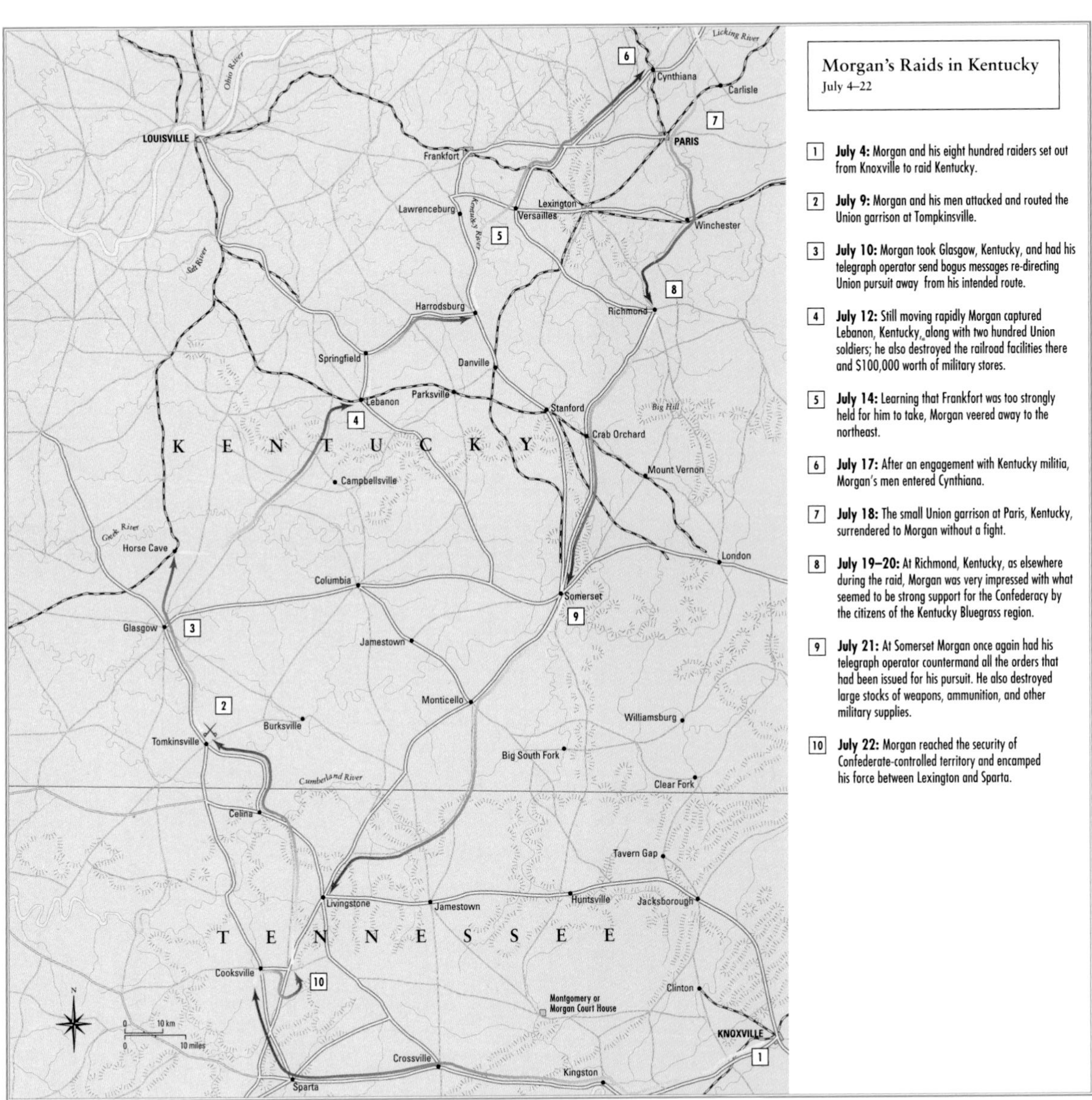

Above: John Hunt Morgan's brave foray deep into enemy territory did not significantly impact the outcome of the war, but did cause the Federals a great deal of inconvenience. It was also the farthest north that any Confederate troops would penetrate throughout the entire duration of the war.

headed north, leaving Bragg to take on Buell by himself.

Part of the reason for Kirkby Smith's decision no doubt lay with the fact that he would have to become subordinate to Bragg should their armies ever combine, but could remain in charge of his own section so long as they remained apart. Whatever the reason, Kirkby Smith's actions turned the momentum in Buell's favor. In fact there was now a real chance that he might be able to take on the two Confederate forces separately and potentially destroy both.

On August 30, Kirkby Smith defeated Union troops at Richmond, Kentucky, before moving on to occupy Lexington. Bragg meanwhile captured the Union garrison of Munfordville and was poised to confront Buell. But, true to his safety-first nature, Buell would not attack, and even more dangerously, Kirkby Smith would not despatch either troops of supplies to aid Bragg's efforts. Without these extra supplies and troops, Bragg could simply not attack. Instead he marched north into the Bluegrass region where he was finally able to take direct control of the—increasingly rogue—Kirkby Smith, but it was too late. Buell had by now reached Louisville where he was able to replenish his forces with significant numbers of reinforcements.

Despite the hopes engendered by Morgan's activities earlier in the year, and Kirkby Smith's fervent belief in the state's latent Confederate tendencies, the Kentuckians nonetheless steadfastly refused to volunteer for the South's cause. The 1,000 rifles packed by Bragg into a wagon train, to be despatched to the volunteers as they came forward, remained unused. Bragg came to the conclusion that the Kentuckians were refusing to step forward because their feared having their property confiscated—or worse—if the Union re-took contol of the state, so he came up with an innovative strategy. He decided to declare the state officially for the Confederate side, by installing a new governor in the state capital of Frankfurt, which would then enable him to enforce conscription. Thus the Kentuckians would be obliged to fight for the Confederate side, but could claim compulsion should the Union ultimately prove victorious.

In the event, there was no time to put his plan to the test. As the new governor was being sworn in, Buell, finally spurred into activity, was marching on Frankfurt. Bragg decided to divide his army. One half would take on Buell's force head on, while the other half, under Major General Leonidas Polk, attacked the flank. But Polk refused to coopearate and the chance was lost.

Bragg would launch one final assault againt Buell at Perryville on October 8. Despite some initial success, he soon realised that his forces were seriously outnumbered—particular as Polk had once again refused to follow orders—and deciding that they had no realistic expectation of victory, withdrew. However, Buell allowed Bragg to escape and pull his forces out of Kentucky.

After the battle, all the commanders associated with the Kentucky invasion, on both sides, would come in for serious criticism from their respective commands.

Today, the town of Perryville has a large interpretive map at the intersection on U.S. Route 150 where the visitor turns onto Kentucky Route 1920 to reach the battlefield. Some of the town's old structures are part of the Civil War experience, including Elmwood Inn and the redbrick Crawford House on State Route 68 (Harrodsburg Pike), which Bragg used as his headquarters. The Confederate cemetery holds nearly 400 bodies collected from the battlefield and buried in mass graves. The Dug Road, which, according to legend, Confederate artillerymen cut into the hillside to facilitate movement of their cannon, remains in use as a dirt road.

On the weekend nearest to the October 8 anniversary, reconstituted Civil War units re-enact the battle. It began during the pre-dawn hours on a hill overlooking Doctor's Creek, but eased off during the morning as 16,000 Confederate troops moved into position for a concerted attack against 22,000 Federals. That movement confused the Union commanders, who thought the Rebels were retreating, and the attack that was finally launched about 2 p.m. by men "yelling like fiends" caught them by surprise. At nightfall, the Confederates held the ridge and thus had the advantage, but Buell had committed only a third of his 61,000 troops, and Bragg believed himself too weak

Left to right: Nathan Bedford Forrest (1821–1877) was a lieutenant general in the Confederate Army.

Braxton Bragg (1817–1876) commanded Confederate soldiers in Kentucky and was eventually promoted to General.

John Hunt Morgan (1825–1864) was a renowned Confederate commander and "raider" whose troops infiltrated Union lines in Kentucky, Indiana, and Ohio.

Opposite page: A map detailing the Confederate invasion of Kentucky.

for victory. Thus, at midnight, Bragg began to withdraw from the battlefield, and soon retreated from the Kentucky. It could be argued that he had won the battle, but what is undeniable is that he had lost the war to control the State. Bragg's aborted invasion was the last major effort to keep Kentucky in the Confederacy.

Both Buell and Bragg had been preoccupied with political matters before the battle began. Buell, who had been dismissed by the War Department in Washington and then reinstated, was beset by command problems as well. Bragg hoped that by installing the secessionist government in Frankfort, the State capital, he would help rally the State behind both his invasion and Confederate cause. Neither General consciously picked Perryville as the site of the battle, maneuvering forces met there primarilay because the Union army was short of water in a hot, dry October and had been informed that Doctor's Creek was a good sources. Neither side would employ all its forces, part of Bragg's army being immobilized by diversionary action near Frankfort. Most of the Union fighting fell on Brigadier General Alexander McCooks' I Corps, while other units were never engaged.

Today, Perryville Battlefield State Park is small compared with many others of its ilk, but it has a number of interesting object packed within 100 acres of the northern end of the battle lines, which at one point during the fighting stretched for three miles. Across the road from the Visitors' Center and Museum, where a slide presentation and Civil War relics relate the story of the battle, stands a tall Confederate monument in a shady fenced-in a grove fronted by two cannon and United States and Confederate flags. At one outside corner is a painting of the battle, along with plaques bearing a map and commentary on the fighting. A short path leads past a tall white column, authorized by Congress in 1928 to commemorate Union participation in the battle; memorials to Michigan units which were among the 61,000 Union troops at Perryville, including Battery A of the First Michigan Light Artillery—whose commander, Coldwater Lewis, refused an order to spike his cannon and retreat and thus prevented the Confederates from turning the Union right flank—and memorials to General Buell and Brigadier James S. Jackson, commanding the 10th Ohio Division, who was killed in the fighting.

A look-out tower on the crest of the ridge provides a splendid view of some of the most important terrain of the battle, as well as the rolling countryside nearby that muffled the sounds of combat so well that Buell did not realize for several hours that a major battle was in progress. A map at the base of the steel-frame tower shows the movements of units.

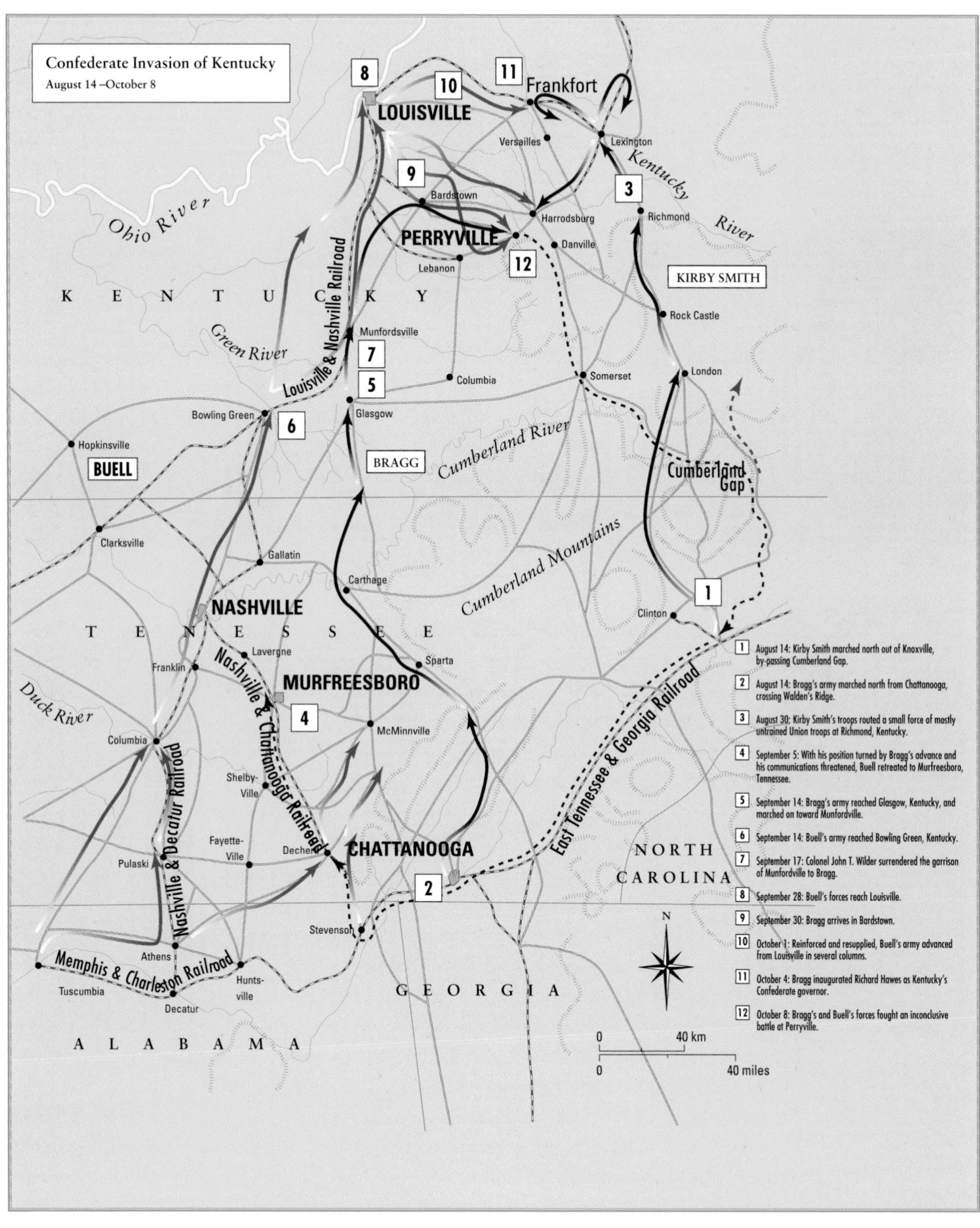
Confederate Invasion of Kentucky
August 14 –October 8
LOUISVILLE
Frankfort
Versailles
Lexington
Kentucky River
Bardstown
Harrodsburg
Richmond
PERRYVILLE
Danville
Lebanon
KIRBY SMITH
Ohio River
K E N T U C K Y
Louisville & Nashville Railroad
Rock Castle
Munfordsville
Green River
Columbia
Somerset
London
Bowling Green
Glasgow
Hopkinsville
BUELL
BRAGG
Cumberland River
Cumberland Gap
Clarksville
Gallatin
Cumberland Mountains
Carthage
NASHVILLE
Clinton
T E N N E S S E E
Lavergne
Franklin
Sparta
Nashville & Chattanooga Railroad
MURFREESBORO
Duck River
Columbia
McMinnville
East Tennessee & Georgia Railroad
Nashville & Decatur Railroad
Shelby-Ville
Fayette-Ville
Decherd
CHATTANOOGA
N O R T H
C A R O L I N A
Pulaski
Stevenson
Athens
Memphis & Charleston Railroad
Tuscumbia
Decatur
Hunts-ville
G E O R G I A
A L A B A M A
N
0 40 km
0 40 miles
1 August 14: Kirby Smith marched north out of Knoxville, by-passing Cumberland Gap.
2 August 14: Bragg's army marched north from Chattanooga, crossing Walden's Ridge.
3 August 30: Kirby Smith's troops routed a small force of mostly untrained Union troops at Richmond, Kentucky.
4 September 5: With his position turned by Bragg's advance and his communications threatened, Buell retreated to Murfreesboro, Tennessee.
5 September 14: Bragg's army reached Glasgow, Kentucky, and marched on toward Munfordville.
6 September 14: Buell's army reached Bowling Green, Kentucky.
7 September 17: Colonel John T. Wilder surrendered the garrison of Munfordville to Bragg.
8 September 28: Buell's forces reach Louisville.
9 September 30: Bragg arrives in Bardstown.
10 October 1: Reinforced and resupplied, Buell's army advanced from Louisville in several columns.
11 October 4: Bragg inaugurated Richard Hawes as Kentucky's Confederate governor.
12 October 8: Bragg's and Buell's forces fought an inconclusive battle at Perryville.

SECOND BATTLE OF BULL RUN

THE BATTLE OF THE SECOND MANASSAS FROM AUGUST 29 TO SEPTEMBER 1, 1862, WAS NOT A RERUN OF THE FIRST ACTION, ALTHOUGH IT WAS FOUGHT OVER THE SAME TERRAIN. A GREAT DEAL HAD CHANGED IN THE YEAR SINCE TWO UNTRIED ARMIES HAD MET FOR THE FIRST TIME.

The first battle was an isolated event expected to end the war quickly; the second was part of an ongoing campaign that followed the failure of Major General George B. McClellan's Peninsular Campaign. It would prove the genius of Confederate General Robert E. Lee in developing strategy, as well as tactics, and in using deception, and reveal his reluctance to impose his will on others, including recalcitrant generals. The carnival air that preceded the first battle was replaced by determination. The second battle was a contest between grimfaced veterans who saw no glory in war but still believed in their causes.

While the second battle did not produce the "firsts" of First Manassas, it was just as important —and much larger and more costly. More than 100,000 troops were involved, 19,514 were killed and wounded—four times the number in the first battle. Confederate victory paved the way for the first Southern invasion of the North.

Confronted with the threat to Richmond posed by the Peninsular Campaign, Confederate forces had pulled back from northern Virginia. Thus, the new Union Army of Virginia under Major General John Pope, numbering 45,000 men, pushed forward to the Rappahannock and Rapidan rivers in a renewed attempt to reach the Confederate capital. General McClellan's refusal to attack Richmond from a Peninsula base without major reinforcements, after a severe pounding by Lee, led to the abandonment of the Peninsular Campaign and to Lee's decision to attack Pope before the two Union armies could unite. Jackson's division struck Pope's forces in the neat farmlands near Cedar Mountain, five miles south of Culpeper just off present U.S. Route 15. Jackson had won the Battle of Cedar Mountain by the time Lee arrived with fresh forces. Lee then used Jackson's well-known "foot cavalry," augmented by additional units, as though it were horse cavalry, sending

Jackson with 24,000 men to cut Pope's communications with Washington. Lee, with main body, would follow and unite with Jackson to trap Pope.

It all came together on almost the same spot where the Battle of first Manassas had been fought. Pope, believing he faced only Jackson, threw caution to the wind in an effort to defeat the famous Confederate general and then mistook a tactical withdrawal for retreat. In pursuing Jackson, he was committing his army to the second battle of Manassas.

Union and Confederate forces occupied positions the reverse of their first encounter. Jackson's forces defended a strong position behind an unfinished railroad grade, still partly visible in wooded areas, until Lee's arrival. The heaviest Union assault occurred at a point known as the Deep Cut. Pope threw units piecemeal against Jackson's front, bending it but never breaking it. Jackson's veterans, low on ammunition, threw rocks to help repel one attack. The arrival of forces under Lee formed a V-shaped line with 160-degree angle. Major General James "Old Pete" Longstreet's masterful use of artillery to support Jackson marked a turning point in the fighting, and when the Confederate wings moved forward they carried everything before them. Fletcher Webster, a grandson of Daniel Webster, died leading the 12th Massachusetts Infantry in the battle. This time, it was Union soldiers who held Henry Hill, and their stubborn resistance provided the time for Pope's beaten army to retreat across Stone Bridge over Bull Run to the prepared defenses at Centreville. Behind the Centreville line, Washington was defended solely by a ring of 68 hastily constructed earthen forts.

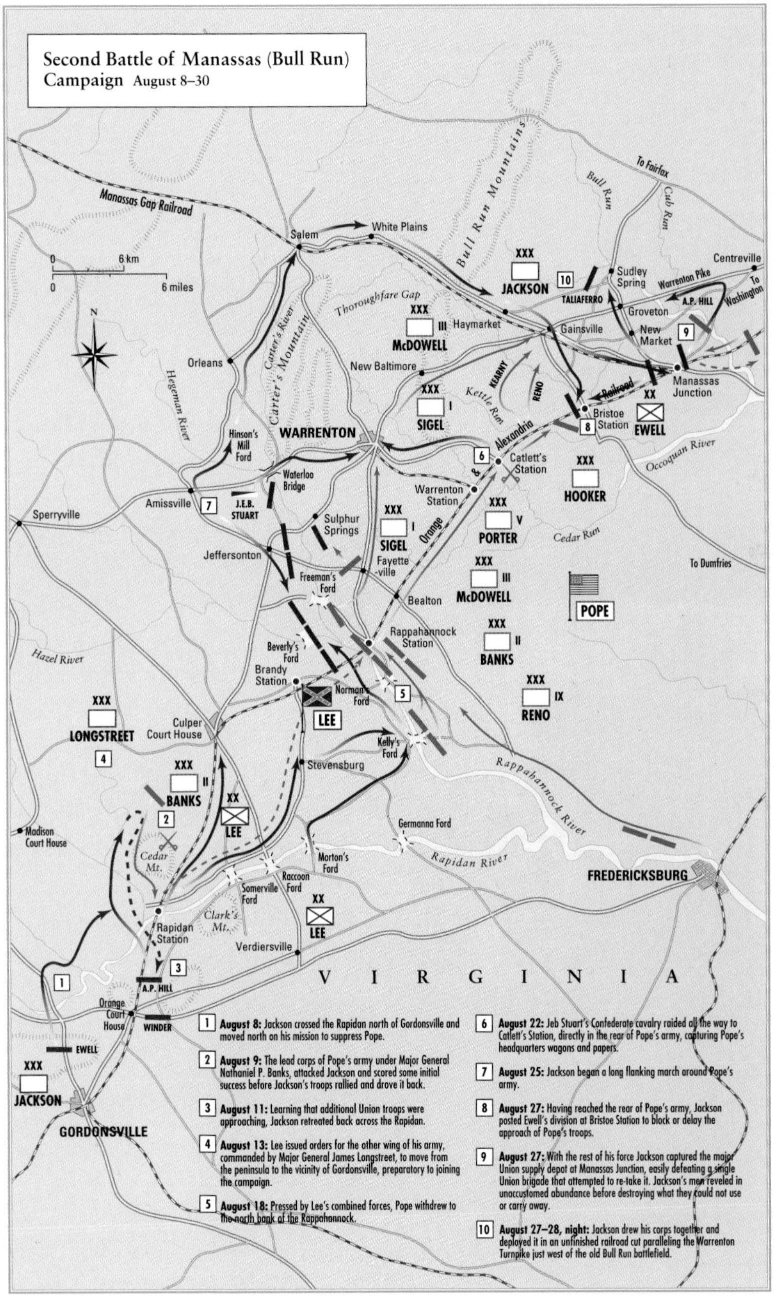
Second Battle of Manassas (Bull Run)
Campaign August 8–30
Manassas Gap Railroad
Bull Run Mountains
Thoroughfare Gap
Salem
White Plains
JACKSON
TALIAFERRO
Sudley Spring
Warrenton Pike
Centreville
To Fairfax
To Washington
A.P. HILL
Groveton
Gainsville
New Market
Haymarket
McDOWELL
New Baltimore
Orleans
KEARNY
RENO
Manassas Junction
Railroad
SIGEL
Bristoe Station
EWELL
WARRENTON
Hinson's Mill Ford
Waterloo Bridge
Catlett's Station
Orange & Alexandria
Occoquan River
HOOKER
Amissville
J.E.B. STUART
Warrenton Station
Sperryville
Sulphur Springs
PORTER
Cedar Run
Jeffersonton
Fayette -ville
To Dumfries
Freeman's Ford
Bealton
POPE
Rappahannock Station
BANKS
Hazel River
Beverly's Ford
Brandy Station
Norman's Ford
LEE
RENO
LONGSTREET
Culpeper Court House
Kelly's Ford
Stevensburg
Rappahannock River
Madison Court House
Cedar Mt.
Germanna Ford
Rapidan River
Morton's Ford
Raccoon Ford
Somerville Ford
FREDERICKSBURG
Clark's Mt.
Rapidan Station
Verdiersville
A.P. HILL
VIRGINIA
Orange Court House
WINDER
EWELL
GORDONSVILLE
6 km
6 miles
N
1 August 8: Jackson crossed the Rapidan north of Gordonsville and moved north on his mission to suppress Pope.
2 August 9: The lead corps of Pope's army under Major General Nathaniel P. Banks, attacked Jackson and scored some initial success before Jackson's troops rallied and drove it back.
3 August 11: Learning that additional Union troops were approaching, Jackson retreated back across the Rapidan.
4 August 13: Lee issued orders for the other wing of his army, commanded by Major General James Longstreet, to move from the peninsula to the vicinity of Gordonsville, preparatory to joining the campaign.
5 August 18: Pressed by Lee's combined forces, Pope withdrew to the north bank of the Rappahannock.
6 August 22: Jeb Stuart's Confederate cavalry raided all the way to Catlett's Station, directly in the rear of Pope's army, capturing Pope's headquarters wagons and papers.
7 August 25: Jackson began a long flanking march around Pope's army.
8 August 27: Having reached the rear of Pope's army, Jackson posted Ewell's division at Bristoe Station to block or delay the approach of Pope's troops.
9 August 27: With the rest of his force Jackson captured the major Union supply depot at Manassas Junction, easily defeating a single Union brigade that attempted to re-take it. Jackson's men reveled in unaccustomed abundance before destroying what they could not use or carry away.
10 August 27–28, night: Jackson drew his corps together and deployed it in an unfinished railroad cut paralleling the Warrenton Turnpike just west of the old Bull Run battlefield.

Above: Fought on the same ground as the First Battle, the Second Battle of Bull Run was a collision of war veterans rather than novices.

ANTIETAM

IT WAS A STRANGE SIGHT. TOUGH, BATTLE-HARDENED VETERANS, LEAN FROM HUNGER AND WEARING TATTERED UNIFORMS, SANG "MARYLAND, MY MARYLAND" LIKE RECRUITS ON THE DRILL FIELD AS THEY STRETCHED OUT FOR MILES ALONG DUSTY ROADS. THERE WAS GOOD REASON FOR THEIR HIGH SPIRITS AND THE SPRING IN THEIR STEP; THEY WERE CARRYING THE WAR TO THE NORTH FOR THE FIRST TIME.

Above: Close to Washington, Maryland was vulnerable to much conflict. Although the state never seceded from the Union, Confederate support was widespread, especially amongst wealthy landowners who had an interest in preserving slavery.

Right and next pages: Map showing military activity in Maryland and at the Battle of Antietam.

Maryland was bitterly divided by the Civil War. Although the State remained in the Union, the decision was made as much by geography as sentiment. At the outbreak of the war, Union troops marching to the defence of Washington were stoned by civilians in Baltimore, which would remain a hotbed of secessionist sentiment throughout the war. Maryland units fought on both sides, but in general, eastern Maryland was more sympathetic to the Southern cause than western Maryland, which was populated by farmers proud of the accomplishments of their own hands and who owned few slaves. Most just wanted both armies to leave them along to work their fields.

This was not to be. Invasion of the Confederate States by Union forces produced a sharp public reaction and a demand for retaliation. The idea of invasion had logistic and strategic appeal, too. An invasion of the North would enable the Southern army to draw supplies from what Lieutenant General James Longstreet called the "bounteous land" of Maryland without further impoverishing areas of Virginia already well worked over. It would bring the war "home" to Northerners who so

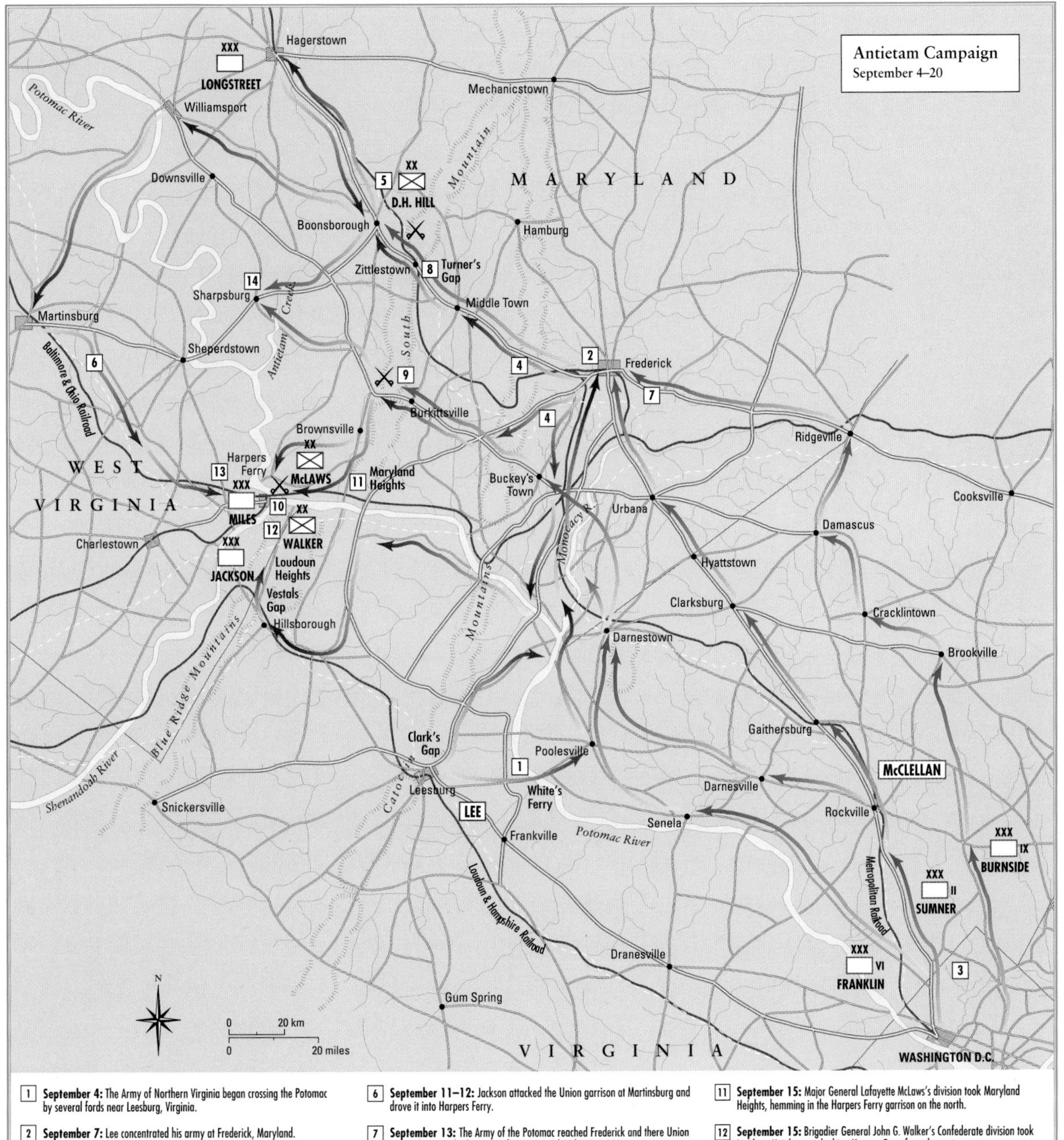

1 **September 4:** The Army of Northern Virginia began crossing the Potomac by several fords near Leesburg, Virginia.

2 **September 7:** Lee concentrated his army at Frederick, Maryland.

3 **September 7:** The Army of the Potomac, once again under the command of McClellan, began a cautious advance from Washington.

4 **September 9:** Lee issued Special Orders No. 191, directing his army to separate into several columns in order to surround and capture the Union garrison at Harpers Ferry.

5 **September 11:** Covering the rear of the Harpers Ferry operation, Lee assigned D. H. Hill to hold the passes of South Mountain and Longstreet to guard the northern approaches.

6 **September 11–12:** Jackson attacked the Union garrison at Martinsburg and drove it into Harpers Ferry.

7 **September 13:** The Army of the Potomac reached Frederick and there Union troops discovered a lost copy of Lee's Special Orders No. 191.

8 **September 14:** The First and Ninth corps of the Army of the Potomac forced their way through Turner's Gap in South Mountain, driving off D.H. Hill's troops.

9 **September 14:** Elements of McLaws's division delayed the passage of the Union Sixth Corps through Crampton's Gap in South Mountain.

10 **September 15:** Jackson moved into position sealing the southern exit to Harpers Ferry and began to bombard the post.

11 **September 15:** Major General Lafayette McLaws's division took Maryland Heights, hemming in the Harpers Ferry garrison on the north.

12 **September 15:** Brigadier General John G. Walker's Confederate division took Loudoun Heights, overlooking Harpers Ferry from the east.

13 **September 15:** Major General Dixon Miles, commanding the Union garrison at Harpers Ferry, surrendered so quickly as to arouse subsequent suspicious that he was not only incompetent but disloyal. Ironically one of the last shots fired mortally wounded Miles.

14 **September 15:** Lee decided to make a stand behind Antietam Creek near Sharpsburg, Maryland.

Sedgwick's Attack
September 17, 1862
Hagerstown Road
Nicodemus Hill
Nicodemus
Miller
Nicodemus Run
XXX
I
HOOKER
S. Poffenberger
West Wood
XXX
XII
MANSFIELD
Mumma
Hauser
Dunker Church
XXX
II
SUMNER
Roulette
XXX
JACKSON
Clipp
Bloody Lane
Hagerstown Road
N

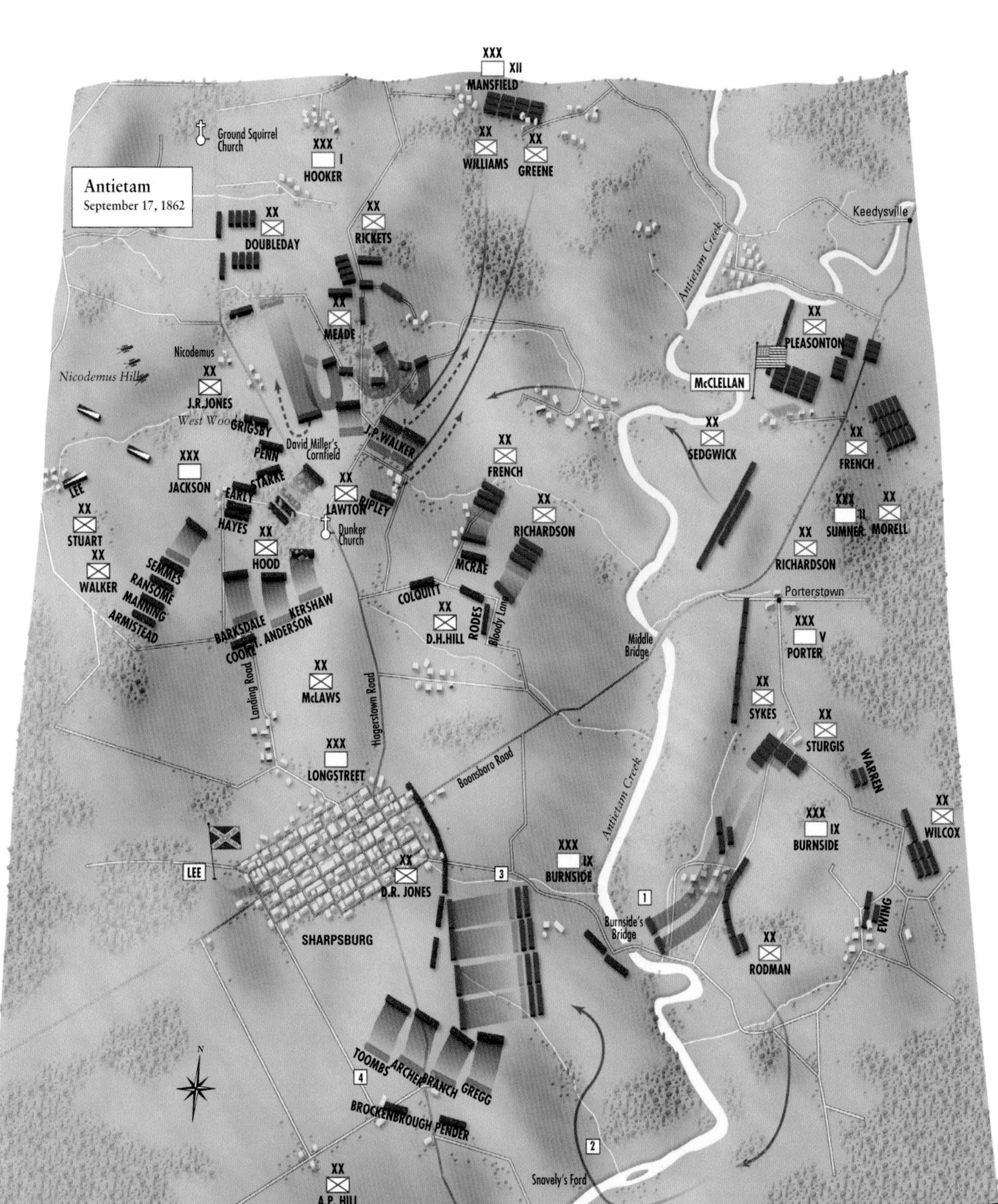

1 After hours of delay, Major General Ambrose Burnside finally launched elements of his Ninth Corps in an assault that captured the bridge that has since borne his name.

2 Brigadier General Rodman's division of the Ninth Corps crossed Antietam Creek via Snavely's Ford and provided cover for the rest of the corps as it crossed the bridge and deployed on the west side of the creek.

3 Burnside's Ninth Corps mounted an assault toward Sharpsburg, driving the Confederate defenders to the outskirts of the town.

4 Ambrose Powell Hill's Confederate division arrived after a day-long forced march from Harpers Ferry, just in time to flank and drive back Burnside's attackers.

far had suffered few ill effects, and would soothe Southern feelings wounded by the deprivations of war. Success might produce good results abroad, too, in the form of recognition by one or more of the major European powers—and that would perhaps enable the South to break the blockade, which was causing cotton and tobacco to pile up in warehouses and hindering the importation of badly needed munitions. General Lee further saw it as an opportunity for Confederate President Jefferson Davis to make a proposal for peace, which, "being made when it is in our power to inflict injury upon our adversary, would show conclusively to the world that our sole object is the establishment of our independence and the attainment of an honorable peace."

Lee's victory at the second battle of Manassas provided the opportunity and the means to carry the war to the North. He moved cautiously across the Potomac near Leesburg, with J. E. B. Stuart's cavalry between his army and Washington. He planned to protect his other flank by clearing the Federal troops from Harper's Ferry and then bringing his army together to continue the invasion, perhaps into Pennsylvania.

Things did not go as well as Lee hoped. On September 13, 1862, while General Jackson was converging on Harper's Ferry, a lost copy of Lee's battle order was found by a Union private and passed on to General George McClellan who had plenty of time to strike at Lee while his army was divided. However, McClellan's continued affliction with the "slows" enabled Lee, who had learned from a Southern sympathizer that McClellan was in possession of the order, to move reinforcements to guard the passes of South Mountain. McClellan attacked the passes on

Right: The Union Army leaves the battlefield. The day after the battle, General Lee prepared to defend an attack that never came, and so withdrew his troops across the Potomac and back to Virginia. President Lincoln was afterwards greatly critical that General McClellan did not pursue them and launch further assaults.

Previous pages: Map of Sedgwick's unsuccessful attack. He was impulsively instructed by Major General Sumner to launch an assault on "Stonewall" Jackson's troops and then found himself almost surrounded.

Above left: Soldiers manning a makeshift lookout post in the Virginian mountains.

Above right: September 17, 1862 became the bloodiest single day in the Civil War. The Federal side sustained losses of 12,410, while the Confederate losses were slightly less at 10, 700.

September 14, and for a time Lee considered withdrawing from Maryland without further contest. However, he changed his mind when he received word that Jackson had captured Harper's Ferry, taken 11,000 Federal prisoners, and would soon be on his way to join Lee.

By then, Lee's army was concentrated on high ground west of Antietam Creek and across the angle formed by the junction of the creek and the Potomac River. Why Lee chose to fight from that position is still something of a mystery; admittedly it was a tactically strong choice, except for the fact that the streams blocked the avenue of retreat, but it was certainly not a good position from which to continue an advance northward. Jackson's arrival on the eve of the September 17, 1862 battle brought Lee's strength to 40,000, far too few to press the invasion as long as McClellan's 87,000 blocked the way.

Antietam is one of the most beautiful Civil War battlefields. The view from the Visitors' Centre on the present Maryland Route 65 looks back across rolling fields toward Sharpsburg; in the other direction lie more undulating fields, sometimes interrupted by sharp breaks that created problems for Union attackers and produced such colourful names as Bloody Lane. The terrain preserved in Antietam National Battlefield Park makes it easy to understand why the Union attack was not as coordinated as McClellan wished. But it is so beautiful and peaceful that the visitor has difficulty realizing that this was the scene of the bloodiest single day of the Civil War. As night fell on September 17, 1862, these fields were strewn with dead bodies and wounded men, pockmarked with shell holes, and littered with smashed equipment. The carnage was "too fearful to contemplate" even for battle-wise General Longstreet. Federal losses came to 12,410 and Confederate losses were only slightly smaller, at 10,700.

An eight-mile self-drive tour of the park covers all aspects of the battle. Cannon between the

Confederate infantry in this area lasted for four hours and caused so many casualties that the road was nicknamed Bloody Lane. The fighting finally petered out in a mixture of confusion and exhaustion.

The third phase of the battle reached a climax late in the afternoon at the Antietam Bridge, now named the Burnside Bridge after the Union general who commanded the assault against more than four hundred well-entrenched Georgia veterans guarding the crossing. The wooded ground which spreads around the bridge today is quite different from the open area which helped the sharpshooters keep Burnside's men from crossing for hours while the battle raged at the other end of the battlefield. At 1 p.m., Burnside finally forced a crossing and gradually pushed the Georgians back, but reforming his lines for a frontal assault took two hours, during which Confederate reinforcements arrived.

Above: Ambrose Everett Burnside (1824–1881) was partially in control of the Army of the Potomac at the Battle of Antietam. After McClellan refused to pursue General Robert E. Lee's retreat, for fear of overextending his resources, Burnside was reinstated.

Although the action in this area was minor compared to the carnage elsewhere, Burnside's crossing created a major threat to Lee's army. Control of Sharpsburg would cut off Lee's line of retreat. The ability of Confederate leaders to move men to the right place at the right time saved the day. About 4 p.m., Major General A. P. Hill's division, which had remained in Harper's Ferry to dispose of captured Federal property and parole prisoners, arrived they immediately drove Burnside back to the heights near the bridge.

The costly battle was over. The next day, Lee ended his first invasion of the North by withdrawing across the Potomac, none of his objectives having been fulfilled. The cautious McClellan licked his wounds and let him go, content to have held the field and forced a Confederate retreat.

President Lincoln inspected the battlefield, consoled the wounded and questioned McClellan about his slow pursuit. The photograph of Lincoln and McClellan sitting and talking in the command tent is one of the most famous of the war; what was said is a mystery.

The Battle of Antietam, the only major battle fought in Maryland, gave Lincoln a great many of the things he desired. McClellan had pressed the attack once he was ready, and his ability to hold the field finally ended the myth of Lee's invincibility, thereby providing a much needed morale boost for the North. It also halted the invasion of Maryland at the outset, and so was a blow to Confederate hopes for recognition by European powers. Thus, although the battle was tactically a draw, it was a strategic victory for the North.

The victory created an atmosphere which permitted Lincoln to issue the Emancipation Proclamation. The proclamation was almost as controversial as the suspension of civil rights. It caused political dispute on the home front and a great deal of dissension in the ranks of the army. Not only did it affect property rights, as people of the period conceived them, but it greatly tarnished the popular image of the war as one to save the Union. It also contained a fundamental paradox: for, while it abolished slavery in Confederate States, it did not do so in those States which remained in the Union. It was certainly much better received abroad, where anti-slavery forces maintained the pressure on the governments of Great Britain and France not to recognise the Confederacy.

The positive results of the battle at Antietam were not enough to save McClellan, however; on November 3, Lincoln replaced him with General Ambrose E. Burnside.

EMANCIPATION PROCLAMATION

AT THE ONSET OF THE CIVIL WAR, ABRAHAM LINCOLN'S INITIAL OBJECTIVE WAS TO PRESERVE THE UNION, NOT TO FREE SLAVES. IN 1862, HOWEVER, THE NORTH'S FORTUNES WERE FLAGGING AND THE CONFLICT NEEDED FRESH IMPETUS. LINCOLN FOUND IT IN THE ABOLITIONISM AND THE WAR NOW BECAME A MORAL CRUSADE AGAINST SLAVERY.

When the Civil War began, the emancipation of slaves was not the first principle on President Lincoln's mind—indeed he even saw it as a potential threat to his aim of saving the Union. A moderate and a pragmatist, he believed that turning the conflict into an abolitionist issue might cause northern Democrats and border-state Unionists to withdraw their support. Constitutionally, he believed he lacked the power to liberate the South's slaves. He even hoped that, if the Southern Rebels thought they could retain their slaves, they would return to the Union—and ignored critics who ridiculed the idea of a victorious North allowing slavery to continue in the South. When Union generals wielded their military powers to undermine slavery, Lincoln overruled them or even relieved them of their posts. When Congress "confiscated" Southern slaves in the first tentative moves toward emancipation, he resisted.

However, as the war dragged on and casualities mounted, Lincoln began to see the many advantages of linking the conflict with the cause of emancipation. He realized that it would add a popular, moral dimension to the Union's campaign and encourage a deeper national commitment to victory. He also hoped that it would generate international support for the Union and deny the Confederacy possible foreign allies—after all, no external power would want to be seen fighting to uphold slavery. Freeing the slaves would also be detrimental to the Southern economy; it would undermine the Confederacy's war effort and weaken its armies, while at the same time—Lincoln expected—to create a new source of military manpower for the North as free blacks and former slaves joined the Union's forces.

During the summer of 1862, Lincoln decided to issue an emancipation proclamation as an "act of justice" and a military measure that was necessary to win the war. The timing of such a

Visitors' Center and the restored Dunker Church stand on the spot from which Confederate artillery swept The Cornfield and East Woods as the Federals attacked. Photographs taken after the battle show clusters of dead Confederate gunners lying around some of their cannon. The cannonading during the battle was furious; indeed, some historians describe Antietam as principally a duel between artillery.

The battle at Antietam had three distinct phases. It began with the dawn attack from Joseph Poffenberger's farm against Jackson's men in The Cornfield. Attackers and defenders charged between head high rows of corn, and the battle surged back and forth until, in the words of Union General Hooker, "every stalk of corn in the northern and greater part of the field was cut as closely as could have been done with a knife, and the slain lay in rows as precisely as they had stood in their ranks a few moments before." The fighting, which proved to be the heaviest of the day, continued for three hours, and the field changed hands no less than fourteen times. The costliest action of the bloodiest day was Union Major General John Sedgwick's attack from the East Woods against Jackson's defensive line in the West Woods. In less than half an hour, Sedgwick lost more than 2,200 men.

Below: President Lincoln with George B. McClellen and other generals outside an army tent after the Battle of Antietam.

The second phase of the battle developed at the Sunken Road. Fighting between Union and

controversial announcement was crucial—it would look like a desperate last measure if issued after a run of defeats. Lincoln read the proclamation to his cabinet in July 1862 but waited until September, when the Confederates withdrew from the North after the Battle of Antietam, to make his announcement.

On September 22, 1862, Lincoln issued his Preliminary Emancipation Proclamation, being careful to justify emancipation as a military necessity under the Constitution. The Proclamation allowed for the liberation of slaves only in areas that were in rebellion and thus under martial law—in other words, only in areas where the North had no power. His Final Emancipation Proclamation, announced on January 1, 1863, specifically listed those rebellious areas where slaves were to be freed. Slave-owners who were loyal to the Union were exempt and allowed to retain their slaves. In 1860, 3,083,614 slaves lived in the rebellious areas, while the loyal, exempted areas were home to 838,817 slaves, which means that twenty-one percent of the entire slave population were excluded and were to remain in bondage. In 1865, one month before Lincoln died, Congress approved the Thirteenth Amendment to the Constitition, which freed all four million slaves.

Although the Proclamation was inadequate, it did declare an intention to end the bondage of slavery and thus, as Lincoln intended, broadened the base of the war and kept Europe out of the conflict.

Below: President Lincoln surrounded by emancipated slaves in Richmond, Virginia. He ensured that black people were considered citizens. Black men were given the right to vote.

FREDERICKSBURG

"A GREAT BATTLE GOING ON" DECLARED A HEADLINE IN THE WASHINGTON STAR ON DECEMBER 13, 1862. AND INDEED IT WAS, BUT NOT FROM THE UNION STANDPOINT. THE BATTLE OF FREDERICKSBURG, WHICH INITIATED A SERIES OF ENGAGEMENTS ALONG THE RAPPAHANNOCK RIVER BARRIER ALMOST HALFWAY BETWEEN WASHINGTON AND RICHMOND, WAS SUCH A DISASTER THAT IT WAS THE ONLY ONE MAJOR GENERAL E. AMBROSE BURNSIDE WOULD LEAD AS COMMANDER OF THE ARMY OF THE POTOMAC.

Burnside did not want to accept the command because he lacked experience. Lincoln had his doubts, too, but they were overcome by his exasperation at the slow movement of General-in-Chief George B. McClellan, who had allowed Lee to withdraw his army uncontested from Maryland after the Battle of Antietam. Burnside must have been influenced by Lincoln's impatience, for he pushed into hostile territory in wintertime and persisted in following his plan of attack even when confronted by Lee in possession of one of the most defensible natural positions used in the Civil War, Marye's Heights and the adjacent hills south of Fredericksburg.

The opening phase of the Battle of Fredericksburg might have been an omen for Burnside. Confederate sharpshooters hidden in the historic prevented his engineers from completing pontoon bridges across the river—one of the innovations associated with the battle—even after he had devastated the town with artillery. Only by using pontoons in the manner of landing craft—another innovation that anticipated modern warfare—was he able to push sufficient forces across the river to clear the city of snipers and skirmishers. The worst was yet to come.

Opposite page: Map of the Battle of Fredricksburg, which took place between December 11–13, 1862

Union skirmishes moved through the narrow streets of the city. Ahead, lay snow-covered fields and Marye's Heights, which at that time were outside the city. Confederates were strongly entrenched along the base and along the ridge, while others entrenched behind the stone wall at the Sunken Road, mowed down Union lines attacking across open fields.

The confederates had total command of the surrounding terrain. The combination of strategically placed artillery units as Louisiana's acclaimed Washington Battery, which raked the attacking Union army and infantry shooting from behind the Stone Wall was so effective that Colonel E.P. Alexander boasted "a chicken could not live on that field." A second Union assault east of Marye's Heights, which should have been coordinated with the main effort but was not, was also unceremoniously beaten back by Lee's triumphant forces. The heights, now a terraced national cemetery where more than 15,000 Union troops are buried amid memorials to many of the units involved,are mute testimony to the effectiveness of the Confederate defence. The Confederate commander watched the battle from a vantage point on what is now known as Lee Hill. It was there, when complete victory became obvious, that Lee allowed himself a little show of ebullience. "It is well that war is so terrible—we should grow too fond of it," he said.

Today, an eight-mile self-drive tour begins at the base of the hill and moves through the wooded terrain to pass the well preserved section of Confederate infantry trench; the point where Major General's George G. Meade's Federals briefly pierced the Confederate line; and Prospect Hill and Major John Pelham's Position, Confederate artillery strongpoints, still fortified with period cannon.

1. December 11, 7:00 a.m.: Brigadier General William Barksdale's Confederate brigade took shelter in the houses of Fredericksburg and fired on Union engineers attempting to construct pontoon bridges over the Rappahannock.
2. December 11: Union artillery on Stafford Heights bombarded Fredericksburg, attempting to drive Barksdale's men out of the town.
3. December 11: Union troops finally succeeded in a cross-river assault in pontoon boats and drove out Barksdale's men in house-to-house fighting, allowing the engineers to finish their bridges.
4. December 13: Using two guns until one of them was disabled Major John Pelham frequently changed positions and held up the Union advance on the southern flank until he ran out of ammunition.
5. December 13, noon–2:30 p.m.: The Union left wing attacked and briefly broke through the defenders' line before a Confederate counterattack drove them back.
6. December 13, 10:00 a.m.–5:00 p.m.: The Union right wing made twelve different frontal assaults across an open field toward an impregnable Confederate position, suffering massive casualties, inflicting few, and failing to accomplish anything.

Battle of Fredericksburg
December 11–13

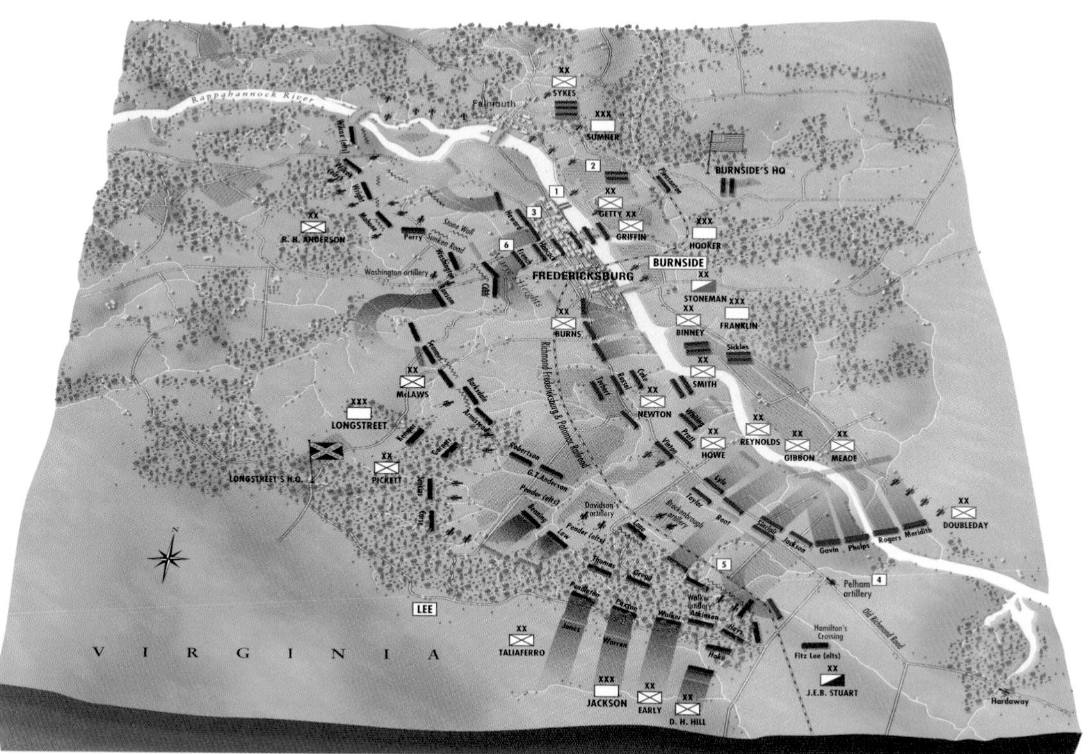

BATTLE OF STONE'S RIVER

THE EVENING OF THE BATTLE OF STONE'S RIVER WAS ALMOST FESTIVE, AS BANDS IN BOTH ARMIES PLAYED UNDER STARRY SKIES. THIS SOON BECAME A CONTEST TO SEE WHICH BAND COULD PLAY THE LOUDEST. THEN, THE HOMESPUN WESTERNERS IN BOTH ARMIES BEGAN SINGING "HOME SWEET HOME." AFTER THE BATTLE MANY WOULD NEVER SEE THEIR HOMES AGAIN.

Union General William Rosecrans had marched out of Nashville in winter to crush the Confederate forces under General Braxton Bragg, who was encamped in winter quarters near Murfreesboro, and then over on to Chattanooga. Bragg's cavalry kept him informed of Rosecrans's progress while his troops prepared for Christmas, most of them thinking of home. Corporal Johnny Green of the 9th Kentucky Regiment dreamed of returning home victorious in a letter to his family, hoping "this joyous season would find us on Kentucky's soil with the invaders... driven north of the Ohio River."

Although Bragg held a strong position, he attacked Rosecran's right wing at dawn on December 31 and drove it back. "Old Rosy" gave orders to contest every inch of ground, while he prepared a new defensive line with his reserves. The costly stand by General Sheridan's forces, along with those commanded by Major General George H. Thomas and the use of cannon at almost point-blank range, bought him the time. Fighting continued until darkness fell, when a silence settled over the battlefield that would continue through the next day. Bragg was so confident that Rosecrans would withdraw that he wrote to his superiors that "God has granted us a happy New Year." His exultation was premature. Rosecrans, with a superior force, stubbornly held his new position.

Bragg ordered a new attack on January 2, 1863, which forced Union troops back across Stone's River, but the offensive was halted by concentrated artillery fire at what is now a detached section of the park distinguished by an artillery monument.

Both armies claimed a victory. Bragg won the battle but did not have the resources to force Rosecrans from the field; so he withdrew to Tullahoma, Tennessee. Another rich farming area was lost to the Confederacy, and Rosecrans had acquired the base from which later attacks on Chattanooga could be launched—Fortress Rosecrans, as the Union General modestly named it.

One of the most obvious parts of the Stone's River National Battlefield is the cemetery, located opposite the entrance to the battlefield park. That would be appropriate for any battle in central Tennessee, which, because of their intensity were bloody affairs, but it is particularly appropriate for Stone's River. More than a third of all the soldiers involved, or 23,000 of them, became casualties during the three days of fighting.

The cemetery should be the last stop on a tour of the battlefield (now at the outskirts of Murfreesboro) because the well-tended lawns and fields and the quiet woods of the battlefield are deceptive. The artillery pieces occupying strategic points in the park, as they did when this was farmland in the strange winter battle in 1862, give only a small indication of the decisive role they played in this battle, where Confederate courage could not match the efficiency of Union artillery units. The well-positioned explanatory markers cannot convey the struggles of the foot soldiers as they fought at close range, often in hand-to-hand combat. The battle comes vividly to life at one place on the preserved battlefield: the rock-strewn wood where Michigan troops under General Philip Sheridan made a desperate stand against advancing Confederates. There in the woods, scattered among the rock outcroppings which provided ready-made rifle pits for the Michigan infantry, are the remains of two demolished rifled cannon. To the troops involved, the area would be known thereafter as the Slaughter Pen.

One of the displays in the Visitors' Centre entitled "Strange Christmas 1862" is indicative of the

Above: General William Rosecrans (1819–1898) took over the command of the Army of Cumberland after Don Carlos Buell was relieved for being too ineffectual.

Left: The Battle of Stone River was the bloodiest battle throughout the entirety of the War. General Rosecrans is pictured here rallying his troops.

tour of the park, starting at the Visitors' Center, follows the progress of the battle. Nearby are the Cedar Forest through which the Confederate attack was launched, and the Chicago Board of Trade Battery (named for the organization which contributed the funds to equip it), which blunted the Confederate attack at that point. A short distance beyond the woods where Sheridan made his stand is the area where Confedertes made their deepest penetration of the battle, and the place where Rosecrans established his new line. At the only poistion which Union forces were able to hold throughout the battle—the Round Forest—stands the oldest Civil War monument in the nation; it was erected in 1863 by the survivors of Colonel William B. Hazen's Brigade, which held the position.

Other detached sections of the battlefield park identify the sites of buildings, since destroyed, whicg Bragg and Rosecrans used as headquarters. The cemetery occupies the hillside where Union artillery stood during part of the battle. Artillery pieces, their muzzles pointed across the 6,100 white headstones identifying Union casualties, are mute testimony to the intensity of the fighting at Stone's River. Handsome monuments to many of the units involved, including the "last shot" memorial to the 15th, 16th, 18th and 19th infantry units and to Battery H of the 5th U.S. Artillery, provide a different perspective.

Opposite page: Movements of both armies throughout the duration of the battle from December 31 1862 - January 2 1863.

Below: A Confederate cannon at the Stones River National Battlefield.

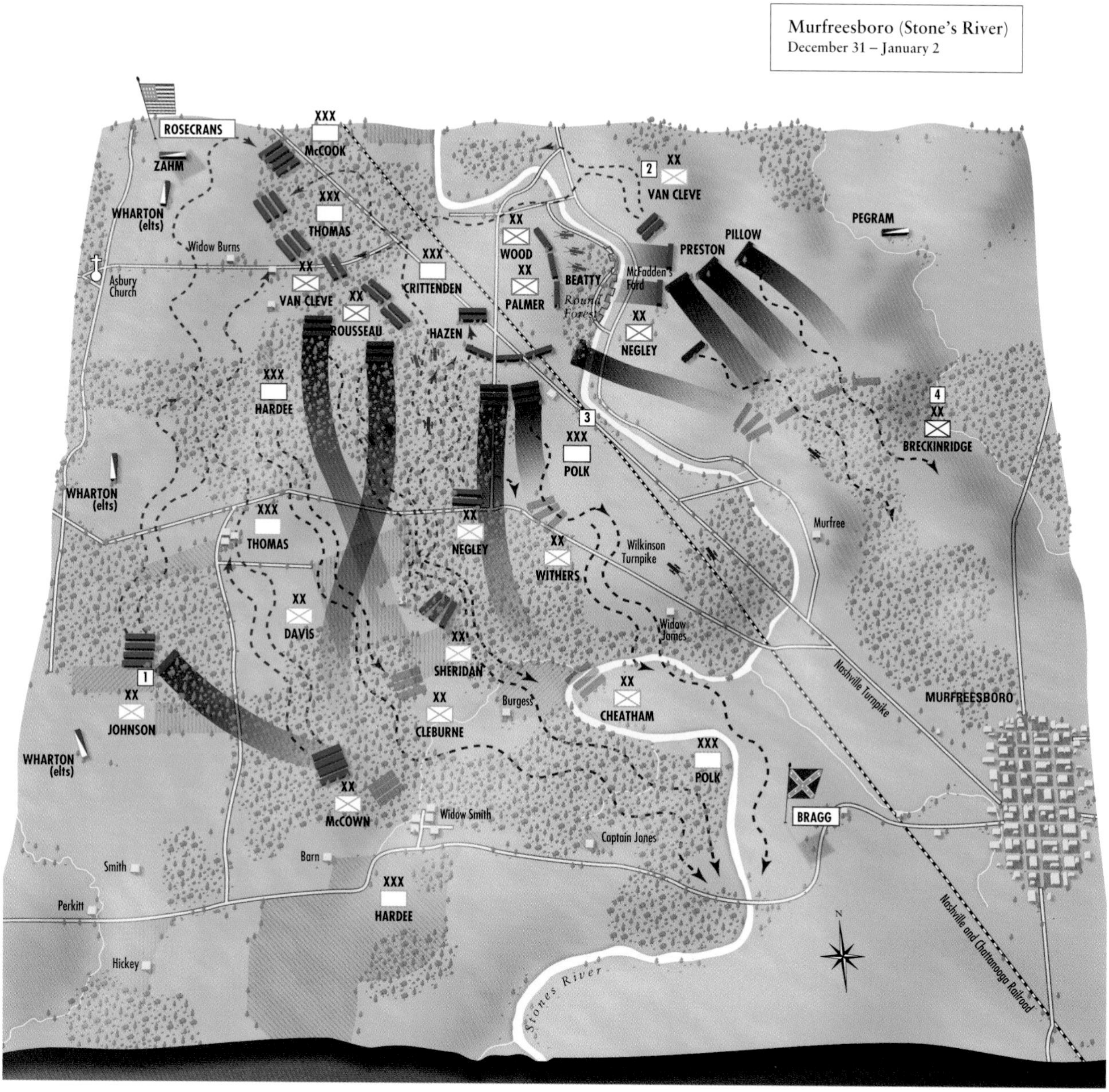

Murfreesboro (Stone's River)
December 31 – January 2

1. December 31, a.m.: Hardee slams into McCook's corps and routs Johnson, but Union resistance stiffens, slowing Hardee's attack. Bragg orders Polk to reinforce Hardee.

2. 6:10 a.m.: Van Cleve's Union division crosses the river, but frantic pleas from McCook for help forces Rosecrans to redeploy entire army to meet massive Confederate attack.

3. 10:00 a.m.–12 noon: Hardee and Polk force McCook back to pike. Sheridan holds Nashville Pike and Federals rally. Unionist corps of Thomas and Crittenden check Confederate advance.

4. January 2: Bragg switches assault to strike Union left but is beaten back by overwhelming firepower at river crossing.

THE FIRST VICKSBURG CAMPAIGN

BY LATE 1862, GRANT HAD IDENTIFIED THE CONFEDERATE STRONGHOLD OF VICKSBURG IN MISSISSIPPI AS A MAJOR TARGET, AND HAD FORMULATED AN ELABORATE PLAN TO TAKE IT. HOWEVER, A COMBINATION OF BAD LUCK AND EFFECTIVE RESPONSES BY HIS CONFEDERATE OPPONENTS WOULD END HIS DREAM—FOR THE TIME BEING.

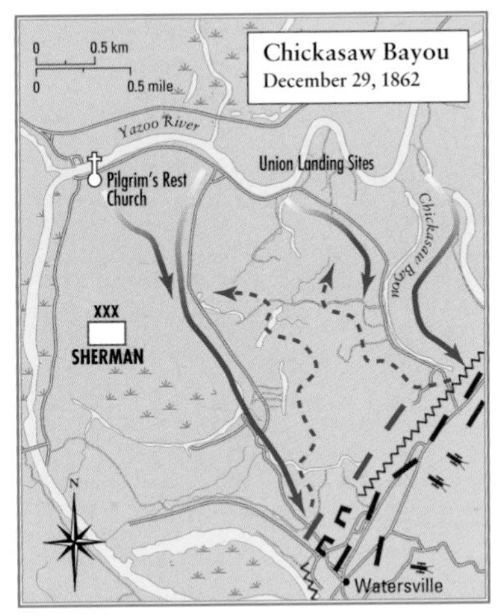

Above: Also referred to as the "Walnut Hills," the Battle of the Chickasaw Bayou was the opening battle of the Vicksburg Campaign. This map shows the thwarted Union advance, and the resulting Confederate victory.

Control of the Mississippi fortress city of Vicksburg was absolutely vital to Confederate strategic interests. Not only could it be used to block Union ships on the Missisippi, but it also acted as a major supply hub, particularly with the states to the west upon whom the Confederates were dependent for the majority of their food. No wonder, it was such a important Union target. However, the Union command knew that the capture of the city would not be without its perils. Vicksburg's nickname, "The Gibraltar of the Conderacy" was well deserved—it was set on high, rocky cliffs above the river and was surrounded by a dense swath of swampland. The Unionist had at first been in favor of a waterborne assault, but a river attack by Admiral David Farragut in the summer of 1862 had been comprehensively repulsed, leading to some serious rethinking by the Union high command. Grant believed that a land assault on the city might ulimately prove successful, so long as the Confederate army protecting Vicksburg could be drawn out and engaged elsewhere.

In early November, 1862, Grant led a force of 31,000 men toward Grand Junction in southern Tennessee. The town was an important rail terminal and could be used, so Grant thought, to provide access into Mississippi to the south. The Confederate forces holding the town were under the command of General John C. Pemberton, who was actually a Pennsylvanian native, but had volunteered to fight for the South. His forces put up little resistance and Grand Junction was taken swiftly by Union troops following minor skirmishing. Pemberton's forces then retreated south of the Tallahatchie River where they held their position. Meanwhile, another Union force of 15,000 men, under the command of General William Tecumseh Sherman, assembled at Memphis to the southwest.

Grant now planned a three-pronged attack against Pemberton: he would lead his troops directly south to engange the Confederate army head on; Sherman's Memphis troops would head southeast to assault Pemberton's flanks; while a third column, under Brigadier General Alvin P. Hovey, would launch an attack from Arkansas, heading eastward toward the town of Grenada where they could severely damage Pemberton's supply line. With Pemberton defeated, the Union army would then march on Vicksburg.

Faced with the prospect of such a concerted—and potentially ovewhelming—assault, Pemberton decided that his best option was to retreat rather than fight, and led his men south deep into the heart of Mississippi.

Thus, the forces of Grant and Sherman were able to link up after a few days' marching in Oxford, Mississippi without having faced any serious opposition. Hovey's division had also successfully completed the first part of its mission, landing at Friar's Ponit on November 27, from where trooops spent the next ten days raiding their way across the countryside to Granada. Union troops were, by now, far into the heart of the state, which would soon provide a new set of probems. The further they marched into Mississippi, the more stretched their supply line would become—something which Pemberton's Confederate forces could possibly take advantage of should they decide to turn and fight.

Grant was so concerned that he decided to alter his strategy. The assault on Vicksburg would be changed from a land offensive to an aquatic one. According to the new plan, Grant would continue his land assault, pushing further into Mississippi in the hope of keeping Pemberton's army busy, and preventing them from turning back towards Vicksburg. Sherman, meanwhile, would return to Memphis, where he was to gather together a force of some 32,000 men. Sherman and his men would then travel in convoy via steamboat down the Mississippi River to Vicksburg. With Pemberton at large in the state, it was assumed by the Union side that Vicksburg would be guarded by a mere token force and that its capture would be relatively straightforward. Grant's troops would prevent Pemberton from rushing back to the fortress's aid once the assault had begun.

In the event, things would turn out very differently from how the Union side had planned it. Although Sherman was able to gather together the required troops at Memphis and set out down the river, Grant's contribution to the campaign was fatally undermined when the Confederate troops of Brigadier General Nathan Bedford Forrest destroyed the Union supply depot at Holly Springs (as Grant had feared they might), making his army's continued presence in the state untenable. He was obliged to disengage with Pemberton and retire, whereupon Pemberton's forces quickly marched back to Vicksburg.

Sherman continued down the river. First he landed at Milliken's Bend on the Mississippi's Lousiana shore, where his troops destroyed the Vicksburg and Shreveport railroad that headed west into Vicksburg. He then pushed north, landing his forces on the banks of the Yazoo River, a few miles north of Vicksburg. He was clearly under the impression that it would be plain sailing to launch a waterborne expedition from here down the local bayous to the town. Unfortunately,

Right: Map of the Union's successful assault at Arkansas Post on January 11, 1863..

Opposite page: Grant's First Vicksburg Campaign did not result in the victory he expected. It would be several more months before the city fell..

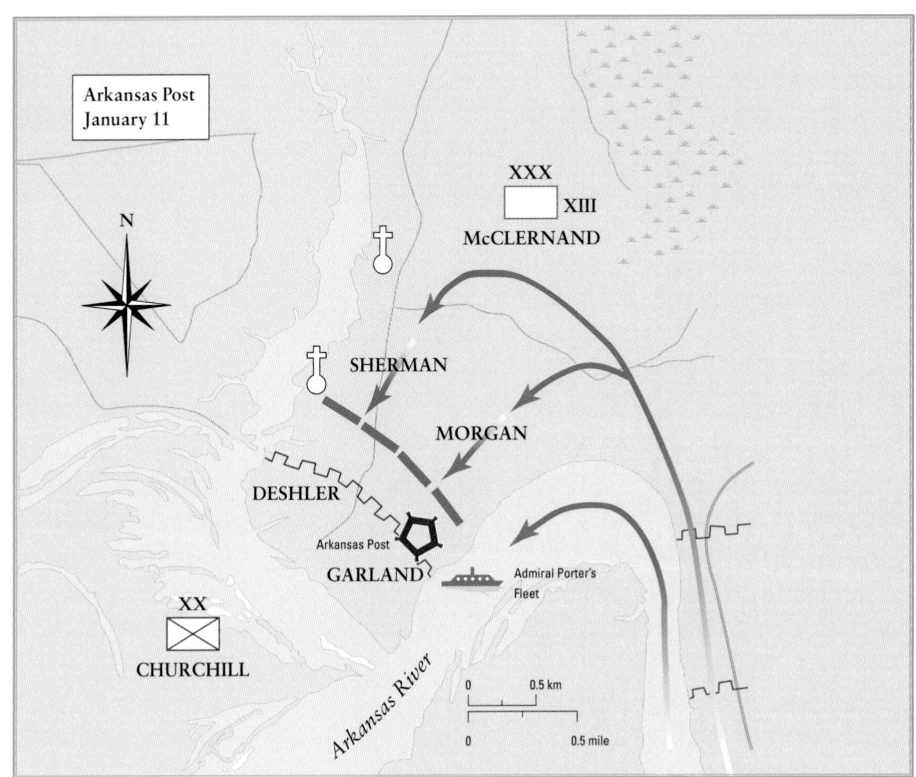

his plans were severely hampered by the geography of the area, which was overwhelmingly swampy and offered no clear way of attacking the heavily defended Confederate line. Despite these disadvantages, Sherman persevered and on December 29, launched an ill-fated assault at Chickasaw Bayou, which was swiftly and comprehensively repulsed by Confederate forces for the loss of just 76 troops. The Union side suffered over 1700 casualties. With no territory gained and the loss of more troops likely, Sherman halted the assault and withdrew on December 31.

Union forces were more successful a few days later when they attacked the Confederate fort at Arkansas Post on the Arkansas River, 50 miles northwest of its confluence with the Mississippi. On January 11, following an artillery barrage and an assault by Union troops, the Confederates surrendered the garrison with minimal resistance. Although the victory boosted morale, and improved Union access to the river, it had no direct bearing on the fate of Vicksburg, which would not fall until the summer of 1863.

Other actions in Arkansas were to prove more significant. In early December 1862, Union Brigadier General James G. Blunt's 5,000 troops were joined by a further 6,000 men under the command of Major General Francis D. Herron. They faced off against the 10,000 troops of Confederate Major General Thomas C. Hindman at the Battle of Prairie Grove on December 7. The subsequent victory for the Union effectively gave them control of Northern Arkansas, and prevented Hindman from going to Vicksburg's aid.

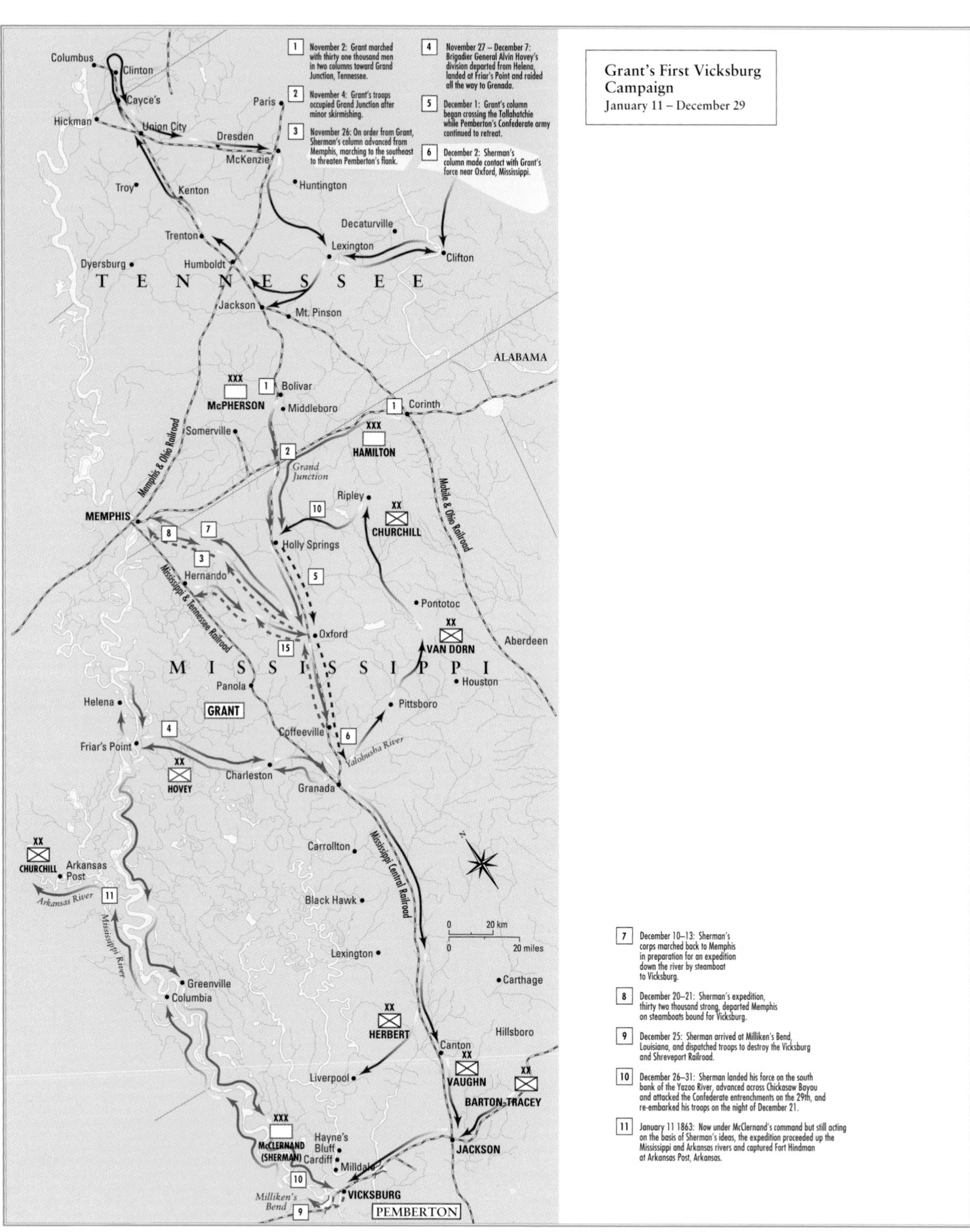
Grant's First Vicksburg Campaign
January 11 – December 29
1 November 2: Grant marched with thirty one thousand men in two columns toward Grand Junction, Tennessee.
2 November 4: Grant's troops occupied Grand Junction after minor skirmishing.
3 November 26: On order from Grant, Sherman's column advanced from Memphis, marching to the southeast to threaten Pemberton's flank.
4 November 27 – December 7: Brigadier General Alvin Hovey's division departed from Helena, landed at Friar's Point and raided all the way to Grenada.
5 December 1: Grant's column began crossing the Tallahatchie while Pemberton's Confederate army continued to retreat.
6 December 2: Sherman's column made contact with Grant's force near Oxford, Mississippi.
7 December 10–13: Sherman's corps marched back to Memphis in preparation for an expedition down the river by steamboat to Vicksburg.
8 December 20–21: Sherman's expedition, thirty two thousand strong, departed Memphis on steamboats bound for Vicksburg.
9 December 25: Sherman arrived at Milliken's Bend, Louisiana, and dispatched troops to destroy the Vicksburg and Shreveport Railroad.
10 December 26–31: Sherman landed his force on the south bank of the Yazoo River, advanced across Chickasaw Bayou and attacked the Confederate entrenchments on the 29th, and re-embarked his troops on the night of December 21.
11 January 11 1863: Now under McClernand's command but still acting on the basis of Sherman's ideas, the expedition proceeded up the Mississippi and Arkansas rivers and captured Fort Hindman at Arkansas Post, Arkansas.
TENNESSEE
MISSISSIPPI
ALABAMA
Columbus
Clinton
Cayce's
Hickman
Union City
Paris
Dresden
McKenzie
Troy
Kenton
Huntington
Decaturville
Trenton
Lexington
Clifton
Dyersburg
Humboldt
Jackson
Mt. Pinson
Bolivar
McPHERSON
Middleboro
Corinth
Somerville
HAMILTON
Grand Junction
Memphis & Ohio Railroad
Mobile & Ohio Railroad
Ripley
CHURCHILL
MEMPHIS
Holly Springs
Hernando
Mississippi & Tennessee Railroad
Pontotoc
Oxford
VAN DORN
Aberdeen
Panola
Houston
Helena
GRANT
Pittsboro
Coffeeville
Yalobusha River
Friar's Point
Charleston
HOVEY
Granada
Carrollton
Mississippi Central Railroad
Arkansas Post
Arkansas River
Black Hawk
Mississippi River
20 km
20 miles
Lexington
Carthage
Greenville
Columbia
HERBERT
Hillsboro
Canton
VAUGHN
Liverpool
BARTON-TRACEY
McCLERNAND (SHERMAN)
Hayne's Bluff
Cardiff
Milldale
JACKSON
Milliken's Bend
VICKSBURG
PEMBERTON

Washington at War

The war effort intruded on everyday life in Washington in numerous ways, small and large. Soldiers were everywhere in the city, with high-ranking officers bustling on duty and enjoying in a relaxed manner the restaurants and soirees of the capital at other times.

Before the war, the national capital of Washington reflected its proximity to the Southern States in both population and outlook. The Southern drawl was more prominent than the sharper tones of the northeast and Midwest on the streets and in the salons frequented by a structured, status-conscious society. Northerners often felt a little strange amid the Southern culture of the city.

The war did not change the atmosphere overnight. Although Southerners who left in droves for the Confederacy, including the senators and representatives of seceding States, were replaced by the aggressive and uncompromising Abolitionists of the new administration of Abraham Lincoln, many of the permanent residents of the city were Southerners by origin and temperament. Citizens of the border slave States, while remaining loyal to the Union, were sympathetic toward the Southern cause.

The first troops from New York to arrive to defend the capital, in advance of any fighting in the area, were met either with indifference or hostility by the public. Southern sympathizers naturally resented their presence, but others fumed at the inconveniences caused by the sudden influx of soldiers and civilians and the raw earthwork fortifications being raised on the occupied Virginia shore of the Potomac River. Police were increasingly involved in altercations with troops.

The inaugural of Abraham Lincoln as sixteenth President of the United States brought an unfamiliar mood to the city. The crowds of outsiders who lounged in hotels and milled about the streets, as well as pre-in-augural pomp at the Capital and elsewhere, prompted a Washington Star reporter to write "a day more un-Sabbath like than yesterday cannot be well imagined." The hundreds of arrives who could not find hotel accommodation used public fountains as "al fresco toilet arrangements." Masses of curious people crowded the entrance to Willard's Hotel, where

Lincoln was staying. The crowd of spectators lining Pennsylvania Avenue for the parade was the greatest ever seen to that time. Lincoln's inaugural address was firm, but conciliatory.

Still, the loss of innocence took time. Crowds of excited citizens followed the Union army to Centreville and freely visited the army camps before the Battle of First Manassas. Many took picnic baskets to sustain them as they watched the "festivities." The rout and subsequent retreat to Washington was a sobering experience, which sowed the seeds of hatred toward the South that would grow in intensity with each defeat and not subside with later victories. Suspicion of the Southerners remaining in Washington replaced earlier cordiality, as stories of spying, real and fancied, made the rounds. This accelerated the departure of Southerners from Washington.

Martial ceremony was impressive but unthreatening. Reviews of troops drew large crowds. In November 1861, the Washington Star reported, droves of people spent half a day getting to Bailey's Crossroads south of the Potomac River to watch a military review. Salutes and salvoes greeted the arrival of the commandant, General McClellan, and as he rode along the line in review "the roars of cheers that went up from seventy-five thousand throats of his army were nearly as deafening as the thunders of artillery."

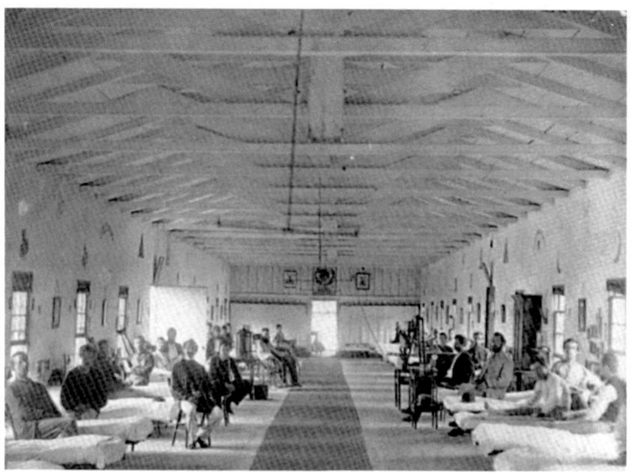

Above: Contemporary photograph of citizens in Washington *(top)*. Lucky soldiers in a Washington hospital *(bottom)* who had the chance to receive medical attention and recover from their wounds. However subsequent infection and disease killed far more people than those who died in combat.

The bucolic side of the city of about 61,000 people persisted. Large fields surrounded the Gothic eminence known as the Smithsonian Institution. Cows grazed on the lawn of the unfinished Washington Monument, then a truncated beginning of the tall spire that ultimately was built. The *Washington Star* reported, but did not object to, an improvised dam on the tiny Tiber River north of New Jersey Avenue which was erected by soldiers defending the capital. The soldiers used the pool for bathing.

Work on the national Capital went on because Lincoln viewed it as a symbol that "we intend the Union to go on." In 1864, the Goddess of Freedom was lowered into place on the dome. Ordinary events continued in the shadow of war. Picnics in Washington Park were a favourite personal and institutional pastime. Carriage accidents continued, and even Secretary of State Seward was involved when a nervous horse bolted while the driver was helping a woman board. In trying to get out of the moving carriage, Seward injured his face and fractured his right arm.

In June 1862, a baseball game was played between the National and Washington clubs, with National winning by 40 runs—62 to 22. In May 1863, a headline fight between Joe Coburn and Mike McCordle for a $2,000 prize had sporting circles "excited." It went 68 rounds and ended with Coburn claiming to be American champion of the prize ring.

The social life of the nation's capital was especially pleasant when good news was heard from the front. Treasured invitations to the White House resulted in people arriving "thick and fast." A

Right and opposite page: President Lincoln insisted that the construction of Washington should continue during the war. He was also vigilant about maintaining its security.

typical event began late, at 10 p.m., and included entertainment. Lincoln and other celebrities naturally were centers of attention. Dancing began at 11 p.m. with Lincoln leading off with one of the ladies. Caterers loaded tables with food—pate de foie gras, chicken, champagne, other wines and liquors. Decorations of spun sugar might include a war helmet, Chinese pagodas, Roman temples, cornucopias and the Goddess of Liberty; even Fort Pickens.

Despite the war, the public had relatively free access to the White House. Lincoln held morning and afternoon receptions during winter, often twice a week, which were attended by civilians and military, including enlisted men. The women were elegantly dressed in silks and satins, with lace feather adornments, and the civilian men wore evening dress. Lincoln stood in the Blue Room or East Room to greet visitors with a handshake, but even close friends described the gesture as perfunctory, with Lincoln staring into space and not even recognizing them. These sessions usually gave Lincoln a swollen hand that would bother him for several hours.

Music was not ignored. The Anchutz Opera Group from Germany entertained in September 1863. Human nature sometimes affected the course of intellectual pleasures; the efforts of a group of young men to serenade with musical instruments a young lady at the United States Hotel was interrupted by a bucket of water on their heads. So many army officers visited Congress in search of political promotions that an unsuccessful attempt was made to limit visitors to those on leave. On one visit to Ford's Theatre, Lincoln could obtain seats only because the manager asked army officers to relinquish their box. When Lincoln requested the names of the officers, the manager said he did not know them because half of them were absent without leave and he did not want to cause trouble for them. At times, paroled Confederate officers walked the streets in their grey uniforms.

The once-quiet streets were crowded with traffic. Cavalry trotted along the thoroughfares, while artillery and quartermaster wagons churned up dust in dry weather and turned the streets into quagmires during inclement weather. Sloping streets sometimes became moving streams of mud, impregnated with litter and garbage.

Washington's five or six first-class gambling saloons and untold numbers of lesser quality establishments continued to be popular. Members of Congress and senior army officers were seen frequently at the faro and roulette tables of the first-class places. A *Chicago Tribune* reporter saw one of them lose $5,000 to $6,000 in a two-hour period one night in August 1862.

Madame Pauline Meyer's place of "agreeable damsels" at 14th Street and North Street was among the numerous institutions anchoring the lower end of the social ladder. Altercations with soldiers who lost watches and other such valuable at these pleasure palaces were not uncommon.

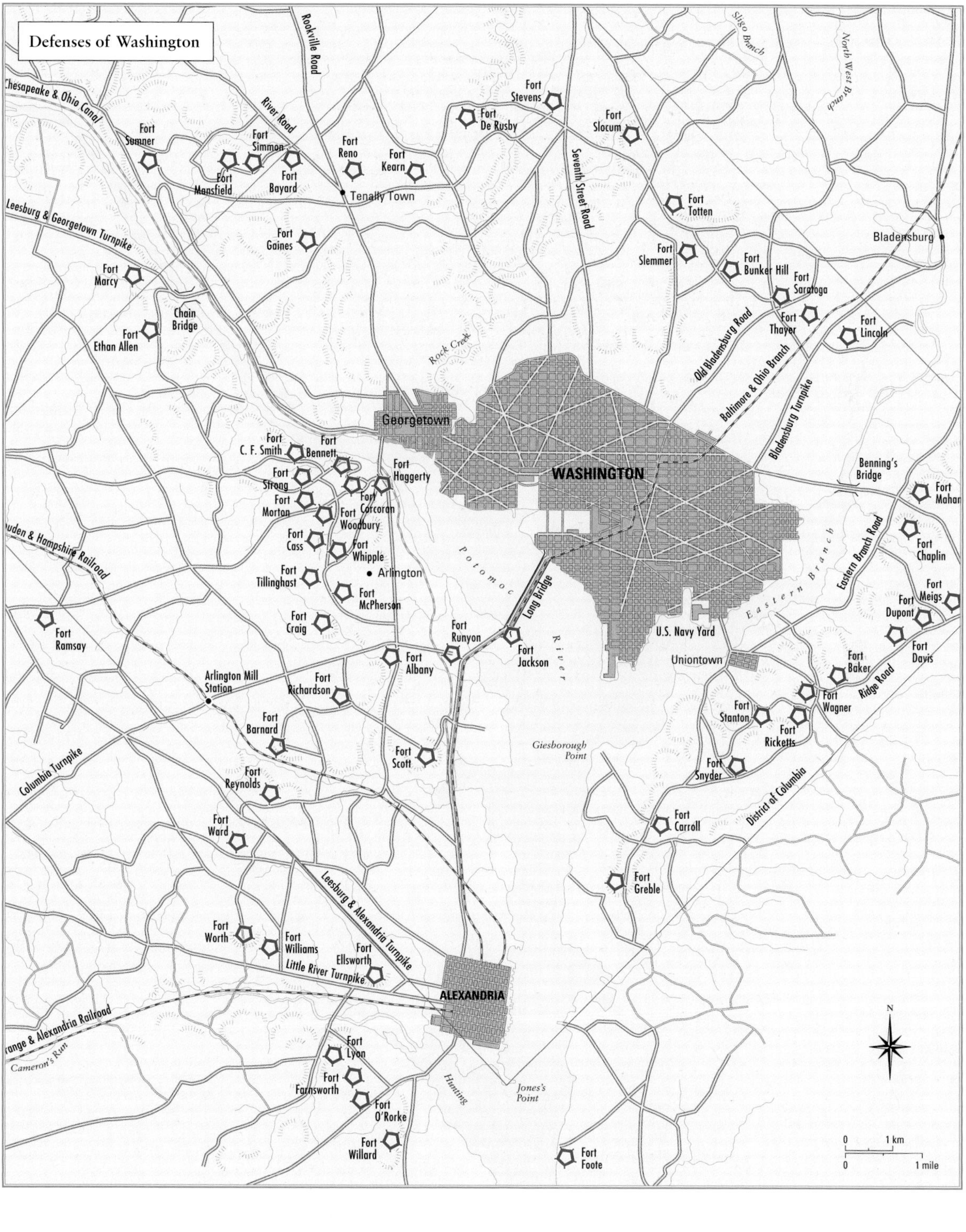

Defenses of Washington

Even the unopposed occupation of Alexandria and the heights across the Potomac in Virginia, which included the former home of Robert E. Lee, Arlington, did not occur peacefully. The first Union officer to die in the war was New York Colonel Elmer Ephraim Ellsworth, who was shot by the proprietor when he charged into an Alexandria hotel to rip down a secessionist banner. It was a sign of the temperament of the times, and a prelude to the bloodletting as yet unanticipated. Alexandria was not integrated into the life of Washington, and passes were required to go back and forth.

In the period immediately following the defeat at First Manassas, near panic gripped Washington. Some newcomers departed and others made plans for a rapid retreat. The fear subsided as Confederates made no move to capture the city and the number of Union troops filling new earth and log forts grew.

Boarding houses and hotels were packed by government workers, businessmen seeking government contracts, relatives of soldiers and refugees. Citizens were called on for various kinds of support, from donating money to conserving water during times of drought.

Drinking houses posed a problem at times, especially during periods of tension. In September 1862, the military governor of Washington ordered the closure of all saloons because recent fighting had caused an 'unsettled state' in the population.

Excursions beyond the limits of the District of Columbia were not allowed and those who violated the ban were picked up and detained by military authorities—even a family on a picnic to the Prince George side of the Anacostia found themselves in trouble.

Right: Mary Surratt, George Atzerodt, Lewis Powell and David Herold were executed after being convicted of plotting to assassinate President Lincoln. They were hanged July 7, 1865, at Fort McNair, Washington D.C.

Above: Portraint of Mrs. Rose O'Neal Greenhow, a notable Confederate spy who passed on secret messages containing crucial information about the Battle of Bull Run and was eventually imprisoned. She is pictured above with her youngest daughter, also named Rose.

Sick and wounded from the battlefields poured into Washington throughout the war. The arrival at Sixth Street dock in May 1862 of the steamer Louisiana with 213 sick soldiers from the Peninsular Campaign brought the number of convalescents sent to Washington from the front to about 1,600. Some were dying of "consumption." In a few instances, the nearest relatives were on hand to greet them. The *Washington Star* noted that only the sick had been sent to Washington's hospitals; the wounded had been sent by boat to other Northern cities.

Washington had 21 hospitals to treat wounded soldiers, some of them located in the Patent Office, churches and public halls. Wounded by the hundreds came by train and boat from savage battles such as Fredericksburg and Chancellorsville in Virginia. The walking wounded, bandaged, disheveled and blackened with gunpowder smoke, often had to fend for themselves until they reached a hospital. They were "so faint and longing for rest" that their plight softened the heart of a veteran newspaper reporter. On occasion, doctors were brought into the city from the nearby States of Pennsylvania, Maryland and Delaware in order to tend the sick and wounded.

Soldiers discharged from the hospitals were sent to Camp Convalescent in Alexandria, where deplorable conditions existed. Some of the 10,000 men often billeted there, including numerous stragglers, had to sleep in tents, even in winter.

Washington was the centre of Southern spying. Security was lax during the Civil War period and military plans often were common knowledge well before they were executed. The society salons of the capital were fertile grounds for intelligence gathering and female spies of the Confederacy were especially effective in this work.

Mrs. Rose O'Neal Greenhow headed one of the numerous Confederate espionage groups in Washington. Her activities, including the information she provided on the Union plans at First Manassas, led to her arrest and brief imprisonment in the Old Capital Prison in Washington before being deported to the South. The famous Belle Boyd was imprisoned for a time at the Old Capital.

The capital was gripped by an uneasiness and a "morbid sensationalism" that saw spies where there were none. The staid Smithsonian Institution came under suspicion of sending signals to the Confederacy because it burned lights late at nights. An amused Lincoln, who was entertaining its director, Dr. Joseph Henry, when an informant came to him with the accusation, turned to the director and asked for an explanation. Weather instruments measuring wind speed, temperature and other data are checked at certain times every day, replied Dr. Henry.

The possibility of assassination was a continuing concern. Even Lincoln got the jitters at times. When Noah Brooks, a newspaper reporter and a friend of the president, reported seeing flitting shadows behind trees during night walks, Lincoln began carrying a heavy cane. But even on expeditions to the front, he traveled without bodyguards. "If anybody wants to kill me," Lincoln said prophetically, "he will do it."

Holidays were generally festive and usually were used by the government to whip up patriotic fervor. The Washington's Birthday celebration in February 1862 featured the ringing of bells and firing of salutes from the navy yard and arsenal and the guns of fortifications around Washington. The Stars and Stripes was displayed from all public buildings and many private residences, and the city was partially illuminated.

WARFARE WITH THE INDIANS

THE CONFEDERATE THREAT TO THE TERRITORY WAS EFFECTIVELY OVER, BUT THE FIGHTING WAS JUST BEGINNING FOR THE CALIFORNIA AND COLORADO VOLUNTEERS. WARFARE WITH THE INDIANS OF THE REGION WAS FREQUENT AND BECAME VERY SAVAGE. MEN WHO LAMENTED HAVING TO DESTROY HORSES THEY COULD NOT TAKE WITH THEM WILLINGLY KILLED INDIANS. LOG FORTS CONTINUED TO SPROUT ALONG THE ESTABLISHED TRAILS IN AN EFFORT TO PROTECT SETTLERS AND TRADERS, BUT THE CAMPAIGNS CONDUCTED BY COLONEL CHRISTOPHER "KIT" CARSON WERE MORE EFFECTIVE IN FORCING THE INDIANS ONTO THE BOSQUE REDONDO RESERVATION.

Above: Christopher Kit Carson (1809–1868) was a frontiersman, fur trapper and guide for renowned explorer John C. Frémont.

Opposite page: Map depicting the Indian Territories.

Carson's campaign against the Apaches in 1862 and the Navahos in 1863-4 were typical. His tactic was to maintain pressure on the Indians by a series of encircling maneuvers that resulted in small engagements and kept the Indians from uniting. Canyon de Chelly National Monument near Gallup, New Mexico, preserves the Navaho stronghold Carson invaded in an effort to break their resistance. Indian guides lead visitors through the rugged, 35-mile long canyon whose walls rise 1,000 feet in places. An attempt to arrest Cochise and his followers resulted in a substantial fight on July 16, 1862, between the Apaches and a detachment of California Volunteers. It was a Hollywood style battle, with the Indians attacking and withdrawing, then ambushing the soldiers from the high ground in the pass. The Indians lost, and were permanently denied one of their favorite haunts by the erecting of Fort Bowie, which continued active until 1894.

The flag in the plaza at Taos flies 24 hours a day because of an incident that occurred during the Civil War. Carson had the Stars and Stripes nailed to the flagpole and set a guard to prevent

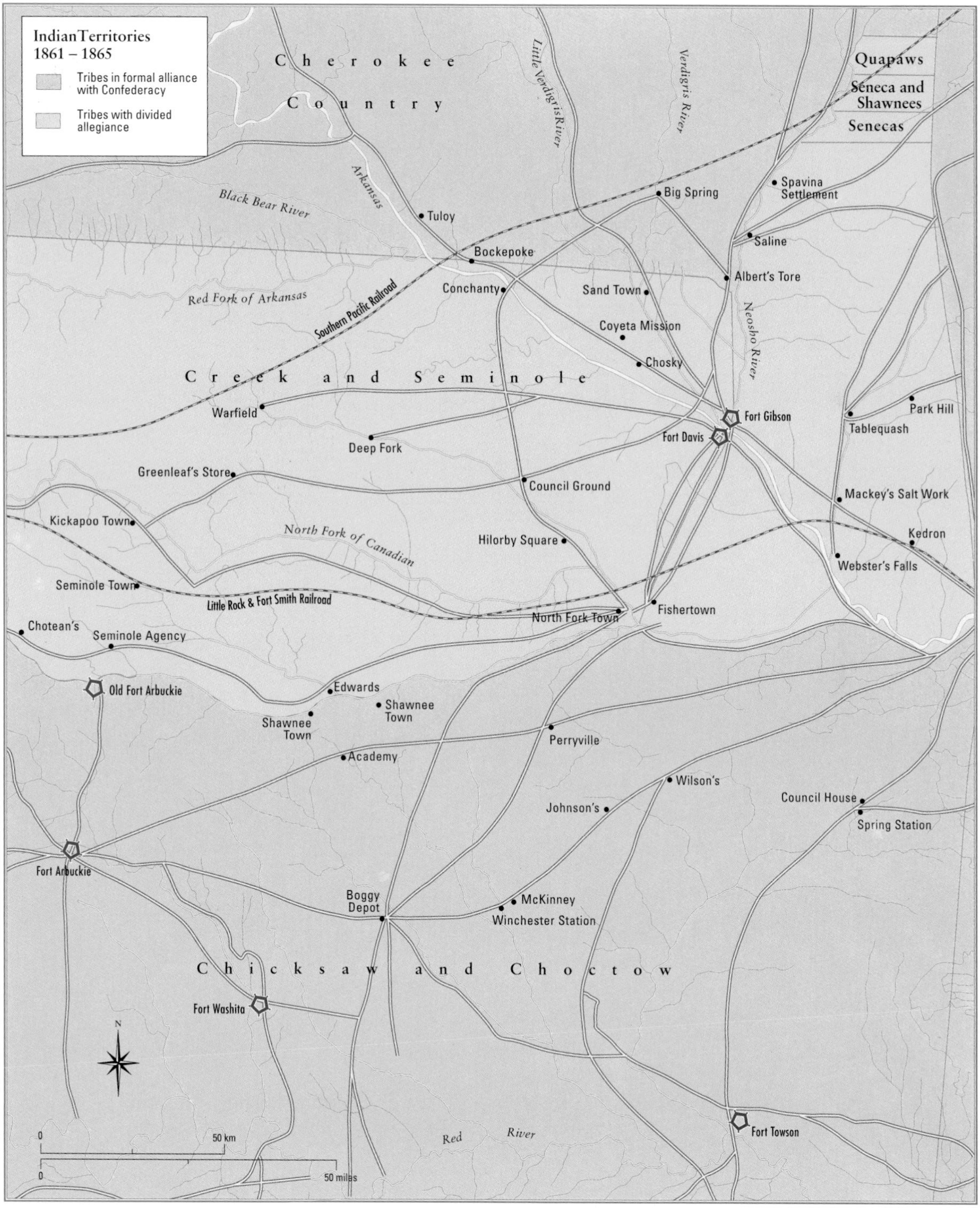

IndianTerritories
1861 – 1865
Tribes in formal alliance with Confederacy
Tribes with divided allegiance
Cherokee Country
Creek and Seminole
Chicksaw and Choctow
Quapaws
Seneca and Shawnees
Senecas
Little Verdigris River
Verdigris River
Neosho River
Arkansas
Black Bear River
Red Fork of Arkansas
North Fork of Canadian
Red River
Southern Pacific Railroad
Little Rock & Fort Smith Railroad
Tuloy
Bockepoke
Conchanty
Big Spring
Spavina Settlement
Saline
Albert's Tore
Sand Town
Coyeta Mission
Chosky
Fort Gibson
Fort Davis
Park Hill
Tablequash
Warfield
Deep Fork
Greenleaf's Store
Council Ground
Mackey's Salt Work
Kickapoo Town
Hilorby Square
Kedron
Webster's Falls
Seminole Town
North Fork Town
Fishertown
Chotean's
Seminole Agency
Old Fort Arbuckie
Edwards
Shawnee Town
Shawnee Town
Perryville
Academy
Wilson's
Johnson's
Council House
Spring Station
Fort Arbuckie
Boggy Depot
McKinney
Winchester Station
Fort Washita
N
Fort Towson
0
50 km
0
50 miles

Right: An American Indian Sioux holy man, Sitting Bull.

Below: Indian Delegates outside the White House. The conflict between whites triggered various Indian uprisings.

it from being taken down. The Kit Carson Museum, a half-block from the plaza, retains numerous mementoes of the famous fighter of the Indians.

Both North and South were accused of fomenting Indian uprisings, but neither government condoned such action, nor did regular forces in the field encourage Indian violence. However, the sight of whites fighting each other was a psychological stimulant to the Indians, and the Civil War divided many Indian tribes in much the same manner as it split white families and clans in the border states. Many Indians saw the white division as an opportunity to reverse the invasion of settlers and opportunists, and periodic uprisings troubled both frontier settlers and the contesting armies. Others counselled peace as a means of retaining the economic gains they had made under a sedentary way of life; for example many well to do Indians owned slaves. Both the Confederates and the Federals recruited Indian soldiers into their regular forces.

Indian conflict was periodic, but it ranged all the way from Minnesota to the New Mexico Territory and even involved the Five Civilised Tribes in Indian Territory, now the state of Oklahoma. The small, intense battles were only vaguely related to the Civil War and more properly should be regarded as portent of the fitful warring that would persist almost to the end of the century as Indian resistance to continued settlement mounted. A number of the conflicts between Indians are included in tabulations of Civil War battles, however, few of the sites have been developed to receive visitors.

The most destructive Indian uprising during the Civil War, and certainly one of the most publicized in the press, was the insurrection of the Sioux in Minnesota in August of 1862. The tribe had signed away its lands in Eastern Minnesota in 1851 in exchange for annual payments and a guaranteed one million acre reserved for their use, but many of the tribe members had been unhappy with the arrangement and the payments were frequently late. Traders took advantage of the financial naivety of the Indians to keep them in debt, and some debt claims were simply fraudulent. The Indians resented white attempts to Christianize them and turn them into farmers. The situation was ripe for violence, but it did not actually begin until some young braves taunted another, saying he was afraid of white men. To show his peers that he wasn't, he shot dead a farmer near Acton, and his taunters followed up by killing four others, including a woman and girl. They fled to the reservation, where their story divided the tribe into two groups, one wanting to surrender the braves and take the consequences and the other willing to take to the warpath. The Indians, apparently following a preconceived plan of driving all whites back across the Mississippi River, attacked some well-defended areas, including Fort Ridgely and New Ulm, where at least a third of the town was destroyed. Some Winnebagos joined the uprising, producing fear of a general Indian insurrection which did not materialise. However, the Sioux rampage was one of the worst massacres in American history, killing at least 800 and driving thousands from their farms and settlements to the safety of St. Paul and Fort Ridgely.

New Ulm preserves a number of relics from the period, including the Frederick. W. Kiesling building on North Minnesota Street (now the offices of the Chamber of Commerce); it was filled with hay so it could be burned to provide light for defence if needed.

Below: This is a portrait of Stand Watie (1806-1871). A three-quarter Cherokee, he lead the Cherokees who allied themselves with the Confederates. At the end of the war he held the rank of brigadier-general in the Confederate army.

Opposite page: A portrait of Christopher "Kit" Carson (1809-1868), who was a military scout and Indian agent *(top)*. During the battle against Mexico at San Pascual, he crawled through enemy lines and got help for the U.S. troops in San Diego. A photograph of a group of Indian tribal chiefs and their white equivalents in the background, during the Civil War *(bottom)*.

Right: A map displaying the numerous Indian Wars in the West between 1850-1900.

Below: An illustration from circa 1850 of Chief Little Crow (1803–1863). Chief Little Crow was a Santee Sioux chief who resisted his tribe's opposition to the settlers for a while before eventually joining them in their raids. He later fled to Canada but returned and was killed by a band of white hunters.

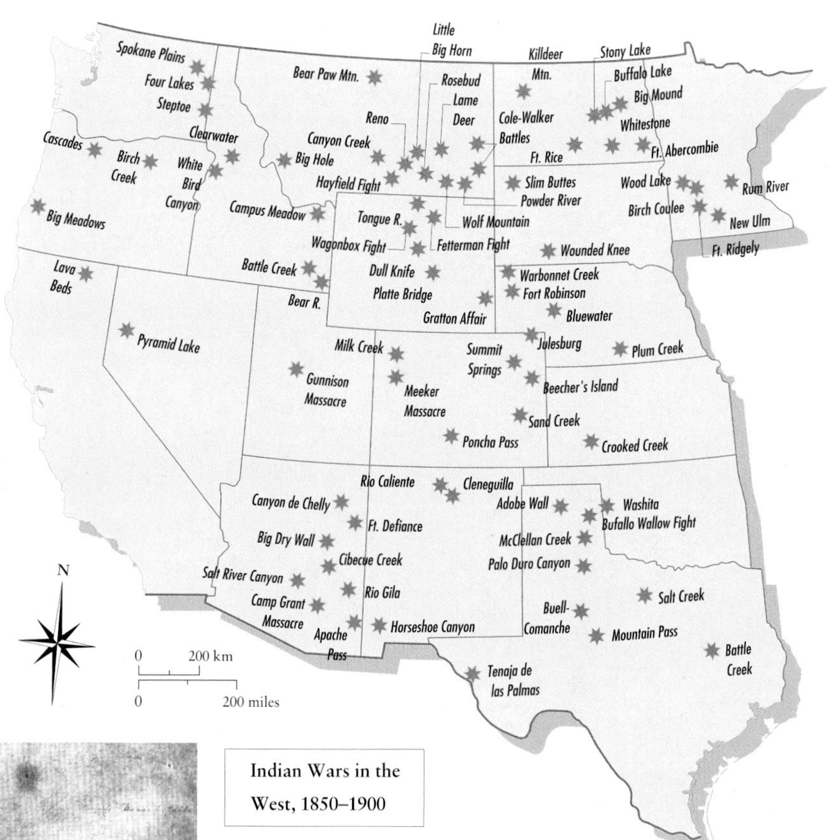

Indian Wars in the West, 1850–1900

Women and children took refuge in the Frank Erd building (part of the original remains). The Frederick Forster building —which along with the Henry Schalk building was a principal defensive point during the uprising —has been altered but retains original features. The ruins of Wajaru Distillery and displays and paintings in the Brown County Historical Museum, together with the Defenders Monument erected by the State of Minnesota in 1891, also recall the heroic defence of the City by its citizens. Fort Ridgely, about 20 miles from New Ulm, has been partly restored and has an interpretive centre. Although the area north of the Minnesota River was most affected, the side-effects extended beyond the Iowa border and into the Dakota Territory. The uprising was broken by a campaign conducted by Brigadier General Henry Hastings Sibley, a former governor, who had lived and traded with the Sioux for 28 years and thus knew them well.

The Battle of Wood Lake on September 23, was actually an Indian ambush that was accidentally discovered. It raged for two hours and included close combat. The rout of the 500 strengthened the hand of the Indians who opposed the warpath, and the warring faction began to dwindle as Sibley pushed up the Minnesota River Valley. War parties continued to operate under Little Crow, the nominal leader of the uprising, but gradually the Indians returned to the reservation.

Little Crow was soon after killed in the fighting, but 306 of the leaders of the uprising were convicted and given the death penalty. President Lincoln noting that the evidence against most of them was unconvincing commuted the sentences of all but 38; who were hanged in a mass execution at Mankato on December 26, 1862.

THE CAMPAIGNS OF 1863

THE SECOND FULL YEAR OF THE CIVIL WAR WAS MUCH LIKE THE FIRST. BOTH SIDES SUFFERED DAMAGING DEFEATS AND WON NO LESS COSTLY VICTORIES, AT THE END OF WHICH THEY LACKED STRENGTH AND WILL TO DRIVE HOME AN ADVANTAGE GAINED. YET THE TREND CONTINUED TO BE TOWARD THE UNION GAINING THE UPPER HAND.

The year began with the Emancipation Proclamation, by which Lincoln changed the Civil War from an acrimonious internecine dispute into a revolutionary struggle. The Proclamation was, among other things, a rallying call to enslaved African Americans in the South, who knew that if they defected to the Federal forces they would be free.

In May 1863, Lee launched a surprise three-pronged attack on Union forces in eastern Virginia at the Battle of Chancellorsville. He drove the enemy back across the Rappahannock River but this was the Confederates' most costly victory; among their dead was General Thomas Jackson.

In the following month, Union commander Ulysses S. Grant besieged Vicksburg, the heavily fortified city on the Mississippi River that had held out doggedly against previous assaults. Six weeks later, the garrison surrendered and, with the capture shortly afterward of Port Hudson, Louisiana, the whole of the Mississippi River was now under Federal control.

As a result of the Vicksburg Campaign, the Confederacy was split into two parts. Lee's response to his side's deteriorating situation was to take the war to the enemy. He marched north, defeating Union forces at Winchester, Virginia, and then pushed on into Pennsylvania, where by chance his men encountered those of General George Meade at Gettysburg in July. The ensuing battle ended in a crushing victory for the Union, but Lee was left to withdraw his forces to Virginia.

Although the tide had turned in favor of the North, there were further setbacks in store. One of the biggest came in September at the Battle of Chickamauga which threw the Northern army back to Chattanooga. There the Union consolidated its position despite being ringed by Southern forces, and iin a November battle forced the Confederate troops to withdraw into Georgia. This victory set the stage for Union General William S. Sherman's decisive Atlanta Campaign the following year.

Opposite page: A map displaying the various campaigns of 1863. Note the larger number of Union battle victories, compared with fewer Confederate wins.

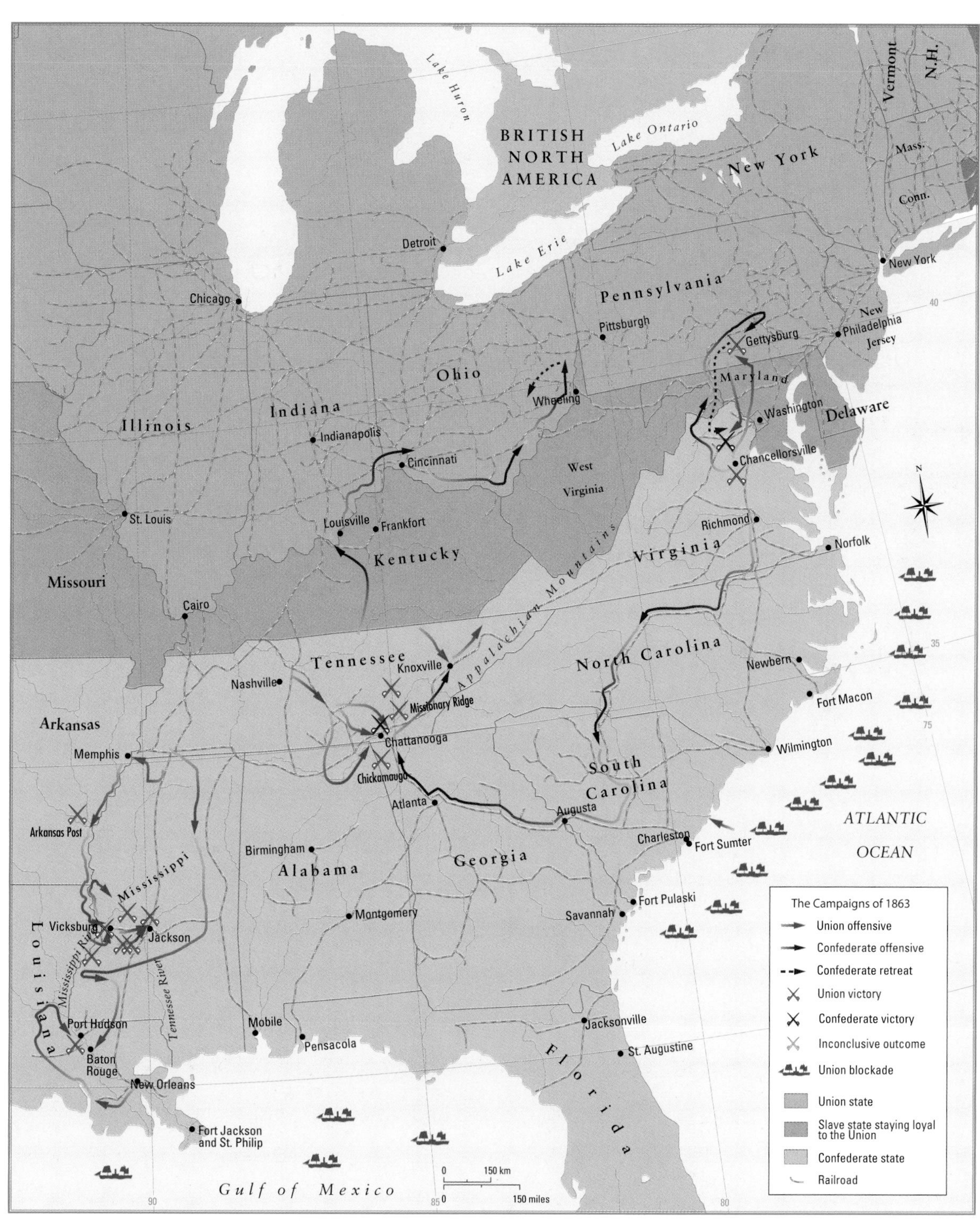

Lake Huron
BRITISH NORTH AMERICA
Lake Ontario
New York
Vermont
N.H.
Mass.
Conn.
Lake Erie
Detroit
New York
Chicago
Pennsylvania
Pittsburgh
New Jersey
Philadelphia
Gettysburg
Maryland
Ohio
Wheeling
Washington
Delaware
Illinois
Indiana
Indianapolis
Cincinnati
Chancellorsville
West Virginia
St. Louis
Louisville
Frankfort
Richmond
Kentucky
Virginia
Norfolk
Missouri
Appalachian Mountains
Cairo
North Carolina
Tennessee
Knoxville
Newbern
Nashville
Missionary Ridge
Fort Macon
Arkansas
Chattanooga
Memphis
Wilmington
Chickamauga
South Carolina
Atlanta
Augusta
Arkansas Post
ATLANTIC OCEAN
Charleston
Fort Sumter
Birmingham
Mississippi
Alabama
Georgia
Fort Pulaski
Montgomery
Savannah
Vicksburg
Jackson
Mississippi River
Tennessee River
Louisiana
Port Hudson
Mobile
Jacksonville
Pensacola
Florida
St. Augustine
Baton Rouge
New Orleans
Fort Jackson and St. Philip
Gulf of Mexico
0 150 km
0 150 miles
90
85
80
75
40
35
N
The Campaigns of 1863
Union offensive
Confederate offensive
Confederate retreat
Union victory
Confederate victory
Inconclusive outcome
Union blockade
Union state
Slave state staying loyal to the Union
Confederate state
Railroad

Vicksburg and Port Hudson

As the war went on, Union activities in Louisiana were designed as much to obtain cotton for the mills of New England, where unemployed workers were becoming restless, and to enrol slaves as workers and soldiers, as they were to engage the Confederates or capture territory.

Confederate forces also spent considerable time living off the land and trying to block Union access to farm products. Nevertheless, sizable battles were fought at Baton Rouge, Vicksburg, Port Hudson, and elsewhere as Union troops pressed deeper into the State, ultimately gaining control of the Mississippi and its tributary, the Red River, thereby inflicting a devasating psychological blow against their opponents.

The fighting for Baton Rouge, which preceded the more intensely fought campaigns for Vicksburg and Port Hudson, and which would result in the devastation of the capital, began innocuously enough with a load of dirty laundry. Guerillas in hiding launched a suprise attack against a laundry boat. In response, a group of citizens rowed to the ships to apologize and explained that they could not control the guerrillas, Farragut agreed not to bombard the city again unless attacked. The next day an occupying force was in the city.

The next fighting was much more serious. On August 5, 1862, Confederate troops led by Major General John C. Breckinridge, a former Vice President of the United States, attacked the camps of the occupying army under cover of morning fog, driving some units in confusion back into the streets of the city. Stiff Federal resistance, and mysterious orders to Confederate units to halt their attacks and fall back, slowed the attack elsewhere. In the river, the Confederate ironclad ram *Arkansas*, which was supposed to support the attack had broken down, and so Union warships were able to supplement Union artillery and provide a sanctuary within the city for defeated units. Breckinridge called off the attack when he learned the *Arkansas* was lost and pulled back to Port Hudson, one of the strongest points on the river.

Opposite page: A Union Navy fleet attacking Confederate batteries at Port Hudson, Louisiana. They were under the command of Admiral David Farragut. This important Federal victory secured their control of the Mississippi River and severed the Confederacy from important states such as Texas and Arkansas.

Breckinridge's attack achieved indirectly what it could not do directly; it caused such concern

about a Confederate attack on New Orleans that General Butler evacuated Baton Rouge to concentrate his forces. Departing troops—in contrast to the disciplined manner in which they had conducted the occupation prior to the battle—plundered and defaced the city.

The Battle of Baton Rouge Monument and a smaller marker on the grounds of the Dufroca School commemorate the battle. A 34-story capitol building has now replaced the turreted structure as the seat of State government. Burned by Union soldiers during their second occupation of the city, the Old Capitol has been restored and operates as a museum and tourist information centre. The Old Arsenal, where strong entrenchments were built by Union engineers against the possibility of another attack, is also a museum.

Following their failure to re-take Baton Rouge, the Confederate forces concentrated instead on holding the fortresses at Vicksburg and Port Hudson. So long as these remained in Confederate hands, so would control of the Mississippi. Vicksburg was key to this control, and, in Union President Abraham Lincoln's view, the war could "never be brought to a close until that key is in our pocket." Pocketing the key would require heavy casualties and inflict untold hardships—but in reality the fate of Vicksburg was decided before the siege began. Indecisiveness, conflicting orders, an appalling lack of intelligence information, and bad judgment enabled Grant to ravage Vicksburg's natural support areas and invade the town from its vulnerable rear.

The fall of Vicksburg began with a fortress mentality, as Confederate Lieutenant General John

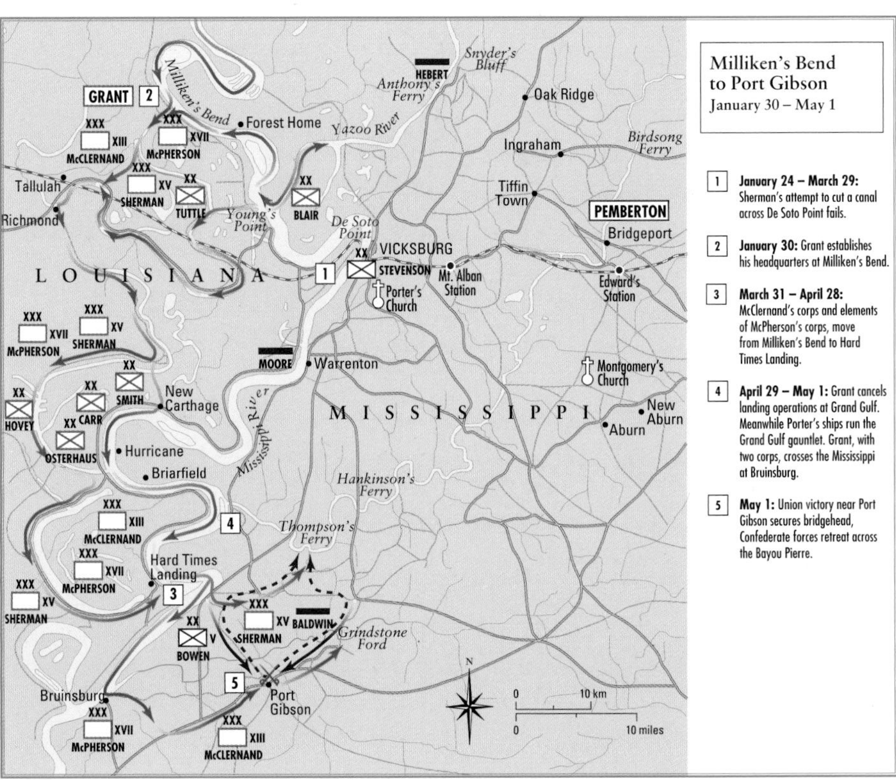

Right: May 1, 1863 saw the culmination of the Vicksburg Campaign at Port Gibson, in the Battle of Port Gibson. This campaign, lead by Union leader Major General Grant, began at Milliken's Bend, situated on the west side of the Mississippi River. Union victory was obtained at the expense of mor than 600 casualties and losses on both sides.

Left: Ships of the Union Navy bombarding Port Hudson.

C. Pemberton demanded reinforcements but did not appreciate the necessity of an active defence; it was abetted by division of forces at a time when concentration might have destroyed Grant's army; and it was confirmed by belated efforts, with inadequate forces, to rectify earlier mistakes.

The first attempts of General Ulysses S. Grant to capture Vicksburg from the north were dismal failures, largely because of impossible terrain. He then spent thousands of man-hours in futile attempts to dig canals through the marshes on the Louisiana side of the Mississippi River in an effort to avoid the well-situated Confederate guns on the heights above the river at Vicksburg. He finally decided to divide his forces and attack the city from the south and east. Confederate General Joseph E. Johnston ordered Pemberton to concentrate his forces and strike at Grant.

"If Grant's army lands on this side of the river, the safety of Mississippi depends on beating it," Johnston wired Pemberton. "For that object you should unite your whole forces." This good advice went unheeded, and Johnston tried again with a similar order, adding, "success will give you back what you abandoned to win it." But Pemberton had orders from Jefferson Davis to hold Vicksburg, and he sent inadequate forces to stop Grant.

While Grant moved his forces southward on the Louisiana shore of the Mississippi, Colonel B. H. Grierson created a spectacular diversion by leading one of the most famous raids of the war through the heart of Mississippi to Baton Rouge. The 17-day raid proved hugely successful, destroying railroads and military targets and evading Confederate pursuers along a 800-mile route.

Grand Gulf Military Monument, ten miles northwest of Port Gibson off U.S. Route 61, preserves the site of a successful attempt on April 29, 1863, to stop Grant from crossing to the east side of the river. The Civil War left Grand Gulf a virtual ghost town, and it was not until 1862 that

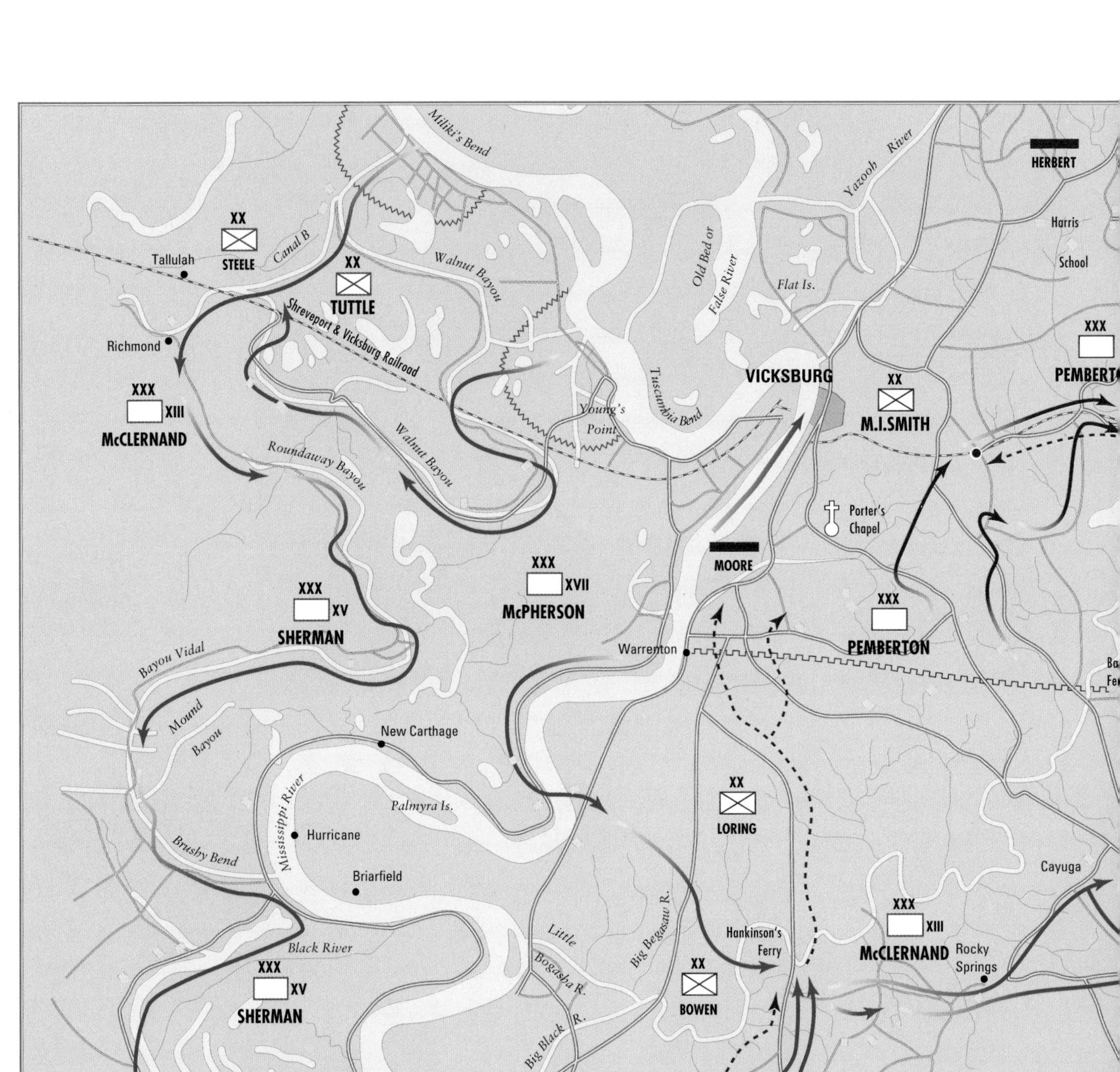

Miliki's Bend
Yazoob River
HERBERT
Harris
School
XX
STEELE
Canal B
Tallulah
XX
TUTTLE
Walnut Bayou
Old Bed or False River
Flat Is.
Shreveport & Vicksburg Railroad
Richmond
XXX
XIII
McCLERNAND
VICKSBURG
XX
M.I.SMITH
XXX
PEMBERT
Tuscumbia Bend
Young's Point
Roundaway Bayou
Walnut Bayou
Porter's Chapel
MOORE
XXX
XVII
McPHERSON
XXX
XV
SHERMAN
XXX
PEMBERTON
Warrenton
Bayou Vidal
Mound Bayou
New Carthage
XX
LORING
Palmyra Is.
Mississippi River
Hurricane
Briarfield
Brushy Bend
Cayuga
Big Begasaw R.
Little Bogasba R.
Hankinson's Ferry
XXX
XIII
McCLERNAND
Rocky Springs
Black River
XXX
XV
SHERMAN
XX
BOWEN
Big Black R.
Hard Times Landing
Coffey's Is.
Grand Gulf
Disharoon
N.Fork Bayou Pierre
Grindstone's Ford
Bayou Pierre
M I S
Port Gibson
Bruinsburg
GRANT

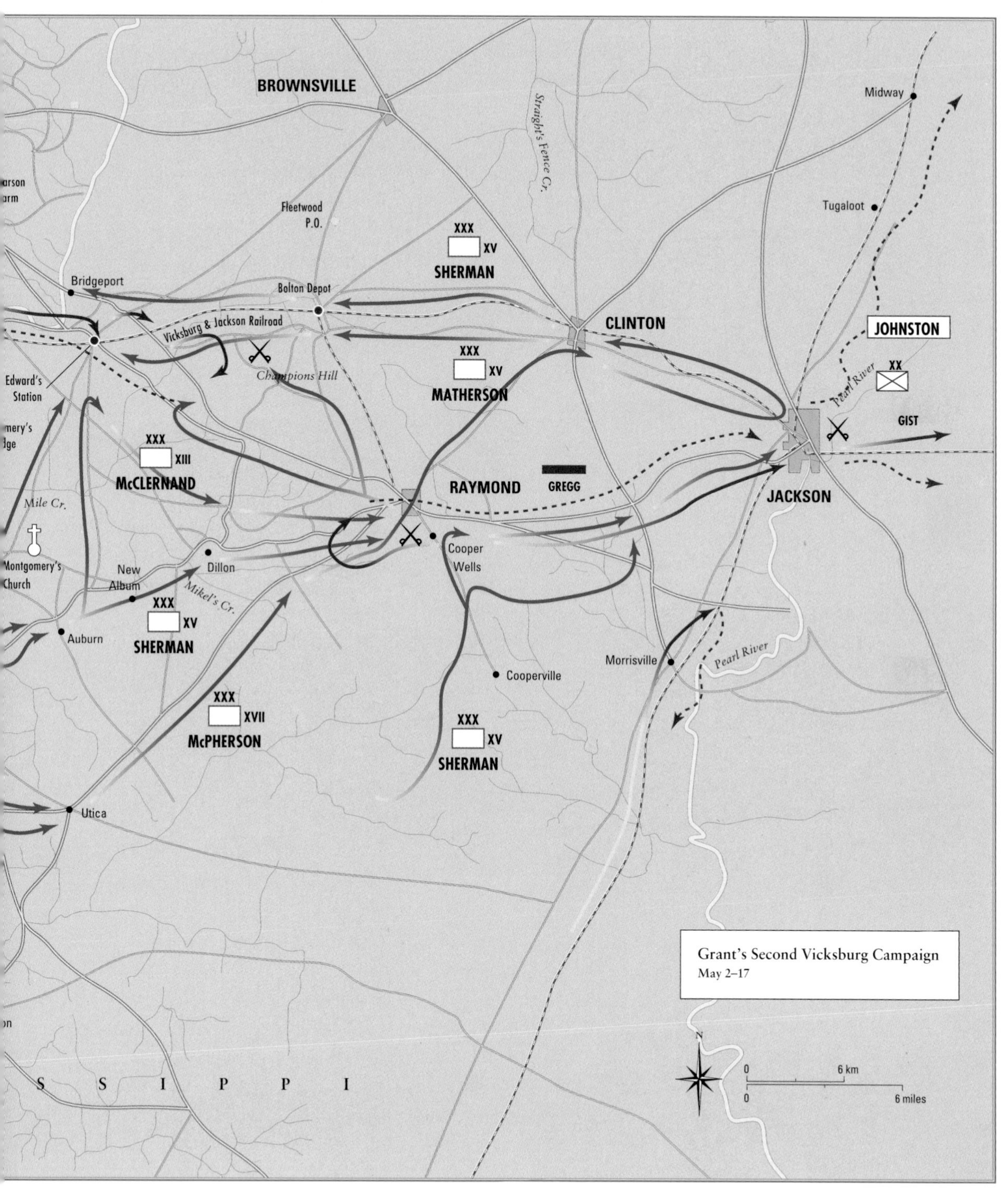

Grant's Second Vicksburg Campaign
May 2–17

Previous page: A detailed map showing Grant's second campaign to capture Vicksburg from May 2–17, 1863.

the importance of the strategic location was recognised by the dedication of the memorial park. Exhibits and relics, including remnants of Fort Coburn and Fort Wade, trace the fighting at Grand Gulf, where the Union suffered heavy losses without dislodging defenders under Brigadier General John S. Bowen. Photographs, maps, scale models, uniforms, muskets, cannonballs, and artefacts recovered in the area are displayed in a museum. Authentic buildings from the region include a frame church and a water mill. Hiking trails and an observation tower, from which mills of the Mississippi River are visible, provide an overview of the battle area.

Grant responded to the stalwart defense of Grand Gulf by moving farther south and attacking Port Gibson, where an outnumbered brigade could not stop his advance. The Shaffer House near Port Gibson, built about 1840, survived the fighting, but Port Gibson's best-known structure is the 1859 Presbyterian church, whose steeple top is a gilded hand pointing toward heaven. Confederate Major General Earl Van Dorn is buried in Wintergreen Cemetery, facing south, along with both Confederate and Union casualties from the Battle of Port Gibson. Other antebellum structures include St. Joseph's Roman Catholic Church of 1849, the 1860 Methodist Church, 1833 Idlewild mansion, 1811 Miss Phoebe's and the Disharoon House, raised in the 1830s and known for its unusual staircase and chandeliers from the steamboat Robert E. Lee. Of the plantation house at Windsor, 12 miles southwest of Port Gibson on Mississippi Route 552, only the handsome columns remain. It was not destroyed in the war, though the plantation house was used as an observation post by the Rebels and as a hospital by the Union; it survived the war only to burn in 1890.

The Battle of Raymond, now listed as a stop along the scenic Natchez Trace Parkway that connects many Mississippi Civil War sites, was an example of how Pemberton sent inadequate forces to confront Grant and how effective the Southern philosophy of attack could be. In the smoke and dust that enveloped the battlefield on May 12, a Confederate brigade stymied an entire Union corps for half a day by repeated attacks. In the end, the greater numbers prevailed and the first Federals into Raymond, the 20th Ohio, sat down to a picnic which the ladies of the town had prepared in anticipation of a Confederate victory.

As Grant marched to destroy Jackson (where the 1857 Manship House, 1846 the Oaks and 1842 Governor's Mansion are among the few buildings to survive), Pemberton missed an opportunity to catch him between two armies and perhaps destroy him. When he finally confronted Grant at Champion Hill and Big Black River, it was a case of too little, too late. Rowen's slashing attack over the rugged terrain at Champion Hill during the May 16 battle bent but could not break Grant's line. Pemberton held the bridges at the Big Black until it was obvious his rear guard had been cut off, then retreated inside his strong fortifications at Vicksburg.

Grant at first demanded unconditional surrender of Pemberton, but decided to soften the terms after Pemberton refused to accept such harsh conditions. At 10 a.m. on July 4—Independence Day—Vicksburg was formally surrendered by Confederates stacking arms and relinquishing colors. Five days later, when Port Hudson surrendered and the Confederacy was divided, Lincoln could proclaim that "the Father of Waters again goes unvexed to the sea."

Lincoln's comment about the importance of control of the Mississippi was justified recognition of the important role of naval power on the rivers in the Western Theatre, which has been

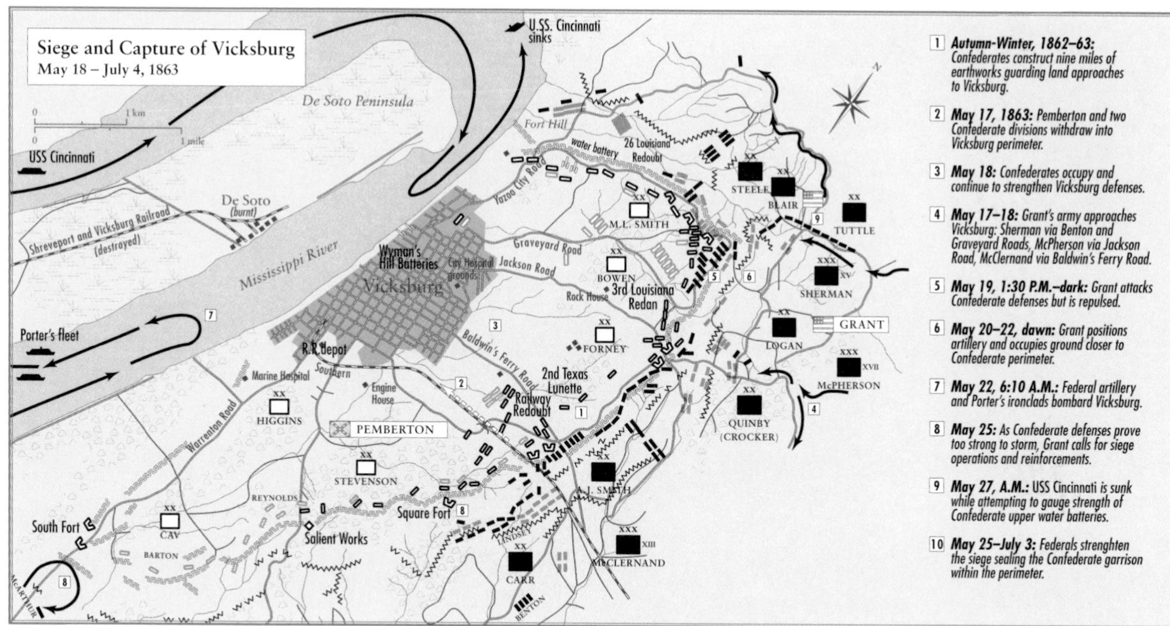

Above: Detailed map of the siege and capture of the city of Vicksburg. An exciting vicotry for Major General Grant. His army crossed the Mississippi River, coercively driving back the Confederates to protect Vicksburg. Confederate forces were soon breached and forced to yield control of the Mississsppi River to the Federal Army.

inadequately covered in memorials because so few relics remain. At long last, that aspect of the war is explored in a museum at Vicksburg national park which includes a partial reconstruction of the gunboat USS *Cairo*, incorporating a 15-ton section of the bow and other artefacts recovered from the bottom of the river. The life of the sailors is shown through personal effects and weapons, such recovered equipment as mess gear and ship fittings, and photographs of Mississippi warships and their crews. Other displays relate the sinking of the US Cairo in 12 minutes—without loss of a single life—and the modern tale of how the parts were located and recovered.

The river war was an important adjunct of the land war. "Tinclads," or lightly armored shallow-draft ships, were the backbone of the Union navy's campaign to control the Mississippi River. They were especially important in bypassing Vicksburg, as well as other fortified river cities. These "turtles" also operated on small rivers. By far the greatest number of warships was engaged in this unglamorous but necessary work.

"To hold both Vicksburg and Port Hudson is necessary to a connection with Trans-Mississippi," Jefferson Davis had said. As Grant closed in on Vicksburg, General Nathaniel Banks edged northward from New Orleans toward Port Hudson, albeit with great caution as an earlier foray against the fortress had proved extremely costly. In March, Admiral David Farragut had tried to sail a fleet of seven ships past the Port Hudson batteries, hoping to block the mouth of the Red River, an important tributary of the Mississippi, along which supplies continued to reach Port Hudson from the west. In the event, the Confederate guns pummelled the Union fleet, severely damaging four ships and even sinking one, the *USS Mississippi*. Still, two ships were able to get through to the Red River where they were able to disrupt the flow of supplies to the fortress.

Banks's campaign later in the year began with some 30,000 Union troops facing off against just

Opposite page: By capturing the Mississippi River, Union forces effectively divided the South and weakened its position. Outlook for the Confederates greatly deteriorated after the Battle of Gettysburg when they were forced to withdraw to Virginia.

6,800 Confederate soldiers holed up in Port Hudson under the command of Major General Franklin Gardner. Although Banks would ulimately prevail, it would require a 48-day siege, the longest in US history, and would see terrible Union losses incurred during two failed assaults.

Wishing to avoid a long, drawn-out campaign in the intense heat of a Louisiana summer, Banks ordered his troops to launch an assault on 27 May. Despite the Union army's vast numerical superiority, they were unable to overcome the Confederate defenders' stubborn resistance. They were also hampered by Banks' tactical approach, with the general ordering piecemeal attacks along the Port Hudson perimeter, rather than a large, sustained assault. When the fighting was over, there were 1,995 Union casualties to 235 Confederate ones.

The assault was nonetheless notable in that it saw the war's first major military contribution by black troops with the First and Third Louisiana Native Guards fighting alongside (and suffering just as severe casualties as) their white counterparts.

Banks continued the siege for another two weeks, and when his calls for a Confederate surrender went unheeded, he ordered another assault for June 14. If anything, this was to prove even less successful than the first with the Union forces suffering 1,792 casaulties, compared with just 47 on the Confederate side. Fatalities were greatly increased by the decision of General Banks not to allow a truce to tend to wounded Union soldiers. The stench of decaying bodies eventually became so great that a flag of truce was arranged by the Confederates so they could be removed. The loss of Union officers was particularly heavy. A Massachusetts soldier called the fate of the wounded 'martyrdom' and said the scene at a field hospital—"here a pile of booted legs, there a pile of arms"—was more trying than the horrors of the battlefield.

Despite their success at repulsing the Union attacks, the siege was taking a mounting toll on the defenders of Port Hudson who, since the fortress's supply lines had been cut, were reduced to eating mules, horses, and rats. Their readiness to survive a third Union assault, planned for July 11, was never put to the test. The mines that had been placed in tunnels dug beneath the Confederate fortress by Union troops were not exploded because, on July 7, news that Vicksburg had fallen reached Port Hudson. Realising that further sacrifice would be meaningless, General Gardner raised the white flag the next day.

Although the Union had paid a heavy price for its victory with 4,363 casualties, compared to Confederate losses of around a sixth of that number, the surrender of Port Hudson, plus the earlier defeat of Vicksburg, had a significant effect on the war's outcome. The Union now had their desired control of the entire Mississippi, from its source to the Gulf of Mexico, which dealt a crippling blow to the Confederates, preventing them from transporting much needed supplies, such as salt, cattle, and horses, from the west, and men and munitions from the east.

Today, in the Port Hudson State Commemorative Area, are four and a half miles of breastworks and redoubts, the physical reminders of one of the war's most intense conflicts. Of particular note are the earthworks at Fort Desperate, a Confederate strongpoint which won its name during some of the fiercest fighing. Other significant points include the Bull Pen, a triangle-shaped low area where Union attackers were caught in a crossfire, and Fort Babock, the most advanced position held by the Union forces, who pushed forward shielded behind cotton bales.

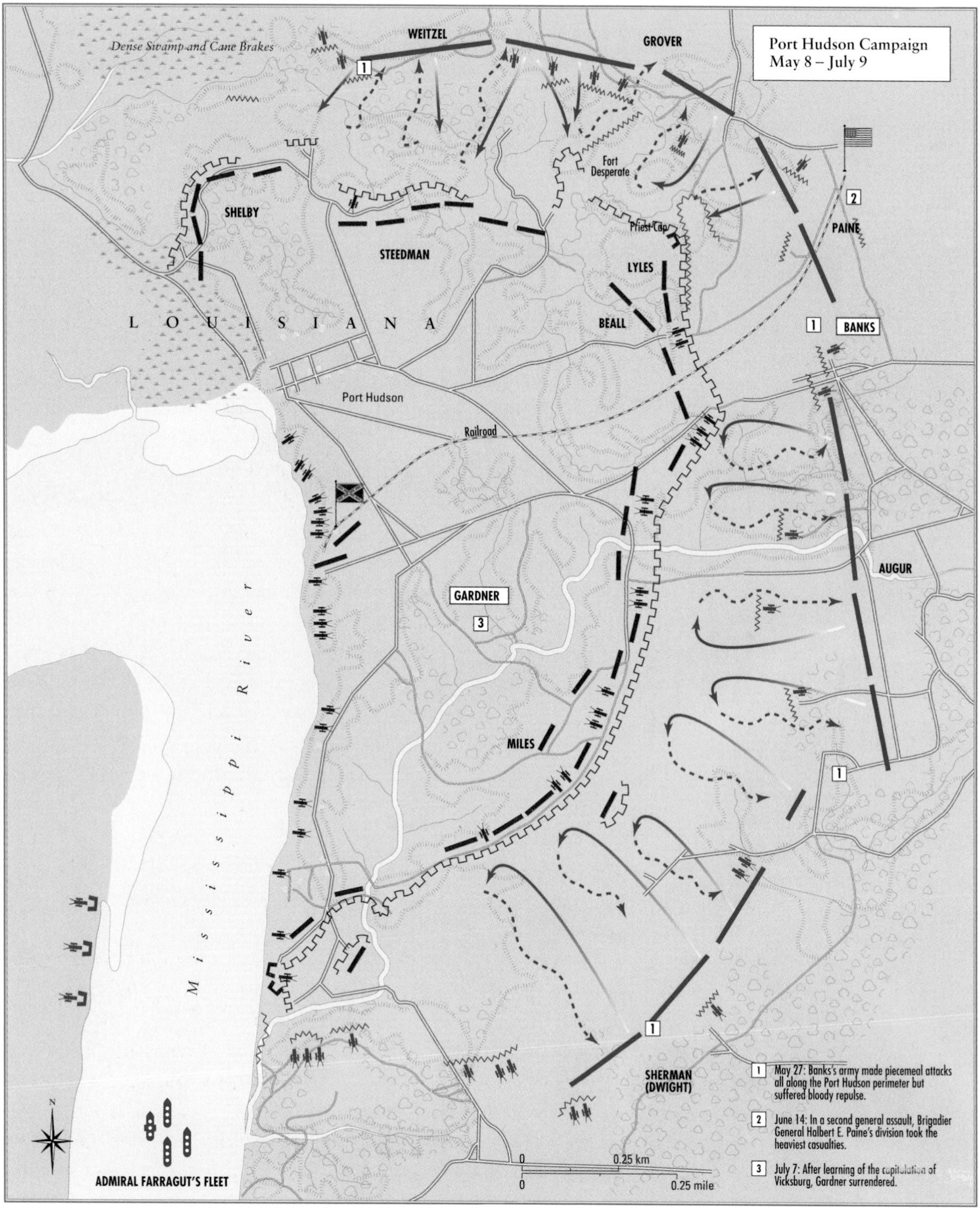

Port Hudson Campaign
May 8 – July 9
Dense Swamp and Cane Brakes
WEITZEL
GROVER
Fort Desperate
SHELBY
STEEDMAN
Priest Cap
LYLES
PAINE
BEALL
BANKS
L O U I S I A N A
Port Hudson
Railroad
AUGUR
GARDNER
MILES
Mississippi River
SHERMAN (DWIGHT)
ADMIRAL FARRAGUT'S FLEET
N
0 0.25 km
0 0.25 mile
1 May 27: Banks's army made piecemeal attacks all along the Port Hudson perimeter but suffered bloody repulse.
2 June 14: In a second general assault, Brigadier General Halbert E. Paine's division took the heaviest casualties.
3 July 7: After learning of the capitulation of Vicksburg, Gardner surrendered.

CHARLESTON

THROUGHOUT THE CIVIL WAR NO FORT ENDURED WHAT FORT SUMTER DID. OCCUPYING A PRIME STRATEGIC POSITION, RIGHT IN THE CENTER OF CHARLESTON HARBOR, IT WAS AN OBSTACLE NO INVADER COULD GO AROUND. IN ORDER TO TAKE CHARLESTON, THE UNION WOULD FIRST HAVE TO TAKE SUMTER.

Sumter had fallen easily enough when the Rebels took it in April of 1861, in the first battle of the Civil War, but back then its defences had been seriously undermanned. By the time the Union forces returned to attempt to retake it, the Confederates had greatly strengthened the fort, adding to its firepower, and ringing the rest of the harbor with guns and fortifications. Thus, when April 1863 arrived, and with it the Union fleet, the Confederates in Fort Sumter were ready.

On April 7 the Yankee ships attacked, steaming straight into the harbor where they passed by a number of bouys which the Confederates had placed as range markers, allowing them to carefully sight their cannons on the Union craft. Once the Confederacy opened fire, it was with telling accuracy. In the two-hour battle the Confederates fired 2,209 shots, of which fully one quarter hit their marks, severely damaging the Union's ships, who between them managed to fire only 154 shots.

The defenders came in for an even more gruelling examination later that year when, for fifteen days in August, General Quincy Gillmore bombarded Fort Sumter with siege guns, hurling tens of tons of iron from long-range guns. Yet, incredibly, the gunners inside the fort held out. They burrowed inside the rubble, finding that it provided a wonderful defence. Indeed the loose mortar and brick absorbed the enemy shells better than had the standing walls. Deep within their tunnels the defenders could sit out the bombardments in comparative safety.

Although the town's other forts, including Fort Wagner, were eventually captured, Fort Sumter kept on holding out until February 1865 when General Beauregard ordered the evacuation of the Rebel forces from Charleston, after every other major Confederate city and fort had been taken.

Opposite: Map showing the Charleston Campaign, April-September, 1863. In order to gain control of the city of Charleston which had good tactical advantage, it was necessary for the Union to defeat Sumter.

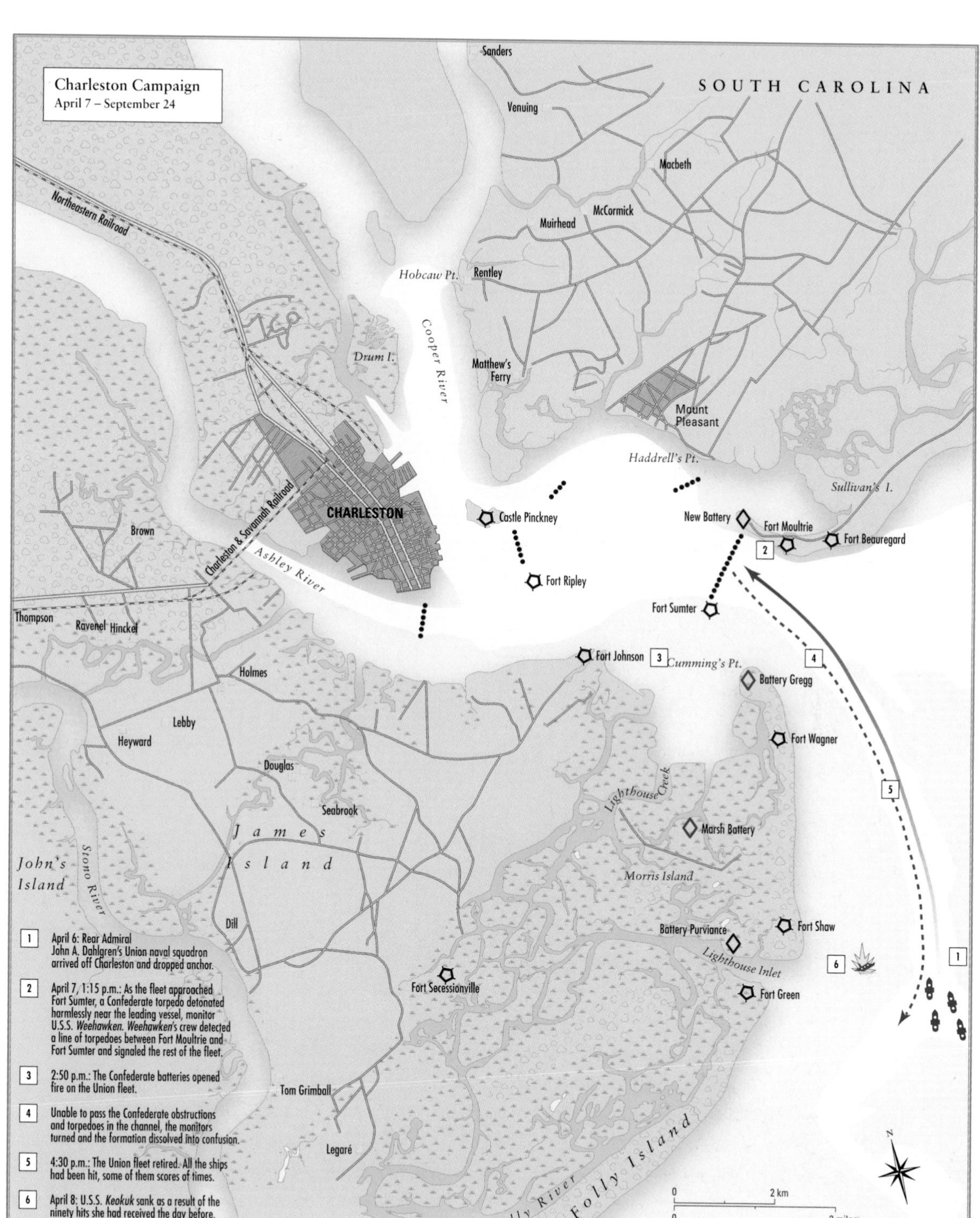
Charleston Campaign
April 7 – September 24
SOUTH CAROLINA
Sanders
Venuing
Macbeth
McCormick
Muirhead
Hobcaw Pt.
Rentley
Cooper River
Drum I.
Matthew's Ferry
Mount Pleasant
Haddrell's Pt.
Sullivan's I.
Northeastern Railroad
Charleston & Savannah Railroad
CHARLESTON
Castle Pinckney
New Battery
Fort Moultrie
Fort Beauregard
Brown
Ashley River
Fort Ripley
Fort Sumter
Thompson
Ravenel
Hinckel
Fort Johnson
Cumming's Pt.
Battery Gregg
Holmes
Lebby
Heyward
Fort Wagner
Douglas
Lighthouse Creek
Seabrook
James Island
Marsh Battery
John's Island
Stono River
Morris Island
Dill
Battery Purviance
Fort Shaw
Lighthouse Inlet
Fort Secessionville
Fort Green
Tom Grimball
Legaré
Folly Island
Folly River
N
0 2 km
0 2 miles
1 April 6: Rear Admiral John A. Dahlgren's Union naval squadron arrived off Charleston and dropped anchor.
2 April 7, 1:15 p.m.: As the fleet approached Fort Sumter, a Confederate torpedo detonated harmlessly near the leading vessel, monitor U.S.S. Weehawken. Weehawken's crew detected a line of torpedoes between Fort Moultrie and Fort Sumter and signaled the rest of the fleet.
3 2:50 p.m.: The Confederate batteries opened fire on the Union fleet.
4 Unable to pass the Confederate obstructions and torpedoes in the channel, the monitors turned and the formation dissolved into confusion.
5 4:30 p.m.: The Union fleet retired. All the ships had been hit, some of them scores of times.
6 April 8: U.S.S. Keokuk sank as a result of the ninety hits she had received the day before.

Chancellorsville, and the Death of "Stonewall" Jackson

Confederates in the heights outside Fredericksburg were attacked again the following spring, and this time the Union forces were successful against the thin grey line. However, the battle was secondary to the main fighting around Chancellorsville, ten miles away. Chancellorsville is regarded as Robert E. Lee's most masterful battle, but it was a costly one resulting in the death of "Stonewall" Jackson.

Relics of the battle are strung out along present State Route 3 (the Orange Turnpike) west of Fredericksburg, but many features of the battlefield are contained within the national park. The Visitors' Centre, located on ground where major fighting took place, is more important in this park than in most others because the circular driving tour does not adequately portray the master stroke that achieved another Confederate victory against far superior Union forces holding strong positions. The centre's excellent museum makes more meaningful the stops at Hazel Grove, now fortified with a few of the three dozen Confederate cannon crowded there at the time, and a painting depicting the artillery duel with massed Union cannon at Fairview, and the trenches and earthworks visible at both sites. Even the foundations of Chancellorsville Tavern, which gave the battle its name, are still visible.

In a way the Battle of Chancellorsville was a follow-up to the Union defeat at Fredericksburg the previous December. Major General Joseph "Fighting Joe" Hooker, who succeeded Burnside as commander of the 130,000 man Arm of the Potomac, made his winter camp near Fredericksburg and resumed the "On to Richmond" drive in the spring. With the lesson of the futile attack on Marye's

Heights burned in his mind, Hooker chose to combine a flanking movement against Lee with a new assault on the hills south of Fredericksburg. Lee anticipated his plan and, although outnumbered nearly three-to-one, took the initiative on May 1. Hooker's units fell back from positions which were crucial to the outcome of the battle. Hazel Grove was one of the few open places in the wooded countryside where cannon had clear fields of fire, but the key to success was Jackson's brilliant surprise flanking attack that collapsed the right wing of Hooker's army. Jackson's winding flank march from the bivouac where he and Lee agreed on the tactic can be duplicated by following the Furnace Road and Jackson Trail, part of it unpaved, to State Routes 613 and 3.

Left: Illustration of Robert E. Lee (*left*) and Stonewall Jackson conferring before the battle.

Below: Map showing Jackson's brilliant surprise attack that was successful even though the Confederate Army was greatly outnumbered.

Jackson was determined to push his success so he rode out the next day at night with a small staff party to reconnoiter. The group was mistaken for enemy scouts and Jackson was badly wounded in the left arm, which was amputated. The loss of Jackson was serious, but the next morning Lee threw his army against the fortified Union line, driving Hooker back to a new position a mile north of Chancellorsville.

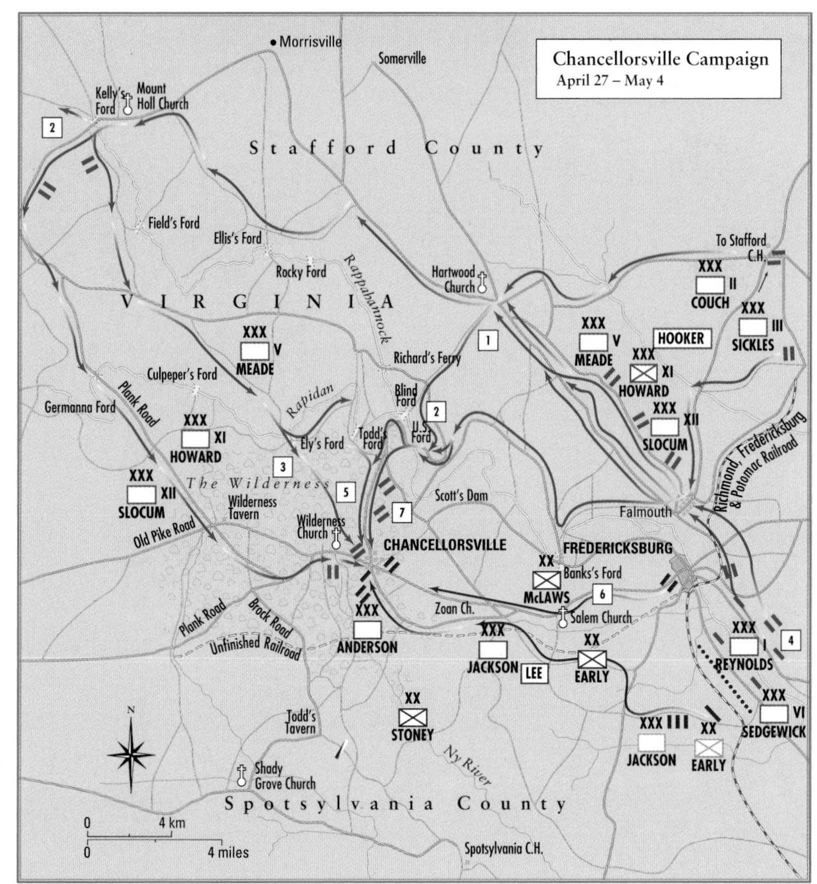

1 April 27: The Army of the Potomac began moving out of its camps around Falmouth, Virginia, moving up the north bank of the Rappahannock to turn Lee's left flank.

2 April 28: Union troops began crossing the Rappahannock at United States Ford and Kelly's Ford.

3 April 29: The bulk of the Army of the Potomac completed its crossing and proceeded into an area of dense thickets and second-growth timber known as the Wilderness.

4 April 29: Major General John Sedgwick, commanding his own Sixth Corps as well as Major General John Reynolds's First Corps, made movements threatening an attack at Fredericksburg in order to divert Confederate attention away from the movement of the rest of the Army of the Potomac.

5 April 30: The main body of the Army of the Potomac, accompanied by Hooker, encamped near Chancellorsville.

6 May 1: Leaving Major General Jubal Early with ten thousand men to cover Fredericksburg, Lee marched the rest of his army to confront Hooker in the Wilderness.

7 May 1: After beginning to advance out of the Wilderness, Hooker inexplicably ordered his troops to fall back into that area, where his army's advantage in numbers was of minimal value.

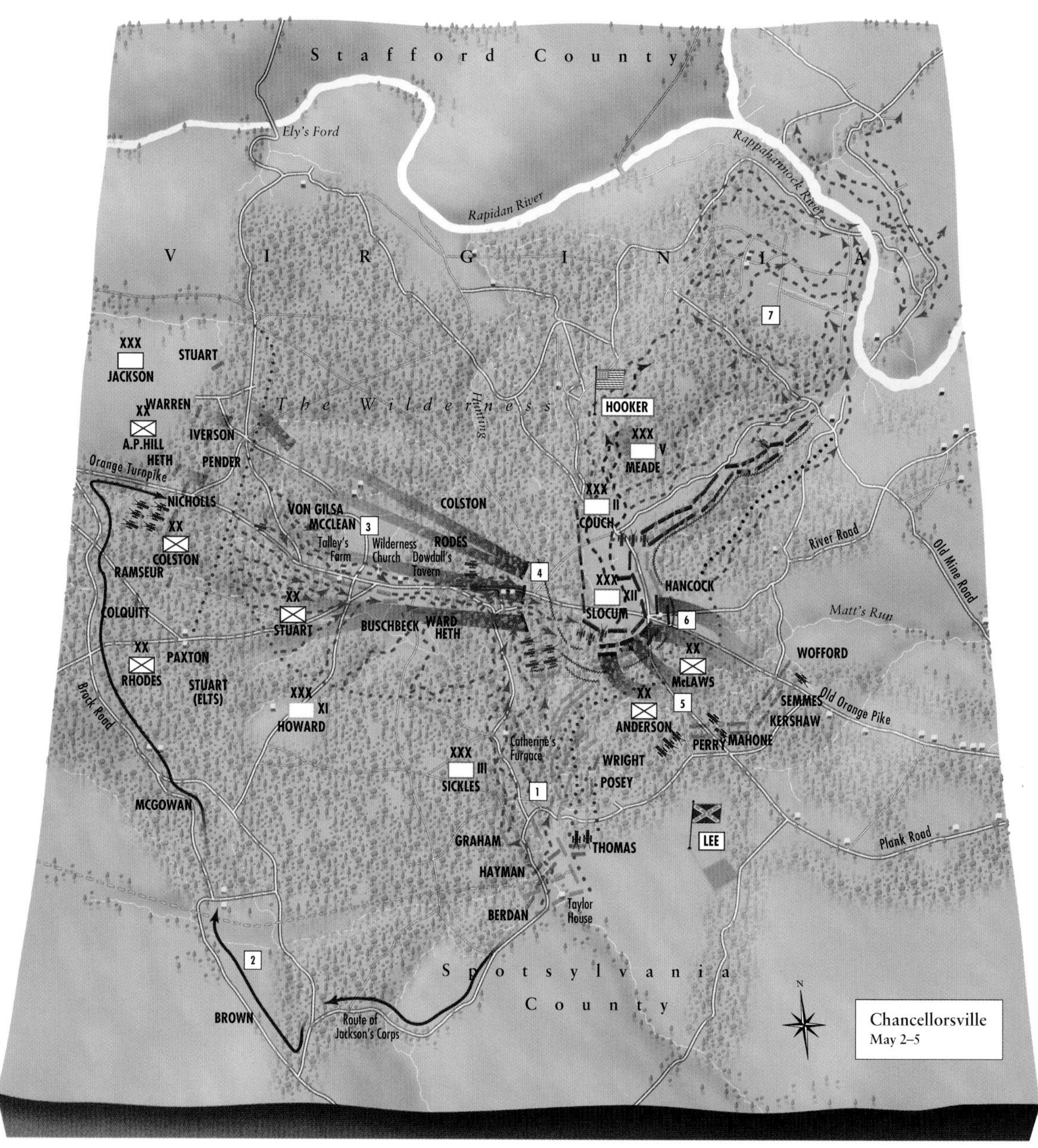

1 May 2, morning: At the start of their long flank march, Jackson's men skirmished with Union troops probing beyond Catherine's furnace.

2 May 2: Jackson's column spent most of the day reaching a position on the Union flank

3 May 2, 6:00 p.m.: Jackson finally launched his flanking attack, crumpling the Union Eleventh Corps.

4 May 2, 9.00 p.m.: Returning from a reconnaissance with his staff after the day's fighting had ended, Jackson was caught in the middle of a flare up of a picket firing and was wounded slightly in the right hand and severely in the left arm. Command of his corps passed to Jeb Stuart.

5 May 3, morning: Confederate artillery occupied a commanding position at Hazel Grove and continued to pound Chancellorsville throughout the day.

6 May 3: Both Lee and Stuart mounted costly frontal assaults against Hooker's lines, pushing them back into a tighter perimeter and linking the two halves of the Confederate army.

7 May 5: Hooker withdrew his forces across the Rappahannock.

1 May 4: Brigadier General Cadmus Wilcox's brigade, fighting a delaying action against Sedgwick's advance, made a stubborn stand at Salem Church.

2 The four brigades of Major General Lafayette McLaws's division, moved into line on either side of Wilcox.

3 Major General Richard H. Anderson's division arrived and confronted Sedgwick from the south.

4 Major General Jubal Early's command, rallied after its defeat at Fredericksburg the day before, moved up behind Sedgwick, threatening him from the east.

5 Sedgwick's troops staunchly fought off the Confederate attacks before withdrawing across the Rappahannock under cover of darkness.

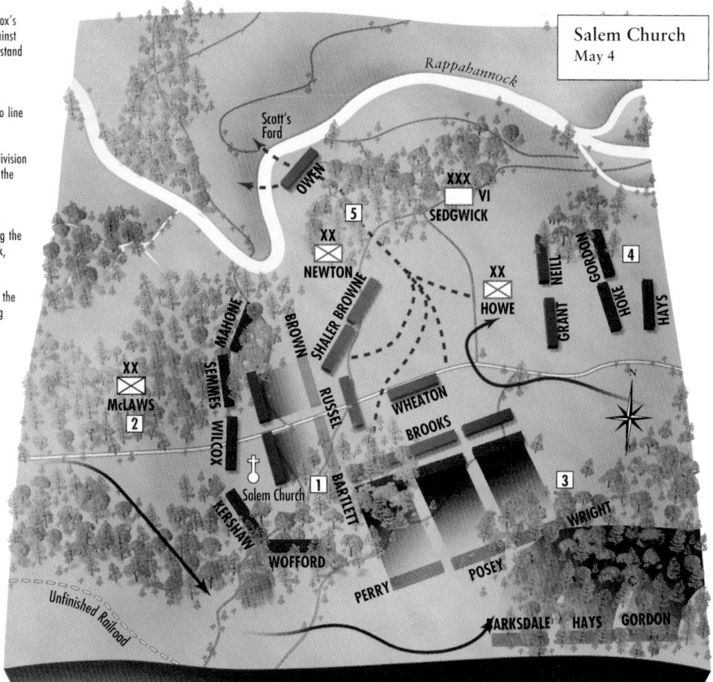

Above: Major General Joseph Hooker, officer of the Federal Army. He was known for his audacious military tactics. However, it was the defeat of General Sedgwick's at the Battle of Salem Church (*left*) made Hooker abandon the entire Campaign of Chancellorsville.

Opposite page: Map of the Battle of Chancellorsville, arguably the greatest victory for the Confederates during the war. It became known as General Lee's perfect battle because he managed to defeat the enemy despite being outnumbered three to one. However, his casualties numbered up to 13, 000 men, and, most seriously, he lost "Stonewall Jackson", his most important general.

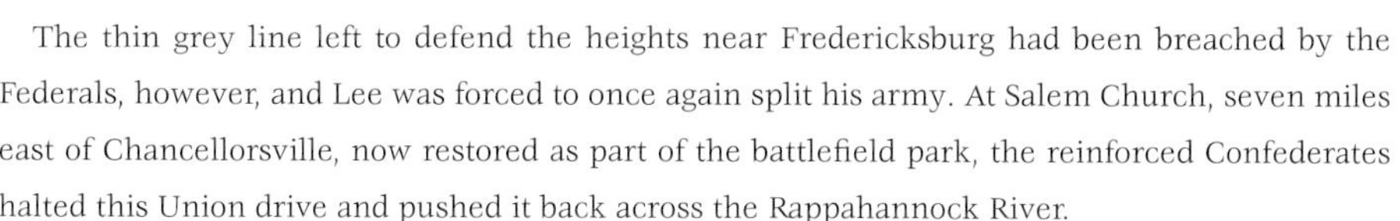

The thin grey line left to defend the heights near Fredericksburg had been breached by the Federals, however, and Lee was forced to once again split his army. At Salem Church, seven miles east of Chancellorsville, now restored as part of the battlefield park, the reinforced Confederates halted this Union drive and pushed it back across the Rappahannock River.

Meanwhile, the wounded General Jackson was taken 27 miles to T. C. Chandler's Fairfield Plantation at Guiney (now Guinea) Station, a key supply centre on the Richmond, Fredericksburg and Potomac Railway line, where it was thought he could receive proper care. The main house was already filled with wounded from the fighting, so Jackson was placed in the nearby white frame plantation office. The days that followed marked alternately optimism and despair as pneumonia set in. On the afternoon of May 10, eight days after his greatest victory, Jackson became delirious and began shouting military commands. Finally he quietened, and then he drew on his knowledge of the Bible as he said: "Let us cross over the river, and rest under the shade of the trees."

Death had claimed the general Lee had called his right arm; Lee would miss Jackson sorely in the battles to come. Many years later, British statesman David Lloyd George would remark "In this little house the Confederacy also died." The frame house where "Stonewall" died is the main feature of the Jackson Shrine, which is five miles off Interstate 95 via State Routes 606 and 607. It is furnished plainly inside, with the bed and blanket and the clock on the mantel (which still works) being original. Another room is outfitted as the doctor's room. A painting, with a recorded commentary, at the entrance to the park depicts the plantation at the time of Jackson's death. Only the foundations of the brick manor house remain.

THE BATTLE OF GETTYSBURG, JULY 1-3, 1863 (PHASE I,II,III)

THE BATTLE OF GETTYSBURG WAS A WATERSHED IN THE CIVIL WAR. IT HALTED THE LAST INVASION OF THE NORTH BY THE SOUTH, AND IT ENDED FOR ALL TIME THE HOPE THAT EUROPEAN POWERS WOULD RECOGNIZE THE INDEPENDENCE OF THE CONFEDERACY. THE WAR WOULD LAST ANOTHER TWO YEARS, AND GENERAL LEE WOULD LEAD HIS ARMY OF NORTHERN VIRGINIA TO VICTORY AGAIN, BUT THE TIDE OF THE CONFEDERACY HAD BEGUN TO EBB.

Above: George Gordon Meade (1815-1872), a Federal Officer who commanded the Army of the Potomac at the Battle of Gettysburg.

Gettysburg became a battlefield more by chance than by design. On June 3, 1863, after his stunning victory at Chancellorsville, against a vastly superior force, Lee marched north again in an attempt to take pressure off Vicksburg, then under siege. He passed through western Maryland and into Pennsylvania, with Harrisburg, its capital, as the objective. Union forces under General Hooker paralleled his route to protect Washington and Baltimore, but Hooker resigned as commander of the Army of the Potomac and was succeeded by General George G. Meade. Lee ordered his army, by then almost at the Susquehanna River, to turn back to Cashtown, and units of the two armies met by chance at Gettysburg on June 30. The next day the battle scene was set as Confederates drove the Federals through Gettysburg to a line formed by Culps Hill, Cemetery Ridge and Little Round Top south of town. Lee moved his forces to Seminary Ridge almost a mile from the Union line, placing them in a north-south arc that stretched almost five miles.

The fighting started late on July 2 and continued until 10 p.m. at night as Lee sought to turn the Union flanks before Meade could concentrate all his forces. General Longstreet, who was to attack the critical

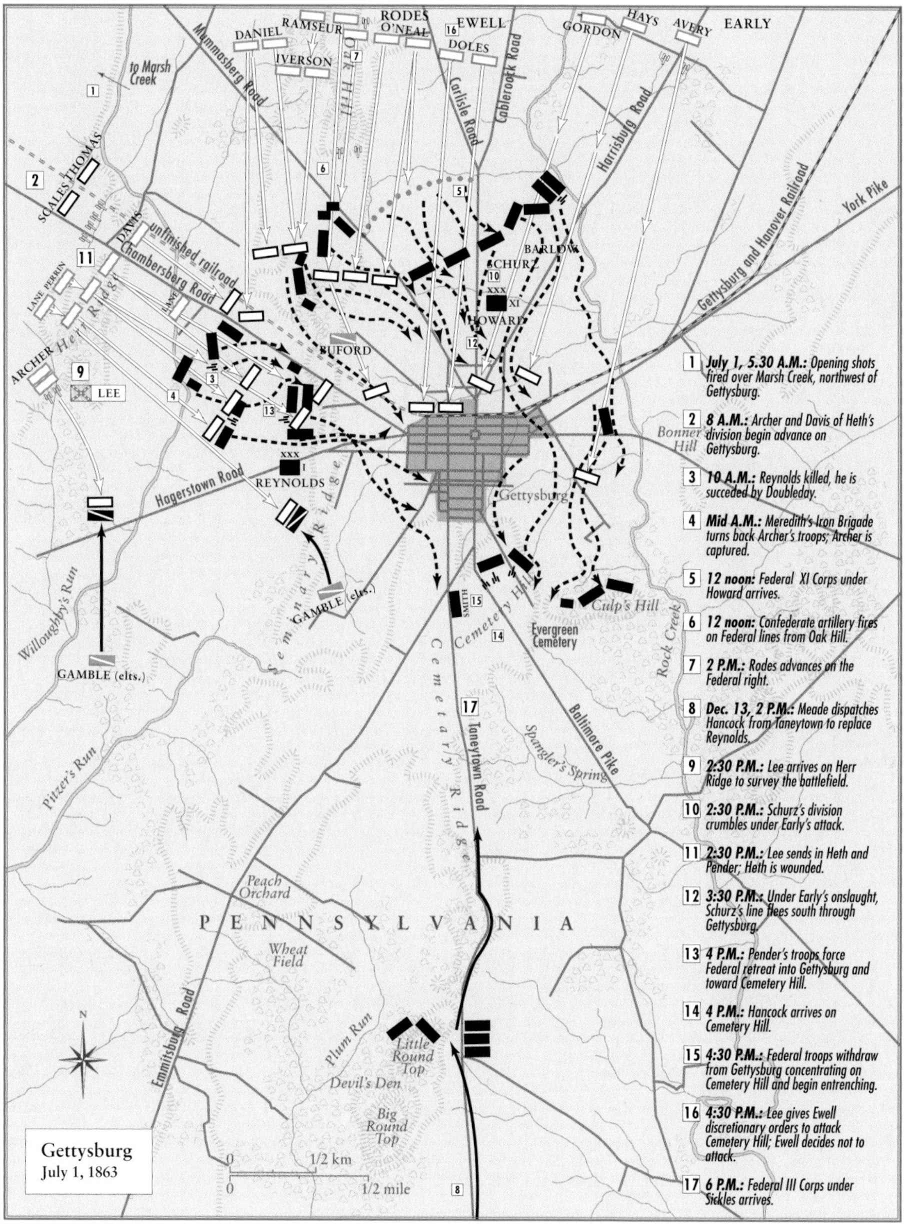
Gettysburg
July 1, 1863
1 July 1, 5.30 A.M.: Opening shots fired over Marsh Creek, northwest of Gettysburg.
2 8 A.M.: Archer and Davis of Heth's division begin advance on Gettysburg.
3 10 A.M.: Reynolds killed, he is succeded by Doubleday.
4 Mid A.M.: Meredith's Iron Brigade turns back Archer's troops; Archer is captured.
5 12 noon: Federal XI Corps under Howard arrives.
6 12 noon: Confederate artillery fires on Federal lines from Oak Hill.
7 2 P.M.: Rodes advances on the Federal right.
8 Dec. 13, 2 P.M.: Meade dispatches Hancock from Taneytown to replace Reynolds.
9 2:30 P.M.: Lee arrives on Herr Ridge to survey the battlefield.
10 2:30 P.M.: Schurz's division crumbles under Early's attack.
11 2:30 P.M.: Lee sends in Heth and Pender; Heth is wounded.
12 3:30 P.M.: Under Early's onslaught, Schurz's line flees south through Gettysburg.
13 4 P.M.: Pender's troops force Federal retreat into Gettysburg and toward Cemetery Hill.
14 4 P.M.: Hancock arrives on Cemetery Hill.
15 4:30 P.M.: Federal troops withdraw from Gettysburg concentrating on Cemetery Hill and begin entrenching.
16 4:30 P.M.: Lee gives Ewell discretionary orders to attack Cemetery Hill; Ewell decides not to attack.
17 6 P.M.: Federal III Corps under Sickles arrives.
DANIEL
RAMSEUR
RODES
O'NEAL
EWELL
DOLES
IVERSON
GORDON
HAYS
AVERY
EARLY
to Marsh Creek
Mummasburg Road
Oak Hill
Carlisle Road
Cablerock Road
Harrisburg Road
Gettysburg and Hanover Railroad
York Pike
SCALES
THOMAS
DAVIS
unfinished railroad
Chambersburg Road
LANE
PERRIN
Herr Ridge
ARCHER
LEE
BUFORD
BARLOW
SCHURZ
HOWARD
REYNOLDS
Hagerstown Road
Seminary Ridge
GAMBLE (elts.)
Willoughby's Run
Gettysburg
Bonner Hill
Culp's Hill
Cemetery Hill
Evergreen Cemetery
Rock Creek
SMITH
Cemetary Ridge
Taneytown Road
Spangler's Spring
Baltimore Pike
Pitzer's Run
Peach Orchard
PENNSYLVANIA
Wheat Field
Emmitsburg Road
Plum Run
Little Round Top
Devil's Den
Big Round Top
N
0 1/2 km
0 1/2 mile

left flank, would spend the remainder of his life denying that his delays cost the Confederacy a victory at Gettysburg; but it was not until 4 p.m. that his cannon roared into action preceding the attack. By then, fresh Union troops had moved into the Wheatfield and Devil's Den, names that by nightfall would become immortalised by the blood of thousands of dead and wounded soldiers. Nor was General Richard Ewell's attack on the other flank successful; it lacked coordination and bogged down as additional infantry units and cannon moved into Meade's line. Delays had cost Lee a decisive victory.

Above left: The events of the first day of conflict at the Battle of Gettysburg.

Above: Soldiers lying dead in an open field at the Battle of Gettysburg.

Opposite page: The second day of battle. General Longstreet's delay cost the Confederacy any chance of victory at Gettysburg.

The third day, July 3, was a classic example of infantry attack. Union regulars regained ground on their right flank, putting both flanks in almost impregnable positions. This forced Lee to make a frontal assault on the centre of the line, where a breakthrough would divide the Union army and win the battle. Longstreet had objections, as he always did, but Lee was determined. "The enemy is there, and I am going to strike him," he said, pointing at Cemetery Ridge. What followed has gone down in history as a symbol of Southern courage, under the name Pickett's Charge.

Seen from either side of the battlefield, from The Angle and the Copse of Trees —at which the charge was aimed—or from the Virginia Monument near the Confederate centre, the heroism of the charge is evident. Almost a mile of open field slopes gradually down from one ridge and up to the other. There is no protection, no place to pause. The 12,000-man grey wave led by soldiers carrying bright regimental flags advanced at walking pace most of the distance, their lines shredded by double canister shells and sharp shooting riflemen in the Union defences. The rebels charged at a run only the last quarter-mile, into a barrier of smoke created by the deadly firing from the ridge ahead. It was a magnificent effort that almost worked. The Confederates breached the Union line near the Copse of Trees but were too few and too exhausted to hold the ground. As they drew back across the open field, their casualties continued

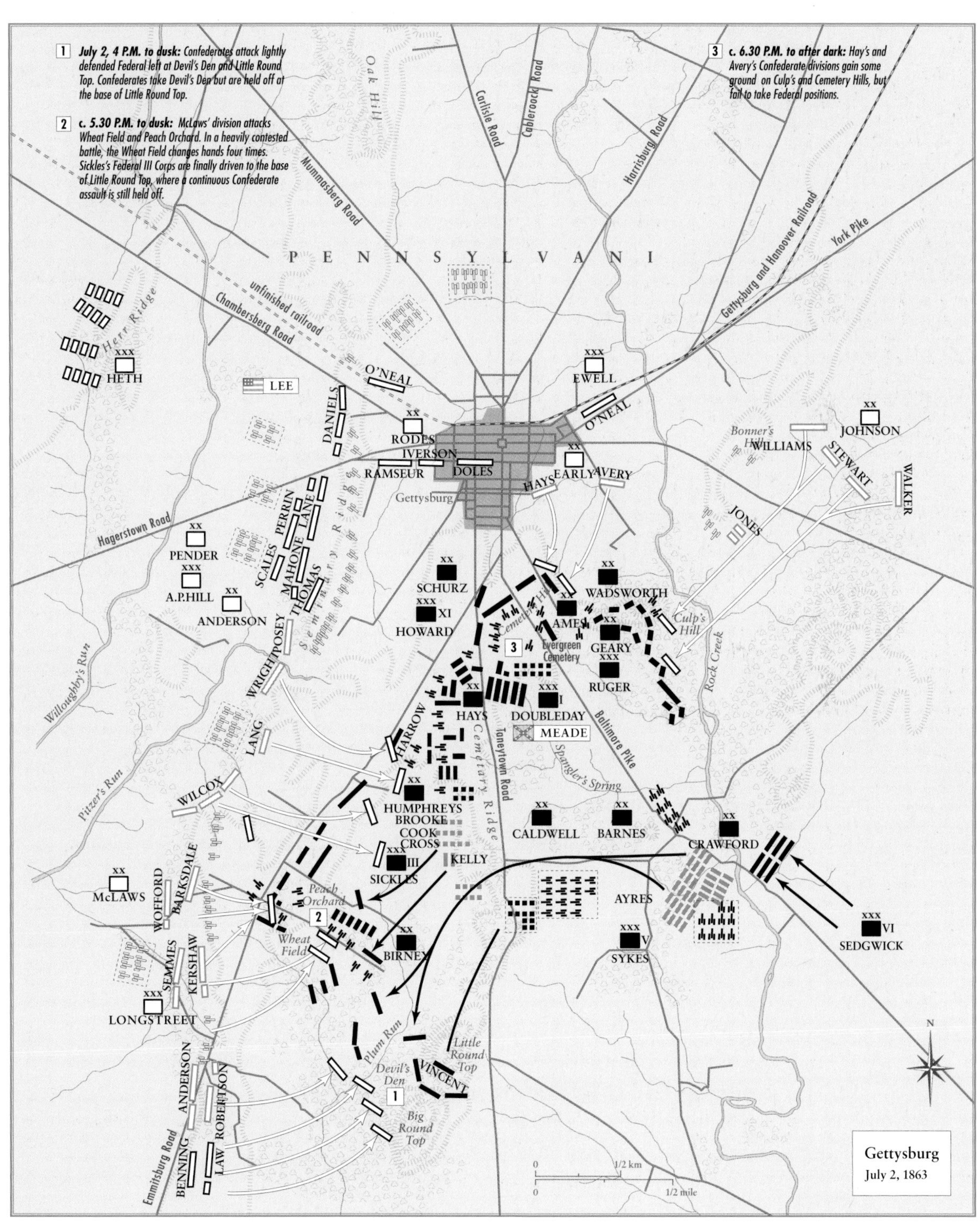
1 July 2, 4 P.M. to dusk: Confederates attack lightly defended Federal left at Devil's Den and Little Round Top. Confederates take Devil's Den but are held off at the base of Little Round Top.
2 c. 5.30 P.M. to dusk: McLaws' division attacks Wheat Field and Peach Orchard. In a heavily contested battle, the Wheat Field changes hands four times. Sickles's Federal III Corps are finally driven to the base of Little Round Top, where a continuous Confederate assault is still held off.
3 c. 6.30 P.M. to after dark: Hay's and Avery's Confederate divisions gain some ground on Culp's and Cemetery Hills, but fail to take Federal positions.
PENNSYLVANIA
Oak Hill
Carlisle Road
Cablerock Road
Harrisburg Road
Mummasburg Road
Gettysburg and Hanover Railroad
York Pike
unfinished railroad
Chambersberg Road
Herr Ridge
HETH
LEE
O'NEAL
EWELL
DANIELS
RODES
IVERSON
RAMSEUR
DOLES
Gettysburg
HAYS
EARLY
AVERY
JOHNSON
Bonner's Hill
WILLIAMS
STEWART
WALKER
JONES
Hagerstown Road
PENDER
A.P.HILL
ANDERSON
PERRIN
LANE
SCALES
MAHONE
THOMAS
Seminary Ridge
POSEY
WRIGHT
SCHURZ
XI
HOWARD
AMES
WADSWORTH
Culp's Hill
Cemetery Hill
Evergreen Cemetery
GEARY
RUGER
Rock Creek
HAYS
DOUBLEDAY
MEADE
Baltimore Pike
Spangler's Spring
Willoughby's Run
LANG
HARROW
Cemetary Ridge
Taneytown Road
Pitzer's Run
WILCOX
HUMPHREYS
BROOKE
COOK
CROSS
KELLY
III
SICKLES
CALDWELL
BARNES
CRAWFORD
McLAWS
BARKSDALE
WOFFORD
Peach Orchard
AYRES
Wheat Field
BIRNEY
SYKES
V
VI
SEDGWICK
SEMMES
KERSHAW
LONGSTREET
Plum Run
Little Round Top
Devil's Den
VINCENT
ANDERSON
ROBERTSON
Big Round Top
Emmitsburg Road
BENNING
LAW
1/2 km
1/2 mile
N
Gettysburg
July 2, 1863

Above: Sculpture showing a scene from the Battle of Gettysburg.

Opposite page: Map of the Battle's third day of fighting. The Union Army regained some minor ground they had lost the day before and forced Lee to attempt a full frontal attack.

to mount; and when the 50 minutes of combat was over, 10,000 of them had fallen.

The next day was the Fourth of July, the birthday of the United States, so the battle did not resume. General Lee's losses during the three days of fighting, which totalled a staggering 28,000, represented 38 per cent of his 75,000 man army, and he could no longer press the fight. Meade, who had lost 23,000 of his 97,000 men, pursued, but the chase was rendered ineffective by Confederate rear guards and by rain. Lee's retreat was made even more bitter by "dispiriting news" that Vicksburg had fallen and the South was cut in two.

Gettysburg today is the most visible American battlefield. Everything about the Gettysburg battlefield is grand. It is the largest contiguous battlefield part in the nation, the most developed and commercialized, and the one which accommodates the greatest number of visitors. It has more than 1,000 monuments and cannon along 40 miles of scenic roads, and has the most impressive monuments—all of which make it easy to follow and understand the decisive battle that occurred there from July 1-3, 1863. It can be viewed in electric map and static display form at the Visitors' Centre, on a cyclorama housed in its own building, and from an observation tower. Airplanes carry visitors on regular flights over the 25 square miles of the battlefield. The most popular method of visitation remains the drive-through tour, which follows both lines of the last two days of the battles and major points involved in the initial day's combat.

The drive begins at the Cyclorama and follows a road named consecutively after Union Generals Hancock, Sedgwick, Sykes, Warren, and Crawford, running among dozens of monuments, large and small, General Meade is memorialized by a large equestrian statue, while a nearby small monument recognizes the 1st Pennsylvanian Cavalry. Pennsylvania and other Union States have raised impressive memorials along this part of the drive.

An artillery battery at The Angle (sometimes called the Bloody Angle) looks out on the ground covered by Pickett's Charge. A copse of trees stands nearby, as it did in 1863, and a tablet identifies the spot as the High Water Mark of the Confederacy. That was where Pickett's men were halted and, although they did not realize it at the time, the days of the Confederacy were numbered.

The drive crosses Little Round Top and skirts Big Round Top, where a one-hour circular walking trail winds through a typical Pennsylvania hardwood forest and passes a stone wall built for defence by Union

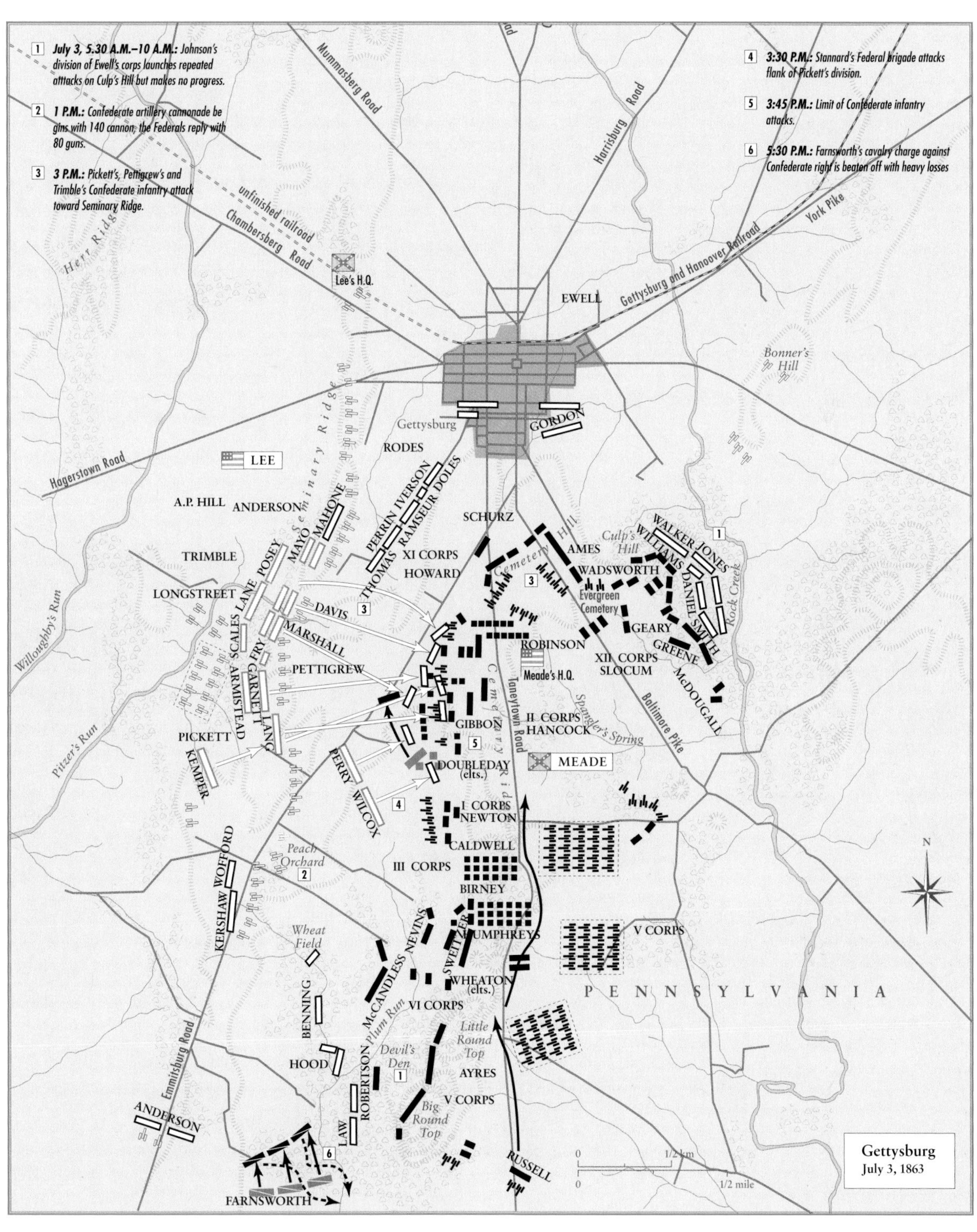
1 July 3, 5.30 A.M.–10 A.M.: Johnson's division of Ewell's corps launches repeated attacks on Culp's Hill but makes no progress.
2 1 P.M.: Confederate artillery cannonade begins with 140 cannon; the Federals reply with 80 guns.
3 3 P.M.: Pickett's, Pettigrew's and Trimble's Confederate infantry attack toward Seminary Ridge.
4 3:30 P.M.: Stannard's Federal brigade attacks flank of Pickett's division.
5 3:45 P.M.: Limit of Confederate infantry attacks.
6 5:30 P.M.: Farnsworth's cavalry charge against Confederate right is beaten off with heavy losses
Mummasburg Road
Harrisburg Road
unfinished railroad
Chambersberg Road
Herr Ridge
Lee's H.Q.
EWELL
Gettysburg and Hanover Railroad
York Pike
Bonner's Hill
Gettysburg
GORDON
RODES
Seminary Ridge
LEE
Hagerstown Road
A.P. HILL
ANDERSON
MAHONE
MAYO
PERRIN IVERSON
RAMSEUR DOLES
THOMAS
XI CORPS
HOWARD
SCHURZ
TRIMBLE
POSEY
LANE
LONGSTREET
SCALES
DAVIS
MARSHALL
FRY
GARNETT
ARMISTEAD
PETTIGREW
LANG
PICKETT
KEMPER
Willoughby's Run
Pitzer's Run
Cemetery Hill
AMES
WADSWORTH
Culp's Hill
WALKER
JONES
WILLIAMS
DANIEL
SMITH
Rock Creek
Evergreen Cemetery
GEARY
GREENE
McDOUGALL
ROBINSON
Meade's H.Q.
XII CORPS
SLOCUM
Baltimore Pike
Spangler's Spring
Cemetery Ridge
Taneytown Road
GIBBON
II CORPS
HANCOCK
MEADE
DOUBLEDAY (elts.)
PERRY
WILCOX
I CORPS
NEWTON
CALDWELL
Peach Orchard
III CORPS
BIRNEY
WOFFORD
KERSHAW
Wheat Field
NEVINS
SWEITZER
HUMPHREYS
V CORPS
McCANDLESS
WHEATON (elts.)
PENNSYLVANIA
Plum Run
VI CORPS
BENNING
Emmitsburg Road
Little Round Top
HOOD
Devil's Den
ROBERTSON
AYRES
V CORPS
Big Round Top
LAW
ANDERSON
RUSSELL
FARNSWORTH
0 1/2 km
0 1/2 mile
N
Gettysburg
July 3, 1863

troops. Then, the driving tour meanders through terrain occupied on the second day by Union units while the Confederates dallied.

Memorials in the Wheatfield and Death Valley recall the terrible toll of the day's fighting. There's also a path which leads onto the rocks called Devil's Den from which sharpshooters poured deadly fire.

Confederate Avenue which lies along Lee's battleline has few memorials and cannons, but the ones there are among the most impressive on the battlefield. Alabama mourns her fallen sons at Biesecker Woods. A feature on the Virginia Memorial, which stands on the spot near the center of the line from which Lee watched Pickett's Charge, is an equestrian statue of Lee on a high pedestal. Figures around the base of the statue, all in action, represent various types of workers who left civilian life to become soldiers. The smaller, but equally impressive, North Carolina Memorial is to Lee's left, in the area where they marshaled to join Pickett's Charge.

The park road also runs along McPherson and Oak Ridges, where the battle began as a chance encounter, to the Eternal Light Peace Memorial, dedicated in 1938 on the 75th anniversary of the battle to "Peace Eternal in a Nation Unified."

A short drive through Gettysburg reveals privately owned attractions ranging from the National Civil War Was Museum to the Lincoln Train Museum. Lifestyles of the Civil War era are recreated during Heritage Days each July. The driving tour then reaches Culp's Hill and Spangler Spring, where seesaw

Below: Photograph of a modern farm close to the where the Battle of Gettysburg was fought.

fighting occurred on the second day of the battle.

Gettysburg National Cemetery, across the street from the Visitors' Centre, commemorates the fallen with with 3,585 plain white headstones and a tall, lean Soldiers Monument acknowledging their supreme sacrifice. But by a curious twist of fate, the cemetery is much better known for a speech that contains just ten sentences. President Lincoln was not the principal speaker at the dedication of the national cemetery on November 19, 1863, and was invited only as a formality. Edward Everett, considered one of the greatest orators of the day, spoke for almost two hours—and nobody today remembers what he said. Lincoln's address, which took only two minutes to deliver and was heard by few in the audience, not only is engraved on a memorial in the cemetery but also is world famous as an expression of hope that good can arise from the sacrifices of war.

Left: The cost of war. Soldiers lying dead at Gettysburg.

Below: Battle of Gettysburg war cemetery..

MORGAN AND QUANTRILL

IN JULY 1863, THE FAMOUS CONFEDERATE RAIDER, JOHN HUNT MORGAN, LED HIS 2,500-STRONG FORCE INTO KENTUCKY. HAVING TAKEN THE TOWNS OF LEBANON AND BARDSTOWN, HE CROSSED THE OHIO RIVER AND HEADED INTO INDIANA, BRINGING THE WAR TO THE MIDWEST FOR THE FIRST TIME, MUCH TO THE UNIONISTS' HORROR.

Above: This painting depicts an example of the increasing brutality of the war. We can see foraging Confederate soldiers taking homemade pies from a farmhouse during Morgans Raid, 1863.

General John Hunt Morgan's raid into Indiana and Ohio took more than two weeks and brought destrucion to many communities not previously involved in the war. Salem, Indiana was taken on July 10, after which he headed towards Ohio. But, by now Union troops were on his his trail. He was finally captured at Salineville, Ohio, near the Pennsylvania line. His harsh treatment by his captors would show had attitudes towards enemy combatants—and particularly raiders—had hardened during the course of the conflict. This was in part understandable, as it had become increasingly clear that some guerrillas who operated as Confederates were more interested in murder and plunder than in serving any cause. Others were motivated by revenge. William Clark Quantrill, one of the Confederacy's most celebrated raiders, led a destructive raid on Lawrence, Kansas, in which most of the men in the town were killed in retaliation for the Confederate defeat at Gettysburg and wrongs committed by Unionists. His men also stripped the community of all its valuables.

Even officers were treated harshly—even capriciously—at times. Before the bitterness of warfare had reduced human feelings on both sides, Confederate General Simon Bolivar Buckner, who surrendered Fort Donelson to Grant, and General Lloyd Tilghman, were imprisoned in solitary

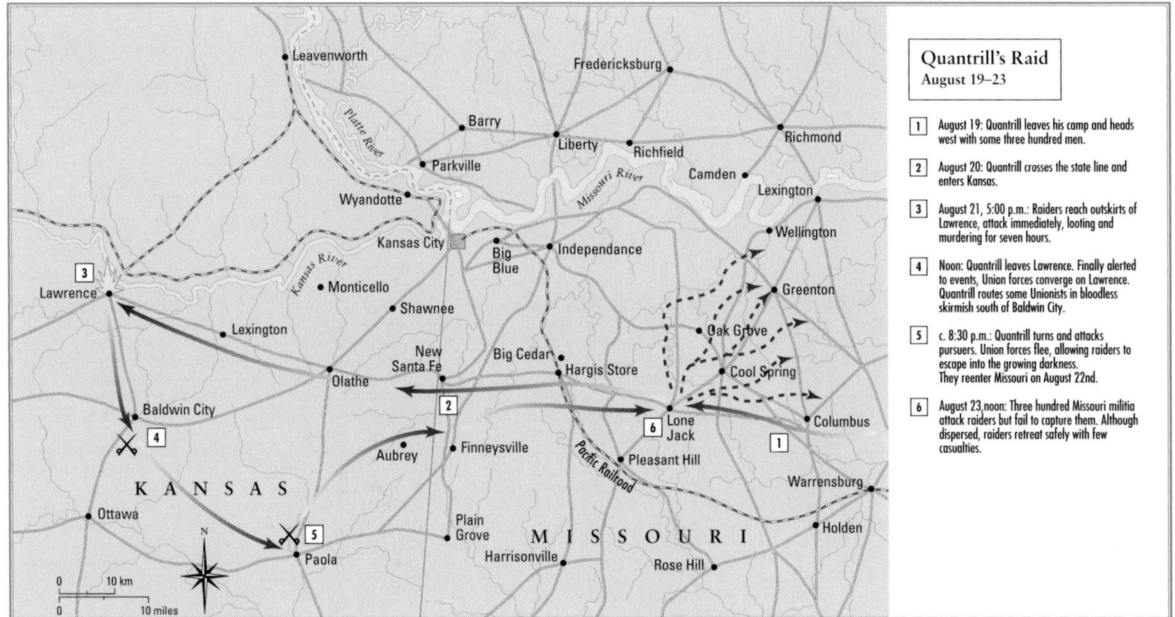

confinement at Fort Warren in Boston Harbor and not allowed to communicate with their families. Only intercession by Lincoln, at the request of Tilghman's mother (who lived in Pennsylvania), got them better treatment. General John Hunt Morgan, meanwhile, was not treated as a prisoner-of-war, but as a common criminal and sent to prison, from which he escaped after a few months.

Above: A map showing the movements of William Clark Quantrill during his ruthless raid (also known as the Lawrence Massacre) on the pro-union town of Lawrence, Kansas, in August 1864.

Irregular fighting of this kind was intensified during the course of the Civil War, and devastated Kansas throughout the war. Union attempts to halt the attacks even extended to the point of arresting the female relatives of Confederate irregulars and jailing them at Kansas City. The deaths of some of them in an accident contributed to one of the most famous raids of the war, the destruction of Lawrence, and an anti-slavery stronghold, in 1863.

While William Clark Quantrill promoted the raid as a way to redress the Confederate defeat at Gettysburg, some of his lieutenants were persuaded to go because of the accident in Kansas City. The 450 raiders were in no mood to be lenient, and Quantrill had given orders to kill all the men and burn every house. This order was systematically carried out in a house-to-house search for valuables and horses. No women were harmed, according to the Bushwhackers code, and few men did manage to survive by hiding out in various ways.

Among the survivors was James Henry Lane, a puzzling politician who had himself been a proficient leader of Union raids behind Confederate lines. In 1861, he had taken delight in destroying Missouri towns that had welcomed the Confederate units victorious at Lexington. His cavalry fired indiscriminately on a charge through Osceola, then set fire to almost all the buildings after finding a cache of lead, powder, and cartridge paper. His men had a more personally satisfying way of destroying barrels of brandy, 3,000 sacks of flour, 500 pounds of sugar and molasses 50 sacks of coffee, and a quantity of bacon.

THE KNOXVILLE CAMPAIGN, AUGUST 15-DECEMBER 4, 1863

THE SLOWNESS OF GENERAL BRAXTON BRAGG AFTER HIS VICTORY AT CHICKAMAUGA GAVE FEDERALS TIME TO REORGANIZE AND FORTIFY THE KEY RAILROAD CENTER OF CHATTANOOGA. ON THE OTHER HAND, BRAGG'S DELAY CREATED SUCH DISSENSION AMONG HIS SUBORDINATES THAT PRESIDENT JEFFERSON DAVIS MADE A TRIP FROM RICHMOND TO MEDIATE.

Above: Canon located in the Virginian mountains. More battles took place in Virginia than in any other state.

Bragg's solution was to send General Longstreet and other dissenters to besiege Knoxville, weakening his forces around Chattanooga at a time when Union forces were being strengthened for the effort to break out. Although the Federals were forced on to quarter rations before an adequate supply line could be established, Confederate chances of successful siege were not good because they could not isolate the city. In November 1863, Union forces under Grant took the offensive.

Cumberland Gap National Historical Park has a display of Civil War weapons at the Visitors' Center and a few preserved artillery sites and rifle pits. Knoxville, occupied by the Union much of the war, recalls the era at Confederate Memorial Hall and the antebellum Bleak House, which General Longstreet used as his headquarters during his unsuccessful 1863 attempt to evict Burnside. The Armstrong-Lockett House dates from 1934. Of the 2,109 Union casualties buried in Knoxville National Cemetery, 1,046 are unknown.

Hale Springs Inn, erected in 1834 on a major stagecoach route, serves as a reminder of the shifting fortunes of Rogersville. Trapdoors probably were installed by owners to provide a quick means of hiding silverware and other valuables every time the city changed hands. The inn was headquarters when Union forces were in town; Confederates preferred the Kyle House across the street when they were in control.

Lincoln Memorial University in Harrogate, established after the war by Union Major General Oliver O. Howard who had been impressed by the patriotism of the people of the region, has a sizable collection of Civil War memorabilia among items related to its namesake.

Dandridge, thirty miles east of Knoxville, was saved from the Confederacy by a mistake of the U.S. Army Corps of Engineers. A Union Army foraging in the area and a Confederate force wintering at Russellville engaged in inconclusive skirmishing along the French Road River in January 1864. Union forces completed what they thought was a bridge across the river and sent cavalry charging across—only to discover that the bridge ended on an island in the stream. Embarrassed, the Union troopers withdrew the next day.

The Knoxville Campaign Union forces under Major General Ambrose Burnside occupied Knoxville, a key town on the railroad corridor between Chattanooga and Virginia. The Campaign relates to a series of battles and maneuvers when Confederate forces were detached from General Braxton Bragg's forces at Chattanooga to prevent Burnside's reinforcement of Union forces there.

Above: Principal Union commander in the Knoxville Campaign, Ambrose Burnside and his troops from Rhode Island entering Knoxville in 1863.

The Campaign ended after the indecisive Battle of Bean's Station in December 14, 1863. Its only real effect had been to deprive Bragg of sorely needed troops in Chattanooga. Burnside's successful held on Knoxville, plus Grant's victory at Chattanooga ensured that this part of Tennessee stayed in Union hands for the rest of the war.

Right Map pinpointing the movements of the Knoxville Campaign which took place August 15-December 4.

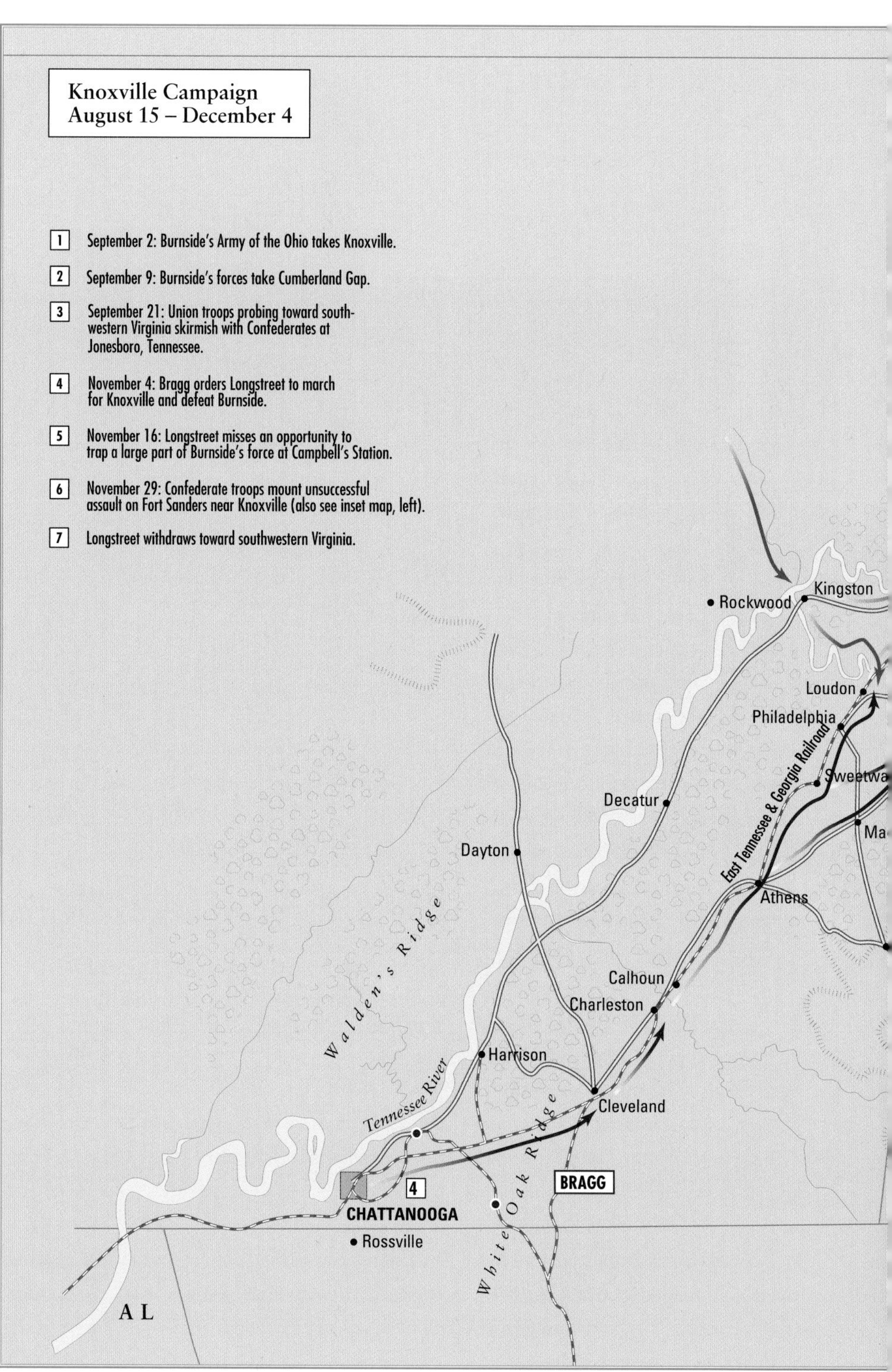

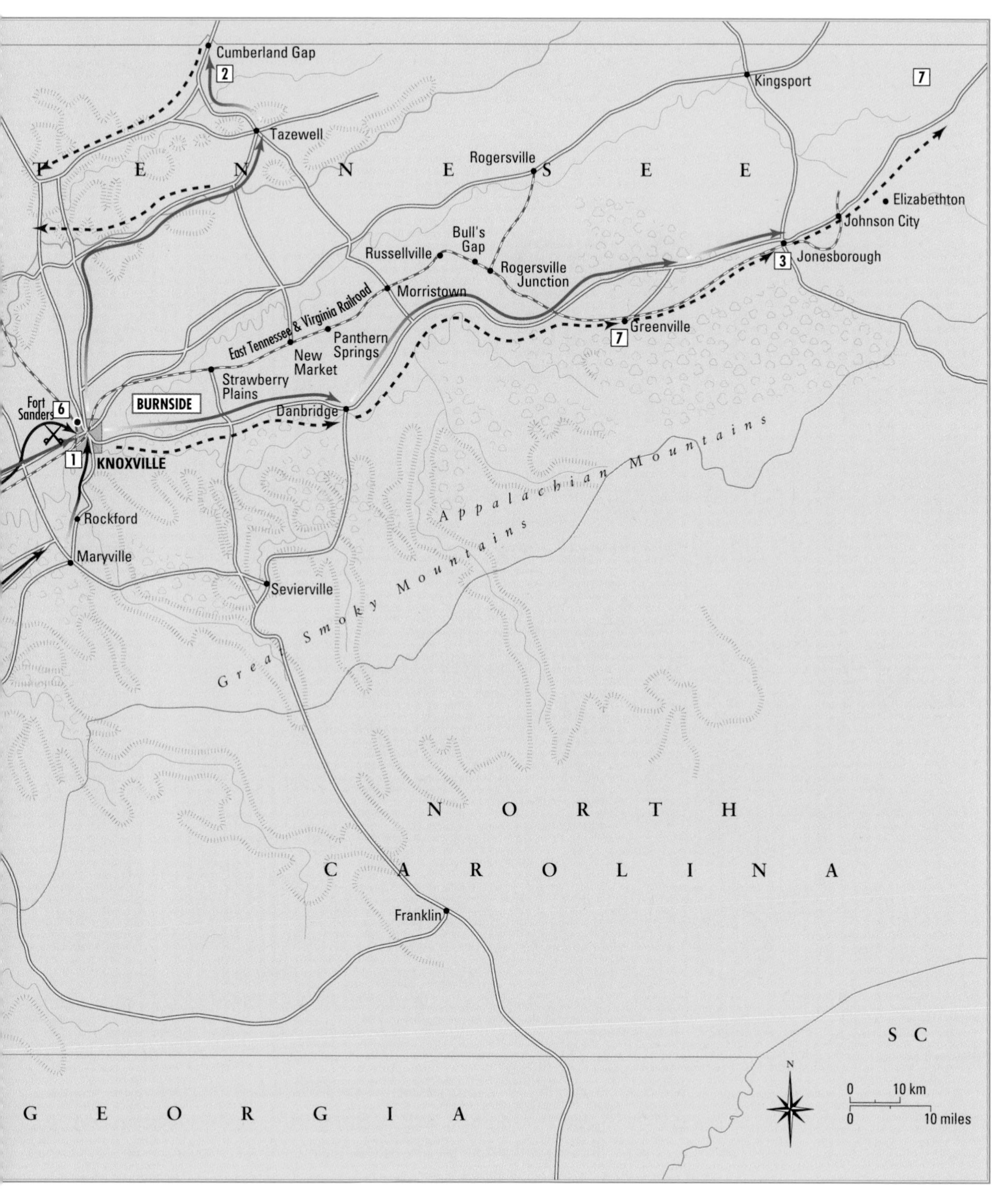
Cumberland Gap
2
Kingsport
7
Tazewell
T E N N E S S E E
Rogersville
Elizabethton
Johnson City
Bull's Gap
Russellville
Jonesborough
3
Rogersville Junction
Morristown
East Tennessee & Virginia Railroad
Greenville
7
Panthern Springs
New Market
Strawberry Plains
Fort Sanders
6
BURNSIDE
Danbridge
1
KNOXVILLE
Appalachian Mountains
Rockford
Maryville
Sevierville
Great Smoky Mountains
NORTH CAROLINA
Franklin
SC
GEORGIA
N
0 10 km
0 10 miles

OPERATIONS IN VIRGINIA, OCTOBER 9 - NOVEMBER 26, 1863

AFTER THE BATTLE OF GETTYSBURG IN JULY, 1863, UNION AND CONFEDERATE FORCES SPARRED WITH EACH OTHER INCONCLUSIVELY IN VARIOUS PARTS OF NORTHERN VIRGINIA. ON OCTOBER 12, A REBEL DIVISION UNDER MAJOR GENERAL RICHARD S. EWELL DEFEATED UNION CAVALRY AT JEFFERSONTON AND THEN ADVANCED ON THE SAME DAY TO FAUQUIER WHITE SULPHUR SPRINGS, SCORING ANOTHER MINOR VICTORY.

Above: Confederate General James Ewell Brown "Jeb" Stuart, (1833-1864) resigned from his post as captain in the United States Army to join the Confederate States Army in 1861. He eventually became Robert E. Lee's right hand man. and was an intimate friend of "Stonewall" Jackson.

Over the next two days (October 13–14), the Battle of Auburn took place after Confederate Major General J. E. B. Stuart's cavalry division had been cut off by Union troops under Major General William H. French. At the end of the first day, Stuart divided his forces, sending most of them to near Warrenton and the remaining two brigades farther south. On the second day, the Confederates cleverly but narrowly avoided encirclement by the Union army and attacked its rearguard as it withdrew.

As the Battle of Auburn ended, A. P. Hill rashly attacked Union forces at the Battle of Bristoe Station, a stop on the Orange and Alexandria Railroad near which General Gouverneur K. Warren had hidden his men behind an embankment. The rebels had already suffered heavy losses before they spotted Ewell's forces approaching from the east to join the fray. They then withdrew, but not before inflicting serious damage on the railroad tracks.

On October 15, Major General George G. Meade drew up a strong defensive line through Centreville. The Confederates declined to engage with it and fell back over the next three days to the southern bank of the Rappahannock River, where they hoped to quarter themselves for the winter. On October 20, Stuart routed the Union cavalry in an isolated incident at Buckland Mills.

Three weeks later, Union forces attacked the rebels again. Meade divided his forces into two, and sent one detachment, under Major General John Sedgwick, to Rappahannock Station, while the other, under Major General William H. French, proceeded to a river crossing five miles downstream to the east.

At noon on November 7, 1863, French drove back Confederate defenders and took his men across the Rappahannock River at Kelly's Ford. Three hours later, Sedgwick opened fire on rebel forces amassed

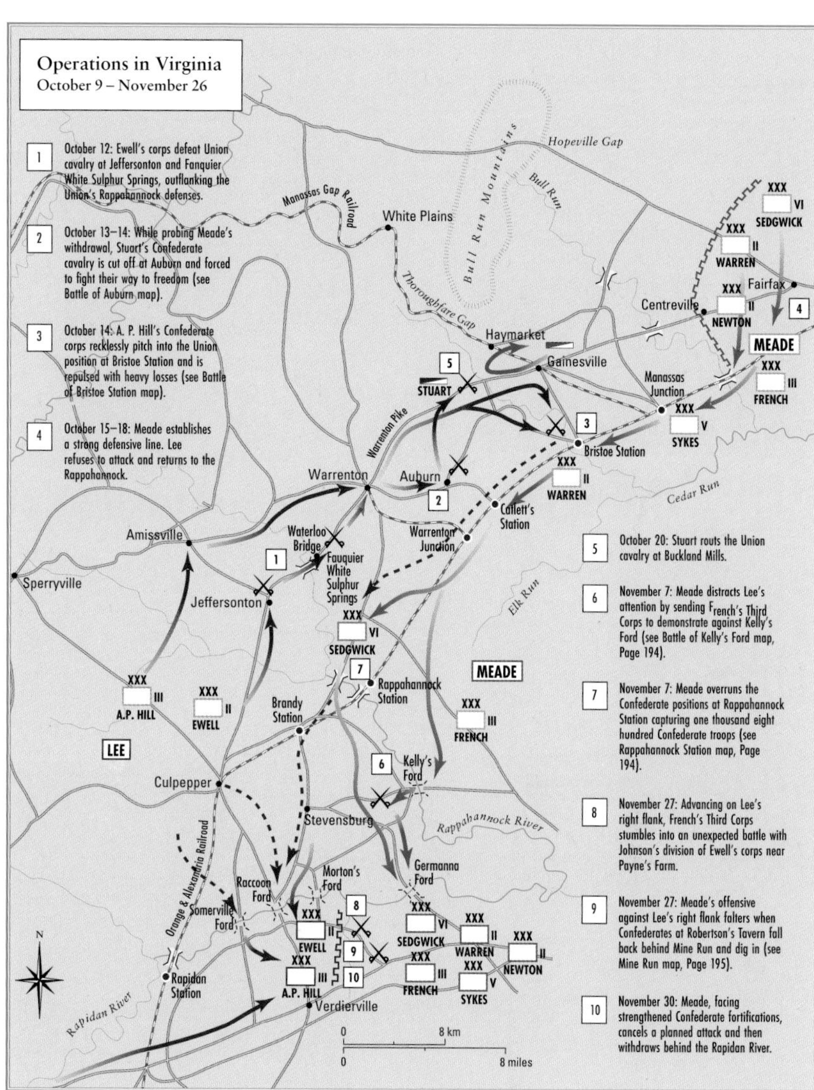

on the bridgehead at Rappahannock. When, by the end of a day of rapid and continuous Federal artillery fire, the Northern forces showed no apparent inclination to cross the river, the Confederates concluded that this was merely a diversionary tactic and that the main attack must be taking place on another part of the river. They were wrong. At dusk the Union army stopped shelling and rushed the pontoon and the adjacent railway bridge; the operation was a complete and quick success.

Above: The operations in northern Virginia were costly on both sides and proved largely inconclusive until a rebel divison defeated Union cavalry at Jeffersonton.

The rebel forces withdrew once more, this time to the southern banks of the Rapidan River. There, on November 27, French's advancing Third Corps ran into a division of Major General Richard S. Ewell's Confederate force near Payne's Farm. The ensuing Battle of Mine Run ended inconclusively. There was then a two-day standoff, at the end of which Meade ordered his forces back to Brandy Station, where they spent the winter. Thus ended the northern Virginia campaign.

CHICKAMAUGA & CHATTANOOGA

THANKS TO MARGARET MITCHELL'S NOVEL "GONE WITH THE WIND," AND THE SUBSEQUENT MOTION PICTURE, GEORGIA'S ROLE IN THE CIVIL WAR IS PERCEIVED TO BE MUCH GREATER THAN IT WAS. OF COURSE, THE BATTLES FOUGHT AT CHICKAMAUGA AND KENNESAW MOUNTAIN WERE OF EPIC PROPORTIONS, AND THE BURNING OF ATLANTA WAS SPECTACULAR, BUT THE PERIOD OF DEATH AND DESTRUCTION IN THE SOUTH'S RICHEST AND MOST POPULOUS STATE WAS BRIEF COMPARED TO THAT OF THE FRONTLINE STATES OF VIRGINIA AND TENNESSEE.

The Union strategies of dividing the Confederacy at the Mississippi and of conquering the Confederate capital at Richmond, even the effort to strangle the South by blockading all its ports, including those in Georgia, existed almost from the beginning of the war. The decision to trisect the South came later, after the early effort at holding the border States and occupying Tennessee had succeeded. The battle at Chickamauga, which is barely inside the Georgia boundary, did not occur until September, 1863 and the State escaped major destruction until 1864.

Opposite page: The Chickamauga campaign fought in Georgia was not as prominent as campaigns in larger neighboring states, but was an important victory for the Confederate Army because it managed to repel a strong Union advance. This map shows the events of the first ten days of battle.

Georgia's late arrival in the demolition derby meant that it felt the full force of a battle hardened Federal army and a war-weary Union, ready to accept wanton destruction and the excesses and improprieties committed by individual soldiers in exchange for an earlier end to the fighting. Furthermore, Federal officers throughout the war demonstrated little talent for maintaining discipline among their soldiers in conquered territory. Thus, the accumulated force of the war fell particularly hard on Georgia, and General Williams Tecumseh Sherman's March to the Sea

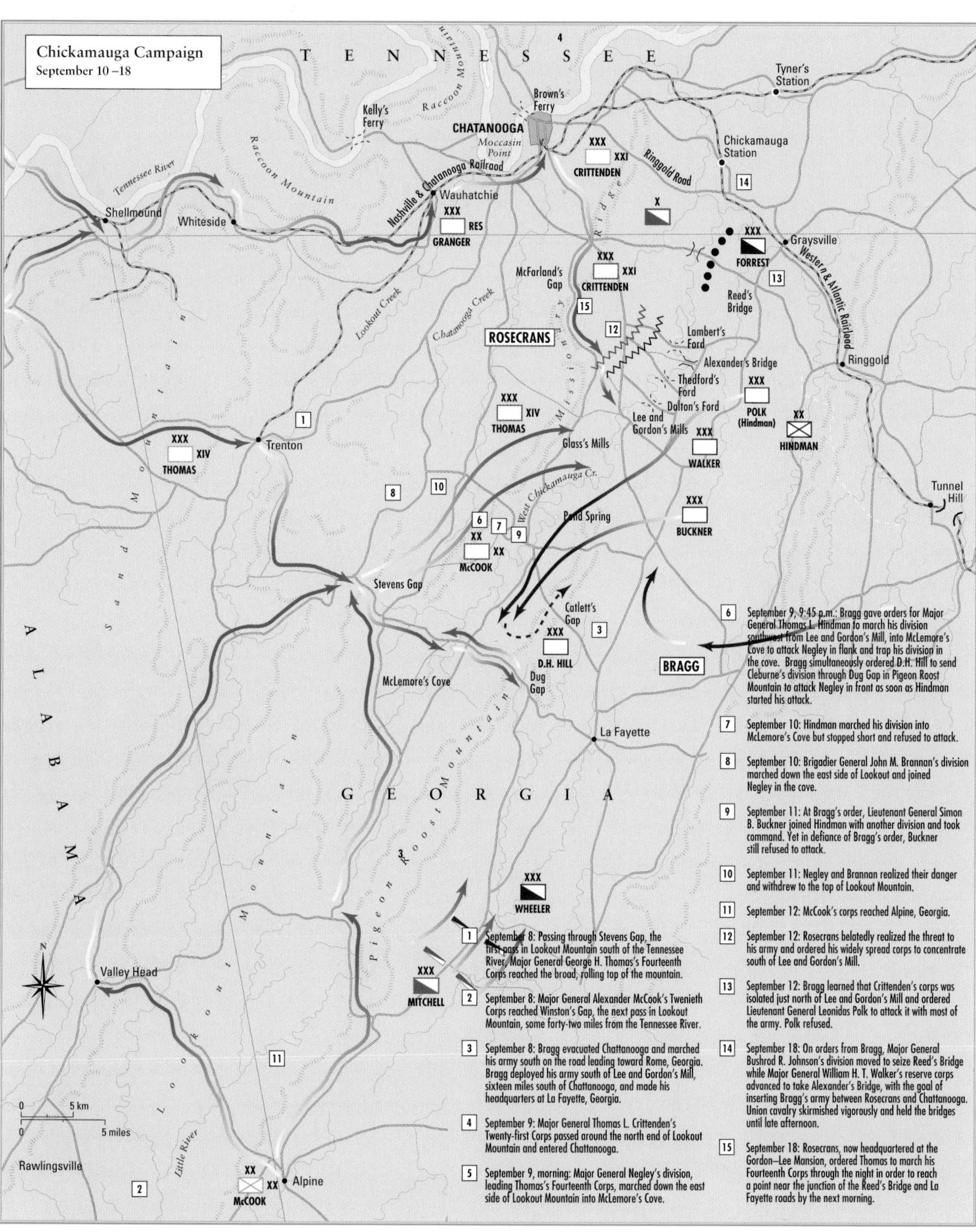
Chickamauga Campaign
September 10 –18
TENNESSEE
GEORGIA
ALABAMA
CHATANOOGA
Moccasin Point
Brown's Ferry
Kelly's Ferry
Raccoon Mountain
Tennessee River
Shellmound
Whiteside
Wauhatchie
Nashville & Chatanooga Railraod
Ringgold Road
Tyner's Station
Chickamauga Station
Graysville
Western & Atlantic Railroad
Reed's Bridge
Lambert's Ford
Alexander's Bridge
Thedford's Ford
Dalton's Ford
Lee and Gordon's Mills
Ringgold
Tunnel Hill
McFarland's Gap
Missionary Ridge
Lookout Creek
Chatanooga Creek
Trenton
Glass's Mills
West Chickamauga Cr.
Pond Spring
Stevens Gap
Catlett's Gap
McLemore's Cove
Dug Gap
La Fayette
Pigeon Roost Mountain
Lookout Mountain
Sand Mountain
Valley Head
Little River
Rawlingsville
Alpine
XXX XXI CRITTENDEN
XXX RES GRANGER
X
XXX FORREST
XXX XXI CRITTENDEN
ROSECRANS
XXX XIV THOMAS
XXX XIV THOMAS
XXX POLK (Hindman)
XX HINDMAN
XXX WALKER
XXX BUCKNER
XX XX McCOOK
XXX D.H. HILL
BRAGG
XXX WHEELER
XXX MITCHELL
XX XX McCOOK
0 5 km
0 5 miles
6 September 9, 9:45 p.m.: Bragg gave orders for Major General Thomas L. Hindman to march his division southwest from Lee and Gordon's Mill, into McLemore's Cove to attack Negley in flank and trap his division in the cove. Bragg simultaneously ordered D.H. Hill to send Cleburne's division through Dug Gap in Pigeon Roost Mountain to attack Negley in front as soon as Hindman started his attack.
7 September 10: Hindman marched his division into McLemore's Cove but stopped short and refused to attack.
8 September 10: Brigadier General John M. Brannan's division marched down the east side of Lookout and joined Negley in the cove.
9 September 11: At Bragg's order, Lieutenant General Simon B. Buckner joined Hindman with another division and took command. Yet in defiance of Bragg's order, Buckner still refused to attack.
10 September 11: Negley and Brannan realized their danger and withdrew to the top of Lookout Mountain.
11 September 12: McCook's corps reached Alpine, Georgia.
12 September 12: Rosecrans belatedly realized the threat to his army and ordered his widely spread corps to concentrate south of Lee and Gordon's Mill.
13 September 12: Bragg learned that Crittenden's corps was isolated just north of Lee and Gordon's Mill and ordered Lieutenant General Leonidas Polk to attack it with most of the army. Polk refused.
14 September 18: On orders from Bragg, Major General Bushrod R. Johnson's division moved to seize Reed's Bridge while Major General William H. T. Walker's reserve corps advanced to take Alexander's Bridge, with the goal of inserting Bragg's army between Rosecrans and Chattanooga. Union cavalry skirmished vigorously and held the bridges until late afternoon.
15 September 18: Rosecrans, now headquartered at the Gordon–Lee Mansion, ordered Thomas to march his Fourteenth Corps through the night in order to reach a point near the junction of the Reed's Bridge and La Fayette roads by the next morning.
1 September 8: Passing through Stevens Gap, the first pass in Lookout Mountain south of the Tennessee River, Major General George H. Thomas's Fourteenth Corps reached the broad, rolling top of the mountain.
2 September 8: Major General Alexander McCook's Twenieth Corps reached Winston's Gap, the next pass in Lookout Mountain, some forty-two miles from the Tennessee River.
3 September 8: Bragg evacuated Chattanooga and marched his army south on the road leading toward Rome, Georgia. Bragg deployed his army south of Lee and Gordon's Mill, sixteen miles south of Chattanooga, and made his headquarters at La Fayette, Georgia.
4 September 9: Major General Thomas L. Crittenden's Twenty-first Corps passed around the north end of Lookout Mountain and entered Chattanooga.
5 September 9, morning: Major General Negley's division, leading Thomas's Fourteenth Corps, marched down the east side of Lookout Mountain into McLemore's Cove.

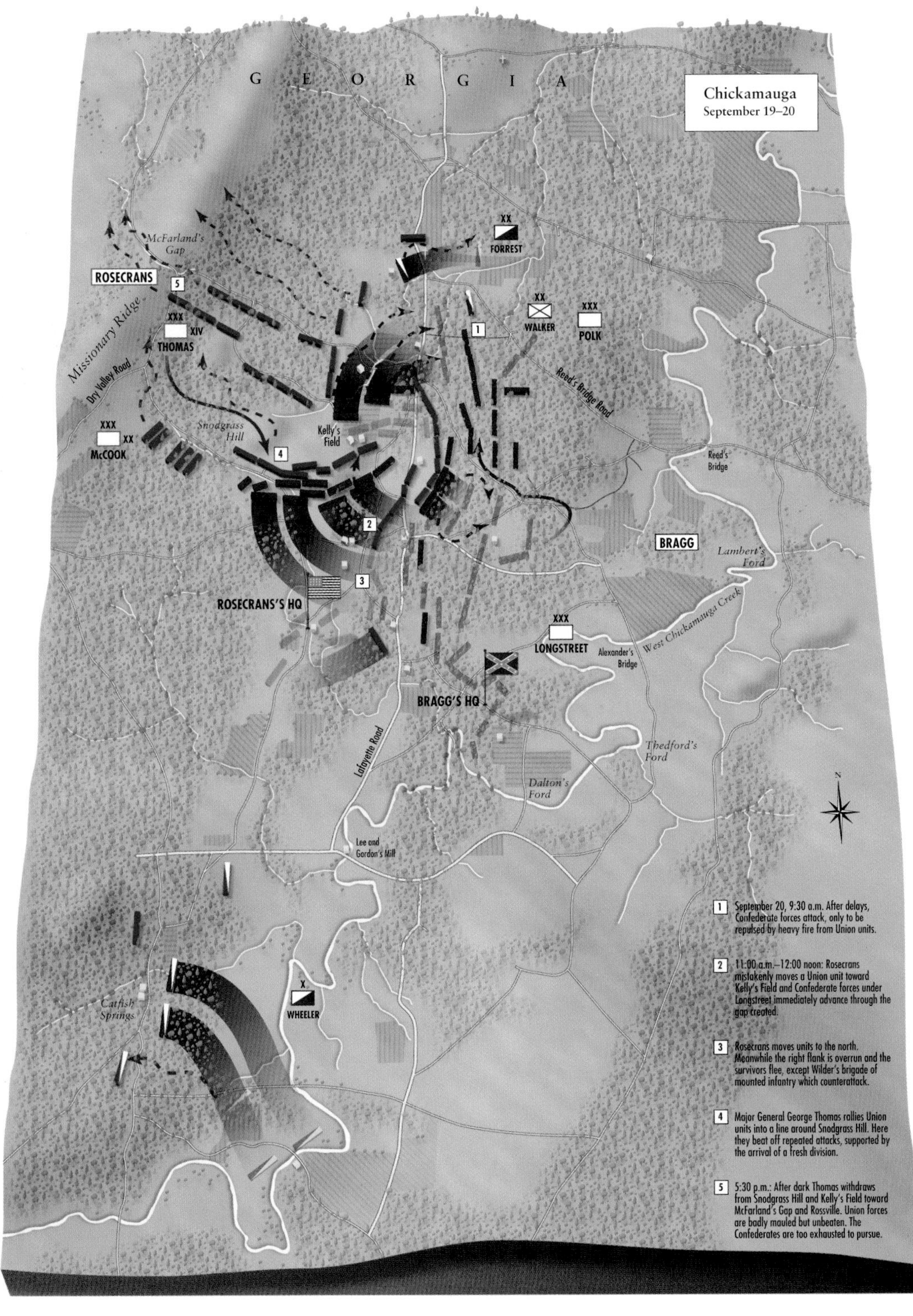

Chickamauga
September 19–20
GEORGIA
McFarland's Gap
ROSECRANS
5
Missionary Ridge
XXX
XIV
THOMAS
Dry Valley Road
XXX
XX
McCOOK
Snodgrass Hill
4
Kelly's Field
XX
FORREST
1
XX
WALKER
XXX
POLK
Reed's Bridge Road
Reed's Bridge
2
3
ROSECRANS'S HQ
BRAGG
Lambert's Ford
West Chickamauga Creek
XXX
LONGSTREET
Alexander's Bridge
BRAGG'S HQ
Lafayette Road
Thedford's Ford
Dalton's Ford
N
Lee and Gordon's Mill
Catfish Springs
X
WHEELER
1 September 20, 9:30 a.m. After delays, Confederate forces attack, only to be repulsed by heavy fire from Union units.
2 11:00 a.m.–12:00 noon: Rosecrans mistakenly moves a Union unit toward Kelly's Field and Confederate forces under Longstreet immediately advance through the gap created.
3 Rosecrans moves units to the north. Meanwhile the right flank is overrun and the survivors flee, except Wilder's brigade of mounted infantry which counterattack.
4 Major General George Thomas rallies Union units into a line around Snodgrass Hill. Here they beat off repeated attacks, supported by the arrival of a fresh division.
5 5:30 p.m.: After dark Thomas withdraws from Snodgrass Hill and Kelly's Field toward McFarland's Gap and Rossville. Union forces are badly mauled but unbeaten. The Confederates are too exhausted to pursue.

has become a symbol of destructiveness. It was also a forerunner of modern concept of "total war."

Historians at the battlefields try to demonstrate both the heroics of combat and the futility of war, but this is difficult in the serenity of park settings where visitors from both North and South come as much to recreate as to experience vicariously the deeds of their ancestors. However, the difficult terrain of northwest Georgia, where the two largest and most decisive battles were fought, combine with cherished memorials and the stark reality of large graveyards at Andersonville and Marietta to create a balanced perspective.

Some historians contend the South almost won the war at the Battle of Chickamauga. A decisive victory for the Confederacy after a string of defeats and retreats in the Western Theatre, it could have had far-reaching consequences if General Braxton Bragg had aggressively pursued the demoralised and retreating Union army under General William Rosecrans. But Bragg was cautious by nature and rejected the pleas of his subordinates that quick and forceful action might make Rosecrans abandon all of Tennessee and fan antiwar sentiment in the North. When Bragg finally followed—four days later—Rosecrans was entrenched in Chattanooga, with reinforcements on the way and General Ulysses S. Grant soon to take charge. While it is doubtful the South could have overcome Northern superiority in manpower and industrial capacity under any circumstances, a successful follow-up after Chickamauga would have changed the strategic situation in the West so much it could have lengthened the war.

Above: Aftermath of the Battle of Chickamauga, and a Confederate victory.

Opposite page: Map showing the outcome of the Chickamauga Campaign.

The battlefield at Chickamauga possesses a balance of beauty and solemnity. Memorials and historic places along the seven-mile, self-guided driving tour are unobtrusively spotted in sylvan settings. This is appropriate because most of the battle was fought in forests. The long-silent cannon are visual reminders of the "thunder of cannon" that erupted along the quiet lanes on a September day in 1863. One historical marker totals the 34,000 casualties of the two-day "sluggish river of death," as Confederate Major General William Bale described the Chickamauga battle. The 22nd Alabama lost 55 per cent of its men.

Buildings on the battlefield, even the white columned Visitors' Centre, contribute to a relaxed atmosphere. The audio-visual presentation is a 20-minute capsule of the overall strategy of the war, including the Chickamauga and Chattanooga battles. The largest section of the museum, an excellent collection of Civil War and earlier rifles, covers the innovations made in firearms during the war.

The Brotherton House, past which the Confederate attack rolled in 1863 to rupture a Union centre thrown off balance by the relocation of units, is as much a curiosity of life style as a battlefield relic. The log cabin stands as it did then, except that marble monuments and historical markers have replaced cattle in the yard and fields. The interior of the cabin reflects the crude conditions and Spartan furnishings that were typical of the area during this period.

The cabin on Snodgrass Hill, whose site dominates the slop where thousands of Confederates fell trying to break the Union flank, has a bloodier history. Here, the stubborn stand earned Union General George H. Thomas and sobriquet "Rock of Chickamauga," but the memorials remembered the sacrifices of his troops, especially the 87th Indiana, 2nd Minnesota, and 9th Ohio Infantry Regiments. Thomas typified one kind of Union Soldier; a Virginian by birth, he had elected to remain with the Union. He was a bold and imaginative leader who was even more aggressive than Grant—his troops pushed past their objective to capture Missionary Ridge at Chattanooga while Grant muttered threats of retribution if the action failed—and whose distinguished record led to command of the Army of the Cumberland.

The 1847 Gordon-Lee House, not far from the battlefield park, was used by the Union first as a headquarters and then as a hospital. Behind its Doric columns, rooms where generals huddled over maps and surgeons sawed off shattered arms and legs are decorated with period furniture, Oriental floor coverings, and brass chandeliers. Chickamauga would prove to be the last Confederate chance to stop the Union invasion.

Lookout Mountain is part of the Chattanooga and Chickamauga National Military Park that stretches across the Tennessee-Georgia border and commemorates two battles and includes a number of separate sites. The oldest and largest non-contiguous national battlefield in the nation includes Point Park on Lookout Mountain, Missionary Ridge, Signal Point on Signal Mountain, Orchard Knob in Chattanooga, and Chickamauga battlefield in Georgia, where a Confederate victory began the series of events commemorated by the park.

Right: Union soldiers under the command of George Henry Thomas capture Missionary Ridge from its Confederate defenders on November 25, 1863.

The slowness of General Bragg after his victory at Chickamauga gave Federals time to reorganize and fortify the key railroad centre of Chattanooga. On the other hand, Bragg's delay created such dissension among his subordinates that President Jefferson Davis made a trip from Richmond to mediate. Bragg's solution was to send General Longstreet and other dissenters to besiege Knoxville, weakening his forces around Chattanooga at a time when Union forces were being strengthened for the effort to break out. Although the Federals were forced on to quarter rations before an adequate supply line could be established, Confederate chances of successful siege were not good because they could not isolate the city. In November 1863, Union forces under Grant took the offensive.

Above: General Ulysses S. Grant on Lookout Mountain. Lookout Mountain was the location for the romantically named Battle Above the Clouds.

Confederate units held the high ground around three sides of the city, which also gave them control of the river. The first Union countermove against Lookout Valley, designed to open a better supply route, was successful largely because Bragg would not believe it was occurring until he was taken to Lookout Mountain to witness the masses of Union soldiers below. This critical mistake was compounded by poor planning, engineering, and leadership, and by overconfidence as the Union plan to break Bragg's flanks on Lookout Mountain and Missionary Ridge unfolded. Confederate defenders on Orchard Knob were tricked and overrun, providing the forward position from which Missionary Ridge could be assaulted.

The site of Grant's headquarters for the battle, which diverged so much from the way he had planned it that he once threatened to wreak the vengeance on those responsible if it did not succeed, is preserved as part of the national park.

The flanking attack under General Sherman was an utter failure; but it produced an 18-year-old winner of the Congressional Medal of Honour, Arthur McArthur. He later became a famous general but his son, Douglas, was destined to become even more famous as commander in the Pacific during World War II and the Korean conflict.

The assault on Lookout Mountain directed by General Joseph Hooker was successful, but it was the frontal assault against Missionary Ridge, intended as a diversion, that swept uncontrolled beyond its limited objective to capture the ridge and drive the Confederates from the field.

Park sites along the scenic drive on Missionary Ridge included the place where Confederates repulsed Sherman's repeated attacks, and other critical points now identified by plaques and period cannon. Many of the 5,824 Union casualties in the battle lie in the city's National Cemetery on Bailey Avenue. Confederate losses totalled 6,667, including 4,146 missing.

Lookout Mountain, which dominates the Moccasin Bend of the Tennessee River, is a hodgepodge of tourist attractions, including Ruby Falls and Rock City, with Point Park and Cravens House at the end of a scenic drive up the steep slopes. Both the drive and visits to the park and house provide an insight into the difficulty of the Federals task of clearing Confederates from the slopes.

From Point Park on the crest, three batteries of Napoleon and Parrott cannon point toward the city and valley. The tall New York Peace Memorial is topped by soldiers of both sides shaking hands, under one flag, and the Ochs Museum and Overlook relate, through pictures and exhibits, the story and significance of the fighting for Chattanooga. The white two-story frame Cravens House, used as a Confederate headquarters, was badly damaged by some of the fiercest fighting on the slopes but has been restored to depict the lifestyle of the period, with hostesses in costume to complete the picture. Park rangers demonstrate weapons and equipment during the warm months. A number of hiking trails extend from the principal Bluff Trail, which descends the mountain from the Ochs overlook.

The three Union divisions attacking Lookout Mountain greatly outnumbered the Confederates. Artillerymen on the heights could not see through the morning fog—later, the event became known as the Battle above the Clouds—but Union forces could not dislodge the Southerners. However, after darkness, the Confederates withdrew from this exposed position.

Exhibits on two acres of Signal Mountain, which gets its name from its use as a Civil War

Right: The Battle of Chickamauga was the most significant and bloodiest ever fought in Georgia. It lasted from September 18–20, 1863 and ended in a Union defeat.

Signaling station, explain other aspects of the fighting. Additional monuments stand along the highways of the region, including those leading to Chickamauga in Georgia. The "Confederama" on Lookout Mountain uses more than 5,000 miniature soldiers and weapons, combined with flashing lights, battle sounds, and smoke, to recreate the four principal battles which occurred in the Chattanooga area; the attraction is billed as the world's largest battlefield display, covering 480 square feet.

Above: House in Kolb's Farm in what is today Kennesaw Mountain National Park. For the period, this house was especially spacious and luxurious, with its double chimneys placed at either end.

When Grant was made commander of all Union armies in 1864, Sherman was put in charge of major military operations in the West. He sent three armies—some 100,000 men—south from Chattanooga with the objective of crushing the Confederate army of 50,000 under General Johnston and capturing Atlanta, a key rail hub and the "workhouse and warehouse of the South."

Bloody fighting—"Hell has broke loose in Georgia sure enough," said one Confederate—would result at Kolb's Farm and Kennesaw Mountain, both of which are preserved in the Kennesaw Mountain National Battlefield Park; but the superior numbers of the Union army permitted Sherman to outflank Johnston on a number of occasions.

Kolb's Farm, six miles south of Big Kennesaw Mountain and thus at one end of the battlefield park, was the first major clash of the two armies. The farmhouse, which Union General Hooker used as a headquarters, has been restored to its mid-nineteenth century appearance. The story of the June 22 attacks by Confederate General John B. Hood's corps is recounted there, where it happened, by a recorded message and exhibition on the trail leading away from the house. The fighting was inconclusive; the their main line.

Five days later, Sherman launched a pair of coordinated attacks on Johnston's defences. Trails and roads leading from the battlefield Visitors' Centre to both Big Kennesaw Mountain and Cheatham's Hill cover the battle area, preserved earthworks, trenches, rifle pits, cannon, and exhibits explaining progress of the fighting, where it was 'only necessary to expose a hand to procure a furlough.' The best example of earthworks is at the top of Cheatham Hill, where 8,000 Union attackers suffered 1,580 casualties but could not dislodge the Confederates. Remains of the trenches they dug with bayonets and mess kits on hard-earned slopes may be seen below the Dead Angle, a Confederate salient where the bloodiest fighting of the battle took place. General Thomas, in command of the assault on the Confederate centre, declared 'one or two more such assaults will use up this army.' Unable to defeat Johnston by assault, Sherman resumed his flanking movement and Johnston had to withdraw.

THE CAMPAIGNS OF 1864

THE LAST FULL YEAR OF THE CIVIL WAR BEGAN QUIETLY, WITH UNION FORCES, WHICH BY NOW HAD THE UPPER HAND IN THE CONFLICT, WINTERING AT BRANDY STATION, VIRGINIA. IN MARCH 1864, THE FEDERAL GOVERNMENT PUT GENERAL ULYSSES S. GRANT IN COMMAND OF ALL ITS ARMIES. AS SOON AS THE WEATHER IMPROVED SUFFICIENTLY TO RESUME THE FIGHTING, GRANT SET ABOUT CONFIRMING TO THE ENEMY THAT HIS BYNAME, "UNCONDITIONAL SURRENDER," WAS A REFERENCE TO WHAT HE DEMANDED, NOT TO WHAT HE WAS OFFERING.

Above: The Battle of Cold Harbor, June 1, 1864. General Lee's last victory in the war.

Opposite page: Map of Union forces swamping the Southern States.

Grant's plan for the year was to immobilize the Confederate army of Robert E. Lee near Richmond, Virginia, while despatching General William Tecumseh Sherman to advance into and through Georgia. In pursuit of the former objective, in May, Union forces engaged the rebels in the three-day Battle of the Wilderness in the heart of Virginia. The confrontation itself was inconclusive, but although the Federal army suffered more casualties than it managed to inflict, it had further resources to call on; Lee, on the other hand, was now running critically short of manpower.

The situation inspired Grant to keep on the attack. He fought for five days at Spotsylvania Court House, and then rushed headlong into the Battle of Cold Harbor, in which he was defeated and lost 7,000 of his men in 20 minutes. Yet this was to be Lee's final victory in the Civil War—win or lose,

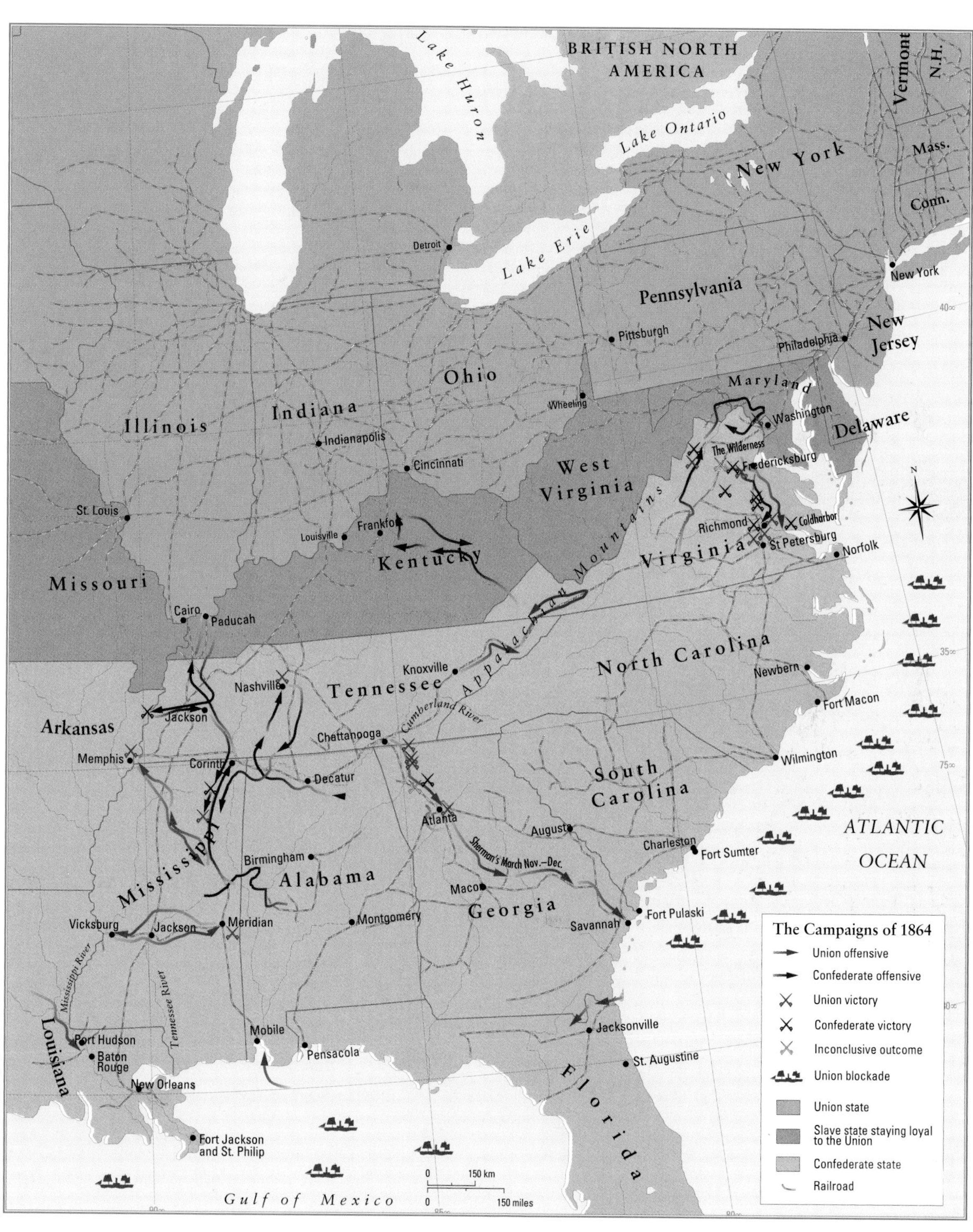
BRITISH NORTH AMERICA
Lake Huron
Lake Ontario
Lake Erie
New York
Vermont
N.H.
Mass.
Conn.
New York
Detroit
Pennsylvania
Pittsburgh
Philadelphia
New Jersey
Ohio
Maryland
Wheeling
Washington
Delaware
Indiana
Illinois
Indianapolis
Cincinnati
West Virginia
The Wilderness
Fredericksburg
St. Louis
Louisville
Frankfort
Kentucky
Richmond
Coldharbor
St Petersburg
Norfolk
Virginia
Appalachian Mountains
Missouri
Cairo
Paducah
North Carolina
Knoxville
Nashville
Tennessee
Cumberland River
Newbern
Fort Macon
Arkansas
Jackson
Chattanooga
Memphis
Corinth
Decatur
Wilmington
South Carolina
Atlanta
Augusta
ATLANTIC OCEAN
Charleston
Fort Sumter
Sherman's March Nov.–Dec.
Mississippi
Birmingham
Alabama
Macon
Georgia
Fort Pulaski
Vicksburg
Jackson
Meridian
Montgomery
Savannah
Mississippi River
Tennessee River
Louisiana
Port Hudson
Baton Rouge
Mobile
Pensacola
Jacksonville
St. Augustine
Florida
New Orleans
Fort Jackson and St. Philip
Gulf of Mexico
0 150 km
0 150 miles
N
The Campaigns of 1864
Union offensive
Confederate offensive
Union victory
Confederate victory
Inconclusive outcome
Union blockade
Union state
Slave state staying loyal to the Union
Confederate state
Railroad

he could no longer stop the Union advancing aganst him in overwhelming numbers.

In June 1864, Grant laid siege to Petersburg, Pennsylvania, with a view to capturing the city and then using it as a base for the final push to the Confederate capital. The attempt ended in failure after 10 months and thousands more deaths on both sides. However, it had the intended effect of pinning down Lee's forces. Meanwhile, Union General Philip Sheridan's cavalry galloped around Virginia, destroying every railroad and enemy supply depot that it encountered. Lee then decided to take the war into Union territory—counterattack at all costs—and in July 1864 he despatched General Jubal Early on his famous Washington Raid, which came within sight of the White House before being driven back into Virginia.

Below: President Lincoln and his wife Mary rode out to watch a night attack of Fort Stephens, on July 11, 1864. They were briefly under enemy fire until ordered to take cover by a commanding officer..

In August, after three and a half months of bitter fighting, the second phase of Grant's grand strategy bore fruit as Sherman advanced from Chattanooga, Tennessee, to Atlanta, Georgia, which surrendered at the beginning of September. News of the fall of the city, and the later destruction of the Confederate munitions' depot there, provoked euphoria in the North.

After 10 weeks' rest and recuperation, in November 1864, Sherman continued his march a

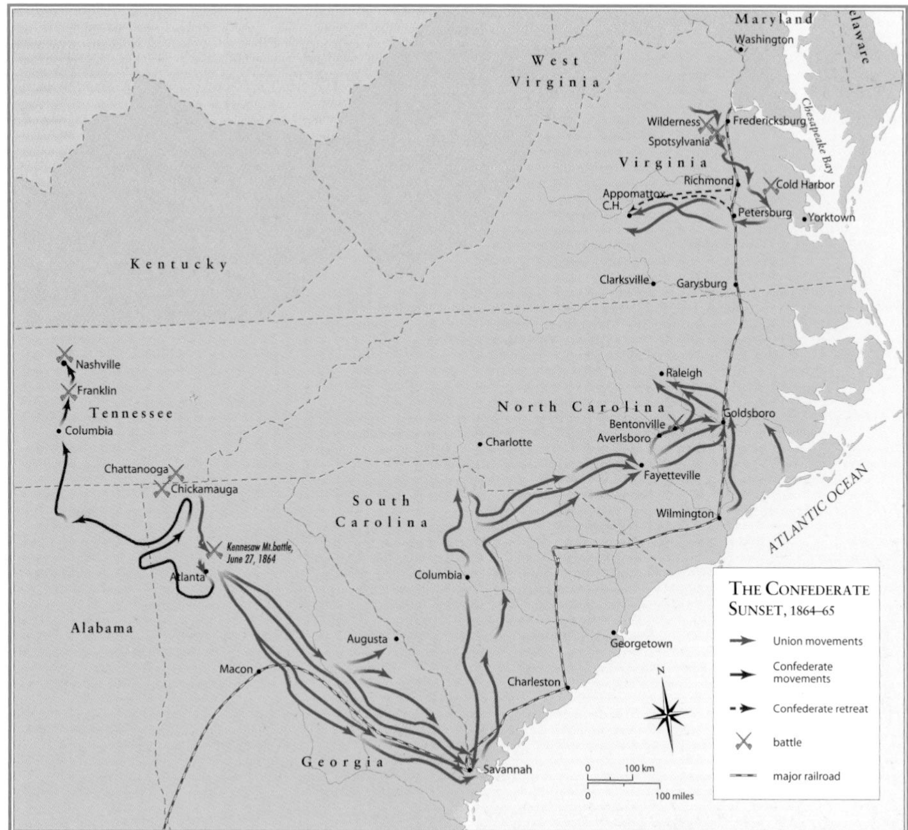

Left: Map showing the Union Army moving confidently through Southern Counties.

further 300 miles southeast through Georgia to the Atlantic coast. Confident that his troops could live off the land, he dispensed with a supply chain back to base. The invaders laid waste to all the economic infrastructure—roads, railroads, bridges, and factories—as they cut a swathe 60 miles wide through the heart of the Confederacy.

In the same month, Abraham Lincoln stood for a second term as U.S. President; his running mate was Andrew Johnson. The Democratic Party ticket was headed by General George B. McClellan with George Pendleton as candidate for vice-president. The result was no foregone conclusion—the incumbent's popularity had been badly eroded by his veto of the Wade-Davis Bill, which had been intended to make the rebel states swear past and future loyalty to the Union as a condition of their readmission after the War. Although radical Republicans were alienated by what they saw as the President's excessive clemency, events in Atlanta swung the vote comprehensively in Lincoln's favor.

On December 15-16, 1864, in the last great battle of the Civil War, Union forces under General George H. Thomas defeated a Confederate attempt to recapture Nashville, Tennessee. On December 21, 1864, Sherman reached the eastern seaboard and captured Savannah, Georgia, finally cutting off the last of the rebels' maritime supply routes.

MERIDIAN & OLUSTEE

FEBRUARY 1864 SAW THE MERIDIAN CAMPAIGN IN MISSISSIPPI AND THE BATTLE OF OLUSTEE IN FLORIDA. THOUGH THE CONFEDERATE VICTORIES WERE SEEN AS TURNING POINTS AT THE TIME, THEY HAD NO GREAT INFLUENCE ON THE OUTCOME OF THE WAR.

In early 1863, Union Major General William Tecumshe Sherman, with a total force of some 30,000 men under his command, was determined to destroy once and for all the rail system and Confederate infrasctructure of the mid-Mississippi region, leaving him free to campaign in the east for the remainder of the year. The plan was to lead his troops to the town of Meridian on the Mobile and Ohio railroad near the Alabama border, which was the site of a Confederate arsenal, its main military hospital and prisoner-of-war camp. There he would meet up with the cavalry General William Sooy Smith, to whom he had given the largest and best-equipped body of Union horseman that had yet been assembled in the western theater: 7,000 troopers all armed with new breech-loading carbines and accompanied by 20 cannon. According to the plan, by the time of their meeting, Smith should have already destroyed all the railroad tracks from Okolona to Meridian. Sherman and Smith's forces would then combine, before rampaging eastward to Selma, Alabama.

Sherman began to make his way across Mississippi in early part of February. Although the Confederate commander of the area, General Leonidas Polk, was aware that Sherman was poised to attack, and had a good number of troops at his disposal, he was still unable to mount a convincing opposition. His plans were particularly hampered by various feinting maneuvers by Sherman, who ordered his troops to launch a number of fake attacks to prevent Polk from guessing his true intentions.

Some skirmishing did take place between Union troops and Confederate forces under the command of Brigadier General Wirt Adams, but despite the Rebels best efforts, they were unable to halt—or even slow down—the advance. On February 5 Sherman's forces marched into Jackson, the state capital, where they quickly destroyed any remaining military infrastructure—of which there was, in truth, little, the town having fallen to Sherman twice already during the course of the

American Civil War.

Sherman kept the Confederates guessing by ordering Union boats in Alabama's Mobile bay to start maneuvers, as if preparing for an attack. Polk became convinced, mistakenly as it turned out, that Sherman's major advance would be in the bay and so stationed the majoirty of his forces there. In the event he even decided to evacuate Meridian, so as to concentrate his forces and equipment in Mobile.

As a result, when Sherman and his forces entered Meridian on February 14, they were more or less unopposed. The troops spent six days in the town, systematically dismantling its arsenal,

Left: Portrait of General William Tecumseh Sherman (1820-1891), Union Commander of the Western Theater, from 1864 onwards

hospital, railroads, bridges, warehouses and any other infrastructure that might be of potential use to the enemy. Of his efforts Sherman said, "Meridian, with its depots, store-houses, arsenal, hospitals, offices, hotels, and cantonments, no longer exists."

The expedition had been a tremendous success, except for one major, but crucial, flaw—the non arrival of General William Sooy Smith and his 7,000 troopers. To begin with, everything had been going well. Although Smith did not actually begin his march until the day after he was due to meet up with Sherman, which meant that he did not arrive in Okolona until February 18, once there his men immediately and enthusiastically set about destroying everything in sight. One officer reported, "During two days the sky was red with the flames of burning corn and cotton."

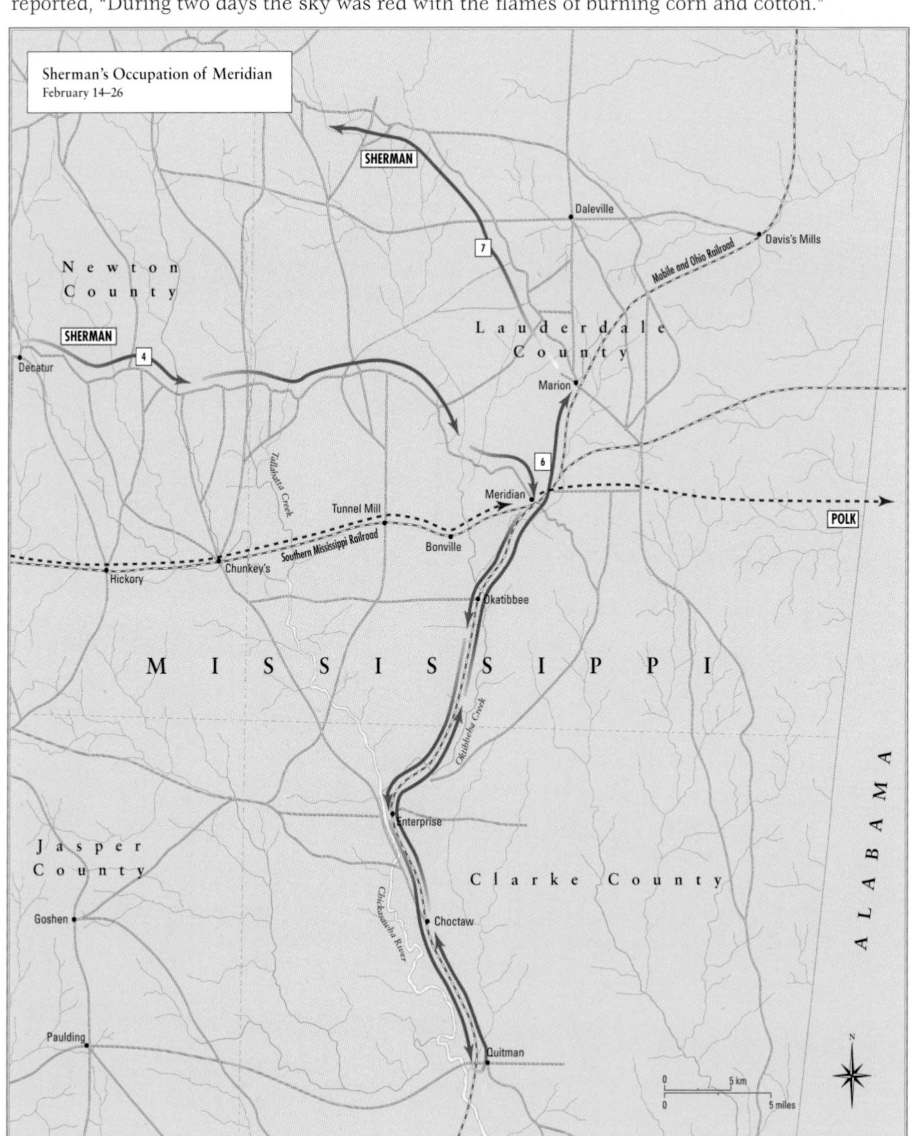

Right: Map showing how Sherman's troops marched on, and destroyed, the town of Meridian in February 1864.

Opposite page: This map shows how Smith's campaign in Mississippi was much less successful than his superior's.

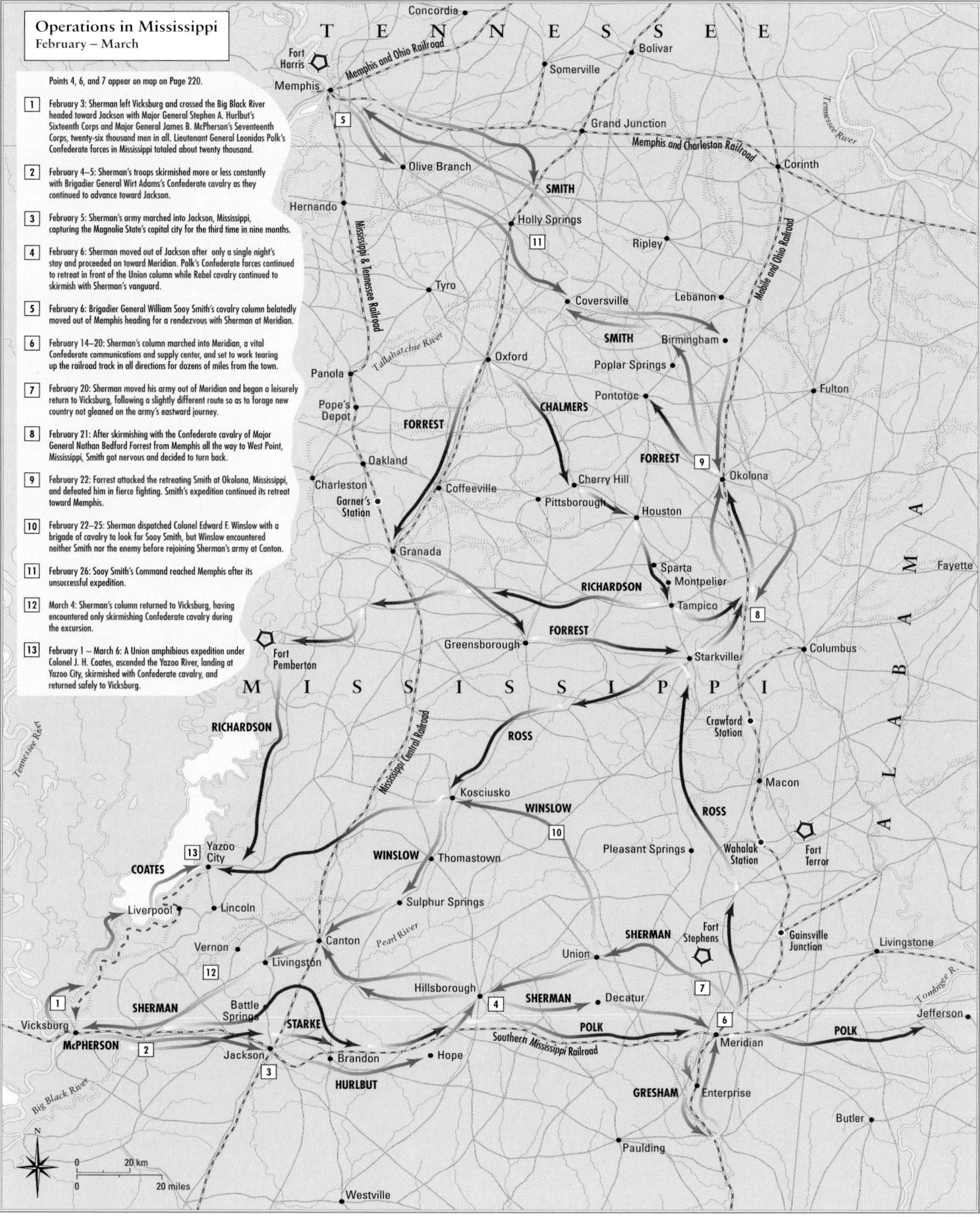

Operations in Mississippi
February – March
Points 4, 6, and 7 appear on map on Page 220.
1 February 3: Sherman left Vicksburg and crossed the Big Black River headed toward Jackson with Major General Stephen A. Hurlbut's Sixteenth Corps and Major General James B. McPherson's Seventeenth Corps, twenty-six thousand men in all. Lieutenant General Leonidas Polk's Confederate forces in Mississippi totaled about twenty thousand.
2 February 4–5: Sherman's troops skirmished more or less constantly with Brigadier General Wirt Adams's Confederate cavalry as they continued to advance toward Jackson.
3 February 5: Sherman's army marched into Jackson, Mississippi, capturing the Magnolia State's capital city for the third time in nine months.
4 February 6: Sherman moved out of Jackson after only a single night's stay and proceeded on toward Meridian. Polk's Confederate forces continued to retreat in front of the Union column while Rebel cavalry continued to skirmish with Sherman's vanguard.
5 February 6: Brigadier General William Sooy Smith's cavalry column belatedly moved out of Memphis heading for a rendezvous with Sherman at Meridian.
6 February 14–20: Sherman's column marched into Meridian, a vital Confederate communications and supply center, and set to work tearing up the railroad track in all directions for dozens of miles from the town.
7 February 20: Sherman moved his army out of Meridian and began a leisurely return to Vicksburg, following a slightly different route so as to forage new country not gleaned on the army's eastward journey.
8 February 21: After skirmishing with the Confederate cavalry of Major General Nathan Bedford Forrest from Memphis all the way to West Point, Mississippi, Smith got nervous and decided to turn back.
9 February 22: Forrest attacked the retreating Smith at Okolona, Mississippi, and defeated him in fierce fighting. Smith's expedition continued its retreat toward Memphis.
10 February 22–25: Sherman dispatched Colonel Edward F. Winslow with a brigade of cavalry to look for Sooy Smith, but Winslow encountered neither Smith nor the enemy before rejoining Sherman's army at Canton.
11 February 26: Sooy Smith's Command reached Memphis after its unsuccessful expedition.
12 March 4: Sherman's column returned to Vicksburg, having encountered only skirmishing Confederate cavalry during the excursion.
13 February 1 – March 6: A Union amphibious expedition under Colonel J. H. Coates, ascended the Yazoo River, landing at Yazoo City, skirmished with Confederate cavalry, and returned safely to Vicksburg.
TENNESSEE
MISSISSIPPI
ALABAMA
Concordia
Fort Harris
Memphis
Memphis and Ohio Railroad
Bolivar
Somerville
Grand Junction
Memphis and Charleston Railroad
Tennessee River
Corinth
Olive Branch
SMITH
Hernando
Holly Springs
Ripley
Mississippi & Tennessee Railroad
Mobile and Ohio Railroad
Tyro
Coversville
Lebanon
SMITH
Birmingham
Tallahatchie River
Oxford
Poplar Springs
Panola
Pontotoc
Fulton
Pope's Depot
CHALMERS
FORREST
Oakland
FORREST
Okolona
Charleston
Coffeeville
Cherry Hill
Garner's Station
Pittsborough
Houston
Granada
Sparta
Montpelier
Fayette
RICHARDSON
Tampico
FORREST
Greensborough
Starkville
Columbus
Fort Pemberton
Mississippi Central Railroad
Crawford Station
RICHARDSON
ROSS
Tennessee River
Macon
Kosciusko
WINSLOW
ROSS
Pleasant Springs
Wahalak Station
Fort Terror
Yazoo City
COATES
WINSLOW
Thomastown
Sulphur Springs
Liverpool
Lincoln
Pearl River
Fort Stephens
SHERMAN
Gainsville Junction
Livingstone
Canton
Vernon
Livingston
Union
Tombigbee R.
Hillsborough
SHERMAN
Decatur
SHERMAN
Battle Springs
STARKE
POLK
Jefferson
Vicksburg
POLK
McPHERSON
Meridian
Southern Mississippi Railroad
Jackson
Brandon
Hope
HURLBUT
Big Black River
GRESHAM
Enterprise
Butler
Paulding
N
0 20 km
0 20 miles
Westville

Above: Photograph of Major General Quincy Adams Gillmore (1825-1888). He is remembered for his expedition into Florida designed to help reconstruct it as a Union state, as well as to recruit more soldiers and sever supply lines to the Confederates.

Dwellings were also burned with such enthusiasm that Smith said that he was "...disgraced by incendiarism of the most shocking kind."

However, when Smith finally set off for Meridian on February 20, he soon encountered Confederate General Nathan Bedford Forrest's newly recruited 2,500-man cavalry force. Although Smith was now two thirds of the way to Meridian, and had a much larger force at his command—not to mention far superior firepower—than his opponent, he was by now ten days behind schedule and was now responsible for the welfare of around 3,000 former slaves who had flocked to him for protection.

In the event, Smith made the extraordinary decision not to fight, but to withdraw. Forrest, however, attacked, defeating Smith's forces who were forced to retreat. Forrest set off in hot pursuit, only calling off the chase when his troopers ran out of ammunition.

Sherman waited patiently for Smith at Meridian for five whole days before reluctantly returning to Vicksburg with his 22,000 men. It was only after he arrived on March 4 that learned of Smith's defeat and ignominious retreat.

Meanwhile, in Florida, moves were afoot to try and reconstruct the state into the Union. The reasoning was that being that as Florida was at that time sparsely populated, of little strategic value, and only defended by a state militia, the state could easily be taken by federal forces. This was largely a political move on Lincoln's part because if the state could be reconstructed in the Republican party mold it would boost Lincoln's support in Congress and in the upcoming presidential election.

Union General Quincy A. Gillmore was delighted to be put in charge of this campaign, which he saw as a sure winner. On February 7, 1864, he arrived at Jacksonville, Florida, with a force of 8,000 men, having traveled by ship from South Carolina. His plan was to push east along the Atlantic and Gulf Central Railroad to the Suwannee River, about 60 miles away, severing Confederate supply routes and recruiting black soldiers for the Union army as he went.

After about 40 miles, having received reports of Confederate forces massing up ahead and suffering severe supply problems, he decided to turn back. He retuned to Jacksonville and put General Truman Seymour in charge, before returning to South Carolina.

Seymour made a number of small-scale but largely successful raids into northern Floridian territory, during which he took a number of Southern bases. Gillmore, however, remained cautious about Confederate retaliation and refused Seymour permission to push further inland into the heart of the state. Indeed, Seymour's actions were proving a source of grave concern to the Confederate command in Charleston, South Carolina—so much so that General Beauregard felt obliged to send troops to bolster Florida's defences who at that time were under the control of Brigadier General Joseph Finegan.

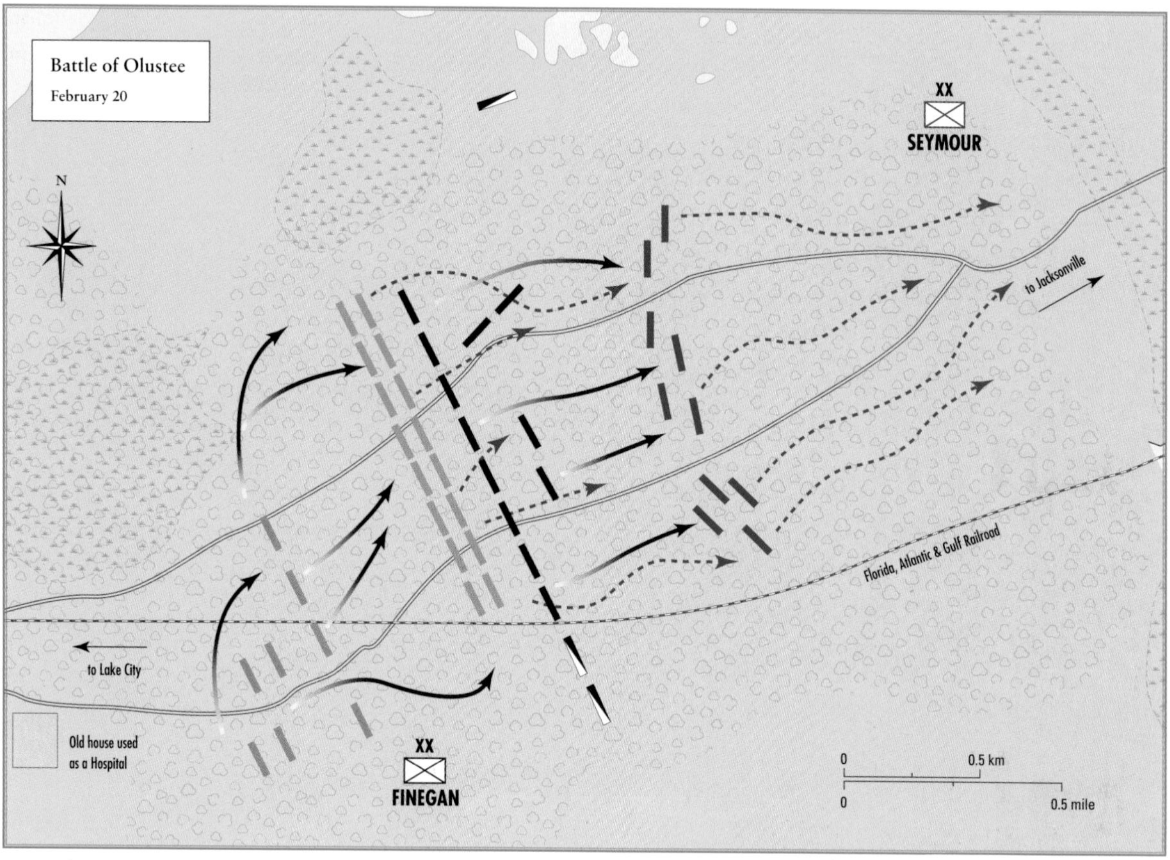

Above: The Battle of Olustee. General Truman Seymour took over control of the Union assault and raided a number of Confederate bases before turning his attentions to Lake City.

On February 20, Seymour was leading his force of 5,500 men on a raid towards Lake City—such had become his frustration with his superior's timidity that he was undertaking without Gillmore's knowledge—when, at around 2.30pm, he was intercepted by Finegan's 5,000-strong force. The troops engaged in a battle lasting most of the afternoon in open pine woods. Momentum shifted backward and forward until eventually Finegan proved victorious, breaking through the Union lines and forcing Seymour to retreat.

The 1,861 casualties suffered by the Union amounted to around 40 per cent of their total force, making it one of the costliest battles for them in the entire war. This high ratio was, it is believed, partly the result of the Confederate side killing captured black Union soldiers. In comparison, the Confederates suffered just 946 casualties, or less than 20 per cent of their total force.

THE RED RIVER CAMPAIGN, MARCH 10 - MAY 22, 1864

THE CAMPAIGNS OF MAJOR GENERAL NATHANIEL P. BANKS WOULD LEAVE DEEP SCARS AT ALEXANDRIA AND PINEVILLE, STRATEGIC CENTRES ON RED RIVER, AND CULMINATED WITH BANKS' DEFEAT IN THE BATTLE OF MANSFIELD, SOUTH OF SHREVEPORT.

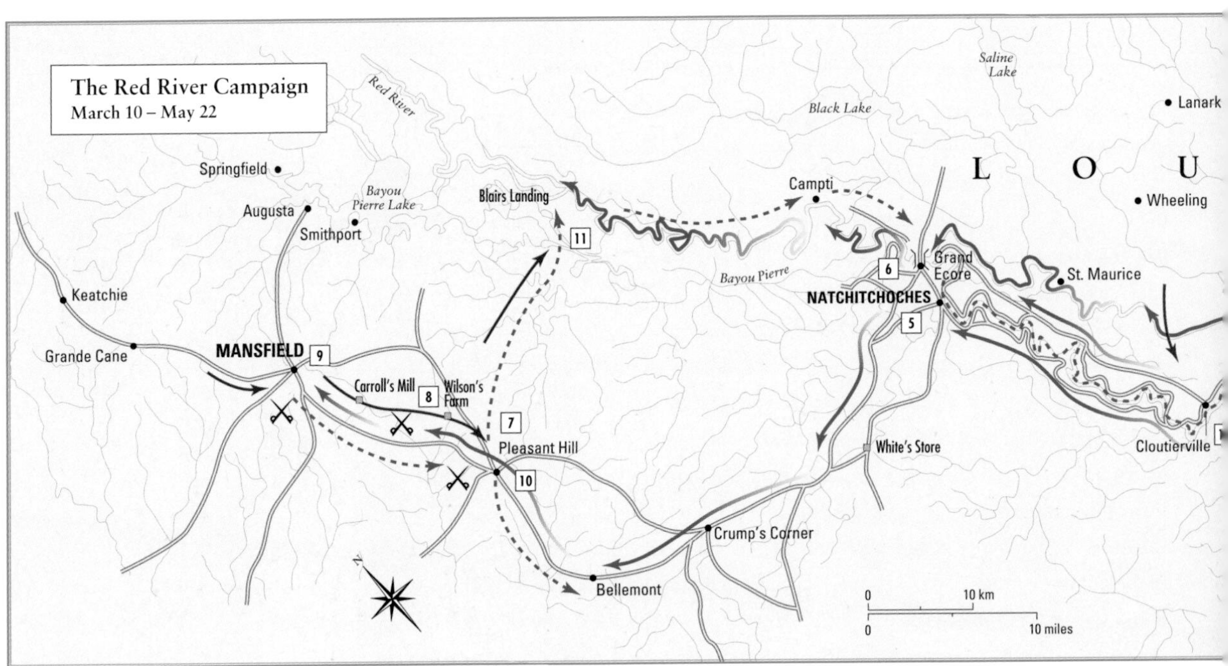

The first, a combined land and naval operation, stopped at Alexandria, a Confederate headquarters and supply base as well as a commercial packing centre. Confederates retreated after only perfunctory defense of the city but the shallowness of the water prevented Union gunboats from going farther. Banks, who disapproved of campaigns in the Red River Valley, destroyed military targets at Alexandria and Pineville, recruited slaves as soldiers, and returned to his base. The second expedition in 1864 met brief resistance at Marksville, better known now for relics of an Indian culture which existed 1,000 years before America was discovered by Europeans. This time the gunboats were able to cross the rapids at Alexandria and move toward Shreveport, the temporary State capital. Occupation of Shreveport would give the Union effective control of Louisiana.

Banks' army of 20,000 men had been strengthened by 10,000 veterans of the fighting at Vicksburg, but Confederate Major General Richard Taylor chose well the place to make his stand. He stopped the campaign in the Battles of Mansfield and Pleasant Hill.

A portion of the battlefield is preserved as a State commemorative area three miles from Mansfield, with a Visitors' Centre and quarter-mile trail through the woods, named after General Mouton, one of the

Below: A detailed map and timeline outlining the key events of the Red River Campaign, which lasted from March 10–22, 1864

1 March 13: Major General A. J. Smith's three-division detachment of the Army of the Tennessee landed at Simsport.

2 March 14: Smith's veterans easily captured Fort De Russy.

3 March 15–16: Union gunboats under the commander of Rear Admiral David D. Porter arrived at Alexander on March 15 and occupied the town the following day.

4 March 21: Several skirmishes occurred as Banks's army continued to ascend the Red River Valley; one of the larger ones was at Henderson's Hill, where Brigadier General Joseph Mower's division of the Sixteenth Corps, along with a detachment of cavalry, captured four guns and two hundred and fifty prisoners.

5 April 2: Banks's troops occupied the old river town of Natchitoches.

6 April 3: A disloyal guide informed Banks that no road paralleled the river above Grand Ecore and he would therefore have to take his army well inland, far from the support of the gunboats. Banks believed him and led his army away from the river.

7 April 7: Banks arrived at Pleasant Hill.

8 April 7–8: Brigadier General Albert L. Lee's cavalry, leading Banks's advance, skirmished intensely with Confederates all along the advance from Pleasant Hill.

9 April 8: Major General Richard Taylor's army caught Banks's column strung out along the road as it approached Mansfield. In a fierce battle Taylor was victorious, and Banks retreated to Pleasant Hill.

10 April 9: Taylor pursued and attacked Banks again at Pleasant Hill. Banks, reinforced by A. J. Smith's troops, repulsed, but nevertheless determined to continue his retreat.

11 April 12: Confederate cavalry, led by Brigadier General Thomas Green, attacked the Union gunboats at Blair's Landing, but the attack was repulsed and Green killed.

12 April 13 – May 13: The Confederates continued to harass the expedition by constant skirmishing as it proceeded down the Red River.

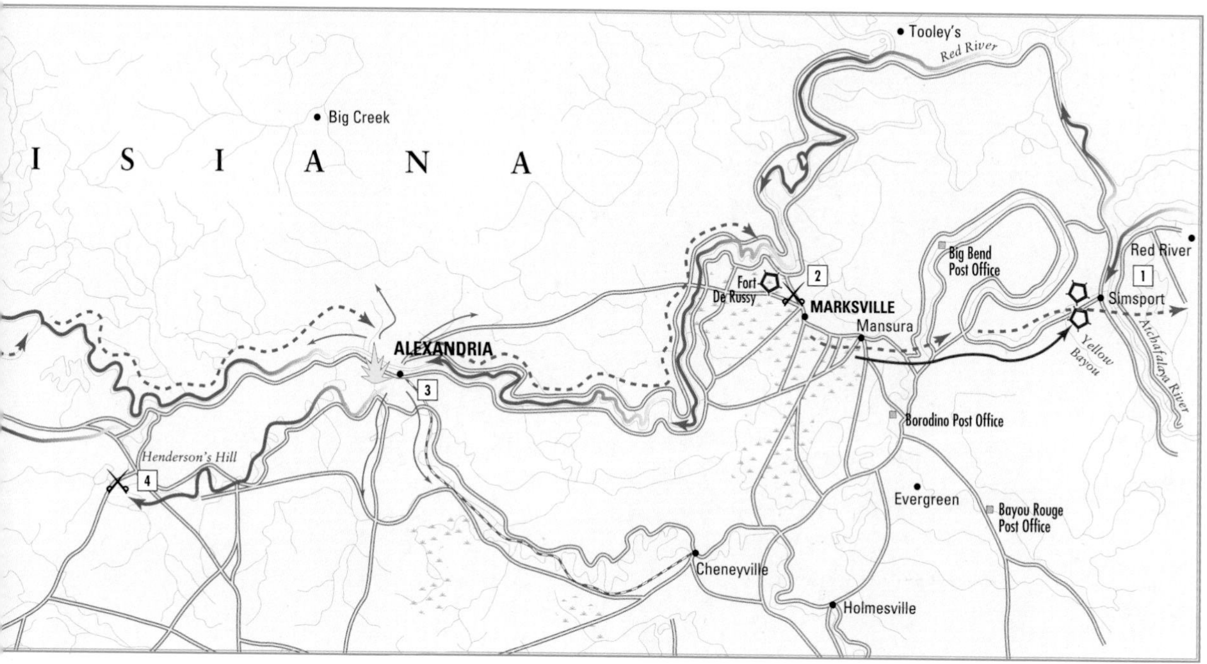

Confederate commanders. Along the trail, a reconstructed rail fence recreates one of the features along which the Union defences were organised; markers identify various phases of the April 8 battle, in which the impatience of General Taylor played an important part. Taylor tired of waiting for Banks to attack and sent his troops against both Union flanks before they could be reinforced. The Union line crumbled and retreated five miles to Pleasant Hill, where a stand by the Union XIX Corps ended the battle.

The Visitors' Centre houses a collection of memorabilia, including a sizable collection of rifles and pistols, a Confederate six-pounder cannon cast in 1861 at Nashville, and good displays on the role of 60 river warships committed to the Red River Campaign. Included are models of the ironclad USS *Corondolet* and the ironclad Confederate ram *Arkansas* and photographs of the riverboats during the campaign.

Monuments at the entrance to the park and elsewhere commemorate the victory and memorialise the officers who were killed in the battle, General Mouton among them. Union losses of 3,000 were about three times those of the Confederates, and Banks retreated first to Alexandria and then to Baton Rouge. His retreat added to the unusual collection of Civil War relics at the cross-river cities of Alexandria and Pineville. Shallow water trapped the Union gunboats above the falls until an ingenious dam enabled them to escape.

The sites of Confederate Forts Buhlow and Randolph, built to protect against further Federal incursions that never came, are preserved. Mount Olivet Chapel, built in 1850, was used as a barracks by Union troops. Kent House, built in 1796 and the oldest remaining structure in central Louisiana, includes separate kitchen, slaves quarters, and milk house. The Rosalie Sugar Mill represents a commodity involved in much of the foraging in Louisiana during the war. Lloyd Hall,

Right: Union warships and transports were trapped by shallow water near Alexandria, Louisiana, during the Red River Campaign of 1864.

Above: A Union Army under General Nathaniel Prentiss Banks crosses the Cane River, Lousiana, on March 30, 1864, during the Red River Campaign.

an 1810 plantation home at Lecompte whose owner was hanged as a spy by the Federals, was used by armies of both sides.

Alexandria has close prewar and postwar associations with two famous Union generals—Major General William T. Sherman and Major General George Armstrong Custer, respectively. Sherman established the forerunner of Louisiana State University at Pineville and resigned as its president to accept a Union commission. Custer, sent to Alexandria in 1865 to direct the "reconstruction," faced one of his most trying challenges—the mutiny of the Third Michigan Cavalry.

The story is told locally this way. As a joke, after having been commended for its soldierly appearance, the 90-man unit turned out with hats on backward, jackets turned inside out, swords on the wrong side, and otherwise in a sloppy condition. Custer, who did not think it funny, courtmartialled the unit and sentenced a sergeant accused of being the ringleader to be shot. When Custer would not yield to a petition from the men, talk of mutiny began to circulate. Custer, aware of it, faced down the prospective mutineers on the morning of the execution of the sergeant and another man, convicted of desertion. The guns of the firing squad roared and both men dropped—the deserter dead and the sergeant fainting. Custer had ordered that he be placed just outside the line of fire. The site of the event is now occupied by St. Francis Xavier Cathedral.

Tyrone House, built around 1840, was spared the torch because its owner was a friend of Sherman's prior to the war. Winter Quarters, a State commemorative site at Newellton, was spared on order of General Ulysses S. Grant while most homes in the region were burned. It was a trade-off: the wife of the owner, a Union sympathizer, offered to feed and quarter Union troops during the siege of Vicksburg. The house, built in sections starting in 1805, demonstrates two architectural styles and houses mementoes of the war and examples of the research on cotton farming done by the plantation owner.

FORREST'S OPERATIONS IN MISSISSIPPI & TENNESSEE

FROM 1862 TO THE END OF THE WAR, ONE OF THE CHIEF THORNS IN THE SIDE OF THE UNION FORCES IN THE MISSISSIPPI-TENNESSEE REGION WAS BRIGADIER GENERAL NATHAN BEDFORD FORREST.

Forrest came from a poor family in rural Tennessee. He was the oldest of twelve children and when his father died when he was 17, he assumed responsibility for the family and went into business, initially with an uncle. He went on to become a very wealthy and successful pillar of Memphis society, chiefly by owning plantations and trading in slaves. It is estimated that at the start of the war he was one of the richest men in the South, with an estimated fortune of around $1.5 million.

Although exempt from military service, in July 1861 he enlisted as a private in the Confederate Army. He had no military training but once he realized the poor state of the Army, he made an offer to use his own money to buy horses and equipment for a regiment of Tennessee volunteer soldiers. As a result he was commissioned as a colonel and in October 1861 he was given command of his own regiment. Forrest made up for his lack of military training by diligent learning. He had strong leadership qualities and an intuition for successful tactics. As a result he soon became an exemplary cavalry officer.

Forrest first made his mark in February 1862 at the battle of Fort Donelson, where he captured a Union artillery battery and broke out of a Union Army siege headed by Major General Ulysses S. Grant. A few days later he took command of Nashville to prevent it falling into Union hands. Forrest rarely lost a cavalry battle during the whole war, but he never got on with his superior, General Braxton Bragg. As a result it was subsequently widely accepted that the Confederate high command never made best use of Forrest's talents. In July 1862 he was promoted to brigadier general, but in December, in spite of his protests, Bragg assigned Forrest's veteran troopers to

Opposite page: Map showing the operations of Nathan Bedford Forrest in Mississippi and Tennessee from 10 March until 4 November 1864.

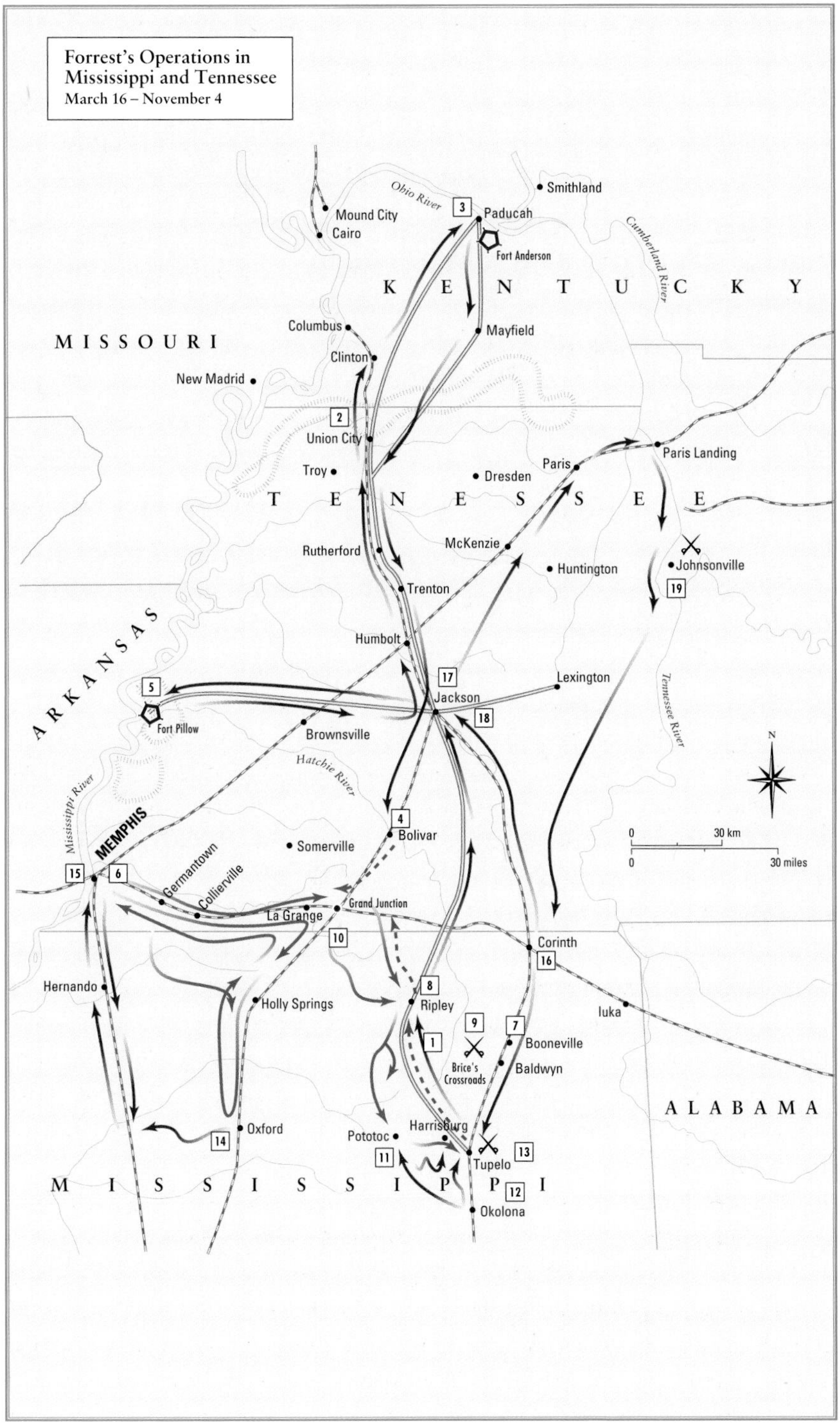

Forrest's Operations in Mississippi and Tennessee
March 16 – November 4

1 March 16: Forrest rode north for another raid into Tennessee and Kentucky.

2 March 24: Forrest captured at four hundred and fifty-man Union garrison at Union City, Tennessee.

3 March 25: Forrest reached Paducah and demanded the surrender of Fort Anderson. When the Unionists refused, he attacked but was repulsed and withdrew the next morning.

4 March 29: Moving rapidly, Forrest reached Bolivar, Tennessee, and drove off a small force of Union cavalry.

5 April 12: Forrest attacked and captured Fort Pillow, where his men slaughtered black troops attempting to surrender.

6 June 2: With orders from Sherman to hunt down Forrest, Major General Samuel D. Sturgis departed Memphis.

7 June 9: Learning of Sturgis's approach, Forrest met with his department commander, Major General Stephen D. Lee, at Booneville to plan a response.

8 June 9: Sturgis's expedition reached Ripley, Mississippi.

9 June 10: Forrest met and defeated Sturgis at Brice's Crossroads.

10 July 5: Sherman dispatched another expedition to hunt down Forrest, this time Major General A. J. Smith with two divisions of infantry and one of cavalry, all from the Sixteenth Corps, and totaling fourteen thousand men in all. They marched out of La Grange, Tennessee.

11 July 11: Smith's cavalry, commanded by Brigadier General Benjamin H. Grierson, met and drove off a force of Confederate cavalry.

12 July 13: The combined forces of Lee and Forrest, numbering nine thousand five hundred men, advanced from Okolona toward Pontotoc. Their advanced forces skirmished with Smith's cavalry.

13 July 13–14: Maneuvering to flank the Confederate position on the Okolona Road, Smith moved east to Harrisburg, near Tupelo. The next morning the Confederates attacked but were repulsed.

14 August 18: Forrest set out on yet another raid, bound this time for Memphis via Hernando. Mississippi.

15 August 21: Forrest and his raiders made an early-morning foray into Memphis before returning quickly the way they had come.

16 October 19: Once again Forrest went raiding, this time setting out from Corinth.

17 October 22: Forrest occupied Jackson, Tennessee.

18 October 29: Using his field artillery from the shore, Forrest captured one gunboat and two transports and began moving them southward, up the Tennessee River, while his troops kept pace on the bank.

19 November 4: Forrest again used his artillery to good advantage, damaging Union transports and supplies at Johnsonville, but he had to abandoned his captured vessels and march back to Corinth overland.

another officer. Forrest had to form a new brigade with 2,000 inexperienced recruits. Against his better judgment he was sent into Tennessee to disrupt the communications of Grant's Unionist forces who were threatening the Mississippi city of Vicksburg.

Forrest was so successful that he returned with more men than he had started out with and all were now fully armed with captured Union weapons. He continued to lead his men in small-scale operations until April 1863 when he was sent to deal with an attack by Union Colonel Abel Streight, who with a cavalry force of 3,000, had orders to cut the rebel supply lines south of Chattanooga. Forrest caught up with Streight on May 3 and although he had fewer men, he persuaded Streight to surrender his 1,700 exhausted troops.

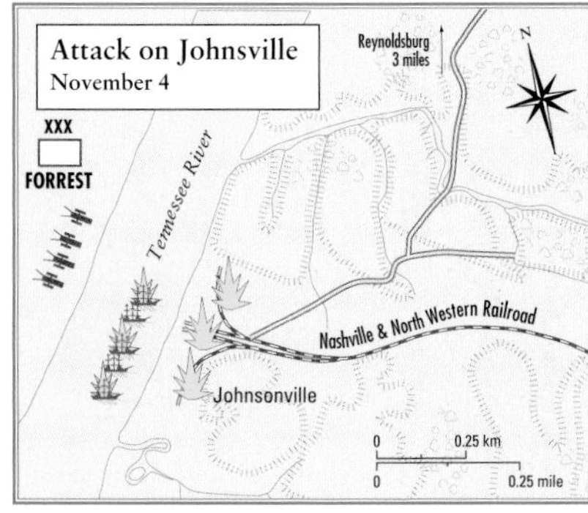

Above: Map of the attack at Johnsville that took place at the Tennessee River.

In September 1863 Forrest served with the main army at the Battle of Chickamauga. He pursued the retreating Union army and took hundreds of prisoners. Chattanooga had fallen a few weeks before and along with a number of fellow officers he urged Bragg to immediately to follow the victory at Chickamauga with an attempt to recapture the city, but Bragg failed to do so. In December 1863 Forrest was promoted to the rank of major general and given an independent command in Mississippi. On March 16 Forrest ordered a month-long cavalry raid with 7,000 troopers into Western Tennessee and Kentucky. The object was to take prisoners, capture supplies and demolish posts and fortifications. The first battle was at Paducah on March 25. His 3,000 men soon dealt with the 650 defenders and Forrest took all the supplies he needed before destroying the rest.

Although this was a Confederate victory, very little was archived that would affect the outcome of the war, other than the destruction of Union supplies. After a number of further skirmishes, April 12 saw the most controversial episode of Forrest's career at the Battle of Fort Pillow. Fort Pillow was 40 miles (64 km) north of Memphis, Tennessee, and was occupied by union troops. Forrest needed horses and supplies, so with a force of between 1,500 and 2,500 men he decided to attack.

The Union garrison consisted of about 600 men, divided almost evenly between black and white troops. A fierce battle raged until mid afternoon when Forrest sent in a note demanding surrender. This was refused and a fresh and devastating assault began. There are conflicting reports as to what happened next. Union sources claimed that after the surviving defenders surrendered they were shot down or bayoneted in cold blood. Subsequent investigations suggest that this was indeed so. However, other sources maintain that the defenders never surrendered, but carried on fighting to the death. Union losses were high; around 80% of the black soldiers and 40% of the whites. Only 58 black soldiers were taken prisoner against 168 white soldiers. In the aftermath of Fort Pillow Abraham Lincoln demanded that Confederates treat captured black Union soldiers as prisoners of war even if they were runaway slaves. This demand was refused and a lasting effect of this battle was the ending of the previous practice of exchanging prisoners of war. The U.S. Congress subsequently cleared Forrest of all responsibility for war crimes at the battle.

By now Union General Sherman was getting increasingly concerned that Forrest's cavalry raids were putting a great strain on the Union's fragile supply and communication lines. To try and put a stop to this he ordered Major General Samuel D. Sturgis to put a halt to Forrest's campaign of

Left: Fort Pillow was under Union control until the Confederate Army attcked and won. Out of 262 Black Union soldiers that engaged in battle, 229 were slaughtered, unarmed, after the Confederate victory. "Remember Fort Pillow!" became a battle cry for black soldiers for the remainder of the Civil War.

destruction of Union supplies and fortifications.

Forrest, with his 3,500-man force met up with Sturgis's 8,500 Union troops at Brice's Crossroads near Baldwyn in Lee County, Mississippi on June 10, 1864. Forrest knew that Sturgis was after him and although heavily outnumbered he decided to attack, choosing the muddy, wooded area around Brice's Crossroads for the ambush. When the Federal army reached the crossroads, Forrest's cavalry attacked. The Union infantry were tired and weary, the line was broken, they were subjected to massive firepower and there was a mass retreat. The Confederates suffered 96 killed and 396 wounded in the action, while Union losses were over 2,000. Forrest captured huge supplies of arms, artillery and ammunition, as well as plenty of stores. Sturgis was demoted and effectively exiled to the far West.

In spite of his run of success, on July 15 Forrest suffered his first tactical defeat. General Sherman was still determined to stop his rampaging activities and this time sent General Andrew J. Smith to deal with him. Smith arrived in Northern Mississippi on July 11, 1864. Forrest was camped nearby with 6,000 troops but under orders not to attack until reinforcements arrived. The following day General Stephen D. Lee arrived with a further 2,000 men. The Confederates attacked on July 14, but Union forces sent Forrest from the field. This was a tactical victory for the Union. Sherman's supply lines had been protected, but Forrest's cavalry were still at large. Smith was criticized for not destroying Forrest when he had the chance since for the remainder of the war he continued to lead raids against Union targets.

STATE OF ARKANSAS, MARCH 29–MAY 3, 1864

THE STATE OF ARKANSAS WAS IN AN UNCOMFORTABLE POSITION DURING THE CIVIL WAR. IT WAS NOT A STRATEGIC PRIORITY FOR EITHER SIDE, YET IT WAS A RUNNING BATTLEGROUND FOR MUCH OF THE TIME. MORE THAN 770 MILITARY EVENTS OF ALL KINDS OCCURRED THERE, FIVE OF THEM CLASSIFIED AS BATTLES.

In early March, 1864, Major General Frederick Steele was ordered to lead an expedition from Little Rock, Arkansas, to Shreveport, Louisiana. Steele had severe misgivings about the mission—particularly about the state of the roads—which caused him to delay his departure until March 23—a delay that would fundamentally undermine the expeditions chances of success.

As soon as Steele had left Little Rock he was set upon by Confederate cavalry and forced to engage in frequent skirmishing which necessarily greatly slowed his pace of advance. Steele pushed on, however, and by March 29 had reached Arkadelphia, 70 miles from Little Rock. The plan had been to join up there were Union troops under the command of Brigadier General John M. Thayer. However, Thayer was nowhere to be seen. Overcoming his natural caution, Steele forged on, finally meeting with Thayer at Eklin's Ferry, Arkansas.

Despite the bolstering of his forces, Steele would soon encounter some serious problems. Union Major General Nathaniel P. Banks' recent defeat at the Battle of Mansfield meant that large numbers of Confederate forces were now free to engage with Steele, which they did forcing him to into a three-day running battle at Prairie D'Ane.

Opposite page: Frederick Steele served as a Major General during the Civil War. He lead a campaign in 1864 to recover secessionist Arkansas for the Northern Army.

To compound his problems, Steele was by now running very low on supplies. Basing himself in the town of Camden, he despatched his troops to forage for supplies using a large wagon train. It was attacked by Confederate forces, who overwhelmed the Union troops, overcoming them and

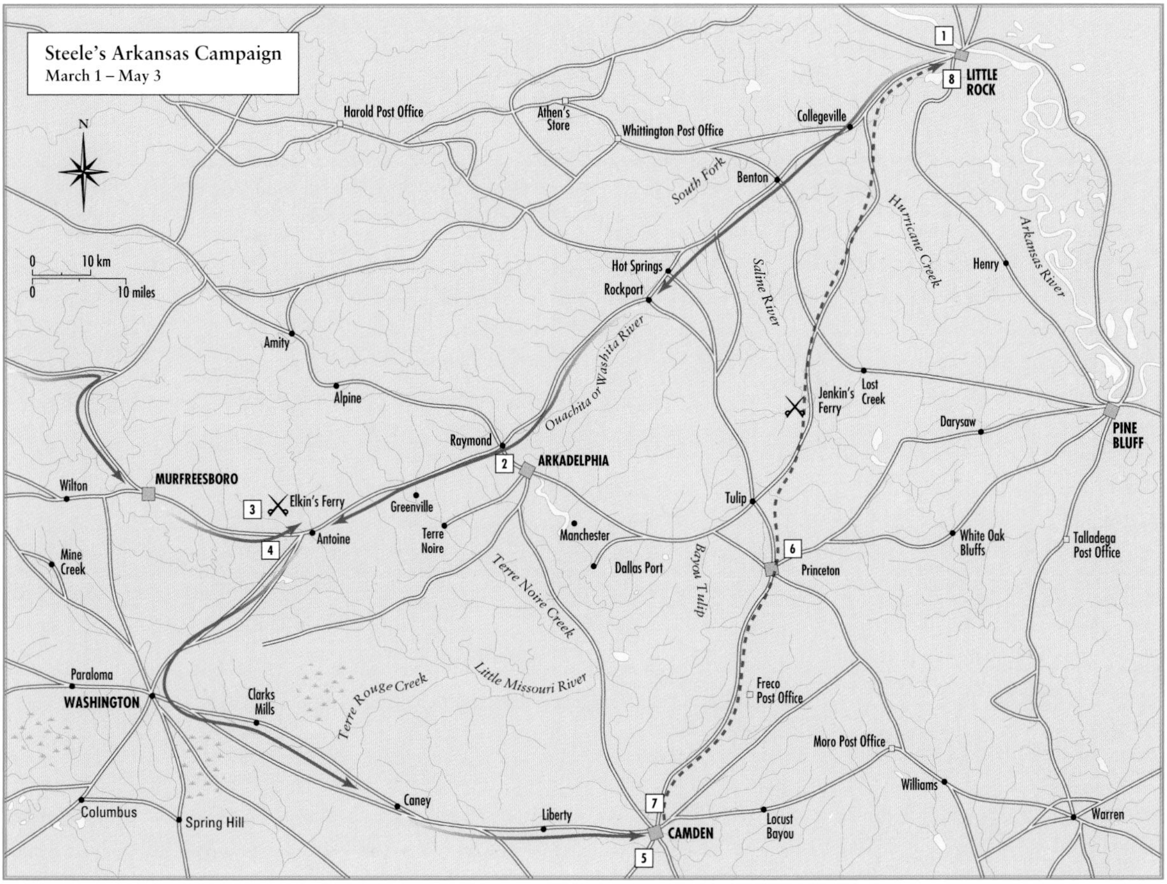

Steele's Arkansas Campaign
March 1 – May 3

destroying 198 wagons.

Another Union supply train was attacked one week later by Rebels at Marks' Mills. Again the Confederate side would prove victorious following heavy fighting, allowing them to capture 240 wagons and take 1300 prisoners.

With little hope of making further progress, and with news of the Union defeat at the Battle of Mansfield having filtered through, Streele felt that his only option was to call off the expedition and return to Little Rock. This was to prove no easy task, however, as bad weather had made the roads, —never that good to begin with—even worse. Progress was slow and Steele was constantly harried by Confederate attacks, the largest of which took place on April 30. He was forced to fight a major engagement at Jenkin's Ferry due to delays in getting his troops across a pontoon ferry. The battle resulted in 528 Union losses to 443 Confederate ones.

It was not until May 3 that Steele finally marched what remained of his weary, hungry, rag-tag troops back into Little Rock. The six-week expedition had been an unmitigated disaster, costing 2,750 Union troops, a great deal of ordnance, and had also greatly restored the morale of the Confederacy.

1 March 23: Steele's column moved out of Little Rock headed southwestward toward a planned junction with Banks's Red River expedition. They had to skirmish with Confederate cavalry almost immediately.

2 March 29: Skirmishing frequently with Confederate cavalry, Steele's vanguard reached Arkadelphia, where it again clashed with the Confederate horsemen.

3 April 4: Confederate Brigadier General John Sappington Marmaduke attacked Steele's column at Elkin's Ferry, on the Little Missouri River but was defeated and had to flee after five hours of hard fighting.

4 April 9: Brigadier General John M. Thayer's division, marching from Fort Smith and joined Steele's expedition.

5 April 15: Steele's troops entered Camden.

6 April 18: Confederates attacked a Union supply wagon train and captured it after a fierce fight with the escort. The victorious Confederates then massacred captured members of the First Kansas Coloured Cavalry.

7 April 26: Harassed by Confederate cavalry and having learned that Banks's campaign had ended in failure, Steele ordered a retreat to Little Rock.

8 May 3: Steele's column arrived back in Little Rock.

SHERMAN'S ATLANTA, PHASE I

DESPITE ITS RELATIVELY SMALL SIZE, ATLANTA WAS THOUGHT TO BE RELATIVELY SAFE FROM UNION HANDS. IN THE EARLY STAGES OF THE WAR IT BECAME A CONCENTRATION POINT FOR THE DISTRIBUTION OF WAR MATERIAL TO THE CONFEDERATE ARMIES OPERATING IN THE WESTERN THEATER.

Above: Painting showing heavy fighting during the Battle for Atlanta in 1864.

However, after the Vicksburg campaign, concerns began to be expressed that perhaps the city was not as safe as had once been thought. A study was commissioned to investigate ways that the city might best be defended. The somewhat depressing finding was that with so many possible approaches and entrances, effective defense of the city would be impossible.

In spite of this it was decided to go ahead and a plan was developed to build a series of 17 redoubts to form a 10-mile (16 km) ring around the city. This would extend one mile (1.6 km) out from the center, and be linked with extensive earthworks and trenches. Work was completed December 1863. Sadly, because of the way the subsequent Atlanta Campaign unfolded, many of these fortifications were never put to the test.

The following year Atlanta's worst fears were realized when it became the target of a major Union invasion. Several fierce battles took place, culminating in the evacuation of the city by Confederate General John Bell Hood on September 1 after a four-month siege. Before he left, Hood ordered all public buildings and possible Union assets to be destroyed. Union General William T Sherman moved in. He ordered a complete evacuation of the civilian population and after occupying the city for several months he ordered every building, apart from churches and hospitals to be burned to the ground. With its dwindling resources the Confederate army was never in a position to re-take the city.

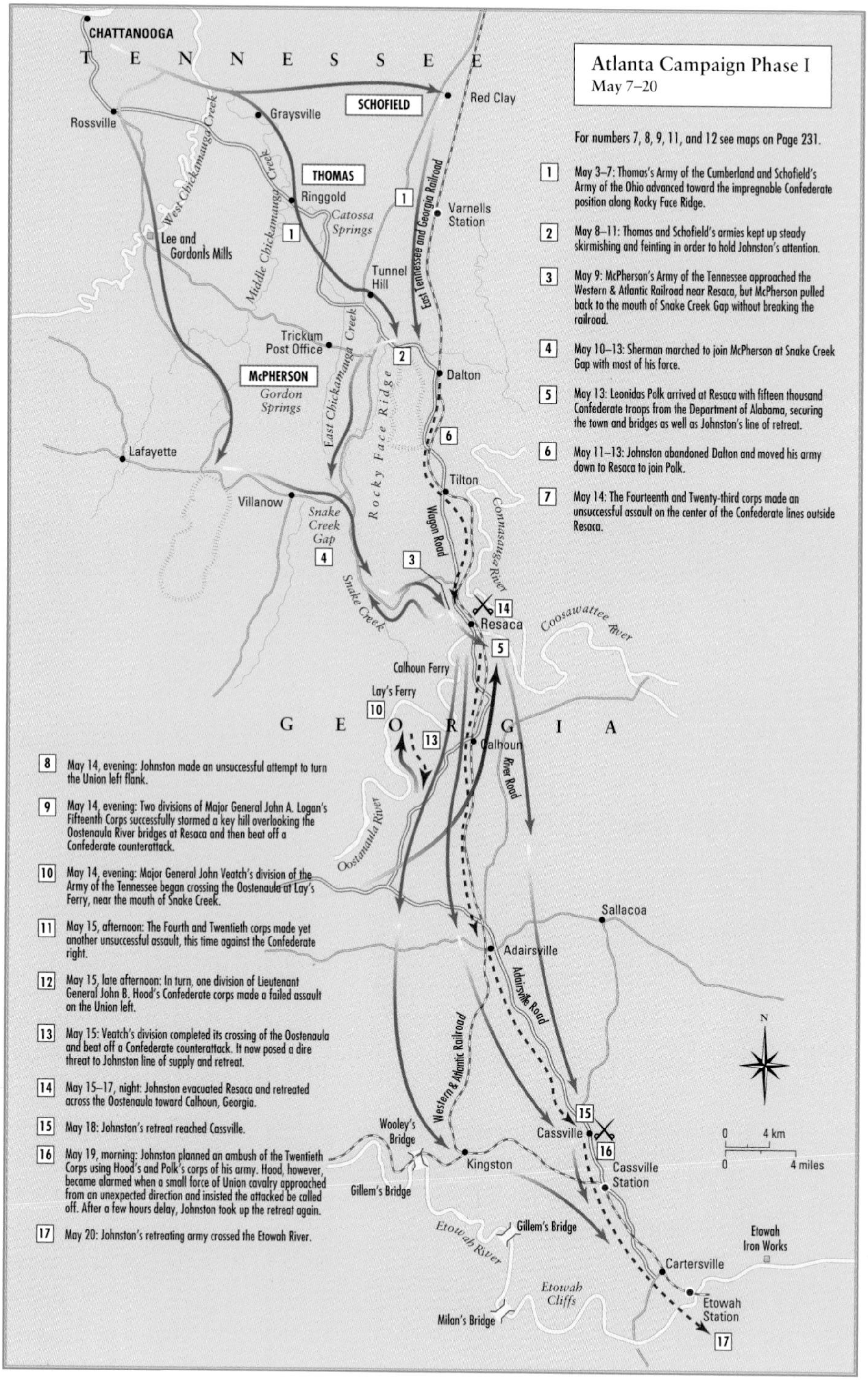
Atlanta Campaign Phase I
May 7–20
For numbers 7, 8, 9, 11, and 12 see maps on Page 231.
1 May 3–7: Thomas's Army of the Cumberland and Schofield's Army of the Ohio advanced toward the impregnable Confederate position along Rocky Face Ridge.
2 May 8–11: Thomas and Schofield's armies kept up steady skirmishing and feinting in order to hold Johnston's attention.
3 May 9: McPherson's Army of the Tennessee approached the Western & Atlantic Railroad near Resaca, but McPherson pulled back to the mouth of Snake Creek Gap without breaking the railroad.
4 May 10–13: Sherman marched to join McPherson at Snake Creek Gap with most of his force.
5 May 13: Leonidas Polk arrived at Resaca with fifteen thousand Confederate troops from the Department of Alabama, securing the town and bridges as well as Johnston's line of retreat.
6 May 11–13: Johnston abandoned Dalton and moved his army down to Resaca to join Polk.
7 May 14: The Fourteenth and Twenty-third corps made an unsuccessful assault on the center of the Confederate lines outside Resaca.
8 May 14, evening: Johnston made an unsuccessful attempt to turn the Union left flank.
9 May 14, evening: Two divisions of Major General John A. Logan's Fifteenth Corps successfully stormed a key hill overlooking the Oostenaula River bridges at Resaca and then beat off a Confederate counterattack.
10 May 14, evening: Major General John Veatch's division of the Army of the Tennessee began crossing the Oostenaula at Lay's Ferry, near the mouth of Snake Creek.
11 May 15, afternoon: The Fourth and Twentieth corps made yet another unsuccessful assault, this time against the Confederate right.
12 May 15, late afternoon: In turn, one division of Lieutenant General John B. Hood's Confederate corps made a failed assault on the Union left.
13 May 15: Veatch's division completed its crossing of the Oostenaula and beat off a Confederate counterattack. It now posed a dire threat to Johnston line of supply and retreat.
14 May 15–17, night: Johnston evacuated Resaca and retreated across the Oostenaula toward Calhoun, Georgia.
15 May 18: Johnston's retreat reached Cassville.
16 May 19, morning: Johnston planned an ambush of the Twentieth Corps using Hood's and Polk's corps of his army. Hood, however, became alarmed when a small force of Union cavalry approached from an unexpected direction and insisted the attacked be called off. After a few hours delay, Johnston took up the retreat again.
17 May 20: Johnston's retreating army crossed the Etowah River.
CHATTANOOGA
TENNESSEE
GEORGIA
Rossville
Graysville
Red Clay
SCHOFIELD
THOMAS
McPHERSON
Ringgold
Catossa Springs
Varnells Station
Lee and Gordonls Mills
Tunnel Hill
Trickum Post Office
Gordon Springs
Dalton
Lafayette
Tilton
Villanow
Snake Creek Gap
Rocky Face Ridge
West Chickamauga Creek
Middle Chickamauga Creek
East Chickamauga Creek
East Tennessee and Georgia Railroad
Wagon Road
Connasauga River
Snake Creek
Resaca
Coosawattee River
Calhoun Ferry
Lay's Ferry
Calhoun
River Road
Oostanaula River
Sallacoa
Adairsville
Adairsville Road
Western & Atlantic Railroad
Wooley's Bridge
Kingston
Cassville
Cassville Station
Gillem's Bridge
Etowah River
Etowah Cliffs
Milan's Bridge
Cartersville
Etowah Iron Works
Etowah Station
N
0 4 km
0 4 miles

Left: By early 1864, with dwindling resources, most Confederates had given up hope of overpowering the Union Armies by force, and opted instead to focus their energies on defending what territories they had left. Atlanta became the target of a major Union invasion.

Right: Compared to their war weary enemies, the Unionists had a solid advantage both in morale and the number of troops. They began to advance on Atlanta with the intention of capturing an important part of Southern territory.

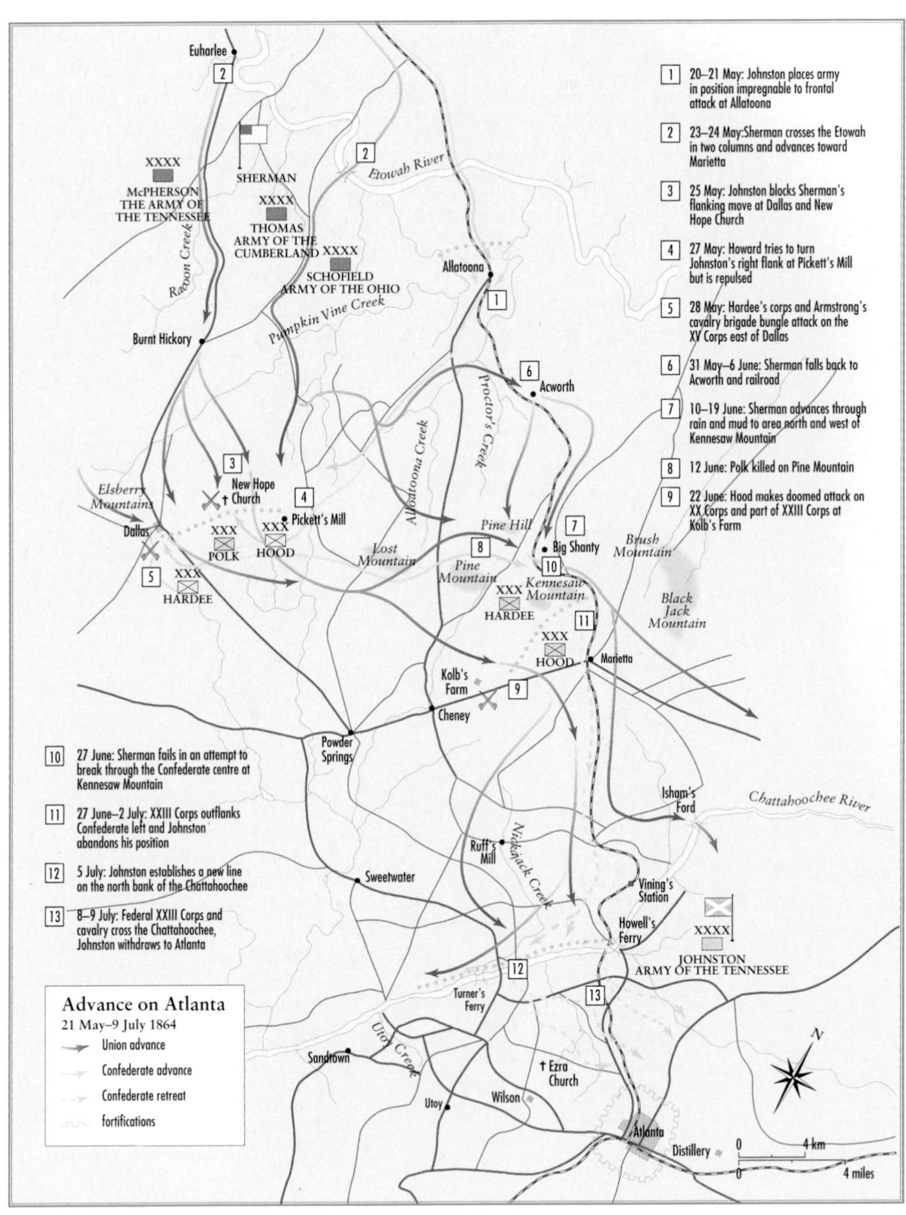

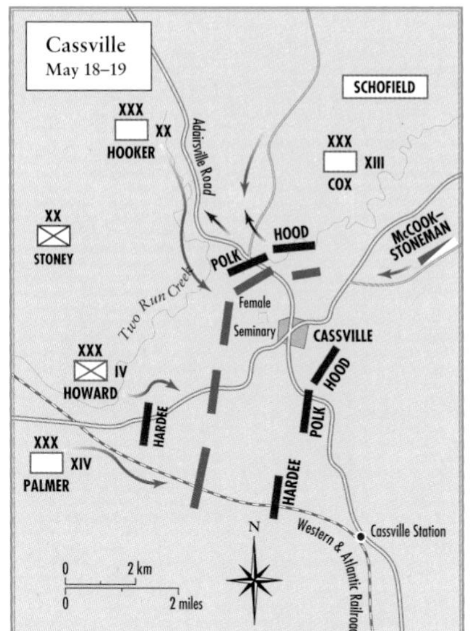

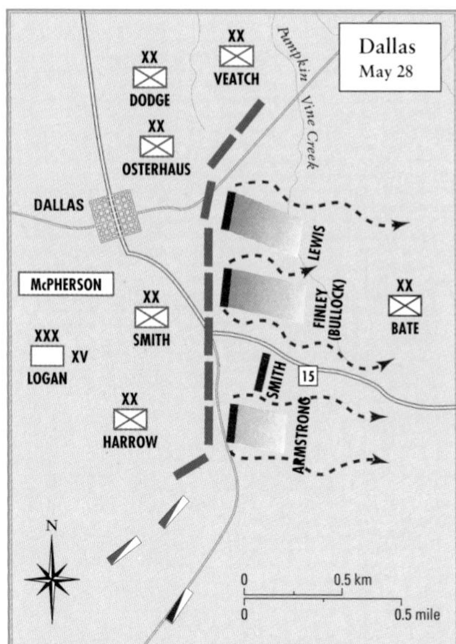

Left: The strategy of the Northern Army was to conquer the surrounding cities in Georgia to make their main target of Atlanta more accessible. These maps show the successful attacks in Cassville and Dallas..

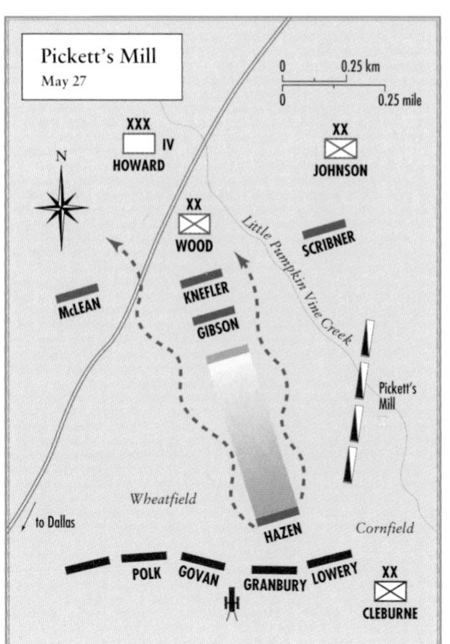

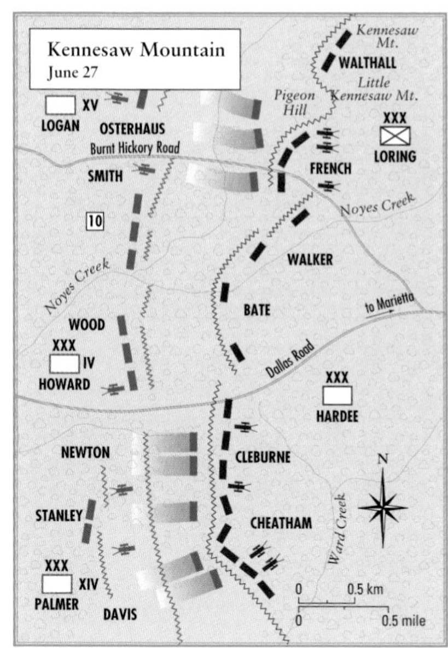

Left: Not all Union assaults were successful, and they were repulsed at the Battle of Pickett's Mill and at Kennesaw Mountain..

THE WILDERNESS

IN MAY 1864, A YEAR AFTER HIS TRIUMPH AT CHANCELLORSVILLE, GENERAL LEE MET GENERAL ULYSSES S. GRANT ON THE FIELD OF BATTLE FOR THE FIRST TIME. THE WILDERNESS BATTLEFIELD, PART OF THE BATTLEGROUND COMPLEX AROUND FREDERICKSBURG, PRESERVES THE SITE WHERE GRANT, AS GENERAL-IN-CHIEF OF ALL UNION ARMIES, BEGAN THE COSTLY STRIKE-AND-FLANK CAMPAIGN OF ATTRITION THAT WOULD END THE WAR.

A drive around the portion of the battlefield owned by the park service shows why the dense thickets and tangled overgrowth deserved the name Wilderness, and why the fighting was so confused that whole units became lost. Heavy firing that set fire to dry underbrush added to the confusion.

The national park lies roughly south of State Route 20, along which Lee moved part of his forces to meet Grant. The Wilderness Exhibit Centre has paintings and written commentaries on the battle, and the road through the park passes landmark farms and remnants of Confederate trenches dug for the battle of May 5–6, 1864. A monument to Hood's Texans, who fought at the Wilderness as part of Longstreet's Corps, recalls an incident which formed a bond between Lee and the Texans in the Army of Northern Virginia that would outlive the war.

At a critical point in the fighting near the Widow Trapp Farm, Lee determined to rally his forces by leading a charge himself. The Texans there were appalled, and shouted to Lee that they would not go unless Lee moved back to safety. "Go back, General, go back!" shouted the Texan soldiers."Hooray for Texas!" shouted Lee, saving his hat. Lee retreated, and the Texans charged. This was not the first time Confederate soldiers had shown concern for their leaders, but ever afterward Lee retained a special affection for the Texans under his command

Opposite page: Map showing details of the initial day of fighting at the inconclusive Wilderness Battle.

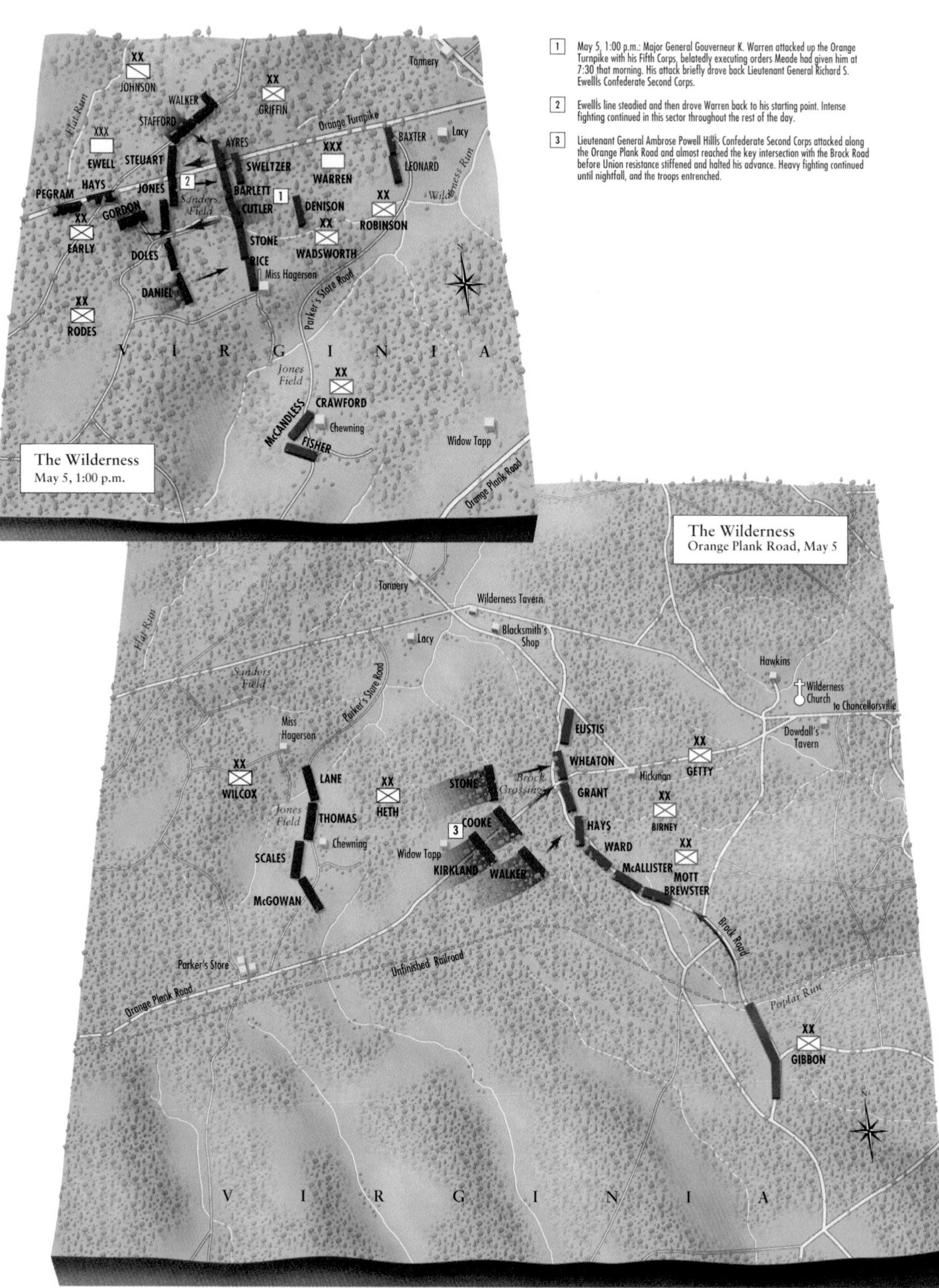
The Wilderness
May 5, 1:00 p.m.
JOHNSON
WALKER
STAFFORD
GRIFFIN
Tannery
Orange Turnpike
Flat Run
EWELL
STEUART
AYRES
SWELTZER
WARREN
BAXTER
Lacy
LEONARD
Wilderness Run
PEGRAM
HAYS
JONES
BARLETT
CUTLER
DENISON
ROBINSON
GORDON
Sanders Field
EARLY
DOLES
STONE
WADSWORTH
RICE
Miss Hagersen
Parker's Store Road
DANIEL
RODES
V I R G I N I A
Jones Field
CRAWFORD
McCANDLESS
Chewning
FISHER
Widow Tapp
Orange Plank Road
1 May 5, 1:00 p.m.: Major General Gouverneur K. Warren attacked up the Orange Turnpike with his Fifth Corps, belatedly executing orders Meade had given him at 7:30 that morning. His attack briefly drove back Lieutenant General Richard S. Ewellìs Confederate Second Corps.
2 Ewellìs line steadied and then drove Warren back to his starting point. Intense fighting continued in this sector throughout the rest of the day.
3 Lieutenant General Ambrose Powell Hillìs Confederate Second Corps attacked along the Orange Plank Road and almost reached the key intersection with the Brock Road before Union resistance stiffened and halted his advance. Heavy fighting continued until nightfall, and the troops entrenched.
The Wilderness
Orange Plank Road, May 5
Tannery
Wilderness Tavern
Blacksmith's Shop
Lacy
Flat Run
Sanders Field
Parker's Store Road
Hawkins
Wilderness Church
to Chancellorsville
Miss Hagerson
EUSTIS
Dowdall's Tavern
WHEATON
GETTY
Hickman
WILCOX
LANE
HETH
STONE
Brock Crossing
GRANT
BIRNEY
Jones Field
THOMAS
COOKE
HAYS
Chewning
WARD
SCALES
Widow Tapp
KIRKLAND
WALKER
McALLISTER
MOTT
BREWSTER
McGOWAN
Brock Road
Parker's Store
Unfinished Railroad
Orange Plank Road
Poplar Run
GIBBON
V I R G I N I A

The Wilderness battle was a draw. The Federals abandoned the field, but this time they did not retreat across the Rappahannock. They turned southward in another flanking movement that would renew the fighting at Spotsylvania Courthouse. From the Wilderness, the drive follows the Brock Road (State Route 613), along which many Federals walked, and turns onto Grant Drive at the entrance to the park.

There is a good view from the exhibit shelter of the Laurel Hill area, where on May 8, 1864, dismounted Confederate cavalrymen fought a determined holding action against a superior Federal force until Confederate infantrymen, hastening from the Wilderness, reinforced them and put Lee once again between Grant and Richmond. Paintings and commentaries at a spot near the shelter provide a good introduction to both the seven mile walking tour of the battlefield, which begins there, and the drive through the park. The principal feature of the park is the Bloody Angle, a salient where the firing was so heavy that it severed the trunk of an oak tree 22 inches in diameter. Monuments to New Jersey, New York, and Ohio troops who assaulted the salient, and a walking trail now occupy the site where some of the most savage hand-to-hand fighting of the war occurred. At the McCoull House site within the salient, Lee once again prepared to lead a charge but was dissuaded by Virginians and Georgians. The incredible bravery displayed by soldiers on both sides did not determine the outcome at the Bloody Angle; not until a new line had been prepared across the base of the salient did the Confederates pull back to Lee's last line, almost parallel to Brock Road. A strong Union assault on this line was crushed by infantry and 30 massed cannon.

Sporadic fighting went on around Spotsylvania Courthouse for almost two weeks, and the battle cost Grant 18,000 men. The number of Southern casualties is unknown, but some of those killed are buried in the Confederate Cemetery off State Route 208 east of Spotsylvania. The battle was another draw, and Grant again abandoned the field to manoeuvre southward. More bloody battles in the war of attrition lay ahead; it was still far from being over.

Opposite page: Map of the Wilderness Battle. Although it was Grant who eventually withdrew his troops, this battle is generally considered a draw.

Right: After the Battle of the Wilderness there were only nine able bodied men left from the original 86 of Company I of the Union's 57th Massachusettes Infantry Regiment.

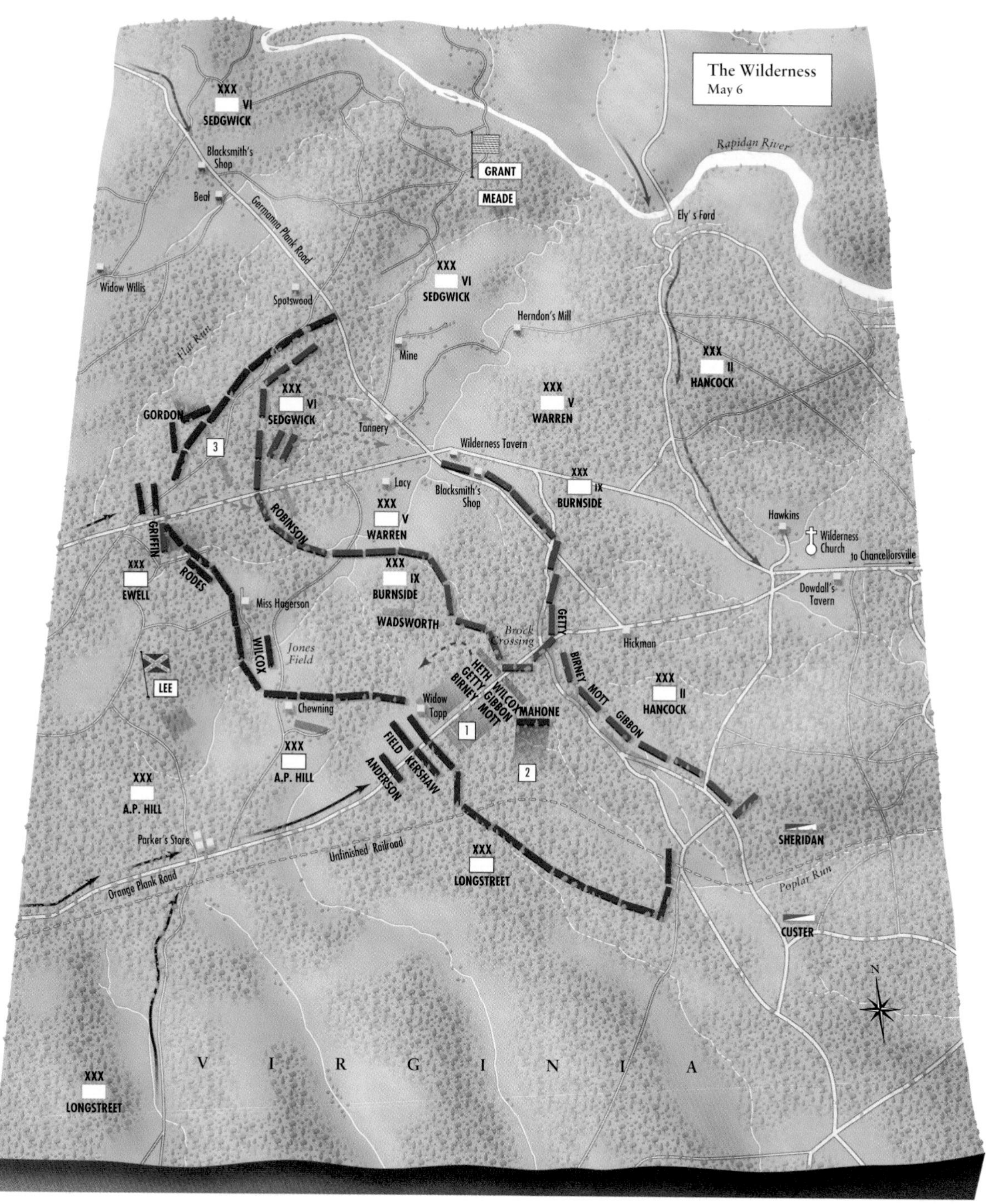

1 May 6: Grant launches masssive attack breaking the Confederate line. Lee, in person, attempts to restore the situation. Longstreet's corps finally arrives and stops the Union advance.

2 Longstreet launches a flanking attack on the Union line, this enjoys only brief success.

3 6:00 p.m.: Lee orders General Gordon to attack the Union right flank despite the protests of Ewell and Hill. Gordon's attack overran the Union flank, advancing to the Germanna Plank Road before nightfall put an end to the attack.

SHERIDAN'S RAIDS

IN 1864 PHILIP HENRY SHERIDAN EXEMPLIFIED THE NEW KIND OF COMBAT REQUIRED TO SUCCEED IN THE CIVIL WAR—GONE WERE THE SLOW, METHODICAL, SAFETY-FIRST TACTICS OF OLD, TO BE REPLACED BY SPEED, MOBILITY AND AGGRESSION.

Sheridan was a career soldier in the U.S.Army. Born in Albany, New York, he was small, only 5 feet 5 inches (1.65 m) tall. and as a boy worked in the town's general stores. When he was 17 he went to study at West Point, where he didn't particularly shine, coming 34th out of a class of 52—his subsequent career was noted for his rapid promotion.

In April 1864 Sheridan was given command of the Cavalry Corps of the Army of the Potomac just before Grant began his massive Overland Campaign against Robert E. Lee.

The traditional role of cavalry had been screening, reconnaissance, and guarding trains and rear areas. When Sheridan was reprimanded by Major General George Meade for not performing his duties of screening and reconnaissance as ordered during the Battle of the Wilderness, Sheridan went above his head to General Grant, who took Sheridan's side, recommending that he be assigned to strategic raiding missions.

As a result, on May 8, 1864, he was ordered to concentrate his available mounted force and proceed against the enemy's cavalry until his supplies ran out.

Sheridan was anxious to demonstrate his command of innovative cavalry tactics and so his advance towards Richmond, Virginia began the following day. His force was well supplied, well armed with breech loading Spencer Carbines, and outnumbered the Confederates by two-to-one.

In the evening of May 9 Sheridan stumbled on Lee's advance supply base on the Virginia Central Railroad at Beaver Dam. The supplies were destroyed along with the station, two locomotives, many wagons and large amounts of track.

Over the next 16 days Sheridan fought battles at Yellow Tavern, Mattapony Church, Jones's Bridge, Haxall's, White House Landing, and Hanover Court House. He marched in a column reputedly 13 miles long, knowing that Confederate cavalry commander Major General J.E.B. Stuart was right behind him trying to find a way to defeat this massive army.

Stuart reasoned that if Sheridan was advancing on Richmond, the Richmond garrison could hold the advance while he attacked from the rear. On the other hand, if Sheridan was only interested in destroying the infrastructure, Stuart could stop him from returning to Union lines.

On May 11 Stuart received word that Sheridan was less than 20 miles from Richmond and there was a brief skirmish at Yellow Tavern, about 11 miles north of Richmond, in which Stuart was shot and killed. The Confederates had, however, managed to slow Sheridan's advance, giving Richmond valuable time to prepare additional defenses. As a result Sheridan decided to return.

This was not helped by the fact that his army had destroyed so much on the first leg of their journey, but eventually he managed to meet up with General Meade at Chesterfield Station on May 24.

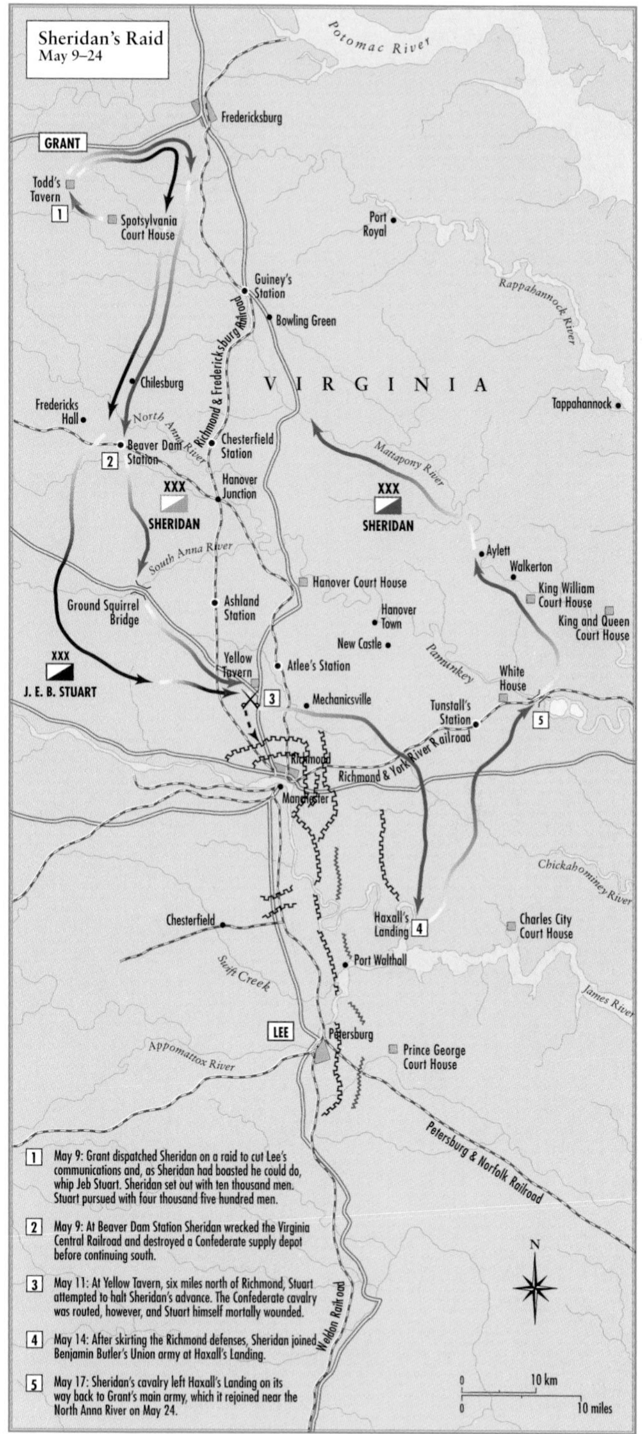

Opposite page: Philip Henry Sheridan (1831-1888) was summoned by Ulysses Grant to command the Cavalry Corps of the Army of the Potomac.

Right: Map of Sheridan's Raid. It is said that Sheridan's army marched a 13-mile-long column—a sure way to intimidate the enemy.

Right: General George Armstrong Custer, best known for his later fateful campaigns against the Indian, was a Union officer during the Civil War during which he commanded cavalry units in notable campaigns such as the Overland.

Opposite page: Map detailing the advance of Sheridan and his cavalry in June 1864.

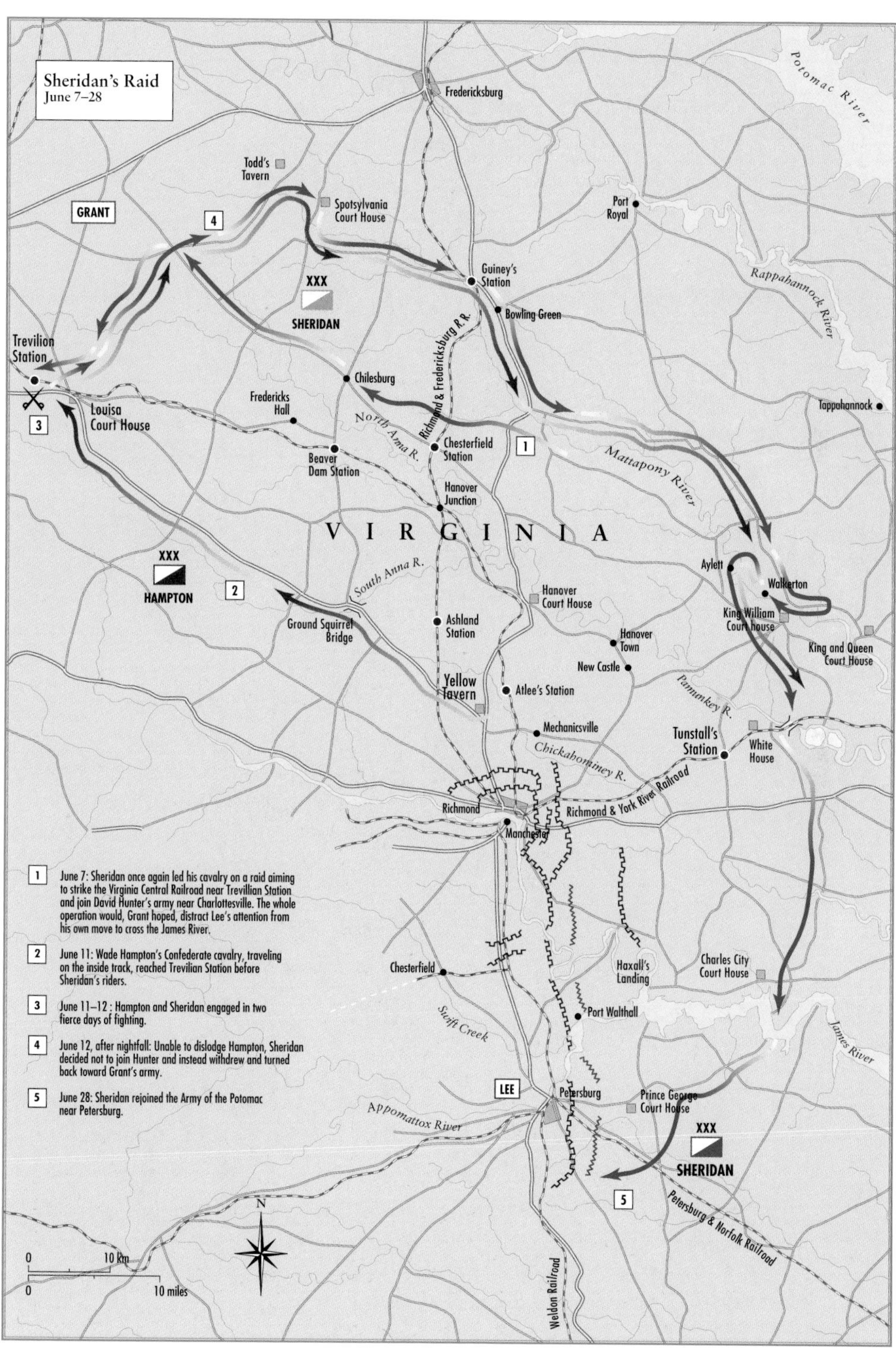
Sheridan's Raid
June 7–28
Fredericksburg
Potomac River
Todd's Tavern
Spotsylvania Court House
GRANT
4
Port Royal
Guiney's Station
XXX
SHERIDAN
Bowling Green
Rappahannock River
Richmond & Fredericksburg R.R.
Trevilion Station
Chilesburg
3
Louisa Court House
Fredericks Hall
North Anna R.
Chesterfield Station
1
Tappahannock
Beaver Dam Station
Mattapony River
Hanover Junction
V I R G I N I A
XXX
HAMPTON
2
South Anna R.
Aylett
Walkerton
Hanover Court House
King William Court house
Ground Squirrel Bridge
Ashland Station
Hanover Town
King and Queen Court House
New Castle
Yellow Tavern
Atlee's Station
Pamunkey R.
Mechanicsville
Tunstall's Station
White House
Chickahominey R.
Richmond & York River Railroad
Richmond
Manchester
1 June 7: Sheridan once again led his cavalry on a raid aiming to strike the Virginia Central Railroad near Trevillian Station and join David Hunter's army near Charlottesville. The whole operation would, Grant hoped, distract Lee's attention from his own move to cross the James River.
2 June 11: Wade Hampton's Confederate cavalry, traveling on the inside track, reached Trevilian Station before Sheridan's riders.
3 June 11–12 : Hampton and Sheridan engaged in two fierce days of fighting.
4 June 12, after nightfall: Unable to dislodge Hampton, Sheridan decided not to join Hunter and instead withdrew and turned back toward Grant's army.
5 June 28: Sheridan rejoined the Army of the Potomac near Petersburg.
Chesterfield
Haxall's Landing
Charles City Court House
Port Walthall
Swift Creek
James River
LEE
Petersburg
Prince George Court House
Appomattox River
XXX
SHERIDAN
5
Petersburg & Norfolk Railroad
N
0
10 km
0
10 miles
Weldon Railroad

DREWRY'S BLUFF

IN THE SPRING OF 1864, GRANT DEVISED A STRATEGY TO CUT RICHMOND'S SUPPLY LINES FROM THE SOUTH. FIVE RAILROADS LED FROM THE CITY OF PETERSBURG TO RICHMOND. DESTROY THESE AND RICHMOND WOULD SURELY FALL.

Above: Contemporary view of the James River in Virginia during the Civil War.

Opposite page: Map of the Battle of Drewry's Bluff fought between the Union and Confederate forces over control of the Richmond and Petersburg Railroad.

Unfortunately, the man Grant chose to take charge of his plans to derail Richmond's transport infrastructure was singularly ill-suited to the task. Major General Benjamin F. Butler was a highly influential political figure with the ear of President Lincoln, but he was, as Grant was acutely aware, no soldier. However, Grant was also extremely aware of Butler's powerful position, his desire to acquire some level of military glory, and his reputation for extreme touchiness. Wanting Butler involved for political rather than military reasons, he concluded that, so long as he assigned him two experienced offers to act as his Corps Commanders—Major Geeral Quincy A. Gillmore would take charge of the 10th Corps, while Major Genral William F. Smith would look after the 18th—no great harm could come of putting the politician in charge; how wrong he was.

On May 5, Butler marched his 30,000 troops to the southern outskirts of Richmond. There he split his forces, stationing one half at City Point on the south bank of the James River and the rest at Bermuda Hundred, the peninsula at the convergence of the James and Appomattox rivers.

It was at this point that things began to go wrong. Butler's plan was to launch an immediate night march along the James River's south bank towards Richmond where his troops would take the Confederate forces by surprise. But his commanders, uncertain of the success of such a scheme, managed to talk him out of it. However, in the morning, Butler, still chomping at the bit, ordered his troops to seize the Richmond and Petersburg Railroad. Still not convinced of the merit of his strategy, his Corps commanders did not fully commit to the assault—Gilmore didn't send any troops and all— and it was quickly repulsed. This lacklustre action started a pattern that would be repeated over the ensuing days, as the Union forces launched a series of tentative, understrength advances that fell back at the first sign of opposition.

All these failed assaults gave the Confederates time to build up their strength. On the Morning of May 16, with the area shrouded in thick fog, Butler's Union foces were attacked by those of the Confederate General P.G.T Beauregard at Drewry's Bluff.

The Confederates seized the early momentum, pushing back Butler's right flank, although his left and center remained steadfast. Still, the Confederates appeared to be in the ascendancy. However, when Beauregard's hoped-for replacements, under Major General W.H. C. Whiting, never arrived, his assault stalled. But rather than seize the initiative, Butler decided to give up the whole show, reatreating all the way back to Bermuda Hundred. Beauregard followed, building defensive works as he went and blocking Butler in at Bermuda Hundred so effectively that Grant described the position "as if it had been in a bottle strongly corked." With Butler and his troops unable to maneuver, the Confederate forces opposing them were now free to to be employed in other arenas.

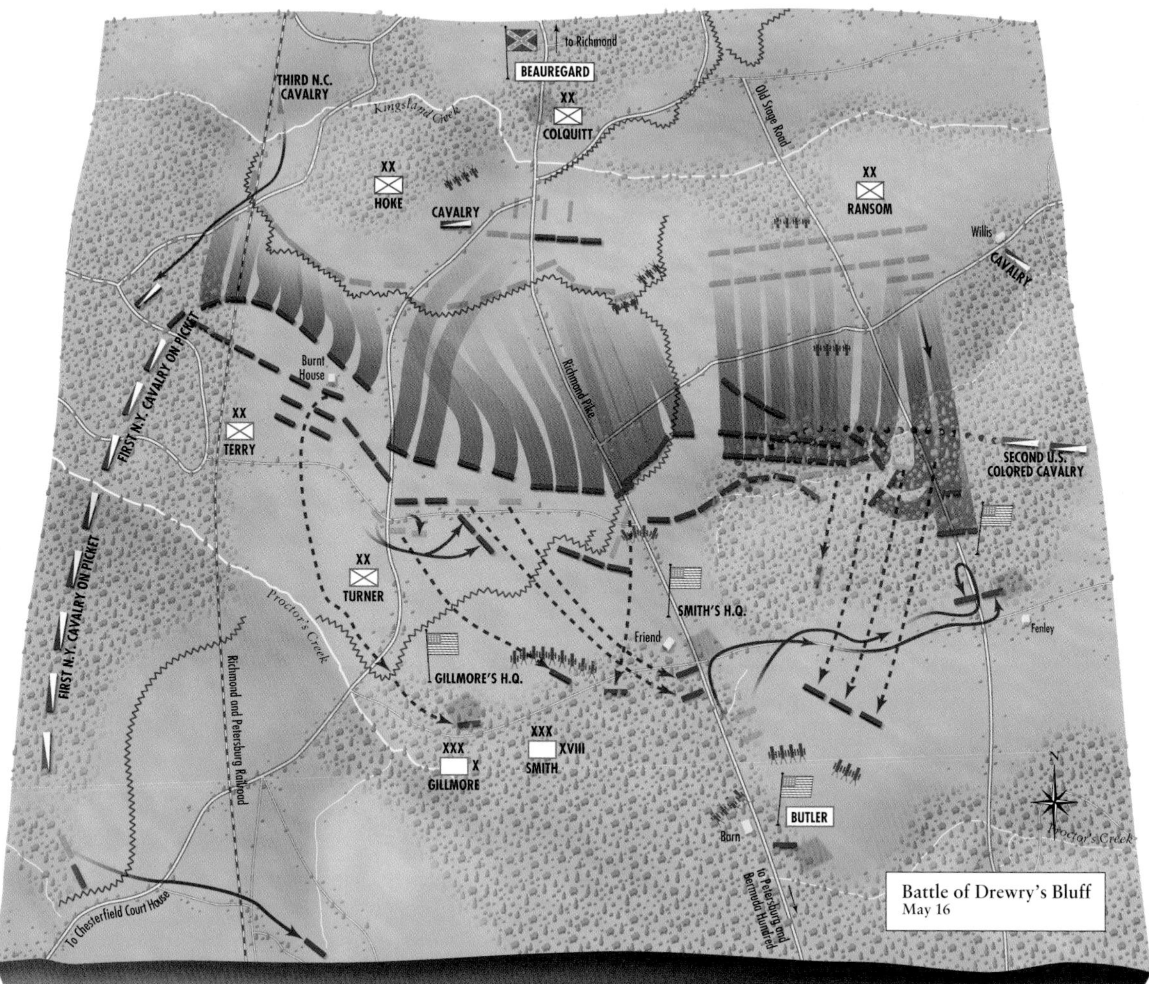

Battle of Drewry's Bluff
May 16

SPOTSYLVANIA PHASE I AND II

SPORADIC FIGHTING WENT ON AROUND SPOTSYLVANIA COURTHOUSE FOR ALMOST TWO WEEKS, AND THE BATTLE COST GRANT 18,000 MEN. THE NUMBER OF SOUTHERN CASUALTIES IS UNKNOWN, BUT SOME OF THOSE KILLED ARE BURIED IN THE CONFEDERATE CEMETERY OFF STATE ROUTE 208 EAST OF SPOTSYLVANIA.

Following the bloody and inconclusive Battle of the Wilderness at the beginning of May 1864, both sides decided to move to Spotsylvania, about 10 miles (16 km) to the southeast.

The Confederates got there first and on May 8 each army began to take up positions north of this small town. Lee deployed his men in a trench line stretching for more than 4 miles (6.5 km), with artillery placed to catch any attacking force. The only weak spot was an exposed salient known as the "Mule Shoe" that extended for a mile or so in front of the main trench. This weakness was taken advantage of by the Union Colonel Emory Upton managed to break through, although they were eventually pushed back.

For the rest of the day there were more futile and uncoordinated frontal attacks, but the following day, May 11, Grant began planning for a new major assault on the Mule Salient. Lee misinterpreted the situation and thought that Grant's inactivity indicated that he was about to pull back and as a result he weakened the critical Mule Shoe sector by withdrawing its artillery support.

Grant attacked before dawn on May 12 with a force of 20,000 and initially this was a great success. The Confederates were without artillery support and due to overnight rain many found that their muskets would not fire because they had not kept their powder dry.

After his initial success, Grant's army became bogged down and Lee was able to shift thousands of men to seal the breach. Because of the seriousness of the situation Lee felt that he should personally lead from the front, but his soldiers, realizing that this would place him in great danger, refused to advance until he moved to a safer position.

The fighting was characterized by an intensity never previously been seen. The entire landscape was flattened and, in many cases fighting was hand-to-hand and both sides moved back and forth over the same corps-strewn trenches. The copses were piled so high that wounded men buried underneath were simply pressed into the mud where they drowned. By 3 a.m. on May 13 the ruined remnants of Lee's Second Corps had finished constructing a fallback line at the base of the Mule Shoe salient, which proved impossible for Grant to break and by May 20-21 both armies were on their way to take up new positions along the North Anna River, 12 miles closer to Richmond.

Grant's losses amounted to 35,000, while the Confederates lost 18,000.

Below: Maps detailing the beginning of the attacks at Spotsylvania where the fighting was particularly intense. Soldiers were forced to engage in hand to hand combat amidst the trenches strewn with corpses.

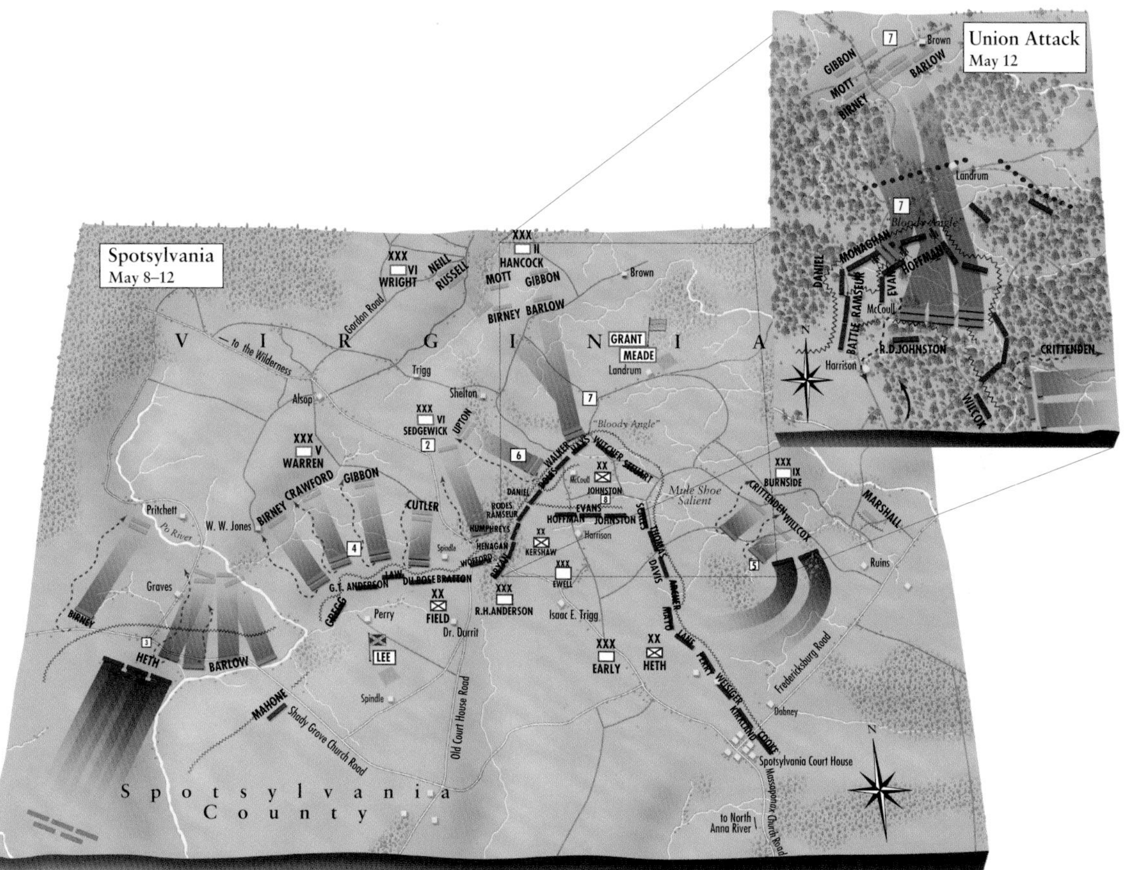

1 May 8, morning: Arriving near strategic Spotsylvania Court House after a night march from the Wilderness, Union cavalry found their way blocked by Confederate infantry and call for infantrysupport of their own. The division of Brigadier General John C. Robinson of the Fifth Corps came up and assaulted the Confederate lines but could not break through.

2 May 9: Major General John Sedgwick, commanding the Sixth Corps, was killed by a Confederate sharpshooter. His replacement was Major General Horatio Wright.

3 May 10: Barlow's and Birney's divisions of Hancock's Second Corps crossed the Po River with a view to flanking the strong Confederate position at Laurel Hill but were driven back by a strong counterattack from Major General Henry Heth's division.

4 May 10: Warren's Fifth Corps mounted poorly coordinated frontal assaults on the Laurel Hill lines but was repulsed.

5 May 10: At the other end of the line, Burnside's Ninth Corps launched an equally unsuccessful attack.

6 May 10, 6:00 pm.: The only success of the day came when Colonel Emory Upton led a carefully prepared attack by a dense column that briefly punched a hole in a section of the Confederate line known as the Mule Shoe. Upton's supports failed to come up, however, and Confederate reinforcements soon drove him off.

7 May 12, 4:30 a.m.: After a day's preparation, Grant sought to duplicate Upton's feet using the entire Third Corps. The attack broke the Confederate line, but Confederate reinforcements plugged the gap through twenty hours of hand-to-hand fighting near the Bloody Angle.

8 While the troops struggled at the Bloody Angle, other Confederates built another line of defenses across the base of the Mule Shoe

Below: Map showing the continuation of the Battle of Spotsylvania.

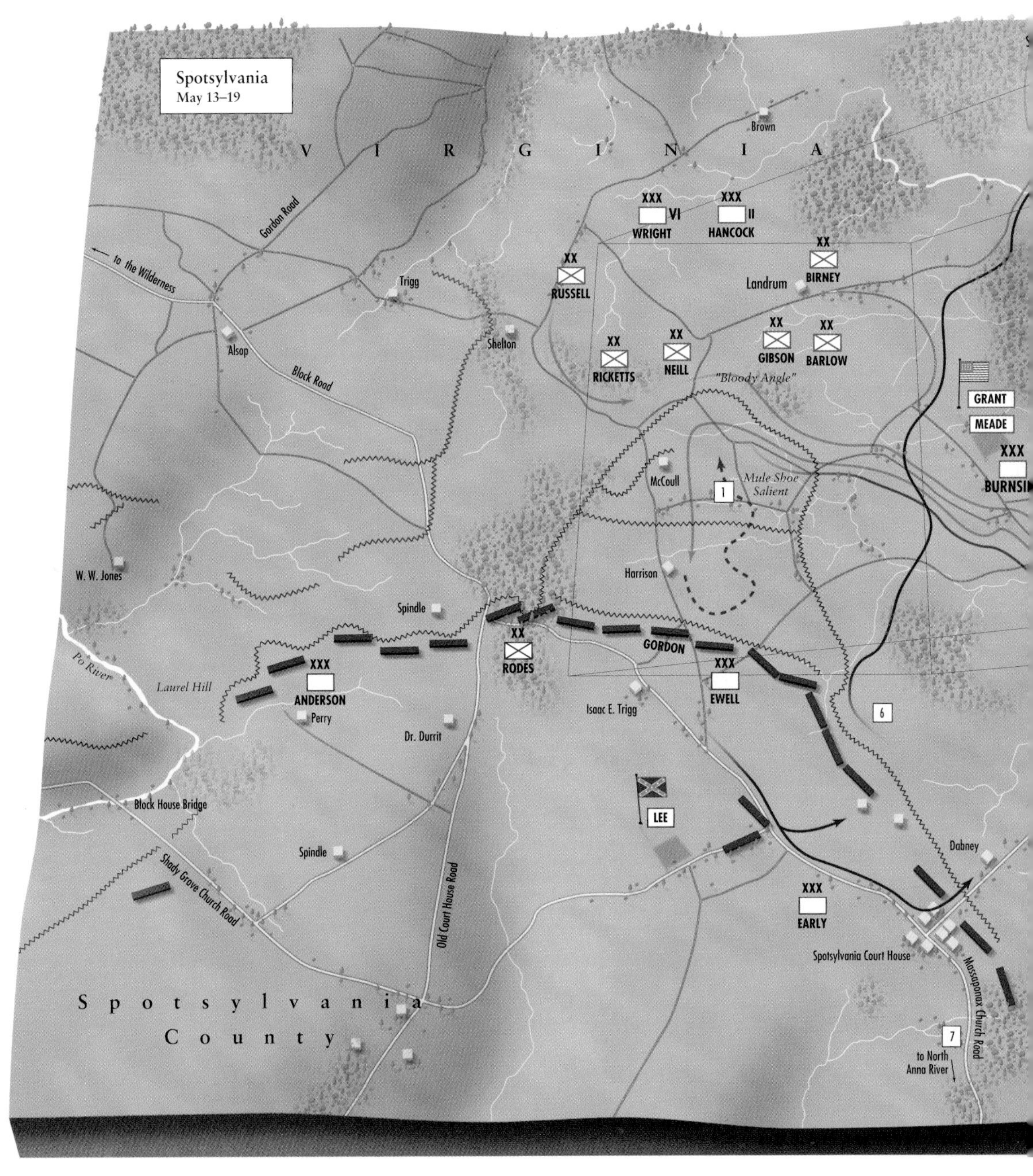

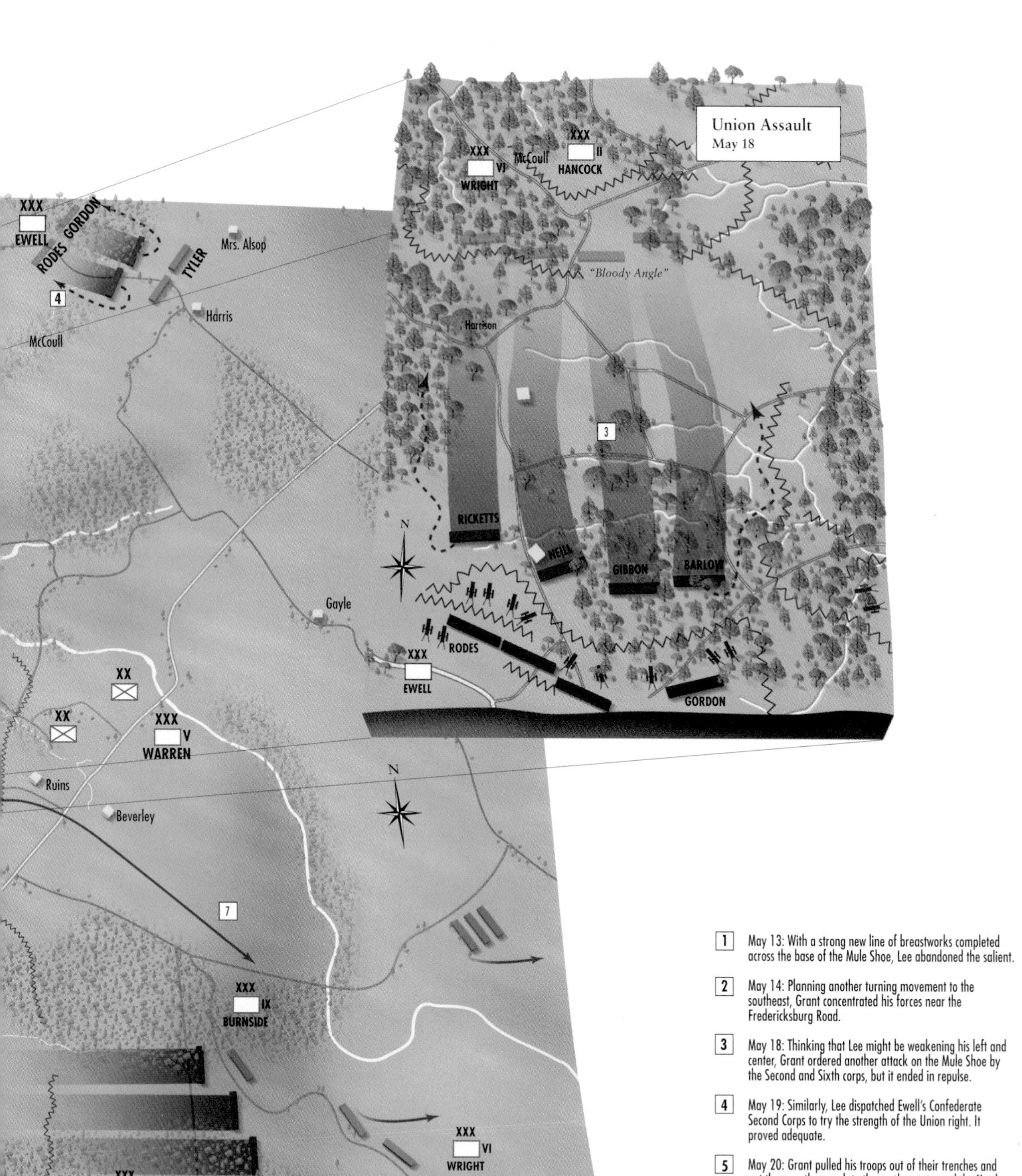

1 May 13: With a strong new line of breastworks completed across the base of the Mule Shoe, Lee abandoned the salient.

2 May 14: Planning another turning movement to the southeast, Grant concentrated his forces near the Fredericksburg Road.

3 May 18: Thinking that Lee might be weakening his left and center, Grant ordered another attack on the Mule Shoe by the Second and Sixth corps, but it ended in repulse.

4 May 19: Similarly, Lee dispatched Ewell's Confederate Second Corps to try the strength of the Union right. It proved adequate.

5 May 20: Grant pulled his troops out of their trenches and put them on the march to the southeast, toward the North Anna River.

6 May 21: Confederate troops advanced and discovered the Unions' absence.

7 May 21: Lee immediately put his army in motion to counter Grant's move.

NORTH ANNA

THIS BATTLE WAS AN EPISODIC ENCOUNTER THAT STRETCHED OVER FOUR DAYS (MAY 23–26, 1864) AND WAS PLAYED OUT ALONG THE BANKS OF THE NORTH ANNA RIVER, A TRIBUTARY OF THE PAMUNKEY RIVER IN CENTRAL VIRGINIA.

After the fighting at Spotsylvania Court House, Robert E. Lee withdrew to the North Anna River where on May 22, 1864, they were joined by reinforcements of perhaps as many as 9,000 more troops, most of whom came from the defense of the James River. The Confederates dug themselves in on the steep southern banks of the North Anna River. Their entrenchments were arrayed in a V-shape, with its north-facing point at Ox Ford, the only defensible river crossing. The forces on the western bar of the V were commanded by Lieutenant General A.P. Hill, while the eastern bar of the V was run by Major General Richard H. Anderson.

The bulk of Grant's forces then proceeded to the North Anna River, reaching it on May 23. They immediately began crossing at Jericho Mill, to the north of Ox Ford under the command of Major General Gouverneur K. Warren. At 6 o'clock that evening, they were attacked by Confederate soldiers from the western bar of the V, but the Federal army held out easily and dug in directly in front of the rebel lines. On May 24, the Federal army's II Corps under Winfield S. Hancock arrived at the North Anna River from a remote position on the west bank of the Mattaponi River, to which Grant had previously despatched them as isolated bait to lure Lee's men in to the open. Hancock attacked Chesterfield Bridge to the east of Ox Ford, crossed the North

Right: The Fifth Army Corps under the command of General Gouverneur K Warren crossed the North Anna River at Jericho Mill, Virginia, on May 23, 1864, during the Overland Campaign.

Anna River, and positioned his men in front of the eastern bar of the rebel V. Then, Major General Ambrose Burnside brought up a third Federal force that tried to cross the river at Quarles Mill, between Ox Ford and Jericho Mill. However, this attempt was successfully opposed by Confederate soldiers and Burnside was forced to set up camp on the northern bank at Ox Ford.

Thus, the Confederate forces had consolidated themselves into a great chevron formation, while the Federal army had been split into three parts, none of which could help either of the others without first crossing and then recrossing the North Anna River.

Having outmaneuvered Grant, Lee should now have been in a position to pick off either Warren or Hancock more or less at will, but he was inhibited by the lack of a fit or capable general. May 25 was a day of minor skirmishes but no significant movement by troops on either side. By nightfall, Grant had confirmed to him what he already suspected – that the Confederate army was impregnable in its current position.

On May 26, Grant ordered Brigadier General James H. Wilson's cavalry division to cross the North Anna River and proceed west in an attempt to deceive Lee into thinking that the Union was about to try to envelop the Confederate left flank. It was during this action that much of the Virginia Central Railroad was destroyed. Then, under cover of darkness on the night of May 26, Grant withdrew his forces to Cold Harbor, 20 miles to the southeast.

By Civil War standards, human cost of the Battle of North Anna was small: over the four days, the Confederacy suffered around 2,000 casualties; Union casualties totalled 1,143, including 186 killed. However, it demonstrated to Grant that the Confederacy was losing its stomach for the fight.

Left: After capturing the Chesterfield Bridge, Federal soldiers from the Army of the Potomac's Second Army Corps under General Winfield Scott Hancock also took the Confederate Fort located on the horizon. May 23, 1864.

COLD HARBOR

THE BATTLE OF COLD HARBOR (JUNE 3–12, 1864) WAS FOUGHT OVER THE SAME GROUND AS THE BATTLE OF GAINES'S MILL (AKA THE FIRST BATTLE OF COLD HARBOR) IN JUNE 1862. SOLDIERS IN THE LATER CONFLICT WERE DISCONCERTED TO FIND IN THE FIELD SKELETONS LEFT OVER FROM THE EARLIER ENCOUNTER.

Above: The Battle of Cold Harbor was the last of the Overland Campaign. Union soldiers were effectively slaughtered in a hopeless frontal assault by General Lee's fortified troops.

Opposite page: Map of the Battle of Cold Harbor June 3, 1864.

However, when battle commenced, such misgivings were soon banished from the combatants' minds by the ferocity of the present fighting. Casualties were heavier on the Union side, for which this was one of the bloodiest and most humiliating defeats in the whole Civil War.

On leaving the banks of the North Anna River, Confederate troops had taken up a new defensive position behind earthworks around 10 miles northeast of Richmond, Virginia. There they waited for the arrival of Grant's Overland Campaign. At first light on June 3, 1864, three Union corps advanced through thick fog toward Confederate lines and into intense gunfire that caused heavy casualties. The first two groups were pinned down, but one division of Hancock's men broke through the Confederate lines However, the most advanced Union troops were soon scattered under fire from the artillery. By 7 o'clock in the morning, it was clear that the Union had no chance of prevailing, but Grant ordered renewed attacks, which Smith described as "a wanton waste of life." The blue divisions held their latest positions until shortly after noon, when Grant admitted that victory was unachievable. Although there were no further all-out attacks, the opposing forces remained lined up against each other for another nine days, during which they engaged in trench warfare—there was much shelling and snipers inflicted many casualties on both sides. By the time the battle ended, on June 12, 1864, the Union had lost at least 10,000 men and possibly as many as 13,000; Confederate deaths numbered just 1,500.

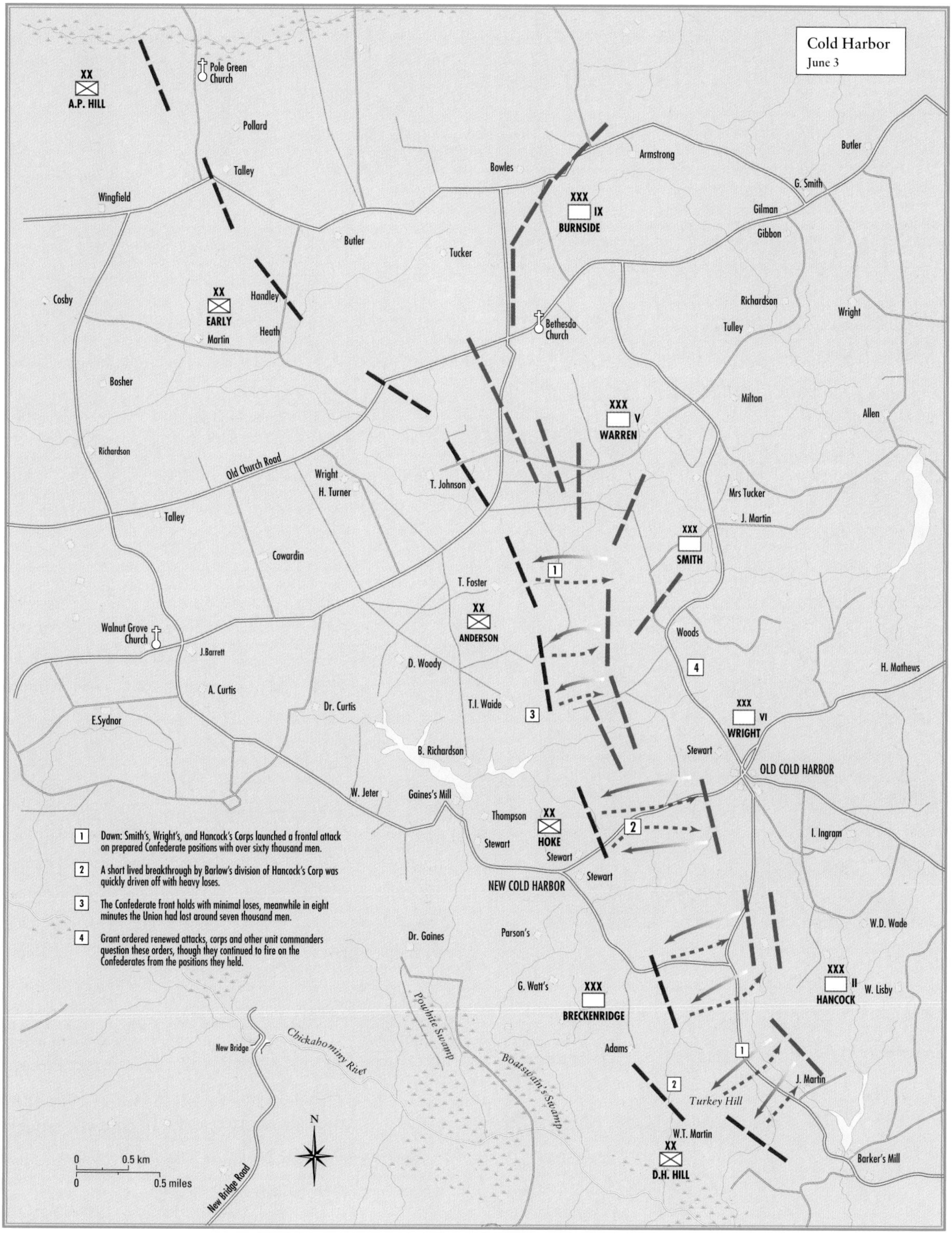

Cold Harbor
June 3

1. Dawn: Smith's, Wright's, and Hancock's Corps launched a frontal attack on prepared Confederate positions with over sixty thousand men.
2. A short lived breakthrough by Barlow's division of Hancock's Corp was quickly driven off with heavy loses.
3. The Confederate front holds with minimal loses, meanwhile in eight minutes the Union had lost around seven thousand men.
4. Grant ordered renewed attacks, corps and other unit commanders question these orders, though they continued to fire on the Confederates from the positions they held.

XX A.P. HILL
Pole Green Church
Pollard
Talley
Wingfield
Bowles
Armstrong
Butler
G. Smith
XXX IX BURNSIDE
Gilman
Gibbon
Butler
Tucker
Cosby
XX EARLY
Handley
Heath
Martin
Bethesda Church
Richardson
Tulley
Wright
Bosher
Milton
Allen
XXX V WARREN
Richardson
Old Church Road
Wright
H. Turner
T. Johnson
Mrs Tucker
J. Martin
Talley
XXX SMITH
Cowardin
T. Foster
XX ANDERSON
Woods
Walnut Grove Church
J.Barrett
D. Woody
H. Mathews
A. Curtis
Dr. Curtis
T.I. Waide
XXX VI WRIGHT
E.Sydnor
B. Richardson
Stewart
OLD COLD HARBOR
W. Jeter
Gaines's Mill
Thompson
XX HOKE
Stewart
Stewart
I. Ingram
Stewart
NEW COLD HARBOR
W.D. Wade
Dr. Gaines
Parson's
G. Watt's
XXX BRECKENRIDGE
XXX II HANCOCK
W. Lisby
Powhite Swamp
New Bridge
Chickahominy River
Boatswain's Swamp
Adams
J. Martin
Turkey Hill
W.T. Martin
XX D.H. HILL
Barker's Mill
N
0 0.5 km
0 0.5 miles
New Bridge Road

THE ADVANCE, ASSAULTS AND SIEGE OF PETERSBURG

THE FATE OF RICHMOND WAS MORE OR LESS DECIDED AT PETERSBURG, AN IMPORTANT RAIL AND HIGHWAY CENTER 25 MILES SOUTH OF THE CONFEDERATE CAPITAL. PETERSBURG NATIONAL BATTLEFIELD'S 1,531 ACRES (6,000 SQUARE METERS) PRESERVE RELICS OF ALL THE PHASES OF THE TEN-MONTH SIEGE OF THE CITY, WHICH BROUGHT GREAT HARDSHIP TO BOTH SIDES.

Above: The fall of Petersburg, April 2, 1865. The Union Army engaged in 10 months of trench warfare surrounding the southern part of the city, cutting off the supply lines. Petersburg and the nearby city of Richmond were major centres of Confederate activity. General Lee eventually yielded to pressure and both cities were abandoned.

The siege that would eventually deliver Petersburg into Union hands began in June 1864 following the Battle of Cold Harbor. Grant believed that taking out Petersburg, the hub of the Confederate supply lines, would make the capture of Richmond itself that much easier.

First, Grant launched a series of diversionary attacks in Virgina, so as to draw Lee's forces away from the city. He then marched on Petersburg. Just 14,000 Confederate soldiers remained to repulse the Union forces, which amounted to almost the entire Army of the Potomac, as Lee was convinced that Grant's pime target would be Richmond, and so had withdrawn the bulk of his forces there.

On June 16 and 17, Union forces launched a series of ferocious assaults on the city, first at Bermuda Hundred and then the next day near Shand House. But despite their vastly superior numbers, Union soldiers made little headway, and it soon became apparent that their narrow window of opportunity was fast closing. By this time Lee had realized Grant's true intentions and had despatched his 1st and 3rd Corps to bolster Petersburg's defenses. He arrived to oversee operations in person on the morning of June 18.

As Union assaults continued to flouder on the determined Confederate defenses, Grant had by the evening reluctantly decided that Petersburg could not now be taken by force, and resolved to besiege it into submission instead—he ordered his men to begin digging great lines of trenches opposite those occupied by Lee's army.

The siege would last for ten months, with Grant slowly and methodically tightening the screw, before launching a final assault which forced the Confederates to abandon the city.

Battery 5, which is located at the rear of the Battlefield Park Visitors' Centre, was one of the nine original strongpoints in the Confederate line. It is a good example of the earthworks fort used throughout the war, and is now outfitted with the period cannon. Nearby, in a shaded glen, is the Dictator, a replica of the 2,000 pound (900 kg) Federal mortar that was used to lob 2000-pound (90-kg) explosive shells into Petersburg, then two miles away.

Fort Stedman, the scene of the General Lee's desperate attempt to break Grant's siege, is now shaded by trees. A nearby painting shows a very different scene in 1865—well defended raw earthworks against which Confederate units were repeatedly hurled, only to be forced back by superior forces.

The Crater, the best known feature of the battlefield, recalls an incident that, tragic though it was, had little effect on the war. There are remnants of a tunnel dug by men of the 48th Pennsylvania Infantry Regiment, many of them coal miners in civilian life, and of the crater created when

Left: United States soldiers in a makeshift breastwork trench outside of Petersburg.

8,000 pounds (3,600 kg) of black powder exploded under the Confederate strongpoint known as Elliott's Salient. Following the explosion, 15,000 Federal troops attacked through and around the gaping, smoking hole in the ground which had destroyed more than 100 feet (30 meters) of the Confederate line; but many were trapped as a Confederate counterattack, led by Major General William Mahone, forced them back into the crater. By the time it was over 5,500 men had been killed, wounded, or captured, 4,000 of them Federals. Ironically, the Confederates had suspected something was afoot and dug an exploratory tunnel themselves, missing the Union tunnel by only a few feet.

Petersburg battlefield has many other outstanding relics, including Battery 9, which was captured by black troops, and Meade Station, an important supply point for Grant's army. A replica of an earthworks system complete with log structures and trenches, located at the entrance to this stop on the self-drive tour of the battlefield, gives a good indication of how primitive life in the field was. The replica is used in living history demonstrations.

Grant's superiority in manpower, transportation, and logistics decided the battle—and the fate of the Army of Northern Virginia. As Grant continued to lengthen his lines, Lee's forces were stretched thinner and thinner. Grant then began to cut the rail and road approaches to Petersburg from the south, one by one, before a final assault on April 2, 1865, compelled Lee to abandon Petersburg. Jefferson Davis, the President of the Confederacy received the sad news while attending church in Richmond's St. Paul's Episcopal Church. The event is recalled today by pew plaques and the Lee memorial window.

Right: Portrait of Confederate General John Brown Gordon. He was one of General Lee's most trusted generals. After the war ended, he was greatly opposed to reconstruction and was also one of the first leaders of the Ku Klux Klan in Georgia.

Right: The railroad mortar "Dictator", a form of siege artillery, outside Petersburg, Virginia, in 1864. Mortars fired shells at a very high trajectory to reach behind walls and buildings.

The day would become even sadder for the Confederacy. People who for the most part had borne up under years of danger and months of siege went wild as the Confederate army began pulling out. To try and prevent the drunken violence, whisky barrels were emptied into the streets; but people scooped it up in pails and sopped it up with cloths. Distribution of food in the government commissary turned into a near riot. An attempt to burn the tobacco at Shockoe

Slip to keep it from falling into Union hands set the city ablaze. The fire spread unchecked until Union forces entered the city and demolished buildings to create fire breaks. Shockoe Slip was reborn after the war as an industrial zone, but today is mainly a chic area of restaurants and speciality shops.

Lee evacuated Petersburg at night to gain time, a ruse that Union forces did not discover until 3 a.m. and Grant then occupied Petersburg without resistance. But the ten month siege had cost him 42,000 casualties and prisoners, while Confederate losses numbered 28,000 men who could not be replaced.

Lee's retreat was southwesterly, with Amelia Courthouse designated as the assembly point, but Lee's lack of supplies proved costly; the need to forage enabled General Philip H. Sheridan's cavalry to get between Lee and Danville, through which Davis passed on the way south, and forced Lee to choose Lynchburg as an alternative. Fear that Lee would escape and unite with the western Confederate army, then falling back through the Carolinas before Sherman's drive, gave Grant extra incentive.

Lee's retreat was marred by the kind of mistakes made by tired officers overwhelmed by the problems confronting them, a combination of events that caused the normally imperturbable Lee to question aloud whether his army was "disintegrating." Sayler's Creek Battlefield Historical State Park, off State Highway 307 and U.S. Route 306 a few miles east of Appomattox, commemorates the last full-scale battle fought by the Arm of Northern Virginia, a battle that occurred only because Lee's rear guard mistakenly followed the wagon train along another route and the rain-swollen creek delayed passage of the Confederate main body. The site, overlooking the small stream where Ewell's Corps successfully drove back the Union centre but became surrounded, has paintings, maps, and recordings that explain the details and stages of the tragic battle, which resulted in the surrender of more than 7,000 Confederate soldiers. Hillsman House, situated on the hilltop from which Union forces attacked, dates from the 1770s and is restored outside to its Civil War appearance.

Next page: Map showing Grant's initial advance toward Petersburg following the Battle of Cold Harbor.

Left: Confederate surrender at Sayler's Creek, Virginia, after the Union Army of the Potomac caught up with parts of General Lee's retreating Army of Northern Virginia.

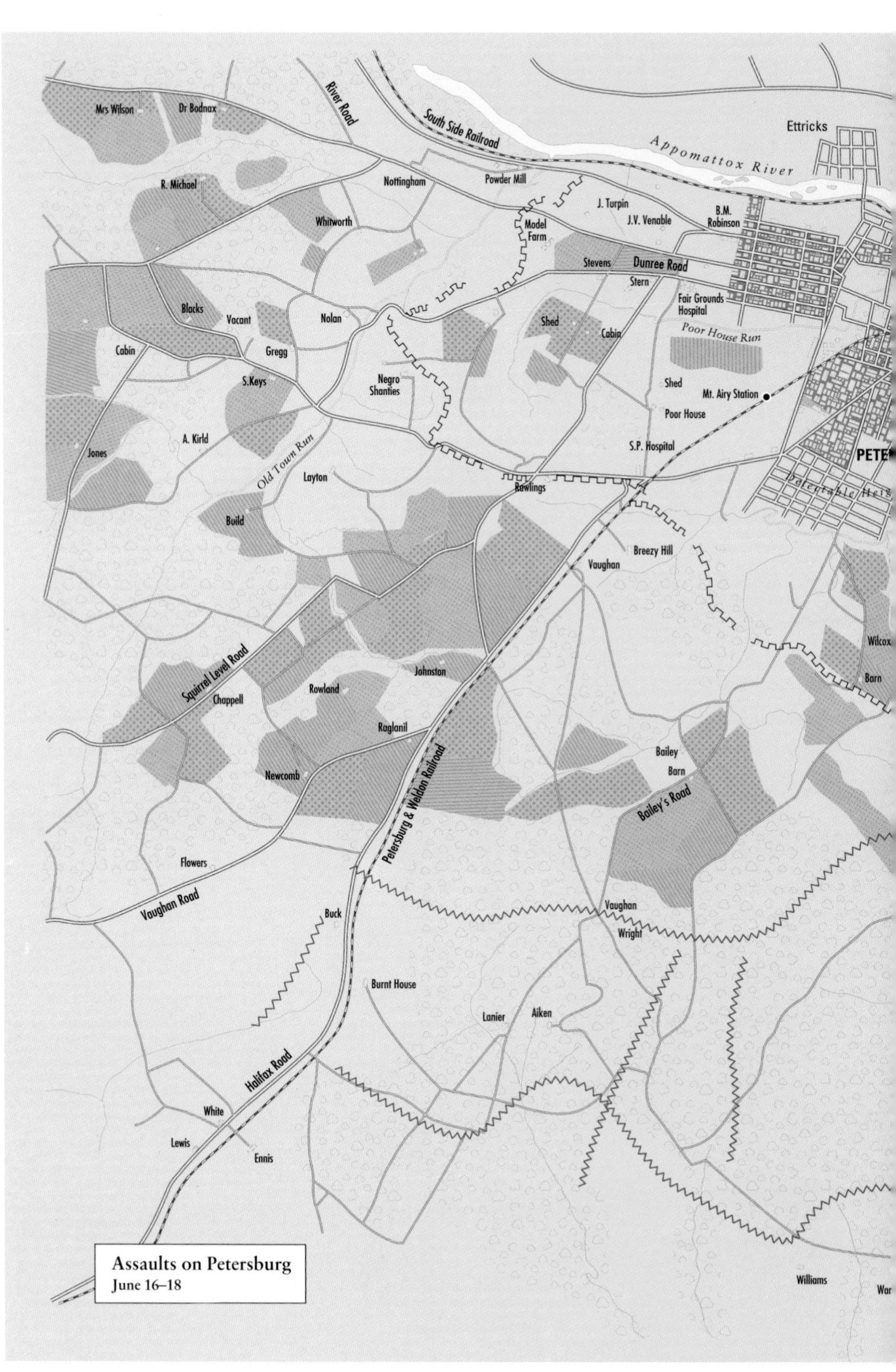

Assaults on Petersburg
June 16–18

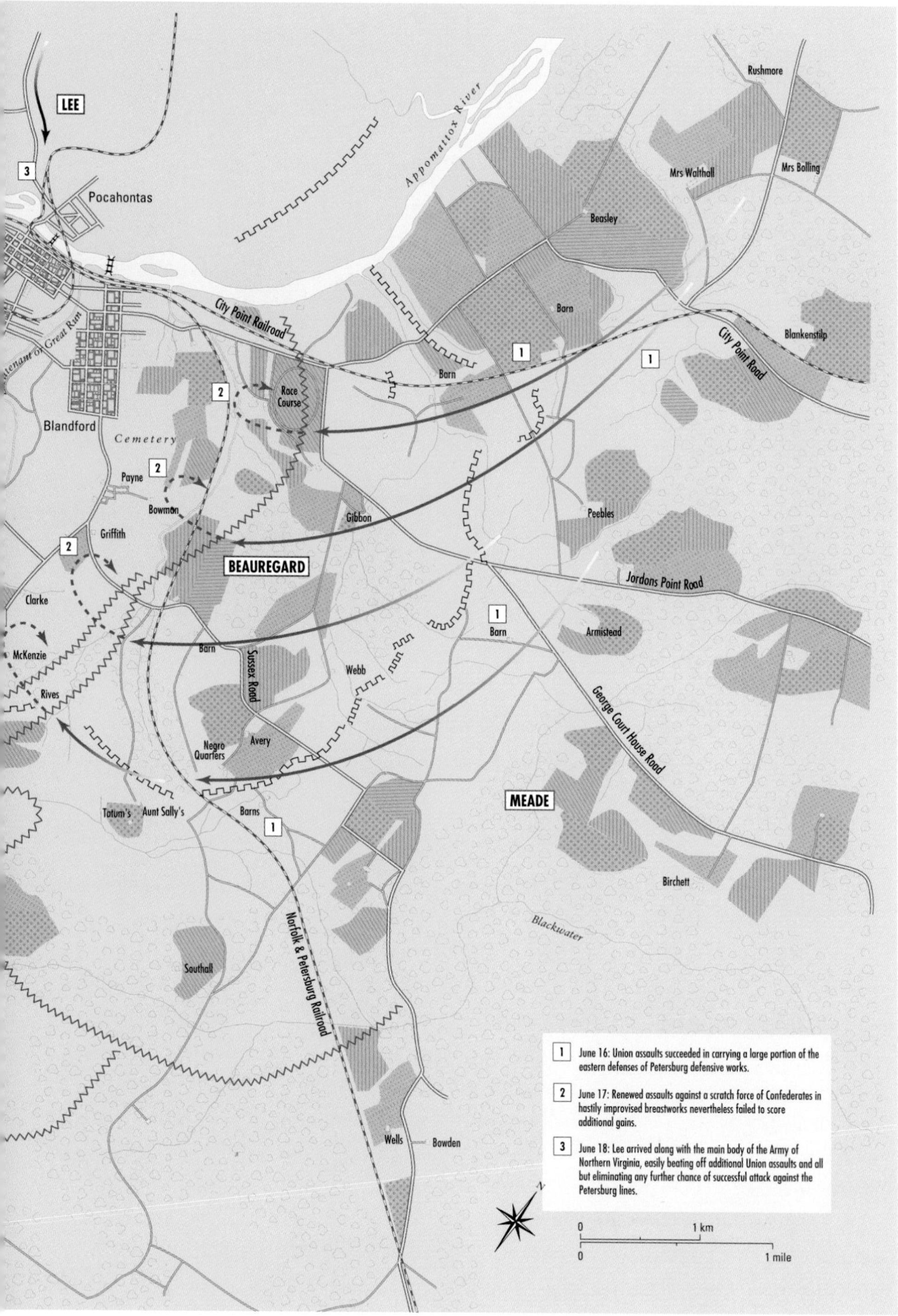

Left: Map showing the Union assaults against the eastern defenses of Petersburg between June 16–18, 1864.

1 June 16: Union assaults succeeded in carrying a large portion of the eastern defenses of Petersburg defensive works.

2 June 17: Renewed assaults against a scratch force of Confederates in hastily improvised breastworks nevertheless failed to score additional gains.

3 June 18: Lee arrived along with the main body of the Army of Northern Virginia, easily beating off additional Union assaults and all but eliminating any further chance of successful attack against the Petersburg lines.

1 June 12: Lee sends Jubal Early's Second Corps west to protect the Shenandoah Valley.

2 Grant prepares to move the Army of the Potomac south to Petersburg. Second and Sixth Corps occupy a revised siege line opposite Richmond.

3 Meanwhile Fifth Corps move to cover the approaches to the James River.

4 June 13: Eighteenth Corps embarks and sails for the Bermuda Hundred.

5 June 14: Second Corps crosses to the south bank of the James River by boat.

6 June 15: A massive pontoon bridge is completed across the James and the rest of the Union army crosses by June 16.

7 Union diversionary tactics keep Lee focused on the front north of the James River.

8 The Union army marches to Petersburg.

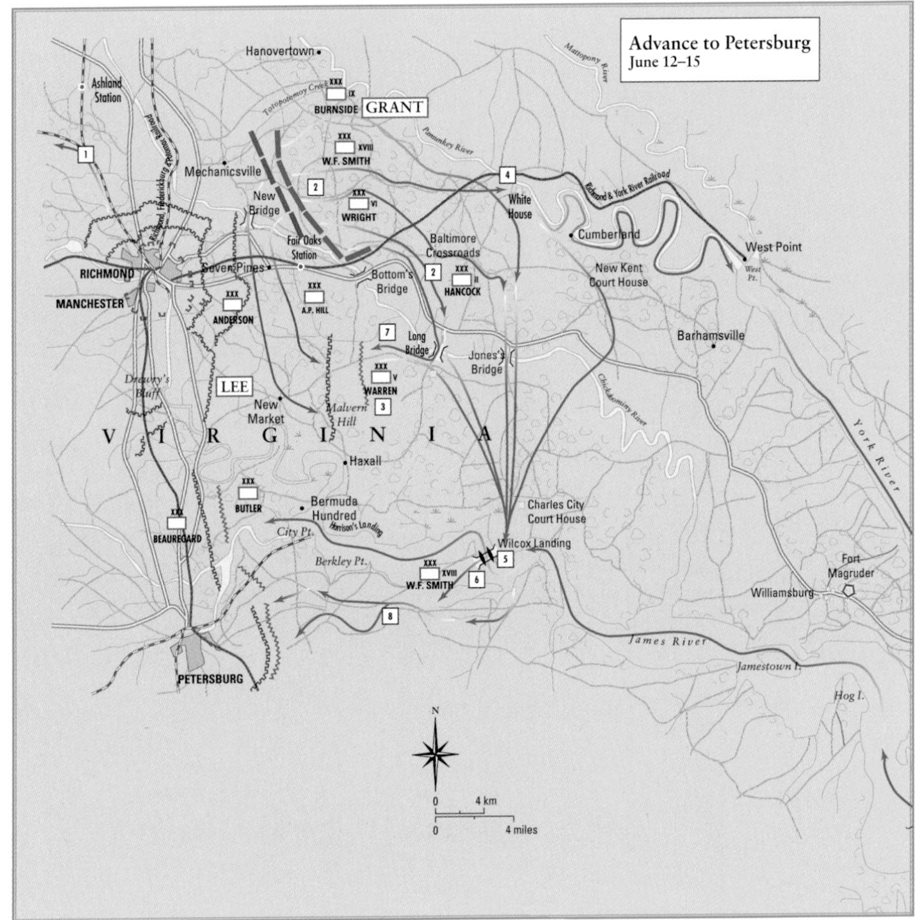

Right: Map showing the Advance to Petersburg, June 12-15

In an engagement not far away, Major General John B. Gordon lost most of the Confederate wagon train and two-thirds of Lee's cannon but was able to prevent capture of his troops.

The loss of such quantities of men and supplies, along with the straggling and desertion resulting from a disjointed retreat, put Lee in an almost untenable position, but despite the long-odds he now faced, he still hoped that his ragged and hungry soldiers could somehow break through Grant's tightening ring and unite with the Army of Tennessee under Johnston. The combined force would then be able to strike first one and then the other of the Union armies and gain more time for the Confederacy. Lee's last chance dissipated when General Gordon's attempt to create an escape route west of Appomattox could not be sustained without reinforcements—a situation that made the loss of 7,000 men at Sayler's Creek critical.

Lee considered courting death by leading a breakout charge, but this appealing alternative to surrender was overcome by his sense of duty. The South would need the leaders that remained to rebuild after four years of destructive warefare; the South could not afford to sacrifice brave men in a futile gesture. Lee swallowed his pride and agreed to meet with Grant to discuss terms.

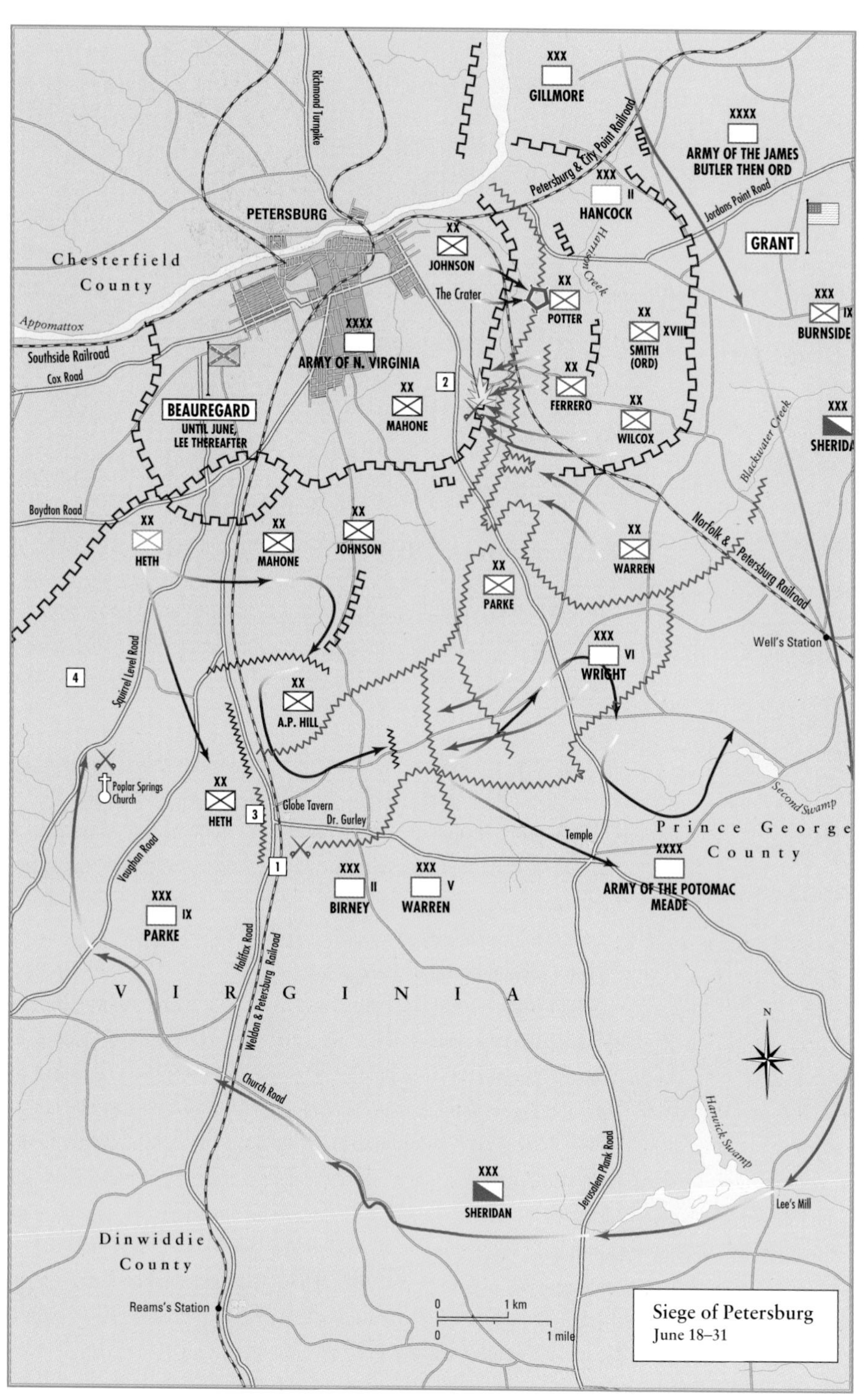

1 June 22: Grant sent the Second Corps, now under the command of Major General David Birney in place of the ailing Hancock, to secure the Jerusalem Plank Road and threaten the Weldon Railroad, but Lieutenant General Ambrose P. Hill's Confederate Third drove the Unions back administering a sharp defeat.

2 July 30: Grant's men detonated a large mine under a Confederate fort, but the subsequent infantry assault by Burnside's Ninth was incredibly bungled and resulted in failure and a Union bloodbath.

3 August 18–21: Warren's Fifth Corps seized a section of the Weldon Railroad around Globe Tavern and fought off subsequent Confederate counterattacks by A. P. Hill's corps

4 September 29–30: Warren's Fifth Corps together with the Ninth Corps, now under the command of Major General John G. Parke, pushed farther west. In the Battle of Peeble's Farm, Hill's Confederate Third Corps drove them back some distance, but the Unions dug in and held at Squirrel Level Road, further stretching Lee's thin lines.

Left: Map showing the continuing Union pressure on Petersburg between June and September, 1864.

ATLANTA

AT THE START OF THE WAR ATLANTA FELT ITSELF TO BE REASONABLY SAFE FROM UNION ATTACK, BUT ALL THAT CHANGED IN THE SUMMER OF 1864. ALTHOUGH MAJOR GENERAL WILLIAM T. SHERMAN WAS THE COMMANDER OF THE UNION FORCES, THE MAIN UNION FORCE IN THE BATTLE OF ATLANTA WAS THE ARMY OF THE TENNESSEE, UNDER MAJOR GENERAL JAMES B. MCPHERSON.

Above: Photograph of General James McPherson (1828–1864), a Federal officer who led the Army of Tennessee at the battle of Atlanta. He was the highest ranking officer to be killed during the conflict.

Opposite page: Confederate fortification during the Atlanta Campaign.

During the months leading up to the battle, Confederate General Joseph E. Johnston had repeatedly had to retreat from Sherman's superior force. Most of this action took place along the railroad between Chattanooga, Tennessee, and Marietta, Georgia. It was cat and mouse. Johnston would take up a position and Sherman would outflank him, so Johnston retreated. This happened over and over again.

Following Johnston's withdrawal after the Battle of Resaca, the two armies clashed again at the Battle of Kennesaw Mountain. Here, even though he had little chance of winning, Johnston was criticized by the Confederate leadership for his reluctance to fight. As a result he was relieved of his command and at the Battle of Peachtree Creek his replacement, Lt. Gen. John Bell Hood, lashed out at Sherman's army. The attack failed and casualties were heavy.

Hood's problem was that although he needed to defend the important and strategic city of Atlanta, his army was small in comparison to the enormous armies that Sherman commanded, so his strategy was to withdraw inwards and entice the Union troops to come forward. His aim was then to encircle the Union troops and win his battle.

Unfortunately for Hood the Union troops regrouped and held their line. Even though some

Confederate troops did manage to break through, Sherman ordered them to be shelled and the Confederate forces withdrew.

The Union suffered 3,641 casualties in this action, but the Confederates lost 8,499. This was a devastating loss for the already weakened Confederates, but they still held the city. Sherman then mounted a siege, repeatedly shelling the city and sending raids west and south to cut supply lines from Macon, Georgia.

Finally, on August 31 Sherman's army captured the railroad track from Macon. Throughout that night explosions could be heard coming from Atlanta and the next morning Hood pulled his troops out of the city, having destroyed all the supply depots to prevent them from falling into Union hands. On September 2 the city formally surrendered to the victorious Union army.

Two days later Sherman issued an order that all inhabitants must leave the city within five days so that the place might be appropriated for military purposes. He regarded this as a humane move, because he expected the Confederates to attack at any time.

When challenged about this he responded, "...was it better to fight with a town full of women and the families of a brave people at our backs, or to remove them in time to a place of safety among their own friends?"

Sherman established his headquarters in Atlanta on September 7 and stayed for two months. The Army then burned every building to the ground and departed east, destroying everything as they went.

Right: Once they had conquered Atlanta, the Federal Army established a base there. After several months of occupation, Sherman ordered the city to be burned and utterly destroyed, except for the hospitals and churches after a plea from the Catholic Church. Union soldiers are photographed here tearing apart the railway tracks.

Opposite page: Map showing the siege of Atlanta.

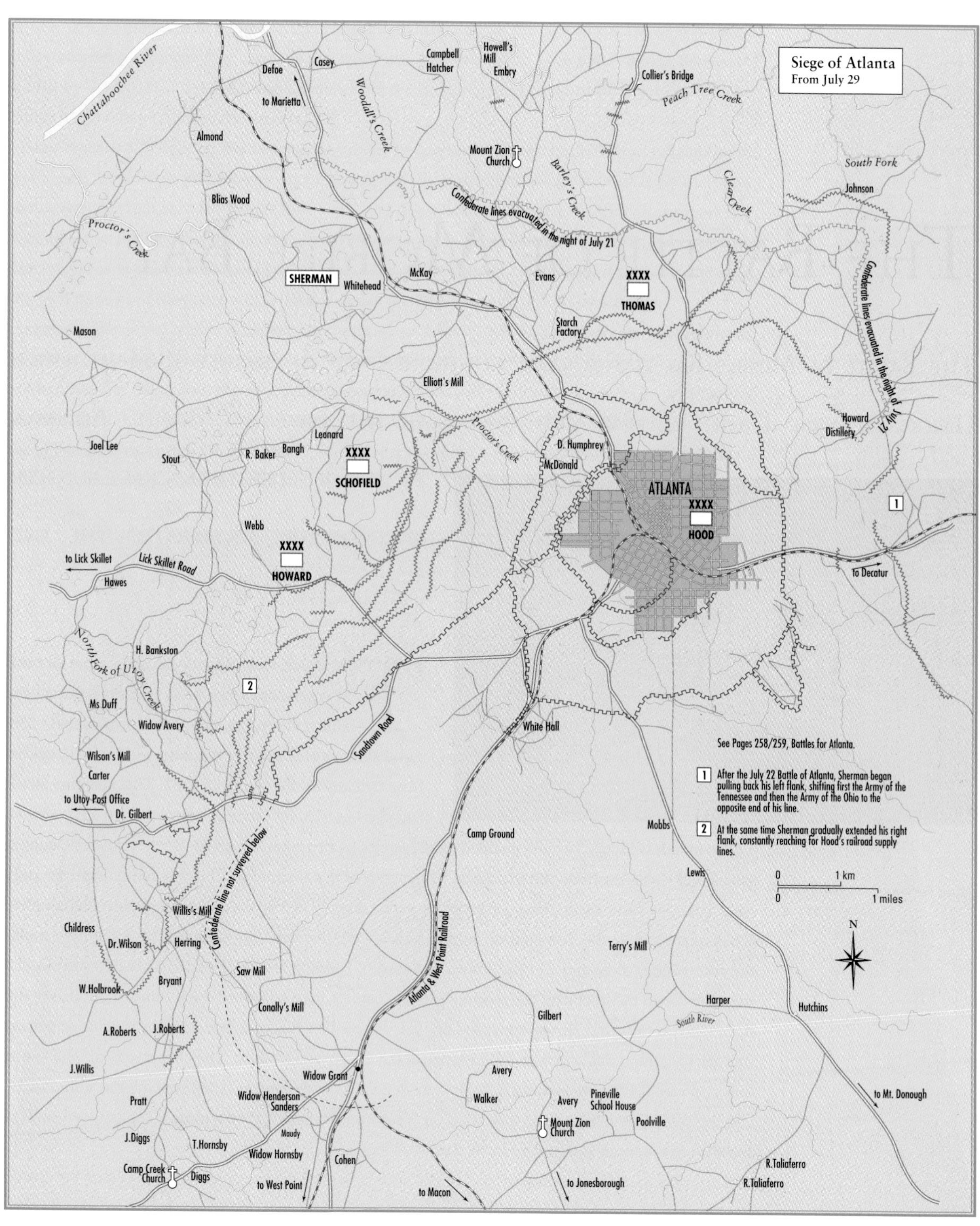

See Pages 258/259, Battles for Atlanta.

1 After the July 22 Battle of Atlanta, Sherman began pulling back his left flank, shifting first the Army of the Tennessee and then the Army of the Ohio to the opposite end of his line.

2 At the same time Sherman gradually extended his right flank, constantly reaching for Hood's railroad supply lines.

MISSOURI

IN AUGUST 1864, THE SOUTHERN COMMAND UNVEILED A BOLD PLAN TO RETAKE THE STATE OF MISSOURI FOR THE CONFEDERACY. IT WAS PARTLY THE WORK OF THOMAS C. REYNOLDS, MISSOURI'S PRO-CONFEDERATE GOVERNOR-IN-EXILE, AND WOULD INVOLVE A FORCE OF 12,000 MEN UNDER THE COMMAND OF MAJOR GENERAL STERLING PRICE.

Above: Confederate guerillas of William Clark Quantrill burn and pillage the town of Lawrence in Kansas, killing more than 150 unarmed civilians.

Price began by dividing his forces, sending one division, under General Joseph O' Shelby, to make a diversionary attack, while he headed west through Arkansas with the rest of his army. By the time Price entered Missouri on September 19, he had been rejoined by Shelby.

They launched their first major engagement against the Unionists at Ironton on September 26, but were driven back. In the morning they discovered that the Union forces had withdrawn in the night. However, this good news was tempered by reports of 4,500 Union cavalrymen fast approaching from St. Louis. This made Price realise that he would have to abandon his ambitious plan of launching assaults on either St. Louis or Illinois. Instead he would concentrate on stirring up popular discontent in the middle of Missiouri where he would hopefully acquire large numbers of new recruits.

He spent the next few days evading Union forces in the Missouri Valley, reaching Boonville

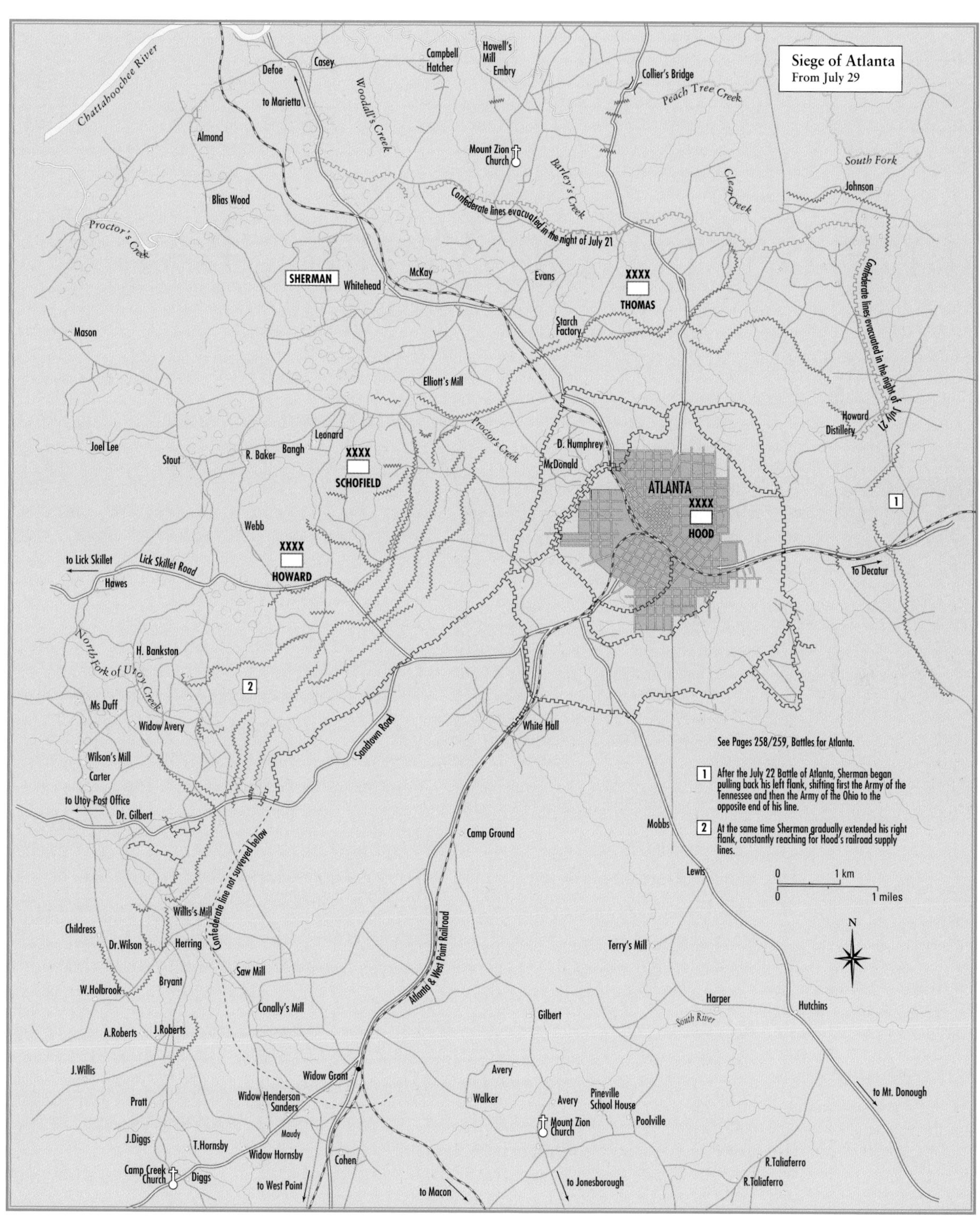

Siege of Atlanta
From July 29
Chattahoochee River
Defoe
Casey
to Marietta
Campbell Hatcher
Howell's Mill
Embry
Collier's Bridge
Peach Tree Creek
Woodall's Creek
Almond
Mount Zion Church
Barley's Creek
Clear Creek
South Fork
Johnson
Blias Wood
Confederate lines evacuated in the night of July 21
Proctor's Creek
SHERMAN
Whitehead
McKay
Evans
XXXX
THOMAS
Mason
Starch Factory
Elliott's Mill
Howard Distillery
Leonard
Joel Lee
Stout
R. Baker
Bangh
XXXX
SCHOFIELD
Proctor's Creek
D. Humphrey
McDonald
ATLANTA
XXXX
HOOD
1
Webb
XXXX
HOWARD
to Lick Skillet
Lick Skillet Road
Hawes
To Decatur
North Fork of Utoy Creek
H. Bankston
2
Ms Duff
Widow Avery
Sandtown Road
White Hall
Wilson's Mill
Carter
to Utoy Post Office
Dr. Gilbert
Confederate line not surveyed below
Camp Ground
Mobbs
Lewis
Willis's Mill
Childress
Dr.Wilson
Herring
Atlanta & West Point Railroad
Terry's Mill
Saw Mill
W.Holbrook
Bryant
Conally's Mill
Harper
Hutchins
South River
Gilbert
A.Roberts
J.Roberts
J.Willis
Widow Grant
Avery
Pratt
Widow Henderson
Sanders
Walker
Avery
Pineville School House
Poolville
to Mt. Donough
Maudy
Mount Zion Church
J.Diggs
T.Hornsby
Widow Hornsby
Cohen
Camp Creek Church
Diggs
to West Point
to Macon
to Jonesborough
R.Taliaferro
R.Taliaferro
See Pages 258/259, Battles for Atlanta.
1 After the July 22 Battle of Atlanta, Sherman began pulling back his left flank, shifting first the Army of the Tennessee and then the Army of the Ohio to the opposite end of his line.
2 At the same time Sherman gradually extended his right flank, constantly reaching for Hood's railroad supply lines.
0 1 km
0 1 miles
N

THE BATTLE OF MOBILE BAY

THE BATTLE OF MOBILE BAY WAS A NAVAL CONFRONTATION IN AUGUST 1864 IN WHICH UNION ADMIRAL DAVID G. FARRAGUT SHUT OFF THE PORT OF MOBILE, ALABAMA, FROM CONFEDERATE BLOCKADE RUNNERS AND THEREBY ACCELERATED THE END OF THE CIVIL WAR.

Above: Painting of the great Union naval victory at Mobile Bay, August 1864.

The action took place at the same time General Sherman was fighting for control of Atlanta—the Union campaign to make "Georgia howl." The naval strategy was roughly the same as that used against New Orleans in the spring of 1862. That surprise attack had also been led by Farragut, who was then a flag officer.

The mouth of Mobile Bay was guarded on either side by two great fortresses - Fort Gaines on Dauphin Island and Fort Morgan on the mainland. The center of the channel was heavily mined, and the only clear passages were two narrow stretches of water directly below the two strongholds' battlements. On August 5, while the Confederate land defenses were distracted by an attack by 2,400 men under the command of Brigadier General Robert S. Granger, Farragut led his fleet of 14 wooden ships and 4 ironclads down the middle of the channel into the bay. As they advanced, they came under heavy fire from the two forts, but Farragut pressed on, calculating that his force had a strong chance of getting through because it was only just within range of the land-based artillery. The Union suffered the loss of only one vessel, the USS Tecumseh, which avoided the gunfire but was holed beneath the waterline by a submerged torpedo (the word then used for what would now be called a mine). The ironclad sank in less than one minute with the probable loss of all hands.

It was then that Farragut uttered the words for which he is best remembered and which have been used as a rallying cry by U.S. forces ever since: "Damn the torpedoes: full speed ahead!" He took the lead

himself, commanding his flagship, the USS Hartford, to head on into the bay. There, the 13 remaining Union vessels confronted four Confederate warships, commanded by Admiral Franklin Buchanan and led by the ironclad USS Tennessee. Throughout the engagement, Farragut's ships continued to be shelled by land-based Confederate forces.

After two hours of fighting, the heavily outnumbered Confederate warships withdrew and the Union fleet joined the army in an attack on Fort Morgan, with its garrison of 600 men. On August 16, Union troops advanced to within 500 yards of the walls, and began bombarding the citadel with artillery. The siege ended on the morning of August 23, when the occupants surrendered. In a vain symbolic gesture, Page broke his sword over his knee, rather than hand it ceremonially to the victors as was customary. The total number of casualties was estimated at 322 on the Union side, 1,500 Confederate.

Although the city of Mobile itself was not captured until April 1865, Farragut's action was significant because it effectively closed the Confederacy's last major port on the Gulf of Mexico.

When news of the Union victory reached Washington, D.C., on September 3, Lincoln – anticipating that the severing of one of the last remaining links between the Confederacy and the outside world would boost his campaign for reelection – immediately ordered a 100-gun salute to honor "the recent brilliant achievement of the fleet and land forces."

Below: Map showing the major engagements during the Battle of Mobile Bay.

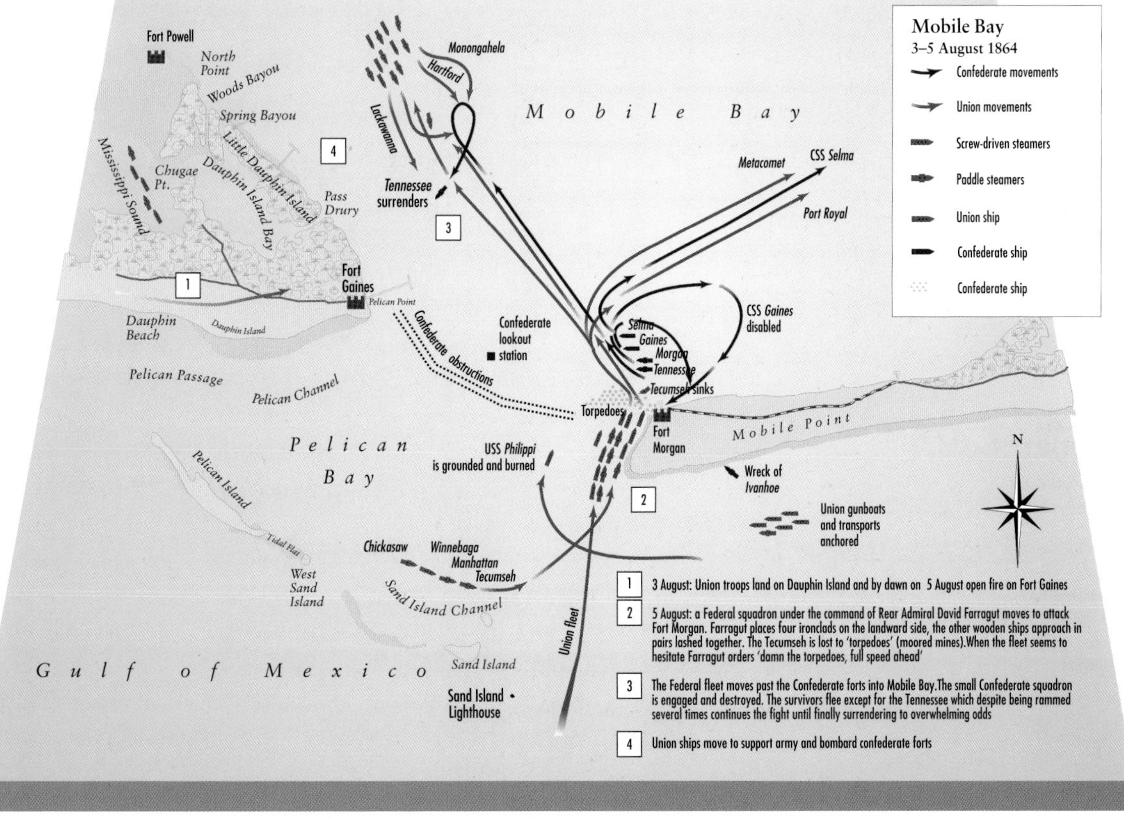

MISSOURI

IN AUGUST 1864, THE SOUTHERN COMMAND UNVEILED A BOLD PLAN TO RETAKE THE STATE OF MISSOURI FOR THE CONFEDERACY. IT WAS PARTLY THE WORK OF THOMAS C. REYNOLDS, MISSOURI'S PRO-CONFEDERATE GOVERNOR-IN-EXILE, AND WOULD INVOLVE A FORCE OF 12,000 MEN UNDER THE COMMAND OF MAJOR GENERAL STERLING PRICE.

Above: Confederate guerillas of William Clark Quantrill burn and pillage the town of Lawrence in Kansas, killing more than 150 unarmed civilians.

Price began by dividing his forces, sending one division, under General Joseph O' Shelby, to make a diversionary attack, while he headed west through Arkansas with the rest of his army. By the time Price entered Missouri on September 19, he had been rejoined by Shelby.

They launched their first major engagement against the Unionists at Ironton on September 26, but were driven back. In the morning they discovered that the Union forces had withdrawn in the night. However, this good news was tempered by reports of 4,500 Union cavalrymen fast approaching from St. Louis. This made Price realise that he would have to abandon his ambitious plan of launching assaults on either St. Louis or Illinois. Instead he would concentrate on stirring up popular discontent in the middle of Missiouri where he would hopefully acquire large numbers of new recruits.

He spent the next few days evading Union forces in the Missouri Valley, reaching Boonville

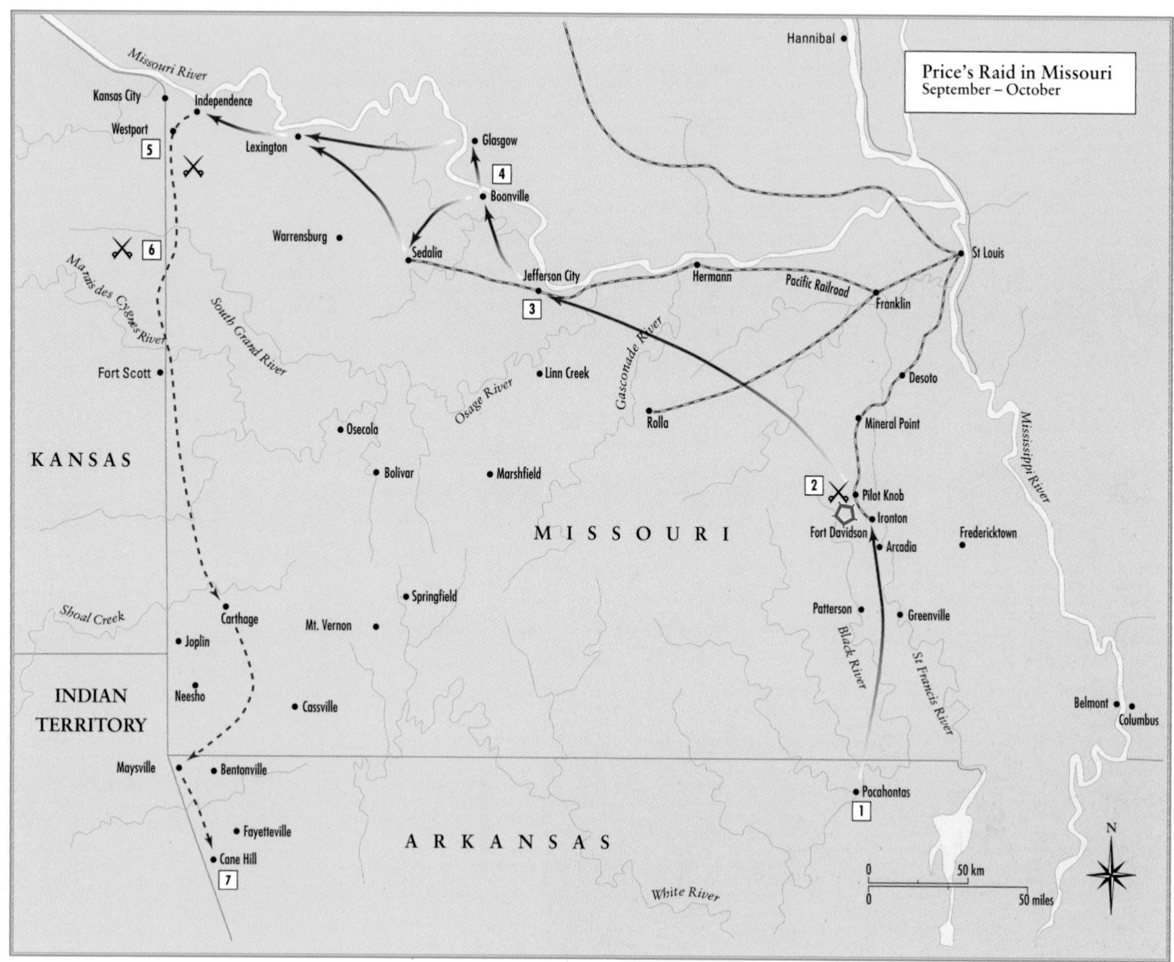

on October 9. Although he was able to acquire weapons from Boonville and the nearby towns of Sedalia and Glasgow, they were insufficient for his needs, while the numbers of new recruits had proved negligible.

Above: Map showing the route of Price's raid through Missouri.

By now, Union forces were closing in from several different directions. On October 21–23 Price was forced to stand and fight at Westport in a two-part battle which covered most of Jackson County and involved about 29,000 men on both sides. The Little Blue Creek was the Union's first defensive line, but it was easily breached, although It took the Confederates four hours of street fighting to clear the area completely. At the Big Blue Creek, Price's forces were situated between two Federal armins, where he planned to hold off one at a strong defensive position while striking the other, and then turn again on his first. The failure of his defensive gorup almost reulsted in his entire force being trapped, and the unanticipated fighting efficiency of the Kansas militia, brought into Missouri against their will, put him at a numerical disadvantage. "Old Pap" Price, who had used only part of his 9,000 men in the battle, escaped the trap and began to retreat.

SHENANDOAH VALLEY, 1864

WHATEVER ELSE MIGHT BE GOING ON IN THE WAR, THE CONFEDERACY COULD ALWAYS LOOK HAPPILY AT THE SHENANDOAH VALLEY—THE SOURCE OF MUCH OF ITS FOOD AND THE SITE OF MANY OF ITS FINEST VICTORIES. THAT WOULD ALL CHANGE IN THE SUMMER OF 1864, ALTHOUGH NOT BEFORE THE CONFEDERATES HAD GIVEN THE UNION AN ALMIGHTY SCARE.

Above: Union General Philip Sheridan rallying his troops in the Shenandoah Valley, Virgina.

Opposite:: A map detailing operations at the Shenandoah Valley, an area long considered to be a prime military target due to its rich farmland.

In the early summer of 1864, Ulysses S. Grant put Major General Franz Sigel in charge of an advance up the Shenandoah Valley, which he had long regarded as prime military target, as it contained some of the Confederacy's richest farmland—destroy this, he reasoned, and the Union would greatly hamper the Confederate army's ability to feed itself. .

In truth, Grant had no great confidence in Sigel who, thus far in the war, had proved himself to be a less than able commander. However, he believed that even someone of Sigel's limited capabilities would be able to march 5,000 troops up the lightly defended valley without mishap—he would come to rue that decision.

On May 15, not long into the campaign, a force of 5,500 Southern toops under the command of General John, C. Breckinridge, attacked Sigel at New Market, defeating him and forcing him to retreat to Strasburg. This was to prove a debacle too far for Sigel who was promptly sacked and replaced with Major General David Hunter. Now in charge of 16,000 troops, Hunter began the re-advance on May 26, defeating Major General W.E. "Grumble" Jones (Breckinridge's replacement) at Covington on June 2 and again on June 5 at Piedmont, killing Jones in the process.

Hunter followed up these successes by occupying Staunton and Lexington. By June 16 he had

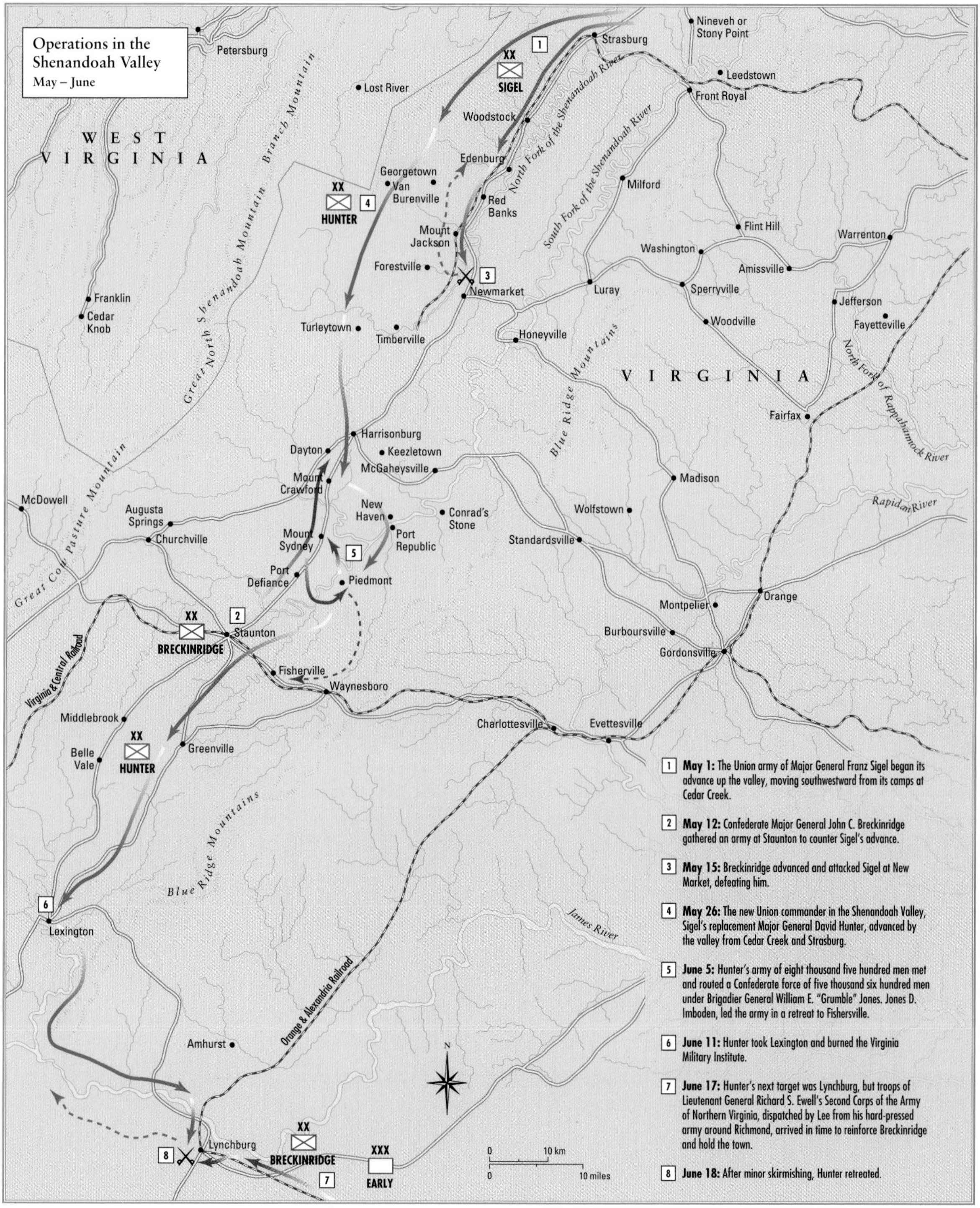

Operations in the Shenandoah Valley
May – June
Petersburg
Lost River
Strasburg
Nineveh or Stony Point
Leedstown
Front Royal
Woodstock
Edenburg
Georgetown
Van Burenville
Red Banks
Mount Jackson
Forestville
Newmarket
Milford
Flint Hill
Washington
Warrenton
Amissville
Sperryville
Luray
Jefferson
Woodville
Fayetteville
Honeyville
Turleytown
Timberville
Franklin
Cedar Knob
Harrisonburg
Dayton
Keezletown
McGaheysville
Mount Crawford
New Haven
Port Republic
Conrad's Stone
Mount Sydney
Port Defiance
Piedmont
McDowell
Augusta Springs
Churchville
Staunton
Fisherville
Waynesboro
Middlebrook
Greenville
Belle Vale
Lexington
Amhurst
Lynchburg
Madison
Wolfstown
Standardsville
Orange
Montpelier
Burboursville
Gordonsville
Charlottesville
Evettesville
Fairfax
WEST VIRGINIA
VIRGINIA
Branch Mountain
Great North Shenandoah Mountain
Great Cow Pasture Mountain
North Fork of the Shenandoah River
South Fork of the Shenandoah River
Blue Ridge Mountains
North Fork of Rappahannock River
Rapidan River
James River
Virginia & Central Railroad
Orange & Alexandria Railroad
XX SIGEL
XX HUNTER
XX BRECKINRIDGE
XXX EARLY
N
0 10 km
0 10 miles
1 May 1: The Union army of Major General Franz Sigel began its advance up the valley, moving southwestward from its camps at Cedar Creek.
2 May 12: Confederate Major General John C. Breckinridge gathered an army at Staunton to counter Sigel's advance.
3 May 15: Breckinridge advanced and attacked Sigel at New Market, defeating him.
4 May 26: The new Union commander in the Shenandoah Valley, Sigel's replacement Major General David Hunter, advanced by the valley from Cedar Creek and Strasburg.
5 June 5: Hunter's army of eight thousand five hundred men met and routed a Confederate force of five thousand six hundred men under Brigadier General William E. "Grumble" Jones. Jones D. Imboden, led the army in a retreat to Fishersville.
6 June 11: Hunter took Lexington and burned the Virginia Military Institute.
7 June 17: Hunter's next target was Lynchburg, but troops of Lieutenant General Richard S. Ewell's Second Corps of the Army of Northern Virginia, dispatched by Lee from his hard-pressed army around Richmond, arrived in time to reinforce Breckinridge and hold the town.
8 June 18: After minor skirmishing, Hunter retreated.

at Lynchburg where Breckinridge was in command of the Confederate forces. Learning that Breckinridge was soon to be reinforced by troops under the command of Lietenant General Jubal Early, Hunter decided to retreat into the mountains of West Virginia rather than attack. His decision left the way clear for Early to begin a dramatic advance, sweeping through the valley and beyond into Maryland. At one point he even reached the very outskirts of Washington before falling back to Virginia.

Grant was by now extremely concerned and sent Major General Philip H. Sheridan into the valley with instructions to combine the federal forces there—which amounted to the 6th, 8th, and 19th corps—into a single fighting force of some 40,000 men, which it was hoped would finally be of a size capable of finally destroying Early's ambitions.

Opposite page: Map showing confrontations between Sheridan and Early in the Shenandoah Valley in September 1864.

Below: The Battle of Cedar Creek was the last instance of the Southern Army attempting to invade a Union state. Their crushing defeat made it impossible for them to ever again pose a threat to Washington, D.C.

In September, having heard reports that Early had sent some of his troops to support General Lee at Petersburg, Sheridan decided to act. On September 19, he led his army into battle against Early's 12,000-strong force at the Battle of Winchester. Despite a huge numerical disadvantage, the battle's preliminary phases favored Early. However, momentum soon swung back to the Union side who succeeded in forcing the Confederates to retreat up the valley.

Early regrouped his forces at Fisher's Hill, but an attack on his flank by Sheridan once again proved

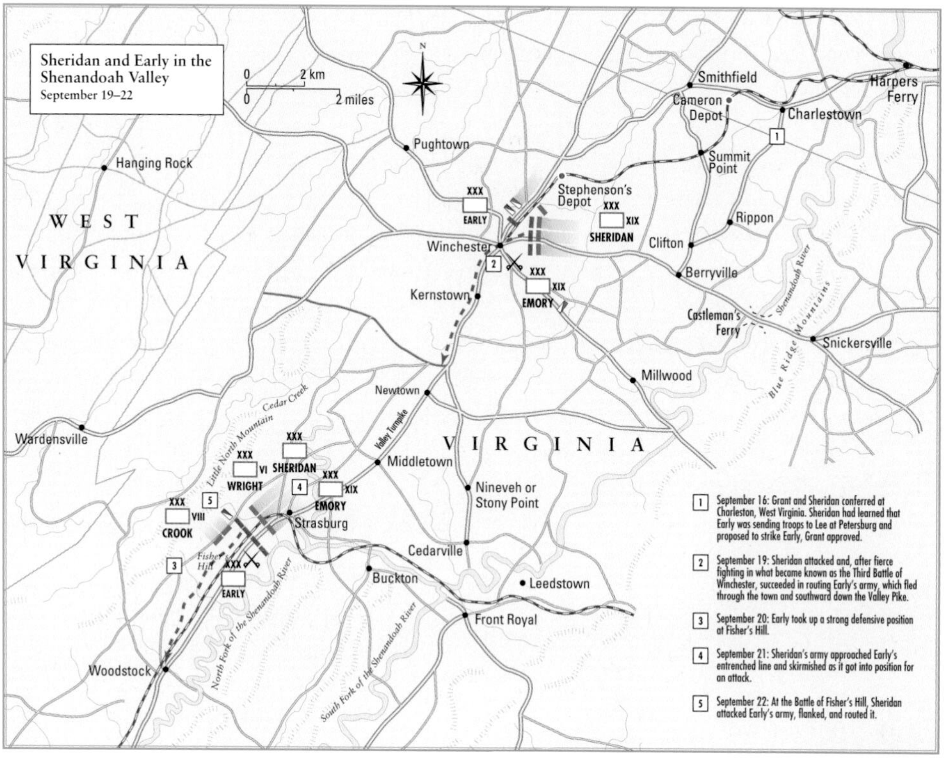

Sheridan and Early in the Shenandoah Valley
September 19–22

1 September 16: Grant and Sheridan conferred at Charleston, West Virginia. Sheridan had learned that Early was sending troops to Lee at Petersburg and proposed to strike Early, Grant approved.

2 September 19: Sheridan attacked and, after fierce fighting in what became known as the Third Battle of Winchester, succeeded in routing Early's army, which fled through the town and southward down the Valley Pike.

3 September 20: Early took up a strong defensive position at Fisher's Hill.

4 September 21: Sheridan's army approached Early's entrenched line and skirmished as it got into position for an attack.

5 September 22: At the Battle of Fisher's Hill, Sheridan attacked Early's army, flanked, and routed it.

successful. The Confederates were routed, losing over a thouand men—the rest fled south up the valley.

Sheridan followed Early to Staunton. However, rather than attacking, he left the Confederate leader to lick his wounds while he sent his men out into the valley with instructions to "ruin" it for the Confederacy—his men carried out their instructions to the letter, destroying crops, burning barns, and killing livestock. Sheridan then assembled his men at Cedar Creek near Middlton before leaving, on October 15, for business in Washington. He was due to return in a few days. However, in his absence, the Confedarates launched a surprise attack on the morning of October 19, driving the Union line back several miles and capturing several Federal camps.

Later in the day, Sheridan, having returned from Washington, learnt of the battle and rode to Middleton where he implored his retreating army to rejoin the fight—that they did, launching a furious counterattack in the late afternoon that retook all the ground they had lost that day. Early's army fled having suffered around 5,700 casualties to the the Union's 2,900.

Cedar Creek was to prove the last battle of 1864 in the Shenandoah, and the last in which the army of the Confederacy stood any chance of victory. In March of the following year, Sheridan's army smashed Early's once and for all at Mount Crawford.

Above: Major General David Hunter. who replaced the disgraced Major General Franz Sigel.

HOOD'S TENNESSEE CAMPAIGN

UNSUCCESSFUL IN HIS CAMPAIGN AGAINST SHERMAN'S ARMY IN GEORGIA, THE CONFEDERATE MAJOR GENERAL JOHN BELL HOOD TURNED HIS ATTENTION TO TENNESSEE. HIS STRATEGY TO ISOLATE AND DEFEAT UNION FORCES THERE ALMOST WORKED—HAD HE AND HIS TROOPS NOT FALLEN ASLEEP ON THE JOB.

Above: Portrait of General John Bell Hood, who notably led a campaign in Tennessee to try and defeat the Union forces.

After the fall of Atlanta in 1864, Hood moved into northwestern Georgia to threaten the supply lines of the Union army, led by Major General William T. Sherman. The two armies maneuvered inconclusively around each other, then turned their attention to other targets. Sherman began his March to the Sea while Hood, as part of a new plan to invade Tennessee, set his sights on Nashville, heading west on October 17.

Speed was of the essence for the Confederates. Tennessee was defended by Major General George H. Thomas, with his Fourth and Twenty-third corps. There were also various garrisons in the state that Thomas needed to bring together to form his army, a task that would take several weeks. This gave Hood a window of opportunity.

Some time was taken up looking for a suitable crossing point over the Tennessee River, which Hood finally found at Tuscumbia, Alabama. A further delay occurred while he waited for supplies, so it was not until November 21 that the Confederates marched north from the river—and by that time, Thomas was in a much better position to receive them.

To delay Hood's advance further, Thomas posted a force of twenty-eight thousand men under

Major General John M. Schofield at Pulaski. Bypassing Pulaski and avoiding them, Hood tried to reach Columbia, Tennessee, ahead of Schofield. Here, the road to Nashville led across the Duck River. If Hood could get to Columbia and the Duck River crossing first, he would cut off Schofield's army—which formed a large part of the Union's strength in the area—and thus come closer to his goal of conquering Middle Tennessee.

However, when Hood arrived there on November 26, he found Schofield waiting for him. In an attempt to trap his opponent's forces, Hood tried another maneuver. But Schofield was ahead of the game, and moved his army back to the Duck River's north bank on the night of November 27. Hood responded with a surprise maneuver—leaving one of his three corps to keep Schofield occupied near Columbia on November 29, he led the others on a wide, flanking march, crossed Duck River east of Columbia, and raced for Spring Hill on the road to Nashville.

Hood's plan almost worked. While Schofield remained largely unaware of the danger, the Confederate troops began arriving at Spring Hill in the afternoon. But as darkness gathered, matters began to go wrong for Hood. He had ordered his generals to take Spring Hill, which was fairly well defended by a small garrison. But it would have been sufficient just to seize the turnpike to the south—a relatively easy task that would have blocked Schofield's escape route. Hood's generals became confused and skirmished unsuccessfully with the Spring Hill garrison, then halted for the night a few hundred yards from the turnpike. During the night, while an exhausted Hood and his generals slept, Schofield and his entire army and wagon train marched across the Confederates' front—within a couple of hundred yards of Hood's campfires.

The following morning of November 30, a furious Hood gave pursuit, catching up with Schofield at Franklin, thirteen miles north of Spring Hill. Without waiting for his artillery and the corps he had left at Columbia to catch up, he launched his entire available force of twenty-five thousand men in a frontal assault against the enemy. Well-entrenched and partially armed with repeating rifles, Schofield's forces convincingly repulsed Hood and, that night, continued on their way to Nashville. Union losses were two thousand three hundred and twenty-six, compared to six thousand two hundred and fifty-two, including six generals, on the Confederate side.

Left: Union soldiers rest and relax in the recently captured Confederate fort outside Atlanta. After a series of battles, General Hood evacuated the city and proceeded to attack General Sherman's supply lines during Sherman's March to the Sea.

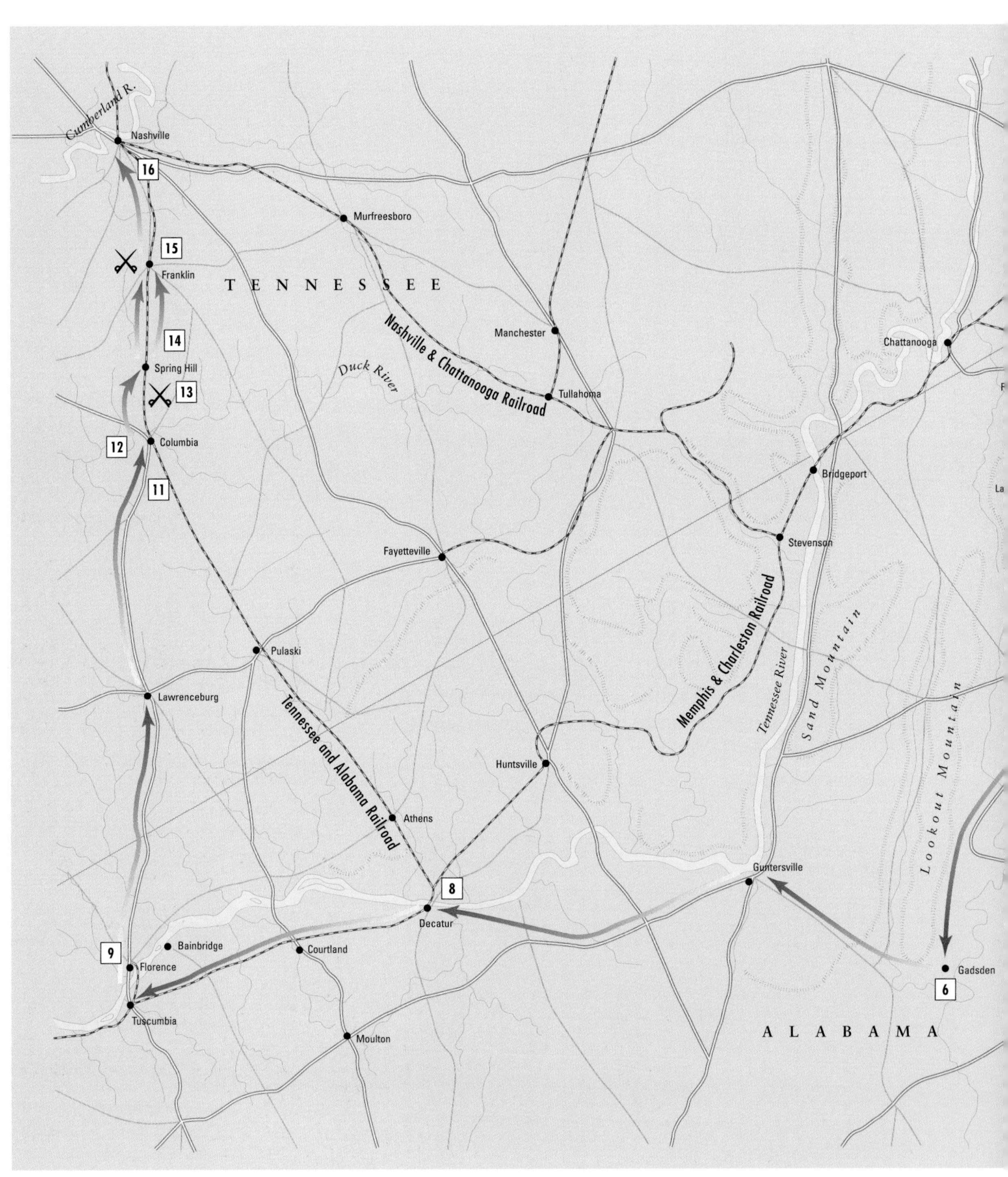
Cumberland R.
Nashville
16
Murfreesboro
15
Franklin
TENNESSEE
14
Spring Hill
13
12
Columbia
11
Duck River
Nashville & Chattanooga Railroad
Manchester
Tullahoma
Chattanooga
Bridgeport
Stevenson
Fayetteville
Pulaski
Lawrenceburg
Memphis & Charleston Railroad
Tennessee River
Sand Mountain
Lookout Mountain
Tennessee and Alabama Railroad
Huntsville
Athens
Guntersville
8
Decatur
Bainbridge
Courtland
9
Florence
Tuscumbia
Moulton
Gadsden
6
ALABAMA

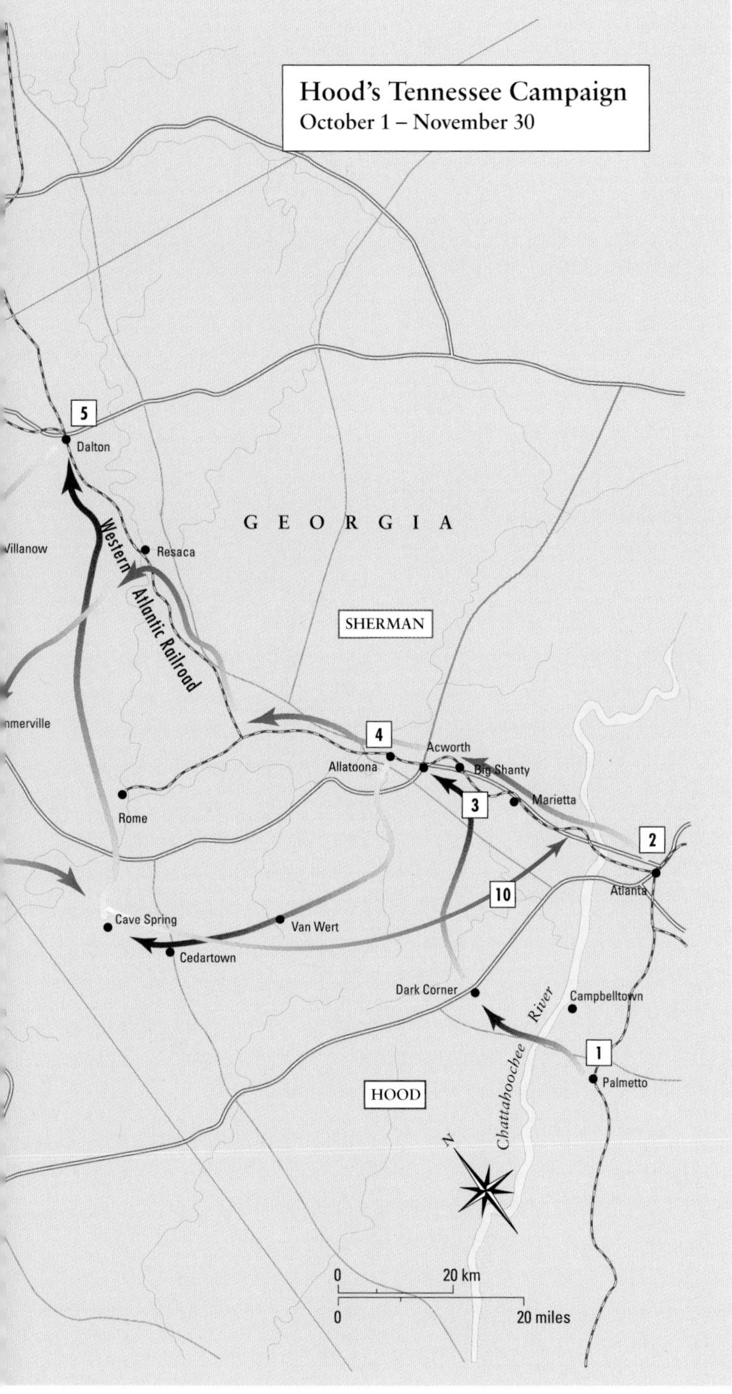

Hood's Tennessee Campaign
October 1 – November 30

GEORGIA
SHERMAN
HOOD
Western Atlantic Railroad
Chattahoochee River
Dalton
Resaca
Villanow
Summerville
Allatoona
Acworth
Big Shanty
Marietta
Rome
Atlanta
Cave Spring
Van Wert
Cedartown
Dark Corner
Campbelltown
Palmetto
N
0 20 km
0 20 miles

1 September 29–30: Intent on a campaign against Sherman's lines of communication in North Georgia, Hood led his army across the Chattahoochee River and marched north.

2 October 2: Sherman left the Tenth Corps to hold Atlanta and pursued Hood with the rest of his force.

3 October 3–4: Hood's Confederates captured Big Shanty and broke the railroad.

4 October 5: The Confederates attacked the supply depot at Allatoona Pass, which was heroically defended by a small Union force under the command of Brigadier General John Corse.

5 October 13: Hood struck again, this time capturing the Union garrison at Dalton, Georgia.

6 October 14–15 : Hood retreated to Gadsden, Alabama.

7 October 14–15 : Sherman pursued Hood as far as Gaylesville and there halted.

8 October 26: Intent on his new plan of invading Tennessee, Hood reached Decatur, Alabama, hoping to cross the Tennessee River there, but found the north bank held by the Union force in too much force to allow a crossing.

9 October 30: Stephen D. Lee's Confederate corps, leading the advance of Hood's army, crossed the Tennessee River and occupied Florence, Alabama.

10 November 15: Having given up on chasing Hood and returned to Atlanta, Sherman this day began his March to the Sea.

11 November 27: Hood's army approached the Union army of Major General John M. Schofield near Columbia, Tennessee.

12 November 28: Concerned that Hood might cut him off from Nashville, Schofield retreated to the north bank of the Duck River.

13 November 29: Hood did indeed plan to trap Schofield and on this day led his army in a hard march around the Union army, beating Schofield to Spring Hill but, incredibly, failing to secure either the town on the pike that ran through it.

14 November 29–30 , night: Schofield's army escaped, marching along the pike in the darkness within a few hundred yards of Hood's camps. Hood had turned in early and slept through the entire episode.

15 November 30: Hood pursued Schofield to Franklin, where the Union troops waited in pre-existing entrenchments while their engineers re-built a bridge over the Harpeth River. Hood attacked but his troops were repulsed with disastrous slaughter.

16 November 30 – December 1, night: Schofield withdrew without difficulty and completed his planned march to Nashville.

Siege of Richmond

Despite the many hardships endured by its citizens, which increased greatly throughout the course of the conflict, and the tremendous desire of Lincoln to capture the Confederate capital, there was never any real danger that Richmond might fall to the Union side until late in the war.

Indeed, when Grant finally ordered the siege of Richmond in June 1864, he did so at the same time as ordering a siege of Petersburg, which in truth he considered at the time a much more strategically important target. In fact, most of the operations against the Capital of the Confederacy during the 10-month siege were aimed not so much at taking the city as tying down Lee's troops, thereby preventing them from reacting to Union attacks elsewhere.

Petersburg was important not just for its own strategic value, but for the knock-on effect its capture would have—once taken it allow the final railroad leading into Richmond from the south to be cut. However, that's not to say that Grant was entirely unconcerned with operations againg the Confederate capital. Although he refrained from ordering a full-scale assault for many months, he continued to oversee minor ones and was always prepared to changed tactics and commit troops to the fray should one of the these minor attacks show signs of turning into something more significant. Indee, it shows the extent to which the pendulum had swung in the Union's favor that they now expected victories on all fronts, and openings to arise from all attacks.

The first operation against Richmond was launched in July. Its ostensible purpose was to create a diversion for Union troops massing for the Battle of Crater at Petersburg on July 30. The Second Corps, under the command of Major General Winfiled S. Hancock, crossed of the James River on July 27 where they joined up with the two cavalry divisions of Major General Philip Sheridan. Together they launched what would amount to little more than a feinting attack against the Confederate New Market Road fortifications—doing just enought to keep the soldiers occupied before falling back to the other side of the river.

Opposite page: Throughout the summer and early fall of 1864, Union forces brought more and more pressure to bear on the Confederate defenders of Richmond.

In September Grant once again ordered his troops to cross the river. Although their ostensible aim

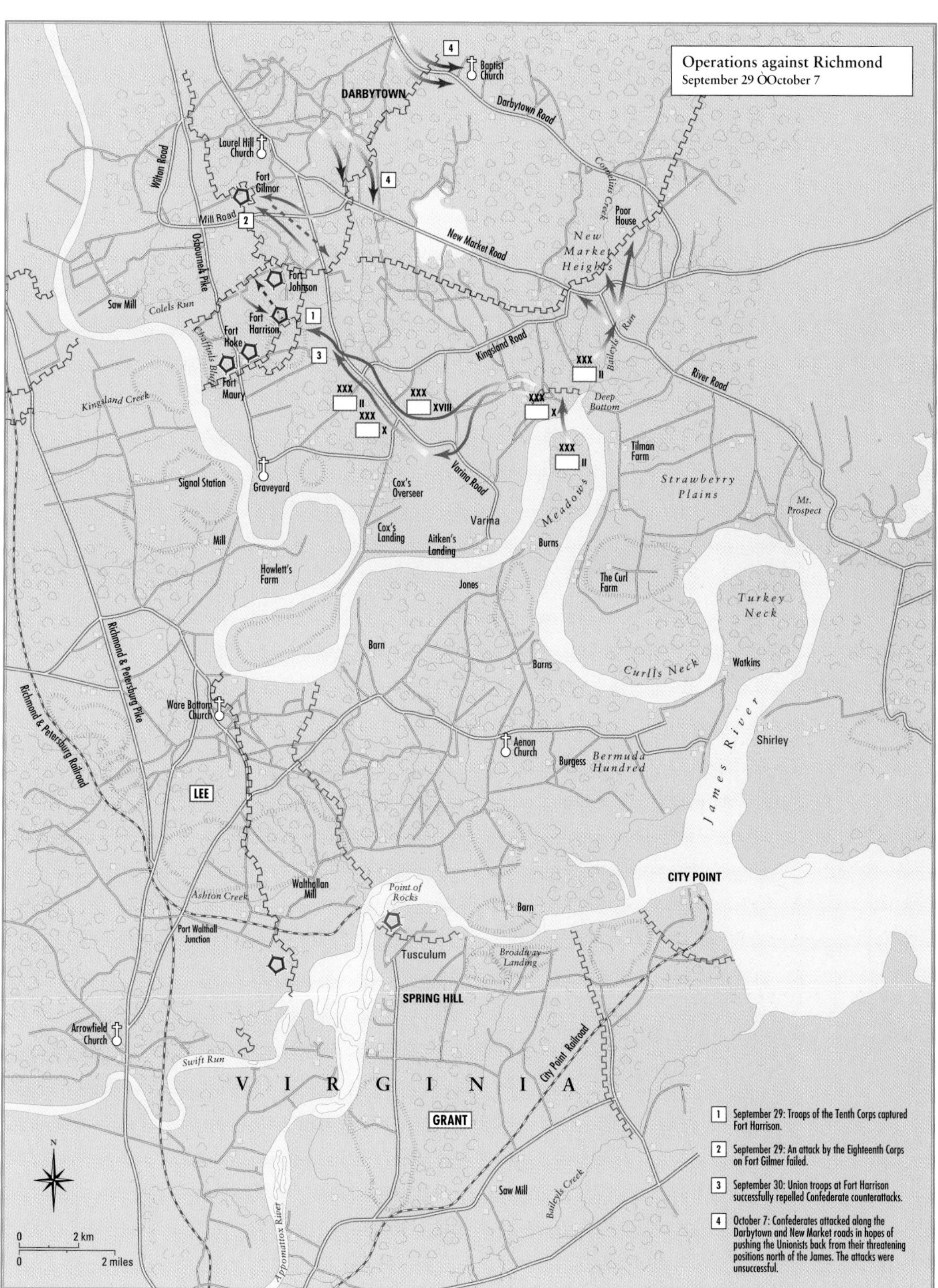
Operations against Richmond
September 29 ÒOctober 7
Baptist Church
DARBYTOWN
Darbytown Road
Laurel Hill Church
Wilton Road
Fort Gilmor
Mill Road
Osbourne's Pike
New Market Road
Poor House
Cornelius Creek
New Market Heights
Fort Johnson
Saw Mill
Coles Run
Fort Harrison
Fort Hoke
Fort Maury
Chaffin's Bluff
Kingsland Road
Baileys Run
River Road
Kingsland Creek
XXX II
XXX X
XXX XVIII
Deep Bottom
Tilman Farm
Varina Road
Signal Station
Graveyard
Cox's Overseer
Strawberry Plains
Mt. Prospect
Varina
Meadows
Mill
Cox's Landing
Aitken's Landing
Burns
Howlett's Farm
Jones
The Curl Farm
Turkey Neck
Richmond & Petersburg Pike
Barn
Barns
Curlls Neck
Watkins
Richmond & Petersburg Railroad
Ware Bottom Church
Aenon Church
Burgess
Bermuda Hundred
Shirley
James River
LEE
Walthallan Mill
CITY POINT
Point of Rocks
Ashton Creek
Barn
Port Walthall Junction
Tusculum
Broadway Landing
SPRING HILL
Arrowfield Church
City Point Railroad
Swift Run
VIRGINIA
GRANT
N
Saw Mill
Baileys Creek
Appomattox River
0 2 km
0 2 miles
1 September 29: Troops of the Tenth Corps captured Fort Harrison.
2 September 29: An attack by the Eighteenth Corps on Fort Gilmer failed.
3 September 30: Union troops at Fort Harrison successfully repelled Confederate counterattacks.
4 October 7: Confederates attacked along the Darbytown and New Market roads in hopes of pushing the Unionists back from their threatening positions north of the James. The attacks were unsuccessful.

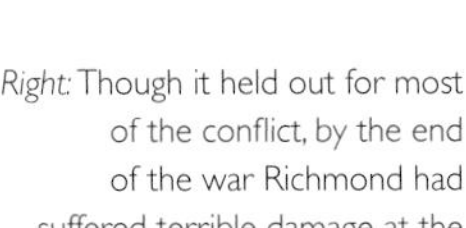

Right: Though it held out for most of the conflict, by the end of the war Richmond had suffered terrible damage at the hands of the Union army.

was to launch attacks on the Confederate forts of Harrison and Gilmer, they also had a secondary objective of preventing Lee from releasing troops to bolster Lieutenant General Jubal A. Early's campaign in Maryland.

On the morning of September 29, the 10th Corps, under the command of Major General David Birney and the 18th Corps of Major General E.O.C Ord crossed over to the north bank of the river and headed toward the forts. The subsequent attacks, known collectively at the Battle of Chaffin's Bluff, were to be much more serious and intense than their predecessors—as demonstrated by the fact that operations were being directed by Grant and Lee themselves, who perhaps sensed that some sort of tipping point in the conflict was at hand.

After fierce fighting, the Union Division of Brigadier General George Stannard took Fort Harrison. The next day a wave of Confederate counterattacks failed to retake it. However, depite repeated and concerted assaults, Union troops were unable to capture Fort Gilmer.

Lee was extremely concerned about the ground gained the the Union side, which he saw as posing a grave, and possibly terminal, threat to the safety of the Confederate capital. He therefore ordered his troops try and retake Fort Harrison, sending his troops out along Darbytown and New Market roads to drive the Union forces back. The two sides engaged at Johnston's Farm and Four-Mile Creek.

For a while it seemed that Confederate effort would prove successful, but ultimately the Unionists held on, further denting Lee's hopes of holding onto Richmond. But the end for the Confederate capital was not yet nigh. Despite the Union gains, the overall strategic situation had actually changed very little. The deadlock would not be broken until the final days of the war in early April 1865.

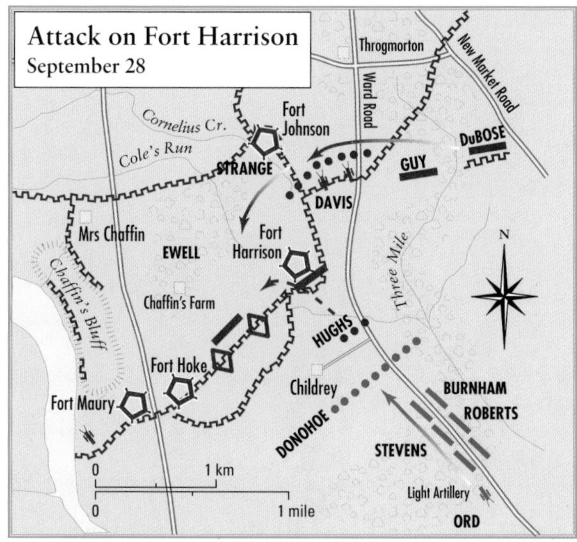

Attack on Fort Harrison
September 28

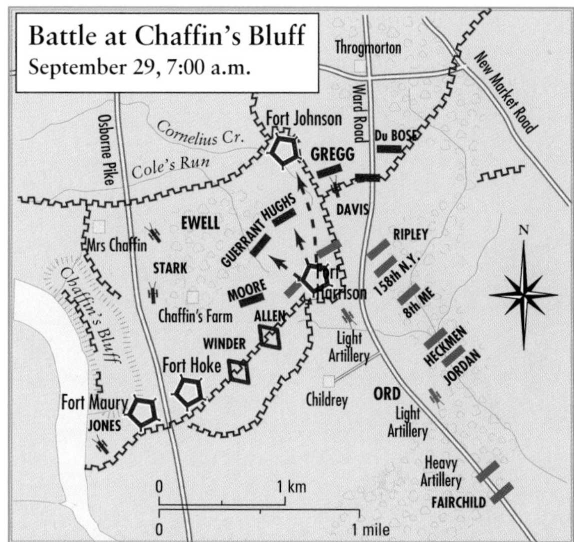

Battle at Chaffin's Bluff
September 29, 7:00 a.m.

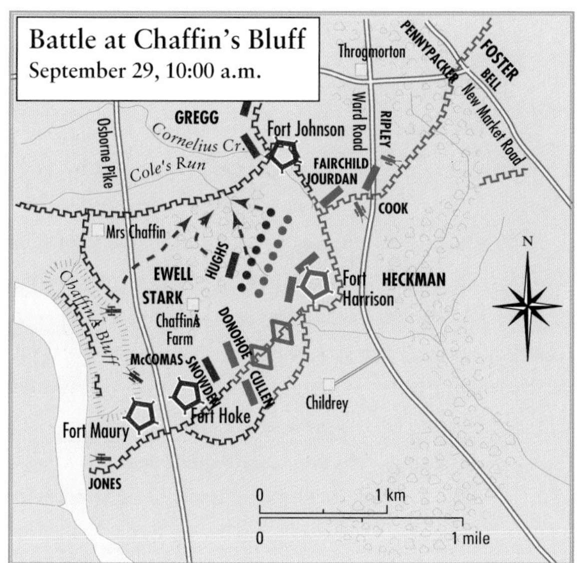

Battle at Chaffin's Bluff
September 29, 10:00 a.m.

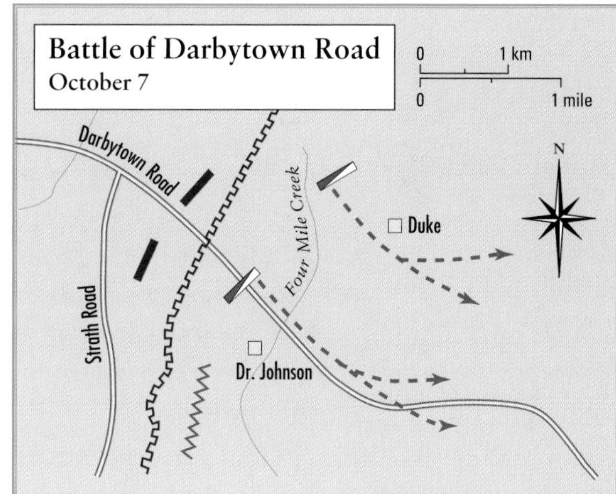

Battle of Darbytown Road
October 7

Above: The September battles on the outskirts of Richmond saw Fort Harrison fall to the Unionists, but little other ground gained.

SHERMAN'S MARCH FROM ATLANTA TO THE SEA

FOLLOWING THE SUCCESSFUL ATLANTA CAMPAIGN BETWEEN MAY AND SEPTEMBER 1864, UNION MAJOR GENERAL WILLIAM T. SHERMAN AND THE U.S. ARMY COMMANDER LIEUTENANT GENERAL ULYSSES S. GRANT BOTH BELIEVED THAT IT WAS NECESSARY TO BREAK THE CONFEDERACY'S STRATEGIC, ECONOMIC, AND PSYCHOLOGICAL CAPACITY FOR WARFARE IF THE WAR WAS EVER GOING TO END.

Sherman's strategy was to move east from Atlanta to the sea and employ a scorched earth policy as he went. He would order his troops to burn all crops, kill all livestock, consume all supplies and to generally destroy all civilian infrastructure along their path. This policy is often considered to be a component strategy of "total war." It also received the tacit approval of newly re-elected President Abraham Lincoln.

Below: General Sherman's March to the Sea campaign left the city of Richmond in ruins. The General also captured the port of Savannah on December 21, 1864.

Sherman's army would live off the land and while most of the troops would be engaged in the destruction of the railroads, manufacturing, and agricultural infrastructure of the state, foragers, known as "bummers" would provide food seized from local farms.

Sherman issued very detailed instructions. According to his rules, soldiers were forbidden to enter dwellings, but were free to help themselves to corn or forage of any kind, meat of any kind, vegetables, corn meal, or anything else that was deemed necessary by the officers in charge. The aim was to keep at least ten day's provisions for the men and three days of forage for the animals at all times.

Only corps commanders had the authority to destroy mills, houses or cotton gins. Union rules stated that in those areas where the army was able to go about its business unmolested, no destruction should take place at all. If on the other hand if the soldiers met with resistance, or even just open hostility, army commanders should order and enforce a more or less relentless devastation according to the measure of the hostility.

Horses, mules, and wagons belonging to the inhabitants could be taken at will, but there should be discrimination between the wealthy who were usually hostile, and the poor who were generally neutral or friendly.

The march to the Sea would cover 300 miles (480 km) and began on November 15, 1864. Early on that day, Union troops left the smoldering ruins of Atlanta and headed in a roughly south-easterly direction. Sherman had divided his 62,000 men into two columns for the march. On the left wing was the Army of Georgia commanded by Major General Frank Blair, Jr., while on the right was the Army of Tennessee commanded by Major General Oliver O. Howard. The two wings of the army attempted to confuse the Confederates, who were not able to work out whether Sherman would march on Macon, Augusta, or Savannah.

Left: General Sherman's men destroying southern railroads as they leave the newly captured city of Atlanta. To damage their enemy's ability to engage in war they also killed livestock and burned crops.

Howard's wing marched south along the railroad to Lovejoy's Station and then onwards towards Augusta, destroying everything as they went.

After issuing proclamations calling on all its citizens to "die free men rather than live as slaves" the state legislature of Georgia promptly fled the capital. By now it was clear to Confederate General William J Hardee that Savannah and not Macon was Sherman's target. He ordered the Confederate cavalry to harass the Union rear and flanks, while the militiamen hurried eastward to protect the seaport city.

The campaign continued relentlessly throughout the rest of November and into December. Sherman's army finally reached the outskirts of Savannah on December 10, but by now Hardee had had time to entrench 10,000 men in good positions. Hardee's soldiers had also flooded the rice fields so that the only way to approach the city was by narrow causeways.

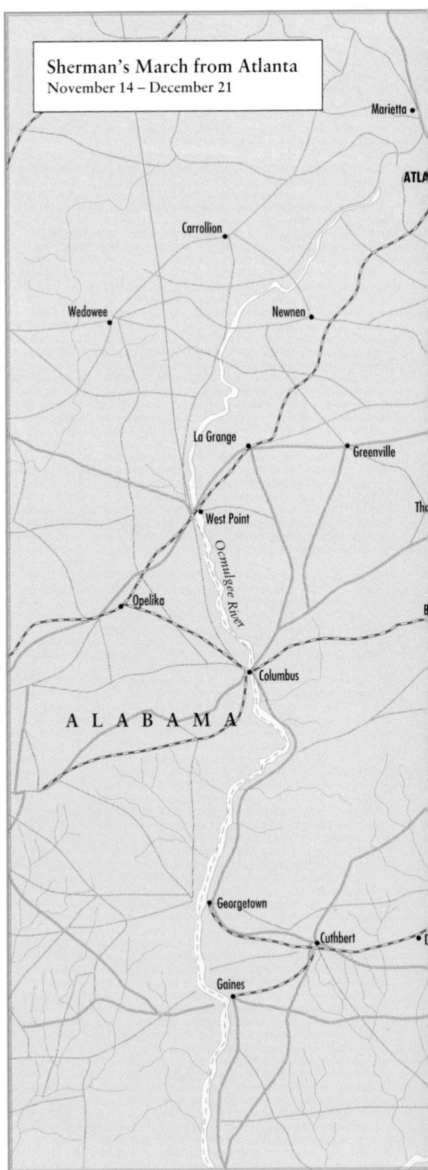

Sherman had planned to link up with the U.S. Navy, but when he found that this was no longer possible he dispatched cavalry to Fort McAllister, which was speedily captured. This provided Sherman with a vital link to obtain supplies and the siege artillery that would be needed to capture the city.

On December 17 Sherman offered Hardee terms of surrender, but Hardee made the decision to escape instead and on December 20 he led his men out of the city across the Savannah River on a hastily constructed pontoon bridge. The following day Savannah's mayor rode out to formally surrender the city.

The surrender meant that the city was not destroyed and, today it retains much of its original appearance. This includes orderly squares mapped out in th e1730s and numerous early-nineteenth-century houses that witnessed the Civil War.

Sherman's scorched earth policies were highly controversial at the time and have remained so ever since. The results of the march to the sea were profoundly devastating, not just for Georgia but for the entire Confederacy. By his own admission Sherman inflicted upward of $100 million's worth of destruction. The army wrecked 300 miles (48 km) of railroad and numerous bridges and miles of telegraph lines. It seized 5,000 horses, 4,000 mules, and 13,000 head of cattle. It confiscated 9.5 million pounds of corn, 10.5 million pounds of fodder and destroyed uncounted cotton gins and mills.

From a purely military point of view Sherman's march was an amazing achievement in that he successfully managed to take a large army deep into enemy territory without lines of supply or communication—something that was previously unheard of.

His scorched earth policy achieved exactly what it set out to do; it knocked the Confederate war effort to pieces and it destroyed much of the South's potential and psychology to wage war.

Below: In General Sherman's March to the Sea Campaign, the enemy was unsure of his target until just before troops arrived in Savannah, where Sherman planned link up with the United States Navy.

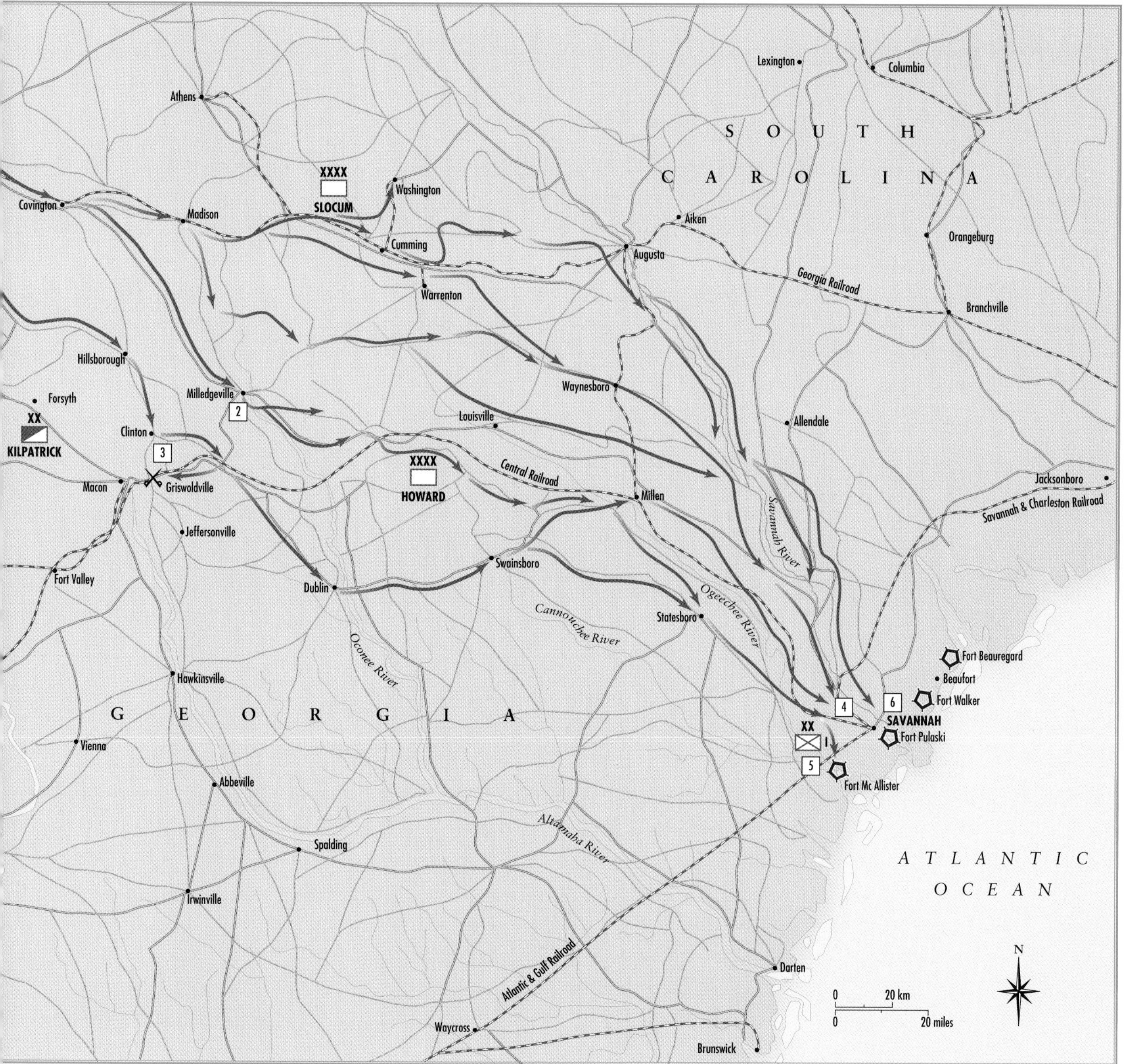

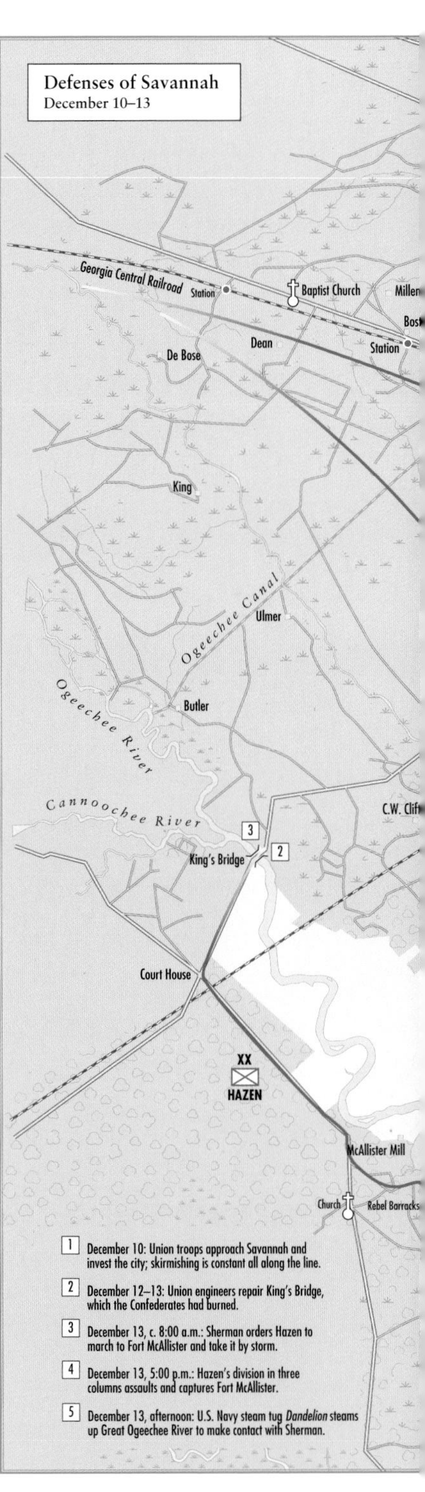

Above: Federal troops fill the streets of Savannah, Georgia, upon its occupation in December 1864.

Right: Confederate defenses of Savannnah. Without this industry to produce naval war ships, the South was overwhelmed by Union forces and eventually crumbled.

Mulberry Grove
Station
Argyle Island
Onslow Island
Taylor
Izard
Smith
Savannah Charleston Railroad
W. Dotson
Savannah River
Hutchinson's Island
White House
Mrs Dolson
SAVANNAH
Fort Lawton
Obstructed by Cribs
Spiles
Fort Tattnall
Fort Boggs
Causton's Bluff
Bonaventure Battery
White Marsh
Wassaw
Fort Thunderbolt
Turner's Rocks Battery
McQueen's Island
Isle of Hope
(Forge) Battery Daniels
Parkersburg
Vernonsburg
Saltworks
Orphan Asylum
Fort Wimberly
Montgomery
Middle Marsh
Back River
Burnside River
Grove River
Little Ogeechee River
Vernon River
Kiddaway Island
Wreck of the Nashville
Great Ogeechee River
Fort McAllister
Hell Gate
Steam Tug Dandelion
Raccoon Key
Florida Passage
Ossabaw Sound
Elements of Union fleet
Little Wassaw Island
Wassaw Island
Wassaw Sound
Wilmington Island
Tybee River
Tybee Island
Tybee Roads
May River Neck
Red Bluff
New River
Hog Island
Wright's River
Jone's Island
Tuhtie Island
Cooper River
Daufuskie Island
Calibogue Sound
Bull's Island
ATLANTIC OCEAN
N
0 2 km
0 2 miles

THE BATTLE OF NASHVILLE

THE BATTLE OF NASHVILLE WAS A TWO-DAY BATTLE IN THE FRANKLIN-NASHVILLE CAMPAIGN. IT WAS FOUGHT AT NASHVILLE, TENNESSEE ON DECEMBER 15 AND 16, 1864 AND THE OUTCOME WAS ONE OF THE MOST IMPORTANT UNION VICTORIES OF THE WAR. THE ARMY OF TENNESSEE, WHICH WAS THE SECOND LARGEST CONFEDERATE FORCE, WAS EFFECTIVELY ANNIHILATED AND WOULD NEVER FIGHT AGAIN.

Above: An illustration of the Battle of Nashville. A two day battle fought on December 15 and 16, 1864, in which the Confederate Army of Tennessee,were brutally defeated.

Following the Battle of Franklin on November 30, the Union forces, commanded by Major General John M. Schofield, concentrated within the defensive works of Nashville alongside the Army of the Cumberland commanded by Major General George H. Thomas, bringing their number to about 55,000. Meanwhile the Confederate Army of Tennessee, commanded by Lieutenant General John Bell Hood, arrived south of the city on December 2 and took up positions facing the enemy.

Hood sat and waited, hoping that Thomas would attack him and give him the opportunity to counterattack and take Nashville. If this plan worked, he would then recruit additional soldiers in Tennessee and Kentucky before pushing on through the Cumberland Gap to relieve Robert E. Lee at St Petersburg.

Although his forces were stronger than Hood's, Thomas knew that he could not ignore Hood's army. Although it had suffered a severe beating at Franklin, by its mere presence and its ability to maneuver, it posed a threat. He knew he had to attack, but he also knew that he must proceed with caution.

Things were not made any easier by the atrocious December weather. A bitter ice storm struck

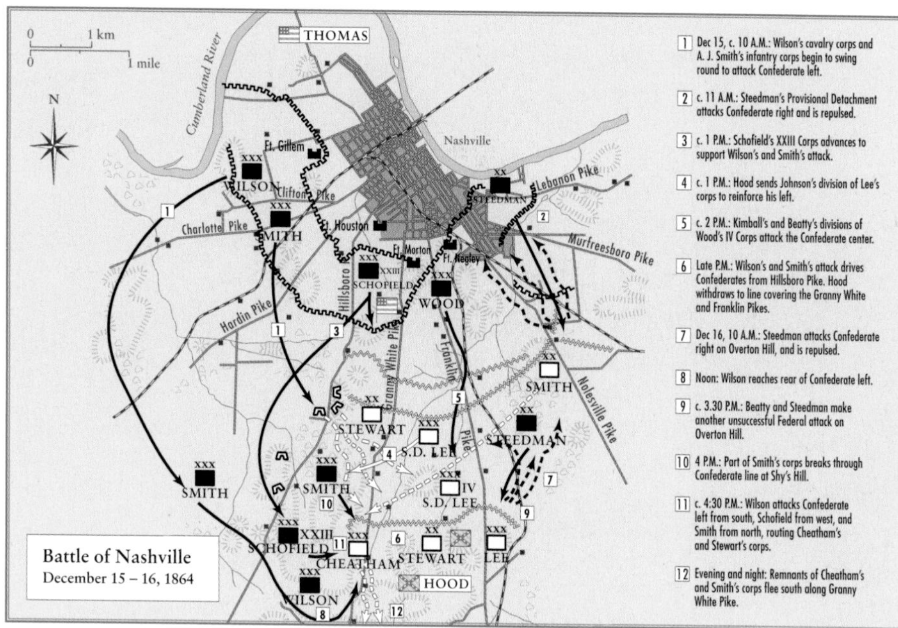

Left: A map detailing the various phases of the Battle of Nashville.

on December 8, which temporarily put a complete stop to the preparations that were being made by both sides. Thomas was under intense political pressure to attack. Lincoln had recently been re-elected and to have a Confederate force so far north was deeply embarrassing. Thomas was even threatened with replacement if he did not soon make a move.

Hood in the meantime made a terrible mistake. On December 5 he sent most of his cavalry, under the command of Major General Nathan B. Forrest, to attack the Union garrison at Murfreesboro. This further depleted his already weakened force so that by December 15 when the weather had improved and Thomas finally decided to emerge from his fortifications on December 15, Hood only had 31,000 men as opposed to the Union's 49,000.

Thomas planned a two-phase attack on the Confederates. The secondary attack was in the manner of a diversion and it was still dark when this was launched against the Confederate right flank by Major General James B. Steedman. The main attack came at first light on the enemy's left. This was led by Major General Andrew J Smith, Brigadier General Thomas J.Wood and Brigadier General Edward Hatch.

By noon the main advance had reached Hillsboro Pike and Wood was preparing to assault the Confederate outposts on Montgomery Hill near the center of the line. Hood was concerned about the threat to his left flank and ordered Major General Stephen Lee to send reinforcements to Major General Alexander Stewart. In the meantime Wood's corps took Montgomery Hill.

In the early afternoon after fierce fighting on Hillsboro Pike, Stewart's corps was overwhelmed and began to retreat towards Granny White Turnpike. Towards nightfall Hood was able to regroup his men in preparation for a continuation of the battle the following day.

On December 16, the second day of the battle, it took most of the morning for the Federals to

move into position against Hood's new line. Once again Thomas planned a two-phase attack, but concentrated on Hood's left.

By 4 p.m. the Confederates on Shy's Hill were under assault from three sides. As light began to fade, Union troops were ordered to fix bayonets, and to refrain from shouting or cheering until they had taken the breastworks on the hill. As the Federals advanced, they soon came under fierce Rebel fire, but they continued, unwavering. They quickly fell upon the line of Rebel skirmishers, who broke under the strain, fleeing to the rear. Wood took this opportunity to renew his attack on Lee on Overton's Hill and it was all over.

As darkness fell, accompanied by heavy rain, Hood collected his forces and withdrew south towards Franklin. The foul weather assisted the Confederate retreat and on December 25 they were safely back across the Tennessee River

The Battle of Nashville goes down in history as one of the Union Army's most stunning victories. The formidable Army of Tennessee, the second largest Confederate force, was effectively wiped out and would never fight again. When Hood arrived in Tennessee he had an army of 30,000 men; when he left he had fewer than 10,000.

Although Hood was not greatly outnumbered, he was simply outclassed by Thomas, who had been able to concentrate his forces at the right time for victory. At Shy's Hill, for instance, 40,000 Union soldiers routed 5,000 Confederates, which was one of the worst defeats of the war.

In fact, the Rebels might have been completely annihilated by Brigadier General James H. Wilson's pursuing troops. However, a skillful rearguard action by Rebel infantry and Major General Bedford Forrest's cavalry insured taht the remnants of the shattered Confederate army were able to cross the Tenneesee River, ten days after the batle.

Lieutenant General John Bell Hood refused to accept blame for the debacle, but he resigned his command on January 13, 1865. He was never given another field command; his career was over.

Opposite page: A painting illustrating Confederate troops making their final advance against the enemy.

Left: A photograph showing the troops in their camp, surrounded by battlefields.

PRISONERS OF WAR

THE SOLDIER WHO WAS CAPTURED WAS NOT IN ANY BETTER CONDITION. ACCEPTED STANDARDS OF CONDUCT IN WARFARE SOMETIMES WERE VIOLATED. IN THE EARLY DAYS OF THE WAR, THE UNION THREATENED TO SHOOT CONFEDERATE OFFICERS AS TRAITORS, BUT BACKED DOWN WHEN THE CONFEDERACY HAD UNION PRISONERS IN RICHMOND DRAW LOTS TO SEE WHO WOULD BE EXECUTED IN RETALIATION.

Above: Andersonville Prison, in Georgia, was the largest Confederate prison during the Civil War

At the start of the Civil War the question of prisoners often did not arise. Captives were simple exchanged on the battlefield on a like for like basis; a private for a private, a sergeant for a sergeant or a captain for a captain.

This system soon broke down, largely because the Confederates refused to treat black soldiers as prisoners of war. This led to the establishment of a system of prisons and holding area.

The prisons in both north and south were for the most part temporary, makeshift, hastily constructed facilities that were seldom suitable for the confinement of human beings, while others were structures that had originally been intended for other purposes, but had been transformed into prisons. By modern standards nearly all would have been condemned for the lack of the most basic sanitary requirements.

Prisons took several forms. Some were in forts or other fortifications, such as Fort Warren in Boston Harbor, Fort Lafayette at New York or Castle Pinckney at Charleston. Generally speaking the more senior officers were kept in the forts, although this was not always the case. Fort Delaware in the Delaware River was a fearsome place that housed a great many private soldiers. No other Northern prison was dreaded so much in the South as this. The ground on which the prisoners were placed was several feet below high water and was always damp and cold.

Some were in former jails and penitentiaries like the old penitentiary at Alton, Illinois. This was nearly always overcrowded, water supply was scanty and drainage was bad. The mortality rate often exceeded 5% per month and was sometimes even higher.

Existing buildings were often turned into prisons, such as the Old Capitol at Washington and the Libby in Richmond. This practice was more common in the South than in the North. Tobacco factories were most common, but also warehouses. They were usually substantial brick buildings with good light and ventilation and since comparatively little machinery needed to be removed, they could easily be converted to prison use. A number of these buildings were also converted for use as hospitals.

Above: At its peak, some 18,000 Union soldiers were held at Florence Military Prison in South Carolina.

A fourth group were enclosures around barracks, such as Johnson's Island, Camp Morton and Rock Island. This group were all in the North and all of them were overcrowded at times, generally having an inadequate water supply and poor drainage.

A fifth group were tented enclosures, such as the ones at Point Lookout, Maryland, and on Belle Isle in the James River, near Richmond. Point Lookout was the largest in the North and at times nearly 20,000 were confined there. The water a first came from shallow wells, but the quality was so poor that a boat was ordered to bring in fresh water. Although tented accommodation seems to have been sufficient, the winter air was cold and damp, as was the ground on which the men had to lie.

Left: Suffering from hunger, disease and exposure. Prisoners from the Union Army held at the notoriously cruel Andersonville were ravaged by diseases such as dysentery, smallpox, measles and scurvy.

Right: Drawing of the Andersonville prison stockade in Georgia. During the summer of 1864 32,899 Union prisoners were held here and 12,912 perished. In the foreground a cart can be seen removing corpses.

Belle Island in the South had the advantage that there was plenty of water, but by the winter of 1863 there were 6,300 prisoners in a camp although tents had only been provided for 3,000. In March 1864 it was reported that one-forth of the prisoners were sick. The final class of prisons were completely open with no shelter at all. These were only found in the South and the most notorious of all the prisons was Andersonville, situated 12 miles (19 km) north of Americus, Georgia.

The stockade at Andersonville, officially named Fort Sumter, was constructed of twenty-foot long tree trunks set five feet into the ground that enclosed an area of 27 acres. A significant area was swamp. The ground sloped down on both sides to a small stream that ran from east to west. The stockade was not completed until February 1864 and the place was soon overwhelmed as the first prisoners began to arrive.

By March the prison contained 7,500 men, which effectively filled the enclosure. By April there were 10,000 men, by May 15,000, by June 22,000 and by July there were 32,000. Rations were issued uncooked and "prisoners were compelled to perform all the offices of life" within the limited space in the camp.

The stream through the camp that was used for drinking and bathing, rapidly became an open sewer. Prisoners were forbidden to construct shelters and were left fully exposed to the elements.

Medical treatment was virtually nonexistent and sunstroke, dysentery, scurvy, malaria and exposure all took their toll. During the summer months more than 100 prisoners died every day.

Although there were many examples of humanity, in the main Prisoners of War were not generally well treated by either side. In most cases this was simply the result of a combination of mismanagement, severe shortages and having to deal with enormous numbers of prisoners.

Left: Illustration of Cuban born Loreta Janeta Velasquez at Johnson's Island Prisoner of War Depot. By her own account she disguised herself as a man and enlisted in the Confederate Army under the false name of Harry T. Buford. In a book she wrote after the war, she claimed to have fought in battles such as The First Battle of Bull Run, and The Battle of Shiloh, but gave little evidence to support this.

THE CAMPAIGNS OF 1865

AT THE START OF 1865, THE CONFEDERACY WAS ON ITS LAST LEGS. THE UNION'S PRINCIPAL REMAINING STRATEGIC AIMS WERE TO CUT THE REBELS' SUPPLY ROUTES AND FORCE THE SURRENDER OF GENERAL ROBERT E. LEE.

As the Civil War entered its final phase, the noose gradually tightened around the neck of the Confederacy. On January 15, 1865, Union General Alfred H. Terry took Fort Fisher in North Carolina by storm after it had been subjected to an intense bombardment from a squadron of ships under the command of Admiral David D. Porter. The fall of this stronghold prevented any further blockade-running by ships from the port of Wilmington.

The closure of the sea routes into and out of the South soon brought the already dispirited rebel forces to an unprecedentedly low ebb. By the end of the month, starving soldiers had begun to desert Lee's army. Jefferson Davis finally approved the arming of slaves to bolster his rapidly dwindling manpower, but events soon overtook him and the executive order was never implemented.

In February 1865, General Sherman moved on from Savannah northward through South Carolina, aiming to come up behind Lee, who was confronted by Ulysses S. Grant's forces in Virginia. Sherman's advance brought a new and terrible meaning to the term "scorched earth policy": the destruction wreaked by Federal troops was even greater than it had been during their march through Georgia at the end of the previous year. On February 3, Sherman's forces were briefly detained by a Confederate force under General Lafayette McLaws that blocked their road ahead, but Federal soldiers quickly erected a series of pontoon bridges across the swamps surrounding the highway and attacked the enemy's right flank. At the end of the day, McLaws withdrew to Branchville, South Carolina. Later that month, the Confederate President Jefferson Davis agreed in principle to a peace conference with Abraham Lincoln, but insisted on Federal recognition of the Confederate States as a precondition to the talks; the U.S. President scorned the suggestion, and no such meeting ever took place.

Opposite page: Map showing the last campaigns of the war and the Union Army strengthening its hold on the South.

On March 4, Lincoln made his second inaugural address to the nation. Two days later, a small band of Confederate volunteers prevented a Union force composed mainly of African Americans from

The Campaigns of 1865
Union offensive
Union victory
Union blockade
Union state
Slave state staying loyal to the Union
Confederate state
BRITISH NORTH AMERICA
Lake Superior
Lake Huron
Lake Ontario
Lake Erie
MICHIGAN
NEW YORK
VT
NH
MA
CT
Detroit
New York
Chicago
PENNSYLVANIA
Pittsburgh
NJ
Philadelphia
OHIO
Wheeling
MD
INDIANA
ILLINOIS
Indianapolis
Washington
DE
Cincinnati
WEST VIRGINIA
Chancellorsville
St. Louis
Richmond
Louisville
Frankfort
Appomattox Courthouse
Norfolk
KENTUCKY
Appalachian Mountains
MISSOURI
VIRGINIA
Cumberland River
Cairo
NORTH CAROLINA
TENNESSEE
Knoxville
Newbern
Nashville
Fort Macon
ARKANSAS
Tennessee River
Chattanooga
Wilmington
Memphis
SOUTH CAROLINA
Columbia
Marietta
Atlanta
Augusta
Charleston
GEORGIA
ATLANTIC OCEAN
MISSISSIPPI
Birmingham
ALABAMA
Macon
LA
Vicksburg
Savannah
Montgomery
Jackson
Mississippi River
Pearl River
Mobile
Pensacola
Jacksonville
FLORIDA
New Orleans
Fort Jackson and St. Philip
N
0 150 km
0 150 miles
Gulf of Mexico
90
85
80
75
40
35
30

Right: As he sat watching a play at the Ford Theatre in Washington, Lincoln was assassinated. He was shot in the back of the head by John Wilkes Booth, a prominent actor of the period and a Confederate sympathiser.

crossing the Natural Bridge over St. Marks River. Their actions prevented the fall of Tallahassee, which thus gained the distinction of being the only Confederate state capital not to fall to the Union during the Civil War. The overall capital, Richmond, Virginia, was, however, not nearly so fortunate: Robert E. Lee was defeated there twice in eight days, on March 25 and April 1. He then made the decision to abandon the city and headed west, hoping to rendezvous with the other remaining rebel forces.

March 27, 1865, marked the beginning of the final phase in the Union's campaign to capture Mobile, Alabama, which had remained in rebel hands after the Battle of Mobile Bay. To that end, after an eight-day siege at the start of April, Federal forces captured Spanish Fort, a heavily armed bastion to the east of the city.

On April 2, three Union divisions under Major General James H. Wilson took Selma, Alabama, in the face of opposition from Lieutenant General Nathan Bedford Forrest. Coming only a day after the fall of Richmond, the defeat of Forrest, whom many Southerners had thought invincible, was another crushing blow.

Lee, having been surrounded by Federal forces, surrendered at Appomattox Court House, Virginia, on April 9. He explained his decision in a report to President Jefferson Davis: "I deemed this course the best under all the circumstances by which we were surrounded. On the morning of the 9th according to the reports of the ordnance officers, there were 7,892 organized infantry with arms, with an average of 75 rounds of ammunition per man; the artillery, though reduced to 63 pieces with 93 rounds of ammunition, was sufficient. These comprised all the supplies of ordnance that could be relied on in the State of Virginia. I have no accurate report of the cavalry, but believe it did no exceed 2,100 effective men. The enemy was more than five times our numbers. If we could have forced our way one day longer it would have been at a great sacrifice of life, and at its end I did not see how a surrender could have been avoided. We had no subsistence for man or horse, and it could not be gathered in the country".

Following his surrender, his men handed over their arms, laid down their flags, and were then sent home. Weary, hungry Confederates broke ranks to kiss the flags they were surrendering, but they obeyed Lee's eloquent surrender order, General Order Number 9, which put into words the thoughts of many of them: "I need not tell the brave survivors of so many hard fought battles, who have remained steadfast to the last, that I have consented to this result from no distrust of them; but feeling that valor and devotion could accomplish nothing that could compensate for the the loss that must have attended the continuance of the contest, I determined to avoid the useless sacrifice of those whose past services have endeared them to their countrymen."

Realizing that the game was up for the Confederacy, an actor named John Wilkes Booth vengefully assassinated Lincoln, shooting him in the back of the head while he was watching a play at the Ford Theatre in Washington, D.C., on the night of April 14, 1865.

While the North mourned the death of its great wartime leader, it did not delay its march to final victory. On April 26, General Joseph E. Johnson surrendered his troops to the unstoppable Sherman at Durham, North Carolina. Jefferson Davis was captured on May 10, and by the end of the month the Civil War was effectively at an end, although the formal ceasefire agreement was not signed until June 23, 1865, at Fort Towson in the Oklahoma Territory. The last Confederate force to surrender was the crew of the CSS Shenandoah, who hauled down the third and final version of the rebel flag on November 4, 1865, while at anchor in Liverpool, England.

Left: The capture of Jefferson Davis, President of the Confederate States of America in May 10, 1865. After the surrender of the South, he attempted to flee and disguised himself as a woman. He was discovered and captured by Colonel Pritchard and the men of Wilson's Corps in Irwinsville, Georgia.

TEXAS AND NEW MEXICO

THE GULF COAST OF THE CONFEDERACY WAS THE THIRD FRONT, WHERE LAND ACTION WAS LIGHT BUT THE NAVY STRAINED TO BLOCKADE THE PORTS OF MISSISSIPPI, ALABAMA, TEXAS, AND FLORIDA. IT WAS AN AREA OF DARING GAMES PLAYED BY BLOCKADE RUNNERS TRYING TO OUTWIT FEDERAL WARSHIPS AND AMPHIBIOUS UNITS HOPING TO DESTROY CONFEDERATE INSTALLATIONS.

Texas escaped heavy fighting during the Civil War, but the State was a major contributor to the Confederate cause. Until the Mississippi was closed by Federal troops and gunboats, Texas was a major source of supplies and manpower. Texans fought on all fronts, from Virginia to Arizona, and saved many a battle by their stalwartness. Colonel Taylor, from his base at Mesilla, redrew the map of the New Mexico Territory as a Confederate territory, with Arizona as a separate jurisdiction. General Sibley's gruelling invasion of New Mexico along the Rio Grande moved from his base in San Antonio through El Paso.

Opposite: Map pinpointing military activity that transpired in Texas during the war.

1 **February 21, 1862:** Confederate troops under Brigadier General Hen Hopkins Sibley won a narrow victory over Union forces commanded by Colonel Edward R. S. Canby and continued their invasion of New Mexico.

2 **March 28:** A mixed force of U.S. Army regulars and Colorado volunteer defeated Sibley's Confederates at the Battle of Glorieta Pass.

3 **January 1, 1863:** Confederate troops under Major General John Bankhead Magruder captured Galveston along with its Union garrison an one gunboat in the harbor. Another gunboat was destroyed and the rest the naval flotilla fled.

4 **September 8:** A Union expedition attempting to land a Sabine Pass met stunning repulse, losing two gunboats that ran aground and were capture by the tiny force of Confederate defenders.

5 **November 6:** Union troops under Major General Nathaniel P. Banks too possession of the important port and border town of Brownsville, Texas.

6 **November 22:** Banks's troops occupied Matagorda Island.

7 **April 8, 1864:** The Confederate army of Lieutenant General Richard Taylor defeated Banks's Red River expedition at the Battle of Mansfield, forcing Banks to abandon his plans of reaching Texas via the Red River.

8 **June 23, 1865:** At Doaksville, Indian Territory (now Oklahoma), Brigadier General Stand Watie surrendered the Confederate Cherokee, Creek, Seminole, and Osage battalion to Union authorities. It was the last surrender of any organized body of Confederate troops.

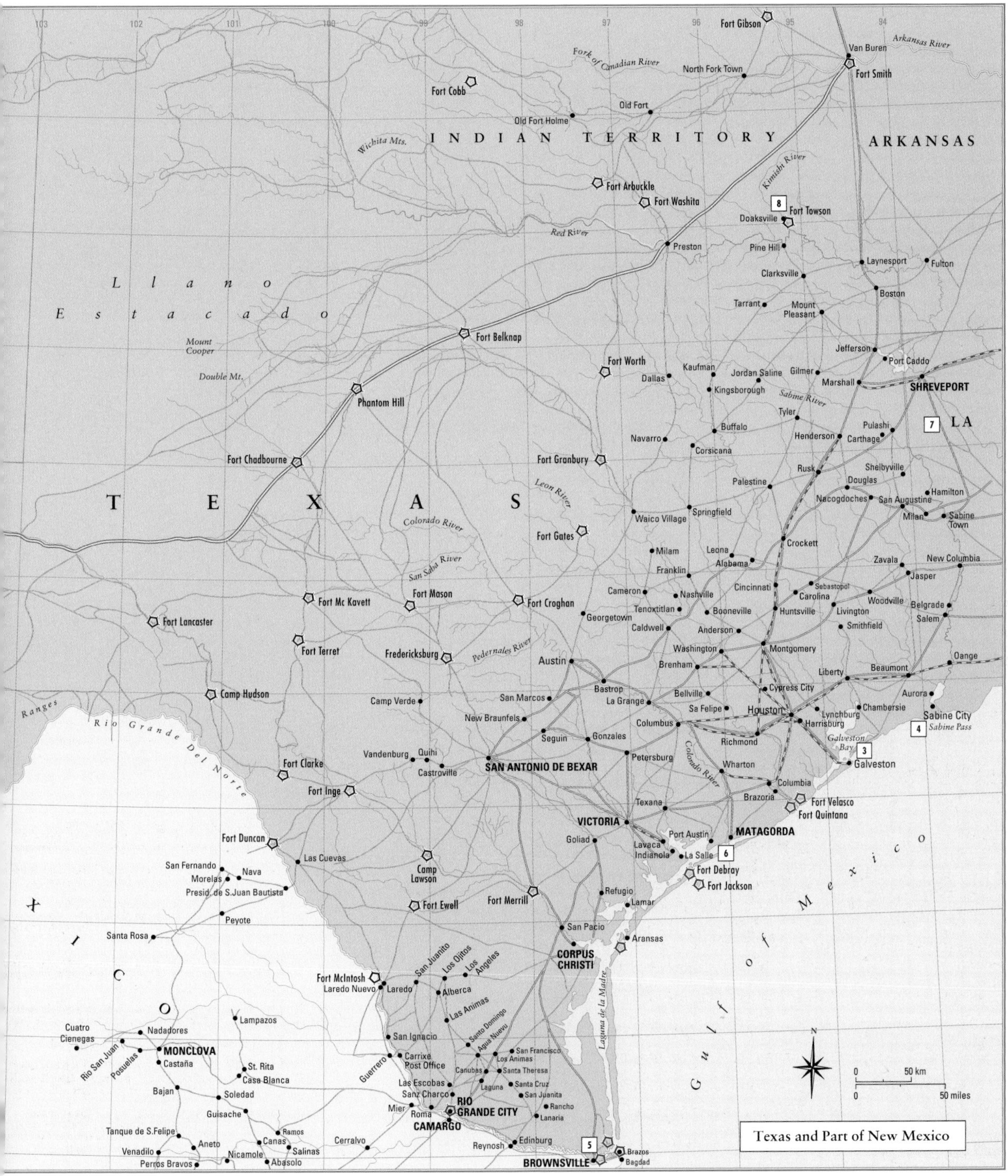

Texas and Part of New Mexico

FORT FISHER

WAR ARRIVED IN NORTH CAROLINA IN EARNEST IN 1865, AS THE CONFEDERACY LAY DYING. WILMINGTON WAS THE LAST MAJOR PORT IN THE EASTERN CONFEDERACY TO REMAIN OPEN, LARGELY THANKS TO FORT FISHER.

An impressively large earthworks fort at the entrance to the Cape Fear River, Fort Fisher was once considered too strong a defensive structure to ever be taken—a view that would eventually be overturned in 1865, although it would take one of the most intensely fought campaigns of the war.

Shortly before the Christmas of 1864, the largest Union fleet of the entire Civil War assembled in the waters off the fort, carrying some 6,500 troops under the command of General Butler. Among the 55 heavily armed and armored warships were an ironclad screw steamer and four monitors. The type of combined bombardment and amphibious operation that had succeeded elsewhere was here to be supplemented by the detonating of a ship laden with explosives near the fort, in the belief that this would damage the fortifications enough to let the assault be a walk-in. In the event, neither the exploded vessel, nor the accompanying bombardment by the warships had the desired effect, and Butler called off the attack on Christmas day after landing a force of some 2,000 men under cover of the naval guns.

A second expedition against Fort Fisher the following month would prove to be the largest sea-land contest of the war, with the Union utilizing no fewer than 60 warships and 8,500 troops under Brigadier General Alfred H. Terry. Although a diversionary attack by 2,000 Navy men and Marines was repulsed with heavy losses, Terry's main attack from the rear finally succeeded in capturing the last Confederate coastal stronghold, thereby closing the North Carolina coast completely to Rebel ships. Confederate casualties numbered 500, and a further 2,083 were taken prisoner, while Union losses came to 691

Nearby Fort Anderson held out for another 30 days, but was abandoned after undergoing heavy bombardment during a three-day siege. Confederate Vice President Alexander Stephens described the loss as "one of the greastest disasters which has befallen our Cause."

Opposite page: Map of the campaign against Fort Fisher, the largest sea-land contest of the war.

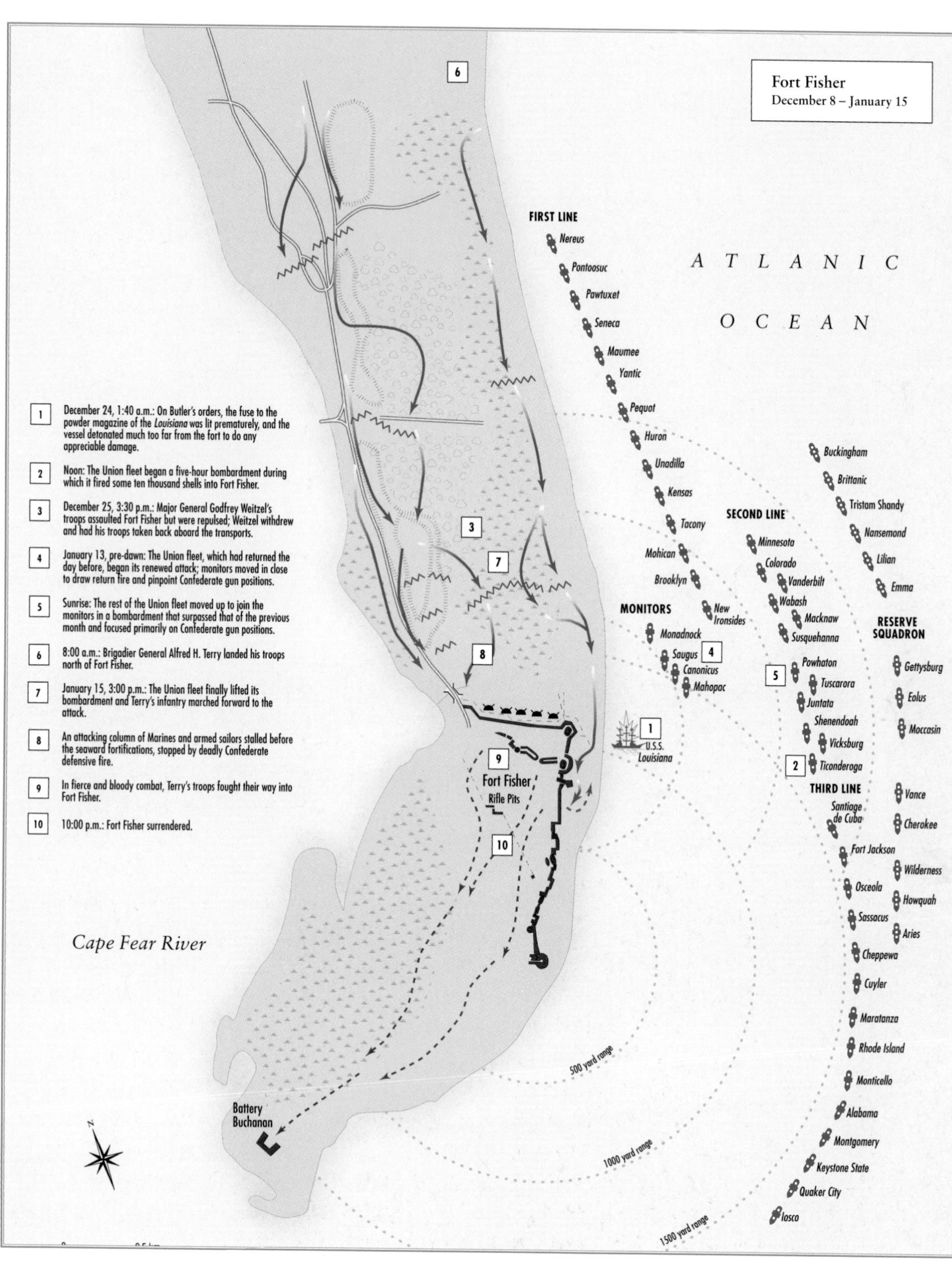
Fort Fisher
December 8 – January 15
ATLANTIC OCEAN
Cape Fear River
FIRST LINE
Nereus
Pontoosuc
Pawtuxet
Seneca
Maumee
Yantic
Pequot
Huron
Unadilla
Kensas
Tacony
Mohican
Brooklyn
SECOND LINE
Minnesota
Colorado
Vanderbilt
Wabash
Macknaw
Susquehanna
MONITORS
Monadnock
Saugus
Canonicus
Mahopac
New Ironsides
Buckingham
Brittanic
Tristam Shandy
Nansemond
Lilian
Emma
RESERVE SQUADRON
Gettysburg
Eolus
Moccasin
Powhaton
Tuscarora
Juntata
Shenendoah
Vicksburg
Ticonderoga
THIRD LINE
Santiago de Cuba
Fort Jackson
Osceola
Sassacus
Cheppewa
Cuyler
Maratanza
Rhode Island
Monticello
Alabama
Montgomery
Keystone State
Quaker City
Iosco
Vance
Cherokee
Wilderness
Howquah
Aries
U.S.S. Louisiana
Fort Fisher
Rifle Pits
Battery Buchanan
500 yard range
1000 yard range
1500 yard range
N
1 December 24, 1:40 a.m.: On Butler's orders, the fuse to the powder magazine of the Louisiana was lit prematurely, and the vessel detonated much too far from the fort to do any appreciable damage.
2 Noon: The Union fleet began a five-hour bombardment during which it fired some ten thousand shells into Fort Fisher.
3 December 25, 3:30 p.m.: Major General Godfrey Weitzel's troops assaulted Fort Fisher but were repulsed; Weitzel withdrew and had his troops taken back aboard the transports.
4 January 13, pre-dawn: The Union fleet, which had returned the day before, began its renewed attack; monitors moved in close to draw return fire and pinpoint Confederate gun positions.
5 Sunrise: The rest of the Union fleet moved up to join the monitors in a bombardment that surpassed that of the previous month and focused primarily on Confederate gun positions.
6 8:00 a.m.: Brigadier General Alfred H. Terry landed his troops north of Fort Fisher.
7 January 15, 3:00 p.m.: The Union fleet finally lifted its bombardment and Terry's infantry marched forward to the attack.
8 An attacking column of Marines and armed sailors stalled before the seaward fortifications, stopped by deadly Confederate defensive fire.
9 In fierce and bloody combat, Terry's troops fought their way into Fort Fisher.
10 10:00 p.m.: Fort Fisher surrendered.

SHERMAN'S CAROLINAS CAMPAIGN

THE SEEMINGLY EVERLASTING SIEGE OF FORT SUMTER ASIDE, SOUTH CAROLINA, THE FIRST STATE TO SECEDE FROM THE UNION, WAS REMOVED FROM THE MAIN BATTLEFIELDS AND THUS ESCAPED MUCH OF THE FIGHTING. THAT CHANGED IN FEBRUARY 1865 WHEN GENERAL SHERMAN LED A 60,000-STRONG INVASION FORCE INTO THE STATE INTENT ON SWIFT AND DECISIVE RETRIBUTION.

Above: General Sherman enters Columbia on February 16, 1865.

Opposite page: Map of General Sherman's activity in North Carolina and South Carolina.

Northern feelings against South Carolina, which many regarded as the birthplace of the conflict, were particularly strong and Sherman swept through the state like an avenging angel. No major battles were fought, but skirmishes between the invading Union forces and what few troops the Confederates could muster were frequent. As fearsome as the Union's wave of destruction had been in Georgia, it was nonetheless eclipsed by what took place in South Carolina. Union soldiers helped themselves to the bounty of the state's farms, raiding storehouses and larders, and even on occasion taking the Confederates' hidden supplies, the locations of which were often as not revealed by slaves. Sherman entered the state capital, Columbia, on February 16. The fire that subsequently destroyed much of the city may have been set by his troops, although there is also evidence to suggest that it may have been the work of departing Confederate soldiers. Either way, it provided a fitting symbol of the

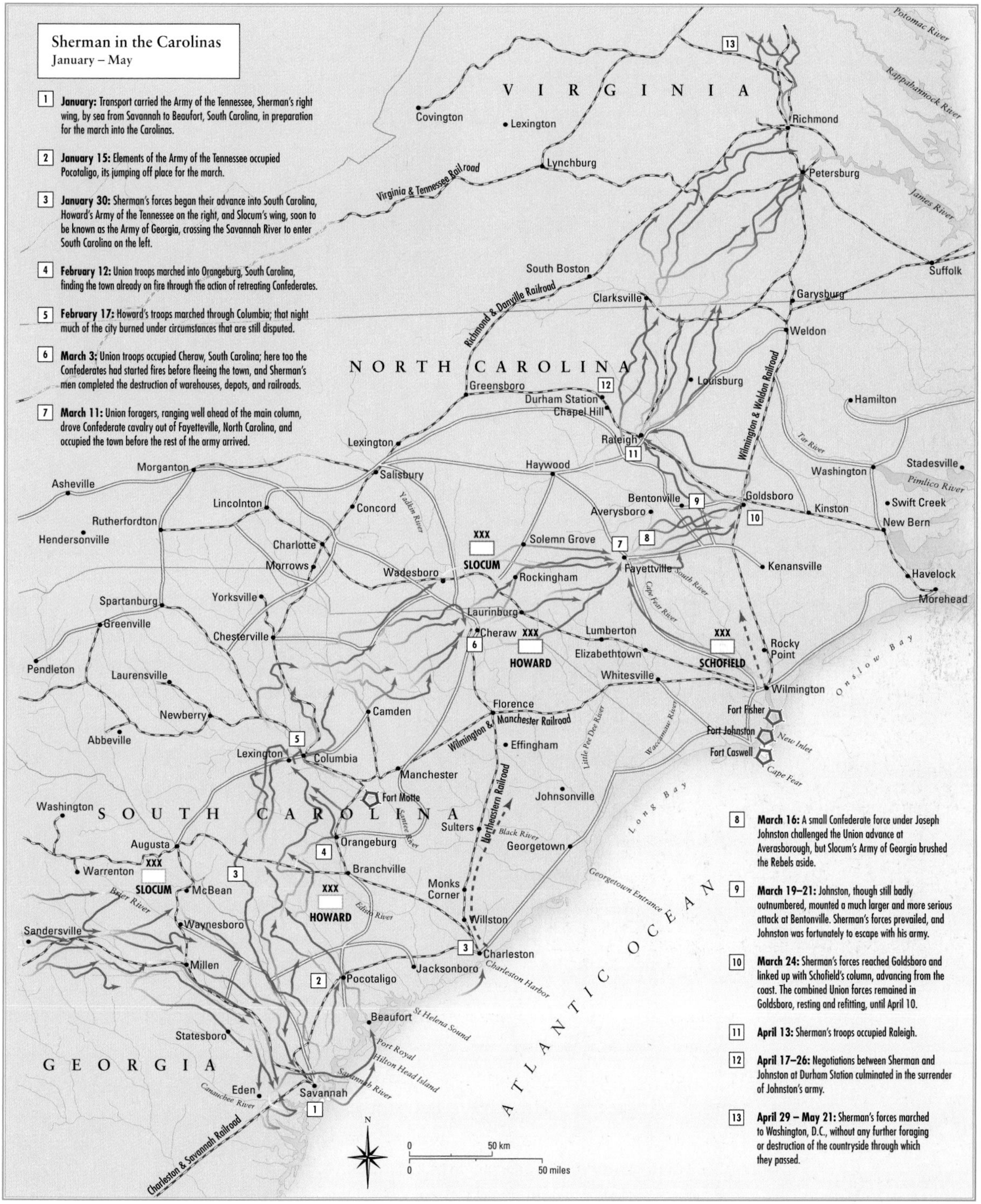
Sherman in the Carolinas
January – May
1 January: Transport carried the Army of the Tennessee, Sherman's right wing, by sea from Savannah to Beaufort, South Carolina, in preparation for the march into the Carolinas.
2 January 15: Elements of the Army of the Tennessee occupied Pocotaligo, its jumping off place for the march.
3 January 30: Sherman's forces began their advance into South Carolina, Howard's Army of the Tennessee on the right, and Slocum's wing, soon to be known as the Army of Georgia, crossing the Savannah River to enter South Carolina on the left.
4 February 12: Union troops marched into Orangeburg, South Carolina, finding the town already on fire through the action of retreating Confederates.
5 February 17: Howard's troops marched through Columbia; that night much of the city burned under circumstances that are still disputed.
6 March 3: Union troops occupied Cheraw, South Carolina; here too the Confederates had started fires before fleeing the town, and Sherman's men completed the destruction of warehouses, depots, and railroads.
7 March 11: Union foragers, ranging well ahead of the main column, drove Confederate cavalry out of Fayetteville, North Carolina, and occupied the town before the rest of the army arrived.
8 March 16: A small Confederate force under Joseph Johnston challenged the Union advance at Averasborough, but Slocum's Army of Georgia brushed the Rebels aside.
9 March 19–21: Johnston, though still badly outnumbered, mounted a much larger and more serious attack at Bentonville. Sherman's forces prevailed, and Johnston was fortunately to escape with his army.
10 March 24: Sherman's forces reached Goldsboro and linked up with Schofield's column, advancing from the coast. The combined Union forces remained in Goldsboro, resting and refitting, until April 10.
11 April 13: Sherman's troops occupied Raleigh.
12 April 17–26: Negotiations between Sherman and Johnston at Durham Station culminated in the surrender of Johnston's army.
13 April 29 – May 21: Sherman's forces marched to Washington, D.C., without any further foraging or destruction of the countryside through which they passed.
VIRGINIA
NORTH CAROLINA
SOUTH CAROLINA
GEORGIA
ATLANTIC OCEAN
Potomac River
Rappahannock River
James River
Richmond
Petersburg
Suffolk
Covington
Lexington
Lynchburg
Virginia & Tennessee Rail road
South Boston
Richmond & Danville Railroad
Clarksville
Garysburg
Weldon
Wilmington & Weldon Railroad
Louisburg
Greensboro
Durham Station
Chapel Hill
Hamilton
Raleigh
Tar River
Lexington
Haywood
Washington
Stadesville
Pimlico River
Salisbury
Morganton
Asheville
Lincolnton
Concord
Yadkin River
Bentonville
Averysboro
Goldsboro
Kinston
Swift Creek
New Bern
Rutherfordton
Hendersonville
Charlotte
XXX
SLOCUM
Solemn Grove
Fayetteville
Kenansville
Havelock
Morehead
Morrows
Wadesboro
Rockingham
South River
Cape Fear River
Spartanburg
Yorksville
Laurinburg
Greenville
Cheraw
Lumberton
Chesterville
HOWARD
Elizabethtown
SCHOFIELD
Rocky Point
Pendleton
Laurensville
Whitesville
Wilmington
Onslow Bay
Florence
Fort Fisher
Camden
Newberry
Wilmington & Manchester Railroad
Fort Johnston
New Inlet
Abbeville
Effingham
Little Pee Dee River
Waccamaw River
Fort Caswell
Cape Fear
Lexington
Columbia
Manchester
Fort Motte
Johnsonville
Northeastern Railroad
Long Bay
Washington
Santee River
Sulters
Black River
Augusta
Orangeburg
Georgetown
Warrenton
Branchville
Monks Corner
Georgetown Entrance
McBean
Brier River
Edisto River
Waynesboro
Willston
Sandersville
Charleston
Millen
Jacksonboro
Pocotaligo
Charleston Harbor
Beaufort
St Helena Sound
Statesboro
Port Royal
Hilton Head Island
Eden
Savannah
Savannah River
Canauchee River
Charleston & Savannah Railroad
N
0 50 km
0 50 miles

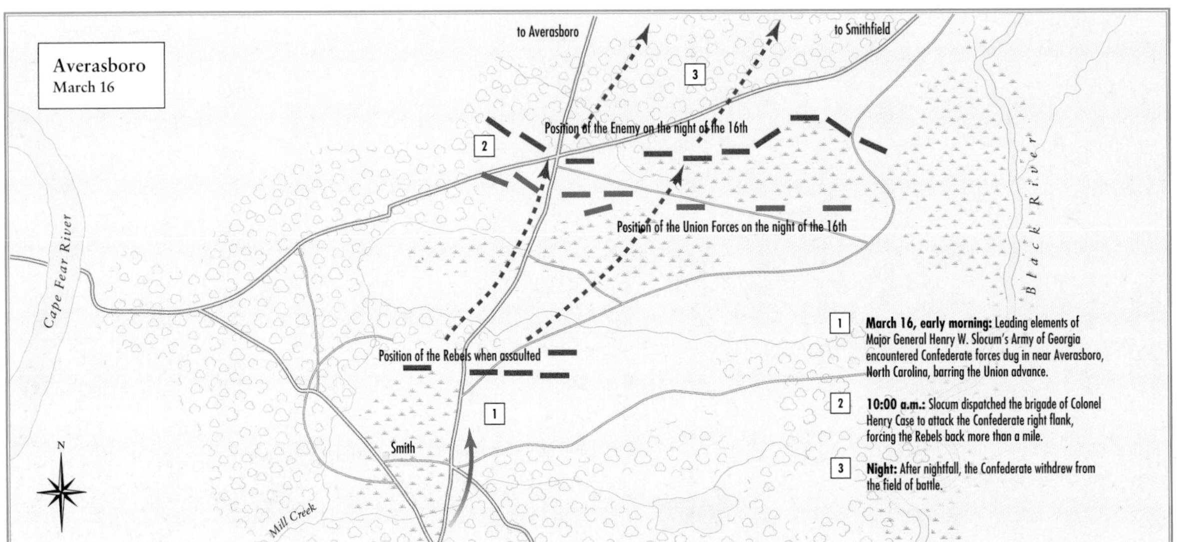

Above: Map of Averasboro in North Carolina, scene of a forlorn attempt by Confederate forces to block the Union advance.

state's ruination.

From here, Sherman turned his attention northward. Although North Carolina was late in joining the Confederacy, being one of the last states to secede from the Union—it even had a rump group meet to try to cancel secession—the State was to become a major source of supplies and manpower throughout the the Civil War. In fact, it ended up contributing more men to the Confederate cause (some 40,000) than any other state. Still, it managed to remain relatively free of fighting until late in the conflict. In the early stages, Union efforts were aimed at controlling the coastline as part of a blockade policy. Fighting on North Carolina soil thus began on the coast, as the Union sought to close the Confederate coastline by blockading ports and capturing strongpoints.

Once the coast had been secured, following the capture of Fort Fisher and Fort Anderson, Sherman turned his attention inland, once againg applying the scorched-earth policy that he had applied so liberally elsewhere. Confederate forces, bolstered by units from Mississippi, were larger than in South Carolina. As a consequence, the fighting here was a good deal fierce, although as before the Union troops ultimately prevailed. Fayetteville fell to Sherman on February 11. Confederate General Joseph E. Johnston then tried to block his path on March 16 at Averasboro when he sent his troops to attack Sherman's left wing, which was under the command of Major General Henry W. Slocum. The Confederates did initially succeed in driving the Union troops back. However, reinforcements soon arrived and the Confederates withdrew.

Johnston tried to halt the Union advance again in a more concerted fashion on March 19 at Bentonville, on the road between Wilmington and Raleigh. Although Bentonville was little more than the dying gasp of a lost cause, it nonetheless proved to be the largest land battle fought in North Carolina during the Civil War, and the first major attempt to stop Sherman after the loss of Atlanta. The Confederates even enjoyed some initial success before, following three days of intense fighing, one again having to admit defeat.

Above: "Bummers" was a term given to groups of foragers who gathered rations for Sherman's troops. They usually ransacked local Southern farms, as is pictured here.

Sherman continued his march to Goldsboro. Raleigh, the state capital, surrendered a short time later.

The Confederacy virtually came to an end 30 days later at a country crossroads farm near Durham, in between Goldsboro and Raleigh, when Johnston surrendered his remaining force to General Sherman. The general negotiated in the living room of the farmhouse, and settled on terms that Washington officials considered too generous. They subsequently had to return for a second meeting to amend them.

The Bennet farmhouse where the two momentous meetings occured burned down in 1921, but has since been restored and is today a visitor center.

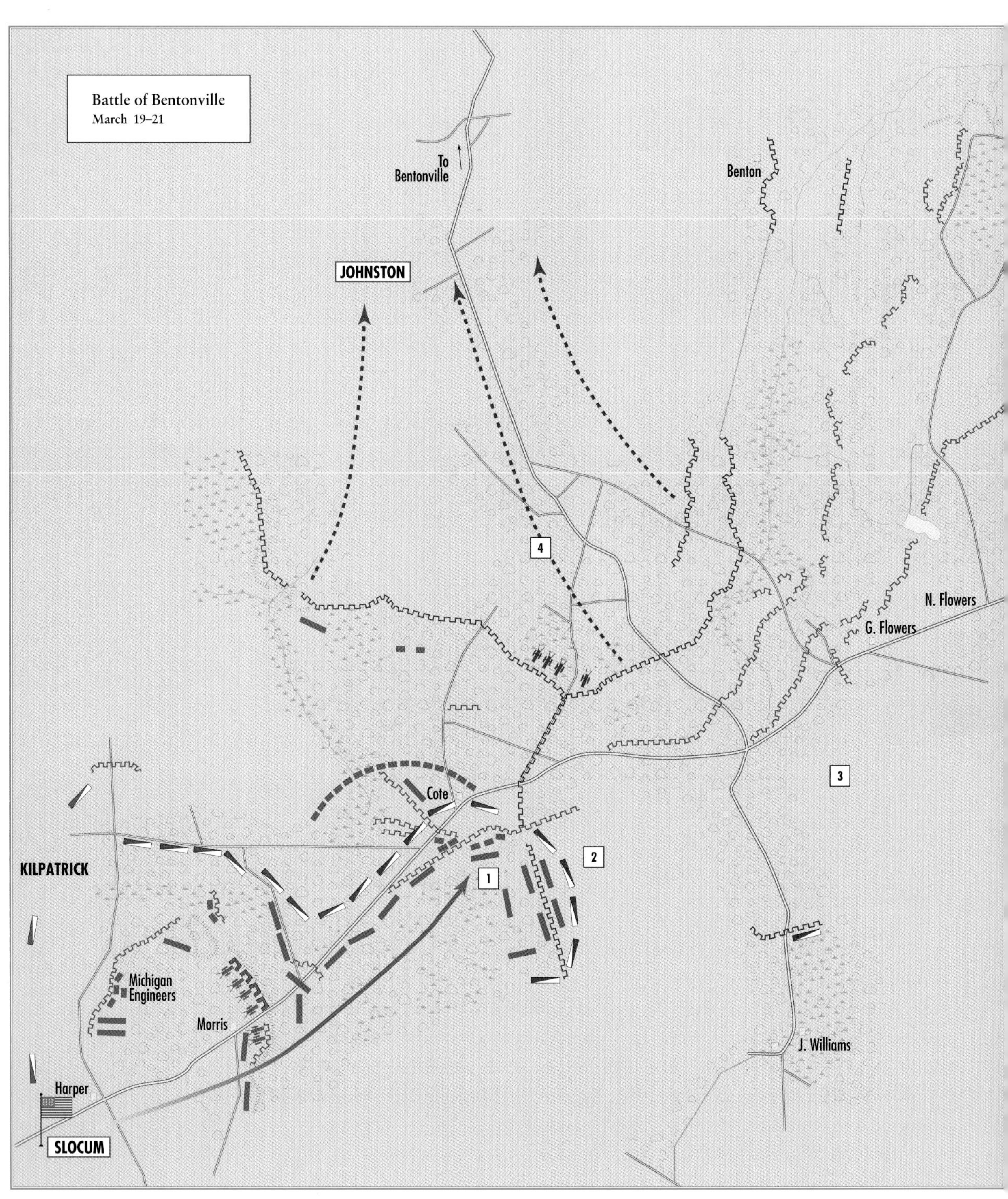

Battle of Bentonville
March 19–21
To Bentonville
Benton
JOHNSTON
4
N. Flowers
G. Flowers
3
Cote
2
1
KILPATRICK
Michigan Engineers
Morris
J. Williams
Harper
SLOCUM

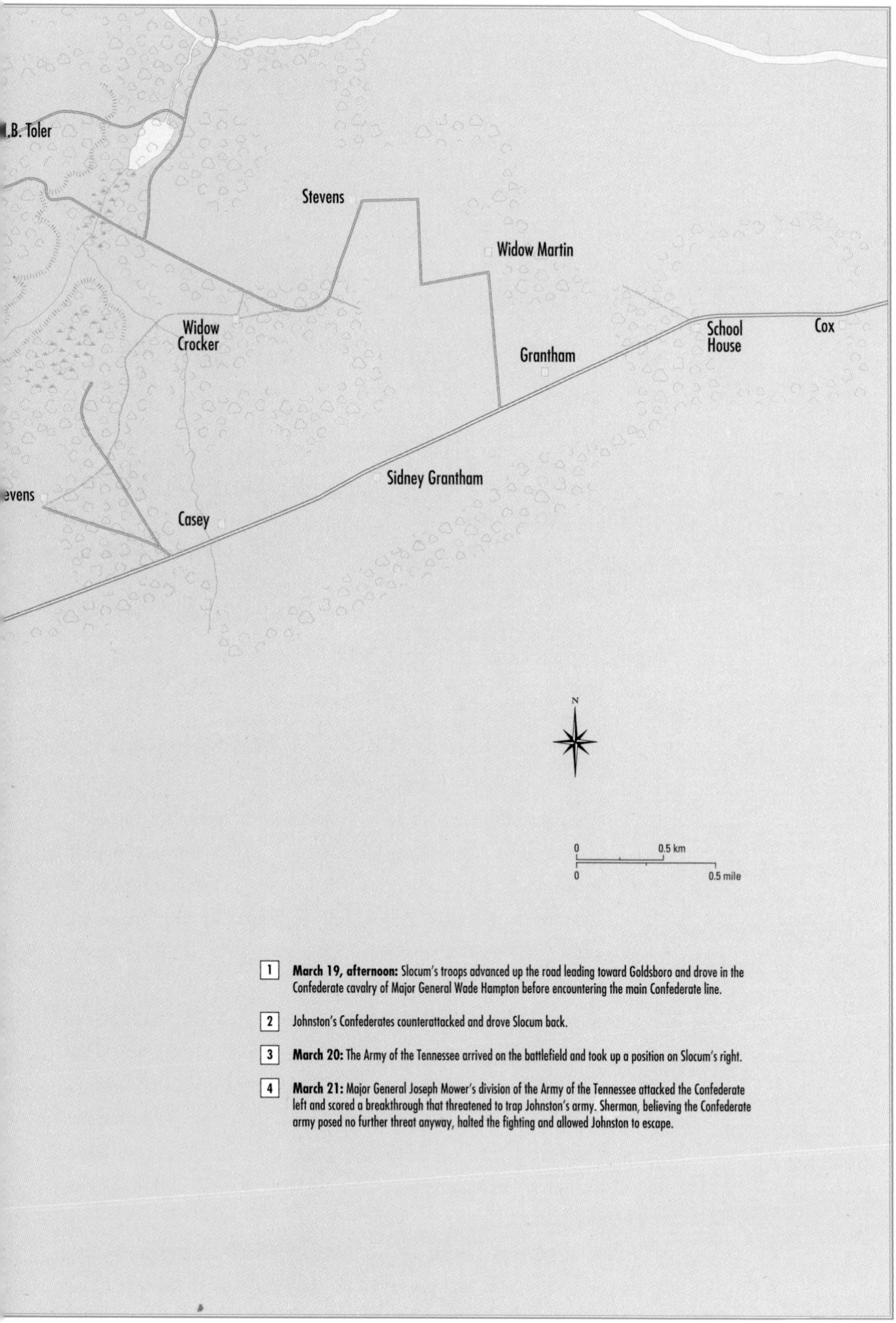

B. Toler
Stevens
Widow Martin
Widow Crocker
School House
Cox
Grantham
Sidney Grantham
evens
Casey
N
0 0.5 km
0 0.5 mile

1 **March 19, afternoon:** Slocum's troops advanced up the road leading toward Goldsboro and drove in the Confederate cavalry of Major General Wade Hampton before encountering the main Confederate line.

2 Johnston's Confederates counterattacked and drove Slocum back.

3 **March 20:** The Army of the Tennessee arrived on the battlefield and took up a position on Slocum's right.

4 **March 21:** Major General Joseph Mower's division of the Army of the Tennessee attacked the Confederate left and scored a breakthrough that threatened to trap Johnston's army. Sherman, believing the Confederate army posed no further threat anyway, halted the fighting and allowed Johnston to escape.

Left: Map of the Battle of Bentonville March, 1865. One of the last battles between the troops of General Johnston and General Sherman.

THE FALL OF PETERSBURG & RICHMOND

IN MARCH 1865, A YEAR AFTER THE UNION ADVANCE ON RICHMOND BEGAN, CONFEDERATE AND UNION FORCES SAT FACING EACH OTHER EITHER SIDE OF A 35-MILE-LONG ARC OF TRENCHES STRETCHING FROM RICHMOND TO PETERSBURG. WINTER HAD TEMPORARILY PUT AN END TO ANY OFFENSIVE AMBITIONS, BUT WITH SPRING FAST APPROACHING BOTH SIDES KNEW THAT THE TIME FOR DECISIVE ACTION WAS AT HAND.

In particular, the Confederate General, Robert E. Lee, was desperately trying to think of a way of extracating himself from an increasingly untenable position. He knew that as soon as the weather improved, his adversary, Lieutenant General Ulysses S. Grant, would be on the move, resuming his westward movement around Petersburg, bolstered by reinforcements from Major General Philip H. Sheridan's Cavalry Corps fresh from a victorious campaign in the Shenandoah Valley.

Lee, who just a few weeks earlier had been elevated, belatedly, to overall command of the Confederate land forces, saw only once course of action open to him: he had to break out of the Federal stranglehold and move south to unite with General Johnston's army in North Carolina, which was trying to stand off a Union advance though the state by General Sherman. Together, Lee and Johnston might be able to beat Sherman, then combine their forces and turn to take on Grant. The odds in favor of such a plan succeeding were long, but it was the only feasible option open to the Rebel commander.

Lee therefore proposed to mount a powerful attack on the Union lines at Fort Steadman, east of Petersburg; the Rebels would breach the lines and sever the military railroad in the rear, along which passed the supplies for the left flank of the Union army. He estimated that, if his plan was

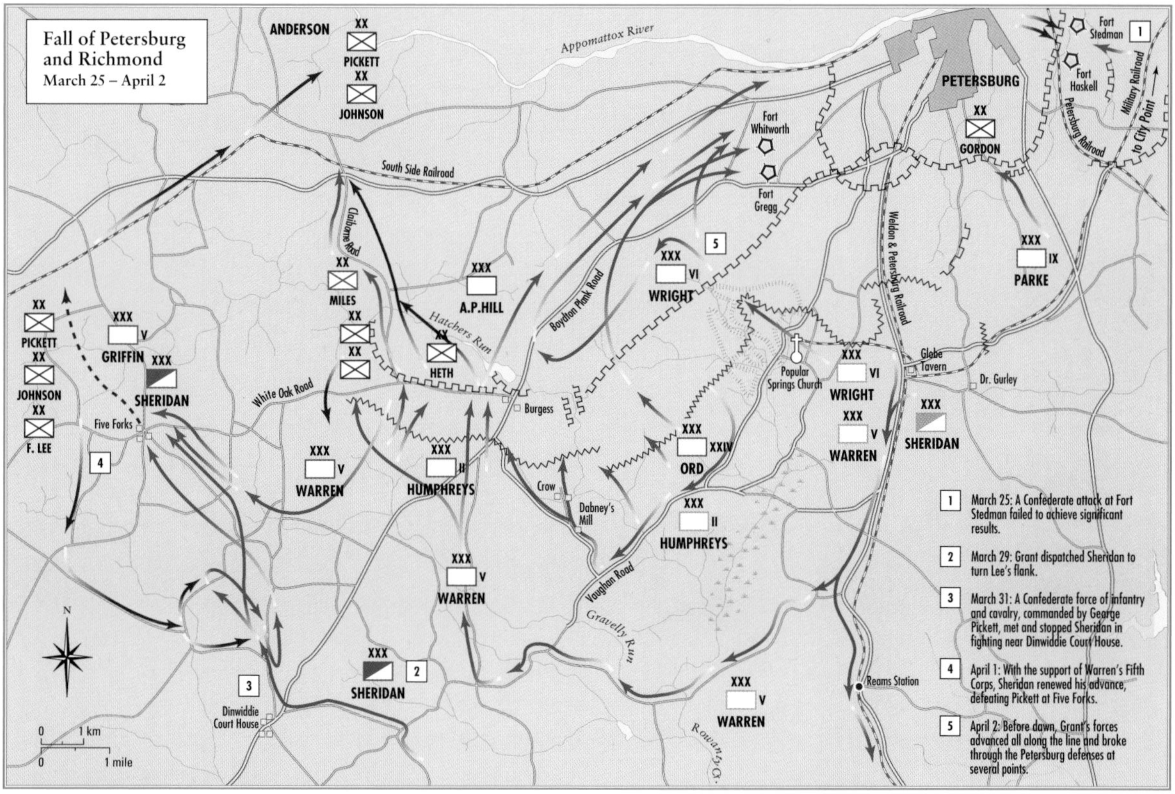
Fall of Petersburg and Richmond
March 25 – April 2
ANDERSON
PICKETT
JOHNSON
Appomattox River
PETERSBURG
Fort Stedman
Fort Haskell
Military Railroad
to City Point
Petersburg Railroad
GORDON
Fort Whitworth
Fort Gregg
South Side Railroad
Claiborne Road
Boydton Plank Road
Weldon & Petersburg Railroad
PARKE
WRIGHT
A.P. HILL
MILES
HETH
Hatchers Run
PICKETT
JOHNSON
F. LEE
GRIFFIN
SHERIDAN
White Oak Road
Five Forks
Burgess
Popular Springs Church
Globe Tavern
Dr. Gurley
WRIGHT
WARREN
SHERIDAN
ORD
WARREN
HUMPHREYS
Crow
Dabney's Mill
HUMPHREYS
Vaughan Road
Gravelly Run
WARREN
SHERIDAN
Dinwiddie Court House
Reams Station
WARREN
Rowanty Cr.
0 1 km
0 1 mile
1 March 25: A Confederate attack at Fort Stedman failed to achieve significant results.
2 March 29: Grant dispatched Sheridan to turn Lee's flank.
3 March 31: A Confederate force of infantry and cavalry, commanded by George Pickett, met and stopped Sheridan in fighting near Dinwiddie Court House.
4 April 1: With the support of Warren's Fifth Corps, Sheridan renewed his advance, defeating Pickett at Five Forks.
5 April 2: Before dawn, Grant's forces advanced all along the line and broke through the Petersburg defenses at several points.

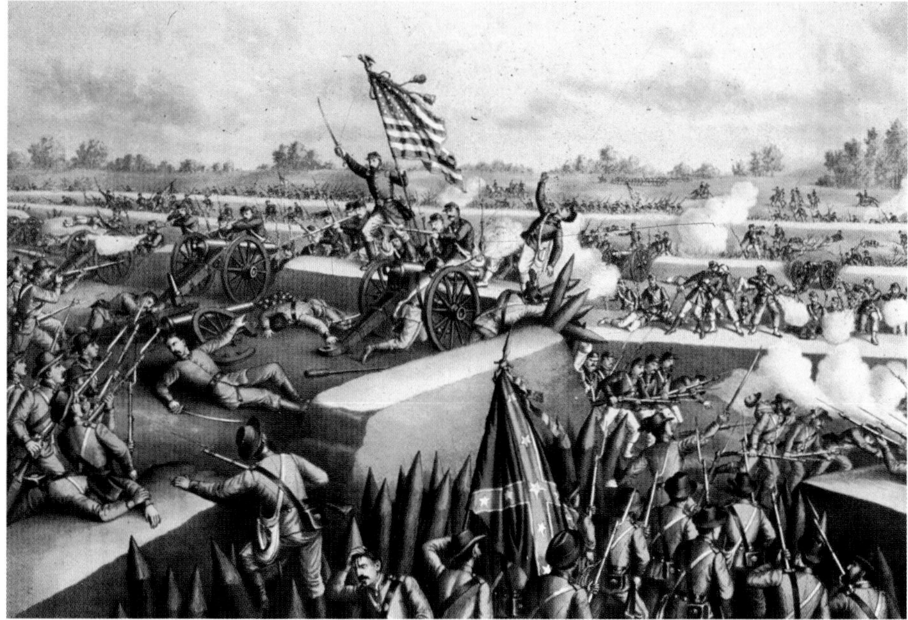

Above: Map of the defeats of Petersburg and Richmond. They fell in March and April of 1865, despite Lee's last desperate attempt to unite with Johnston in North Carolina and repel further invasion.

Left: The victorious Union Army and the doomed Rebel soldiers during the fall of Petersburg.

successful, Grant would then have no alternative but to pull back his exposed left, leaving the way clear for the Army of Northern Virginia to march south.

Just before dawn on March 25, Major General John B. Gordon's corps took the Federals by surprise and carried Fort Steadman. Despite this initial success, the assault was badly coordinated, however, and Gordon withdrew with heavy losses in the face of a strong Federal counterattack. Lee's best hope had been dashed.

Four days later the Union side launched their own offensive when Grant dispatched Sheridan to take an important junction called Five Forks, well beyond the Confederate right wing's fortifications. Lee hurriedly sent to Five Forks a mixed force of cavalry and infantry of an estimated 7,000 to 10,000 men under Major General George E. Pickett, of Gettysburg renown, with the following orders: "Hold Five Forks at all hazards. Protect road to Ford's Depot and prevent Union forces from striking the South Side Railroad."

Pickett ran into Sheridan's troopers on their approach to Five Forks and, in a sharp engagement, drove them back to Dinwiddie Court House. Sheridan, however, was not unduly perturbed by the day's events. He was already looking forward to the next day and the prospect of victory, noting to one of Grant's staff officers: "This [Pickett's] force is more in danger than I am—if I am cut off from the Army of the Potomac, it is cut off from Lee's Army, and not a man in it should ever be allowed to get back to Lee."

His judgment was proved correct when, on April 5, his troops, bolstered by the Fifth Corps of Major General Gouverneur K. Warren, decisively routed the Rebels following an intense day of fighting. As darkness approached, Sheridan found himself in possession of the important Five Forks crossroads and several thousand Confederate prisoners, with the way now clear to the South Side Railroad.

Estimates of numbers are difficult to calculate, but at the Battle of Five Forks, the Confederates may have had up to 10,000 men, with total casualties of about half that number. Sheridan's force was in the region of 25,000 effectives, and suffered about 2,000 caulaties.

Grant, on hearing the good news, ordered a general assault all along the Confederate line for April 2. Lee, at last, had been overstretched, and the days of the Army of Northern Virginia now looked to be numbered.

On April 3, following an intense all-night Union artillery barrage of the Confederate lines, Federal forces advanced deep into enemy territory. Petersburg fell, after which Lee informed the Confederate government that Richmond would have to be evacuated. The President of the Conderacy, Jefferson Davis, fled with his cabinet to Georgia where he was captured just over a month later.

In a highly symbolic gesture, his departure from Richmond was followed the next day by the arrival of the Union President, Abraham Lincoln, who toured the captured Confederate capital, thereby sending a powerful signal to the Confederate forces that the end of their resistance was fast approaching.

Lee, meanwhile retreated westward with the remainder of his forces, always with the hope of eventually striking south to unite with General Joe Johnston. But it was not to be.

Above: Union soldiers stand among the wreckage of a steam locomotive on the Richmond and Petersburg railroad following the fall of Richmond, Virginia.

Left: The fall of Richmond. Fleeing Confederate soldiers were under orders to set fire to buildings and bridges as they left.

MILITARY DISCIPLINE

SUBMISSION TO MILITARY REGIMENTATION WAS NOT EASY FOR YOUNG MEN FROM THE FARMS AND CITIES OF EITHER THE NORTH OR SOUTH. THESE YOUTHS—OFTEN DESCRIBED DURING THE PERIOD AS "FREE, HONEST AMERICANS"—WERE ACCUSTOMED TO A LESS RIGID LIFE STYLE; CONSEQUENTLY, MANY OF THEM CAME FACE TO FACE WITH THE THEN TRADITIONAL DISCIPLINARY SYSTEM OF THE SERVICES.

Above: A cartoon taken from Harper's Weekly, June, 1862, illustrating a camp punisment. This particular soldier is being punished for drunken behaviour; note that the caption around the barrel reads "too fond of whisky".

Soldiers could be punished for a wide range of offences, including thievery, being drunk on duty, or failing to perform an assigned task when ordered to do so. First offenders usually were "shamed" rather than actually punished—they might be required to wear boards around their necks citing their minor offences. Indeed, even something as relatively serious as cowardice in battle might result in no more than a drumming out of camp in disgrace. For insolence toward an officer, a soldier could expect to receive much harsher treatment, perhaps being forced to stand on the head of barrel or to be tied in a sitting position with a pole between knees and arms. for several agonising hours. Many units kept a blacklist of offenders, who were assigned the most tedious and odious tasks.

One of the most serious offences of all was sleeping on guard duty, which was punishable by death, but the sentence was not often invoked. Lincoln himself commuted the sentence of one youth thus accused.

Absenteeism and desertion were major problems in both armies, and it was not always easy to distinguish one from the other. As much as a quarter of an army might be missing at any given time, according to some estimates.

Many men in the ranks simply left their units and went home when their families needed them—some more than once—especially in the South, where the protection of the home hearth was uppermost in the minds of most soldiers. Deserters who were caught were sometimes brought back to be executed in front of their regiment. This was more likely to happen if desertion was a problem at the time.

Commanders used their imaginations a bit more when it seemed necessary for the punishment to fit the crime. For several hours messmates saw one Federal cavalryman walking about their camp carrying a saddle on his back, only to learn that this was his sentence for stealing the saddle. Insurbordination could bring several hours of the ball and chain, usually a thirty-pound cannon ball on a few feet of heavy chain attached to the offender's leg. Wherever he went he had either to carry the ball or else drag it behind him, an exhausting excercise after a surprisingly short time, even for the most robust of officers.

Ironically, what most soldiers dreaded more than other forms of punishment was being ordered to perform extra hours of guard duty, and yet it is the punishment that they actually received most infrequently.

But what soldiers feared most of all was being shown the "white feather" of cowardice. But even those who fought bravely might be wounded or captured—a dangerous situation in itself.

Above: In this illustration we can see an offending soldier being marched through the streets of Washington, surrounded by armed guards.

FIREPOWER OF THE ARMIES

THE CIVIL WAR MADE THE INFANTRY "QUEEN OF BATTLE" IN FACT AS WELL AS IN NAME. THE SIMPLE IMPROVEMENT OF RIFLING THE MUSKET BARREL EXTENDED THE EFFECTIVE RANGE OF INFANTRY FARTHER THAN PREVIOUSLY THOUGHT POSSIBLE, WHILE QUICK, ONE-STEP RELOADING GREATLY INCREASED THE FIREPOWER OF SHOULDER WEAPONS.

Above: Cannons capable of smashing even the sturdiest fort's walls to rubble, were used by both sides during the conflict.

Land combat became a contest between manpower and firepower—a concept that still exists in conventional warfare. The war was a testing ground for modern arms, especially crew-operated weapons like machine guns and breech-loaded artillery. The breech-loading rifle, which was later to become standard in armies around the world, came of age.

Weapons and tactics were inextricable linked. Massed formations, so favoured in the conflicts of previous centuries, became obsolete when the firepower, accuracy, and killing distance of the infantryman was increased. Greater accuracy meant infantrymen could no longer effectively engage in stand-and-fire tactics. The primary example where this occurred, in the early stage of the Second Manassas, became an object lesson to all who participated. Frontal assaults were deadly; casualties in many battles were so heavy that they demoralized troops.

New infantry tactics stressed mobility, protection, and surprise. Battlefields became deeper and maneuver was essential to the conservation of force. Armies had to prepare for combat at distances farther apart than ever before. Formations were spread out and redesigned. Usually attack lines were preceded by widely separated skirmishers, who fired at will as they advanced and used whatever cover they could find.

Two or more lines with men several feet apart was a particularly popular arrangement. These formations would stop at some point during the assault to fire at the defenders or would proceed in a succession of rushes, hugging the ground between moves.

One formation that is considered an American innovation involved double lines of two close ranks each, with considerable distance between each pair of lines to reduce the effects of defensive firepower.

The increased firepower of the infantryman practically ended the use of the bayonet, which until then was regarded as the final shock weapon. In close-quarter fighting, soldiers preferred to use their rifles as clubs. Only one percent of Union battle casualties were bayonet wounds; eighty percent came from rifle bullets.

Increased infantry firepower gave defense a substantial advantage over offense, especially when combined with makeshift defensive installations. Defenders utilized hastily improvised breastworks and rifle pits or natural terrain features to evade the increased firepower of the enemy. The longer a unit remained in one place, the more elaborate its defences became. Even attackers learned quickly to put earth and logs between them and the incoming bullets when pinned down or when counterattacking.

Cavalry charges were no longer decisive when infantry could drop horsemen from 250 yards (230 meters) away and fire their weapons up to two to three times as fast as previously. Infantry

Below: Use of the rifle made the American Civil War a war like no other, where for the first time most of the killing was done at long range.

did not even have to mass in close formation, as it had done during the Napoleonic Wars, to meet the once-fearsome cavalry charge. A charge by the First Pennsylvania Cavalry Battalion to cover the Union retreat at Cedar Mountain, near Culpeper, Virginia, in 1862, was shattered by the fire of advancing Confederate infantry. So devastating was the barrage that only 71 of the 164 men in the unit escaped unharmed.

Some commanders never learned the lesson that battlefield conditions had changed, but instead became obsessed with recreating the now obsolete battle conditions of the past. Their ignorance cost the lives of untold thousands on both sides. The Union Second Corps, which used a massed column formation to attack Confederate defences at Spottsylvania in 1864, sustained 6,642 casualties in just a two-week period. Others, although schooled in tactics that had been developed in the era of musketry, learned to "rewrite the book" and improvise according to the current conditions. Although drillmasters continued to instruct recruits to remain in close order, the brutal lessons of combat on the ground and the irregularity and confusion of battlefields nearly always served to move them farther apart.

The development of techniques on the battlefield went hand in hand with the development of new and more deadly weaponry.

Right: The 12-pound "Napoleon" cannon, named after Napoleon III of France, was one of the most popular cannons with both sides.

Handguns were very popular. The chief American producers were Colt, Remington, and the Starr Arms Company Foreign produced handguns were also used, especially by the Confederacy. Most of these were produced in England and Belgium.

The most widely used shoulder arm was the Springfield Model 1861. This was particularly favored for its range, accuracy, and reliability. The rifle had an effective range of about 600 yards and cost $20 each, compared to the $12 for a colt revolver.

Second to the Springfield was the Pattern 1853 Enfield Rifled Musket, which was used by both sides in the war. It has been estimated that more than 900,000 P53 Enfields were imported during that time, but many had to be bought by the South from private contractors and gun runners after Britain refused to sell any more when it became clear the Confederacy could no longer win the war.

Nothing showed quite how much technology had moved on from the days of the one-shot muskets and muzzle loaders than the development of the fearsome Gatling Gun, a multi-barreled repeating machine gun that was capable of firing an incredible 1000 rounds a minute, Strangely, in spite of its terrible efficiency it was never as popular as common rifles and saw little action in the war.

Left: Mortars would be loaded on to —and sometimes fired from—railroad cars during battle.

GUERRILLA TROOPS

GUERILLA, OR IRREGULAR WARFARE, PLAYED AN IMPORTANT ROLE IN THE CONFLICT, PARTICULARLY FOR THE CONFEDERATE SIDE, WHO MAINTAINED SPECIAL PARTISAN UNITS CHARGED WITH MOUNTING OPERATIONS BEHIND ENEMY LINES. SO SUCCESSFUL WERE THESE ACTIONS THAT THEY HAVE BEEN CREDITED WITH KEEPING THE SOUTH IN THE WAR FOR MUCH LONGER THAN HAD IT RELIED ON CONVENTIONAL WARFARE ALONE.

Above: John Mosby photographed in his military uniform. After impressing General Lee with his scouting abilities, he was promoted and assisted in forming attack strategies. Postbellum, he continued his career as an attorney.

Opposite page: This photograph is of a group of Confederate partisan Colonel John S. Mosby's raiders. The men were from the 43rd Virginian Partisan Rangers.

In the early stages of the war, most guerilla activities were ad hoc and unofficial in nature, launched by civilians, often as not against other civilians, with few strategic or political goals. In 1862, however, the Confederate Congress passed the Partisan Ranger Act with the specific intention of officially organizing guerrila activity against the Union. As many as 10,000 men may have acted as guerillas under Confederate sponsorship.

The Confederate cavalry officer, John Singleton Mosby, founded a particularly effective partisan unit, which engaged in numerous successful raids behind Union lines during the last three years of the war. The Federal high command became so concerned about the unit's activities that at one stage Grant ordered that any of Mosby's men who were captured should be hanged without trial rather than treated as prisoners of war. Mosby responded in kind, executing several Union prisoners, after which both sides agreed to resume treating prisoners according to the conventions of war, regardless of the nature of their activity.

Such was Mosby's renown that he earned himself the nickname the "Gray Ghost of the Confederacy" and his actions have been credited by some authorities with extending the war by up to six months after the South's cause looked lost.

Other units lead by Lieutenant General Nathan Bedford Forrest and John Hunt Morgan also led highly effective raids into Union and Border territory where they usually engaged in activity designed to disrupt Federal infrasctructure, such as taking up railroads, destroying bridges, and disrupting supply lines.

Above: The recapture of a Federal wagon train seized by General Mosby's guerrillas in 1863.

However, as the war continued and Confederate losses continued to mount, the South's high command became increasingly wary of using valuble, and largely irreplaceable, cavalry forces to undertake such risky operations.

In Border areas, where many of the Confederacy's guerilla activities were targeted, Union military commanders had real problems with spying—both professional and amateur. Confederate sympathizers eagerly awaited the return of their Boys in Gray and offered choice intelligence to them when they could. On occassion they were suspected of doing a bit more for The Cause. General Paine complained to Grant that snipers were picking off Federal guards while they walked their posts at Hinds Point in Missouri. Grant authorized him to remove the citizens within a six-mile circumference, if he could prove civilians were doing the sniping. Anyone who returned would be liable to execution. Aware of Paine's reputation for harsh methods, Grant cautioned that the purpose of the order was not to take political prisoners but "to cut off a dangerous class of spies."

Despite Grant's caution, in trying to prevent guerilla activity, official or impromptu, Union commanders often imposed harsh and arbitrary rules on civilians in Border States and occupied areas of the South. Military commissions were set up to assess Confederate sympathizers, innocent or not, for the cost of any damage to property of loyal citizens. Anyone found guilty of aiding guerillas was subject to the death penalty. Furthermore, any pro-Confederate found within five miles of a guerilla raid could be arrested and ejected from the country.

Above: Federal troops capture a wagon train from Mosby's Confederate guerillas.

THE WAR AT SEA

THE HIGH SEAS AND COASTLINE OF THE CONFEDERACY WERE ONE OF THE DECISIVE BATTLEGROUNDS. AS A RESULT, MARITIME EXPLOITS MATCHED THOSE ON LAND IN INTENSITY AND IMPORTANCE, BUT NOT IN SIZE. THE NAVIES OF BOTH COUNTRIES REMAINED SMALL, BUT THEY HELPED DETERMINE THE FATES OF SOLDIERS FIGHTING IN THE FIELDS AND CIVILIANS SUPPORTING THE WAR AT HOME.

Above: Painting of a Confederate ship sinking after an assault from naval forces.

The importance of the slow-developing naval conflict cannot be overrated. It affected the lifestyle of both nations as much as the land war. It assured Northerners of continued plenty and helped devastate the South.

At the start, the Union possessed a small navy of 90 vessels, about half of them in operating condition. Twenty-eight were on foreign station, some as far away as China. However, most of the shipbuilding facilities, including seven of the nine naval yards, were located in the North. Naval yards at New York, Boston, Philadelphia, Washington, Portsmouth, New Hampshire, Sackett's Harbor, Maine, and Mare Island, California and numerous private yards immediately began a crash program to build vessels and convert peacetime ships to wartime use. Captured Confederate craft were put back into service, sometimes after alteration.

A total of 626 vessels were constructed and purchased by the Union during the war. Even after losses, the Union navy reported 671 ships on duty at the end of 1864, including ironclads of various designs.

The Northeast had a far stronger seafaring tradition than the South and thus possessed a much larger pool of skilled manpower. Furthermore, the North had control of virtually the entire naval

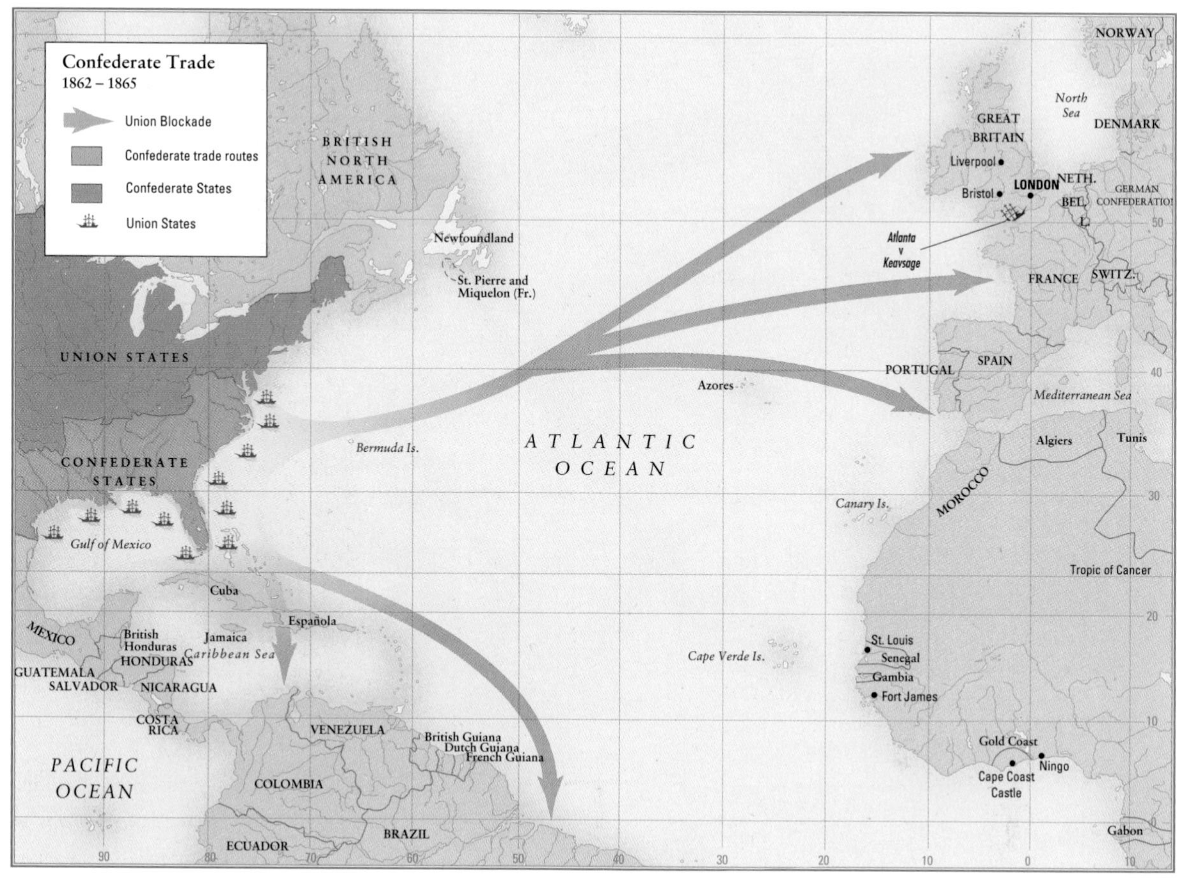

force of about 8,900 men, including about 1,300 officers, and the U.S. Naval Academy at Annapolis. The Union navy reached a peak of about 52,000 during the war, at lease a third of whom had been born abroad.

About a third of the officers in the U.S. Navy—322—resigned their commissions to enter Confederate service or return to their homes in southern States. This created a temporary surplus of officers in the Confederacy since the new nation had few ships. The reverse was true of enlisted seamen; since it takes up to three years to produce skilled mariners, the Confederacy struggled throughout its existence with a shortage of capable seamen. At its peak, the Confederate navy had about 5,200 officers and men. Only the use of foreign mercenaries, principally English and Scandinavian, enabled the Confederate navy to man its newly constructed cruisers. Members of the crew of the CSS *Alabama*, for example, were mostly Englishmen.

The Confederacy's greatest naval asset was the existence of a few bold and imaginative leaders. Secretary of Navy Stephen R. Mallory was an energetic chieftain with imagination to encourage development of new designs and weapons, and a facility for overcoming endemic shortages. Matthew Fontaine Maury, already famous as the "Pathfinder of the Seas," added innovative design

Above: Map showing Confederate trade routes. Union strategy from the very beginning of the War was to split the Confederate States into more defeatable parts and to strangle their abilty to trade overseas, the profits on which they were heavily reliant.

and use of mines (called torpedoes at the time) to his many laurels. More than 40 Union vessels were sunk or heavily damaged by mines; many naval historians regard this as the Confederacy's most effective naval defence. Commanders of raiders, including Captain Raphael Semmes of the Alabama, were experienced and courageous sailors who captured and sank more than 1,000 vessels—295 steamers, 44 large sailing vessels and 683 schooners. A naval academy was created from scratch in 1863 aboard the steamer *Patrick Henry*, anchored near Richmond.

Opposite page: Confederate submarine The Hunley was the first to successfully sink an enemy warship. It was thought lost after an enemy attack but was recovered on 8 August, 2000. Photographed here suspended in conservation tank, scientists found the bodies of 8 crew members still inside.

The Confederacy had virtually no combat vessels at the start of the war. The Confederate government issued letters of marque to privateers, authorizing the seizure of Union vessels, as soon as war broke out. It took control of ships in Southern ports, including a warship which sailed into New Orleans shortly after the war began, and captured others during the war. However, most of the deepwater Confederate navy was acquired abroad. Sleek and speedy warships like the CSS *Alabama* and CSS *Florida* were constructed or purchased abroad, often using subterfuge to evade neutrality laws. States also procured and operated naval fleets and turned them over to the Confederate navy.

The Confederacy captured the naval yards at Norfolk, Virginia, and Pensacola, Florida, and had small facilities at a few other sites. For the most part, however, the Confederacy had to build new shipyards to provide the vessels to protect its vulnerable rivers and coastline. The Norfolk naval yard remained in Confederate hands only long enough to raise the burned USS *Merrimack* and reconstruct it as the ironclad CSS *Virginia*. Further Federal encroachment on the coastline and along the rivers took away other facilities. Despite a shortage of skilled labor, the Confederacy continued to produce vessels to end, including components in places as remote from water as Charlotte, North Carolina.

The Confederacy attempted to counter the Union's superiority in numbers, many of them wooden ships, constructing ironclads—and thus advanced the science of marine engineering. Overall the records of the ironclads was patchy; they were too unseaworthy to break the Union blockade, one of the main Confederate objectives, and too unwieldy to engage effectively in combat in confined coastal waters. Ironclads were more suited to the Union objective of obtaining command of the Mississippi River because they could run past Confederate shore batteries.

The Confederacy led in experimentation with submarines. The most successful was the HL *Hunley*, named after its inventor who was killed in a test dive. The Hunley sank the Union warship *Housatonic* at Charleston, but unfortunately was dragged down by its victim. Confederate officials canceled further submarine research.

Sailors who served during the Civil War spent almost all of their enlistments aboard crowded ships, with no organized recreation and little time ashore. The sailor of the period ate unpalatable food, learned his craft on the job, stood watch and performed repetitious tasks at other times. Photographs taken during the period show sailors lounging on packed decks, scraping and painting, hauling ropes, polishing weapons and doing other tiresome chores. On long voyages abroad, all of the hardships of shipboard life were aggravated by the problem of scurvy. Sailors on blockading duty or manning warships in rivers and coastal waters at least had an occasional opportunity to obtain fresh vegetables, meat and soft bread.

Right: Crew of a Union gunboat on deck.

Battles were noisy and confused affairs as ships closed to point-blank range or tried to out maneuver each other in waters spiked with mines. Exploding and solid shells ripped sails and sent masts crashing down, blasted holes in hulls and left decks coated with blood. Gun decks were hot, smoky, smelly and slippery; parched throats, smoke and putrid air made the gunners fast for precious air. Self-induced fire was almost as dangerous as an enemy cannon and combat always carried the possibility of drowning. Battles might be brief or lengthy, intense or cat-and-mouse but they left the sailors exhausted and bleeding and their vessels sinking or badly damaged.

Sometimes fire from shore could be deadly; the first naval officer killed in the war, Commander James H. Ward, was shot aboard his ship by a Confederate sniper firing shots from the banks of the Potomac River.

On the other hand, sailors had certain advantages over soldiers. They seldom had to walk into combat and they had a permanent, indoor home. Personal effects of sailors aboard the USS *Cairo* recovered from the Mississippi River—watches, polished eating and cooking utensils, untattered uniforms and photos in frames—reveal a more settled life than that of soldiers on land.

The adventures of warships spread across the Atlantic and Pacific Oceans were more romantic. A deadly cat-and-mouse game was played on the high seas, with Confederate cruisers searching for Union merchant vessels to capture, and Union warships trying to locate and engage the Confederate raiders.

The Confederacy constructed and purchased most of its seagoing fleet, which created hope in the Confederacy and fostered a saga of heroism and effectiveness seldom matched, in Great

Left: The bombardment of Port Royal in South Carolina.

Britain, France and Portugal. Seven cruisers were among the raiders put into Confederate service, including the CSS *Shenandoah*, which took 36 prizes during the war; CSS *Georgia*, an iron-hulled vessel; and most famous of all, the CSS *Alabama*.

The construction of the CSS *Florida* demonstrates the method frequently used to evade the British Foreign Enlistment Act which established British neutrality. The vessel, built ostensibly as a merchant vessel under the name *Oreto*, sailed from Liverpool for Nassau under a British captain. A British vessel transferred two seven-inch rifles and size smoothbores to the *Oreto* in Nassau. Despite a protest from the United States consul, the vessel was allowed to depart and was commissioned CSS *Florida* at Green Cay. It picked up additional crew in Havana, and then flew a British flag to reach Mobile unmolested. The vessel slipped back through the Union blockade and, after taking three prizes, returned to Nassau without disguise to land the crews of the prizes.

The *Florida* ultimately went to the South Atlantic and was shadowed into port at Bahia, Brazil, by the USS *Wachusett*, which had been searching for it. Both the captain of the *Florida*, Lieutenant Charles M. Morris, and the United States consul, assured Brazilian authorities that the ships would not engage in hostilities in the harbor, but Commander Napoleon Collins of the *Wachusett* rammed and fired on the *Florida* while most of its crew was ashore, and captured it. It was taken to Hampton Roads under a prize crew.

The CSS *Alabama* was designed for speed and was lightly armed. Constructed in Britain, it sailed prematurely to the Azores to prevent impoundment by British authorities. There, the vessel was armed and officers were brought on board to begin a career which in less than four months included the capture of 21 prizes. Captain Semmes then sailed into the Gulf of Mexico to assist beleaguered Galveston and sink the USS *Hatteras*. Later, when trapped in the harbor at Cherbourg, France, he boldly sailed out to engage the USS *Kearsarge*; the *Alabama* was sunk.

Right: The U.S.S. *Washington Irving*, a Federal transport vessel shown on the Appomattox River, Virginia

Opposite page: Admiral David Farragut (top left) oversees the conflict on his flagship, *The Hartford*, on August 5, 1864, during the Battle of Mobile Bay.

The cruiser *Shenandoah*, attacking Union whaling ships in the Pacific, was the last Southern unit to fly the Confederate flag. When the ship's commander, Lieutenant James I. Waddell, learned of the end of the war from newspapers obtained from a British vessel, he stowed his guns in the hold and sailed 122 days without stop to intern his vessel in Britain on November 6, 1865. The war had been over for more than six months.

Quite a few Confederate vessels were destroyed while under construction or being repaired as the Union pushed ever deeper into the South. However, Southern inexperience in naval operations caused many vessels to be mishandled or run aground in combat and a large number to be abandoned, scuttle or burned to prevent capture. On February 25, 8363, Confederates abandoned efforts to salvage the Union ironclad *Indianola* because of a ruse directed by Rear Admiral David Dixon Porter. The Union "warship" which frightened off the Confederates was simply a barge with dummy stacks, superstructure and guns.

Nevertheless, Confederates loved their naval heroes, whose exploits were examples of personal honour and bravery. One of the boldest was Lieutenant Charles W. "Savez" Read, who sailed the captured Union schooner *Archer* into the harbor of Portland, Maine, and sailed out with the Revenue Cutter *Caleb Cushing*. Read wasn't able to escape with the vessel, but his exploit caused consternation along the coast of New England. Confederates also operated on the Great Lakes. In September 1864, a naval unit operating from Canada burned the steamers *Philo Parsons* and *Island Queen*. A Confederate army-navy team hijacked the steamer *St. Nicholas* on its regular run between Baltimore and Washington and used it to capture several prizes in Chesapeake Bay.

The North's greatest naval hero was Admiral David G. Farragut, who commanded the West Gulf Squadron. Farragut boldly sailed his ship past forts protecting the entrance to the Mississippi River and captured New Orleans. Subsequently, his fleet operated effectively on the Mississippi, primarily in support of land operations. Farragut's lasting fame rests on the Battle of Mobile Bay.

MEDICAL FACILITIES

MEDICAL TREATMENT WAS APPALLING AT THE START OF THE WAR AND MILITARY COMMANDERS SHOWED LITTLE INTEREST IN THE PROBLEM. IN THE NORTH, THE CIVILIAN SANITARY COMMISSION AND CHRISTIAN COMMISSION WORKED DILIGENTLY TO IMPROVE FACILITIES AND THE CARE OF THE WOUNDED BY MILITARY MEDICAL PERSONNEL, BUT WITH LIMITED SUCCESS.

Above: This painting, from circa 1861, provides us with a snapshot of the conditions at a field hospital. during the Civil War.

In the Union army, each regiment was authorized two surgeons and each corps had a fleet of four-wheel and two-wheel ambulances, but wounded were also carried by stretcher bearers and on mule litters. Illnesses were treated on the spot, and wounded were treated at makeshift hospitals near the battlefield. Generally, forward aid stations were established in tents or under trees close to the fighting and field hospitals were set up in nearby churches, schools, or houses. The Harper farmhouse at Bentonville Battlefield in North Carolina was used as a hospital during the last major attempt to stop Sherman's drive through the South.

Field physicians were mostly country doctors, ill suited for coping with wounds and epidemics of dysentery, measles, and diphtheria. Young doctors were in short supply; older ones had difficulty keeping up with the military pace, and this affected their work. Doctors in the field treated large numbers of wounded, sometimes having to continue operating for days after a battle under terrible conditions—often without anaesthetic and in the dim light of lanterns or candles. "Sawbones" became a common nickname as doctors quickly acquired a reputation for amputating wounded

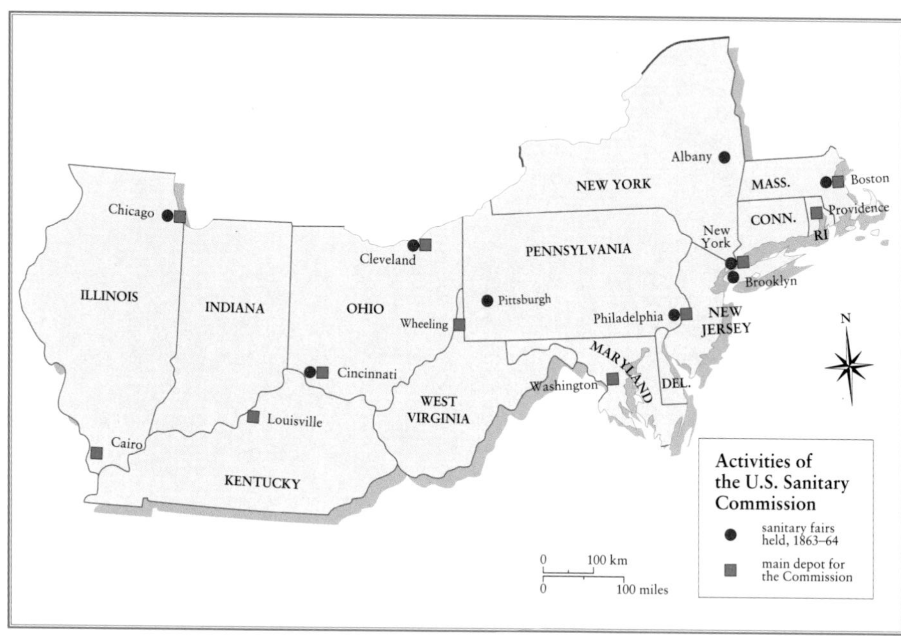

Left: A map pinpointing the key areas of U.S. Sanitary Commission activities.

limbs. Complications following amputations were often more serious than wounds. Sometimes these operations were unnecessary. Although most soldiers submitted, a few determined their own fates. A veteran in the 1st Massachusetts Heavy Artillery pointed a gun at a doctor and would not surrender it until the doctor promised not to amputate his leg. The obstinate soldier recovered but was demoted and dismissed from the service.

After initial treatment, seriously wounded men were sent to hospitals in major cities, sometimes traveling by railway hospital car and hospital ship as far as New York and Boston. Soldiers who reached a rear hospital had a good change of survival, even though conditions there were not always the best. The large numbers of wounded necessitated setting up makeshift hospitals, which often were dirty, poorly ventilated, and ill equipped. In addition, as a result of the need to resort to "contract doctors," unqualified men were appointed as physicians in some of these hospitals. By the end of the war, 350 army general hospitals were in operation.

The Confederate army professed a similar organization, but the medical corps, like all sections of the army, was plagued by substantial shortages of personnel and supplies. Local hospital relief and soldiers' aid societies existed in most cities; but sick and wounded soldiers did not get enough food and medicine, especially in the last years of the war, despite efforts which included clandestine trade with the North.

For soldiers in both armies, bullets and artillery shells were not the worst danger. Disease killed at least two soldiers for every one that died of combat wounds. At times, whole units were decimated by measles, diphtheria, or malaria; but yet more lethal were the various forms of diarrhoea and dysentery that afflicted the soldiers. Even when men did not die, such ailments as bowel complaints put commanders and even whole units out of action temporarily.

AFTERMATH OF WAR & RECONSTRUCTION

THE BLACK FUNERAL CORTEGE THAT CARRIED THE BODY OF PRESIDENT ABRAHAM LINCOLN THROUGH THE STREETS OF WASHINGTON, TO BEGIN THE LONG TRAIN RIDE TO ILLINOIS FOR FINAL HIS BURIAL, BODED ILL FOR THE FUTURE. A NEW PALL WAS DESCENDING ON A NATION WHICH ALREADY HAD BEEN TORN ASUNDER BY FOUR BITTER YEARS OF CIVIL WAR.

The end of the war brought great rejoicing in the North. Bells rang from Maine to California, not in alarm as might have been the case during the war but in happiness. If many doubted the wisdom of certain wartime act—the denial of constitutional rights or the emancipation of the slaves—at least the Union had been saved. Husbands and sons returned home in triumph, their test of strength and courage behind them.

A different situation existed in the South. Once magnificent cities were now burned out shells; the great plantations that had been the region's major source of wealth stood in a state of devastation or decay; the infrastructure, like the railroads and bridges, was in ruins; and the spectre of poverty and starvation stalked the land. Tens of thousands of half-starved soldiers and civilian refugees had to make their way home as best they could, nourished by what little good generous people along the route could give them. Defeated Southerners remained defiant, but at least gave a sigh of relief that the fighting was over.

The socio-economic structure was in a shambles, too. White manpower had been depleted by the casualty lists of war, and emancipation had eliminated the slave labour which had underpinned the old South. Economic chaos ruled vast areas of the South as soldiers returned home to a non-functioning economy and freed blacks congregated in groups or wandered aimlessly. Wartime labour shortages had taught many blacks the (hitherto neglected) value of their services, but not how to benefit from the knowledge.

The immediate postwar attitude was reminiscent of the naivety that had existed in 1861. Neither

side understood that reuniting the nation would be as great a tribulation as the war itself had been.

Above: April 14 1865, at Ford's Theatre in New York City, Abraham Lincoln, the 16th President of the United States, is assassinated by John Wilkes Booth.

The Reconstruction era was not a happy one. The North was beset by a new debate on the status of the freed slaves and by the economic recession that followed the war. The Democrats waned reconstruction left to individual States; the Radical Republicans wanted to destroy the South's ruling class and replace it with a cadre of their own choosing. A majority of the citizens probably sided with the martyred Lincoln in wanting to temper retribution with compassion.

Republican regulars exerted a moderating influence on events during the emotional release that immediately followed the collapse of the Confederacy, but they lost control after the 1866 election increased the strength of Radical Republicans. Their disillusionment with the leadership of President Andrew Johnson was also a factor. A Tennessee Democrat, Johnson despised the Southern planters because of their wealth and power, not because of slavery. He shared Lincoln's opinion that the war had been a rebellion rather than a war between separate nations, and that the States thus remained part of the national union.

President Johnson undertook to direct the Reconstruction by executive order. His first proclamation offered amnesty and restitution of property to Southerners who would take an oath of allegiance, with the exception of former Confederate government officials, senior army and naval officers, anyone arrested for military crimes, men who had resigned Federal positions at the start of the war, and people whose worth exceeded $20,000. Other proclamations recognised the governments in Tennessee, Arkansas, and Louisiana and appointed provisional governors of six Southern States with authority to call elections—in which only whites who had taken the oath of allegiance could vote—to select delegates to a convention to draft new State constitutions nullifying secession, repudiating debts incurred during the war, and abolishing slavery.

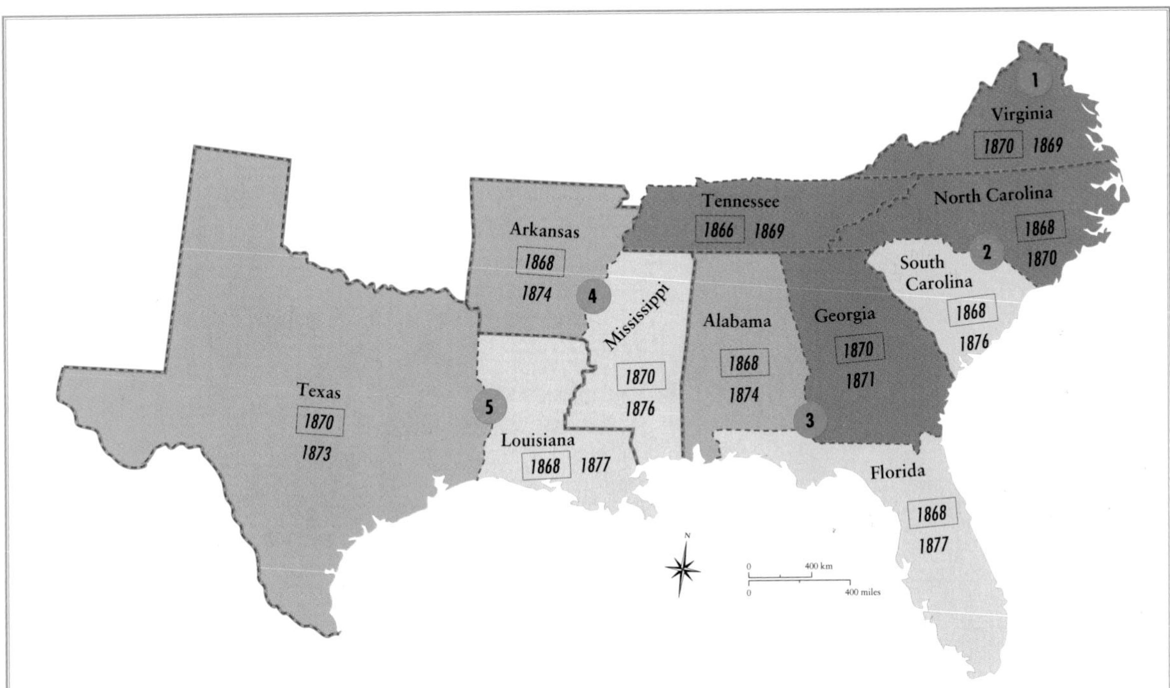

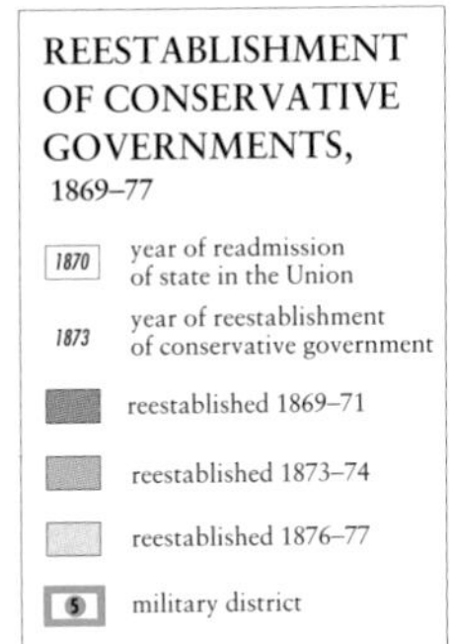

Above: Map of the southern states that re-established a conservative government in the years after the war.

This did not satisfy the Radical Republicans. They suspected Johnson was trying to create a new coalition of Northern Democrats, Southern Unionists, and conservative Republicans that would end their own domination of national affairs. They immediately counter-attacked with a campaign for universal male suffrage. Senator Thaddeus Stephens of Pennsylvania urged that land owned by wealthy ex-Confederates be confiscated and given to freed slaves. General Oliver O. Howard, head of the Freedmen's Bureau, disobeyed a presidential directive and refused to return land and property to pardoned Confederates.

Johnson was stern on one matter, accommodating on the other. He ordered return of property to their owners but sought to diffuse the voting issue with suggestions to governors and delegates that they enfranchise literate blacks and those who owned property worth $250. None of the new State constitutions provided black suffrage, but that was not as unusual as it sounds. At the same period, voters in three New England States where only a few blacks lived rejected proposals to give them the vote.

Congress gradually took the initiative away from the President. Vindictive Northern radicals grasped the reins of power and, ignoring Lincoln's expressed wish to avoid malice, wreaked vengeance on the South. In the process, they completed the economic impoverishment that four years of Civil War had begun. The Reconstruction era, as much as the war, embittered the South to such an extent that it would not forget for at least seventy years. In 1866, Congress passed over presidential veto a law which established special courts to function as military tribunals, in lieu of State courts, until the ex-Confederate States were admitted back into the union. Although many Freedmen's Bureau commissioners did not enforce this law, it nevertheless became a symbol of despotism to many Southerners, as did the suppression of laws that were designed to segregate the races. The status of the conquered States separated the President and

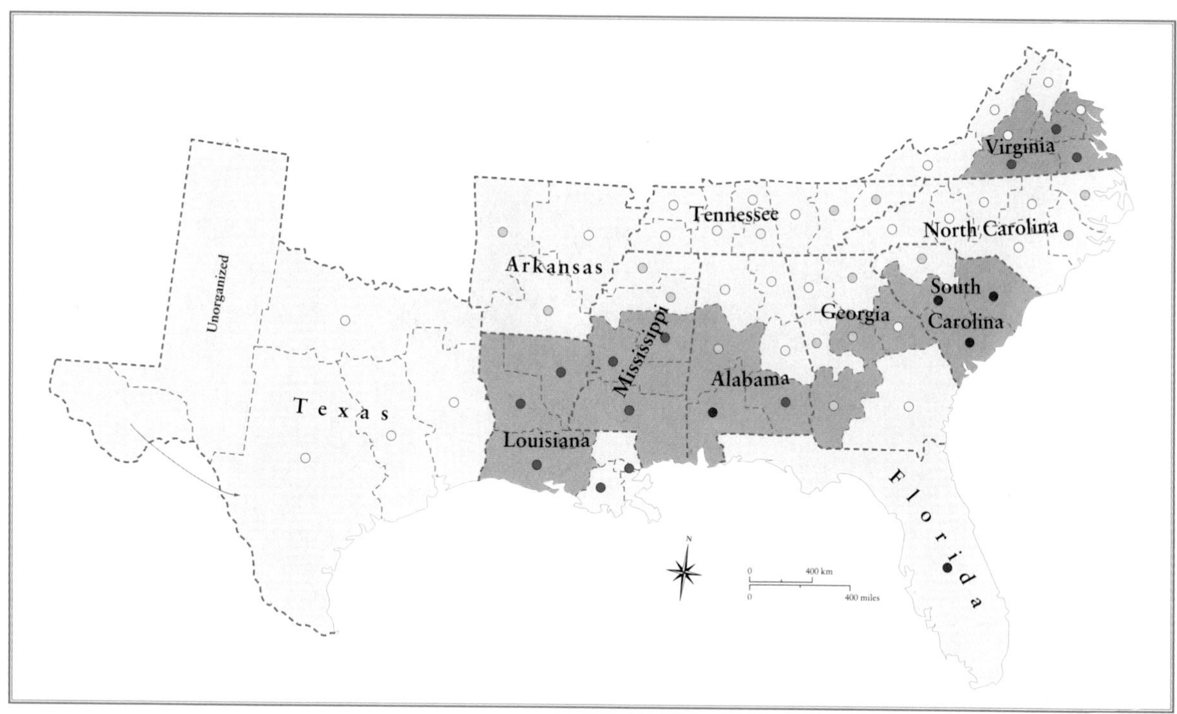

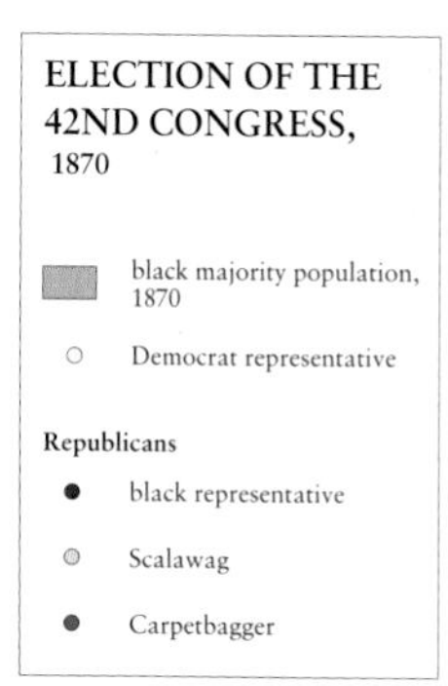

Above: Map of the separate southern states where black people made up the majority of the population.

Congress. The Republican majority in Congress refused to admit the representatives chosen under the new State constitutions enacted pursuant to Johnson's proclamations. They enacted laws defining the rights offered blacks and giving Federal courts jurisdiction over civil rights cases. These laws were twice vetoed by Johnson on the grounds that representatives of the Southern States were being denied seats in Congress and that the court provision discriminated against whites. Congressional leaders took their case to the States in the 14th Amendment, which established blacks as citizens, reduced the congressional representation of any State that denied the vote to a portion of its adult male population, prohibited States from denying any person equal protection of the law, and disqualified from holding public office anyone who, having once taken an oath to defend the national Constitution, had broken the oath. While the proposed amendment gave constitutional recognition to blacks it also reduced Southern representation and disenfranchised senior Confederate military officers and government officials.

Southern States which ratified the amendment were to be readmitted, Tennessee was the first to do so, and its representatives were seated in Congress in 1866, even though the ratification process was far from complete. Such generosity was short-lived. Congress delayed the return of other Southern States by requiring new constitutional conventions, with delegates elected by male suffrage, and approval voting by blacks. Over Johnson's veto, Congress divided the ten remaining ex-Confederate States into five military districts and subjected all civil authorities to military supervision.

Military occupation of the Confederate States was a mixture of benevolence and harshness. The 200,000-man occupying army was, for a time after the fighting stopped, the only source of food and medical assistance for displaced whites and freed blacks. The military also enforced laws through military courts,

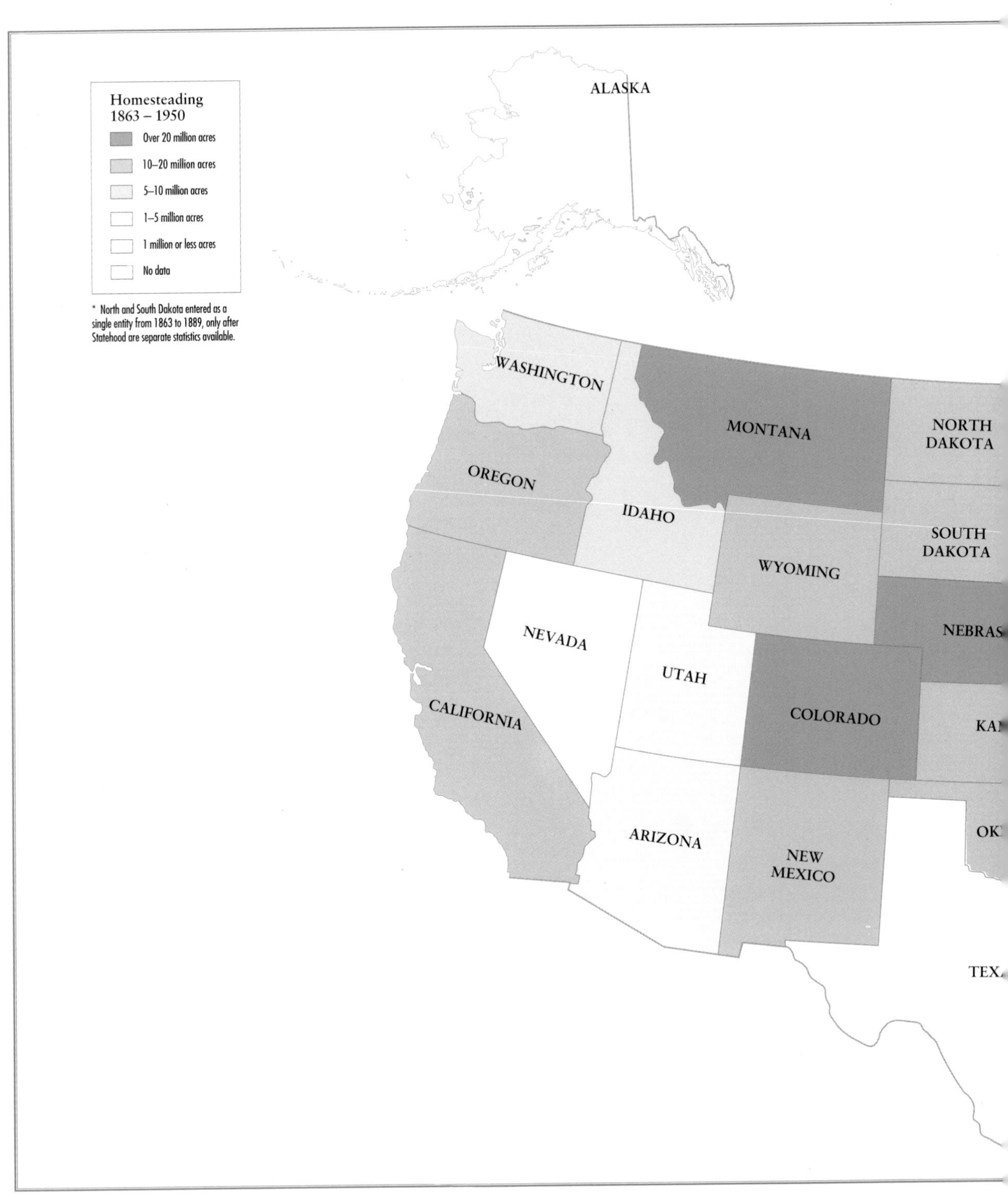
Homesteading
1863 – 1950
Over 20 million acres
10–20 million acres
5–10 million acres
1–5 million acres
1 million or less acres
No data
* North and South Dakota entered as a single entity from 1863 to 1889, only after Statehood are separate statistics available.
ALASKA
WASHINGTON
MONTANA
NORTH DAKOTA
OREGON
IDAHO
SOUTH DAKOTA
WYOMING
NEBRAS
NEVADA
UTAH
CALIFORNIA
COLORADO
KA
ARIZONA
NEW MEXICO
OK
TEX

Left: Although the end of the war brought joy and relief throughout the nation, the reconstruction era was difficult and unhappy. The socio-economic structure had been ravaged by four years of war, especially in the South. Many people, especially emancipated slaves, decided to revert to living independently on homesteads. Often they were squatters and occupied whatever space they could find. This map shows what is known about the numbers of congregations in all the different states.

Right: A common practise after the war was Sharecropping. Black people, though free, were prevented by whites from owning any land. The once wealthy Southern land owners in former slave counties could not afford to employ workers. Therefore a compromise had to be reached. Land that had once been worked by slaves, was divided into smaller plots. Tenants were provided with a house, tools, and seed in return for a generous share of the crop. Many black people found this way of life preferable to wage labor as it was more liberated.

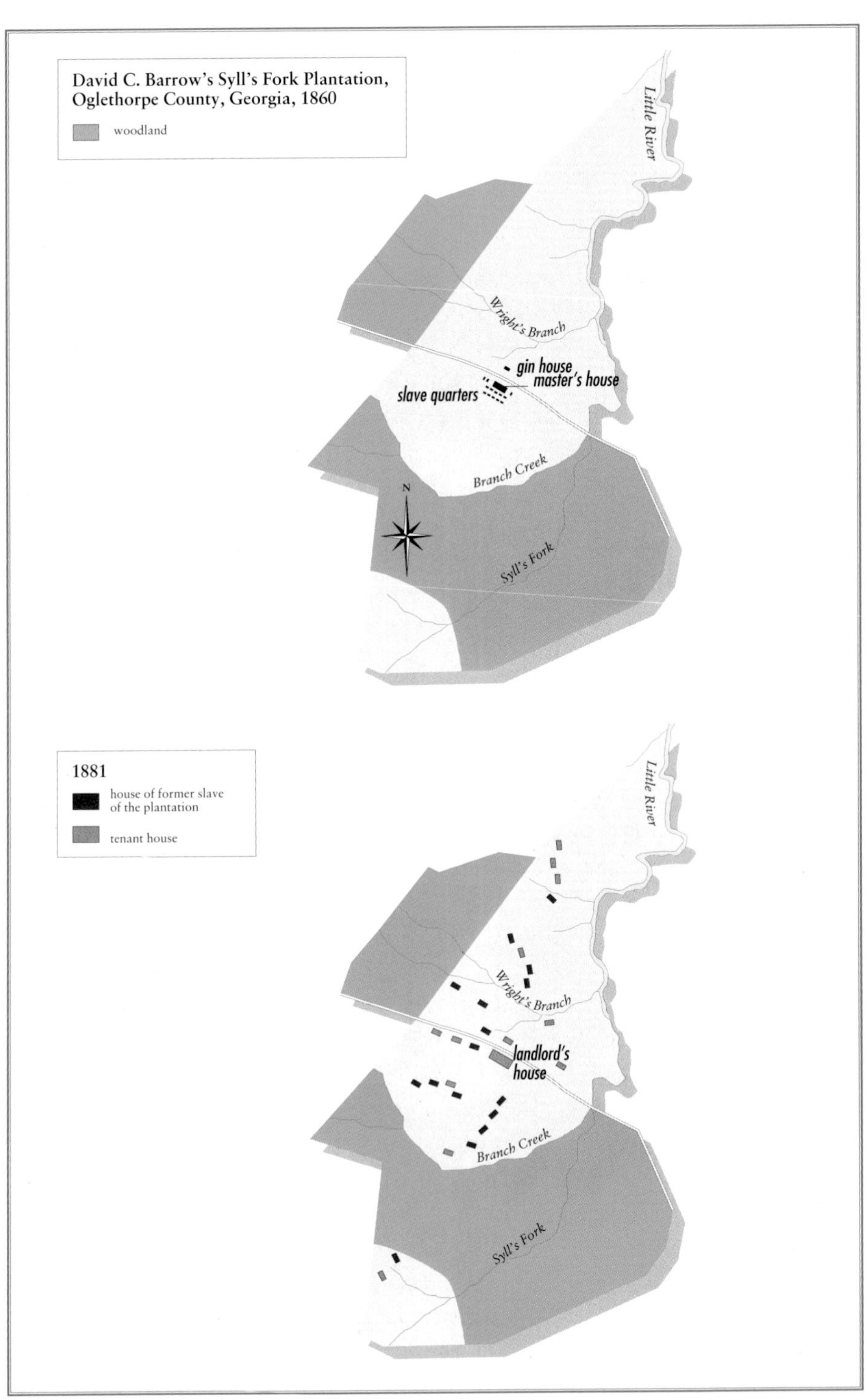

not always with wisdom and justice. The purpose of the Freedmen's Bureau was to assist blacks, but it also aided a few needy whites. About a third of the rations issued in 1865 went to poor whites.

At the same time, the South was inundated by agents of the Federal government who used their unusual powers to oppress or plunder. These men were called "carpetbaggers" because many of them arrived in the South carrying cheap suitcases made of thick, rough cloth like old rugs. Southerners who worked with them, principally Unionists, were called 'scalawags.'

Many began with a legitimate purpose. The Federal government laid claim to the cotton that had been purchased by the Confederate government and sent agents to identify it and ship it North. The agents did not restrict themselves to legitimate prizes, though. Privately owned cotton was seized and sold by the agents on the open market, or owners were forced to pay bribes to keep their property. The number of honest agents may well have exceeded the number of dishonest; but under the conditions that existed, the blatant excesses of the latter coloured the minds of the people of the South.

Farms and land were taken from owners through a variety of devices, including claims that taxes paid during the lifetime of the Confederacy were invalid and that back taxes had to be paid—in Union dollars. The Freemen's Bureau leased to free blacks nearly a million acres of land whose owners had fled during the war or which had been confiscated. In some instances, the bureau was also able to provide ploughs and mules, financed by the proceeds of crops.

Most Southerners submitted to the whims and vagaries of the Union soldiers and civilians on the scene and the politicians in Washington, but some remained unreconstructed. They resented the loss of the war and the subsequent occupation, and they showed their distaste for Northerners in various ways, even in outbreaks of violence. It was during this period that the Ku-Klux-Klan came into existence.

Congress showed its distrust of Johnson by limiting his authority to remove officials whose appointments were confirmed by Congress—the Tenure of Office Act—and requiring that all Presidential orders to military commanders be issued through General Grant.

Another act of Congress required generals in command of the districts to register voters and initiate procedures leading to constitutional conventions. The disenfranchisement of former Confederate soldiers and the enfranchisement of blacks was a blatant attempt to establish political and economic control of the Southern States. When registration of Southern voters was completed in 1867, blacks outnumbered whites—735,000 to 635,000, respectively—and represented a majority in five States. Three quarters of the constitutional convention delegates elected were Republicans and, of these, 45 per cent were Southern whites who were Unionist in sympathy, 25 per cent were Northern whites who had gone South after the way (many of them former Union army officers or Freedmen's Bureau commissioners) and 30 per cent were blacks.

The constitutions they drafted conformed to the wishes of Congress, but Congress imposed a new requirement. Afraid the 15th Amendment, prohibiting State denial of voting rights on grounds of race, colour, or previous condition, would not receive the required approval in Northern States, Congress insisted the last four Southern States readmitted also had to ratify the amendment. It was not until 1870 that the last Southern State was allowed to take its seats in Congress.

In the meantime, congressional imposition of taxes on cotton, designed to make Southerners pay for the Union war effort, helped further impoverish the region.

The conflict between Johnson, undaunted by reverses, and a Congress drunk with power finally flared openly: Johnson, who tried to circumvent the Tenure of Office Act and fire Secretary of War Stanton for siding with Congress against the President, became the only President in American history to be impeached. Only one courageous vote saved him from being removed from office.

In the State elections which followed re-admission, Republicans capitalised on their popularity with freed slaves to gain majorities in the legislatures of most Southern States. The record they compiled helped establish the South as a Democratic Party bastion for almost a century. The duplicity of the politicians was a far cry from the honest emotion and mutual respect the soldiers had shown for each other at Appomattox.

The destruction caused by the Civil War extended far beyond the battlefield, even beyond the civilian areas engulfed in warfare. The "Southern way of life"—the thing the war was supposed to preserve—was sacrificed. Confederates had begun the process themselves by centralizing the government and curtailing individual freedoms in an effort to create a new nation. Reconstruction finalised the process.

The South had made its case on the field of battle and had failed. A hush descended on Dixie. The war sharply altered Southern society. The dominance of the cavalier evaporated in the smoke of the modern battlefield. The egalitarian nature of combat and the stresses of adversity weakened the exclusionary nature of planter society. New people were admitted to the social and power structure with an influx of Northern immigrants after the war accelerated the process. While the domination of the planters did not end, it was weakened. The trend was accelerated by the growth of industry and increasing importance of the cities.

Most Southerners accepted the new situation, and the "Lost Cause" replaced "The Cause." The Statue of a Confederate soldier in the town square became the new symbol. The South would remain loyal to its memories and its heritage—no section of the nation devotes so much attention to history—but at the same time be as loyal as any section of the nation in two world wars.

The military influence, not strong in the North prior to the Civil War, dominated Northern politics for a long time afterward. It catapulted General Grant into the Presidency and General Benjamin Butler into the governor's office in Massachusetts. The comradeship of soldiers who fought on the bloody battlefields lasted as long as one of them could don a faded blue uniform and answer muster at the Grand Army of the Republican buildings that still stand in many Northern cities.

Although the Civil War solidified sectionalism, it also—curiously—ended a sort of national provincialism. The war that uprooted more Americans than any previous event in the nation's history gave restless young men a glimpse of life beyond their native horizon. They never forgot the glimpse and soon began a great migration to the western territories. Southerners who had lost everything turned that way to restore their fortunes; Northern youth seeking to fulfil their dreams joined them.

Finally, the Civil War touched the psyche of the nation and initiated a great change as competition within one society replaced competition between two societies.

Left: Monument to Confederate soldiers topped with a statue of an individual soldier in Monroe, Georgia.

THE COST OF WAR

THE CIVIL WAR EXACTED A HEAVY TOLL ON BOTH SIDES. LOSS OF LIFE WAS HIGH AND THERE WAS A LARGE ECONOMIC PRICE TOO—RUNNING THE WAR WAS A COSTLY BUSINESS. THE SOUTH SUFFERED PARTICULARLY BADLY. WITH THE END OF SLAVE LABOR AND ITS AGRICULTURAL BASE IN RUINS, IT WOULD NOT RECOVER UNTIL THE TWENTIETH CENTURY.

Of all the wars in America's history, its own Civil War—fought mostly by volunteers—was the bloodiest. Losses were greater in the South, with the deaths of 20 per cent of Confederate soldiers, compared with around 16 percent on the Union side.

The odds were stacked against the Confederacy from the beginning. The more prosperous, populous North had three times as many men of military age to call upon. The South, in contrast, was shorter on manpower, so Confederates enrolled for the duration of the war and were thus on the battlefield, facing possible death, for longer. The South also suffered more through disease, which accounted for 50 percent of all Confederate fatalities. To put the losses into historical perspective, 665,850 men died in the American Civil War as opposed to 116,516 in World War I, 405,399 in World War II, 54,246 in the Korean War, and 57,777 in Vietnam.

There was also a tremendous economic cost. The Union's total military spending was $2.3 billion. The South spent less overall—$1.0 billion in total—but because the population was smaller in the Confederate states this represented $111 per capita compared with $98 per capita in the North.

For the South, war damage exacted an even higher price, amounting to a total figure of $1.1 billion. Some 98 percent of all engagements took place on Confederate soil, and there was enormous—and sometimes deliberate—destruction of Southern property. The South's economy had been based on agriculture, especially the growing of cotton, yet two-fifths of its livestock and half of its farm machinery were destroyed. In addition, the prewar dependence on slave labor meant that emancipation cost former slave-owners $1.6 billion. By 1900, thirty-five years after the war's end, the agriculture of the South had reached only 75 percent of its earlier production levels, and in the post-war years the average Southerner was only half as wealthy as the average Northerner.

Opposite page: April 24, 1865. This illustration depicts the body of Abraham Lincoln, the assassinated 16th President of the United States of America, arriving outside of City Hall in New York, to a large crowd in mourning.

impending civil war. All dreaded it, all sought to avert it. While the inaugural address was being delivered from this place, devoted altogether to saving the Union without war, urgent agents were in the city seeking to destroy it without war—seeking to dissolve the Union and divide effects by negotiation. Both parties deprecated war, but one of them would make war rather then let the nation survive, and the other would accept war rather than let it perish, and the war came.

One-eighth of the whole population were colored slaves, not distributed generally over the Union, but localized in the southern part of it. These slaves constituted a peculiar and powerful interest. All knew that this interest was somehow the cause of the war. To strengthen, perpetuate, and extend this interest was the object for which the insurgents would rend the Union even by war, while the Government claimed no right to do more than to restrict the territorial enlargement of it. Neither party expected for the war the magnitude or the duration which it has already attained. Neither anticipated that the cause of the conflict might cease with or even before the conflict itself should cease. Each looked for an easier triumph, and a result less fundamental and astrounding. Both read the same Bible and pray to the same God, and each invokes His aid against the other. It may seem strange that any men should dare to ask a just God's

Epilogue

After his first term in office, Abraham Lincoln was re-elected president in 1864 and, on March 4, 1865, he swore his Oath of Presidential Office. In his celebrated address to his "fellow countrymen," he spoke of "binding up the nation's wounds." Little more than a month later, he would be dead.

"At this second appearing to take the oath of the presidential office there is less occasion for an extended address than there was at the first. Then a statement somewhat in detail of a course to be pursued seemed fitting and proper. Now, at the expiration of four years, during which public declarations have been constantly called forth on every point and phase of the great contrast which still absorbs the attention and engrosses the energies of the nation, little that is new could be presented. The progress of our arms, upon which all else chiefly depends, is as well known to the public as to myself, and it is, I trust, reasonably satisfctory and encouraging to all. With high hope for the future, no prediction in regard to it is ventured. On the occasion corresponding to this four years ago all thoughts were anxiously directed to an

Opposite page: President Lincoln meets with his General George B. McClellan and other officers at Antietam on October 3, 1862, to discuss the strategy for a war that had yet to turn in the Union's favor.

assistance in wringing their bread from the sweat of other men's faces, but let us judge not, that we be not judged. The prayers of both could not be answered. That of neither has been answered fully.

The Almighty has His own purposes. "Woe unto the world because of offenses; for it must needs be that offenses come, but woe to that man by whom the offense cometh." If we shall suppose that American slavery is one of those offenses which, in the providence of God, must needs come, but which, having continued through His appointed time, He now wills to remove, and that He gives to both North and South this terrible war as the woe due to those by whom the offense came, shall we discern therein any departure from those divine attributes which the believers in a living God always ascribe to Him? Fondly do we hope, fervently do we pray, that this mighty scourge of war may speedily pass away. Yet, if God wills that it continue all the wealth piled by the bondsman's two hundred and fifty years of unrequited toil shall be sunk, and until every drop of blood drawn with the lash shall be paid by another drawn with the sword, as was said three thousand years ago, so still it must be said the 'judgements of the Lord are true and righteous altogether.'

With malice toward none, with charity for all, with firmness in the right as God gives us to see the right, let us strive on to finish the work we are in, to bind up the nation's wounds, to care for him who shall have borne the battle and for his widow and his orphan, to do all which may achieve and cherish a just and lasting peace among ourselves and with all nations."

Further Reading

Alexander, General E.P. *The American Civil War Siegle*, Hill & Co, London, 1908

Boatner, Mark *The Civil War Dictionary* David Mackay Co, Inc, New York, 2nd ed, New York, 1991

Davis, William C. (Ed), *The Image of War:* 1861-1865 (6 vols) Doubleday & Company, Inc, New York, 1984

Grimsley, Mark, *The Hard Hand of War* Cambridge University Press, 1995

Hood, J.B. *Advance and Retreat: Personal Experiences in the United States and Confederate State Armies* Hood Orphan Memorial Fund, New Orleans, 1880

Humble, Richard *The Illustrated History of the American Civil War* Multimedia Publications (UK) Ltd, London, 1986

Longstreet, James *From Manassas to Appomattox: Memoirs of the Civil War in America* J.B. Lippincott Co, Philadelphia, 1896

Parish, Peter J., ed., *The Reader's Guide to American History* Fitzroy Dearbon, 1997

Stockesbury, James L., *A Short History of the Civil War* Morrow, 1995

Time Life Books *The Civil War* (27 vols), Amsterdam BV; Alexandria, Virginia, 1988

Wheeler, Richard *Voices of the Civil War* Thomas Y. Crowell Co, New York, 1976

Wordsworth, Steven E., ed., *The American Civil War: A Handbook of Literature and Research* Greenwood Press, 1996

INDEX

Page numbers in italic type refer to maps and illustrations.

A

Abolitionist movement 17–19, 26, 51, 64, 180–1, 192
absenteeism 348–9
Adams, General Wirt 250
Adams-Onís Treaty 31
African Americans
  combatants 17, 64–7, 66, 67, 99, 204, 214, 257, 262, 290, 330
  Confiscation Act 65
  contrabands 64, 65, 65
  Emancipation Proclamation 14, 65, 94, 100, 179, 180–1, 204
  homesteading 372–3
  Militia Act 65
  population 38, 41
  prisoners of war 326
  racial segregation 49
  Reconstruction period 369
  sharecropping 374
  slavery see slavery
  Southern states 370, 371
  suffrage 370
agriculture 42, 44–9, 44–5
  crops 47
  sharecropping 49
  see also cotton production
Alabama 18, 21
Albuquerque 103–4
Alexander, Colonel E.P. 183
Alexandria, Louisiana 256–9
Alexandria, Virginia 74, 196, 197
Alton Penitentiary 326–7
American Revolution 16, 26, 28
  African American soldiers 64
  Loyalist emigration following 38
Ames, Adelbert 82
Anaconda Plan 72, 74–7, 74, 75, 77, 146
Anderson, General Richard H. 284
Anderson, Robert 55–6, 56
Andersonville Prison 326, 327, 328, 329
Anti-slavery Society 18
Antietam, Battle of 65, 69, 72, 172–9, 173, 174–5, 176, 177, 178
Appomattox 131
Appomattox Court House 332
Arizona 37, 41, 102, 334
Arkansas 18, 19, 21, 110–13, 112, 113
  Arkansas Campaign 264–5, 265
Arkansas, CSS 148–9
Arkansas Post 190, 190
army camps 138, 153, 156–9, 157, 158, 159, 325
Army of the Cumberland 242, 322
army diet 157–8, 157
Army of Georgia 317
Army of the Potomac 132, 138, 160–1, 182–3, 218, 222, 274, 288

Army of the Shenandoah 130–2
Army of Tennessee 294, 296, 317, 322–5
Army of Virginia 137, 170, 222
Ashby, Colonel Turner 150
Atlanta, Georgia 12–13, 238, 248, 266, 267, 268–9, 317, 317
Siege of 296–8, 297, 298, 299
Auburn, Battle of 236
Augusta 318
Averasboro 340, 340

B

badges, corps 101
Baja California 37
Bale, General William 241
Balloon Corps 82, 88, 90, 91
Ball's Bluff 72
Baltimore 172
Banks, General Nathaniel Prentiss 132, 213–14, 256–8, 259, 264
Bardstown 230
Bates, Edward 20
Baton Rouge, Battle of (1862) 72, 146, 148–9, 148, 206, 208
Battle above the Clouds 244
battle sites 12–13
major African American battle sites 67
Virginia 15
bayonet 351
Bean's Station, Battle of 233
Beauregard, General P.G.T. 56, 79, 82, 122–5, 142–4, 216, 255, 279
Beaver Dam Creek 138
Bee, General Bernard 79
Bell, John 18, 19, 20
Belle Isle 327, 329
Benjamin, Judah P. 20, 70, 130, 135
Bentonville, Battle of 340, 342–3, 366
Bermuda Hundred 279, 288
Big Bethel 74, 76, 137
Big Black River, Battle of 212
Birney, General David 314
Blair, General Frank, Jr. 317
Bleeding Kansas 35
blockade of Southern seaports 46, 48, 68, 69, 74–7, 74, 75, 77, 126, 135, 176, 330, 331
blockade runners 334
Bloody Angle 272
Bloody Lane 179
Bloody Pond 143
Blunt, General James G. 111, 113, 190
Boatswain's Creek 160
Boonville 302–3
Booth, John Wilkes 332, 333, 369
Bosgue Redondos Reservation 198
bounty payments 60
Bowen, General John S. 212
Boyd, Belle 70
Bragg, General Braxton 58, 88–9, 109, 165–8, 168, 184, 232–3, 260, 262
Battle of Chickamauga 241–3
Brandy Station 246
Brannan, Captain James M. 58
Breakthrough Point 138
breastworks 139, 289, 351
Breckinridge, John C. 18, 19, 20, 148–9, 206, 208, 304, 306
breech-loading rifle 350, 351
Brice's Crossroads 263
Bristoe Station, Battle of 236–7
Brown, Joe 62
Brown, John 70
Buchanan, Admiral Franklin 301
Buchanan, James 54, 56
Buckland Mills 237

Buckner, General Simon Bolivar 115, 230
Buell, General Don Carlos 109, 142–4, 165–8
Bull Run, First Battle of 15, 68, 69, 72, 78–82, 80–1, 83, 88, 91, 101, 130, 158, 193, 196
Bull Run, Second Battle of 15, 72, 170–1, 171, 176, 350
bummers 316, 341
Burnside, General Ambrose E. 73, 77, 120, 179, 179, 182–3, 233, 285
  Knoxville Campaign 232–3, 233, 234–5
Butler, General Benjamin F. 278–9

C

Cahill, Colonel Thomas 149
California 18, 36, 41, 198
Camp Convalescent 197
Camp Dick Robinson 108
Camp Morton 327
canal network 43
Canby, Colonel Edward R.S. 102–3
Cane Hill, Battle of 113
Carolinas Campaign 338–41, 338, 339, 340, 341, 342–3
Carson, Colonel Christopher "Kit" 198, 198, 203
Carthage, Battle of 86
casemates 58–9
Cassville, Battle of 269
Castle Pinckney 326
casualties 14, 20, 185, 378
  African American 67
  bloodiest single day 177
  Gettysburg 224, 226, 228, 229
  through disease 157, 193, 327, 329, 367
  The Wilderness 272
cattle trails 23, 198
cavalry 274, 351–2
ceasefire 333, 368
Cedar Creek, Battle of 306, 307
Centreville 171
Chaffin's Bluff, Battle of 314
Champion Hill, Battle of 212
Chancellorsville, Battle of 93, 204, 218–21, 219, 220, 221
Chandler, T.C. 221
Charleston 54–9, 55, 165, 326
  Charleston Campaign 216, 217
Chase, Salmon P. 20, 50
Chattahoochee Arsenal 57
Chattanooga 88, 109, 165, 184–5, 204, 232, 238, 241–5, 262
Cherokee 201
Chickamauga, Battle of 88, 204, 238–45, 239, 240, 241, 244, 262
Chickasaw 100
Chickasaw Bayou 190
Choctaw 100
Christian Commission 366
Clausewitz, Karl von 92, 93–4, 93
Clay, Henry 30, 31, 34
Clem, Johnny 98, 145
Cobb, Howell 67
Cochise 198
Cold Harbor, First Battle of see Gaines' Mill, Battle of
Cold Harbor, Battle of 246, 246, 285, 286, 287, 288
Collins, Napoleon 363
Colorado 19, 198
Colt firearms 353
Columbia 309, 338
Columbus 107, 108, 115
communications 82, 88–91, 89, 90, 91, 92
Confederate Army of the West 110–11
Confederate states 20, 25
  army 100–1, 101, 156–9, 161
  cabinet 20
  conscription 61–3
  Constitution 52

flag 25, 110
foreign assistance 14, 48
guerrilla warfare 354–6, 355, 356, 357
impressed black labor 29
Native American soldiers 100, 201, 201
navy 126–9, 149, 358–65
recruitment of slaves 67, 330
sea trade 359
slavery 25
strategic tactics 92–4
see also Southern states
Confederate Sunset 249
Confederation, Articles of 16
Confiscation Act 65
Congress 16
Connecticut 17
conscription 60–2
Constitutional Convention 17–18, 30
contraband camps 65
contrabands 64, 65
Corinth 142, 144
Siege of 98, 122–5, 123, 124
cotton production 18, 28, 29, 42, 44–9, 47, 96
cotton belt 27
slavery 18, 27, 29, 46, 49
Union activities in Louisiana 206
Crater, Battle of 312
Creek Indians 100
Cross Keys, Battle of 152
Curtis, Samuel R. 110–11
Custer, General George Armstrong 99, 259, 276
Cynthiana 164

D

Dallas, Battle of 269
Dandridge 233
Danville 291
Dauphin Island 300
Davis, Charles H. 146
Davis, Jefferson 20, 20, 48, 50–3, 51, 54, 67, 91, 93, 134, 176, 213, 232, 243, 290, 330, 346
capture by Union forces 333, 333
Death Valley 228
Delaware 21, 64
Democrat Party 20, 35, 40, 49
desertion 348–9
Devil's Den 223, 228
The Dictator 289, 290
diseases, communicable 157, 193, 327, 329, 367
Douglas, Stephen A. 18, 19, 20, 34, 34, 50–1
Douglass, Frederick 18, 64
Drewry's Bluff, Battle of 278–9, 279
Dug Springs 86
duration of War 14

E

Early, General Jubal 248, 306–7, 314
economy
and abolitionism 26
agriculture 42, 44–9, 44–5, 47
cotton production 18, 27, 28, 29, 42, 44–6, 47
industrialization 18, 42–5, 47
Northern states 18, 26, 28, 42, 44–5
post-Revolutionary recession 16, 16
post-war 378
Reconstruction 14, 49, 368–76
Southern states 18, 26, 27, 28, 42, 45–9, 47, 378
trade tariffs 18
Elizabeth City 120, 129
Elkhorn Tavern, Battle of see Pea Ridge, Battle of
Ellsworth, Colonel Elmer Ephraim 196
Emancipation Proclamation 14, 65, 94, 100, 179, 180–1,

204
Emerald Guards 101
equipment, army 101, 158
Ericsson, John 128
espionage 70, 86, 137, 164, 197, 197, 356
Evans, Colonel Nathan "Shanks" 79
Everett, Edward 229
Ewell, General Richard S. 152, 223, 236–7

F

Fair Oaks 138
Farragut, Admiral David 96–7, 146, 146, 148, 188, 206, 213, 300–1, 364, 365
Fauquier White Sulphur Springs 236
Fayetteville 340
Finegan, General Joseph 255
firepower 350–3, 350, 351, 352, 353
Fisher's Hill 306
Five Civilised Tribes 201
Five Forks 346
Florence Military Prison 327
Florida 18, 21, 25, 57, 250, 254–5, 255
Forrest, General Nathan Bedford 62, 114, 165, 165, 168, 189, 254, 260–3, 261, 262, 323, 325, 332, 354
Fort Anderson 336, 340
Fort Barrancas 57
Fort Bliss 104
Fort Buhlow 258
Fort Coburn 212
Fort Delaware 326
Fort Donelson 71, 114–19, 116–17, 118–19, 230, 260
Fort Fillmore 102
Fort Fisher 330, 336, 337, 340
Fort Gaines 300
Fort Gilmer 314
Fort Harrison 314
Fort Henry 71, 114–19, 115, 116–17
Fort Jackson 96–7, 146
Fort Jefferson 58
Fort Johnson 58
Fort Lafayette 326
Fort McAllister 318
Fort Macon, Siege of 120
Fort McRee 58
Fort Marion 57
Fort Monroe 137, 157
Fort Morgan 300–1
Fort Moultrie 58
Fort Pickens 57, 58
Fort Pillow 125
Fort Pillow, Battle of 67, 262
Fort Randolph 258
Fort Ridgely 202
Fort St. Philip 96, 146
Fort Steadman 344, 346, 289
Fort Stephens 248
Fort Sumter 54–9, 54, 55, 57, 58, 59, 64, 100–1, 216, 338
Fort Towson 333
Fort Union 104
Fort Wade 212
Fort Wagner 66, 216
Fort Walker 77
Fort Warren 326
Fortress Monroe 74, 128
Fortress Rosecrans 185
Four-Mile Creek 314
Frankfurt 167
Franklin, Battle of 309, 322
Franklin-Nashville Campaign 322–5
Frayser's Farm, Battle of 161
Fredericksburg 150, 270
Fredericksburg, Battle of 69, 73, 182–3, 183, 218

Free Soil Party 34
Freedman's Bureau 370, 375
Frémont, General John C. 64, 132, 150–2, 155
French, General William H. 236–7
Fugitive State Law 18, 19
furloughs 157

G

Gadsden, James 36
Gadsden Purchase 23, 25, 25, 36–7
Gaines' Mill, Battle of 138, 286
Gardner, General Franklin 214
Garfield, General James A. 144–5
Garrison, William Lloyd 18
Gauley Bridge 70–1
Georgia 21, 62, 238–45, 239, 240
  Andersonville Prison 326, 327, 328, 329
  Atlanta see Atlanta
  battle sites 12–13
  March to the Sea 316–19, 316, 317, 318–19, 320–1, 330
Gettysburg, Battle of 15, 204, 222–9, 223, 224, 225, 226, 227, 228, 229, 230
Gillmore, General Quincy Adams 216, 254–5, 254, 278
Glasgow 303
Glendale, Battle of 161
Glorieta, Battle of 102–3, 102
Gold Rush 41
Goldsboro 341
Goldsborough, Louis M. 120
Gordon, General John Brown 290, 294, 346
Grand Gulf 209, 212
Grand Junction 188
Granger, General Robert S. 300
Grant, General Ulysses S. 29, 99, 108–9, 115–16, 142–4, 246, 259, 260, 330
  Battle of North Anna 281, 284–5, 284
  Battle of Spotsylvania 272, 280–1, 281, 282–3
  Battle of The Wilderness 246, 270–2, 271, 272, 273
  Chickamauga and Chattanooga 241–5, 243
  Overland Campaign 270–86
  Siege of Petersburg 288–94, 288, 289, 292–3, 294–5, 344–6, 345
  Siege of Richmond 312–14, 344–6, 345, 347
  strategic tactics 93, 94, 114–19, 246, 316
  Vicksburg Campaigns 188–90, 188, 190, 191, 204, 209–14, 210–11, 213
Granville Rifles 101
Great Compromise 18
great hog swindle 109
Green, Johnny 184
Greenhow, Rose O'Neal 197, 197
Grierson, Colonel B.H. 209
Guadalupe Hidalgo, Treaty of 25
guerrilla warfare 354–6, 355, 356, 357

H

Halleck, General Henry 125
Halleck, Henry H. 165
Hammond, James Henry 45
Hampton Roads 126–9, 126, 127, 128, 129
Hampton, Virginia 74
Hancock, General Winfield S. 284–5, 312
Hanover Court House, Battle of 275
Hardee, General William J. 318
Hardee's Tactics 62
Harper's Ferry 70, 130, 176, 179
Harris, Isham G. 142
Hart, Nancy 70
Hatch, General Edward 323
Hatteras, Battle of 76, 76
Hatteras Inlet 120
Haxall's, Battle of 275

Hemp Bales, Battle of the 87
Herron, General Francis D. 190
Hickman 107
Hill, General A.P. 179, 236, 284
Hill, General Daniel 160
Hilton Head Island 77
Hindman, General Thomas C. 111, 113, 190
Holly Springs 189
homesteading 372–3
Hood, General John Bell 245, 266, 296, 298, 308, 322–5
  Tennessee Campaign 308–9, 310–11
Hooker, General Joseph 178, 218–19, 222, 243
Hornet's Nest 143
hospitals see medical facilities
Hough, Daniel 56
Hovey, General Alvin P. 189
Howard, General Oliver O. 317–18, 370
Hunter, General David 64, 304, 306–7, 307

I

Illinois 18, 302
Indian Territories 199
Indian Wars 22, 23, 198–203, 202
Indiana 18, 230
industrialization 18, 42, 47
insignia 101
Iowa 19
Irish Brigade 99
iron and steel industries 42, 44, 47
Ironton 302
Island No.10 122–3, 123, 125

J

Jackson 250
Jackson, Andrew 25
Jackson, Claiborne Fox 84
Jackson, General Thomas J. "Stonewall" 68, 70, 72, 78–9, 78, 88, 131, 132, 150, 152, 160, 212, 219
  Battle of Antietam 176–9
  Chancellorsville Campaign 218–21, 219
  character 78–9, 130–1
  death 204, 218, 221
  Jackson's Valley: Phase I 130–2, 131, 133
  Jackson's Valley: Phase II 150–3, 152, 153, 154, 155
  Second Battle of Bull Run 170–1
  strategic tactics 95, 153
Jackson, James S. 168
Jefferson, Thomas 34, 35
Jeffersonton, Battle of 236
Jim Crow laws 49
Johnson, Andrew 249, 369–71, 376
Johnson's Island 327, 329
Johnston, Colonel William Preston 144
Johnston, General Albert Sidney 140–2
Johnston, General Joseph E. 82, 88, 138, 209, 294, 296, 333, 340–1, 344, 346
Johnston's Farm 314
Jomini, Antoine Henri 92–3
Jones, General W.E. 304
Jones's Bridge, Battle of 275

K

Kansas 19, 25, 231
  Bleeding Kansas 35, 84
Kansas-Nebraska Act 30, 34–5, 35, 36
Kearny, General Philip 101
Kelly, Colonel B.F. 70
Kennesaw Mountain, Battle of 238, 245, 269, 296
Kentucky 21, 50, 53, 64, 106–9, 107, 108, 115
  Commonwealth of 106
  Confederate invasion 164–8, 166, 169
  Morgan's Raid 230–1, 230

Natchez 146
Native Americans 200, 201, 202, 203
Indian Territories 199
Indian Wars 22, 23, 198–203, 202
Native American combatants 99, 100, 201, 201
naval warfare 330, 358–64, 358
Battle of Mobile Bay 300–1, 300, 301
blockade of Southern seaports 46, 48, 68, 69, 74–7, 74, 75, 77, 126, 135, 176, 330, 331, 334
Charleston Campaign 216, 217
cottonclads 129
Fort Sumter 54–9, 54, 55, 57, 58, 59, 64, 100–1, 216
Hampton Roads 126–9, 126, 127, 128, 129
ironclads 126, 126, 128–9, 129, 146, 148
mines (torpedoes) 76, 77, 300, 361
Mississippi River 146–9, 147, 148, 206–14, 206, 208, 209, 210–11, 213, 215
Red River Campaign 256–9, 256–7, 258, 259
submarines 361, 361
technological innovations 126, 128
tinclads 213
Nebraska 19
Kansas-Nebraska Act 30, 34–5, 35, 36
Nebraska Territory 25
Nelson, General William 62
New Bern 120
New Hampshire 17
New Jersey 18
New Madrid 122, 125
New Market 304
New Mexico Territory 23, 25, 37, 41, 334, 334–5
New Mexico Campaign 102–4, 103, 104, 105
New Orleans 36, 72, 100, 208
Confederate re-occupation 149
fall of 96–7, 97, 148
New Ulm 201–2
New York 18
New York Highlanders 101
newspapers
army 157
newspaper coverage 10
North Anna, Battle of 281, 284–5, 284
North Carolina 21, 120, 121, 336
Carolinas Campaign 338–41, 338, 339, 340, 341, 342–3
North Dakota 19, 25
Northern states 10
abolition of slavery 65
economy 18, 26, 28, 42, 44–5
opposition to slavery 17–18, 100
population 60
see also Union states

officers 62, 98–9
Ohio 18, 230
Oklahoma 19, 25
Old Glory 25
Old Spanish Trail 23
Olustee, Battle of 250, 254–5, 255
Ord, General E.O.C. 314
Oregon Trail 23
Orleans Grand Battalion 101
Osceola 231
O'Shelby, General Joseph 302
O'Sullivan, John L. 22
Overland Campaign 270–86
Oxbow Route 23

Paducah 108
Paducah, Battle of 262
Paine, General E.A. 109, 356

Hemp Bales, Battle of the 87
Herron, General Francis D. 190
Hickman 107
Hill, General A.P. 179, 236, 284
Hill, General Daniel 160
Hilton Head Island 77
Hindman, General Thomas C. 111, 113, 190
Holly Springs 189
homesteading 372–3
Hood, General John Bell 245, 266, 296, 298, 308, 322–5
  Tennessee Campaign 308–9, 310–11
Hooker, General Joseph 178, 218–19, 222, 243
Hornet's Nest 143
hospitals see medical facilities
Hough, Daniel 56
Hovey, General Alvin P. 189
Howard, General Oliver O. 317–18, 370
Hunter, General David 64, 304, 306–7, 307

I

Illinois 18, 302
Indian Territories 199
Indian Wars 22, 23, 198–203, 202
Indiana 18, 230
industrialization 18, 42, 47
insignia 101
Iowa 19
Irish Brigade 99
iron and steel industries 42, 44, 47
Ironton 302
Island No.10 122–3, 123, 125

J

Jackson 250
Jackson, Andrew 25
Jackson, Claiborne Fox 84
Jackson, General Thomas J. "Stonewall" 68, 70, 72, 78–9, 78, 88, 131, 132, 150, 152, 160, 212, 219
  Battle of Antietam 176–9
  Chancellorsville Campaign 218–21, 219
  character 78–9, 130–1
  death 204, 218, 221
  Jackson's Valley: Phase I 130–2, 131, 133
  Jackson's Valley: Phase II 150–3, 152, 153, 154, 155
  Second Battle of Bull Run 170–1
  strategic tactics 95, 153
Jackson, James S. 168
Jefferson, Thomas 34, 35
Jeffersonton, Battle of 236
Jim Crow laws 49
Johnson, Andrew 249, 369–71, 376
Johnson's Island 327, 329
Johnston, Colonel William Preston 144
Johnston, General Albert Sidney 140–2
Johnston, General Joseph E. 82, 88, 138, 209, 294, 296, 333, 340–1, 344, 346
Johnston's Farm 314
Jomini, Antoine Henri 92–3
Jones, General W.E. 304
Jones's Bridge, Battle of 275

K

Kansas 19, 25, 231
  Bleeding Kansas 35, 84
Kansas-Nebraska Act 30, 34–5, 35, 36
Kearny, General Philip 101
Kelly, Colonel B.F. 70
Kennesaw Mountain, Battle of 238, 245, 269, 296
Kentucky 21, 50, 53, 64, 106–9, 107, 108, 115
  Commonwealth of 106
  Confederate invasion 164–8, 166, 169
  Morgan's Raid 230–1, 230

Kentucky Rifles 164
Key West 58
Kirby Smith, General Edmond 165–7
Know-Nothing Party 35, 40
Knoxville Campaign 232–3, 233, 234–5, 243
Kolb's Farm, Battle of 245

L

Lane, James Henry 231
Lawrence 230, 231, 302
Lebanon 164, 230
Lee, General Robert E. 65, 72–3, 79, 93, 115, 130–2, 135, 138–9, 160, 204, 219, 246, 330, 344
  Battle of Antietam 176–9
  Battle of Fredericksburg 182–3
  Battle of Gettysburg 222–8
  Battle of North Anna 281, 284–5, 284
  Battle of Spotsylvania 272, 280–1, 281, 282–3
  Battle of The Wilderness 246, 270–2, 271, 272, 273
  Chancerllorsville Campaign 218–21, 219, 220, 221
  Siege of Petersburg 288–94, 322, 344–6, 345
  Siege of Richmond 314, 344–6, 345, 347
  surrender 332–3
Lee, General Stephen D. 263, 323
Letcher, John 135
Lexington 166, 304
Lincoln, Abraham 14, 19, 50–3, 51, 53, 54, 57, 72, 74, 91, 101, 178, 179, 181, 208, 248, 316, 330, 346, 381
  anti-slavery position 20
  assassination 332, 333, 369
  electoral victories 19, 20, 249, 323
  Emancipation Proclamation 14, 65, 94, 100, 179, 180–1, 204
  funeral 368, 379
  Gettysburg Address 229
  inauguration 192–4
  plots against 196, 197
  strategic tactics 93, 94, 170–1
Lincoln, Mary 248
Little Crow 202, 203
Longstreet, General James 88, 171, 172, 177, 222–4, 232, 243
Lookout Mountain 242–5
Loring, General W.W. 70
Louisiana 18, 19, 21, 96, 206–14
  Lower Mississippi Valley 146–9, 147, 148
  Red River Campaign 256–9, 256–7, 258, 259
Louisiana Native Guards 214
Louisiana Purchase 19, 22, 30
Louisville 109, 167
Lovejoy's Station 318
Lowe, Thaddeus 82, 90, 91
Lynchburg 291, 306
Lyon, General Nathaniel 84, 84, 86

M

McArthur, Arthur 99, 243
McClellan, General George A. 99
McClellan, General George Brinton 77, 99, 128, 132–9, 135, 153, 160–1, 170, 176–9, 178, 182, 193, 381
  presidential campaign 249
McCook, General Alexander 168
McCown, General John P. 122
McCulloch, General Ben 111
McDowell, General Irvin 68, 79, 82, 132, 150, 152–3
McIntosh, General James McQueen 111
McLaws, General Lafayette 330
Macon 298
McPherson, General James B. 296, 296
Mahan, Dennis Hart 94–5, 94
Mahone, General William 290
Maine 18, 31, 31, 34

Mallory, M. 20
Mallory, Stephen R. 359
Malvern Hill, Battle of 161
Manassas 153
battles of see Bull Run
manifest destiny 22
Mansfield, Battle of 256, 257, 264–5
March to the Sea 119, 238, 308, 316–19, 316, 317, 318–19, 320–1, 330
Mark's Mills 265
Marksville 257
Marmaduke, General John S. 62, 113
Marye's Heights 182–3, 218–19
Maryland 64, 65, 172–9, 173, 174–5, 314
Mason-Dixon line 21, 28
Massachusetts 44
abolition of slavery 17
Shay's Rebellion 16, 16
Mattapony Church, Battle of 275
Maury, Matthew Fontaine 76, 359, 361
Meade, General George Gordon 183, 222–3, 222, 237, 274, 275
medical facilities 139, 144, 193, 197, 212, 366–7, 366
Memminger, C.S. 20
Memphis 125
Mennonites 130
Meridian Campaign 250–4, 252, 253
Mesilla 102
Mexico
Gadsden Purchase 23, 25, 25, 36–7
Mexican War 25, 34, 41
Michigan 18
Middle Creek, Battle of 108
military discipline 348–9, 348, 349
Militia Act 65
Milliken's Bay 67
Milliken's Bend 189, 208
Mine Run, Battle of 237
mines (torpedoes) 76, 77, 300, 361
Minnesota 19, 201
Missionary Ridge 242–3, 242
Mississippi 18, 21
Forrest's operations in 260–3, 261
Meridian Campaign 250–4, 252, 253
Mississippi River 122–5
battles for control 12–13, 146–9, 147, 148, 188–91, 206–14, 207, 208, 210–11, 213, 215
Missouri 19, 21, 30, 64, 84, 86
clashes in 84, 86–7, 87, 112
Price's Raid 302–3, 303
Missouri Compromise 19, 30–5, 31, 32, 84
Mobile Bay, Battle of 300–1, 300, 301, 332, 364, 365
Monitor, USS 128–9, 129
Monroe, James 34
Montana 19
Montgomery, Alabama 52, 54, 134
Morgan, Colonel John Hunt 164–7, 166, 168, 230–1, 354
Morgan's Raid 230–1, 230
Mormon Trail 23
Morris, Lieutenant Charles M. 363
Morris, Lieutenant George U. 128
Morse Code 91, 91
Morse, Samuel Finley Breese 91, 91
Mosby, John Singleton 354, 354, 355, 356, 357
Mouton, General 258
Mule Shoe 280–1
Murfreesboro 165, 184, 323
Murfreesboro, Battle of see Stone's River, Battle of

N

Nashville 42, 260, 308–9
Nashville, Battle of 67, 249, 322–5, 322, 323, 324, 325

Natchez 146
Native Americans 200, 201, 202, 203
Indian Territories 199
Indian Wars 22, 23, 198–203, 202
Native American combatants 99, 100, 201, 201
naval warfare 330, 358–64, 358
Battle of Mobile Bay 300–1, 300, 301
blockade of Southern seaports 46, 48, 68, 69, 74–7, 74, 75, 77, 126, 135, 176, 330, 331, 334
Charleston Campaign 216, 217
cottonclads 129
Fort Sumter 54–9, 54, 55, 57, 58, 59, 64, 100–1, 216
Hampton Roads 126–9, 126, 127, 128, 129
ironclads 126, 126, 128–9, 129, 146, 148
mines (torpedoes) 76, 77, 300, 361
Mississippi River 146–9, 147, 148, 206–14, 206, 208, 209, 210–11, 213, 215
Red River Campaign 256–9, 256–7, 258, 259
submarines 361, 361
technological innovations 126, 128
tinclads 213
Nebraska 19
Kansas-Nebraska Act 30, 34–5, 35, 36
Nebraska Territory 25
Nelson, General William 62
New Bern 120
New Hampshire 17
New Jersey 18
New Madrid 122, 125
New Market 304
New Mexico Territory 23, 25, 37, 41, 334, 334–5
New Mexico Campaign 102–4, 103, 104, 105
New Orleans 36, 72, 100, 208
Confederate re-occupation 149
fall of 96–7, 97, 148
New Ulm 201–2
New York 18
New York Highlanders 101
newspapers
army 157
newspaper coverage 10
North Anna, Battle of 281, 284–5, 284
North Carolina 21, 120, 121, 336
Carolinas Campaign 338–41, 338, 339, 340, 341, 342–3
North Dakota 19, 25
Northern states 10
abolition of slavery 65
economy 18, 26, 28, 42, 44–5
opposition to slavery 17–18, 100
population 60
see also Union states

officers 62, 98–9
Ohio 18, 230
Oklahoma 19, 25
Old Glory 25
Old Spanish Trail 23
Olustee, Battle of 250, 254–5, 255
Ord, General E.O.C. 314
Oregon Trail 23
Orleans Grand Battalion 101
Osceola 231
O'Shelby, General Joseph 302
O'Sullivan, John L. 22
Overland Campaign 270–86
Oxbow Route 23

P

Paducah 108
Paducah, Battle of 262
Paine, General E.A. 109, 356

Parker, Ely S. 99
Parrot guns 59
partisans see guerrilla warfare
Pea Ridge, Battle of 110–11, 112
Peachtree Creek, Battle of 296
Pelham, Major John 183
Pemberton, General John C. 188–9, 208–9, 212
Pendleton, George 249
Peninsula Campaign 72, 77, 128, 134–9, 135–6, 139, 157, 170
Pennsylvania 42, 44, 204
abolition of slavery 17
Battle of Gettysburg 15, 204
Pensacola Forts 57–8
Peralta, Battle of 104
Perryville, Battle of 109, 167–8
Petersburg, Siege of 67, 100, 248, 288–94, 288, 289, 292–3, 294–5, 312, 322, 344–6, 345
Philadelphia 61
Constitutional Convention 17–18, 30
Philippi, Battle of 70, 70, 71
photographic records 10
Pickett, General George E. 346
Pickett's Charge 224, 226, 228
Pickett's Mill, Battle of 269
Pickins, Francis 54
Pierce, Franklin 36, 36
Pigeon's Ranch, Battle of 103, 104
Pineville 257–9
Pittsburg Landing, Battle of see Shiloh, Battle of
Pleasant Hill, Battle of 257
Point Lookout 327
Polk, General Leonidas 167, 250–1
Pope, General John 122, 125, 170–1
population 60
growth 38–41, 39
immigration 38, 40, 40, 41, 60, 99, 100
territorial expansion 22–5, 23, 24, 34, 36–7
Port Gibson 212
Port Hudson, Battle of 67, 206–14, 207, 215
Port Republic, Battle of 152–3, 155
Port Republic Skirmish 155
Port Royal 363
Port Royal, Battle of 77
Port Royal Sound 77
Porter, Admiral David Dixon 330, 364
Porter, General Fitz John 138–9, 160, 160
Porterfield, Colonel G.A. 70
Prairie D'Ane, Battle of 264
Prairie Grove, Battle of 113, 113, 190
Price, General Sterling 86, 87, 110, 302–3, 303
prisoners of war 115, 139, 177, 231, 262, 326–9, 326, 327, 328, 329
African American prisoners 326
profiteering 109
Pulaski 309

Q

Quantrill, William Clark 230–1, 302
Quantrill's Raid 230–1, 231

R

railroads 23, 34, 36, 37, 42, 43, 44, 92
destruction 316, 317
Morse Code 91, 91
mortars fired from 290, 353
use in Civil War 88–9, 89, 156, 165
Raleigh 341
Rappahannock 237
Raymond, Battle of 212
Reagan, John H. 20
Rebel Yell 79

Reconstruction 14, 49, 368–76
recruitment 60–1, 61, 63, 98–101, 99
African Americans 64–7, 66, 67, 204
army pay 67
bounty payments 60
Red River 206
Red River Campaign 256–9, 256–7, 258, 259
Remington firearms 353
Renshaw, William B. 129
Republican Party 19, 20, 35, 40
Resaca, Battle of 296
Reynolds, Thomas C. 302
Rhode Island 17
Richmond 28, 48, 68, 72, 77, 94, 128, 132–9, 153, 158, 160, 166, 170, 218, 316, 327
Siege of 312–14, 313, 314, 315, 332, 344–6, 345, 347
rifling 350, 351
Rio Grande 22, 25
Roanoke Island 76–7, 120, 129, 135, 158
Rock Island 327
Rosecrans, General William S. 71, 184–5, 185, 241
Rousseau, General Lovell 143
Ruffin, Edmund 56, 56, 82
Ruggles, General Daniel 143

S

St. Louis 302
Salem Church, Battle of 221, 221
Salineville 230
Sanitary Commission 366, 367
Santa Anna, Antonio Lopez de 36–7, 37
Santa Fe 103–4
Savage's Station 160
Savannah 249, 318–19, 320–1
Sayler's Creek, Battle of 291, 291, 294
Schofield, General John M. 111, 309, 322
scorched earth policy 316, 318–19, 338–41
Scott, Winfield 25, 72, 146
Secession states 20, 21
Sedalia 303
Sedgwick, General John 174, 178, 237
Selma 250, 332
Seminole 100
Semmes, Captain Raphael 361
Seven Days' Battles 72, 139, 160–1, 162–3
Seward, Frederick William 20, 193
Sewell's (Seawell's) Point 70
Seymour, General Truman 254–5
Shand House 288
sharecropping 374
Sharpsburg 179
Sharpsburg, Battle of 28
Shay's Rebellion 16, 16
Shenandoah, CSS 333, 363–4
Shenandoah Valley
1864 operations 304–7, 304, 305, 306, 307
Jackson's Valley: Phase I 130–2, 131, 133
Jackson's Valley: Phase II 150–3, 152, 153, 154, 155
Sheridan, General Philip Henry 184–5, 248, 274–5, 274, 291, 312, 344
Shenandoah Valley 304, 305–7
Sheridan's Raids 274–5, 275, 277
Sherman, General Thomas W. 77
Sherman, General William Tecumseh 56, 119, 157, 243, 245, 246, 248–9, 251, 259, 262–3, 296, 298
Atlanta Campaign 204, 248, 266, 266, 267, 268–9
Carolinas Campaign 338–41, 338, 339, 340, 341, 342–3
March to the Sea 119, 238, 308, 316–19, 316, 317, 318–19, 320–1, 330
Meridian Campaign 250–4, 252, 253
Vicksburg Campaigns 188–90, 188, 190, 191, 208–14, 210–11, 213

Shiloh, Battle of 69, 71–2, 101, 140–5, 140, 141, 143, 145
Shockoe Slip 290–1
Shreveport 257
Sibley, General Henry Hastings 103, 202–3, 334
Sigel, General Franz 86, 304
Signal Mountain 242–5
signalling 82, 88
Sioux 200, 201, 202–3, 202
Sitting Bull 200
Slaughter Pen 185
slavery 10, 17, 26–9, 38, 49, 206
 Abolitionist movement 17–19, 26, 51, 64, 180–1, 192
 American Revolution 26, 28
 cotton production 18, 27, 29, 46, 49
 Fugitive State Law 18, 19
 Great Compromise 18
 importation banned 18, 38
 Native American slave owners 201
 Northern opposition 17–18
 Northern states 26, 28, 65, 181, 206
 slave emancipation 14
 Southern states 18, 26, 27, 28–9, 46
 strongholds of slavery 27
 trade in 18, 28, 28, 96
 Underground Railroad 19
 US Constitution 17–18
Slocum, General Henry W. 340
Smith, General Andrew J. 263, 323
Smith, General William F. 278
Smith, General William Sooy 250–2, 254
Smith, Major Leon 129
Sonora, Republic of 37
South Carolina 21
 Carolinas Campaign 338–41, 338, 339, 340, 341, 342–3
South Dakota 19, 25
Southern states 10
 African American population 370, 371
 agriculture 27, 29, 44–9, 47, 49
 economy 18, 26, 27, 28, 42, 45–9, 47, 378
 Reconstruction 368–77
 reestablishment of conservative governments 370
 slavery 10, 14, 18, 26, 28–9
 see also Confederate states
Spanish Fort 332
Spotsylvania, Battle of 272, 280–1, 281, 282–3
Spring Hill 309
Stand Watie 100, 201
Stannard, General George 314
Stanton, Edwin 50
Starr Arms Company 353
Starr, Belle 86
Stars and Bars 25
states, independence of 16
Staunton 304, 307
Steedman, General James B. 323
Steel, General Frederick 264–5, 265
Stephens, Alexander Hamilton 20, 336
Stewart, General Alexander 323
Stewart, Thaddeus 370
Stone's Rive, Battle of 184–5, 185, 186, 187
Stonewall Brigade 131
Strasburg 150
strategic tactics 92–5, 114–19
Streight, Colonel Abel 262
Stuart, James Ewell Brown 176, 236, 236, 275
Sturgis, General Samuel D. 262–3
submarines 361, 361
suffrage 370
Sumner, General Edwin Vose 161
Sunken Road 143
sutlers 158
Sweatt, Leonard 109

T

Tallahassee 332

Tallmadge, James, Jr. 30

Tappan, Arthur 18

Tariff of Abominations 18

taxation 16

  Shay's Rebellion 16, 16

Taylor, Colonel 334

Taylor, General Richard 257–8

Taylor, Sarah Knox 51

Taylor, Zachary 51

technological innovations 10, 88–91, 126, 128

telegraphy 88, 91, 92, 113, 164

Tennessee 21, 42, 114–19, 122–5, 165, 165

  Army of Tennessee 294, 296, 317, 322–5

  Battle of Nashville 67, 249, 322–5, 322, 323, 324, 325

  Forrest's operations in 260–3, 261

  Hood's Campaign 308–9, 310–11

  Knoxville Campaign 232–3, 233, 234–5

Terry, General Alfred H. 330, 336

Texas 21, 25, 41, 334, 334–5

  annexation 18, 34

  slavery 18

Texas, Republic of 25

Thayer, General John M. 264

Thomas, General George H. 184, 242, 242, 245, 308–9, 322–5

Thomas, Jesse B. 34

Thomson, General M. Jeff 122

Tilghman, General Lloyd 230–1

Tiptonville 122

tobacco 44, 47, 158

Tompkinsville 164

Toombs, Robert 20

torpedoes see mines

total war 94–5, 119, 241, 316, 338–41

training 62, 101, 156, 158–9

trench warfare 10, 138, 139, 245, 266, 288, 289, 290, 344

Tullahoma 184

Tupelo 125

Tuscumbia 308

U

unconditional surrender 119, 246

Underground Railroad 19

uniforms

  Confederate states 101, 101

  Union states 101, 151

Union states 25

  African American soldiers 17, 64–7, 66, 67, 99, 204, 214

  army 98–100, 100, 101, 138, 151, 156–9, 157, 158, 289

  flag 25

  Native American soldiers 99, 201

  navy 67, 74–7, 126–9, 126, 206, 258, 358–65, 362, 364

  objectives 180–1, 206

  recruitment and conscription 17, 60–2, 60, 61, 63, 64–7, 66, 67, 74, 98–100, 99

  Sanitary Commission 366, 367

  strategic tactics 94–5

  see also Northern states

United States of America

  Articles of Confederation 16

  Constitution 16–18, 30

  establishment 16

  following Civil War 14

  Reconstruction 14, 49

  territorial expansion 22–5, 23, 24, 34, 36–7

United States Colored Troops (USCT) 66

Upton, Colonel Emory 280

Utah Territory 25

V

Valley Campaigns see Shenandoah Valley
Valverde, Battle of 103–4, 103
Van Buren, Martin 25
Van Dorn, Earl 110–11, 111, 148, 212
Velasquez, Loreta Janeta 329
Vermont 17
Vicksburg 146, 148
  Vicksburg Campaigns 188–90, 188, 190, 191, 204, 206–14, 209, 210–11, 213, 222, 226
Virginia 21, 44, 204, 232, 236–7, 237, 246, 248, 330
  Army of Virginia 137, 170, 222
  Battle of Drewry's Bluff 278–9, 279
  Battle of North Anna 281, 284–5, 284
  battle sites 15
  Battle of Spotsylvania 272, 280–1, 281, 282–3
  Battle of The Wilderness 246, 270–2, 271, 272, 273
  Peninsula Campaign 72, 77, 128, 134–9, 135–6, 139
  Richmond see Richmond
  Sheridan's Raids 274–5, 275, 277
  Valley Campaigns see Shenandoah Valley
volunteer units 60–1, 62, 74, 98

W

Waddell, Lieutenant James I. 364
Wade-Davis Bill 249
wagon trails 23, 198
Walker, Leroy Pope 20
Walker, General Lucius M. 62
Walker, William 37
War of 1812 64
Ward, Commander James H. 362
Warren, General Gouverneur K. 236, 284–5, 346
Warrington 58
Washington 134, 137, 157, 171, 192–7, 193, 194, 196, 327
  defences 195
  White House 194, 200
Washington Battery 183
Washington Raid 248
Washington Territory 25
Webster, Fletcher 171
West Virginia 21, 25, 64, 68, 70–1, 73
Wheatfield 223, 228
Whig Party 35, 50
White House Landing, Battle of 275
White Oak Swamp, Battle of 161
Whiting, General W.H.C. 279
Whitney, Eli 44
Whitney's Lane, Battle of 111
Wilderness, Battle of The 246, 270–2, 271, 272, 273, 274
Williams, General Thomas 148–9
Williamsburg, Battle of 137, 138
Wilmington 336
Wilson, General James H. 285, 325, 332
Wilson's Creek, Battle of 84–7, 85, 87
Winchester, Battle of 132, 204, 306
Winnebagos 201
Winton 120
Wisconsin 18
Wise, General Henry A. 135
Wolsey 58
women 135
  female spies 70, 86, 197, 197
Wood, General Thomas J. 323
Wyatt, Henry Lawson 76
Wyoming 19

Y

Yellow Tavern, Battle of 275
Yorktown 137

ACKNOWLEDGEMENTS

The publishers would like to thank the following picture libraries for their kind permission to use their pictures and illustrations:

Getty Images 51,83,93,119, 151, 160, 181, 202, 209, 224, 263, 314, 317, 316, 347, 345, 358, 360

Istock photolibrary p6,8,9,95, 228, 226, 229

Corbis UK Ltd p29,36,37,49,56,58,70,74,90,101,110,126,149, 161, 168, 150, 153, 155, 186, 232, 242, 245, 246, 248, 254, 258, 272, 285, 288, 289, 291, 290, 296, 300, 306, 309, 332, 333, 338, 341, 347, 355, 366, 377, 381

Northwind /photolibrary 61,111

Every effort has been made to contact the copyright holders for images reproduced in this book. Any omissions are entirely unintentional, and the details should be addressed to Quantum Publishing.